A HISTORY OF
UKRAINE

BY

MICHAEL HRUSHEVSKY

Edited by

O. J. FREDERIKSEN

Preface by

GEORGE VERNADSKY

Published for the
Ukrainian National Association

ARCHON BOOKS
1970

ISBN: 0-208-00967-1
[Reproduced from a copy in the Yale University Library]
Library of Congress Catalog Card Number: 72-120370
Printed in the United States of America

ACKNOWLEDGMENT

THE publication of this book has been made possible by the Ukrainian National Association. It meets a vital need for an authoritative work in English on the main developments in the history of Ukraine, a country whose centuries-old struggle for independence is beginning to have an important bearing on the course of European events. The preparation of the manuscript for publication has been accomplished under the direction of Dr. Luke Myshuha, editor-in-chief of the daily *Svoboda,* official organ of the U.N.A.

The translation of this one-volume *History of Ukraine* by Michael Hrushevsky represents the coöperative efforts of several persons. Wasyl Halich, author of *Ukrainians in the United States,* Omelian Revyuk, managing editor of *Svoboda,* Dr. Luke Myshuha, and Stephen Shumeyko, editor of the *Ukrainian Weekly,* English-language supplement of *Svoboda,* made a first draft. A final, complete editing of the manuscript was done by Professor O. J. Frederiksen of Miami University, Ohio, who also wrote the last chapter. Professor George Vernadsky of Yale University, author of *Political and Diplomatic History of Russia* and other historical works, has contributed the Preface on Hrushevsky and offered valuable suggestions.

PREFACE

SLAVONIC studies have made considerable progress in this country during the last two decades. The American reader has now at his disposal bookshelves of publications in English dealing with Russia, Poland, and Czechoslovakia as well as the Balkan countries. There has been one important gap, however—Ukraine.* Yet the Ukrainians are the second largest Slavic nation, and some familiarity with Ukraine and her history is essential to an understanding of the present developments in Eastern Europe. Ukraine may become before long the pivot of Eastern Europe, and in a sense is that already. The fact has not yet been clearly realized because of the lack of information on the subject. People used to speak for example of the annexation of "Eastern Poland" to "Russia," not realizing that the country in question is neither Poland nor Russia proper but Ukraine.

For the understanding of the tangled conditions in Central and Eastern Europe, of the manifold nationalistic and political combinations and rivalries of its peoples, knowledge of its historical background is indispensable.

Michael Hrushevsky was the leading Ukrainian historian, whose authority has been widely recognized both in and outside of his country. His ten-volume *History of Ukraine* is the standard work on the subject; he worked on it throughout his whole life. Volume I appeared in 1898; the subsequent parts followed at intervals of a couple of years, and Volume IX was published in two parts in 1928–31. Volume X is said to have appeared posthumously. It is the work of a great scholar, based upon exhaustive research, pervaded by the spirit of keen criticism, and displaying a wealth of information with regard not only to the history of the Ukrainian people but to the

* An abridged English edition of D. Doroshenko's *History of the Ukraine* has recently appeared and fills the gap to a certain extent.

general history of the period as well. Hrushevsky succeeded only in bringing his narrative down to the hetman-
ship of Vyhovsky (1657–59). But when he was still in the
middle of his work he wrote a condensed *Outline of a History of Ukraine* to supply the reader with a manual of
Ukrainian history and civilization. It was first published
in Russian in 1904; there have been several editions since.
In 1911 Hrushevsky published a popular one-volume *Il-
lustrated History of Ukraine,* in Ukrainian. For the present English translation a copy of the Ukrainian edition of
this history printed at Winnipeg, Canada, has been used
by the editors.

While deeply interested in the Ukrainian past, Hrushevsky was no less responsive to the realities of contemporary Ukraine. He combined the spirit of a scholar with
that of a political fighter. His whole life was closely inter-
woven with that of the Ukrainian nation, and the vicissi-
tudes of his personal fortune are in a sense representative of the lot of Ukrainian intellectuals at large.

Hrushevsky was born September 29, 1866, in Kholm, a
city in the northwestern corner of Ukraine, which was
within what then was known as the Government General
of Warsaw, that is, Russian Poland. Thus his very birth-
place was symbolic of the historical triangle of Russia,
Poland, and Ukraine. At the time of his birth the territory of Ukraine was divided between the Russian and the
Austrian empires, the former controlling the larger part
of Ukrainians. The Russian Imperial Government, while
making no distinction between Great Russians and
Ukrainians with regard to their personal rights, privileges of civil and military service, and so on, denied the
use of the Ukrainian language in schools and governmental offices and even forbade the publication of books and
newspapers in Ukrainian.

The situation was more involved in Austrian Galicia,
due to the fact that Poles were allowed by the Austrian
Government to control not only the western, or Polish,

part of the province, but the whole of it. Eventually a compromise was reached between the Poles and a group of Ukrainians, and as a result of this it was decided, in 1891, to establish a chair of the history of Eastern Europe, with special attention to Ukrainian history, at the University of Lviv. The chair was offered to Volodimir Antonovich, then professor of history at Kiev University. He did not choose to accept, referring to his advanced age, and recommended in his stead Michael Hrushevsky as one of his ablest pupils. Hrushevsky had been graduated from Kiev University in 1890 and had devoted himself under Antonovich's guidance to extensive research in the field of Ukrainian history. He accepted without hesitation (1894). Hrushevsky's decision proved to be of great importance both to himself and to the Ukrainian movement. He became a kind of living bridge between the Great, or eastern, Ukraine (then Russian), and the smaller western Ukraine (then Austrian). Both sides benefited by this contact. The intellectuals of Austrian Ukraine were apt to concentrate on their local problems, since most of them were out of immediate touch with the larger portion of their nation. On the other hand, they had better chances of political training since Austria was a country of constitutional government, limited though it was.

With his background of a native of Great Ukraine and the political opportunities of a resident of western Ukraine now open to him, Hrushevsky became before long one of the leading men in the Ukrainian movement. In 1897 he was elected president of the Shevchenko Scientific Society which was then the center of Ukrainian cultural life. The publications of the society contributed immensely to promoting research in Ukrainian history and literature. Among other materials the society published many volumes of important historical documents under Hrushevsky's editorship.

After the Russian revolution of 1905 more liberal poli-

cies were inaugurated in the Russian empire and a limited
constitutional regime was established. Restrictions on
Ukrainian publications were revoked, and Hrushevsky
now decided to come back to Kiev to promote the national
movement in Great Ukraine. During the following decade
he spent part of his time in Kiev and part in Lviv, attempting to bring the two Ukrainian groups more closely
together. When the World War broke out in 1914 Hrushevsky was spending his vacation in a summer resort in
the Carpathian Mountains. He first went to Vienna but
later decided to make his way to Kiev. By that time the
Russian Government already suspected the Ukrainian
leaders in Galicia of pro-German inclinations, and upon
his return to Kiev Hrushevsky was arrested and deported
to the town of Simbirsk on the Volga River. At that juncture, however, the Russian Academy of Sciences intervened in his favor and he was allowed to proceed to Moscow and to continue his research work in the Moscow archives.

When the Russian revolution began in March 1917,
Hrushevsky immediately made for Kiev and plunged
headlong into politics. A Ukrainian National Council
(*Rada*) was organized in Kiev and Hrushevsky was
elected its first president. The so-called Provisional Government which established itself in Petrograd under Alexander Kerensky hesitated to confirm the Ukrainian autonomy before the convocation of an all-Russia Constituent Assembly. Struggling desperately to maintain its
equilibrium in the midst of war and revolution with the
hopeless deterioration of economic conditions, the Provisional Government was unable to stop the rapid ascend-
ancy of the communist movement, and in November 1917
Lenin and Trotsky seized power in Petrograd.

The Ukrainian Rada answered by the declaration of independence of Ukraine. The Bolsheviks did not recognize
the Rada Government, however, and set up a Communist
Government of their own for Ukraine. The Rada applied

to the Central Powers for aid and on February 9, 1918, a treaty was concluded at Brest-Litovsk between the Ukrainian Republic and the Central Powers. While the latter were at the same time negotiating with the Soviet Government and put the recognition of Ukrainian independence as a prerequisite for peace, Soviet troops entered Kiev. In fires which broke out in the city Hrushevsky's house with its invaluable library was burned among other buildings.

Following the signature of the peace treaty at Brest-Litovsk, German troops were sent to Ukraine to rid it of the Bolsheviks. The Rada Government was restored and Hrushevsky once more accepted the presidency. After a while, however, the Germans withdrew their support from the Rada Government; General Skoropadsky became the head of the new government with the historic title of Hetman. Hrushevsky left the country for Prague and Vienna. He now gave up politics and concentrated again on scholarly work. Meanwhile Ukraine went through the horrors of civil war and finally was controlled by the Soviets. It became one of the constituent republics at the formation of the Soviet Union, in 1923.

The next year the Ukrainian Academy of Science at Kiev elected Hrushevsky one of its members and invited him to return to Kiev. The Soviet Government was ready to grant him the necessary permission and to guarantee him the opportunity to pursue his scientific work on condition that he refrain from political activity. He accepted and undoubtedly meant to keep his word. For several years the government did not interfere with his work. While busy with the continuation of his *History of Ukraine* he also published, in 1923–26, a five-volume *History of Ukrainian Literature*. Meanwhile the period of the so-called NEP, or new economic policy, came to a close, and a new drive of militant communism was started both in Russia and in Ukraine. Pressure was exerted on Hrushevsky to make him join the Marxist group of historians, and since he refused to do so, a violent campaign was opened against him in the Soviet press. In 1930 he was arrested and interned in a small town near Moscow. There he spent four years, under strict police supervision, denied any facilities for research and forbidden to correspond with his friends. His health was broken and he was growing blind. Finally, the Moscow authorities agreed to send him to a home for Soviet scholars in Kislovodsk, northern Caucasus, for recuperation, but it was already too late. He died in Kislovodsk on November 26, 1934. His body was brought to Kiev and buried there at state expense with impressive solemnity.

From Hrushevsky's life we have now to turn to the consideration of some general aspects of Ukrainian history and the Ukrainian question, to which Hrushevsky's life was dedicated.

If the reader of this book has seen previously some of the general outlines of Russian history, he will no doubt be struck by the fact that the subject matter of that part of Hrushevsky's book which deals with the early period of Ukrainian history is almost identical with the corresponding chapters in the outlines dealing with the so-called "Kievan Period" of Russian history. The explanation is that both the Ukrainian and the Russian peoples had a common period of their political and cultural life at the dawn of their respective histories. The Kievan princes succeeded in uniting most of the East Slavic tribes and organized them along similar lines both politically and culturally. Since the city of Kiev had been the center of their state, we may assume that the south then was the leading force, and the north only followed suit. It was the Kiev area which was then known as Rus, and the name only gradually spread over the rest of the country which was to be known as Russia later on.

The unity between south and north was cemented by many common religious and cultural bonds. Christianity came to Kiev from Byzantium, and so it was the Greek Orthodox Church which became the church of old Rus-Ukraine. The see of the metropolitan was in Kiev which thus became the ecclesiastical as well as the political capital of the entire country. Church Slavonic was the language of religious service and became likewise the foundation of the literary language of the period, both in the south and in the north. Thus Kiev is still considered the ancient metropolis by both the Ukrainians and the Russians; the old legal code known as the Rus Law (*Pravda*), the Primary Chronicle, the epic song of Prince Igor's campaign are claimed by both Ukrainians and Russians as precious documents of their common past.

It was in the twelfth century that the characteristics of the Ukrainian language first became evident; the process of consolidation of each of the three branches of the East Slavic family—the Ukrainian, the Great Russian, and the White Russian—was further accelerated by the political events of the thirteenth and fourteenth centuries—the Mongol invasion and the expansion of both Poland and Lithuania. By the end of the sixteenth century most of the Ukrainian lands were controlled by Poland. Ukrainian peasants became serfs of the Polish or Polonized landowners. Difference of religion—the landowner being a Roman Catholic and the serf Greek Orthodox—accentuated the social cleavage. The Greek Orthodox clergy now assumed spiritual leadership of the Ukrainian people. In order to break the independence of the Church, the Polish Government adopted the plan of subjecting the Ukrainian Church to the authority of Rome. In this way the so-called Uniate Church was organized (1596). The plan worked for a while, but failed in the long run, since eventually the Uniate Church identified itself with the national movement in western Ukraine, while eastern Ukraine remained loyal to the Greek Orthodox Church.

Another national force which the Polish kings attempted to tame was the Ukrainian Kozak Host. The

Kozak revolution of 1648 led by Hetman Bohdan Khmelnitsky resulted in the formation of a Kozak state, which subsequently looked for assistance to the Tsar of Moscow and became a Russian protectorate (1654).

We must have in mind all this historical background in order to approach the fundamentals of the Ukrainian question in modern times. Bohdan Khmelnitsky's objective was to restore the independent Ukrainian state, following the traditions of the early Kievan princes. He was only half successful in his effort, but in spite of this we must not underestimate the importance of his legacy. Traditions of Ukrainian statehood were kept alive, and a new Ukrainian ruling class emerged to replace the old Ukrainian gentry, by now Polonized or half-Polonized. This new ruling class consisted of the officers of the Kozak Host (*starshina*). Due to their efforts as well as to those of the Ukrainian clergy there came about an important cultural revival. In the second half of the seventeenth and the first half of the eighteenth century Ukraine was probably the leading Slavonic nation culturally.

Due to the union of Great Russia and Ukraine, Ukrainian culture influenced profoundly the development of Russian civilization at that time. Many of Peter the Great's assistants in the fields of the church, education, and general administration were Ukrainians. In a sense the new westernized Russian empire was the creation of the Ukrainians as much as that of the Great Russians. This Ukrainian expansion had certain drawbacks from the point of view of the Ukrainian nationalist. While Ukrainians helped Peter and his successors to build up the empire, their own autonomy was being gradually curtailed and finally was canceled altogether. In 1764 the office of the hetman was abolished and in 1780 Ukraine was incorporated into the empire; Ukrainian provinces were organized according to the Russian pattern. The old Kozak Host was disbanded and its remnants transferred to the banks of Kuban River in the northern Caucasus.

The Ukrainian gentry were made equal with the Russian nobility, and the formerly free peasants became serfs, to be freed only in 1861 together with the Russian serfs.

The southward expansion of the Russian empire in Catherine II's time brought the Imperial frontier to the shores of the Black Sea; rich steppes of the south were now thrown open for agriculture, and Ukraine became the granary not only of Russia but of Europe as well. It was the Russianized Ukrainian gentry who first profited by this; but the opening of the south for colonization meant more "living space" for the Ukrainian nation as a whole. Consequently, we must admit that this period was in a sense one of material progress and consolidation. It was, however, quite unfavorable to the preservation of Ukrainian culture as such, especially since the educated upper strata of the Ukrainian nation were being rapidly Russianized.

Thus we see that twice in history the upper classes of the Ukrainian nation lost their old national traditions: first, under the Polish regime, in the sixteenth and seventeenth centuries, and secondly, under the Russian regime, in the eighteenth and nineteenth centuries. This explains the thoroughly democratic foundations of the modern Ukrainian movement. Started by a few idealist intellectuals, it soon became primarily a peasant movement. Peasant life is the chief subject matter of modern Ukrainian literature. Likewise the Ukrainian literary language of our times is essentially an adaptation of the folk speech to modern requirements. This has given the Ukrainian language its peculiar charm but it has also imposed on it certain limitations, which have been met by coining new terms as in science, technology, and so on, or by borrowing such words from other languages. At present, this process may be considered as completed and the Ukrainian language is fully equipped for all its needs. The Soviet Government has given it its full recognition. The Ukrainian language has become the official language in

Soviet Ukraine, its schools, offices, and courts. New generations have during the two decades of the Soviet regime received all their education in the Ukrainian language, and it has thus been firmly entrenched throughout the country.

As a result of the international policy of the Soviets, western Ukraine, which was controlled by Poland from 1920 to 1939, and partly by Rumania from 1918 to 1940, has recently been merged with Soviet Ukraine, and the whole Ukrainian nation is now united except for fractions of it remaining in the German-controlled part of Poland, and in Hungary. The results of this Ukrainian reunion are far-reaching. For the first time since the early Kievan period the Ukrainian people are gathered together. Legally, Soviet Ukraine is not only autonomous but, according to the Constitution of the Union, even has a right of secession. Whatever future developments may bring in their wake, the strong determination displayed by the Ukrainian people in their age-long struggle for the defense of their unity, their freedom, and their civilization is in itself an evidence of the tremendous vitality of the nation.

GEORGE VERNADSKY

New Haven, Connecticut,
  March 12, 1941.

CONTENTS

PREFACE BY GEORGE VERNADSKY   v

LIST OF MAPS   xix

I. THE DAWN OF CIVILIZATION   1
History and Prehistory. Ancient Times. The Coming of Man.
Neolithic Culture. Copper, Bronze, and Iron.

II. GREEKS AND SCYTHIANS   11
The Greek Colonies. The People of the Steppes. Life among
the Steppe Tribes. The Slavic Settlements.

III. THE FIRST UKRAINIANS   20
The Ukrainian Migrations, the Antae. The Ukrainian Tribes.
Ukrainian Customs. Characteristic Traits, Customs, and Be-
liefs. The Family, Clan, and Community. Commerce. The
Princes and Their Retinues.

IV. THE FOUNDING OF KIEV   39
Kievan Traditions. The Kievan Chronicle. Rus. Early Rus
Campaigns. Prince Oleh. Ihor and Olha. Sviatoslav and His
Sons.

V. THE KINGDOM OF KIEV   63
Volodimir. The Adoption of Christianity. Cultural Developments. War with the Pechenegs. The Heirs of Volodimir.

VI. THE DECLINE OF KIEV   76
Yaroslav. The Successors of Yaroslav. The Polovtsian Raids.
Provincial Self-Government. The Principalities. The Down-
fall of Kiev.

VII. THE KINGDOM OF GALICIA   96
Prince Roman (1189–1205). The Dynasty of Roman. The
Tatar Raids. Under the Yoke of the Tatars. King Daniel.
Galicia-Volynia under Daniel's Heirs. Political Organiza-
tion in the Period of Decline. Culture and Education.

VIII. UKRAINE UNDER POLAND-LITHUANIA   123
Lithuanian Expansion in Ukraine. The Partition of Galicia-
Volynia. The Union of Poland and Lithuania. The New Pol-
icy in the Grand Duchy of Lithuania. The Struggle for
Equal Rights. The Intervention of Muscovy.

IX. The Rise of the Kozaks   144

Attempts at Revolt in Galicia and the Beginnings of Ukrainian Nationalism. Rise of the Kozaks. The Kozak Host and the Early Kozak Expeditions. Founding of the Sich. The Kozak Organization.

X. National Revival in the Steppes   165

Reunion under Poland of Eastern and Western Ukraine. Social and Political Effects of Polish Annexation. Political Changes and the Growth of Population in Eastern Ukraine. Growth of the Kozak Host at the Close of the Sixteenth Century. The Kozak Wars.

XI. The First Kozak Uprisings and the Church
      Union   188

The War of 1596. Decline of Ukrainian National Life and Efforts at Revival. Educational Progress. The Brotherhoods. The Church Union. The Struggle against the Church Union.

XII. The Kozaks and the Revival of Kiev   217

The Kozak Host after the Battle of Lubny. The Kozak Organization. The Sea Raids. Polish Negotiations with the Kozaks; Hetman Sahaidachny. The Revival of Kiev as the Center of Ukrainian Cultural Life. The New Hierarchy in the Church.

XIII. The Kozak Wars   246

The Khotyn War and the Death of Sahaidachny. Strife with the Government. The Ukrainian Project and the War of 1625. The War of 1630. The Interregnum. Sulima and Pavliuk. The Ostrianin War and the Oppression of the Kozaks.

XIV. Khmelnitsky's Rebellion and the Liberation of Ukraine   277

The Revolution of 1648. The Ukrainian War of Liberation. Foreign Alliances. The Muscovite Protectorate. Between Muscovy and Sweden. The Hetman State. The Union of Hadiach. The War with Muscovy.

XV. Dissolution and Decline   319

The Partition of Ukraine. Doroshenko's Aims. The Downfall of Doroshenko. "The Ruin." The Great Eviction and the New Kozak State in Western Ukraine. Events in the Hetman State.

XVI. Ivan Mazepa 347

The Officers and the People. Mazepa's Administration. On the Eve of the Break. The Alliance with Sweden. Mazepa's Defeat. Philip Orlik.

XVII. The Dissolution of the Kozak Host and the Decline in Ukrainian National Life 374

The Curtailment of the Hetman's Power. The First Abolition of the Hetmancy; Polubotok. Revival of the Hetmancy; Hetman Apostol. The Second Abolition of the Hetmancy.

XVIII. Eastern Ukraine 398

The Hetmancy of Rozumovsky. Political and Social Organization of the Hetman State. The Land of Free Communes (*Slobidshina*). Culture in Eastern Ukraine—Literature and Education. National Life in Eastern Ukraine.

XIX. The Last Rebellions 422

The Decline of Ukrainian Culture in Western Ukraine. Carpatho-Ukraine. Western Ukraine. The Haidamak Rebellion. The Revolt of the Kolii.

XX. The Dispersion of the Kozaks 446

The Final Abolition of the Hetmancy. Destruction of the Sich. The Last Years of the Hetman State.

XXI. The National Renaissance 462

The Austrian Annexation of Galicia and Bukovina. The Destruction of Poland and the Annexation of Western Ukraine by Russia and Austria. Beginning of the Renaissance in Western Ukraine. Beginning of the Renaissance in Eastern Ukraine. Ideas of Nationalism and the Beginnings of Enlightened Democracy.

XXII. The National Idea 483

Ukrainian Literary Circles in Russian Ukraine and the Brotherhood of Saints Cyril and Methodius. The National Rebirth in Galicia and the Year 1848. The Year 1848 in Bukovina and Carpatho-Ukraine, and the Reaction of the 1850's. The New Movement in Russian Ukraine. Nationalism and the Russophile Movement in Galicia.

XXIII. The National Struggle 500

The Beginnings of National Aspirations in Bukovina. The Kievan *Hromada* and the Decree of 1876. Ukrainian Activity in Galicia. The Political Movement in Galicia in the 1890's. National and Cultural Progress in Austrian Ukraine. Ukraine under Russia on the Eve of the First World War.

XXIV. Ukrainian Independence   514
The First World War. The Russian Revolution and the Liberation of Ukraine. The Struggle for Ukrainian Autonomy within a Federation. The Ukrainian National Republic. Independent Ukraine. The Insurrection in Kiev. The War for the Preservation of Independence.

XXV. Recent Ukraine   551
Skoropadsky and the Germans. Western Ukrainian Independence. Civil War. The Ukrainian Soviet Socialist Republic. Rumania and Czechoslovakia. Poland. Ukraine under the Soviets from the Postwar Treaties to Munich. Ukraine under Poland from the Postwar Treaties to Munich. Carpatho-Ukraine. The Reunion of Ukraine under the Soviets.

Appendix   575
1. Kievan Princes and Kings. 2. Princes of Galicia and Galicia-Volynia. 3. Genealogy of Ukrainian Princes of the Kievan Dynasty. 3a. Descendants of Volodimir Monomakh, Princes of Kiev, Volynia, and Galicia. 4. Genealogy of Ukrainian Princes of the Lithuanian Dynasty. 4a. Descendants of Olgerd. 5. Hetmans of Ukraine.

Bibliography   585

Index   601

MAPS

Ukraine in the 17th century.   152

Volynia (based on Beauplan's map). (1665).   226

Western Ukraine (based on Beauplan's map). (1665).   268

Ukraine. Boundaries as of June, 1941.   *preceding index*

A HISTORY OF UKRAINE

CHAPTER I

THE DAWN OF CIVILIZATION

History and Prehistory: This history of Ukraine aims at presenting a history in the old Greek sense of the word: the story of a land and of a people. The earliest source of information about Ukraine, as about other ancient lands, was the oral tradition handed down from father to son. Later more accurate methods of transmitting knowledge of the past appeared with written chronicles and verses intended to be memorized. Then came a time when historians consciously put the earlier materials into permanent form and added to them a record of their own times.

The stories thus recorded contain many gaps and are not all equally old. Ancient manuscripts and chronicles have been destroyed or lost, and peoples have varied widely in their success in preserving records of their past.

In the country which was later on to be known as Ukraine the art of writing began to be diffused some time before A.D. 1000, simultaneously with Christianity itself. For the period following the development of writing there are manuscripts to tell the story. But even so, records dating from the tenth century A.D. are dependable only to a slight degree; to a large extent they represent merely the recording of a memory of earlier times. Our information regarding the early history of Ukraine comes chiefly from the writers of neighboring lands, especially the Greeks; but the Romans, the Arabs, and finally the Germans have also made their contributions.

The oldest descriptions of the region of Ukraine date back to the seventh century before Christ, and begin to appear in some detail in the fifth. They have, however, to do only with the Black Sea coast itself, for there was as yet no Ukrainian people. Written records of foreign writers concerning the people begin considerably later, about four hundred years after Christ. This may be called the dawn of their history. The history of the Ukrainian people is thus fifteen hundred years old, or approximately fifty human generations, counting about thirty years to a generation, whereas the history of Ukraine, at least of its coastal region, is a thousand years older.

As to the life of the people who inhabited Ukraine before the beginning of recorded history, there is a wealth of relics to be found in caves or buried underground. These include articles of handiwork, tools, dishes, the ashes of wood fires, remains of human shelters, food, bones, and other remnants. An idea of the main features of their life can be gained from ancient Ukrainian customs which have been handed down to this very day, or which are described in early writings. Such customs persist for many years, occasionally until the people have forgotten their origin and significance and why they have kept them, except that they consider them proper because their parents observed them. Some information can be gleaned from the origin of words. For example, the word *skot* (cattle) in earlier days meant money or wealth because formerly human wealth was counted in terms of cattle, which were bartered for other articles and would buy anything.

The historian can thus tell with fair exactitude, though only in general terms, how human life developed ten, twenty, thirty thousand years ago; how the early inhabitants of Ukraine lived; and how they provided for their needs, even in the dim past before they had acquired a knowledge of iron or other metals or knew how to sow grain and to raise domestic animals. He can tell further the hardships they had to endure and how, slowly but surely, they attained to a richer and easier life.

Ancient Times: The oldest records of the past are those engraved upon the surface of the earth itself. A river cuts deeply into a high bank and makes a gorge. One who knows how to interpret the writing of the precipice can read from it as from a book the story of the life which developed there and passed away.

At the surface such an observer would see black earth, resulting from the decomposition of grasses and other plants, and sometimes a few traces of human life itself, such as long-lost implements. Beneath the black earth lies a stratum of yellow clay, or loess. Occasionally there occur several layers of various kinds of clay, separated by strata of sand or stone. In these so-called Diluvial strata there sometimes come to light great bones, tusks, and other remains of ancient animals, or charcoal, flint, and bone left by human hands. Beneath the strata of clay are strata of light and porous limestone, containing various crustaceans, the so-called Tertiary layers. Still farther down there often appear pure chalk deposited by an ancient sea, a layer of crumbly calcite, and below that a layer of coal. And finally, at the very bottom, a layer of hard, lifeless stone, the solid rind with which the earth became covered when its once-molten mass began to cool.

These various layers of stone and clay and sand and the remains of plants and animals tell us whether at any particular spot there was once sea or land: they inform us what plants and animals lived there, what they looked like, and on what they lived. Each area has undergone vast changes. Where today there is dry steppe, there once rolled the waves of a deep sea, teeming with a variety of marine life: later, as the bottom of the sea rose, the waters receded. The relics of the sea life remained in the form of heaps of bones and shells, which became compressed into a layer of limestone, overlaid by the mud of rivers or by wind-borne dust and layers of decomposed vegetable and animal matter.

At the time when human life was first appearing on the earth, the sea was in process of receding from Ukraine. Formerly it had covered almost the entire region, but toward the end of the Tertiary period it extended barely beyond the present shore lines of the Black Sea, the Sea of Azov, and the Caspian Sea; these three at that time constituted a single sea, as is evidenced by the great salt swamps (*solonchaks*) lying between the Sea of Azov and the Caspian, as well as by other signs. The Carpathian, the Crimean, and the Caucasus mountain ranges raised themselves slowly above the plain, so that the landscape of Ukraine at the beginning of the Diluvial period began to take on its present appearance. But it had still to pass through one final transmutation which was to have a profound influence upon its life and form—the glacial ages.

In the first half of the Tertiary period the climate in Europe was as warm as it now is in central Africa. The flora were unusually luxuriant, more abundant than in the tropics of today. There were many species of land animals of large size and strange aspect. Among them were immense lizards, several kinds of elephants, and huge birds. In time these animals disappeared, leaving only their bones buried in the earth. As the air grew cooler the plants and animals which could not accustom themselves to the cold began to die off: only those, such as the mammoth and the woolly rhinoceros which could adapt themselves to the change, survived. As the Northern Hemisphere began to freeze over, a great mass of ice gathered in present-day Sweden and Finland and spread southward. For thousands of years this ice sheet covered the northern part of Ukraine. Then, as the climate became warmer, it melted and receded northward, leaving behind thick layers of clayey loam, layers of sand and stone, and broad, deep river beds carved out by the water that flowed from beneath the glaciers.

The Coming of Man: The first signs of human life in Ukraine date from the period when the ice was receding. Such traces are met with less often than in France or in Germany, where man lived in dry stone caves in which bones and other relics of human life could be preserved intact; in Ukraine there were few such caves. Nevertheless, as more careful search is made, relics are discovered in larger and larger numbers.

Among the oldest signs of human life yet found in Ukraine is the famous Cyril Street site in Kiev, discovered during the excavation of clay for making bricks. The relics lay under a thick layer of yellow clay, in a layer of sand forty to seventy feet below the surface, and occupying an area of two or more acres. At the bottom were found a large number of bones of mammoths, including more than a hundred tusks. In higher levels were unearthed the bones of other animals now long extinct in Ukraine, such as the lion, the hyena, and the cave bear. Some of the bones were burned and crushed and bear other signs of human touch, and with the bones were found pieces of charcoal and flint tools fashioned by man in that far-off time.

Of somewhat more recent origin is the settlement discovered later on the Desna River, near the village of Mizyn in the province of Chernihiv: it lay buried beneath two layers of yellow clay in a stratum of stones deposited by glaciers. Another typical find is that on the Udai near the village of Hontsi in the province of Poltava. It lies above a layer of yellow clay and dates from the period following the disappearance of the glacier.

The best-known and most authentic finds thus furnish us with evidences of man dating from long ago, as far back as the second half of the Diluvial period.

From these discoveries in Ukraine and from the richer ones in Western Europe we know that man had already made considerable progress in his ways of living and had risen high above the animals. He knew how to produce fire and to use it in cooking his food. He was no longer satisfied with a stick or an unworked stone, but had learned to fashion bones and stone itself: a sharp-pointed stone to be held in the hand for attacking, or a blade of some kind to be mounted on a pole to form a spear, or a scraper for skinning or for scraping leather. He even knew how to adorn bones with sketches and drawings. Decorated bones of this kind were found in the sites at Kiev and at Mizyn, and the French caves often yielded beautifully carved figurines.

In this so-called Paleolithic or Old Stone Age, however, man still lacked domestic animals. He did not yet know how to sow grain, and had to depend upon hunting for his food. He lived on meat and fish and clams. He had not learned how to make dishes, and in many other respects still had far to go.

Neolithic Culture: The Stone Age culture of the period when man was still ignorant of metals and had to make even his finest tools of stone gave way little by little to a new type. So-called Diluvial times passed into an era in which the older species of animals died out, the glaciers melted and ran off in streams, and life in Ukraine changed to something very much like that of today. Man still continued to make his implements chiefly of stone, but he learned to manufacture much better tools than had his predecessors. He was no longer satisfied to use a rough piece of rock; now he sharpened his tools with delicate taps, polished them to a fine smoothness, and learned how to drill holes in order to mount his ax-heads, hammers, or maces upon wooden or bone handles. Today one is struck with amazement that without the aid of iron man was able to drill such perfect holes with stone or bone tools, to polish his stone ax or wedge or chisel with sand alone, and to fashion a finely pointed arrowhead, knife, or sickle of flint.

There were other advances in the art of living. Man in the more ancient period had kept no domestic animals or household pets. But in the New Stone Age he kept cattle and could live on the meat and milk of his herd. He tamed the dog, his guardian and faithful companion. He learned how to make dishes of clay and to bake them in fire: he shaped them by hand, without the aid of the potter's wheel, but nonetheless he was able to make well-shaped pots and vases and to adorn them with beautiful designs. He began to build a better shelter for himself. First he excavated a shallow pit and piled up the earth around the sides; the walls he made of sticks and wattle evenly smeared with clay, covering the structure with a roof. He began to cultivate the soil, to sow grain and to grind it in a hand mill, to bake bread and to cook porridge.

The New Stone Age did not last as long as the Old, but it has left its marks everywhere in Ukraine. Clearly the number of inhabitants had grown, and the traces of their life are accordingly more plentiful. Their tools and weapons are also easier to identify than the older flints; it is often difficult to say whether these were the work of human hands or received their shape by mere chance. Dating from New Stone times there are various tools and dishes, cemeteries, and in some places traces of large villages consisting of huts and workshops and strongholds to which people could repair in time of danger. The remains of such fortresses are in some places fairly extensive, which indicates that the number of people living in the neighborhood was large.

The dead were sometimes buried in stone cists made of several slabs, sometimes in graves over which high mounds were raised. Sometimes the whole body was buried; sometimes it was cremated and the ashes and cinders were placed in a clay pot for burial. Beside the body of the dead some of his possessions were often placed, and food was provided in clay pots. Sometimes the body was smeared with a powder of red ochre, which settled onto the skeleton after the body had decomposed. Graves containing these red-stained bones occur throughout Ukraine, from the Kuban River to Bessarabia.

Of especial interest is the life in Ukraine at the very end of the period of New Stone culture, when the first metal objects, chiefly of copper, began to penetrate from neighboring countries in the south. People now lived in small huts made of wood or of plaited withes plastered with clay, and took delight in pottery of strange forms, richly decorated in red, white, rust, or polychrome. It is scarcely believable that these beautiful vessels can date from such a distant time, when people were in other respects just beginning to rise above the status of savages.

Besides the various kinds of pottery in the clay huts there are also to be found figurines made of well-baked clay, little images of men and women and domestic animals. The tools of these settlements were chiefly of flint, but by this time tools of copper and of bronze were also beginning to appear.

Villages of this type stretch from the Dnieper River at Kiev, across the district of Kiev to Podolia, into Galicia and on into Moldavia and the Balkan peninsula. They are technically known as pre-Mycenaean.

Copper, Bronze, and Iron: It has already been said that the first metal used was copper. This is because copper is the easiest metal to melt from the ore. Pure copper, however, is very soft and unfit for hard use, but it was discovered that by adding about one part of tin to ten of copper a much harder metal, bronze, could be obtained, suitable for making all kinds of utensils, weapons, and tools. In some districts this bronze was employed for a long time, until the use of iron was discovered. In Western Europe copper and bronze first appeared about 2000 B.C. About a thousand years later iron came into use. Gold became known much earlier, silver later.

In Ukraine copper and bronze arrived from the Danubian countries and from the Black Sea coast to the south. No copper mines have been found in Ukraine;* hence the use of bronze spread only along the seacoast and on the

---

* Old copper mines were found in 1903 by the Russian archaeologist, V. A. Gorodtsov, in the vicinity of Bakhmut (Editor).

more important trade routes along the Dnieper. Before it had become widely known, articles of iron began to be imported. These were not only much stronger but, what was even more important, much cheaper.

As Ukraine possessed deposits of iron ore in several localities, and the process of smelting the metal is comparatively easy, in the course of time it came into general use, though not everywhere at once. In the districts bordering on the Mediterranean Sea a knowledge of metals and of their uses had come from the countries to the south—Babylonia, Syria, and Egypt. Those lands had long had implements of bronze, and later of iron, when people in Ukraine were still using wood and stone. Thus it was only in the districts located near important trade routes that the inhabitants were acquainted with metals. In more remote regions they remained a luxury known only to the rich, and the people lived for a long time under a stone culture, although stone had elsewhere fallen into disuse.

To judge from the form and design of the objects and from other indications, it would seem that the cultural influences in this period of the early use of metal in the second and first millennia before Christ were all foreign and chiefly Mediterranean. They reached Ukraine by a variety of paths. Some came from the south (from Asia and the Mediterranean Sea) via the Black Sea coast; or by way of the Black Sea steppes from Hither Asia and Turkestan and what is now Iran. Others came from the Danubian region, from present-day Hungary and the Alpine area where various art forms had developed under Mediterranean influence. Finally, much was brought in from the west, from the Germans, for example: this is attested by words in the ancient Ukrainian language adopted from the German tongue. The Germans themselves had acquired them partly from the Romans and partly from Celts.

From these regions by various routes, especially following the rivers, new products and new skills passed into the Ukrainian country, spreading slowly into the most remote regions. Most is known of the influences which reached Ukraine by the Black Sea coast through the Greek colonies.

CHAPTER II

GREEKS AND SCYTHIANS

The Greek Colonies: As early as the seventh century B.C., or possibly even the eighth, Greek colonists began to settle along the Black Sea coast. They came from a number of different cities, fleeing from strife and warfare to seek peace and a livelihood in these outlying regions. Their countrymen had come even earlier to carry on commerce, bringing with them trinkets to exchange for local articles. In time some of them permanently settled in Ukraine.

In this manner Greek colonial settlements sprang up all along the Ukrainian coast of the Black Sea. Among the most important of the early settlements were Tyras at the outlet of the Dniester, Olbia on the estuary of the Dnieper, Chersonesus near what is now Sevastopol, Theodosia where the city of the same name lies today, Panticapaeum at Kerch, Phanagoria across the Straits, and Tanais on the site of Rostov, not to mention many other less important cities.

Wherever they settled, the Greeks introduced their own ways of life. They sowed grain, planted grapevines, caught fish, and at the same time entered into commercial relations with their neighbors. They sold them Greek wines and olive oil, Greek cloth and clothing, exquisite articles of gold and silver, and richly decorated Greek vases. In return they acquired from the natives grain, leather, furs, and other products of the land and the people, including slaves, and exported all these to parent cities in Greece. They penetrated deep into the interior with their goods, reaching far to the north. In the neighborhood of Kiev, Poltava, and Kharkiv there have been unearthed from ancient mounds the coins of the Greek colonial city-states as well as jars for wine and oil, vases, and various gold and silver products of Greek craftsmanship.

Accompanying these articles to Ukraine came the Greek arts themselves. Master craftsmen of that age, the Greeks passed on to the local inhabitants their knowledge and their skills, and even their customs and habits. Herodotus, who spent some time in Olbia in the middle of the fifth century B.C., tells the story of a Scythian ruler by the name of Scylas. His mother had come from a Greek city and had taught her son to speak and to write Greek. He had acquired so great a liking for the Greek way of life that after becoming ruler he often went to Olbia. Leaving his retainers in the suburbs, he lived among the Greeks of the city like a Greek, took part in all their activities, and then returned to the Scythians. He even built himself a home in Olbia and, without the knowledge of his people, had a wife there. In time, however, the people learned of his double life, revolted against him, and made his brother their ruler. They seized Scylas and killed him because he had renounced his native customs.

Many tribes on the other hand completely accepted the Greek ways, intermarried with the Greeks, and adopted their beliefs and habits. Thus many of the innovations brought by the Greeks were carried throughout the land as long as the Greek cities existed. And when the Greeks were themselves subjected to Rome, Roman influences penetrated into Ukraine through the Greek cities. This process went on until the Greek colonial settlements on the Black Sea fell before the onslaughts of the warlike tribes which arrived in the third and fourth centuries A.D.

The People of the Steppes: The Greeks have rendered a great service in handing down some knowledge of the tribes living in their time in the Ukrainian steppes along the Black Sea. They called the earlier inhabitants of the coast Cimmerians, but knew very little about them and their country. Homer's *Odyssey* (IX, 14), for example, describes Ukraine as a land of eternal frost and fog:

> There in a lonely land, and gloomy cells,
> The dusky nation of Cimmeria dwells;

The sun ne'er views the uncomfortable seats,
When radiant he advances or retreats;
Unhappy race! Whom endless night invades
Clouds the dull air, and wraps them round in shades.

And in the *Iliad* (XIII, 1) he says of the nomadic tribes of the Ukrainian steppes: "Zeus gazed afar on the land . . . of the lordly Hippemolgi who live on milk, and the Abii, the most just of men."

Later writers report in greater detail on these dwellers of the steppes. Tribes of Iranian origin, related to the Persians, had been living there. Some had long been settled in the Black Sea and Caucasus steppes and were being joined by new tribes, when bands of Turkish peoples from central Asia began to press upon Turkestan. Some of the steppe tribes were made up of farmers who sowed grain and lived on it. Others were genuine nomads who migrated with their herds of cattle: their food was meat, mare's milk, and cheese, and they lived in tents like the modern Kalmucks and Nogais.

In the seventh and sixth centuries B.C., and late into the fifth, when Herodotus described Olbia from a personal visit, the tribes of that neighborhood were under the control of Scythians, who gave their name to all other steppe tribes. Later on the Scythians weakened and the Sarmatians gained the upper hand. Consequently, in the fourth and third centuries B.C. the steppe tribes all became known as Sarmatians. Afterward, about the time of the birth of Christ, the supremacy passed to the Alan tribe, and in the first and second centuries A.D. their name was generally adopted.

Constant internecine warfare weakened the tribes, who had to give way before incoming hordes from Turkestan being pushed on by Turkish bands. Under this pressure the steppe dwellers were forced to keep moving westward, from the Caspian Sea to the Don River, from the Don to the Dnieper, from the Dnieper to the Danube. Some migrated into the plains of Hungary on the middle course of the Danube, others moved northward along the Dnieper. They were unable, however, to penetrate far into the forest belt, for they were accustomed to the life of the steppes with its nomadic migrations.

Thus these steppe tribes from Iran roamed about the Ukrainian steppes some thousand years, from the arrival of the Scythians to the time when they were vanquished by the Goths from the west and the Huns from the east. Eventually their remnants could be found in isolated groups only, along the Don, in the Caucasus Mountains, and in Crimea. In the Caucasus there still exists a people known as the Ossetes, the descendants of these early steppe races driven for refuge into the mountains.

Life among the Steppe Tribes: Although the steppe tribes were known by various names, they had a common origin and were alike in many ways. The ruling bands were usually savage and warlike, and the mild and submissive were subject to them. Herodotus described many of the warlike customs of the Scythians which he had learned from the Greeks living along the Black Sea coast.

A Scythian drank the blood of the first enemy killed in war. The heads of enemies were brought to the ruler, only those who presented him with heads being entitled to a share in the spoils. The warrior who killed the largest number of enemies received high honors and was handed a double portion of wine at public festivals. The Scythians scalped their enemies and, after tanning the scalps, attached them to their horses' reins or made ornaments of them. In every district was a sanctuary dedicated to the god of war, with an old iron sword as his symbol. The Scythians held an annual celebration in his honor, at which they sacrificed animals, as well as one out of every hundred prisoners taken in war, over a drinking bowl. The blood collected in the bowl was poured over their swords.

Cruel toward foreigners, they were also harsh toward their own kind. If a quarrel arose between two Scythians, particularly if they were of the same clan, they went to their ruler and fought a duel in his presence. The victor killed his opponent and made of his skull a memorial drinking bowl, which he adorned with gold and silver and displayed before his guests on special occasions.

Whenever a chief of the Scythians fell ill, sorcerers were called to determine who was responsible. The accused was seized and questioned to discover if he had caused the sickness by swearing falsely before the god of the chief's hearth, who was supposed to watch over the chief's abode. If he refused to plead guilty, other sorcerers were called in, and if they too accused him, he was put to death. If the defendant was acquitted, the sorcerer who had made the original accusation was slain by placing him upon an oxcart loaded with brush which was then set afire and the oxen turned loose on the steppe.

At the funeral of a chieftain many members of his tribe were sacrificed. His body was disemboweled and stuffed with aromatic herbs to prevent decomposition and then taken on a cart through the subject districts. At each village to which it was brought the subjects came out to meet it. Each was obliged to cut off his hair, gash one of his ears, cut or scratch his arms, forehead, and nose, and pierce his left arm with an arrow. After making the rounds of his domains the chieftain was buried on the bank of the Dnieper, not far from the rapids. At the same time one of his wives was killed and one of each class of servants and courtiers, to be buried beside their master. His horses were also killed and buried with him, and gold and silver dishes were interred. At the first anniversary of the chief's death, fifty of his finest servants and fifty horses were slaughtered, disemboweled, and stuffed with chaff, after which the corpses were placed on the dead horses around the chief's place of burial, to act as his guards. This story is no invention by Herodotus, for on the Dnieper there can be found the mounds in which chiefs were buried in the manner he describes.

In addition to these barbaric habits the steppe people also had, of course, their better qualities. Scythian friendship, the loyalty of Scythian friends, was famous. It was a fine thing to have a faithful friend in those warlike and barbarous times, and every dweller of the steppes strove to possess one. When he had found one who was faithful, loyal, and brave, he joined with him in a ceremony of brotherhood: into a cup of wine each dropped blood drawn from the veins of his arm and sprinkled his weapons with the potion. Both then drank from it with clasped hands, and thereafter the warriors considered themselves bound closer than brothers.

The Greek author Lucian collected a number of tales about such Scythian friends. He tells of a poor Scythian who courted the daughter of a king of Bosporus. In pressing his claims against those of others who prided themselves on their riches, this suitor boasted of having no herds or tents but two faithful friends. Ridicule was heaped upon him, and the princess was married to another suitor, who had gold cups, many wagons, and great herds, "valuing cattle and useless cups and heavy carts higher than good people," as the author comments. But the friends proved their worth by kidnaping the princess and killing both the bridegroom and the father.

Lucian also tells the story of a man who agreed to have his eyes gouged out in order to free his friend from slavery. Another of his accounts describes the decision of a man trapped in a burning hut with his wife and children and a wounded friend. His first act was to save his friend, leaving his wife to save herself with great difficulty, while the children perished. The Scythian, however, remarked, "I can still have more children, and there is no knowing how these might have turned out; but another friend like the one who has proved his love for me would be hard to find."

The Slavic Settlements: For centuries various bands of Scythian, Sarmatian, and Alan origin roamed the Ukrainian steppes. The Carpathian Mountains were settled by small tribes related to them, the so-called Thracians, from whom developed the later Wallachs (Rumanians). Among these were the Besses, the Kostoboks, and the Carps, from the last of whom the Carpathians took their name.

At the foot of the Carpathian Mountains in Galicia there lived Germanic tribes known as Bastarnians, who had moved in from their original homes farther north. Slavic tribes at that time lived farther to the east and north, along the Dnieper River, in the neighborhood of Kiev and farther upstream, possibly also in Volynia and Polisia, and perhaps also beyond the Dnieper. It is possible that the tribes of Neuri and Androphagi mentioned by Herodotus were Slavic peoples living in ancient settlements, for he remarks that they were non-Scythian tribes living north of the Scythians. In the writings of other chroniclers the tribes living on the middle course of the Dnieper in what is now the region of Kiev were called Amadokians. On the whole, little news reached the literate Greeks and Romans from those distant lands.

From Roman writers of the first and second centuries A.D. it is learned that Slavic villages at that period extended as far north as the Baltic Sea, to the vicinity of the Lithuanians and the Germans. The people of these settlements were known as Venetes, a name given them by the Germans. The Germanic tribe of Goths were their neighbors on the west, occupying the left bank of the Vistula River.

To the east of the Slavs were Lithuanian tribes along the Baltic shore, and beyond them various Finnish tribes. Finns at that time occupied almost all the lands along the Volga River. They later interbred with Great Russian settlers of the Slavic race, adopted their language, and finally merged with them into a single race of Great Russians. In the neighborhood of Kiev and farther west there have remained from that period extensive cemeteries known as funeral fields. In some graves complete skeletons are found, in others only ashes. With the dead were buried dishes and many other kinds of utensils. Occasionally there occur Roman coins dating from the second or first centuries B.C. and later.

The Slavs had lived in these areas since the earliest of times, and it is possible that as their neighbors moved toward the west or south they also moved. The great Slavic resettlement took place, however, later, beginning with the fourth century A.D. when the Germanic tribes left their home in the west, and the Huns cleared a space for the Slavs in the south, on the steppes and in the forest border of the steppes.

The Germanic tribes living on the Vistula, Oder, and Elbe rivers, for a long period of time advanced slowly in a southerly direction. About the third century B.C. the Germanic tribe of Bastarnians began a migration toward the Carpathian region and from there continued toward the Danube. In the second century A.D. the Goths moved from the Vistula toward the south. Unable to find a suitable home near by, they migrated as far as the Black Sea, where, dispersing the Alan tribes, they settled along the coast from the Danube to the Sea of Azov. They were a warlike people and often caused unrest by their marauding expeditions against the Roman provinces and the Greek cities on the coast.

The Goths too came to grief when the Turkish tribe of Huns broke into Europe toward the end of the fourth century. The Huns defeated and destroyed the Alans, settled about the Caspian Sea and the Sea of Azov, and attacked the Goths. Hermanaric, the old King of the Goths, was so terrified by their threats that he killed himself rather than witness the defeat of his people. As a matter of fact the Huns spread terror far and wide, contemporaries describing them as unusually savage and barbarous, hardly resembling human beings. The Goths attempted to defend themselves, but after the first disasters lost their courage and many took flight across the Danube, while others surrendered. The Huns then pushed farther westward into the plains of what is now Hungary, and with them went most of the remaining Goths, though a few lingered about the Sea of Azov, in the Crimean peninsula, and on the Caucasian coast.

Wide areas of land were thus opened up for the Slavs simultaneously to the west and to the south. These they began to occupy. The west-Slavic tribes, from which are descended the Poles, the Czechs, the Slovaks, and the now almost extinct Polabian and Pomorian tribes on the shore of the Baltic Sea, pressed against the Germanic areas along the Vistula, the Oder, and the Elbe rivers. The south-Slavic tribes, from which developed the present Bulgarians, Serbs, and Slovenes, migrated beyond the Carpathians toward the Danube and past it toward the Balkans. The southeastern Slavs, ancestors of the present Ukrainians, left their villages for the adjacent districts abandoned by the western and southern Slavs. They also went southward into the steppe region and the adjoining lands made vacant by the havoc created by the Huns. It is at this time that the ancestral Ukrainian tribes are first heard of as a separate people, apart from the Slavic tribes in general.

CHAPTER III

THE FIRST UKRAINIANS

The Ukrainian Migrations; the Antae: As long as the Slavs were living in their old homes in close proximity to one another they spoke a more uniform language, had more similar customs, and led a more common type of life than later after they had spread out over a larger territory. Yet certain differences already existed among them and these differences grew more striking after their expansion. Greeks who wrote about the Slavs as far back as the time when they were only in process of establishing colonies differentiated between those who lived in the south in the neighborhood of Byzantium, on the Danube, and in the Balkan areas, whom they called the Slavs, and others whom they named the Antae, who lived on the Dniester, farther east on the Dnieper, and on beyond to the shore of the Sea of Azov.

The oldest accounts of the Antae given us by Byzantine writers date from the fourth century, in the period following the Hunnic invasion. For the Ukrainian tribes the emergence of the Antae marks the beginning of historic life. Jordanes, the historian of the Goths, has preserved an interesting account of how the Gothic King Vinitar, one of the successors of Hermanaric, made war against the Antae. The very name Vinitar is, by the way, probably a nickname for the "conqueror of the Venetes," that is, the Slavs. In the first battle, says Jordanes, the Antae defeated the Goths, but Vinitar was undaunted and continued the war. In the end he defeated the Antae and captured their prince, Bozh, and their chiefs. To terrorize the tribe he ordered the captives put to a horrible death by crucifixion. The Huns, however, intervened, took the Antae under their protection, and defeated Vinitar.

Vinitar's war may have been the first contact of the

Antae with the Goths, a result of the colonization of the
Black Sea steppes by these first Ukrainians. At any rate
the war with the Goths failed to put a stop to their movements, nor did encounters and clashes with other local
tribes succeed in halting them. Living among the warring
tribes of the steppes, they undertook marauding expeditions in association with the Huns. They also joined the
Bulgarians (Bolgars), tribal relatives of the Huns who
later settled in the Balkan peninsula among Slavs, mingled with them, and passed on their name to them.

Among these warlike peoples the Ukrainians neglected
their farming, as did the Kozaks in a later period. They
gave up raising grain and lived wretchedly in miserable
huts. Like the earlier Greeks, they had in this period no
iron cuirasses and used whatever arms they could secure.
They were not accustomed to attack in a solid mass but to
hide in ambush, launch a sudden assault, and then scatter
in order to entice the enemy to follow them. They were
active and accustomed to hardships, and their ability to
conceal themselves, even in water, aroused the admiration
of the Greeks. They went on expeditions to the Byzantine
provinces in search of plunder, and Byzantium sometimes
hired them to attack her other enemies. It is possible that
the war which broke out in the 530's A.D. between the
Antae and their neighbors the Danubian Slavs was begun
at the instigation of the Byzantine government, which
suffered greatly from Slavic invasions. Later Greek historians relate how Byzantium incited the Antae against
the Slovenes toward the end of the sixth century.

In connection with this war between the Antae and the
Slovenes, the Byzantine historian Procopius describes
many fascinating incidents in the lives of both tribes.
Among the most interesting is the story of Chilbudius.
This famous Greek warrior ably defended the Byzantine
provinces against the attacks of the Slovenes and the
Antae but was believed to have perished in one of his ex-
peditions against the Slovenes, who thereupon renewed

their attacks. Some time later a Greek slave held by the Antae told his master that Chilbudius had not died but was living as a slave among the Slovenes, though the Slovenes did not know of it. The slave's master at once purchased Chilbudius and took him to his home, where he questioned him as to whether he was really the famous warrior. The newly purchased slave replied that he was no Greek but a member of the Antae by origin, that his name was Chilbudius, and that he had been taken prisoner during the last war. Although his master was skeptical he reported the facts to his neighbors. They were convinced of Chilbudius' identity and greatly rejoiced at having in their midst so famous a warrior. They called a council meeting such as they were accustomed to hold to settle important matters; for, as Procopius says, not having a single prince at their head, they decided everything jointly. At the meeting they enjoined upon Chilbudius to keep secret the fact that he was not the well-known soldier and they themselves notified the Byzantine emperor.

The Emperor Justinian then invited the Antae to settle in Byzantine territory and to defend Byzantium against his enemies, promising them payment for their services. The Antae agreed on condition that Chilbudius be allowed to live among them. He was sent to Constantinople in connection with these negotiations, but on his way was seized by the Byzantine general Narses and put in irons as an impostor. His arrest put an end to negotiations between the emperor and the Antae.

In the writings of Menander, another Greek historian of the time, there is an account of the struggle of the Antae against the tribe of the Avars, who invaded the Ukrainian steppes in the middle of the sixth century. They defeated the Antae, took many captive, and began to plunder their lands. The Antae sent one of their leaders by the name of Mezamir to negotiate the release of the captives and to conclude terms of peace. Mezamir was a bold and proud man who could not endure the boastful words of the Avar khagan but returned a sharp answer. One of the khagan's favorites suggested that he was evidently very influential among the Antae and might incite them against the Avars, so the khagan killed Mezamir and the Avars renewed their plundering of the Antae districts.

This disastrous invasion was long remembered by the Ukrainian people. The Kievan Chronicle contains an account of how the Obri (Avars) mistreated the Dulibs, a Ukrainian tribe living in Volynia, even hitching Dulib women to their carts. "Those Obri were large in stature, and proud in spirit, but God destroyed them; they all died and not one was left behind, so that a saying originated, 'they perished like the Obri,'" says the chronicle. As a matter of fact the Obri did not perish but passed on farther west, into Hungary.

The Ukrainian Tribes: Such misfortunes of the steppes as this Avar onslaught could not dismay the Ukrainians, accustomed as they were to every kind of hardship. They stayed on in the steppes and continued to expand eastward toward the Sea of Azov and westward as far as the Danube River. Their colonization was greatly facilitated by the fact that the Caspian steppes were dominated in the seventh century by a new tribe, the Khazars, who were less ferocious than their predecessors. As they enjoyed profitable trade relations with the towns of the Caspian and Azov coasts, the Khazars found it to their interest to maintain peace and stability. They held back fresh Turkish tribes who were pressing upon the Ukrainian steppes, and life there became more tranquil and secure. The Ukrainians began to prosper in their new villages, to develop agriculture and commerce, and to become less warlike. This development was partly for the better, but not entirely so; for when the Khazar tribe in turn began to weaken and aggressive Turkish tribes appeared in the steppes, the peaceful life of the Ukrainians had made them unable to withstand the invaders. They were forced

to abandon the steppes anew and to retire to safer regions, either into the forests on the north or into the
mountains on the west. There life was not so bountiful as
it had been on the fertile plains.

Few accounts of this period have survived. What is
known of the earlier epoch is found in the writings of the
Greeks; but in the beginning of the seventh century the
Greeks gave up their defense of this northern frontier,
as they were unable to cope with the Slovenes and the
Avars, and consequently they ceased to write about it.
For three hundred years very little was heard of the region. The last mention of the Antae is in A.D. 602, and by
the seventh and eighth centuries their very name is lost.
The accounts collected by Constantine Porphyrogenitus
in the middle of the tenth century concerning life in the
steppes do not speak of the Antae but do mention a number of separate Ukrainian tribes living in the south: these
are said to be the Uliches, the Derevlians, the Luchans,
and the Rus* in the neighborhood of Kiev.

More complete information about these tribes is given
by the Kievan chroniclers writing a hundred years later
in the eleventh century. From them it is known that east
of the Dnieper, along its branches the Desna, the Seym,
and the Sula, there lived a large tribe of Sivers, or Siverians. They already possessed important cities, Chernihiv,
Novhorod-Siversky, Lubech, and Pereyaslav. On the op-
posite shore of the Dnieper near Kiev there lived the
tribe of the Polians, also known as the Rus. Farther east
beyond the Polians, in the dense forests which in those
days stretched along the Teterev, the Usha, and the Horyn, there lived the Derevlians, that is, the "forest dwellers," and beyond the Pripet River the Drehoviches, the
"bog people." In Volynia beyond the Sluch lived the Dulibs. On the Black Sea coast near the Dnieper lived the
Uliches and farther west on the Dniester the Tivertses.
What tribes lived on the Don and the coast of the Sea of

* The *s* in "Rus" is to be pronounced softly (Rusï, Ruś).

Azov or at the foot of the Carpathian Mountains in Galicia the chroniclers do not say. But they were also Ukrainian tribes, or perhaps rather southeastern Slavic tribes, out of which developed the later Ukrainian people. Their tribal names are not known.

Ukrainian Customs: The Ukrainian tribes are said by the annalist to have differed from one another in their habits and modes of living: "each tribe had the customs, the laws, and the traditions of its own forefathers." These differences, however, were not great, and in fact the various tribes had much in common. From the accounts of the chroniclers and other Kievan sources, from descriptions by foreigners, from the finds in ancient burial mounds, and finally from the language itself there can be gleaned a fairly accurate knowledge of the mode of living of the Ukrainian tribes after they settled in what is now Ukrainian territory. Their customs differed, of course, in large and wealthy commercial cities and in remote farmsteads located in deep forests far from the world's marts of trade, just as today the customs of city people differ widely from those of dwellers in the country. These differences, however, which the annalists are prone to point out, are of no great significance. Then, as today, the people of one district loved to poke fun at those of another because of a variance in words, or pronunciation, or dress, though such matters are after all mere trifles.

It is evident that the Ukrainian people throughout the country were engaged in the growing of grain, and for the most part they made their living in this way. This may be seen from the language itself, the word *zhito,* which they used to denote grain, really meaning "the source of livelihood." The raising of grain in Ukraine dates far back to the period before metal tools came into use: the Derevlians, for instance, lived in a remote region, and the annalist of Kiev said of them that "they live like wild animals or cattle," yet they plowed and sowed the land and supported themselves with grain. In the graves of the

Derevlians and the Siverians there have been found sickles, and grains of various kinds including rye, oats, barley, and wheat. In the records almost all the present varieties of grain are mentioned except buckwheat, also many agricultural implements such as the plow, the harrow, the hoe, the spade, and the flail. The manner of tilling the soil is also described as well as that of sowing, reaping, threshing, and winnowing. The process of raising grain and making flour would thus appear to resemble that of today but for the fact that hand mills were used instead of power mills.

Several kinds of livestock were raised, but little poultry. Many Ukrainians kept bees; they used a large amount of honey, sold both honey and wax, and paid their taxes to the princes in them. Those who lived in forested regions kept bees in hollow trees, making holes in the stems so high that the bees hived in them could not be reached from the ground. Hunting, which had been an important means of subsistence, lost its primary importance as agriculture developed. The people trapped animals now more for the furs than for meat, and hunting became an amusement of the wealthy nobles and the princes.

Wild animals were, however, still plentiful. Volodimir Monomakh, the Prince of Kiev, tells of his hunting exploits in his instructions to his children. In Chernihiv, he says, "I lassoed a hundred and twenty mustangs along the Ros River; I caught horses with my bare hands; I had many adventures, two buffaloes once lifted me and my horse on their horns, a stag once attacked me with his antlers, a moose trampled me underfoot, another tried to impale me on his horns, a wild boar once tore my sword from my side, a bear ripped away a part of my saddle from beneath my very knee, a wildcat leaped upon me and threw both me and my horse to the ground."

Since wild animals and fowl were plentiful and it was easy to keep cattle in the many pastures and meadows, the people probably ate more meat than they do now.

Even so, a vegetarian diet prevailed, being composed largely of such foods as bread, porridge, and cooked vegetables. Bread was leavened with yeast and baked in ovens. Meat was usually stewed. The chief drink was mead, and all, from the poor to the princes, drank it in great quantities. A chronicler tells how Prince Volodimir ordered his servants to distribute among the poor quantities of bread, meat, vegetables, barrels of mead, and the unfermented *kvas*, the beverage of the people. How the rich gorged themselves can be inferred from an order of Prince Yaroslav concerning the fare to be provided his tax collectors: the tax gatherer and his servant were to receive daily a loaf of bread, a measure of millet and peas for porridge, two chickens, a lump of salt, and a pail of malt for beer; each week a young calf or beef; and on fast days, instead of meat, cheese and fish.

People dressed simply in shirts and trousers of linen, covered by a short jerkin or a long cloak. On their feet they wore knitted socks and leather boots or sandals, and on their heads fur or knitted caps.

In old burial grounds dating from that period there have been found remnants of linen garments. The linen is made of flax or hemp and ranges from fine to coarse. There are leather belts, and attached to them are knives, combs, and leather bags containing various tools such as flints and small whetstones. For the feet there are low, sharp-pointed little boots with tops of saffian or of a similar finely tanned leather. Women wore necklaces and neckpieces of coins threaded on wires and on their heads little caps or headdresses adorned in various ways. From their temples they suspended rings sewed to leather straps, and they also plaited rings into their braids, which still lie in rows on their bones, from the temples to the breast, following the original form of the braids.

The wealthy wore silk dresses of Greek or Arabian cloth spun with gold, of brocade, or of cloth of gold; and they further adorned themselves with chains, medallions,

gold and other metal buttons, and hammered belts. When
the Ukrainian princes entered into closer relations with
the Byzantine court they adopted from it a number of
costumes and fashions, in which they were imitated in
turn by the nobles (*boyars*) and the other wealthy people.

Characteristic Traits, Customs, and Beliefs: Foreigners praised the Ukrainians of that period for their generosity and friendliness. Especially interesting is the account of the Antae and the Slovenes (the Ukrainians and
their neighbors) given by Procopius. He described them
as being kind to foreigners, whom they received with hospitality and accompanied for a distance lest any harm befall them. Their wives were faithful and many killed
themselves on the death of the husbands. They loved freedom and resented serving others or being subject to another's authority. They were stubborn and refused to
listen to the opinions of others, and as they clung to their
own beliefs they had many quarrels and bloody contests.
Later writers described the Ukrainians and other Slavs
in similar terms: they were spoken of as a brave and warlike people who would be irresistible if only they knew
how to take common action.

They liked to make merry and to amuse themselves,
and celebrated all occasions with songs, dances, and
games. The chronicler speaks in angry tones about the
games in which villages joined and complains of the
"dancing and devilish singing" which occurred at them,
for in his mind these were connected with the old pagan
beliefs. Weddings were celebrated with "dancing, music,
and clapping of hands." A Byzantine historian relates
that Kievan soldiers amused themselves with dancing and
carousing for many nights on end. "Rus finds joy in
drinking. Without it she cannot live," says Prince Volodimir in the story of his baptism. The chronicler had evidently placed in the prince's mouth a contemporary proverb. Pagan and, later on, Christian festivities were usually
accompanied by great drinking bouts.

This generous and sunny disposition was also reflected in customs and laws. In the ancient Ukrainian law there was no capital punishment or mutilation of the guilty, no cutting off of legs, ears, or noses, as was customary among the Byzantines and early Germans. Later on the clergy, who had adopted from Byzantium not only church books but Byzantine codes of law, attempted to introduce into Ukraine corporal and capital punishments after the Greek pattern, but the people refused to accept them. They sentenced the condemned to pay fines, to imprisonment, or at worst to be surrendered into servitude so that the culprit might repay his crime with labor, but they would not shed blood or deprive a man of his life, as to do so was contrary to their convictions. The rule did not apply in war, for when killing was to be done in such a time, they considered it the will of God.

No sullen boors who envied others their happiness, they looked upon the world with clear and gay eyes. Above all, they glorified and revered the light and warmth of the world which manifest themselves in the sun, in heat, in the rank growth of plants, in all the life of nature. Procopius says that the Antae and the Slovenes of his time worshiped only one god Svaroh, the god of heaven, who sends down light and lightning. In later times various manifestations of the same god of light were known by different names. To the sun they gave the name of Khors and Dazhd, meaning "the giver of all good." To the menacing power of thunder, which rumbles and flashes during a storm, they gave the name of Perun. To fire was given the name of Svarozhich, the son of the great god Svaroh, god of heavenly light and of fire, sun, and lightning. To the senior gods belonged also Veles or Volos, the "god of cattle" and protector of animals.

Each of these gods was called *boh*, which means "good" or "weal." Of the same origin are the words *bohaty* (rich), *zbizhe* (grain), and *ubohy* (poor). Boh also denoted the bestower of every kind of welfare. The people

continued to worship all these gods even after the introduction of Christianity, except that their identities were
concealed by the names of saints. Thus various beliefs
pertaining to Perun passed from him to St. Elias, those
about Volos to St. Vlasius, and so on.

Besides these supreme deities the ancient Ukrainian
saw about him a great number of elf-like beings called
bisy. This word did not of necessity connote anything evil
at that time, though later the Christian clergy attached
the name to evil spirits. The ancient Ukrainians thought
that such beings, whom they worshiped and to whom they
made sacrifices lest they should do harm, lived in bogs,
forests, fields, and fountains; mention of this worship is
made by the clergy of the first period of Christianity, who
wrote that the people made offerings to the bisy, the bogs,
and wells, and prayed in the forests and around waters.
A great many elements of those beliefs have survived to
our day in the form of tales about water sprites, nixies,
and forest spirits, and even now in some places food is
regularly placed at wells. At present, however, these old
beliefs about devils and the like have become confused
with others pertaining to spirits of the dead who are supposed to live in houses and courtyards, while the spirits
of drowned persons become water nymphs, and so on.

There were neither special temples nor special priests
to serve these gods. Each person made his offerings personally and prayed to the gods for himself and for his kin.
An Arabian writer of the ninth century has handed down
to us the harvest prayer of the ancient Ukrainians. They
took millet in a pail, raised it to the sky, and prayed,
''Lord, Thou wast wont to give us food: give it to us now
in abundance.'' They liked to pray in secluded, quiet spots
such as over water, where man can best feel the breath of
the mysterious power which animates nature. Idols were
rare, to be found only in larger settlements.

They believed that human life does not end with death.
Those who have died in reality keep on living, and at

times make their appearance among people. Hence one should curry the favor of the deceased by arranging a splendid funeral for him, lest the dead annoy and harm one. They buried a man with various household utensils and domestic animals, and the wife of the deceased often killed herself on her husband's grave.

One such funeral is described by an Arabian who witnessed it when traveling among the Khazars and the Volga Bolgars in 922. The mourners dressed the deceased, a merchant from the country of Rus, in his very best, laid him in his boat, set up a tent over him, and placed at his side his arms, as well as food and drink. They then asked his slave women, whom he probably had brought with him to sell, if any of them cared to die with him, so that she might live with him and the souls of his parents in a beautiful green garden in Paradise. One of them consented and they killed her and placed her with the dead man. They also cut to pieces two horses, two cows, a dog, a rooster, and a hen and put them into the boat. After all these were burned the mourners erected a mound over the site of the pyre.

This account is in accordance with what is found in Ukrainian burial mounds dating from the ninth and tenth centuries. In some sections of Ukraine the bodies were buried in mounds, in others they were cremated and covered with soil, and in still others they were burned, the relics collected in a jar, and a mound erected above it. Various articles were placed beside the corpse and burned with it. Memorial services were held at the grave, with drinking, dancing, and sometimes, chiefly among the rich, with games. At such celebrations more earth was piled on the grave. Food was left, often after each meal, as is still the custom in Polisia. One's life in the hereafter was thought to be an exact counterpart of his life on earth.

The Family, Clan, and Community: A Kievan chronicler, describing the ancient Ukrainian tribes, boasted that only his fellow countrymen, the Polians, had proper customs, lived peacefully and modestly, and had regular marriages, the bride being brought to the bridegroom and her dowry delivered on the day following the wedding. Other tribes, he declared, lived like beasts, the Derevlians, the Siverians, and others having no regular wedding ceremonies but kidnaping their wives at watering places or at games arranged among the villages. Such kidnapings were usually the result of collusion with the victim. In general, however, there was but little difference between the customs of the Polians and those of the other tribes.

It was customary not only then but even later, after the introduction of Christianity, for the rich and the prominent to keep two or more wives, and often the utmost the clergy could do to limit this custom was to arrange for the legally married wife to be the chief wife. Men were divorced merely by sending the wife away and taking another in her place. It was considered proper for a wife to be faithful to her husband, and the loyalty of Ukrainian wives, and of Slavic wives in general, was widely known.

The man usually took a wife either by purchase or by kidnaping. In early times the latter method had been widely favored, but in more recent times, contemporary with the chronicler, it was merely a rite, and the kidnaping was arranged between the kidnaper and the kidnaped-to-be. Traces of this rite remain in the present-day wedding ceremony, in which the bride's relatives guard the girl and the bridegroom's best men take her by force and flee with her. In old games played among Ukrainians this form of kidnaping was even more clearly recalled. The purchase of a wife is also reënacted in the wedding ceremony of today.

The wife, purchased or kidnaped, was considered as much the husband's property as any other part of his husbandry. That is why the wife, together with his horse and hound, was killed at her husband's funeral. Later on, in more humane times, the wife was allowed to kill herself as proof of her fidelity to her husband. Evidently, however, even this custom died out during the tenth and eleventh centuries, as the Ukrainian chronicles of that period make no mention of it. In these later times the wife was highly regarded by the ancients, and for killing her a husband was obliged to pay the same penalty as for killing a man. Upon her husband's death, furthermore, the wife assumed the first place in the family and conducted the household. When the widow remarried, her children received a guardian.

Families were larger then than now. As late as a hundred years ago, and in some parts of Ukraine down even to more recent times, there were families that numbered twenty or thirty persons. The sons did not leave the household upon the death of their father, but worked the land in common, under the leadership of the oldest or the most capable member—the mother if she was still alive. Such a family, and perhaps any kind of family, was called a *rid* (clan). "Everyone lived with his clan, each clan in a place of its own, managed by the clan," wrote the Kiev chronicler in his description of ancient Ukrainian life. In still older times the clans had been larger, for even families dwelling far off were considered to be members, as Ukrainian wedding songs still recall.

In time these broad clans broke up, the ancient ties grew weak, and blood relationship began to be superseded in importance by neighborliness, by proximity not of origin but of abode. Families living close to one another, even though of different origin, conducted the various affairs which affected their region by means of a common council (*viche*) of the elders (*startsi*) of all the families. The villages were not compact settlements like those of today but each clan lived separately, "by itself," as the chronicler says, after the fashion of the Ukrainian *khutor* (homestead) in later eastern Ukraine or of villages in the Carpathian Mountains. The people were accustomed to gather on the game grounds or on the court grounds where cases were tried.

By common effort they erected for their protection a *horod* (stockade), surrounded by moats and ramparts, where in a moment of danger they could bring together their old and young, their wives and children, and their property. All Ukraine is strewn with ancient stockades which served as havens of safety in Stone Age times of danger, and there are more recent ones dating from the period of the princes. Among them are found small forts, capable of housing a single family clan, whereas the larger could shelter many people. Most of them usually stood empty, except in time of danger, but some became important centers of settlement. Thus around a horod there grew up an *ostroh,* a town protected by fortifications. Merchants moved into them and introduced market days, and many degrees of officials, the wealthy, and the prominent also made their homes there. In time the horod became the chief town of the entire region; its decisions became binding upon the adjoining villages, and its name came to be applied to the inhabitants of the whole surrounding district. The ancient clan of "Dulibs" disappeared, to be replaced by the Buzhans and Volynians, whose names came from the towns of Buzhsk and Volyn. The tribes of Chernihiv and Pereyaslav came into being about the towns of those names in the former region of the Siverians, and the Turiv and Pinsk tribes in the land formerly known as that of the Drehoviches.

Commerce: Among the factors which raised some cities to positions of greater importance than others were commerce and commercial routes. It has been noted that there had been a well-established trade between the interior and the Greek cities on the Black Sea and also with certain Caspian and Turkestan areas. This trade fell into the hands of the Ukrainians when they finally occupied Ukraine. At first they traded with the Greek cities remaining in Crimea and on the Danube, but soon began to enter into commerce with Byzantium and its capital Constantinople, or Tsarhorod, as it was known. They exported furs, wax, honey, and slaves, and imported from the "Greeks," as the Byzantines were called, fine cloths, gold and silver objects, wine, and pottery. The trade routes, however, became dangerous when the steppes were invaded by nomadic tribes of Pechenegs, and consequently commerce could be carried on only in large caravans under the protection of strong guards.

A description of the method by which a trading caravan of this kind made its way to Constantinople is given by the Greek emperor Constantine Porphyrogenitus. In the winter timber was cut in the extensive forests on the Dnieper and boats were built, which were floated in spring on high water to cities farther downstream, particularly to Kiev, where rudders and other rigging from boats used in previous years were attached and preparations were made for the main journey. Meanwhile the merchants had been gathering their wares.

In June the flotilla left Kiev. It made a three-day stop at Vitichev to wait for the belated, and then set sail down the Dnieper, always on the lookout for marauding Pechenegs who lay in ambush for them. Especially dangerous was the portion of the route which lay near the Dnieper rapids. As it was impossible to take the boats through the various cataracts without wrecking them, the merchants were obliged to carry both their wares and their boats on their backs. The slaves who were being taken along for sale, in chains to prevent their escape, assisted in making the portage, while the merchants kept an eye on them and also kept watch against the Pechenegs.

Once the caravan had safely passed the rapids it rested for a time at the island of St. George, upon which the Kozak fortress of Khortitsia was later to be erected. Here under a tall oak tree offerings, usually of bread and meat, were made to the gods in thanksgiving, and prayers sent up for a continued safe journey; chickens were also offered and lots were drawn to decide whether to kill the chickens as a sacrifice or to set them free. Another overnight stop was made on the island which is now called Berezan, in the estuary of the Dnieper near the Black Sea. Hugging the coast, the party then proceeded to Constantinople, where a suburb located in the port near the Church of St. Mamant was set aside for the Ukrainian traders, of whom, at times, there were hundreds present.

Commerce had to be conducted by men who knew not only how to trade but how to fight in defense of themselves and their wares. These men were therefore both traders and warriors, who did not hesitate to engage in plundering on the side. The Greek emperors did not like to trade with them but dared not stop because of their fear of the Kiev princes. The emperors demanded of them, however, credentials to show that they were actually traders and not merely warriors, and kept a strict watch over them. They were permitted to enter the city only by a certain gate, in groups of no more than fifty persons under the supervision of Byzantine officials.

Ukrainian trade also extended in another direction. Considerable commerce was carried on with the ancient capital of the Khazars at Itil, situated on the estuary of the Volga on the site of modern Astrakhan, where Arabian and Persian goods were obtainable. Due to the efforts of the Khazar khagans, their capital had become a great commercial center, frequented by merchants from many lands. Here could be bought in great quantities luxurious cloths, clothing, and many kinds of glass and metal objects, all brought in from distant regions on the backs of camels or by boat across the Caspian Sea. As the trade with Itil and the other large center of Bolgar on the Volga, near modern Kazan, was not extensive enough to suit the Ukrainian traders, they pushed farther down the Caspian Sea to the Persian cities, and from there to the famous market places of the Arabian Caliphate. They sold much the same goods as to the Byzantines, receiving in exchange oriental goods which they carried to their own land as well as to the towns of the western Slavs and even of the Germans. By this means a large quantity of Arabian money came into Ukraine.

The Princes and Their Retinues: In view of the methods of carrying on commerce and the warlike character of the traders, it can be readily understood that the commercial centers of Ukraine became at the same time military and political centers. For the protection of commerce in those turbulent and dangerous years military power was indispensable; where commerce developed there also developed military power, for without it no journey was possible, and even to remain at home was unsafe. Kiev thus became the largest center in Ukraine, its location enabling it to become the focus of trade flowing down the Dnieper and its main tributaries, the Pripet and the Desna, both of which enter the river above Kiev. The report of Constantine Porphyrogenitus indicates that all river traffic converged upon Kiev, which also became the military and political capital of Ukraine.

There is a dearth of information as to the exact steps in the process of consolidation of the power of Kiev. It is not discussed in the chronicles and narratives, for reports of the expansion of this power did not reach the Greeks, and Ukrainian literature did not develop until later. The oldest chronicles of Kiev were not written until after the memory of the first princes had been dimmed by time, and the chroniclers could present only their conjectures as to how they rose to power.

The Greek writers of the sixth century do say that the Antae were not ruled by a single head but by a general council. When leaders appeared they lacked military power and so had no real authority. A book on Byzantine military science generally credited to the Emperor Maurice and written in the second half of the sixth century declares that the Slovenes and the Antae had a large number of chiefs, called *rix*, which in the ancient language meant a chief or master and was of the same stem as the Latin word *rex*. These chiefs did not live in harmony with one another, and were able to unite and to delegate supreme authority to one of their number, even for a definite period, only in the face of danger.

A Kiev chronicler commenting about Mal, the Prince of the Derevlians, and his struggles with the princes of Kiev, refers to various petty princes of the time as rulers in name only because they had no military forces at their disposal. They had to depend upon the commune and the "elders," who were the leaders of prominent clans. Thus the neighboring centers of population and trade were unable to offer any serious resistance to the expansion of Kiev when this city acquired an army in the form of the retinue of its prince.

Whether other Ukrainian localities produced leaders as strong as those of Kiev is not known. Masudi, the Arabian author who was writing in the time of Prince Ihor in the first half of the tenth century, refers to a powerful nation among the Slavs called the Valinana. It is generally believed that he was speaking of the Volynians, who at that time had strong rulers but were later conquered by the Kievans. Still, there is some uncertainty since the very name differs in different copies of the manuscript. But one fact is certain: Kiev had strong princes as its rulers.

CHAPTER IV

THE FOUNDING OF KIEV

Kievan Traditions: Various accounts of the origin of Kiev
were recorded in the ancient Kievan chronicles. According to one version there was a ford across the Dnieper
River, in charge of a man named Kiy, and it was from him
that the town received its name. One legend was that he
and two of his younger brothers, Shek and Khoriv, built
the first settlement on the site of Kiev and named it after
the oldest brother. Kiy is said to have lived in the old
quarter of the city where the Tithe Church was later
erected, Shek lived on the site of Cyril Street on a hill
named after him, and Khoriv on the so-called Khorivitsia
Hill. The Lebed Stream near Kiev was believed to have
been named after a sister, Lebed. For their common protection the men built a fort on the hill where Kiy lived,
and named it Kiev. The princes of the Polians were said
to have been descended from these brothers.

Because the Polian tribe at Kiev had no princes and no
armed forces, it suffered from the attacks of the neighboring Derevlians and others. The Khazars who exacted
tribute from tribes east of the Dnieper also collected from
the Polians, each householder of Kiev being obliged to
contribute a sword. The Khazar elders, however, did not
take kindly to this form of payment; they considered the
swords an ill omen and predicted that the Polians would
eventually gain supremacy over them and other tribes because they had the advantage of using two-edged swords,
while the Khazars used single-edged.

It is clear that there was no definite knowledge as to the
origin of the Kievan dynasty, the names of Kiy and his
descendants were probably taken from the names of
Kievan villages, just as legends have grown up about
other places, of which the origins are not known. Simi-

larly, Kharkiv was said to have been founded by a man named Kharko, Chernihiv by a certain Cherniha, and so on. Such an imaginative reconstruction of the past has been common not only in Ukraine, but in many other countries as well.

Of the ancient Kievan princes, Askold, Dir, and Oleh (Oleg) were remembered because their graves were preserved. All that was known about Prince Ihor (Igor) was that he was the father of Sviatoslav and the grandfather of Volodimir, and that his wife's name was Olha (Olga, Helga). The princes and other rulers of the later period were known, but as to the early ones, nothing could be said with certainty about their dynasty or when it reigned. Of some there were legends, of others nothing remained but a name and a grave.

Some of the legendary accounts assert that the first prince was Kiy; then came Askold, Dir, Ihor, and Oleh, Ihor's military governor. On the basis of these legends and traditions an ancient chronicler attempted to write a history of the Kiev state, but even this oldest chronicle has not been accurately preserved. Many changes were introduced, while the accounts of the early princes vary considerably. The work of these early chronicles is, therefore, not to be greatly relied upon.

Apparently all Kievan traditions traced the Kievan dynasty back to Kiy as the founder of the city. In the tenth century, however, there were so many Scandinavian warriors at the royal palace in Kiev that a few writers conceived the idea that members of this Norse band, known in Kiev as Varangians, had been the first princes. One of the chroniclers so altered the records as to support a new theory that not only the dynasty of Kievan princes but even the name of Rus had originated from these Scandinavians. The name Rus was first applied to the land occupied by the tribe of the Polians, but later to the whole territory ruled by Kiev, to be at last superseded by the

name Ukraine.* This particular chronicler wrote that the
Varangians who accompanied the princes of Kiev were
called "Rus" (people of Rus) and that for this reason the
name Rus came to be applied to Kiev and to the Polian
districts.

The Kievan Chronicle: The Kievan Chronicle, in the
form in which it has been preserved, describes the beginning of Rus-Ukraine and her princes as follows. The dynasty of Kiy ruled over the Polians but finally died out,
leaving Kiev without a ruler. Two brothers, the Varangian warriors Askold and Dir, who had come from Novgorod, seized power and made themselves princes. Varangians were at this time ruling over Novgorod and holding
in subjection a number of northern Slavic and Finnish
tribes. They received tribute from the Kriviches and the
Meres, but in time these tribes revolted and drove them
out. Because of the ensuing anarchy, the northern Slavic
tribes finally invited the Varangians to send them a new
ruler. In reply to the invitation, three brothers—Rurik,
Sineus, and Truvor—arrived from Scandinavia and settled down with their warriors to rule over Novgorod. To
extend their sway they sent out bands of followers to
seize adjacent territory. Among these followers were
Askold and Dir, who went down the Dnieper River as far
as Kiev, learned that the city was without a ruler, and
seized power. They were not to rule long, however, because Ihor (Igor), the son of Rurik, and his captain Oleh
conquered a number of towns along the Dnieper and finally reached Kiev. By means of treachery both Askold
and Dir were slain, the assassin Ihor explaining, "You
are neither princes nor of royal blood; I am a prince and
should rule." The tomb of Askold is still to be seen on a
hill on the bank of the Dnieper not far from Kiev. Ihor
now began to reign in Kiev; thus the Varangians became

* The name Ukraine is first mentioned in the chronicles under A.D. 1187
(Editor).

rulers not only over Novgorod but also over Kiev, and from them, the chronicler says, the name of Rus was derived.

Though the foregoing account is given by an annalist who made alterations in the original Kievan Chronicle, it has been accepted at face value by later historians. But the story calls for questioning. For several of his statements the annalist evidently had no definite knowledge and merely guessed at the facts. For instance, he did not know that Oleh was the Prince of Kiev and not merely a military captain under Ihor. How then can his statements that Askold and Dir were Varangian warriors and that Ihor was the son of a king of Novgorod of the Varangian dynasty be believed? It is not likely that the name of Rus was brought to Kiev by the Varangians of Novgorod, for, if so, why was it not applied to Novgorod as well as to Kiev, the country of the Polians? Moreover, it is difficult to believe that the dynasty of Kievan rulers came from Novgorod in two contingents in rapid succession, Askold and Dir coming first, and then Ihor and Oleh a few years later to replace them.

Since we cannot wholly accept the accounts of the Kiev chronicler and have no other records, the early history of Ukraine remains obscure. It is better to admit that there are gaps in our knowledge than to accept mere conjecture as truth. In this respect the history of Ukraine is not unique: for many other countries the remote past is not precisely known, as it is not until a country is well developed and a literature has appeared that chroniclers undertake to keep exact records and to try to account for the events of their own times and those of the recent past. For the time of Volodimir and for part of the period of his father there are accurate records, but for the more remote past there are only legends and scanty descriptions by foreigners.

*Rus:** Foreigners of the ninth and tenth centuries, as

* As the following constitutes one of the fundamental arguments of

well as the people living in and about Kiev, called the Ukrainian princes and their armed followers Rus or Ruski, and their country Rus. The conjecture of the ancient chronicler that the name Rus was brought by the Varangians from Sweden cannot be correct, for in Sweden there were no such people, and the Swedes themselves were never known by such a name in Ukraine. We do not know the origin of the word, and should not attempt to guess at an answer; but it is important to note that the name was closely attached to Kiev, and that reports concerning Rus and the Rus band of warriors in the foreign sources of the ninth and tenth centuries refer to the Kievan rulers, to the princes and retainers whose capital was Kiev.

An Arabian author of the ninth century describes Rus as follows; "It has neither land, nor villages, nor farms, but the inhabitants live from the fur trade, chiefly in sables. Rus attacks the Slavic countries, takes prisoners, and sells them as slaves in Itil and Bolgar. Whenever a son is born to Rus parents, his father lays a naked sword beside him and says, 'I shall leave you no wealth: your wealth shall be whatever you can gain with this sword.' "

The neighboring peoples knew the Kievan state of Rus as a country of soldiers and merchants: her people attacked neighboring lands, plundered them, took slaves and traded them at the market. There was a close connection between war and trade: the merchant was a warrior, and the warrior a merchant who brought his spoils of war to the market to sell them or to exchange them for ornaments and weapons. Kiev, the center of Ukrainian trade, was also the military center of the country. Constantine Porphyrogenitus, who lived a hundred years later than the Arabian writer, left a description of the course of life in Ukraine at this period: "At the beginning of No-

Ukrainian nationalists, and the whole problem of "the Rus" is still being debated, Professor Hrushevsky's statement appears here in its original form (Editor).

vember the princes with all their officials leave Kiev and
go south to collect taxes from the Slovenes, the Derevlians, the Drehoviches, the Kriviches, the Siverians, and
other subject Slavic tribes. In this way they spend the entire winter, and in April when the ice thaws on the Dnieper they return to Kiev. Here they equip boats and sail
down the Dnieper to the Byzantine markets.''

The Kievan warrior bands of the ninth and tenth centuries were made up of both local inhabitants and immi-
grant Varangians. In the first half of the tenth century
there were so many Varangians at the court of the Prince
of Kiev as agents and as military chieftains that they
quite overshadowed the local inhabitants. Among the lists
of envoys and other agents of the Prince of Kiev, as recorded in the official documents of Byzantium of the
years 907, 911, and 944, there were more Scandinavian
names than Slavic, and there were also many Varangians
in the prince's retinue at home. At this time anarchy
reigned in Norway and Sweden, and the resultant spirit
of restlessness caused many chiefs and their followers to
move into other lands to establish themselves as rulers or
to enter the service of others.

Until the death of Prince Yaroslav in the eleventh century, we find Scandinavians in the service of the Ukrainian rulers. They were brave, bold, and eager warriors,
and since they were not connected in any way with the
country or its inhabitants, were loyal to their sovereigns
and could be relied upon for both foreign and domestic
warfare. Because there were so many Scandinavians in
the Kievan state the entire country was often regarded as
Scandinavian or Norse; and for this reason the Kievan
chronicler, as already said, invented the fiction that the
name Rus had been brought over from Sweden.

Early Rus Campaigns: Frequent reference to the campaigns of the Kievan rulers against neighboring lands begin to appear in the ninth century. The invaders plundered the southern shore of the Black Sea and the coast

of Asia Minor, from Constantinople to Sinope, and attacked the city of Amastris. A report of the expedition
has been preserved in the *Life of St. George of Amastris*.
In the *Life of St. Stephen of Surozh* there is an account of
how the Rus army under the leadership of Prince Bravlin
plundered the southern coast of Crimea. As such attacks
upon Byzantine cities along the Black Sea coast were
probably frequent, the Byzantine government made a
treaty with the Kievan princes in 839. After the treaty
was signed the Byzantine emperor sent the Rus envoys on
to Germany and asked the German emperor to provide
for their safe return home, as the direct route from Byzantium was blocked by enemies. In spite of the treaty the
Rus attacks on Byzantium were soon renewed, the most
severe coming in 860, when ten thousand men sailing in
two hundred boats hurled themselves upon Constantinople.

The Byzantine emperor was waging war in Asia Minor
and had left his capital unprotected. When the invaders
began to plunder the countryside the terrified populace
sought refuge behind the walls of the city; in order to
lessen their fears the Patriarch directed that a sacred relic
of the Virgin Mary be carried ceremoniously around the
city walls. The procession and the prayers are said to
have caused a miracle, for the Rus departed. In later
years the legend arose that when this relic was lowered
into the sea a terrible storm came up and drove the enemy
away, but the fact of the matter was that the army had
learned that the emperor was returning from Asia Minor
and to avoid battle had decided to retire.

This bold attack upon Constantinople induced the
Greeks to seek the favor of the people of Rus. They sent
envoys to the Rus princes with precious gifts of silk and
gold-embroidered garments. The bishop who accompanied
the envoys converted a number of the Rus to Christianity.
According to a Greek account the people demanded a
miracle: they asked the bishop to place his Gospel in a

fire, and if it remained intact they would allow themselves
to be baptized. The bishop did as he was asked and the
Gospel remained unharmed; as a result many people were
baptized. It is noteworthy that similar stories of miracles
involving the Gospel recur frequently in the chronicles.

Besides the expeditions undertaken against Byzantine
cities, the bands of Rus also invaded the Caspian coast
from time to time. An onslaught upon the southern coast
of the Caspian Sea in 870 is mentioned by one of the later
Arabian writers in his history of Tabaristan. Another
took place in 910, and after this there were still others.

There is plenty of material describing the type of life
of Rus, but neither the Byzantine nor the Arabian writers
indicate by what title the warriors and princes called
themselves. Ninth-century Arabian sources and the German chronicler who mentioned the arrival of the Rus envoys at the court of the emperor in 839 spoke of the
Ukrainian princes of that time as khagans, a Khazar title
frequently applied both then and later to Kievan and
other Ukrainian princes, including Volodimir.

When the Kievan chronicler came upon the Byzantine
sources describing the campaign of 860 against Constantinople he assumed that it was led by Askold and Dir, in
the belief that they were the rulers of Kiev; there was
some justification for this, for whether all the expeditions
originated in Kiev or not, the fact remains that Kiev was
powerful enough to undertake such campaigns. The Patriarch Photius declared in a sermon at Constantinople
that the raid of 860 was the result of overweening pride
on the part of the Rus after their conquest of neighboring
tribes.

The treaty of 944 between the Byzantine emperor and
Prince Ihor states that besides Ihor himself twenty "noble and grand princes and great boyars" had sent their
envoys to Constantinople. Several decades later a delegation of about the same number accompanied Princess
Olha on a mission to the Byzantine capital. The large

number of nobles and officials "subject to the Prince in Kiev" referred to in Oleh's treaty itself indicates that he ruled over a large domain. It is known that in the decade following the year 940 there was a prince in Kiev whose name was Ihor and that his young son Sviatoslav was made ruler of Novgorod, at the northern end of the Dnieper highway. The southern end was also in the hands of the Kievan rulers, as would appear from their expeditions against Crimea and the coast of the Black Sea and from the presence of princes of Rus in Tmutorokan on the Straits of Kerch. The Turkish invasions and the resulting annihilation of the people in the Black Sea steppes subsequently put an end to Kievan control over the southern trade route.

At the beginning of the tenth century the ruler of Kiev had his governors in the country of the Siverians: even the Don region was gradually conquered and the way opened to the Caspian Sea. All the eastern Slavs and even a few Finnish settlements in the Volga region and the Lithuanian lands in the west were then governed by the Prince of Kiev. The entire territory which later belonged to the Kievan state was already under the rule of Prince Oleh, although his grip over it was not as yet firm.

Prince Oleh: There is but scant information concerning such early rulers as Bravlin, Askold, and Dir. The Kievan chroniclers had heard of the last two but could furnish no reliable information about them. Even the story that they were brothers who came to Kiev from Novgorod, led the expedition against Constantinople, and finally perished at the hands of Oleh or Ihor is no more than conjecture. It seems certain that Askold and Dir were not brothers and that they did not rule jointly. The fact that a church was built over the grave of Askold may indicate that he was ruling over Kiev at the time when the Greek bishop accompanied the envoys to Ukraine and "baptized many." Some years later the Arabian writer Masudi mentions Dir, who apparently outlived Askold, but who had been forgotten by the time of Yaroslav, when the chronicles were being written. The memory of Prince Oleh, however, who ruled in Kiev at the beginning of the tenth century, remained fresh in the minds of the people, his name being commemorated in song and story. The people not only made of him a great warrior but also attributed to him a magical ability to turn himself into an insect, a bird, or a beast: thus the real Oleh was lost sight of.

Historical ballads, known as *bylini,* sang of Prince Oleh as Volha Vseslavich (son of Vseslav), thus combining stories about Olha and Oleh with others concerning the "miracle worker," Prince Vseslav. One such song runs as follows:

> The red sun had gone to rest
> Behind the dark forests and the wide seas;
> The stars were planted thickly over the clear sky
> When Volha Vseslavich was born
> In Holy Rus.
> There grew Volha Vseslavich until his fifth year;
> Then went Volha Vseslavich out over the earth.
>
> Mother Earth trembled;
> The wild beasts in the forests fled;
> The birds under the clouds flew away;
> Fishes in the blue seas were dispersed.
> So went Volha Vseslavich
> To study all the secret wisdom—
> All the languages, different tongues.
> When Volha grew to be seven
> And looked as though he were twelve,
> He learned this secret wisdom—
> Many languages, different tongues.
> He had selected a bold druzhina [retinue],
> Good and brave soldiers,
> Thirty youths less one;
> Himself took the place of the one.
> "Oh, my brave and good soldiers,
> Listen to me, your elder brother Otaman,

Obey my orders:
Spin the silk threads,
And tie the strings in the dark woods,
Set the nets over the land
And catch me martens and foxes,
Wild beasts, black sables,
Jumping white rabbits,
The white jumping rabbits.''
They hunted for three days and three nights. . . .
The orders of their elder brother Otaman were obeyed;
They tied the silk threads
And set them in the dark forests, over the land.
Though they hunted three days and three nights,
They could not catch a single beast!
Therefore Volha himself became a lion.
He ran over the dark forests and the land,
Chasing the foxes and the martens,
The wild beasts, black sables,
The jumping white rabbits.
He was in the city of Kiev
With his brave soldiers.
So said to them Volha Vseslavich:
''You are good and brave soldiers!
Listen to your elder brother Otaman,
Obey the given orders—
Make the traps of silk threads,
Set them in the dark forests,
In the dark forests on the tops of the trees.
Catch geese, swans, and bright falcons,
And all the small birds.
Catch them three days and three nights.''

They listened to their elder brother Otaman,
Obeyed the given order,
Made the silk traps,
Set them in the forest over the tops of the trees,
Snaring birds three days and three nights
But could not catch any!
Therefore Volha became a bird himself.
He flew under the clouds,

Chasing the geese, swans, and falcons,
And the small game.
Again they came to the city Kiev,
Volha and his brave soldiers.
Thus addressed them Volha Vseslavich:
"Oh, my good and brave warriors!
Listen to your elder brother Otaman,
Obey the given order—
Take ye the hatchet to chop wood,
Build a boat out of an oak tree,
Tie to it the silk nets,
Sail in it on the blue sea,
Catch the fish big and small,
The very rare pike.
Catch ye them three days and three nights."
They listened to their elder brother Otaman,
Executed the given orders,
Took the axe to chop wood,
Built the oak boat,
Tied to it silk nets,
Sailed on the blue sea,
Fishing three days and three nights—
But could not catch any fish.
Volha became a rare pike himself,
He went swimming all over the blue sea,
Chasing the fish big and small,
The very rare pike.

The ancient chronicles contained many legends about Oleh, all portraying him as a man of great wisdom. Fortunately there is documentary evidence in the form of a fully preserved treaty made by Oleh with Byzantium in 911, that he ruled over Kiev at the beginning of the tenth century. The chronicles also give portions of another treaty made in 907.

The chronicler informs us that these treaties were made after Oleh's successful attack upon Constantinople; that Oleh with his entire army, together with the reinforcements sent him by his subject tribes, marched on Constantinople in 907; and that the Byzantines, in order to prevent his landing, tied chains across the Bosporus; but that Oleh outwitted them. He ordered his soldiers to set "the boats on wheels," and when the wind blew into the sails, the boats moved forward on land toward the gates of the city. The Byzantines became so alarmed at this sight that they pleaded with Oleh to take any kind of tribute but not to destroy the city. Thereupon Oleh demanded six pounds of silver for each soldier and for the princes who were left in Kiev, Chernihiv, Pereyaslav, and the other cities. He also ordered the Byzantines to make him new sails of the famous Byzantine sailcloth. As a sign of victory he and his chiefs suspended their shields over the gate of Constantinople.

Too much reliance should not be placed upon such stories. Judging, however, by the generous concessions made by the Byzantines in the treaties of 907 and 911, it seems probable that there must have been successful Rus attacks upon Byzantium, though they may not have been against Constantinople itself. In return for these treaties Prince Oleh promised to permit his warriors to enter the service of the Byzantine emperor.

From the Arabian writer Masudi it is learned that as soon as Rus made peace with Byzantium, she immediately turned east in search of further conquests and plunder. Near the close of 913 she sent a great expedition into the Caspian Sea region. In five hundred ships carrying a hundred men each the Rus sailed down the Don, portaged their boats to the Volga, entered the Caspian Sea, and plundered the rich commercial region of Tabaristan on its southern shores. As the local garrisons were not at home to defend the district, the invaders overran and sacked it without encountering resistance. On their journey home, however, they met disaster at the hands of a force of Khazars who ambushed and defeated them. The chronicle does not mention this event, but recollections of this and similar expeditions were preserved in a song telling

of the expedition of a Prince Volha against "India"
(Persia):

> Volha was then fully alert;
> With his brave warriors
> He marched at once upon
> The famous Indian kingdom.
> The soldiers fell asleep, but Volha did not.
> Like a wolf he ran and leaped in the forest,
> Springing in the dark thickets
> And, killing the beasts,
> Would not permit wolf or bear to pass by.
> There were sables in great abundance;
> He also saw rabbits and foxes.
> He watered and fed his brave army.
> He gave to his brave youths shoes and clothing;
> They wore sable cloaks
> In place of their coats of horse hide.
> The soldiers fell asleep, but Volha did not sleep;
> He became a falcon,
> Flying far away over the blue sea,
> Killing the geese and white swans;
> And the little gray ducks he would not let go either.
> He watered and fed the brave army,
> Giving them various foods.
>
> Thus began Volha his discourse:
> "Oh, handsome and brave youths,
> You are indeed many, seven thousands.
> Is there among you a man
> Who would become a brown bison,
> And run into the Indian kingdom,
> To learn of that land?"
> Like grass and leaves
> All his soldiers bowed down.
> The handsome and good youths said to him,
> "No, there is not among us such a youth—
> Except you, Volha Vseslavich."
>
> Now Volha Vseslavich
> Became a buffalo with golden horns.

He ran away into the Indian kingdom.
With a bound he cleared a mile,
The second bound removed him from their sight.
Then he became a falcon,
And flew into the Indian kingdom.
He sat on the top of a white palace,
At the window of the Indian king—
The king was talking to his queen.
Thus spoke the Queen Asbiakivna:
"Oh, thou famous Indian king,
Thou desirest to attack the distant Rus,
But thou dost not know
When the moon lightened the clear sky
In Kiev was born a mighty hero.
He will oppose thee, O king!"
Now Volha was full of comprehension.
He listened to all of this conversation.
He became now a sly weasel
And entered into the armory.
He bit and weakened the bowstrings;
He extracted all the arrowheads,
Then buried them in the ground.
Again he became a gray wolf.
He leapt to the horse stable,
Selected the better horses
And tore their throats straightway asunder.
Once more he became a falcon,
Ascended high into the sky,
Flew away into the open fields,
Then to his brave army.
"Wake up, handsome, good boys,
Oh, my brave and loyal army!
This is not the time to sleep, wake up.
Let us go into the Indian kingdom."
So they advanced as far as the white stone wall,
A strong, white stone wall
Containing iron gates;
The beams and crossbars were of copper.
The gates were like fish teeth,
Cunningly designed.

Through the spaces only an ant could pass.
Here all of the youths became saddened:
"We shall lose our heads in vain.
How can we cross these walls?"

Youthful Volha, full of understanding,
Became an ant,
Then changed his youths into ants,
Until they found themselves within the walls,
In the famous Indian kingdom—
Here he made them soldiers again,
And they stood in the spirit of war
Ready to receive his orders.
"Oh, ye brave soldiers!
March over the Indian kingdom,
Kill both the old and young,
Do not leave the least of the seeds,
Leave only what you choose—
Not much, not little, seven thousand
Beautiful souls—maidens."

Here Volha became a king,
Took for his wife Asbiakivna,
And his brave army
Married all the maids.
He gave them much gold and silver,
Numbers of horses and cows,
For each soldier hundreds of thousands.

Ihor and Olha: Ihor (914–945) succeeded Oleh as Prince
of Kiev. His treaty with Byzantium, like Oleh's, has been
preserved and with it much historical information pertaining to the remaining years of his reign. There are detailed descriptions of his attacks upon Constantinople and
his expedition to the Caspian Sea. The first years of a
prince's reign were spent in strengthening his position
and subduing disloyal officials, provinces, and tribes. After
these things were accomplished and the prince had raised
a strong and loyal army, he attacked wealthy and distant
countries in order to gain military fame and booty.

After Oleh had signed his treaty with Byzantium, the two nations were on friendly terms for many years. The Kievan army aided Byzantium on a few occasions, both in suppressing uprisings at home and in assisting in foreign wars. The memoirs of Constantine Porphyrogenitus contain an account of the payment of a hundred pounds of gold to seven hundred Rus soldiers who took part in a Byzantine expedition against Arabia in 910. This incident became the basis of a ballad.

By 940 the Byzantine-Rus treaty had terminated and in the following year Ihor directed a large naval expedition against Constantinople. The Byzantines estimated that there were ten thousand Rus vessels, but this was no doubt an exaggeration. Ihor selected as an appropriate occasion for the expedition a time when the Byzantine navy was fighting against the Arabs. He was able to advance without interference nearly to Constantinople but the Byzantines collected enough ships to block the passage through the Bosporus and then fought Ihor with the aid of Greek fire.* Repulsed by the Byzantines the Rus vessels departed from the vicinity of Constantinople and went off to plunder the shores of Asia Minor, where they sacked cities, tortured the inhabitants, and seized booty. In the end their good fortune deserted them, for the returning Byzantine navy defeated them. Though the expedition was unsuccessful it was proclaimed in Kiev that the frightened Byzantines had paid a heavy tribute. The new treaty signed with Byzantium in 944 indicates that the emperor took advantage of his victory to limit the privileges of the Rus merchants; at the same time Ihor promised that he would not attack the Byzantine towns in Crimea.

In 944 another, more successful expedition was directed against the coast of the Caspian Sea. Much was written at the time about this campaign by the local scribes. Later

* A flame thrower, the exact nature of which is not known; it is thought to have involved the use of petroleum or gunpowder (Editor).

on, in the twelfth century, a famous Persian poet, Nizami, described it in a fantastic poem. On one side was the Prince of Kiev with an army of nine hundred thousand mounted on elephants; opposing him was Alexander the Great, who had come to punish him for the sack of his cities, and who, after seven battles, expelled the invaders. As a matter of historical fact, the Rus army was inferior in numbers, but succeeded in obtaining heavy booty and departing unpunished. Remembering their previous experience of being attacked from ambush, they returned home overland by way of the northern Caucasus, going up the River Kura into the region now known as Karabah, at that time a possession of Arabia. They attacked this province, subdued it, settled there, and became masters of the capital Berdaa, on the River Kura. From there they plundered the neighboring districts for many months until disease broke out among their warriors, caused, it was reported, by eating too much local fruit; as a result they were forced to return home.

Descriptions of life in Ukraine in this period would be of greater interest than the lengthy records of expeditions against foreign lands, but unfortunately such information is very scarce. From the treaty of Ihor and the writings of Constantine Porphyrogenitus, however, it is evident that the Kievan princes ruled over a vast territory extending as far north as Novgorod and east to the cities on the Volga River. In the early chronicles some information has been preserved about the Kievan princes and their wars with neighboring tribes who were forced into obedience and the payment of tribute, and about subject princes and governors who frequently revolted against their Kievan rulers. In addition, some descriptions of the everyday life of a warrior have been preserved in Ukrainian and foreign folk songs. Old Ukrainian Christmas carols tell of winter expeditions into the hinterland to collect tribute: each settlement was canvassed and the spoils divided. The prince selected the best, while the warriors complained that they had to take what was left. The old Kievan Chronicle, which was written a hundred years after most of these events, is fresher, but is to be taken rather as a poetical portrayal of the past than as fact.

The success of the expedition of Ihor against Byzantium has been noted. Equally profitable were the later expeditions of his son Sviatoslav. At the same time changes were taking place in the interior of the Kievan state. We do not have the facts before us, but we do have a poetical picture of the past to give us a general conception of what took place.

According to the chronicle, Ihor waged wars with the tribes of the Uliches and the Derevlians. The Uliches defended themselves for a long time; their city of Peresichen held fast for three years and refused to surrender to Ihor, but at the end of the third year was starved into submission. The tribute which he received from the conquered tribe he gave to his military chieftain Sveneld, whereupon Ihor's personal following complained that he had given too much to Sveneld. "Now," they said, "Sveneld's soldiers have new uniforms and arms, while we go about naked." They urged Ihor to go with them to collect more tribute from the Derevlians and to share it with them.

Ihor listened to their plea and returned. Because the Derevlians had been so submissive, he decided to exact even more than on the first occasion. According to Sveneld's soldiers he sent many of his warriors home, apparently to have fewer with whom to divide the spoils. As soon as the Derevlians heard that Ihor was coming back for more tribute, they held a conference, led by the chief of their tribe, Mal. They said, "When a wolf gets used to stealing sheep he will soon destroy the herd, if no one kills him. So it is with Ihor; if we do not kill him, he will ruin us." Thereupon they sent him a delegation to warn him not to oppress them further. "Why do you come again? We have just paid you your tribute,'' they complained. Nevertheless he did not heed them, and when he began to make his collections, the Derevlians of the city of Iskorosten sallied out, attacked his small force, and dispersed it. They seized Ihor and tore him asunder by tying him to the tops of bent trees and letting the trees spring back.

Ihor's widow, Olha (945–960?), becoming regent in the name of her infant son Sviatoslav, considered it her first duty to avenge her husband. "Whoever does not avenge himself, God will not avenge," ran the old Slavic proverb. Many legends grew up around her clever and savage punishment of the Derevlians for her husband's death.

In one of these tales she is said to have buried their deputies alive when they came to offer her the hand of their prince. In a second she caused the deputies to be smothered in a bathhouse. In a third she treated the deputation very hospitably, but when they had become intoxicated she had them killed. Another story tells how she organized an expedition against the Derevlians, plundered their country, killed some of the people, took others as slaves, and imposed on the rest an even heavier tribute than had been laid in the time of Ihor. Two parts of the tribute she ordered to be paid to the Kievan treasury and the third to her personal treasury as widow. She besieged the Derevlian city of Iskorosten and destroyed it by treachery. She offered the inhabitants peace on payment of a tribute of three pigeons and three sparrows for each house. After the people had paid this tribute, she ordered her soldiers to tie lighted tow to the feet of the birds and set them free. The birds flew home to the old straw roofs and set the city on fire. Similar tales of the burning of cities by birds and animals are, however, common in various countries.

According to the custom of the time, Olha religiously fulfilled her duty as a widow. She educated her children, governed the state wisely, and was not eager to marry again, though even the Byzantine emperor proposed to her. In Ukrainian tradition Olha became the model of a shrewd princess, just as Oleh became the typical adroit prince.

The church groups respected and supported her because she had accepted Christianity. She kept a clergyman at her court and asked to be buried according to the Christian rite; because of this she was canonized after her death.

Sviatoslav and His Sons: Sviatoslav (960–972), the son of Ihor and Olha, is as well remembered by the people through national legends and traditions as were Oleh and Olha. He was not considered a magician or a master of cunning, but a daring and honest knight who was frank and open in all his dealings. Not caring for plunder and wealth, but valuing military reputation above all else and dedicating himself to a life of martial glory, he became a hero prince to his soldiers. A legend declares:

When Prince Sviatoslav grew up and became a man, he began to gather about him brave soldiers because he too was a bold warrior, as light of tread as a leopard, and eager for war. When campaigning he took neither abundant supplies nor cooking utensils. He did not boil his meat but whether it was horse meat, game, or beef, he cut it into thin strips, roasted it over an open fire, and ate it. He had neither tent nor bedding, but used the blanket from under his saddle to cover himself at night, and pillowed his head on his saddle. His soldiers did likewise. Whenever he decided to attack a country, he warned it of his coming by sending messengers ahead to inform it, "I am marching against you."

The chronicle tells of Sviatoslav's expedition eastward against the Khazars, the Kasohi (Circassians), and the Yasians (Ossetes), who inhabited the northern Caucasus and part of southeastern Ukraine. He also waged war against the Viatiches and forced them to pay their tribute to Kiev instead of to the Khazars. From Arabian writers we learn that the Rus warriors then ravaged the country districts and the commercial centers of the Khazars and

Bolgars, including the rich cities of Itil and Bolgar. Thus Rus became mistress of the mouth of the Don and of the region about the Sea of Azov and gained an open road to the Caspian Sea.

New expeditions against the Persian and Arabian cities might have been expected, but Sviatoslav decided to wage war against Bulgaria in the Balkan peninsula. He was persuaded to do this by the Byzantine Emperor Nicephorus, who wished to destroy Bulgaria and made use of Sviatoslav for that purpose. At his instigation a native of Chersonesus named Kalokir approached Sviatoslav with a proposal for a joint campaign. Sviatoslav was to conquer Bulgaria for himself, while Kalokir would attempt to seize the Byzantine crown. The ambitious Prince of Rus snapped at the bait, believing that if he could conquer Bulgaria he would be able to control the entire Balkan peninsula and eventually extend his dominion to the gates of Constantinople, as the famous Bulgarian Tsar Simeon had done a century-and-a-half earlier.

Bulgaria was itself a prize worth fighting for. "I do not wish to live in Kiev," said Sviatoslav, according to the chronicle, after he had settled in Bulgaria. "I prefer to live in Pereyaslavets [Preslav] on the Danube. This is the center of all good things, and will be the capital of my kingdom. From the Byzantines I will get silk, gold, wines, and fruit; from the Czechs and Hungarians silver and horses; from Rus furs, wax, honey, and slaves."

In 968 Sviatoslav assembled a large army and invaded Bulgaria. At Dorostol (Silistria) on the Danube he defeated the Bulgarians, and occupied the eastern part of the country, making Pereyaslavets near Tulcea his capital.

At this juncture he received from Kiev an urgent summons to return home, since the nomadic Pechenegs had surrounded Kiev and were besieging it. Upon his arrival the Kievan nobles (boyars) rebuked him for not staying at home and attending to the affairs of the kingdom. "Thou, O prince," they complained, "seekest foreign

lands while thine own land is forgotten: we have barely
escaped falling into the hands of the Pechenegs, and thy
mother and children likewise.''

As soon as he had driven off the Pechenegs, Sviatoslav,
in spite of the prayers of his followers, made preparations to return to his beloved Bulgaria. His aged mother
Olha, who had ruled as regent for him, feeling that her
time was short, begged her son to stay at her side; soon
after making her plea she died.

Sviatoslav made his oldest son, Yaropolk, Prince of
Kiev, and his second son, Oleh, ruler over the Derevlians
as Prince of Ovruch. The inhabitants of Novgorod, where
Sviatoslav had earlier lived as a prince, begged for one of
his sons as prince of Novgorod, but none of them cared to
go there. Finally one of the Kievan nobles, brother of
Sviatoslav's concubine Malusha, persuaded the citizens
of Novgorod to ask for her minor son Volodimir as ruler.
Sviatoslav agreed, and Dobrinia was sent to Novgorod to
rule as regent for Volodimir, while other regents ruled
over Kiev and Ovruch in behalf of Yaropolk and Oleh,
who were also minors.

After making these arrangements Sviatoslav departed
for Bulgaria. Upon his arrival he equipped a new army
for the purpose of conquering additional territory in the
Balkans. But the Byzantines, under the rule of the soldier-
emperor John Tzimiskes, intervened in the role of guardians of Bulgaria. When the emperor demanded of Sviatoslav the same tribute as that paid by his predecessors in
Bulgaria, the Kievan prince undertook a campaign against
Constantinople; but Tzimiskes sent a fleet equipped with
Greek fire up the Danube to cut off reinforcements from
Kiev, slipped past the Rus army through an undefended
mountain pass, and captured Pereyaslavets.

After a long siege at Dorostol, Sviatoslav decided to
risk his fate on a battle in the open field, but in the ensuing encounter his army was crushed. In the terms of peace
he agreed to return captives taken in earlier campaigns,

to evacuate Bulgaria, to refrain from attacking the Greek cities in Crimea, and to become an ally of the Byzantine empire. He was then supplied with food for his journey and allowed to depart for Ukraine.

According to an eyewitness of the ceremony following the signing of the treaty, Sviatoslav was of medium height, but sturdy, with a short nose, blue eyes, and bushy eyebrows. He was clean-shaven except for a mustache, and, in the style of the steppes wore a tuft of hair on his shaven head. He was simply dressed, differing from his followers only in wearing a gold ring in one ear. His bearing was austere.

Sviatoslav doubtless had plans for recouping his loss, but he found a band of Pechenegs lying in wait for him at the portage of the Dnieper. He wintered at the mouth of the river; in spring lack of supplies forced him to attempt to fight his way through the nomad horde. He fell in an ambush, and the Pechenegs made a drinking cup of his skull; on it they engraved the legend, "He sought foreign lands, but lost his own."

CHAPTER V

THE KINGDOM OF KIEV

Volodimir: The death of Sviatoslav in 972 marked the outbreak of a struggle among his sons, each of whom was eager to inherit the whole kingdom. Yaropolk (972–978) of Kiev waged war against Oleh of the Derevlians and in a battle near Ovruch put his brother's army to flight. Oleh fell from his horse in the rout and was trampled to death by men and horses; he was buried near Ovruch. Yaropolk then annexed the province of the Derevlians.

When the news of Yaropolk's successes reached Volodimir he fled to Scandinavia to hire a Varangian contingent to save him from the fate of Oleh. In his absence Yaropolk captured Novgorod and installed boyar vassals there to rule over the city and the surrounding districts. Soon after, Volodimir returned from abroad with Varangian warriors, expelled Yaropolk's governor from Novgorod, and prepared himself for a campaign against his half brother.

After conquering the near-by principality of Polotsk and giving it to his son Iziaslav, Volodimir marched against Yaropolk, who surrendered but was treacherously put to death. With the river road from Novgorod to Kiev in his hands, Volodimir (978–1015) then set out on an ambitious program of empire building.

First, he conquered a number of other tribes and added their territories to his dominions. In this way he annexed the districts of the Viatiches and the Radimiches and the territory of Galicia. Within a few years he had united under his rule all the provinces that had at any time belonged to the Kievan state. To strengthen his personal control he removed the princes of the conquered principalities as he conquered them and replaced them with his sons. As he had many concubines, there was no lack of sons for these positions, even when his empire assumed vast proportions; during the minority of the sons, he entrusted the administration of the provinces to loyal boyars.

As Prince of Novgorod he installed his son Yaroslav, later succeeded by Visheslav. Iziaslav took Polotsk, Smolensk was given to Stanislav, Turiv to Sviatopolk, and the western principalities of Volodimir (Volynia), and probably Galicia as well, to Vsevolod. The Don, Crimean, and Caucasus regions, with their capital at Tmutorokan, fell to Mstislav. Rostov, with its control of the upper Volga, was first awarded to Yaroslav and later to Boris; in the Murom region along the Oka River the rule was assigned to Hlib. Volodimir himself took charge of the heart of Ukraine in the middle basin of the Dnieper, and probably also all newly conquered and unassigned territory.

Volodimir's work in creating this empire went down in the chronicles as the "gathering of the lands of Rus." It had cost many lives and much bloodshed. Especially in his youthful days, Volodimir is portrayed as harsh and even cruel. The pious monks who wrote the chronicles may have overemphasized these qualities in order to draw attention to the change in his character after he accepted Christianity, but it is true that he built his empire on foundations of force, intimidation, assassination, and war.

Once the empire was established, Volodimir gave his attention to the problem of organization. By placing his sons rather than unrelated princes, nobles, or governors in charge of the various parts of his dominion he gave birth to the idea of a dynasty in the Kievan state. Thereafter the princely heirs of Volodimir on the one hand and the townspeople and warriors on the other found it to their common advantage to promote the theory that the unification of the Rus state was a task laid upon the dynasty of Volodimir. There was general agreement that he and his descendants should rule and that there should be no other princes than the heirs of Volodimir.

The "dynastic idea" strengthened the country internally, for it led to a feeling of unity and solidarity. Volodimir further added to the consolidation of his empire by introducing Christianity, which became a state religion binding together the parts of his far-flung empire.

The Adoption of Christianity: Christianity reached the coast of the Black Sea and the lower Danube in the early years of the Christian era. From there it spread slowly northward, carried by merchants and other travelers. There is no doubt that in the course of the ninth century the Christian faith was well rooted in the chief commercial cities of Ukraine. Greek Orthodox missionaries sent to Rus in the 860's baptized so many people that shortly after this a special bishop was sent to care for their needs. In the first part of the tenth century mention is made of a Church of St. Elias in the lower town in Kiev, and in the treaty made between Ihor and the Byzantine empire it was stated that Ihor's army consisted of both pagans and Christians of Rus.

In the capital and at court there were large numbers of Christians. According to tradition, even Princess Olha, the wife of Ihor, went to Byzantium and was baptized, although neither the chronicles nor any of the records at Constantinople, which fully describe her visit, mention this fact. It is probable that she was baptized at Kiev. After she herself had accepted Christianity she attempted to persuade her son Sviatoslav to follow her example, but he refused; his children, however, who remained at Kiev and grew up at the court of their Christian grandmother, were imbued from their earliest years with Christian ideas. Among them was Volodimir, but it was many years before he had completed his task of organizing an empire and had time to devote to Christianizing it.

As the chronicle tells it, missionaries from many lands came to Volodimir and pleaded the merits of their respective faiths. The Volga Bolgars expounded Mohammedanism, the Khazars Judaism, the Germans Catholicism, and the Byzantines Greek Orthodoxy. Volodimir decided to find out for himself which was the best religion and sent out envoys to many lands to gather information and report to him. Those sent to Constantinople found Greek Orthodoxy the best; the boyars also said, "The Greek religion is clearly the best, for it was accepted by your grandmother Olha, who was the wisest of all people."

Volodimir, the story goes, decided to be baptized, but was too proud to beg for baptism at the hands of the Byzantines, preferring to gain by his victories the right to demand it. He thereupon attacked the Greek cities in Crimea and conquered them. Made bold by his conquest, he sent an embassy to the joint Byzantine emperors, Basil and Constantine, to demand their sister Anna in marriage; in case of refusal he threatened to march on Constantinople. The emperors consented on condition that Volodimir be baptized. He replied that he would gladly accept Christianity, as he had already been favorably inclined to it.

The emperors then sent Anna to Volodimir at Chersonesus, but the Kievan prince delayed the ceremony. As he was suffering from inflammation of the eyes, the princess was able to persuade him that as soon as he accepted Christianity he would be healed; accordingly he was baptized, his eyes were miraculously cured, and he celebrated his marriage with Anna. On his return to Kiev he took with him several Greek Orthodox clergy to baptize the people of Kiev and the rest of the country.

In this rather fanciful account there are embedded a number of actual facts. During the time of Volodimir's negotiations for the hand of the Princess Anna he was engaged in reorganizing his empire. In his search for aid in strengthening the structure of his government, and especially his personal authority, he turned to Byzantium. The Byzantine empire and its capital Constantinople went by the name of the New Rome, and were considered the center of culture, fame, and power, as Old Rome had been at the zenith of her greatness. Many nation builders of the time were eager to become connected with Byzantium by marriage and to receive their regalia from it. The memoirs of the Emperor Constantine, who was a contemporary of Ihor, indicate that the Hungarian, Khazar, and Rus rulers frequently presented requests for a crown and other emblems of royalty and for the hand of a princess, in return for some favor. Volodimir followed suit.

The emperors themselves gave him the opportunity. The Byzantine general, Vardas Phocas, headed a revolt and marched his army against Constantinople; in desperation the emperors appealed to Volodimir for aid. He promised assistance on condition that they give him their sister in marriage, and also a crown and other insignia of royalty. Long afterward the tradition lived on that Volodimir had received from Constantinople the crown with which he was invested, and the Muscovite tsars claimed to be the heirs to this crown. The same crown was probably used several decades later by Volodimir's great-grandson Monomakh, whose given name was also Volodimir; and it came to be known as the Hat of Monomakh.

Volodimir sent to Byzantium an army of six thousand men who helped to suppress the revolt and then remained in the service of the emperors. As soon as the danger had passed, however, the emperors forgot their side of the bargain, considering it beneath their dignity to give their sister in marriage to one whom they still looked upon as a barbarian in spite of the fact that he had been baptized. Volodimir then attacked the Greek cities and villages in Crimea. Previous princes of Rus had often stretched their hands in that direction, and treaty after treaty contained clauses forbidding the Kievans to disturb these centers. Volodimir, with a large army, laid siege to the Byzantine capital in Crimea, the city of Chersonesus, known to the Rus as Korsun. Unable to take the stoutly walled city by storm, Volodimir diverted its water supply and thus forced the inhabitants to surrender (989). As Byzantium was again involved in a rebellion and was unable to send aid, Volodimir thus became master not only of Chersonesus but of all Crimea. In order to regain the territory the Byzantine emperors were obliged to fulfill their earlier promise and send Anna to Chersonesus, where the marriage took place. Volodimir then returned Chersonesus "as the bridegroom's gift for the princess."

Amid these events the formal baptism of Volodimir took place unnoticed. According to various sources it was performed at Chersonesus, Kiev, or Vasilev—now Vasilkiv—near Kiev, although it is possible that he had already been baptized three years before his expedition against Crimea. As his Christian name he took that of his brother-in-law, Basil.

Cultural Developments: After Volodimir had accepted Christianity he devoted all his efforts to extending it to his dominions. He wished to draw his realm as close as possible to that of Byzantium, and to clothe it in Byzantine culture and glory. As a wise statesman he realized that if the new faith, with its colorful ritual and its priesthood, could become firmly established, new literature, education, and art would follow. Under his protection Greek Orthodox Christianity spread rapidly. As in other countries, the state church necessarily became a potent political ally of the authority of the state and of the power of the grand prince himself.

The chronicle declares that after Volodimir returned to Kiev from his Crimean expedition he ordered all the pagan idols and the statues of pagan gods on the hill near his palace destroyed. Some were ordered hacked to pieces, others burned. The chief idol, that of Perun, was tied to the tail of a horse, dragged through the streets, flogged by the populace, and finally thrown into the Dnieper. Following the destruction of the idols he commanded the citizens to appear at the river bank on the next day. After they had gathered he ordered them to undress and to enter the stream. The priests stood on the shore and read the baptismal liturgy, and thus the entire city was Christianized. Similar mass baptisms were, according to the Kievan chronicler, performed in many other cities, but probably not without some instruction in the new faith, which could easily be given, since there were already priests living in the larger centers before this time. A number of inhabitants must already have had at least a vague knowledge of Christianity.

Several authors, some of them contemporaries, state that during the lifetime of Volodimir the "entire nation" was converted; "if not because of love, then of fear they were baptized." As soon as Christianity was officially introduced, churches were built and priests appointed to take charge of education. "Volodimir gathered the children of prominent men and set them to getting knowledge from books." Greek craftsmen were imported to build and decorate the new churches, and thus a new class of society appeared. Masters of many trades immigrated—architects, painters, and goldsmiths—and from them the natives acquired new skills. Byzantine learning, especially that connected with the Church, began to take root.

Obviously this cultural awakening occurred at first only in the larger cities; outside the more important centers, and particularly in the remote villages, the new faith made slow progress. But the state became officially Christian, and culture as a whole developed side by side with political organization. From this time on, the tribes were bound together not only through one dynasty, one army, and one law propagated by deputies of the princes, by local police officials, and by justices, but through Christianity as well. The empire was consolidated by the new faith, by the Church organization, and by the priestly hierarchy subject to the metropolitan of Kiev. Through the coöperation of all these agencies learning was promoted, which at first was of a religious character. Before the acceptance of Christianity, Persian and Arabian influences had been strong in Ukraine, but with the introduction of the Greek Orthodox faith, Greek learning gained the upper hand, for it was supported by the new state Church. For many years the new Rus-Byzantine culture dominated the East European lands united under the state of Kiev.

The new cultural influences introduced by Volodimir not only bound together the Ukrainian districts and tribes, but spread to White Russia as well and even north to Great Russia. The new religion soon knit them more closely together, and a more friendly feeling resulted. Deliberately the clergy and the ruling dynasty worked together to uproot differences of every kind and to create unity.

Politically and culturally the reign of Volodimir proved to be a most important epoch in the history of Ukraine. Fortunately the task begun by him was carried on by his son Yaroslav.

Contemporary writers stress the fact that after Volodimir accepted Christianity his character completely changed and he became a different man. More important, he laid down a solid cultural and spiritual foundation for his kingdom. He saw to it that relations between the government and the subjects became more amicable, and that a greater degree of order was established than had previously existed.

In the latter part of his reign Volodimir did not wage many wars but lived on friendly terms with his neighbors, devoting more time to the internal affairs of his realm than he formerly had done. Frequently he held council with his army officers, with the clergy, and with the "elders," as the prominent city dwellers were known. In these meetings they discussed improvements in the laws and ordinances.

Every day, whether he was present or not, there was a banquet at his court attended by the nobles, army officers, civil officials, and wealthy citizens. On holidays great national feasts were provided, at which hundreds of kettles of mead were brewed, the festivities lasting several days. To the poor money was given, to the sick and the invalids food. At other times the needy were invited to the palace; the crippled were supplied at home with bread, meat, fish, honey and kvas.

Though the chronicle attributes this generosity to Volodimir's new Christian spirit, there was in it a strong political purpose and a new trend in government. People were led to remember his kind deeds, while his wars and harsh acts were forgotten. Even in far-off Muscovy he was recalled in popular songs as a generous king, a "bright sun." He feasted his people at his capital in Kiev and left all affairs of state in the hands of the "rich and mighty":

> In the hospitable city of Kiev,
> The benevolent King Volodimir
> Gave a banquet, a notable feast
> For the wealthy princes and boyars;
> All "the elect" were his guests;
> Strangers were also invited.
> All at the banquet ate,
> All at the banquet drank,
> All at the banquet made boasts:
> One praised his beautiful horse,
> Another his garment of silk
> Yet another his towns and villages,
> His cities and their environs.
> So it was until noonday,
> When the feast was half over.
> King Volodimir made merry.

War with the Pechenegs: The period of Volodimir the Great, or, as the Church proclaimed him, St. Volodimir, remained in popular memory as a bright and happy era. In reality, however, despite successful wars, extensive annexations, intermarriage with Byzantine royalty, the establishment of the Church, and the spread of Greek culture—despite all these, his last days were shrouded in gloom. A bitter enemy invaded Ukraine; and Volodimir, with all his skill and power, was unable to prevent the devastation of his country.

From the beginning of the ninth century Turkish and other bands from the east had overrun the Ukrainian steppes. In the middle of the century the barbaric and rapacious Magyars crossed the land, destroying, burning, and pillaging as they went, and taking with them the inhabitants to be sold to Greek traders as slaves. In the years from 860 to 880 another band, the Pechenegs, leaving their home east of the Volga, crossed the realm of the Khazars, who were unable to withstand them. The Pechenegs were even more savage than the Magyars, whom they expelled from the Ukrainian steppes and forced to migrate into the middle Danubian region, where they settled in what is now Hungary. After the Pechenegs had established themselves upon the steppes from the Don to the Danube they laid waste the Ukrainian villages more completely than had the Magyars.

At the beginning of the tenth century, during the reigns of Oleh and Ihor, the Ukrainians were driven out of the Black Sea steppes and forced west and north in search of peace and refuge. It is not known whether the Kievan princes failed to give adequate attention to this Ukrainian migration resulting from the inrush of Pechenegs, as it took place far from Kiev itself, or whether they were powerless to prevent it. In any case, during the reign of Sviatoslav, the Pechenegs not only displaced the Ukrainians along the north shore of the Black Sea but followed them north. During the first expedition of Sviatoslav against Bulgaria in 968 the Kievan nobles complained that the Pechenegs were taking them captive at the very walls of Kiev. Their bands blocked navigation on the Dnieper so completely that traders could not go north even in heavily armed caravans, as Sviatoslav traveled.

Sviatoslav had led a number of expeditions against foreign lands but failed to devote himself to subduing the Pechenegs. Even in the time of Volodimir the Great matters did not improve. As the chronicle puts it, "the wars with them were unending." Some of these encounters were long retold in popular legends, as in the following tales.

When the Pechenegs besieged Kiev, Volodimir met them on the Trubezh at the spot where Pereyaslav is now located. Instead of a pitched battle, picked warriors from each side fought a duel. A Ukrainian youth overcame his mighty Pecheneg opponent, and Volodimir named the place Pereyaslav, the place where his warrior had "won over the glory."* When the Pechenegs besieged Bilhorod near Kiev, the inhabitants broke the siege by convincing the nomads that the city held supplies of food to last for ten years. In one campaign Volodimir with a small band was suddenly faced by a great throng of Pechenegs. After a sharp fight he had to flee, and saved himself by hiding underneath a bridge. In gratitude for his escape he built a church at Vasilkiv.

It is clear that even the vicinity of Kiev was rendered unsafe, the inhabitants having often to seek refuge in the forests. To better the defense of his capital, Volodimir constructed three lines of heavy ramparts, remnants of which are still visible near Stuhna and Pereyaslav. A Czech missionary who passed through Kiev on his way to the Pechenegs wrote that there were iron gates in the walls, at which guards were stationed; that strong fortifications were also built along the rivers Stuhna, Seym, Trubezh, and Sula; and that people from the north were brought to guard them. Apparently the local population was decreasing and the lower region of the Dnieper, a vitally important district, was becoming a desert.

In the midst of this threat to his realm, Volodimir died. He was already confined to his bed when a report arrived

---

* Allusion to the meaning of the name in Slavonic (Editor).

that the Pechenegs were crossing the Sula. He sent his son Boris at the head of an army to oppose them; without learning of the outcome of the battle he died, in 1015.

The Heirs of Volodimir: By dividing the provinces of his dominions among his many sons, Volodimir believed that he could bind the whole empire more closely to Kiev, and in some degree he succeeded. But he had himself seized territory from his brothers, and his sons followed his example. Each sought to grasp the portion belonging to his brothers and to gain control of the whole land for himself as his father had done. Even during the lifetime of Volodimir several of his sons were disobedient and rebellious, especially Sviatopolk (Prince of Kiev 1015–1019), who ruled in Turiv over the Drehoviches, and Yaroslav (Prince of Kiev 1019–1054), who held Novgorod. After their father's death, their ambitions led them into war, in which each hoped to take the place of Volodimir and become sole ruler over all Ukraine.

Sviatopolk, who at the time of his father's death was in Vishorod just outside Kiev, began the slaughter. First he killed Boris, whom Volodimir had always kept at his side and who had been expected to inherit the crown of Kiev. Sviatopolk's followers then murdered Hlib, a brother of Boris, and overtook Sviatoslav in the Carpathian Mountains as he was fleeing to Hungary; he was killed near Hrebenev, where there is a monument to him. Both Boris and Hlib were later canonized as martyrs.

Yaroslav, proclaiming himself the avenger of his fallen brothers, now marched with an army of Varangians on Kiev and forced Sviatopolk to seek foreign aid. He called his brother-in-law, King Boleslav the Brave of Poland to Kiev, and also hired bands of Pechenegs. After a war of three-and-a-half years, in which the city of Kiev changed hands several times and suffered severely from fire and pillage, the decisive battle was fought on the Alta River near Pereyaslav. Yaroslav was victorious, and the defeated Sviatopolk fled west "to the Czechs and the Liakhs

[Poles]," never to return, and Yaroslav became master in Kiev. The fame of this battle spread to far-off Iceland, where one of the sagas tells the story of a Varangian adventurer, Eimund, who took part in the fratricidal wars in Ukraine.

Yaroslav's victory was not long unrevenged. Another brother, Mstislav, Prince of Tmutorokan, raised an army augmented by hired Khazar and Yasian tribesmen and overran the regions beyond the Dnieper. Yaroslav with his Varangian mercenaries attacked him in a terrible battle near Chernihiv in which Mstislav was victorious. Mstislav now proposed to his brother that they divide the empire between them. Kiev, with the territory west of the Dnieper, would be ruled by Yaroslav and Mstislav would reign over the districts east of the river. An agreement was made, and the two brothers lived side by side in peace, united by an alliance. Mstislav made his capital at Chernihiv, where he began the construction of the Church of the Holy Saviour, the oldest church still standing in Ukraine. He was greatly respected, and described in song as "powerful in frame, with rosy cheeks and large eyes; bold in battle, but gentle in private life. He loved his warriors, and did not spare his wealth, but permitted all to eat and drink."

In 1036 Mstislav died suddenly, leaving no heir. Once more all Ukraine came into the hands of Yaroslav, except for the western principality of Polotsk, where a brother reigned as a vassal.

CHAPTER VI

THE DECLINE OF KIEV

Yaroslav: Just at the time when Yaroslav by the death of Mstislav gained control over the whole of his father's realm, other events occurred further to strengthen his kingdom; in the south the power of the Pechenegs was broken, and in the west that of the Poles. The Pechenegs were attacked by new bands of nomads arriving from the east, the Torks and the Polovtsians, whom they were unable to withstand; as Kiev lay in the way of their retreat they attacked it in great force in 1036, the year of Mstislav's death, and in a great battle near the city suffered a crushing defeat. Where the Cathedral of St. Sophia now stands, Yaroslav founded a new Kiev on the battlefield. The remnants of the Pechenegs emigrated beyond the Danube and were seen no more in the Ukrainian steppes; their places were occupied at first by the Torks, and later by the Polovtsians.

With more peaceful neighbors on the south, Yaroslav was free to devote his attention to the western frontier, where a large Polish state had been established during the latter part of the tenth century. Not content to rule over the lands inhabited only by the Poles, the Polish kings attempted to enlarge their boundaries to include the Ukrainian provinces, especially those with a mixed Polish-Ukrainian population.

Volodimir the Great had already waged war against the Polish king, Boleslav the Brave. Later, during the civil wars among Volodimir's sons, Boleslav had assisted Sviatopolk and at the same time had seized a few western Ukrainian cities, the "Cherven towns," as the chronicle calls them; when Yaroslav emerged victorious from the civil wars he at once set about regaining this lost territory.

In 1025 Boleslav died, and Poland fell into a state of anarchy similar to that in Ukraine after the death of Volodimir. Yaroslav and Mstislav joined in seizing back the lost territory, and in plundering Poland and taking captives. In the decade following 1030 Poland was swept by a revolution: kings, princes, and priests were expelled and Christianity was wiped out; and it was not until 1039 that Casimir, the grandson of Boleslav, returned to Poland and began gradually to restore order. This he accomplished with the aid of the German emperor and of Yaroslav, who took Casimir under his protection, gave him his daughter in marriage, and on various occasions sent armies to assist him in quelling rebellious leaders. Poland appeared to be so helpless that Yaroslav did not realize he was strengthening a potentially dangerous enemy.

Yaroslav was now one of the most powerful rulers in Europe, and was in friendly relationship or alliance with many sovereigns. With the Scandinavian countries from which he had frequently sought aid, he was on a most amicable footing. He became related to the crown of Sweden by marrying King Olaf's daughter Ingigerda, who adopted the Christian name of Irene. The Crown Prince of Norway, Harold the Bold, a famous warrior who had long lived in Ukraine and who was later to become King of Norway, married Yaroslav's daughter Elizabeth. Another of Yaroslav's daughters, Anna, became the second wife of the French king, Henry I. She outlived her husband, and stayed on with her son, King Philip I, taking part in political councils and signing her name in Cyrillic characters on one document as "Queen Anna."

Many members of the Kievan dynasty married into German, Hungarian, and Byzantine royal families, the relationship with Byzantium being of especial importance. In the 1040's a dispute arose, caused, according to a contemporary Greek author, by the killing of a Rus merchant in Constantinople; Yaroslav seized the opportunity to threaten the Byzantines with reprisal and thus sought to gain for Ukraine the commercial privileges she had formerly enjoyed. He dispatched his son Volodimir with a combined Rus and Varangian army to attack Constantinople; the expedition, the last Rus expedition against Constantinople, failed when the Byzantines destroyed a large number of ships with Greek fire, Volodimir being forced to return home empty-handed. In the course of time, however, friendly relations were reëstablished.

Although Yaroslav was successful in his foreign relations, his outstanding achievements were in internal affairs. He continued the work of strengthening the country begun by his father, his skill in this regard gaining for him wide renown. He aided in the propagation of Christianity, strengthened the organization of the Church, and furthered the extension of education and Byzantine culture. After his victory over the Pechenegs, he had founded a new citadel at Kiev, fortified with great walls and a strong gate; beside the gate he erected the Church of Annunciation with a gold-plated roof. In accordance with custom he built in the new town monasteries dedicated to St. George and St. Irene, the patron saints of himself and his wife.

He then began the construction of the immense Cathedral of St. Sophia, the most imposing monument of his reign, using Greek artisans to erect and to decorate it. The altar and the central dome were ornamented with designs in mosaic, and other portions were covered with beautiful paintings. Much of the original structure, the most outstanding example of Byzantine architecture in Ukraine, remains standing to the present day, though it was unskillfully remodeled in the middle of the nineteenth century. Later churches were the work of native students of Greek art and are therefore of more interest in the history of Ukrainian style; unfortunately, however, they are less well preserved than the Cathedral of St. Sophia, of which the exterior and most of the interior have remained intact.

Of Yaroslav's interest in religion the Kievan Chronicle says:

With him began the spread of the Christian faith in Rus and monks and monasteries came into existence. Yaroslav admired the church ceremonies; liked the clergy, especially the monks; and read books day and night. He gathered together many scribes who translated into the Slavonic tongue the Greek books written for the instruction of the faithful. As one farmer plows the land, another sows the seed, and yet others harvest and eat the crop, so it was with Yaroslav. His father plowed and harrowed the soil and enlightened the country by baptism; Yaroslav sowed the seed in the hearts of the faithful by means of books; and later generations reaped the harvest.

Upon his arrival at Novgorod, Yaroslav assembled three hundred children of the upper classes and "had them taught from books." Similar education was probably instituted in all the larger cities.

In regard to civil life Yaroslav was remembered for his reforms in the enforcement of justice and for his ordinances and laws. To protect the people against corrupt officials he clearly specified the amounts that tax collectors could demand, and issued many similar beneficial decrees. The entire "Ruska Pravda," or the Rus Law Code, was attributed to Yaroslav. Only the first clauses, however, those in which the right of revenge is limited and fines are imposed for murder or bodily injury, belong to his period. Even these provisions were not the creation of Yaroslav but were a written codification of the legal practices of the time. The fact that the Code is assigned to Yaroslav testifies, nevertheless, to his activity as a lawgiver and to his efforts to establish better law and more order and to reform the courts. These reforms were of great significance, for his laws were in force for many centuries.

Yaroslav was also important as the founder of a dynasty. His reign as a whole was a bright period in comparison with the troubles that later befell Ukraine.

The Successors of Yaroslav: Yaroslav, like his father, after uniting the Rus provinces divided them among his sons. Death did not find him unprepared, for he had issued detailed orders as to the inheritance of the various provinces. He willed the throne of Kiev to his eldest son Iziaslav, though one account has it that he hoped that his favorite son Vsevolod would eventually succeed to Kiev by peaceful means.

The chronicle states that when Yaroslav divided the kingdom among his sons he urged them to live at peace with one another, as was proper for children of the same parents, and also urged them to obey their eldest brother, the King ("Grand Prince") of Kiev. This story probably reflects not the express command of the dying king but the desire on the part of the people for peaceable rulers: it was hoped that the related princes would help each other and join in defending the fatherland; and that instead of seizing each other's possessions, they would allow the titles to pass legally from older to younger.

The sons of Yaroslav failed to live up to these desires. All were dissatisfied with their shares, and each hoped to unite the entire country under his rule, as his father and grandfather had done. As none was willing to wait until the eldest should die and it should become his turn to reign in Kiev as king, bloody civil wars flared up. The inhabitants became discouraged and complained that the princes did not look after the interests of the country or cherish it, and that they furthered anarchy by hiring enemies, especially the Polovtsians, to take part in their strife. In vain the people of the towns attempted to bring the princes to their senses. Yaroslav's great accomplishment, "the gathering of the lands of Rus," could not be achieved again by any of his sons, and his grandsons accomplished even less.

In the course of time the number of princes increased by the tens and hundreds, and they divided and redivided the empire. They were ashamed, however, to murder their brothers brutally as Volodimir and Sviatopolk had done; and, besides, Christianity had taught that murder was both unlawful and sinful. It was still permissible, nevertheless, to kill on the battlefield. Meanwhile it had become more difficult than formerly to uproot the numerous local princes, because each found refuge and aid among the townspeople of his district. The time had passed when each city lived its own life apart, had its own administration and its own courts, and submitted to its prince only to the extent of paying him tribute. Now the authority of the prince and of the judges and bailiff, directed by his assistants, was firmly entrenched in the lives of the townspeople and difficult to replace. Therefore the townspeople took a lively interest in the affairs of their prince and ceased to be mere onlookers in the quarrels of the princes and their constant shifting from province to province; they had become opposed to frequent changes of rulers, and valued a local dynasty that took to heart the affairs of the town and watched over its inhabitants. In order to avoid new rulers and changes in administration, they defended their princes to the utmost of their power and prevented other princes from driving them out. Consequently, old Ukraine was soon broken up into fragments, each governed by its local princely dynasty. The Prince at Kiev was recognized as senior only in name, each prince carrying on his life and administering his province in practically complete independence of him.

The sons and nephews of Yaroslav did not fully realize the difficulties of the situation but did strive to bring about some unity. Yaroslav's oldest son Iziaslav, who had inherited the principality of Kiev, the traditional capital, was neither capable enough nor bold enough to undertake the task alone. Consequently, the three older brothers— Iziaslav as the senior; Sviatoslav of Chernihiv, energetic and fearless; and Vsevolod of Pereyaslav, shrewd and unscrupulous—attempted to combine their strength for the purpose of seizing the other districts from the younger brothers and cousins. But once they had succeeded in robbing the others, a struggle ensued among themselves. Sviatoslav and Vsevolod, quickly learning of the insecurity of Iziaslav's position at Kiev, made an agreement for joint action at his expense, and within a short time a favorable opportunity appeared.

In place of the Pechenegs, the Torks now occupied the southern Ukrainian steppes; but they were a weak tribe forced westward by the Polovtsians, who had overwhelmed them in 1060 and then begun an advance toward the Ukrainian towns. In 1062 the Polovtsians attacked Pereyaslav and defeated its prince, Vsevolod. When they came again in 1068, Vsevolod learned of their plan of attack and this time invited his brothers to assist him; all joined in opposing the common enemy, but the invaders were victorious and began to plunder the whole Dnieper region.

The inhabitants of Kiev, who had supported Vsevolod in this ill-fated campaign, hastened home after the defeat. They called a public meeting in the market place at which a decision was made to undertake a fresh campaign against the Polovtsians, who were still ravaging the countryside. When they asked King Iziaslav to give them horses and weapons for the purpose, he refused, either because he feared an uprising or because he was displeased with them, having already imprisoned a number of townspeople for treason. Another public meeting was then called, at which feeling ran high against both the king and his military commander, Kosniachko, when it was learned that no arms were forthcoming.

Riots broke out, some of which were directed toward freeing the Prince of Polotsk from imprisonment in Kiev and making him ruler. Iziaslav fled, but returned in the next spring with help obtained from his brother-in-law, the Polish King Boleslav. He still lacked the courage to face the Kievans in battle, but when the latter discovered that neither Sviatoslav nor Vsevolod would accept the position of king, they invited him back. He returned and inflicted severe punishment upon the leaders of the revolt.

Sviatoslav and Vsevolod now realized the extent of the weakness of Iziaslav's position, and united to attack him. They expelled him from Kiev in 1073 and divided his kingdom between themselves.

The rule of Sviatoslav II (1073–1076) was cut short by his death. Iziaslav again returned with Polish help, but his reign came to an end with his death in 1078. It was characteristic of the times that he died in a battle with his nephew, Oleh, a son of Sviatoslav.

Vsevolod (1078–1094) now succeeded to Kiev; he attempted to assemble in his own hands as many of the principalities as possible, thus leaving to the sons of his deceased brothers as few as possible. His nephews, however, refused to surrender their rights without a struggle: led by Oleh, the most active of their group, they called in the Polovtsians to aid them in regaining their lands, and also received help from the townspeople of their old provinces. During his sixteen years as king, Vsevolod was never free from strife with the so-called "dispossessed" princes.

The Polovtsian Raids: After Vsevolod's death, his son, Volodimir Monomakh, became Prince of Chernihiv; and Sviatopolk (1094–1113), the son of Iziaslav, took over Kiev. They hoped to restore peace and order by returning each district to its legitimate heirs. Meanwhile, taking advantage of the unsettled conditions, the Polovtsians had laid waste the land so thoroughly that in the southern steppes there was not a moment's peace; it had become impossible for the inhabitants to till the soil and to live normal lives. These new nomad bands proved to be even more rapacious and destructive than the Pechenegs.

The new king had hardly been crowned in Kiev after the death of Vsevolod when he suffered a "visitation" by the Polovtsians, who at Tripillia overwhelmed the combined forces of Sviatopolk, Volodimir Monomakh, and the brother of the latter, Rostislav. During his flight Rostislav was drowned in the River Stuhna.

The Polovtsians wrought havoc throughout the neighborhood of Kiev. They besieged the town of Torchesk for many months, until the inhabitants surrendered, and then departed laden with booty and captives. Encouraged by their success, Oleh allied himself with them and marched against Chernihiv. Monomakh came out to meet him but retreated to Pereyaslav under the blows of the Polovtsians delivered upon himself and Sviatopolk from both sides of the Dnieper. The countryside was emptied as whole villages migrated northward to more secure regions. Finally Monomakh and Sviatopolk decided to make peace with the "dispossessed" princes. In 1097 they called a conference of all the princes at Lubche Lake, and it was there decided that each dynasty should retain its patrimony and should reign undisturbed by others. Peace, however, did not result. Immediately after the conference another civil war broke out, which lasted several years. Then the threat of the nomads again brought united action. From 1103 to 1111 yearly campaigns were directed against the Polovtsians so successfully that they were thoroughly subdued. Many of their bands were driven far into the steppes and the others ceased marauding.

The nomad invasions, however, had left an indelible mark upon the life of Ukraine. The Pechenegs had already seriously disrupted the region of the middle Dnieper, the center of Ukrainian political and cultural life. The Polovtsian raids had added to the confusion; many people had been torn away from their homes and others had lost everything they owned. The peasants (smerd) suffered the most heavily: they lost their property, became heavily indebted, and many became enslaved. For those who fell into debt the times were hard; interest was high, and the debtor had great difficulty in freeing himself of his burden. He was obliged to work out the interest or the principal, but a low value was set upon his labor, and

the master took advantage of every opportunity to increase the debt or even to make the debtor his slave.
Through this process many formerly free peasants became either slaves (*kholop*) or indentured laborers (*zakup*). Small farms disappeared, to be replaced by large
estates owned by princes and nobles and worked by large
numbers of people wholly or partially enslaved. When a
princely estate in Putivl was attacked and seized, seven
hundred slaves were taken by the victors.

A legal code of about 1120 clearly reflects the state of
affairs in this respect. On every page are found decrees
having to do with slavery: legal and illegal methods of
enslavement, legal and illegal usury, debt-slavery and
methods of working off the debt, enslavement and liberation, fugitive slaves and repossession. Debt and enslavement were the vital issues of the day. These conditions led
to great discontent. After the death of Sviatopolk II a
revolution broke out in Kiev: Jews were beaten because
they had had dealings with him; civil officials and wealthy
individuals were attacked. The frightened nobles invited
Volodimir Monomakh (1113–1125) to become the king of
Kiev, because of all the princes he was the best liked by
the people, and it was hoped that he would be able to restore order. Monomakh accepted the invitation. His first
official act as the king of Kiev was to reduce the rate of
interest on loans, making clear what lay at the bottom of
the disaffection and the hatred for the rich; yet the rate
still remained excessive, probably averaging about 20 per
cent.

Under such circumstances the prosperity of the Dnieper region declined, the decline being accompanied by the
cultural and political decay of the main centers of Ukrainian life.

Provincial Self-Government: Though the Lubche conference of 1097 did not improve conditions, it did recognize their existence. In acknowledging the right of each
prince to retain his inheritance, the older princes also ac-

knowledged the rights of their younger brothers to their respective shares. Some of the more selfish rulers, of course, did not live up to this agreement and continued to prey upon the lands of their weaker brothers and neighbors; but in spite of this it was recognized that each son of a ruler had the right to derive his living from and to inherit a part of his father's domain. The system was of great value to the principalities which had able princes whom the people wished to retain; it also tended to make these principalities more nearly independent. From this time many of the local princes and their officials attempted to adjust their administrations to the needs of the people in order to ensure their good will and support.

As the princes increased in number and settled down in remote districts, their relations with the local townspeople underwent a change. The prince was no longer able to rely altogether upon his mercenary following, especially of Varangians and other foreigners, and with their aid to extort from the people whatever he pleased. Because he had less funds at his disposal, his army was now smaller and consisted chiefly of local inhabitants. In place of the old merchant-warriors, it was now made up mainly of landowning gentry. Commerce had fallen off because of the loss of the steppe route to the south, but the economic depression furnished slaves and indentured laborers for the cultivation of the soil. Members of the prince's military retinue began to intermarry with the native gentry, and to form a new upper class of civil society. The prince realized the importance of this class and tried to maintain good relations with it.

The town increased its power over the prince, and whenever it was dissatisfied with his policies demanded reforms; if he failed to comply, it expelled him. In some of the principalities this authority was vested in both the town merchants and the country gentry jointly, while in others the gentry alone held power, the merchants being relegated to a position of secondary importance. The agency of control over the prince was the general assembly, or *viche*. All freemen of both town and countryside were entitled to attend, but the most influential element was of course the gentry. The general assembly decided all important matters and presented requests to the prince; frequently it deposed him and selected a successor. This selection was a comparatively simple problem, as there were always many princes awaiting an opportunity to rule. As was natural under these conditions, the princes obeyed the will of the people. The uprising in Kiev against King Iziaslav was the first example of bold action on the part of a general assembly, but many others were to follow.

In some of the principalities the citizens deliberately changed their princes as frequently as possible to prevent them from becoming firmly seated. When such a change was effected the general assembly and its elected officials became the real governing authorities, while the prince was merely the commander-in-chief of the army; this was true in Novgorod, in the north. In many of the provinces of Ukraine the prince controlled through his officials the courts and the administration of other civil matters, but the general assembly acted as a supervising body and frequently presented him with their grievances, to which he gave careful consideration in order to avoid arousing civic animosity. There are many reports of the activities of the general assembly in Kiev, and apparently the assemblies in other principalities played a similar role. In some places, as in Galicia, the gentry gained control over the prince and reduced the power of the town as well.

Though each of the many provinces was independent politically, they had many features in common. Kievan law had been carried by the princes and their bands of followers to the most remote districts and adopted there by the local courts. If Kievan law as found in the "Ruska Pravda" of the late eleventh century and the edition of the time of Monomakh is compared with later laws in force in the other provinces, a great similarity appears, which similarity indicates that the principles of Kievan legislation had been widely adopted. Especially noteworthy are the similarities between the Ruska Pravda and the later Lithuanian Statute, which was based upon the law of Polotsk, the most autonomous part of the kingdom of Kiev.

Law and administration were thus uniform throughout Ukraine. Equally so were literature, culture, and the whole Byzantine-Rus complex of customs which for two centuries prior to the fall of Kiev were continuously propagated from the capital. In addition one faith and one Church, united in a single hierarchy, also greatly contributed to internal unity. All churches were subordinated to the metropolitan of Kiev, who sent out from Kiev large numbers of the higher Church officials as well as of the village priests; some thirty or forty bishops were furnished by the Monastery of the Caves (Pechersky Monastir) alone. This great institution had been founded in the middle of the eleventh century and had enjoyed especially vigorous growth under the energetic Abbot Theodosius, whose administration caused it to become the most important monastic center in the entire Kievan kingdom.

Thus in spite of political disintegration there remained a deep internal unity among all the lands of Rus, particularly those inhabited by Ukrainians, bound as they were by tribal relationship, geographical proximity, and many other ties. For two centuries, from the latter half of the eleventh to the middle of the thirteenth, this cultural unity continued to develop in spite of political disunity, administrative disintegration, and the decreasing power of the king of Kiev.

The Principalities: The sons and grandsons of Yaroslav who succeeded him upon the throne of Kiev in the second half of the eleventh century and the first half of the twelfth made every effort to halt the decline of the power of Kiev and thus impede the disintegration of the kingdom. Their efforts sometimes delayed and sometimes hastened the process, but in either event it went on inevitably to its tragic end.

The first and most complete separation was that of Galicia (Halichina), where the dynasty of Rostislav reigned. Rostislav had probably inherited the province of Galicia after the death of his father, but had soon been driven out; and Galicia, together with the neighboring province of Volynia, had passed into the hands of Yaropolk, son of the Kievan King Iziaslav. As soon as Rostislav's sons— Volodar, Vasilko, and Rurik—grew up they caused so many difficulties for Vsevolod that he finally (1084) regained their patrimony for them from Yaropolk. After this the dynasty of Rostislav firmly established itself in Galicia and divided the province among its members. The western portion about Peremyshl fell to Rurik; the central districts, with Zvenihorod as their capital, went to Volodar; and the south, under the city of Terebovl, was assigned to Vasilko. Yaropolk opposed them and lost his head, thus showing what lay in store for those who interfered with the fearless heirs of Rostislav, who proved to be able statesmen, capable of defending their share of Ukraine from the attacks of covetous neighbors. The most troublesome of these were the Poles, the Hungarians, and their own relatives, the princes of Kiev-Volynia, who attempted to reunite Galicia to their principalities.

Volodimirko (1124–1153), the son of Volodar and an astute politician, strengthened the position of his dynasty by expelling his nephews from the other western districts and thus uniting the whole region under his rule. Even before this union, Galicia had been a large and thickly inhabited territory. Free as yet from the attacks of the Polovtsians, it had been able to prosper in peace; and once united under a single ruler, it soon became the strongest of the Ukrainian regions. Its rulers refrained from interfering with the affairs of their neighbors and saw to it that neighboring princes did not interfere with them. At the same time the nobles in Galicia gained steadily in strength, outstripping both the common people and the princes.

Yaroslav (1152–1187), the son of Volodimirko, was especially renowned among the Ukrainian princes; to him were dedicated some stanzas of the *Song of the Legion of Ihor,* the most famous epic of medieval Ukraine. In this epic he is portrayed as "seated on a lofty golden throne, defending the Hungarian [Carpathian] Mountains with his iron regiments, blocking the way to a king, and closing the gates of the Danube." In Galicia, however, Yaroslav was forced to submit to the nobles, who even interfered in his private family affairs.

Following in the footsteps of Galicia, the region of Chernihiv seceded from the kingdom of Kiev, the secession occurring during the reign of Sviatoslav II of Kiev. The chief dynasty of Chernihiv became that of Oleh, a son of this Sviatoslav. As his was a family of energetic and competent rulers, the inhabitants gave it their full support. The greatest weakness of Oleh and his successors was their ambition, for they were never satisfied with the possession of Chernihiv alone but constantly strove to become masters of Kiev, Pereyaslav, and later even of Galicia. From these efforts arose wars in which Chernihiv frequently suffered heavy losses.

Since the dynasty at Chernihiv increased rapidly in numbers, its princes were constantly forced to redistribute their holdings in smaller and smaller units. Fortunately they were able to do this by peaceful means. The leading city, Chernihiv, was the oldest; second in importance was Novhorod-Siversky. On the two occasions when a prince of Chernihiv conquered Kiev he made this ancient city his capital, and gave to the next prince in line the city of Chernihiv, while the third took Novhorod-Siversky.

In the middle of the twelfth century, as the result of a struggle for the possession of Kiev, two more principali-

ties that had previously been subordinated to Kiev seceded—Pereyaslav and Turiv-Pinsk (Polisia on the Pripet). Pereyaslav was small and was in a state of ruin as a
result of repeated attacks by the Polovtsians. Unable to
withstand the attacks of their stronger sister principalities of Kiev and Chernihiv, the people of Pereyaslav decided to select for their rulers members of the northern
dynasty of Suzdal, who were descendants of Monomakh;
Suzdal, however, was so far removed from Pereyaslav
that it was impossible to unite the two regions, and the
people of Pereyaslav remained independent under the
princes of Suzdal. There was one great disadvantage in
their new position: in their struggle with the nomads of
the steppes they could no longer rely upon the aid of their
Ukrainian neighbors; but even so the people preferred to
be politically independent, even at the cost of suffering at
the hands of the Polovtsians.

The people of the remote province of Turiv-Pinsk, with
its poor land lost in swamps and forests, led a more tranquil existence, experiencing neither domestic disorders
nor foreign attacks. In the decade of the 1150's the inhabitants, dissatisfied with their princes, invited a descendant of Sviatopolk to be their ruler, since Sviatopolk
had once been Prince of Turiv. The King of Kiev soon
directed two expeditions to force the young ruler out of
Turiv, but failed to do so. After their successful defense,
the people of Polisia were free from further invasions
until the Lithuanians began their sporadic attacks.

At about the same time the large, rich, and strongly defended region of Volynia also became independent of
Kiev. Its princes, after secession, made several attempts
to conquer Kiev; whenever these attempts met with temporary success, the senior prince established his capital
there and left Volynia to be ruled by a younger brother.
But in the second half of the twelfth century, when the
Kievan kingdom was badly crippled by dismemberment,
the princes of Volynia were not so eager to own Kiev as

to defend their own territory from the attacks of the
Poles and Lithuanians. Eventually Volynia was also subdivided into the principalities of Volodimir and Lutsk,
and later into even smaller districts. The anarchy resulting from this repeated parceling came to an end at the
close of the twelfth century, when Prince Roman of Volodimir again united the province. Still better days were to
come when his descendants rejoined Volynia to Galicia
and so created a single powerful state.

The Downfall of Kiev: The city and principality of
Kiev, also deciding to become independent of the other
provinces, were ready to accept the princes of the senior
branch of the Monomakh dynasty as their rulers. The
founder of the dynasty, Volodimir Monomakh (1113–
1125), was a strong ruler and skilful statesman; he kept
Kiev firmly in hand, as did his son Mstislav (1125–1132)
after him. But after the death of the latter his heirs were
opposed in a three-cornered struggle by the younger sons
of Monomakh and their strife reduced the province to a
state of anarchy. The Prince of Chernihiv, Vsevolod of
the Oleh dynasty, took advantage of the situation to capture Kiev. The more confused the struggle became, the
more pretenders there were to the throne, all eager to
rule in this ancient seat of the senior princes of Rus. The
very fame of Kiev thus contributed to its downfall.

At first the people of Kiev gave their full support to
the sons of Mstislav—Iziaslav and Rostislav; they even
undertook several campaigns in their behalf. But as they
saw the princes continually quarreling among themselves,
they refused to interfere, and this in itself made the situation worse. Whenever a capable prince gained the throne
of Kiev there was peace for a time, because the weaker
claimants did not dare to oppose him. At other times,
however, chaos was so complete that princes were dethroned not merely every year but every few months or
weeks.

All these changes in the occupancy of the throne were

brought about by force of arms. The country was pillaged, and farming and commerce were ruined, especially after the competing princes began to call to their aid bands of Polovtsians. These pitiless nomads ruthlessly ravaged the countryside, killing many inhabitants and carrying off great numbers as slaves. Once invited into the country as mercenaries by the pretenders to the throne, they returned of their own accord for the sake of booty, their incursions being frequent in the 1170's and 1180's when the provinces of Kiev and Pereyaslav suffered the most destructive raids. Living conditions in Ukraine became desperately hard. In order to protect the merchants and their caravans from the nomads it became necessary to send a large army into the steppes and to take drastic measures to defend the frontier.

The younger and more daring princes attempted, as in the time of Monomakh, to subdue the Polovtsians by sending military expeditions against them. In 1185 Prince Ihor of Novhorod-Siversky accompanied his brothers and a large force into the steppes, but the campaign ended in the disaster described in the *Song of the Legion of Ihor,* and Ihor himself was taken prisoner. Sviatoslav III and Rurik also undertook campaigns against them, as did Rostislav II, the son of the latter. These kings, however, were not so powerful as their predecessors Monomakh and Sviatopolk, behind whom the whole population of Ukraine had poured forth. Ukraine too was weak: her trade and commerce were reduced and her inhabitants, especially the wealthy, constantly on the move to safer regions in the north or in Volynia and Galicia. The words of the *Song of the Legion of Ihor* echo like a funeral march over the dying political life of Ukraine: "Darkness covered the light on the River Kayala; like a brood of panthers, the Polovtsians spread throughout the land of Rus. Already dishonor has taken the place of glory; already woe has been loosed."

Further troubles beset Ukraine. The princes of Suzdal,

descendants of the younger George (Yuriy) Monomakh
and founders of the later Muscovite dynasty, had settled
in the Volga region. From there they made deliberate attempts to lessen the power and prestige of the Kievan
kingdom in order to make themselves supreme. Andrew,
the son of George, for example, took advantage of the dis-
sentions among the Ukrainian princes to send an army in
1169 to destroy Kiev. The attack was successful, and for
many days the victors pillaged the churches and monasteries; the soldiers carried away icons, rare books, vest-
ments, and church bells, which they carried into the northern regions; they killed many of the inhabitants or led
them away into captivity. Following his conquest of Kiev,
Andrew saw to it that only mediocre princes ruled over it,
thereby lowering still further its power and prestige. In
the 1180's some degree of order was restored among the
princes of Ukraine, and the kingdom of Kiev was divided
between Sviatoslav of Chernihiv and Rurik of the dynasty
of Rostislav, who were able to live at peace with one another. In 1203 Vsevolod, the brother of Andrew, introduced another period of disorder and destruction by dispatching his son-in-law Roman to attack Kiev.

On account of these internal conflicts and later attacks
by the Tatars, the Kievan kingdom fell to pieces, as is
well described in the *Song of the Legion of Ihor:*

For now, brothers, sad days are come;
Desolation has spread over the land. . . .
The princes ceased warring against the pagans, for brother spake
    unto brother,
"This is mine, and that too is mine,"
And the brothers began to call petty things great,
And to forge plots against one another
While from all sides, victorious, the pagans pressed upon the
    land of Rus;
Now groaned the land of Rus,
Remembering the past, and famous kings,
And Volodimir of old, and his renown. . . .

So, brothers, Kiev lamented its sorrow, and Chernihiv its afflic-
    tions:
Woe poured out upon the land of Rus,
Grief overflowed the land of Rus,
And the princes forged plots against one another,
But the pagans, victorious, overran the land of Rus. . . .

CHAPTER VII

THE KINGDOM OF GALICIA

Prince Roman (1189–1205) : Though the princes of Suzdal in the north made serious efforts to destroy the importance of the princes of Kiev and thus to disrupt the Kievan kingdom, their plans were not fully realized. While they were inflicting their blows, new centers of political power were arising on western Ukrainian soil. The new state that arose there did not embrace all Ukraine as the kingdom of Kiev had done; yet for another century it remained a united and politically independent power in densely inhabited western Ukraine. This strong state was created by the grandson of Iziaslav II and son of Mstislav II of Kiev, Prince Roman of Volodimir in Volynia.

Roman entered political life when Kiev had already lost its significance. Because of this he did not at first attempt to gain the crown of Kiev for himself as his predecessors had done; instead, he directed his gaze toward the neighboring province of Galicia. There the powerful and wealthy nobles were struggling with the reigning sons of Yaroslav. Roman made an alliance with the nobles, who raised an insurrection, expelled their prince, Volodimir, and in 1189 invited Roman to take his place. Roman was so delighted with Galicia that he turned over to his brother his own province of Volynia. His harsh treatment of the Lithuanian tribes was known far and wide; a Lithuanian historian later wrote that he punished the defeated Lithuanians by harnessing them to the plow. Songs celebrating his campaigns against the Polovtsians are still sung in Galicia.

Meanwhile the exiled Volodimir sought military aid of the King of Hungary, who had for years coveted the rich and beautiful country of Galicia, with its ample resources in salt and other minerals. He escorted Volodimir to Galicia, ostensibly to restore him to his position, but upon their arrival at the capital, Halich, he imprisoned the prince and placed his own son Andrew upon the throne. Volodimir escaped and succeeded in regaining his seat with the aid of the Poles and Germans and of the Galician inhabitants who had found the yoke of the Hungarians heavier than the rule of the easygoing native princes. Volodimir reigned until his death in 1199. Though Roman was a candidate for the succession, the nobles did not welcome him, as they had once before felt the weight of his heavy hand. He invaded Galicia with the aid of relatives among the Polish princes, and this time was more careful not to renounce his control over his patrimony Volodimir-in-Volynia. He did not live to see the complete unification of Galicia and Volynia, but laid the groundwork for it, and the task was accomplished later by his sons.

After he became ruler of Galicia the second time, Roman fought for a long time against the nobles. The contemporary Polish chronicler, Kadlubek, describes in forceful language how Roman confiscated their estates and killed the owners, saying, "You can't eat honey in peace, without first killing the bees." Kadlubek may have invented many of the acts of terror that he ascribes to Roman, although among the people this severe handling of the nobles gained for Roman wide popularity. Until then these nobles of Galicia with their great power had been able to oppress the people at will, and could not be brought to justice. They controlled the army, the courts, and the important civil offices, and feared nothing and no one. They often changed rulers in order to keep the government in their own hands. The Galician Chronicle, written, it is true, from the prince's point of view and not without prejudice against the nobles, contains numerous complaints against them and names as their leading characteristics a love of intrigue, selfishness, and pride. There is a story of a noble named Dobroslav who, clad only in a shirt, rode through Halich on his way to see the king; he was so proud of himself that he would not even look down while "the people ran at his stirrup." The sympathy of the people was entirely with Roman in this conflict.

The fame of Roman as a powerful, conscientious prince who would permit no one to infringe upon his rights was widespread. According to contemporary Polish and Byzantine writers his popularity extended not only to all Ukraine, but into the neighboring countries as well. This reputation awakened in the people of Ukraine the hope that in Roman they had at last found a man who could restore order, curb the petty princes, put an end to intrigues and quarreling, subdue the Polovtsians and other foreign enemies, and ensure better living conditions.

With his position firmly established at home, Roman turned his attention to Kiev, where the plotting of Vsevolod and the general chaos promised an easy conquest. When he directed a campaign against his father-in-law Rurik, the King of Kiev, the Kievans departed from their usual policy of noninterference in the quarrels of the princes and opened the gates of the city to him, in the belief that so powerful and ambitious a prince would restore the old preëminence of the city. Their hopes, however, were not realized. Under the existing conditions of unrest Roman did not consider it advisable to remain in Kiev but appointed to reside there first his brother Yaroslav and later Rostislav, the son of Rurik. Kiev remained subject to Roman, nevertheless. Contemporary writers entitled him "Grand Prince," "Tsar," and "Autocrat of All Rus." Yet the broader projects of Roman did not materialize, for in 1205 he died suddenly while fighting against the Polish princes. Hopes for the resurrection of Ukrainian political power perished with him, and the Galician-Volynian dual principality tottered.

The Dynasty of Roman: Roman was survived by two small sons—Daniel, who was three, and Vasilko, only a year old. The government was left in the hands of their young mother, who placed herself under the protection of King Andrew II of Hungary, who had been a friend and ally of her late husband. Hungary had for many years desired to cross the Carpathian Mountains and to annex Ukrainian Galicia, as she had already annexed Carpatho-Ukraine. Taking advantage of an invitation from the family of Roman, the Hungarian king became protector of Galicia. He brought to the capital, Halich, a Hungarian garrison and assumed the title of "King of Galicia and Volodimiria (Volynia)." Under his protection Galicia was to be ruled for the heirs by Roman's widow and the Galician nobles.

As soon as the stern Roman had passed from the scene, the nobles of Galicia began to raise their heads. They communicated with various princes who were eager to sit on the throne of Galicia and began to invite them to Halich. Among the ambitious candidates were the two sons of Ihor, of the dynasty of Sviatoslav. With the aid of the nobles they became joint rulers of Galicia, but were unable to live in peace with their proud supporters.

When the nobles began to conspire against them, the princes discovered their intentions and decided to kill the conspirators. They assassinated a large number of the chief plotters—several hundred, according to the author of the chronicle. The remaining nobles rallied, and in 1211 with the aid of the Hungarian king, whom they invited to come to their assistance, captured the two princes and hanged them. Such an event had never before occurred in Ukraine, where even during revolutions the person of a prince had been respected. After this experience, the nobles decided to remove their rulers whenever they threatened to become too strong. Thus they hoped to keep the government in their own hands and to remain all-powerful. A few of the Galician nobles felt that they were better off under the Hungarian protectorate, since the Hungarian king permitted them to administer the territory in his name. There were others who hoped to become rulers of Galicia themselves, and on at least one occasion a noble did so.

Upon discovering that the heirs of Roman were unable to oppose him, King Andrew II of Hungary decided to annex Galicia. For this purpose he entered into an alliance in 1214 with the Polish Prince Lieszko. Koloman, the son of King Andrew, was married to a daughter of Lieszko and was crowned king in Halich, with a crown sent by the Pope. Lieszko then seized for himself the provinces of Peremyshl and Bereste (Brest), permitting the family of Roman to keep a part of Volynia. This arrangement was of short duration; Andrew of Hungary soon quarreled with his ally, and attempts to unite the Ukrainian Church with Rome caused a revolt in Galicia.

Andrew had promised the Pope that he would bring about a union of the Churches in return for the crowning of Koloman, but the people were unwilling to accept Roman Catholicism. Lieszko now induced Mstislav, the nephew of Rurik and a noted warrior, to attack Koloman; Mstislav drove the Hungarians from Galicia.

The short-lived Hungarian protectorate had not, however, been entirely without result. A century later Poland and Hungary renewed their alliance for the purpose of partitioning Galicia-Volynia, and Poland actually seized Galicia, which she kept until her own dismemberment in the first partition of Poland in 1772.

Daniel and Vasilko, the sons of Roman, grew up amid these unceasing wars, uprisings, and intrigues. More than once they had to flee from home and seek asylum at foreign courts. Those nobles, however, who remained faithful to the memory of Roman had implicit faith in their future, and reared them with great regard for their name and their rights. As soon as they had come of age and had assumed their responsibilities as rulers of Galicia, they devoted all their energies to the task of reuniting their fatherland. In the accomplishment of this purpose they encountered many obstacles, but nothing daunted them.

By the Polish-Hungarian treaty there was left to Daniel and Vasilko only a part of Volynia, but there they were firmly established. The local nobles were loyal to them, and the people held in deep respect the memory of their father, Roman, and supported his sons. The other princes of Volynia died or lost their provinces in struggles with Roman's heirs. By 1230 they were in possession of almost all of Volynia, and after the death of Mstislav the Daring they began a serious struggle for Galicia, opposed by the King of Hungary and the hostile nobles.

The people of Galicia supported Daniel because they hated the autocracy, misrule, and selfishness of the nobles. Following the example of their father, the young rulers endeavored to extend their rule eastward in the direction of Kiev. During the Tatar attack on Kiev in 1240, a representative of Prince Daniel took part in the defense, and shortly afterward Daniel himself led an army against the Tatars in an effort to free Kiev and the rest of Ukraine from their raids. Having successfully reunited Galicia and Volynia, he next sought to reunite all Ukraine. In this ambitious program he had hopes of success, for in holding all the Volynian lands he was much more powerful than his father had been, and in the last quarter-century the princes in eastern Ukraine had grown much weaker. The Tatars, however, blocked his project.

The Tatar Raids: The barbaric nomads of the central Asiatic steppes had long hindered the development of Ukrainian progress and culture by pouring westward in ever fresh bands whenever earlier hordes had become civilized or weakened by contact with Ukraine. Once more a rapacious army pressed into Europe, this time made up of Mongolian Tatars. The details of this latest invasion are much better known than those of earlier movements, as there are complete reports written by the invaders themselves. It had its origin among the Mongolian tribes of the southern Amur basin. For a long time these tribes were of little importance, as they were vassals of their western neighbors, the Turks; but at the end of the twelfth century they were united by a great military leader named Temuchin, who began to overcome the near-by Turkish and Tatar tribes.

In 1206 Temuchin was proclaimed Genghis-Khan, the "heavenly emperor." He conquered the kingdom of Tangut, northern China, and Turkestan, and went on to invade southeastern Europe. His commanding general, Subuday, ravaged Transcaucasia in 1220 and invaded Georgia by way of Derbent. The Polovtsians rallied the Yasians, Circassians, and others to oppose him, but Subuday defeated the Polovtsians in 1222 and destroyed their settlements on the lower Don.

The Polovtsians then appealed for aid to the princes of Ukraine, with whom they were at the time on peaceful terms. Mstislav the Daring, who had married a daughter of Khan Khotan of the Polovtsians, used his influence to persuade other princes to aid them against the Tatars. He declared that if they did not aid the Polovtsians, the latter would have to join with the Tatars, who would thus gain fresh forces for their invasion of Ukraine. There was an element of truth in this argument, but the Ukrainian princes, in their efforts to aid the Polovtsians, became too deeply involved themselves: they assembled an army from all Ukraine and advanced far into the steppes to seek out the Tatars. In 1224* there was a great battle on the Kalka, a small river flowing into the Sea of Azov. The Ukrainian contingents fought bravely, but the Polovtsians were seized with panic and disrupted the whole army by their flight.

Mstislav III of Kiev, who had not taken part in the battle, was besieged in his fortified camp on the banks of the Kalka. Though abandoned by the other princes, he de-

---

* The date 1224 is given in some chronicles; other chronicles have 1223, which is now generally accepted (Editor).

fended himself stubbornly, but finally surrendered to friendly contingents among the Tatars. They, however, turned him over to other Tatar chieftains, who smothered Mstislav and the other captured princes under a platform of planks upon which the Tatars feasted and danced.

After this victory the Tatars turned back to the east, ravaged the Volga region, and then disappeared into Turkestan. For several years nothing was heard of them. Meanwhile they were planning the conquest of the Black Sea area and were merely awaiting the opportune moment. In 1227 Temuchin died, and his domain was divided among his sons, who were to govern the empire under the supervision of a Great Khan whom they were to select from among themselves. The western part of the empire was assigned to a grandson of Temuchin named Batu, whose ambition it was to carry out the projected conquest of the Black Sea region. In 1236 he and the aged Subuday set out. Their army consisted of a few Mongols and a large body of Turks, whom the Ukrainian chroniclers designated as Tatars.

The expedition set out from the steppes between the Caspian Sea and Lake Aral. The invaders first attacked and laid waste the land of the Volga Bolgars; then they went up the Volga destroying villages belonging to Muscovy. After this raid they decided to push into the Black Sea region and settle accounts with the Polovtsians once and for all. This campaign occupied about two years, by the close of which the remnants of the Polovtsian bands had fled westward, chiefly to Hungary.

Next the Tatar hordes conquered the territories of the northern Caucasus, and in the autumn of 1239 opened their attack upon Ukraine. They took by storm Pereyaslav, on the Dnieper below Kiev, sacked the town, and killed without mercy all who fell into their hands. Even the bishop was murdered, though as a rule the nomads spared the clergy. Another Tatar army attacked the province of Chernihiv. The prince there rallied his forces and fought a battle against them, but was defeated with heavy losses and forced to retreat. The Tatars sacked and burned the city of Chernihiv.

Khan Manke then marched to attack Kiev, which, according to the Galician Chronicle, aroused his deep admiration as he gazed at it from across the Dnieper. He offered the Kievans terms of surrender, which the inhabitants refused, though the prince lost courage and fled. During the first Tatar invasion the princes had presented a bold and united front, but during the second all took to flight, each in his own direction.

A year passed. At the end of 1240 the Tatars again moved westward, making the capture of Kiev their first objective, and encamped near the hills of the city. The siege is vividly described in the chronicle. The nomads presented a frightful aspect; the grinding of their wooden axles, the cries of camels, and the neighing of horses made it impossible to hear one's own voice in the city. Disregarding the danger of the situation, although they knew of the fate of the people of Pereyaslav and Chernihiv, the Kievans bravely defended the city under their military governor, Dmitro. Batu decided to attack the walls from the side facing the Dnieper.

The Tatars were skilled in besieging cities. Day and night they hammered ceaselessly at the walls with their battering rams. As the fortifications began to fall, the inhabitants, led by Dmitro, manned the breaches. In the end the enemy gained control of the wall but were so exhausted from the battle that they were forced to rest for twenty-four hours. Taking advantage of this opportunity, the Kievans made a final effort to defend themselves by fortifying the old Cathedral of Prince Volodimir, into which they retreated, determined to continue the struggle. The fortifications, however, were so weak that the Tatars took the Cathedral with ease. Then the people fled to the balcony of the church, but the structure could not hold the weight of all who crowded upon it, and when the balcony collapsed they perished in its ruins. The capture of Kiev took place on December 6, 1240, a date which marks the close of the history of the medieval kingdom of Kiev. As to the fate of the remnants of the Kievan army, there is no record. Mention is made, however, of the fact that Batu pardoned Dmitro "on account of his bravery." In later times many disasters were suffered from Tatar raids, but although Kiev endured two terrible pillages and many lesser ones, the worst of all was that of 1240.

To make up for the time lost in the siege of Kiev, the Tatars, following in the footsteps of the Polovtsians, hastened unopposed across the provinces of Kiev, Volynia, and Galicia on their way to Hungary. The very news that the city of Kiev had fallen and that the terrible Mongols were moving westward caused princes, nobles, and the common people to seek refuge wherever they could find it. Some of the cities along his way Batu captured by treachery, and as soon as he had gained possession he slaughtered the inhabitants. But if the cities opposed him, he avoided them and went on. He took by storm Volodimir, the capital of Volynia, and put the whole population to death. Its churches, says the chronicle, were filled with corpses and not a living soul was left. Halich and many other cities fell into the hands of the marauders.

Other Tatar bands plundered Poland, Silesia, and Moravia, defeating every army that dared to oppose them. Batu, with his main army, finally invaded Hungary at the Solona River, defeating the Hungarian army and gaining control of their country. He wished to remain there, but news reached him that the Great Khan had died, and being ambitious to succeed him, Batu returned to Asia in order to influence the election. In the spring of 1242 he rapidly crossed Ukraine on his way east.

Failing to become Great Khan, Batu settled down on the Caspian and Azov steppes. He and his bands occupied the lower Volga, where he founded the city of Sarai, near later Tsarev. Vassal groups spread out as far to the west as the Dnieper. Batu then ordered the Suzdalian and Ukrainian princes to come to his capital and pay him homage. He also sent officials to collect tribute in all the lands which he considered his dependencies. Both Ukraine and Great Russia (Muscovy) had entered upon a dark period in their history.

Under the Yoke of the Tatars: When the princes and nobles abandoned the land upon the arrival of the Tatars the people took advantage of the opportunity to free themselves from the cruelty and oppression of the old order. Not infrequently entire villages surrendered to the Tatars as early as Batu's first march across Ukraine in the winter of 1240–41. They promised to pay tribute in grain, to recognize Tatar sovereignty, and to pledge their loyalty to it. They had had enough of princes and wished to be governed by elders of their own choice.

This arrangement suited the Tatars, as they too wished to be rid of the Ukrainian princes. Any lessening of the power of the princes would make peaceful control over the subject provinces easier, for without rulers or armies the separate communities were incapable of resistance. Therefore from the free cities the Tatars collected their tribute in the form of grain and left the people to govern themselves in peace.

It is not known with certainty how widespread this revolutionary movement was. There is a reference to these so-called "Tatar people" in connection with a campaign which Daniel of Galicia undertook against them in an effort to put down their uprisings with their threat to the princely order. The revolts broke out in the border areas of Volynia and Kiev, along the rivers Sluch, Horyn, Teterev, and Buh (Bug), where Daniel made campaigns to suppress them. It is probable that the movement extended to the lower Dnieper as well, but there is no information as to whether it also affected the upper Dnieper valley. Wherever possible the Tatars encouraged its spread.

The rebellion against the princes and nobles destroyed the already decaying system of princely government along the Dnieper. Some of the princes appealed to Batu to permit them to rule over Kiev. Yaroslav of Suzdal was the first prince to turn to Batu for confirmation of his rights and received authority to rule not only in his own lands but also in Kiev. When this became known, princes from other provinces vied with one another in reaching Batu to ask him for special rights to coveted districts. Possibly they feared the popular movement or dreaded the possibility that the Tatars might abolish the principalities and take the lands under their direct control. One of the petitioners was Prince Michael of Chernihiv, who asked to have his claims to Chernihiv recognized, but who was slain by the Tatars when he refused to cleanse himself with fire and bow down before the images of the khan's ancestors according to Tatar custom.

For a long time Kiev was left without a prince while the inhabitants governed themselves; the princely thrones in Pereyaslav and Chernihiv were also vacant. The princes of the region migrated northward away from the Tatars into the old land of the Viatiches. In the latter part of the thirteenth century and in the fourteenth, however, they again became numerous but lacked political power, having been reduced to the status of great landlords. In the upper Dnieper valley the Ukrainian princes, nobles, and higher clergy also found it advisable to emigrate. The common people, on the other hand, did not suffer any more under Tatar sovereignty than they had under their own princes and nobles, especially as the khans still had great authority in the horde and carried on government in an orderly way, permitting no harm to be done to those who submitted, and levying lighter taxes than had the Ukrainian princes and nobles.

The emigrating upper classes moved to the provinces where the old regime still prevailed, as it did in the north and in western Ukraine. As they went they carried with them books, icons, works of art, and other products of their local culture; as a result of this emigration the cultural development of the lower Dnieper valley became greatly retarded, and what culture was left was chiefly restricted to the monasteries. The common people devoted all their efforts to supporting themselves and took little interest in esthetic matters, as there was no one to patronize art and literature. Interest in local history also died out, and for this reason we know little about the period of Tatar domination.

King Daniel: While political and cultural life was thus decaying in the Dnieper region, it was flourishing in the country of Galicia-Volynia, which emerged from its domestic confusion and became powerful and independent. In 1245, immediately following the invasion of Batu, Daniel and Vasilko defeated the last usurper of the Galician crown, Prince Rostislav, the son-in-law of the Hungarian king, whom the Hungarians had supported against the heirs of Roman. After this there was peace in Galicia. Daniel took charge of Galicia and his brother Vasilko of Volynia, as before; the brothers lived in amity and in such close alliance that in reality there was no boundary between their dominions.

The Tatar invasion caused great destruction but did not undermine the local social and political order. There was for a time even some question whether the khan and the Tatars had any sovereignty over this part of western Ukraine, but this doubt was not of long duration. In about 1245 the Tatars requested Daniel to surrender his capital, Halich, to another prince who had been granted the right to it by the khan. Daniel realized that if he did not recognize the supremacy of the Tatars they would continually support other pretenders and cause him endless difficulty. In humiliation and sorrow he went to the capital of the horde and did homage to the khan, who received him with great respect but gave him to understand that he was only a vassal. The chronicler, deeply moved by his loyalty to

Daniel, tells how the khan offered Daniel the fermented mare's milk, *kumys,* which was the common beverage of the Tatars and other steppe people. "You are now a Tatar," he said; "drink what we drink!" Daniel was given recognition as the lawful ruler but in return had to acknowledge himself a slave of the khan. "When he returned to his native land his brother and his sons came to meet him. They all wept because of his humiliation, but were glad that he had returned alive."

Though Daniel's homage to the Tatars had brought him tears and shame, his visit to the horde had greatly strengthened his position, as none of his neighbors dared to antagonize him for fear of inviting retaliation by the Tatars. All Europe trembled before the nomads in fear lest they renew their march westward.

Daniel was unable to reconcile himself to the "Tatar yoke" and awaited only an opportune time to free himself from their sovereignty and also to liberate the Kievan region from their control. The popular movement at Kiev held great dangers for him, for the Tatars were making attempts to encourage a similar trend in Galicia-Volynia and were finding supporters there. Daniel therefore decided to suppress it and with it the Tatar protectorate. On his way east to visit the Tatars he met papal delegates who were also en route to the khan. They told him, among other things, that the Pope was organizing all the Christian powers of Europe to make war upon the Tatars. When they counseled Daniel to recognize the supremacy of the Pope, he and his brother opened negotiations with the papacy in order to gain military support.

The granting of such aid, however, was beyond the Pope's power. Instead, he tried to persuade the Galician princes to accept Catholicism, and promised in return to crown Daniel king. Daniel hesitated to accept this proposal, for he feared to offend the Tatars; but his family persuaded him to agree. A papal legate accordingly came to Galicia in 1253 and crowned him in the city of Dorohichin; as soon as King Daniel discovered, however, that the Pope was unable to give him any actual military assistance, he severed relations with him. The plan of uniting the Ukrainian Church with Rome was also arousing a rebellious spirit among his subjects. To antagonize Daniel against the Pope, they recalled a story to the effect that the Pope had also promised Daniel's father, Roman, a crown and the "sword of St. Peter," whereupon Roman had drawn his own sword and showed it to the papal delegate, declaring that while he had this he needed no other.

Meanwhile Daniel's relations with the Tatars became so strained that, losing hope of receiving aid from his neighbors, the Poles and the Hungarians, he decided to undertake war against them alone. In 1254 he sent his forces against the Tatars and the "Tatar people" of Ukraine. The towns refused to surrender; or if they did, they revolted as soon as he had left. Daniel feared that if he did not suppress this popular movement it would spread throughout Ukraine and wreck all political life. He therefore decided to destroy its centers by burning the towns and enslaving the people who refused to submit to him. With the aid of an ally, the Lithuanian King Mendovg, he made preparations to march against Kiev; but the Lithuanians were not ready in time and the campaign was postponed. By the time he was able to make fresh preparations conditions had so changed that it was useless to think of attacking the Tatars.

To punish Daniel the Tatar military governor in charge of the frontier sent a force into Volynia; it was, however, so weak that it was easily repulsed. Later the horde sent another commander, Burundai, with a larger army. Burundai announced that he was on his way to attack Poland. Daniel and his brother were dancing at the wedding of Vasilko's daughter when Burundai sent an ultimatum from the border of Volynia. To escape destruction the sons of Roman were obliged to make another visit to the khan to renew their allegiance to him. This time the khan ordered them to destroy the fortifications of all their cities in order to prevent future defense against the horde. Only Kholm, the favorite city of Daniel, was saved by a pretended misunderstanding of the order.

The loss of his fortresses was too great a blow for Daniel to endure: all his projects had failed; the neighboring Christian powers had given him no help against the Tatars; his efforts to enlarge his domains by annexing Polish and Lithuanian cities had also come to nothing. Unlike the Muscovite princes, Daniel could not accommodate himself to the rule of the Tatars, and under this humiliation he fell ill and died in 1264.

Galicia-Volynia under Daniel's Heirs: What Daniel had failed to accomplish, his successors also failed to do. The kingdom of Galicia-Volynia did not long endure, though while it lasted it enjoyed great power and played an important role. It was unable to conquer the rest of Ukraine or to expand at the expense of its western neighbors, though on several occasions its rulers made serious attempts to do so. In the east the Tatars blocked the way, while the western countries were too foreign in nature to be easily assimilated.

Daniel's sons coveted the Lithuanian throne. One of them, Shvarno, succeeded in making himself Grand Duke of Lithuania but died shortly after doing so. In the course of time the Galician princes lost their power over Lithuania, and its rulers became in turn dangerous neighbors, casting hungry eyes upon the lands of Galicia-Volynia. The Tatars also caused frequent disturbances, especially when anarchy reigned in the horde itself because of internal struggles for supremacy. On the whole, the Tatar yoke was not as oppressive as in eastern Ukraine or in Muscovy. The Tatars did not intervene in the internal affairs of the state but were satisfied with the periodical collection of tribute.

Daniel's younger son, Vasilko, succeeded him but did not live long after his succession. Upon the death of Vasilko, peace was at an end. Among the sons of Daniel the most ambitious and energetic was Leo, after whom the city of Lviv (Lwow, Lemberg) was named. He dreamed of conquering the near-by Polish provinces and even planned to make himself ruler in Cracow, but his projects came to naught. He was also unsuccessful in his attempts to take advantage of anarchy in Hungary to regain Carpatho-Ukraine.

Volynia was now governed by Vasilko's son, Volodimir, an able ruler and a lover of books; "such a philosopher," says the chronicle, "has never lived in the land before nor will again." Yet he was a man of passive disposition and handicapped by ill health. By the beginning of the fourteenth century the dynasty of Roman had died out in Volynia and all Galicia and Volynia again fell into the hands of a single ruler, Prince George (Yuriy), the son of Leo. His royal seal bore the inscription "King of Rus," as had that of his grandfather, Daniel. He was a strong prince and a capable administrator, under whose hands the unruly country settled down to peace and prosperity, as both Polish and Ukrainian sources testify.

At about this time, or possibly as early as the reign of Leo, an important event took place—the division of the Rus Church into two metropolitan dioceses. On account of the constant Tatar attacks upon Kiev, the metropolitans preferred to stay in Suzdal-Muscovy, and by 1299 the metropolitan had left Kiev for good. The princes of Galicia then sought and obtained in 1303 from the Patriarch of Constantinople and the Byzantine emperor special authority to found a new diocese in Galicia; the religious bonds uniting the Ukrainian people were seriously weakened by this act, for the Dnieper region remained subject to the former metropolitan.

King George was succeeded by his two sons, Andrew and Leo, who reigned until 1320, when both died without male heirs. Their deaths created a dangerous situation for Galicia-Volynia, surrounded as it was by greedy neighbors only awaiting an opportunity to dismember it; there was, however, no internal disturbance. The nobles selected a close relative of the last rulers, a Polish prince named Boleslav, who had been baptized in the Catholic Church but now accepted the Greek Orthodox faith and a new Orthodox name, George (Yuriy) II, in honor of his grandfather, George (Yuriy) I. He was crowned Prince of Galicia-Volynia in 1325.

The position of the new prince was difficult; he was a foreigner and for this reason was viewed with suspicion. At the same time, the nobles considered that since he was indebted to them for his crown, they were his patrons and entitled to govern in his name. As he disliked this situation he surrounded himself with foreigners, chiefly Czechs and Germans. This conduct, of course, added to the dissatisfaction; rumors spread that he was working in the interests of the Catholics with the aim of establishing Catholicism and uprooting the Greek Orthodox Church. Dissatisfied with George-Boleslav and his refusal to be their tool, the nobles themselves encouraged these rumors and stirred up further ill-feeling against him.

Noting this dissension in Galicia-Volynia, Poland and Hungary decided to seize the country. Accordingly, in 1339, a secret treaty was signed between Casimir, the King of Poland, and Carol, the King of Hungary, in which they agreed to conquer and divide Galicia. This was a renewal of the Polish-Hungarian alliance of 1214. The King of Hungary believed that Galicia should belong to him because during Daniel's boyhood the King of Hungary had been its protector. But the agreement now made between the two rulers provided that if either of them died without male heirs, the other should inherit the kingdom. The King of Hungary also promised his ally military aid in conquering other Ukrainian provinces.

Meanwhile, the discontented nobles communicated with Grand Duke Liubart of Lithuania, who had married the Princess of Galicia-Volynia, and plotted to make him their prince. After entering into an agreement with him, they poisoned King George on April 7, 1340. Uprisings immediately followed, and many foreign Catholics who had been brought in by the king were killed. Liubart was crowned Prince of Volynia in the city of Volodimir; Galicia was to be governed by the nobles, who recognized Liubart as their prince. The actual administration was in the hands of one of their own number, Dmitro Dedko.

As soon as news of George-Boleslav's death reached Hungary and Poland, these powers attacked Galicia in accordance with their secret agreement. The Polish army was led by the king himself, and the Hungarian army by the palatin, Willerm. When Dedko, the governor of Galicia, learned of the Polish-Hungarian invasion, he immediately appealed to the Tatars for assistance. The Hungarians, in all probability, returned home at once. Learning of possible Tatar aid to Galicia, Casimir became frightened and retreated so rapidly that he had to abandon the spoils he had captured during his advance. News now came that the Tatars were preparing a great expedition against Poland because of her attacks on Galicia. This information so alarmed the Polish ruler that he opened negotiations with Dedko, asking him to dissuade the Tatars. Dedko agreed, Casimir swore not to molest Galicia again, and for some time it seemed that the Galician-Volynian state had escaped danger. As soon as the Tatar threat had been removed, however, Casimir broke his oath and went to the Pope for absolution; then he awaited the hour when he could attack Galicia. He began his campaign in about 1345, and took Sianok and other districts, but was forced to sign a peace with Liubart, who nominally ruled over Galicia until 1349. Then Casimir persuaded the Tatars not to interfere, and when the latter had agreed he launched an unexpected attack which gave him Galicia and part of Volynia. In this manner war began between him and Liubart, which finally resulted in the loss of the independence of Galicia-Volynia and opened a new period in the life of the Ukrainian people, the Lithuanian-Polish period.

Political Organization in the Period of Decline: The independence of the Ukrainian lands thus came to an end in the middle of the fourteenth century. The Poles had seized Galicia, Volynia had temporarily become a province of Lithuania, and the other principalities in the regions of Kiev and Chernihiv, as fast as they freed themselves, had also fallen under the control of the dukes of Lithuania. Thus the Ukrainian state foundered.

The main outlines of the political and civil organization of the Ukrainian state have already been described.* Ukraine was divided into principalities, some large and some small, but all tending to become subdivided as the number of members in the princely families increased. The King, or Grand Prince, of Kiev was considered the senior among the royal princes; all the others were expected to obey him and to live at peace with one another. For a time they did, especially when there was a strong and energetic prince on the throne of Kiev, but during the second half of the twelfth century the Prince of Suzdal claimed to be the senior and weakened the supremacy of Kiev. After the close of this century the Galician princes claimed seniority over all of western Ukraine. For a short time Kiev still retained its leadership in the Dnieper region, but even there it soon lost its importance.

As far as the domestic affairs of his own principality were concerned, each prince was entirely independent, and none was permitted to interfere in the affairs of another. The prince governed with the support of his retinue (*druzhina*) of warriors, who were paid out of the funds which he was able to take in from contributions and income from his personal possessions. At first the retinue was very mobile, migrating with or without its prince from one province to another. Later the warriors settled down, took root in the soil, and occupied themselves with

* See pp. 85 ff.

the management of their estates. All the functions of lo-cal government—the trial of cases and enforcement of justice, the making of laws and determination of policy, the levying and collection of taxes—were in the hands of the prince and his retinue, who administered them in his name. The townspeople sometimes interfered when they observed abuses: in some provinces the city *viche* or gen-eral assembly made investigations and discussed reforms, frequently presented petitions—a right which the prince recognized—proffered complaints, and even changed princes. But when the prince felt strong enough he paid no attention to these infringements upon his authority and attempted to suppress the general assembly; this re-mained, however, a significant expression of the wishes of the townspeople, not to be sure of the ordinary people, but of the upper class, and especially of the merchant no-bility.

The common people on the whole had no influence, and merely looked on passively. The prince's administration was primarily under the influence of the nobles, while the misfortunes which overwhelmed Ukraine forced the vil-lagers and smaller tradesmen into ever greater depend-ence upon the nobility. Many of the people became so im-poverished that they lost their freedom and became serfs. The laws and administration provided by the prince fa-vored the rich and powerful nobles rather than the com-mon people, and if anything at all was done for them it was out of fear of revolt. The free population was re-placed by an ever-increasing number of unfree people—slaves and domestics—and half-free people—tenants and indentured laborers—who often descended into slavery. The Church also failed to raise its voice in defense of the poor and oppressed devoting itself largely to advising them to be loyal and obedient rather than to rebuking those in power for misuse of authority.

Oppressed by economic slavery and lacking a voice in the government, the masses of the people did not place any high value upon the existing political order. It was for this reason that the cities accepted without protest control by the Tatars and later raised no objection to the authority of the grand dukes of Lithuania. Nor under the circumstances did they value political independence for the nation as a whole. National independence had been of importance only while the national government had been able to defend the people from political and economic enslavement at the hands of foreign powers, and to preserve and foster a national culture.

Culture and Education: In its earlier stages the Kievan state had served the cultural interests of the masses of the people. As long as the governing system was native to the soil, the governing classes—king, nobles, and Church—were in close contact with the common people and made use of the power of the government to develop and propagate an indigenous national culture. Later on learning, literature, and art fell under the strong influence of the Byzantine Church and lost contact with the actual life of the people. Underneath the foreign and superficial modes of thought the native culture based on the life of the people continued to develop, always more and more in conflict with the foreign elements, until its course was blocked by the revolutions and disruption accompanying the collapse of the political order.

It has already been pointed out that Greek Orthodoxy and other Byzantine cultural influences had been introduced into Ukraine prior to the time of Volodimir. During his reign and that of his successors these movements spread to the far corners of the country. Byzantine customs and culture conquered the earlier types which had been primarily southern, especially Persian and Arabian. With the introduction of Christianity cultural life acquired a religious flavor which was especially noticeable in education, literature, and art. Books and education were considered essential in the extension of Christianity: learning and literature were thus chiefly in the hands of the clergy, and art was applied chiefly to the service of the Church. This situation, it is true, was not restricted to Ukraine alone, being equally prevalent in Western Europe. Much time was to pass before secular culture would take preëminence over that of the Church.

Education was poorly organized and not available to the masses so long as the Ukrainian clergy used educational methods adopted from Byzantium. Only the larger monasteries and cathedrals conducted regular schools; wealthy parents who did not send their sons to the monastic schools usually had them taught in private lessons by the clergy, and this system of tutoring also restricted learning to the few.

What education existed was generally limited to reading, less frequently including writing and arithmetic. A knowledge of other subjects was obtained from books, but these were few, and for the most part of a liturgical character. Only in the larger centers was it possible to acquire a higher education, which consisted of learning to write in a correct "literary" style and to read Greek in order to understand Greek books in the original. Men who had reached this highest level of Greek enlightenment were present in the first generation after the introduction of Christianity: among the most noted were Metropolitan Ilarion, Bishop Kyrilo of Turiv, and the authors of several anonymous works. The number of these highly educated writers was very small; the majority of the authors were self-taught men who wrote as best they could.

Most of the Greek books translated into Slavonic in Ukraine or imported in translation from Bulgaria or Serbia were the work of priests or monks, intended for the propagating of the Christian faith and the nurturing of religious folk in the Christian life. Most native literature was of this type, and was produced in the eleventh century by such men as Ilarion, who wrote the *Eulogy to Volodimir the Great;* St. Theodosius, the author of sermons; Jacob, the monk, and Nestor, coauthors of biographies of Volodimir the Great, of Boris and Gleb, and of St. Theodore; and the Abbot Daniel, who wrote of his pilgrimage to the Holy Land. The best-known authors of the twelfth century were Metropolitan Klym; Kyrilo, the bishop of Turiv, who wrote prayers and sermons; and George Zarubsky. Outstanding writers of the thirteenth century were Simon and Policarp, who described the monastic life, and the preacher Serapion. These authors are known by name, but there were many others whose names are unknown and whose works have been lost. Most of the Slavonic works that have come down to us are from the pens of authors who migrated north and settled down in Great Russia, and thus were removed from the field of Ukrainian literature, especially as in the twelfth century, particularly its second half, relations with Kiev were rapidly becoming weaker. Literary production in Ukraine itself fell off during the decline of Kiev. For this reason little is known of early Ukrainian literature.

Next in importance to strictly religious literature were the chronicles. Though they were written by churchmen and have much to do with Church affairs, they reveal many aspects of the life of the time. What information is available regarding cultural, economic, and civic life has been found in these chronicles, which contain fragments of popular legends, songs, literary productions, and official documents; they are the archives of Ukrainian cultural life. Several annalists displayed considerable originality of thought and a deep interest in the events of the time, and few peoples can pride themselves upon such fascinating chronicles. Unfortunately only small portions have been preserved.

A collection of annals known as the Primary Chronicle was put into literary form in Kiev during the first quarter of the twelfth century; it included fragments dating back as far as the beginning of the eleventh. At the end of the thirteenth century another collection of chronicles was made in northern Volynia. At the same time the Primary Chronicle was supplemented by the Kievan annals of the twelfth century; then there followed the Galician Chronicle of the period of Daniel, and the Volynian Chronicle of the last half of the thirteenth century, down to the 1280's. Without the aid of these precious collections very little would be known of Ukrainian history.

Of the secular literature of the period one of the most valuable examples is the *Instructions of Monomakh to His Sons,* with its illustrations drawn from his own life. In poetry the most important contribution is without a doubt the *Song of the Legion of Ihor,* composed in 1185. It is characterized by deep poetic feeling and is at the same time important as a witness to the strong and broad spring of secular military poetry, in which were united a national literary creativeness and the influences of Greek literature. In its poetic imagination the *Song* is unique in Ukrainian literature; on the other hand, it has much in common with other writings of the end of the twelfth and the beginning of the thirteenth centuries which combine the feeling of poetry and the artistry of prose, such as the sermons of Kyrilo of Turiv, the sermon on the raising of the wall at the Vitebsk Monastery in the year 1200, the *Prayer of Daniel,* and the Galician Chronicle. In these works a deep literary tradition is given the polish of a scholarly and mature style.

Especially notable in the fine arts are examples of church architecture, a few paintings, rare miniature illuminations in manuscripts, and a rich variety of goldwork decorated with designs and enamel. In all these arts the native craftsmen worked with Greek masters, and frequently excelled their Byzantine models in originality and skill.

The least native originality during the Kievan period was displayed in architecture, although even here the local craftsmen departed freely from the Greek models, as appears in the few examples still existing in Galicia. Especially great artistry was achieved in the illumination 'of books in Kiev. The most original and distinguished work was that of the goldsmiths; in this field the local artisans succeeded from the very beginning in freeing themselves from Byzantine influences; the creations of the native goldsmiths compare favorably with those of contemporary craftsmen in Western Europe, and the same statement would hold true in general of Ukrainian culture of the eleventh to thirteenth centuries. Although this culture differed from that of the west, it was on an equally high plane.

In time, with the weakening of communications, the influence of Byzantium lost its original force; and as the center of Ukrainian political life moved from Kiev to the cities of Volodimir and Halich in the west, other phases of life also fell under western influences. The existing examples of Galician culture of the twelfth to fourteenth centuries show clear evidence of a merging of western elements with the basic Ukrainian and Byzantine styles. This merging explains why there was in Galicia so little fear of Catholicism. The Ukrainian townspeople, living as they did in close contact with their Catholic western neighbors, had none of that aversion for Romanism which the Greek clergy attempted to instill in eastern Ukraine. The princes made use of the Latin language in their official correspondence with western countries, and used Latin seals. In the larger cities German immigrants settled down, introducing German law and bringing western influences to bear on Ukraine. In the inventories of the churches are mentioned time and again objects of western origin or style. The rulers, however, retained their basic Ukrainian-Byzantine ideals, the population clung stubbornly to its own culture, and in the Latin writings the princes define their national identity by entitling themselves "princes of all Little Rus."*

* Little Rus, it should be noted, was the name applied in the Greek manner to the original core of a land, in contrast with the name Great Rus given to its extensions, as today one would speak of New York proper as against Greater New York (Editor).

Generally speaking, the cultural life of Ukraine from the eleventh to the fourteenth centuries had a great fascination; it was teeming with life, vigor, and energy, and bore high promise of contributing richly to its own nation and to human civilization as a whole. It is highly unfortunate that it was hampered at the very outset by the loss of political independence, and that its progress was thus halted in infancy. It is true that before the loss of political independence the common people had suffered abuses from their kings, princes, and nobles; but their lot failed to improve under foreign rule. With the collapse of the economic and social order the national cultural life suffered a blow, from the effects of which it has never recovered.

CHAPTER VIII

UKRAINE UNDER POLAND-LITHUANIA

Lithuanian Expansion in Ukraine: During the second half of the thirteenth century and the whole of the fourteenth the power of the princes of Lithuania expanded with extraordinary rapidity and success, at first over the neighboring territory of White Russia and then over the Ukrainian lands beyond. The Lithuanians, for long the most backward and neglected among the peoples of Europe, had been threatened by German expansion. In their determined struggle for survival they developed a remarkable organizing ability and tried to extend their sovereignty over the more highly civilized neighboring Slavic countries. The program of expansion was initiated in the middle of the thirteenth century in the reign of the Lithuanian Prince Mendovg and called forth opposition on the part of King Daniel of Galicia, who was also bent upon extending his power over his neighbors. Daniel made an alliance with the Teutonic Knights and the Poles for the purpose of subduing Mendovg, and then declared war upon him. To save himself, Mendovg permitted Daniel's son Roman to annex a few Lithuanain towns. A few years later Mendovg's son Voishelk recognized Shvarno, another son of Daniel, as his successor to the Lithuanian throne; but Shvarno died soon thereafter in 1264, and Daniel's other sons failed to take advantage of the situation. Mendovg's lands passed into the hands of other Lithuanian princes, who undertook a new campaign of expansion.

In the first quarter of the fourteenth century most of White Russia was seized by Lithuanian princes, who were now prepared to annex parts of Ukraine. During the last years of the dynasty of Daniel, the Lithuanians annexed districts in the vicinity of the upper Buh, the Pripet, and the Pinsk rivers, and a Lithuanian prince by the name of Vid seized the Ukrainian province of Polisia. During the reign of Gedymin in the 1320's, even Kiev fell under Lithuanian control, although the local princes still recognized the sovereignty of the Tatars. The election by the Ukrainian nobles of Liubart, the son of Gedymin, as Prince of Galicia to succeed Boleslav hastened Lithuanian expansion into Ukraine, and was also clear evidence that there was no ill feeling against the Lithuanians.

The petty Lithuanian princes, after acquiring White Russian and Ukrainian territories, quickly adapted themselves to the local customs and culture. They tried to introduce as few changes as possible, proclaiming, ''We neither destroy the old customs nor introduce new.'' They accepted the Greek Orthodox faith, adopted the Ukrainian or White Russian language and habits, and carried on the old forms of government, although under their own local dynasties. Many communities which had grown tired of the civil strife of their old princes and the corrupt rule of the Tatars welcomed the change, for the Lithuanian rulers were powerful enough to assure safety from invasion. The Ukrainian princes disliked the loss of their sovereign rights, but were frequently allowed to retain their posts on condition of recognizing the Lithuanian prince who reigned in their capital. Thus, almost imperceptibly and without bloodshed, the Ukrainian provinces fell one after another under Lithuanian control. The change took place so quietly that even the Ukrainian sources do not always mention this skilful Lithuanian penetration.

Liubart, it has been noted, was chosen prince of Galicia in 1340. He ruled there only until Galicia was seized by Poland in 1349, but reigned in the neighboring province of Volynia until his death more than forty years later. In the 1350's Grand Duke Olgerd of Lithuania expanded his possessions to the east and south by conquering Briansk in northern Chernihiv, and the southern principalities of

Novhorod-Siversky and Starodub, where he installed Lithuanian princes as rulers.

In about 1360 Olgerd deposed the last Ukrainian prince of Kiev, Theodore, annexed the province, and placed his own son Volodimir on the throne. The principality of Kiev was in a state of economic ruin after a long period of rule by the Tatars, but as one of the largest it still had some importance. The Tatars, who looked upon Kiev as one of their possessions, attempted to protect Theodore as their vassal, but the horde was so disorganized and demoralized by internal strife that it was unable to offer serious resistance. Olgerd marched south with his army, defeated the Tatars, and seized not only Kiev but also Podolia, which had also been under the control of the horde. The nephews of Olgerd were made local princes in the cities of Podolia and began to fortify their capitals against the Tatars. The chronicle of the second half of the fifteenth century describes these events as follows:

While the great Olgerd was ruling over Lithuania he led his army into the Ukrainian steppes and at the Blue Water defeated the three Tatar brothers—Kochubey, Kutlubuh, and Dmitro— who had ruled over Podolia and collected taxes there. Olgerd's brother, Koriat, who ruled over Novhorod-Litovsky, had three sons—George, Alexander, and Fedir—who were now made the rulers of Podolia. In this province not a single city had been fortified, as the Tatars had not permitted it. The Lithuanian princes put a stop to the payment of tribute to the Tatars and successfully defended the province. They built fortifications on the River Smotrich and founded the city of the same name. Monks dwelt on one of the hills, and there the city of Bakot was founded. On an island where their hunters had often driven deer, they built the city of Kaminets. At last all the cities of Podolia were fortified and the land was occupied.

For some time the people of Podolia continued to pay occasional tribute to the Tatars in order to avoid trouble, and the province was still considered subject to them. The

same was true of other provinces, and for this reason the
royal coins of the Kievan Prince Volodimir, the son of Olgerd, bore the Tatar insignia. But the Mongols ceased to
interfere in the internal affairs of the old Kievan principality, which was governed by princes of the Lithuanian
dynasty.

The Partition of Galicia-Volynia: The Lithuanian
princes were fortunate in meeting with no powerful opposition to their acquisition of east Ukrainian territory.
They were able to annex only provinces that submitted
readily, as they did not have formidable forces for carrying on a severe struggle, and as their kingdom in spite of
its vast area was very poorly organized. Taking advantage of this situation, the Teutonic Knights and the Livonian "Brothers of the Sword" of the Baltic region, who
had already conquered and enslaved the Lithuanian tribes
of Prussians and Letts and now desired to acquire Lithuania, made continual attacks upon the country. In the east
the Lithuanian princes waged wars with the Muscovite
princes who wished to annex the cities along the border.
Because of these circumstances the Lithuanians were unable to render much assistance in defense of Ukraine, and
when Liubart was engaged in a bitter struggle with Poland and Hungary for possession of western Ukraine, the
other princes gave him only occasional help. Galicia, left
between the two fires of Poland and Hungary and lacking
sufficient support from Liubart, fell victim to Poland.

Although under the nominal rule of Prince Liubart, Galicia continued to be self-governing until 1349, when King
Casimir of Poland suddenly attacked it, drove out the Tatars, and annexed it as well as a part of Volynia. Con-
fronted by this new danger, the Lithuanian princes came
to the aid of Liubart and reconquered the Volynian cities.
It was a more difficult task, however, to reconquer Galicia from the Poles, and failing in this they harassed
Casimir by a continuous plundering of Poland. In order
to defend his possessions, the Polish king renewed his al-

liance with King Louis of Hungary, and with financial support from the Pope at Rome he and his ally Hungary attempted to annex to Poland at least the Ukrainian territories of Belz and Kholm. Especially noteworthy was their siege of Belz in 1352, which encountered heroic resistance from the townspeople, undaunted by the large Polish and Hungarian forces. Negotiations for surrender were opened with the local governor, who temporized in order to gain time to fortify the city and to obtain aid from Lithuania. He managed to drag out the negotiations for an entire week while he constructed more effective fortifications and filled the moats with water. Finally informing the enemy that he would not surrender, he faced an attack which lasted from early morning until noon. The Polish and Hungarian soldiers, forced to fight in the moat in water up to their necks, sustained heavy losses; and Louis, suffering a blow on the head, fell from his horse and almost perished. Louis and his Hungarians, having lost all desire to fight on, abandoned Casimir and returned home, an example which the Poles followed.

After this unsuccessful expedition, Casimir came to an understanding with Lithuania according to which Galicia was to remain in the hands of Poland, while Liubart was to keep Volynia. The attempts to free Galicia from Poland had failed and were to fail again in the future. After Casimir occupied Galicia, he rooted out the anti-Polish factions and invited large numbers of Poles to settle there; for their benefit and that of other foreigners he dispossessed the Ukrainian nobles of their official positions and their large estates. He also induced Poles and Germans to move to the cities by granting them special concessions and privileges. With all his power he defended Galicia from the encroachments of Liubart, and was aided in his endeavor by the Hungarians, the Pope, and occasionally the Teutonic Knights. As a result, Liubart was unable to free Galicia from Poland.

The struggle continued over thirty years. In the meantime the Lithuanian princes harassed Poland by their many attacks and by inciting the Tatars to plunder the country, although Casimir eventually succeeded in gaining the friendship of the Tatars and in turning them against Liubart. Meanwhile Casimir made a secret alliance with the Teutonic and Livonian Knights for the purpose of attacking Lithuania from two directions, and in 1366 Poland attacked Volynia in the south, while the Germans fell upon Lithuania from the north. The Poles seized the cities of Belz, Kholm, and Volodimir; Belz and Kholm succeeded in freeing themselves, but Casimir retained Volodimir until his death in 1370. After Casimir's death, Liubart recaptured his capital, Volodimir, and again ravaged a part of Poland. Louis of Hungary, the new King of Poland, therefore declared war on Liubart, the struggle ending with the annexation to Galicia of the provinces of Belz and Kholm.

Louis did not intend to give Galicia to his Polish heirs but wished to keep it in Hungarian hands, in accordance with the old Polish-Hungarian alliance of 1214 and the secret treaty of 1339. He therefore gave Galicia as a Hungarian province to Volodislav, one of the Silesian princes, who governed the province from 1372 to 1378 under the supervision of the Hungarian government. Louis then transferred him to another post, and Galicia passed completely into the hands of the Hungarian officials and their army. After the death of Louis in 1382 the Polish nobles elected as their queen his younger daughter Yadviga; and since Hungary was undergoing a revolution, the Poles sent the young queen with an army to recapture Galicia. The attempt was successful, and Galicia was again united with Poland in 1387. The Hungarian government protested against this act but did not dare to oppose Poland by force of arms.

The Union of Poland and Lithuania: No one could have predicted how the struggle between the Lithuanian and Polish princes for the possession of the Ukrainian territories of Galicia and Volynia would end, but it reached an unexpected termination when Poland and Lithuania were united under the rule of the Grand Duke of Lithuania, who became King of Poland and permanently incorporated Lithuania into that country. This clever scheme originated with the Polish nobles. In order to free themselves from Hungarian influence, they had selected as queen the younger daughter of Louis. Now they were seeking a husband for her, and wanted someone who would not interfere with their interests. It is true that Yadviga was already engaged to marry an Austrian prince, Wilhelm, but he did not meet with their approval. They kept their eyes on Yagello, the young Grand Duke of Lithuania, in the expectation that if he were made king of Poland he would be so grateful that he would submit to their dictation. They were not disappointed, for he acceded to all their requests. He promised to make Lithuania Roman Catholic, and himself abandoned the Greek Orthodox faith for the Roman Catholic; he also promised to reconquer at his own expense the territory lost by Poland. The most important part of the agreement was that he would "unite Lithuania and his Ukrainian possessions with Poland for ever." The compact, signed in Krevo, Lithuania, August 15, 1385, is known as the "Krevo Union," and was of unusual significance to Eastern Europe.

After the agreement was made, the Polish nobles devoted their efforts to arranging the marriage of Yagello to Yadviga, but they encountered many obstacles. In the first place the mother of Yadviga notified Wilhelm, who hastened to Cracow, married Yadviga, and lived with her as her husband at the castle of Cracow. In order to separate them the nobles expelled Wilhelm from Cracow; Yadviga followed her husband in the hope of overtaking and bringing him back, but she was compelled to return home. Her marriage was proclaimed void and the Polish priests tried to persuade her that for the sake of Poland

and Catholicism she should marry Yagello; in the end
they were successful and Galicia was thus united to Poland. The nobles then awaited the fulfilment of Yagello's
promise to unite permanently to Poland the White Russian and Ukrainian lands belonging to Lithuania.

The great Lithuanian grand duchy now ceased to exist
as an independent state, and all the foreign territories belonging to it became a part of Poland. At the bidding of
the Polish nobles, King Yagello (1386–90) requested all
the Lithuanian princes who ruled the White Russian and
Ukrainian provinces to pledge allegiance to him, to his
wife, and to his children, and informed them that from
that time on their lands were a part of the kingdom of
Poland. As these princes had already recognized Yagello
as their sovereign, they drew up a document in which they
pledged their loyalty to him.

Later the princes and nobles discovered that they would
lose all their rights by the transaction and were much disturbed at the possibility. Vitovt, a cousin of the king, put
himself at the head of the malcontents. Twice before he
had waged war against Yagello in an effort to regain his
patrimony, and in 1392 Yagello had finally granted him
Lithuania and the title of grand duke. Taking advantage
of the dissatisfaction among the princes and nobles because of the Polish claims, Vitovt now proclaimed himself Grand Duke of Lithuania and prepared for another
war against Yagello. Meanwhile, Vitovt went on a campaign against the Tatars and at the battle of Vorskla in
1399 suffered a severe defeat. This catastrophe so blocked
his plans that instead of completing the separation of Poland and Lithuania he made an agreement with Yagello
in 1400, according to which Lithuania remained an independent state ruled over by Vitovt, who in turn recognized the claims of Yagello and his successors to the Polish throne. The union of the two nations was not so close
as that foreseen by the Union of Krevo; nevertheless,
Lithuania still remained bound to Poland and this connec-

tion had unfortunate results upon the internal conditions in all the Lithuanian lands, and the Ukrainian provinces in particular.

The New Policy in the Grand Duchy of Lithuania: The first move on the part of Yagello and Vitovt was an attempt to weaken the larger principalities subject to Lithuania. Almost all Ukraine consisted of such principalities, and the new policy therefore affected it most drastically. After the death of Liubart, Volynia passed into the hands of his popular son Fedir; Podolia was governed by Prince Fedir of the dynasty of Koriat; Kiev and the region beyond the Dnieper were governed by Volodimir of the family of Olgerd; Yagello's nephew governed the Ukrainian territories of Polisia, Ratno, Pinsk, and Chortoreisk; and Chernihiv was divided into the principalities of Chernihiv, Briansk, and Starodub, each ruled by a different prince. These extensive provinces led independent political lives and felt but little bound to Lithuania. The people were acquainted with their own princes, who, though of a Lithuanian dynasty, were frequently born in Ukraine, adopted Ukrainian culture, and became entirely assimilated. Under their supervision the local nobles governed the country according to the old laws, and therefore the masses were not much better off than before; but the national culture on the other hand was not suppressed, and the Ukrainians enjoyed the right to their own language and literature as well as freedom of assembly, while the Lithuanian princes even did all they could to foster the Orthodox Church.

Vitovt and Yagello next removed the chief princes from their thrones and transferred them to small and insignificant principalities where their power and influence were limited. The possessions thus freed they either governed directly or transferred so frequently from prince to prince that none of them could gain power; and in the end, royal appointees were installed in these provinces to rule in place of the hereditary princes.

In 1393 the province of Chernihiv was taken away from Dmitro Koribut. Prince Fedir lost first Lutsk and finally the whole of Volynia; in exchange he was offered principalities in Chernihiv, but refused to accept the change, and Vitovt therefore set out with an army to take Podolia from him. On his way he passed by Kiev and expelled Volodimir. Fedir attempted to defend himself with the aid of the Hungarians and the Wallachians, but in 1394 Vitovt attacked Podolia in the absence of Fedir, took the chief cities, and left viceroys in charge.

Within two years all the important princes were deposed in this manner. The province of Kiev was assigned to an able administrator, Prince Skirhailo, but he died shortly after taking office. At the beginning of the fifteenth century, there were left intact only such smaller principalities of Ukraine as Ratno, Pinsk, Chortoreisk, Starodub, and Ostroh, and even these resembled large estates more than they did the former principalities: they covered large areas but had no political significance. Ukraine thus became a province of Lithuania, subject to its direct administration and guided by its policies. After the Union these policies led to the introduction of drastic changes by which the Ukrainian system was reconstructed according to the Polish model.

After converting heathen Lithuania to Roman Catholicism, Yagello announced that in the future special privileges would be given only to nobles of that faith. He attempted to create a privileged Roman Catholic class of nobles (*pan*), the members of which were given a monopoly of high governmental offices by the Charter of Horodla of 1413. All the princes and nobles who clung to the Greek Orthodox religion lost their positions in Ukraine and White Russia. A German type of municipal self-government, the Magdeburg Law, like that already in use in Poland, was introduced into the cities. Because of their religion the Greek Orthodox Ukrainians were not even permitted to sit in municipal councils, nor could they be considered citizens with full rights because such rights were reserved for Roman Catholics only. Although the Orthodox Church was still tolerated, it had lost all government support. In some provinces the Greek Orthodox population suffered great mistreatment, the priests of Galicia, Kholm, and Belz suffering the most seriously. In 1412 Yagello, to show his zeal for Catholicism, seized the beautiful Ukrainian Orthodox cathedral in Peremyshl, Galicia, and gave it to the Roman Catholics; the bodies of the princes buried there were exhumed, and both Orthodox clergy and people wept over this insult and injustice. King Yagello also forbade the baptism into the Orthodox Church of the children of mixed Roman Catholic and Orthodox marriages, and those who had already been so baptized he forcibly made Roman Catholic. Neither Yagello nor Vitovt persecuted the Orthodox believers in Lithuania as harshly as they did those in Ukraine, but there, too, many limitations were placed upon them.

The Struggle for Equal Rights: The Ukrainians and White Russians, embittered by these political changes, placed their hopes in Svitrihailo, the younger brother of Yagello, who, though baptized a Roman Catholic, was a friend of the Ukrainian and White Russian princes and nobles. He was displeased because Vitovt had been made Grand Duke of Lithuania, and being ambitious himself, he led frequent uprisings against Vitovt. In these he was ably aided by the nobles and people of White Russia and Ukraine, who hoped that when he became ruler over Lithuania he would restore to the Orthodox believers rights equal to those of the Roman Catholics. Svitrihailo was not successful as a military leader or as a politician, but regardless of this fact he had many followers among the malcontents.

In 1409, while at the court of Vitovt, Svitrihailo opened secret negotiations with the Teutonic Knights who were hostile to Vitovt, but the plot was revealed and he and his German friends were imprisoned. The princes were eager

to free him, and to forestall a rescue he was secretly transferred from one prison to another. When he was brought
to Kreminets in Ukraine, two of the Ukrainian princes,
Dashko Ostrozky and Alexander Nos, learned of it and by
previous arrangement attacked the prison, killed the
guards, and freed Svitrihailo. They gathered a small
force and attacked and captured Lutsk, but when Vitovt
pursued them with his army they fled to Wallachia, and
from there to Hungary. The Hungarian king, Sigismund,
was not in a position to give them military aid, but reconciled Svitrihailo with Yagello and finally with Vitovt. The
discontented prince was permitted to return and rule over
the province of Chernihiv, where he remained to brood
over his wrongs, as did the oppressed Orthodox princes
and nobles of White Russia and Ukraine.

The princes saw their opportunity in 1430, when the
harsh Vitovt died, but Yagello and the Poles also planned
to use this occasion to put an end to the Lithuanian grand
duchy and to gain more complete possession of Ukraine;
they therefore spread the rumor that on his deathbed
Vitovt had willed his kingdom to Yagello. In Lithuania no
attention was paid to these false reports, the people proclaiming Svitrihailo as their grand duke; he was supported not only by the Lithuanians, but by the White Russians and the Ukrainians also. Yagello was compelled to
recognize Svitrihailo as grand duke, though relations between them continued to be so unfriendly that everyone
expected the Polish-Lithuanian union to come to an early
end.

The Poles had entertained high hopes that after Vitovt's death they would be able to annex Lithuania to Poland; but as they were uncertain of success, they decided
to seize at least the Ukrainian territory that had formerly
belonged to the state of Galicia-Volynia, and other provinces which Casimir had made unsuccessful attempts to
seize from Lithuania. Yagello was especially eager to an-

nex Podolia. Some feared that as soon as the Polish nobles who had been given estates in Podolia learned of
Vitovt's death they would seize the castles of Kaminets
and of other cities and turn them over to Yagello's garrisons, and this was actually done. The Polish nobles at
Vitovt's side informed their friends in Podolia of his approaching end; as soon as he was dead the Podolian nobles seized the custodian of the castle of Kaminets, who
had not heard the news, and took not only Kaminets, but
many other cities of Podolia. When Svitrihailo learned of
this he became greatly aroused, rebuked Yagello and the
Polish nobles, and finally declared that he would hold Yagello in Lithuania unless Podolia were returned to him.
Yagello promised to give orders for the return of Podolia,
and so departed unmolested from Lithuania; but the Polish nobles refused to comply and retained the cities. Then
the friends of Svitrihailo captured Smotrich and other
border cities such as Zbarazh, Kreminets, and Olesko,
which Poland had previously seized from Volynia. War
thereupon broke out between Lithuania and Poland for
the possession of the Ukrainian provinces.

The Polish nobles who had taken possession of Podolia
decided to take advantage of the war to seize Volynia as
well. In the summer of 1431 Yagello crossed the Buh
River with a large Polish army, took Volodimir, the capital of Volynia, advanced toward Lutsk, drove Svitrihailo's forces from the city, and laid siege to the citadel,
which was defended by a strong force under the command of Yursh. The Poles attempted to take the castle by
storm, but failed. Yursh then asked for an armistice, during which he strengthened his fortifications, and continued the struggle; he succeeded in repeating this strat-
egy several times. The siege consequently lasted for a
long time, and Svitrihailo was able to get aid from his
allies; the disheartened Poles finally signed an armistice
for two years and went home empty-handed. The Lithua-

nians, however, had missed a golden opportunity by granting this armistice, because their allies, the Teutonic Knights, were attacking Poland at the same time.

The terms of the Polish-Lithuanian armistice provided that Poland was to retain the territory which she had seized in Podolia and Lithuania was to keep Volynia. The agreement remained in force for nearly a hundred years.

The Poles, however, did not leave Svitrihailo in peace. When they realized that they could not conquer him, they determined to rid themselves of him in some other way. They knew that the Lithuanian nobles, accustomed under Vitovt to hold the Ukrainians and White Russians in utter subjection, were not content with Svitrihailo and his curbs on their authority; they consequently sent Polish agents to promise aid in case of revolt. These agents persuaded the Lithuanian nobles to proclaim Vitovt's brother Sigismund grand duke. Sigismund attacked Svitrihailo at night without warning and almost succeeded in capturing him, but he escaped to the city of Polotsk. All of Lithuania proper joined Sigismund, while the Ukrainian provinces remained loyal to Svitrihailo. The Lithuanian kingdom was divided in its sympathies, the Ukrainian and White Russian provinces remaining so loyal to the grand duke that no promises by Sigismund could break their allegiance, even though he assured them that Ukrainian nobles of Greek Orthodox faith should have the same privileges as Roman Catholics. The fortunes of war again went against Svitrihailo. Finally, concentrating all his forces and aided by the Teutonic Knights he invaded Lithuania in 1435, but suffered a severe defeat in a battle near Vilkomir. Almost the entire German army was lost; forty-two princes were taken prisoner and many others were killed, Svitrihailo barely escaping with his life. Sigismund immediately directed his army against White Russia, where he easily captured one city after another; only Ukraine remained loyal to Svitrihailo.

Svitrihailo settled down in Volynia and reached an un-

derstanding with the nobles of Galicia, who after gaining
Polisia were eager to seize Volynia. He made an agreement with them that if they would use their influence to
induce Yagello to abandon Sigismund and join him, he
would surrender Volynia to Poland. As Yagello's advisers did not approve of breaking the alliance with Sigismund, the Polish nobles of Galicia sent their own forces
into Volynia with the purpose of annexing it. When the
nobles of Volynia learned that Svitrihailo had betrayed
them, they decided to surrender to Sigismund and to remain under the sovereignty of Lithuania; they thereupon
sent delegates to Sigismund in the autumn of 1438, asking him to take Volynia under his protection.

At this juncture, in 1440, the Ukrainian princes John
and Alexander Chortoreisky, who were friendly to Svitrihailo, assassinated Sigismund, "at the wish of all the
princes and nobles," as reported by one chronicler. They
accused Sigismund of having crushed the innocent nobles, whom he had punished and even killed in large numbers, while attempting to raise the common people. He
had imprisoned many of the nobles and princes and had
invited others to banquets with the intention of killing
them; it was in order to put a stop to these abuses that the
princes had made a plot against him. They conspired with
the captain of the royal guard and smuggled soldiers concealed in a load of hay into the castle. By bribing the
grand duke's Kievan servant Skobeiko, the conspirators
were able to enter the castle, and reach Sigismund's room.
After they had enumerated to Sigismund a long list of his
faults, Skobeiko attacked him with a heavy iron fork and
killed him.

This at least was the story told by the chronicler in an
attempt to justify the assassination. By killing Sigismund the nobles had intended to restore Svitrihailo to his
former position; and as soon as his opponent's death became known, Svitrihailo went to Lutsk in Volynia, where
he was received with honor as sovereign. In his official

papers he again entitled himself grand duke of Lithuania and attempted to gain recognition as such in Polish circles. The Lithuanian nobles, however, refused to recognize him, for they wished to retain the important offices themselves rather than to share them with the Ukrainians. In place of Sigismund they chose Casimir, the younger son of Yagello, as their ruler; Svitrihailo remained prince of Volynia until his death.

The Intervention of Muscovy: In leaving Volynia to Svitrihailo and the Ukrainian princes who had supported him, the Lithuanian nobles who governed in the name of the young Casimir had made a significant concession to the Ukrainian people: the princes and nobles of Volynia were permitted to govern their lands in complete freedom. The principality of Kiev was also allowed autonomy under the rule of Alexander, son of the Volodimir who had been expelled by Vitovt. He was docile and maintained close contacts with the Lithuanian nobles. His son Semen, who succeeded him about 1454, continued these close relations and married the daughter of Hashtovt, the regent for Casimir. Semen became so well liked by the Lithuanians that when Casimir was elected king of Poland, leaving the Lithuanian throne vacant, he was considered the leading candidate. On the basis of equal rights his candidacy was justified, because most of the Lithuanian grand duchy was at this time composed of Ukrainian land, and there was nothing unusual in the fact that one of its princes should be a claimant to the Lithuanian throne.

The rulers of Lithuania at this time were in need of the support of Ukraine, as their relations with Poland were strained because of the attempt of the Poles to take the province of Dorohichin. Later on a dispute arose over Volynia, as the Poles desired to take this province also. At one time, in 1451, the Polish nobles planned to make war upon Lithuania in order to acquire Volynia, but Casimir dissuaded them.

In the course of time the quarrel over Volynia was forgotten, and relations between Poland and Lithuania again became peaceful. Casimir would not permit the crowning of an independent grand duke of Lithuania but left the government of the country almost completely in the hands of the nobles, merely visiting them at long intervals. The Lithuanian nobles took full advantage of this neglect, monopolized all the offices, and ignored the wishes of the majority of the inhabitants—the Ukrainians and White Russians—although for a time the province of Volynia, where either Ukrainians or Lithuanians were appointed as governors, was an exception to the rule.

When Semen, the Prince of Kiev, died in 1470, his relatives were not permitted to succeed him; all efforts on the part of Semen himself, his relatives, and the Kievans to retain the principality were in vain. The Lithuanian nobles made an ordinary province of Kiev and sent a native Lithuanian, Martin Hashtovt, to govern it, the family of Semen receiving Slutsk, an estate in White Russia. When the Kievans learned of this decision, they informed the Polish king that they would not receive Hashtovt because he did not belong to the royal family and, in addition, was a Roman Catholic. They swore to suffer death rather than to accept him, and twice when he came they refused him recognition. Meanwhile they pled with Casimir to give them a prince of the Greek Orthodox faith; or if this desire could not be fulfilled, to give them, out of regard for the old glory of Kiev, one of royal blood—especially one of his sons. But the Lithuanian nobles stubbornly supported Hashtovt with a large army, and forced the people to submission and humiliation.

This conflict over the Kievan throne caused great bitterness in Ukraine and White Russia against Lithuania, for the people sorrowfully recollected that Lithuania had once been an insignificant territory paying tribute to the kings of Kiev. Michael Olelkovich, the heir of Alexander, deprived of Kiev, began to conspire with his relatives and with other princes. He solicited the support of his brother-in-law, Stephen of Moldavia, and of the Grand Prince Ivan of Muscovy, who was also related to him. The local princes apparently desired to place on the grand ducal throne of Lithuania their own candidate, perhaps Michael himself or his brother. They relied chiefly upon the aid of the Grand Prince of Muscovy, but it is not known whether it was he who conceived the plan for an uprising. In 1481 the plot was discovered ahead of time. One of the chief participants, the Prince of Bilsk, fled to Moscow, leaving behind his personal belongings and his young wife who was not permitted to leave the country to join her husband. The other conspirators were accused of intending to assassinate Casimir and were beheaded.

How many others took part in the conspiracy is not known. In any case the idea of securing aid from Muscovy for revenge against Lithuania did not die; whenever the Lithuanians, relying on the Catholic Polish forces, oppressed the people of the Orthodox faith too severely, the latter sought aid from Greek Orthodox Wallachia and Muscovy. For some time there had been competition for the possession of Kiev between the Lithuanian and Muscovite rulers, both of whom were eager to annex all Ukraine. As long as the Lithuanian kings were favorably inclined to the old Ukrainian culture, left undisturbed the local Ukrainian and White Russian customs, and adapted themselves to local conditions, the people willingly endured them; and as long as they furthered the interests of the Ukrainian people there was no danger of Muscovite intervention. But when their administration became oppressive, the Ukrainians and White Russians turned to Muscovy for aid against them, and their appeals aroused in the government at Moscow a fresh willingness to undertake the struggle against Lithuania. The Lithuanian nobles were aware of this, but did not take the trouble to change their policies or to curb their selfish desires.

This policy affected in particular the province of

Chernihiv, which was situated on the border between Lithuania and Muscovy. The northern part of this province was, it will be recalled, by this time made up of small principalities reduced to the status of great landed estates and held by the princes of the old Chernihiv dynasty. At one time they had willingly submitted to the rule of Lithuania, reserving only the right of "transference," or of changing their allegiance; but when Lithuania changed her internal policy toward the Ukrainian provinces and people in 1470 and more radically in the 1480's these petty principalities began to transfer their allegiance to Muscovy. The Lithuanian government attempted to put a stop to these secessions and war ensued in the course of which the cities along the border surrendered of their own volition to Muscovy. In an attempt to prevent the disruption of his empire Alexander, the new Grand Duke of Lithuania, married a daughter of the Grand Prince of Muscovy, and obtained in 1494 a pledge that Muscovy would accept no more districts that might be dissatisfied with the rule of Lithuania. The marriage, instead of ending conflicts between the two powers, only introduced new complications in the form of religious differences. At about this time the Grand Duke Alexander appointed a compliant metropolitan named Joseph and set about forcing the Greek Orthodox churches in his dominions into Roman Catholicism. The question even arose whether the queen would be able to remain Greek Orthodox. Rumors that the Orthodox subjects of Lithuania were being persecuted and forced to accept Roman Catholicism caused many of the Ukrainian princes to denounce the Lithuanian government in 1500 and to recognize once more the sovereignty of Muscovy. Since a question of religion was now involved, the government of Muscovy abrogated the treaty of 1494 and promised to protect the oppressed Ukrainian princes and their lands; in a short time all Chernihiv had transferred its allegiance to Muscovy. The Grand Prince of Muscovy now

informed Lithuania that he was going to attack it in defense of the faith, "to fight for Christianity with the help
of God." He annexed the Siverian province and from this
time on dreamed of "liberating" all Ukraine from Lithuania. Meanwhile the Lithuanian government gave up the
idea of forcing the Orthodox Church to become Catholic,
but it was now too late.

A few years later the petty princes and nobles of
Ukraine began an insurrection, instigated by the influential Prince Michael Hlinsky, owner of large estates in
the region of Kiev and a man of great ability and courage; in his youth Michael had visited Western Europe,
lived for many years at the court of the Emperor Maximilian, and later entered the military service of Prince
Albrecht of Saxony, whose army he had accompanied to
Friesland, Italy, and Spain. In the course of his travels
he had acquired a good education, especially in military
science. When he returned to Ukraine the Grand Duke
Alexander of Lithuania took such a liking to him that they
shortly became close friends. A Ukrainian, Hlinsky made
use of this friendship to acquire high offices for his relatives and other Ukrainian nobles; while Lithuanian nobles were vexed, they feared to oppose him. One of
Hlinsky's brothers received Kiev, another became governor of Bereste, and other relatives received lucrative offices and estates; it was long since the Ukrainians and
the White Russians had been so generously treated under
Lithuanian rule.

When the Grand Duke Alexander unexpectedly fell ill
and died in 1505 at a comparatively young age, the Lithuanian nobles elected his brother Sigismund to succeed him.
Immediately after the election they made efforts to undermine the position of Hlinsky by saying he had shortened
the life of Alexander and was seeking to become grand
duke. These accusations were false, but Sigismund pretended to believe them and deprived Hlinsky and his relatives of their high offices. Hlinsky sought for justice in

vain, until finally, deciding that justice under Sigismund was impossible, he resolved to lead a rebellion. He went to his estates in Turiv, reached an understanding with the princes and nobles there, and preached war against Lithuania, arousing the people by telling them that they would be forcibly baptized into Roman Catholicism, and that whoever rejected that religion would suffer death. At the same time he sought to persuade the Grand Prince of Muscovy and his ally, the khan of Crimea, to attack Lithuania at the same time as he revolted. Hlinsky's exact plans are not known, but presumably he intended with the aid of Moscow and the Crimean horde to separate the Ukrainian provinces from Lithuania and to create an independent state under the protection of Muscovy. This could have been easily accomplished if Hlinsky's allies had given him aid, but the khan failed him, and the Grand Prince of Muscovy did not send an army until the autumn of 1507. Hlinsky, relying on the support of the Muscovites, began the uprising, but as the main forces of the Muscovites left Ukraine and went into White Russia Hlinsky was left unaided. When the local princes saw his precarious situation they refused to join him. The common people meanwhile were not at all interested, and no one knew how to arouse them, for no one understood them. Only the city of Mozy surrendered to Hlinsky, its priests receiving him with religious ceremonies as their ruler. The other cities, such as Slutsk, Ovruch, and Zhitomir, did not surrender; and Hlinsky could only harass his Lithuanian enemies by frequent attacks and by plundering their estates. To oppose Hlinsky, Sigismund and his ally Poland sent a powerful army under Prince Constantine Ostrozky. Hlinsky and his friends, unable to face such formidable forces, departed for Muscovy, and the revolt thus came to an end. In the next war Hlinsky gained some satisfaction, for Muscovy seized Smolensk from Lithuania, but the status of Ukraine was in no way improved.

CHAPTER IX

THE RISE OF THE KOZAKS

Attempts at Revolt in Galicia and the Beginnings of Ukrainian Nationalism: At the time when the nobles of eastern Ukraine were looking for help from Muscovy, western Ukraine, especially Galicia, was seeking the aid of Moldavia in an effort to improve its unhappy position. The principality of Moldavia, closely related to Ukraine by religion and Slavic culture, had been founded in the middle of the fourteenth century. During the next century, under the leadership of the hospodar Stephen the Great (1457–1504), it expanded its boundaries and succeeded in repelling the attacks of the Turkish Sultan Mohammed. The Rumanian population of Moldavia was under the influence of Bulgarian culture, which closely resembled the Ukrainian in religion, education, and art; therefore Podolia and Galicia, especially southern Galicia, had always maintained friendly relations with Moldavia and in time of distress had sought aid from it. At the close of the fifteenth and the beginning of the sixteenth centuries Moldavian princes were ruling over the Ukrainian province of Bukovina and keeping their eyes on the southeastern corner of Galicia known as Pokutia, which they tried to detach from Poland. The Ukrainians of Galicia inclined toward Moldavia, just as eastern Ukraine was leaning toward Muscovy. Songs sung in Galicia and neighboring regions record a high esteem for Stephen of Moldavia. The following extract from a song written down and printed by a Czech in 1571 was called forth by an attempt by Stephen of Moldavia to seize Pokutia with the aid of Turkish and Tatar allies; it is the oldest printed Ukrainian song:

> O Danube, Danube, why dost thou flow in grief?
> Oh, how can I, Danube, escape the grief?

At the Danube three armies stand,
In the Turkish ranks the sabres flash,
In the Tatar ranks the arrows fly,
In the Wallachian ranks Stephen is duke.

In 1490 under the leadership of Mukha there began a very important movement, of which the minor details are unknown. Contemporaries relate that "a certain Mukha of Wallachia" instigated revolts among the peasants of Pokutia and organized among them an army numbering nine thousand men, with the aid of which he ravaged the estates of the Polish nobles. He was supported not only by the peasants, but by the townspeople and the Ukrainian nobility as well, as is clear from a document recording the confiscation of the estates of the Ukrainian gentry because they had participated in Mukha's revolt. He conquered the country as far as Halich and crossed the Dniester River, aiming at the city of Rohatyn. The Polish gentry were terrified at his advances and the king appealed not only to all his own gentry but even to Prussia for aid. As Mukha was crossing the Dniester, the Polish army attacked him, threw his army into confusion, and defeated it; many of the soldiers were drowned and Mukha took to flight. A later writer adds that he tried to stir up another revolt, but the Poles, learning of his whereabouts, bribed a woman at whose home he was staying and captured him.

One account has it that Stephen supported a pretender who claimed to be the rightful ruler of Ukraine and instigated revolts in Galicia, expecting with the aid of the sultan to free it from Poland. In 1509, when the Moldavian duke (*voyvoda*) Bohdan invaded Galicia, a large number of the local Ukrainian gentry joined him, as they had previously joined Mukha. When the expedition failed, they accompanied the Wallachian army to Moldavia, and in the meantime their estates were confiscated. This incident reveals the fact that here, too, was a Ukrainian irredentist movement aimed at the freeing of Galicia from the

Polish yoke with the aid of Moldavia. The attempts failed because Moldavia was too weak, and in consequence the Ukrainians of Galicia were oppressed more severely than ever. Efforts were made, however, to organize in defense of their rights, and thus were laid the foundations of an organized national life.

The conditions under which the Ukrainians of Galicia lived at this time were unusually discouraging. There were no wealthy Ukrainian lords like those in Volynia or Kiev who might have helped to sustain cultural life, all the wealthier ones in the province having either disappeared during the fourteenth and fifteenth centuries or lost their property through confiscation by the Poles. Others had become denationalized, frequently as a result of marriage to Poles, in which event both parties accepted Catholicism. As all roads were closed to the Orthodox, even oaths by Orthodox citizens not being readily accepted by the courts, it is no wonder that many at last washed their hands of the matter and became converted, while small landlords and country gentry who clung to the Greek Orthodox faith remained uneducated, unorganized, and lacking in influence. The Orthodox Church, the only representative of Ukrainian national life, was subjected to severe repression. In the middle of the fifteenth century when the metropolitan see of the Ukrainian Church in Galicia became vacant, the Polish king entrusted its property to a Galician elder, and the direction of religious affairs was assumed by the Polish Catholic archbishop of Lviv (Lemberg), the protests of the Orthodox clergy being met by intimidation and actual force. It was the attempt to reëstablish the Orthodox hierarchy that brought about the beginning of a Ukrainian national revival in Galicia, accompanied by hopes of aid from abroad. The movement had gained considerable strength by the 1520's, when the demand was made that the Orthodox metropolitan of Kiev appoint a bishop for the Galician diocese. Approval for this request was secured only by bribing some of the nobles; even the king and queen accepted gifts for the granting of this religious concession. It was a costly victory. For the privilege of having their own bishop, the people of Galicia had to promise Queen Bona 200 oxen; afterwards, in order to abolish the right of the Roman Catholic archbishop of Lviv to intervene in the affairs of the Orthodox Church, they had to give 110 more oxen to the king, the queen, and various noblemen; and finally, before the king issued the permit, they were required to give him 140 more.

The chief credit for this achievement is due the Ukrainian citizens of Lviv. From that time on they presented repeated petitions for the abolition of all unjust restrictions against them, such as those excluding them from local municipal offices and artisans' guilds, forbidding them to engage in business or to own property in the city outside the Ukrainian quarters, and denying them the right to conduct religious ceremonies in public. As has been stated, even the oath of an Orthodox believer had not been recognized in court.

The Ukrainians of Lviv presented their requests for the abolition of religious discrimination through a few influential lords, among others being the well-known Volynian magnate Constantine Ivanovich Ostrozky, a Lithuanian general who was highly respected at the royal court because of his military services and as a reward had been made military governor of Troki, one of the most important regions. The Ukrainians spared neither gifts nor bribes in their efforts to win their old civic rights in their own country, and yet their success was negligible; the old abuses continued to weigh heavily upon them.

Nevertheless the people continued the struggle, and won a victory of great value for the national movement by acquiring an Orthodox bishop in Lviv in 1539. The Church again became a self-governing institution able to defend the rights of the people, and the church brotherhoods now became national organizations.

The brotherhoods were old associations dating back to ancient ceremonies of pagan times. With the introduction of Christianity, the old pagan brotherhoods had attached themselves to the Church and had celebrated all the national festivals—the so-called *bratchiny,* for which they brewed mead and beer and charged their guests admission; the money thus collected went to the support of the Church. Later, when the Polish-Lithuanian government reorganized the city governments on the German model, the Ukrainian citizens reformed the old church brotherhoods in order to gain legal recognition for them. The oldest constitutions of such reorganized brotherhoods are those of Vilna in White Russia and Lviv in Ukraine. The latter brotherhood, associated with the Church of the Assumption in the Ukrainian quarter of the city, was reformed about the time the diocese was established in Lviv. After 1540 there were granted many constitutions of church brotherhoods attached to other churches in Lviv; they were modeled after that of the Church of the Assumption, according to which gentry belonging to the Church were admitted but no one could leave the organization at will. These brotherhoods served as organizers of the Ukrainian nation. The merchants of Lviv, especially the most progressive and influential ones, were attracted to these city organizations: and being also the most embittered by their lack of privileges, they best furnished the impulse for the national organization, breathing new life into the few remaining Orthodox gentry and Ukrainian clergy. The peasants, who had no rights whatever, were quite unable to play a part in this cultural movement.

The brotherhoods of Lviv, especially that of the Church of the Assumption, were active in establishing similar organizations in other cities. Even the Moldavian dukes who were protectors of Galician Ukraine showed their interest and sympathy by sending money for mead and beer and gifts of lambs to the churches and to "their friends" the brotherhoods for their festivals. In the course of time the organizations spread over the whole country, serving as a center for national unity. The final program was not yet complete, but its outlines had been drawn.

Rise of the Kozaks: After their unsuccessful uprising against Lithuania, the princes and gentry of eastern Ukraine remained quiet for a time in order to gain favor with the government; but the people of western Ukraine, in spite of the failure of the Moldavian rebellion, began to organize for new activities. At first it was impossible to foresee the significance of this new movement, and apparently no one predicted that it would become a national force which would accomplish a task that the Ukrainian princes and nobles had failed in because of the lack of mass support. Neither was it apparent that this new movement in the eastern corner of the country would march forward on the road which the townspeople of western Ukraine had been unable to follow because of the opposition of the Polish nobility. Yet it was this new element in Ukrainian frontier life, the Kozaks, that was to provide the initiative for a strong national movement.

The people were forced into new activity by a change in circumstances, especially by a renewal of the old Tatar raids upon Ukraine at the end of the fifteenth century, this time by the Crimean horde. The Tatar horde under Batu's leadership, it has been noted, did not retain its strength for any great length of time. Toward the close of the thirteenth century it began to disintegrate, and the process went on at a more rapid pace through the fourteenth century, with members of the khan's family fighting among themselves for supremacy. As this internal strife continued, the largest horde, the so-called Golden Horde inhabiting the Volga region, became seriously weakened during the fifteenth century, and its western bands, which had occupied Crimea and the lower Dnieper and Dniester regions, broke away in about 1430 and organized a separate horde, centered on Crimea. The first to sever himself from the main horde was Hadji-Gerai. In doing so he sought aid from the neighboring Grand Duke of Lithuania, but as the latter was occupied with other projects and failed to see the importance of the movement, he neither gave the Crimean horde assistance nor forsook his alliance with the Golden Horde. Therefore, the son of Hadji-Gerai, Mengli-Gerai, found new allies by cultivating friendly relations with Muscovy and by submitting to Turkish suzerainty. Muscovy utilized the new friendship by inducing Mengli-Gerai to attack Lithuania. He began by plundering the Ukrainian states that were subject to Lithuania and Poland, and met little opposition because of internal strife and the Lithuanian war with Muscovy. The local Ukrainian princes defended themselves as best they could, but without aid from the central government they could not repel the Tatars. Thus in the spring of 1482, inspired by promises of gifts from the Grand Prince Ivan of Muscovy, Mengli-Gerai was able to move north, attack and capture Kiev, destroy the fortifications, plunder the neighboring country, and triumphantly send to Ivan a golden chalice taken from the Cathedral of St. Sophia.

Following this success he ravaged Podolia several times over a period of many years. The Polish king, because of his unsuccessful attack on Bukovina, had also antagonized the Turks; so the Tatars, the Turks, and the Wallachians pillaged the Ukrainian districts of Polisia and Galicia that were subject to Poland. The Tatars sent expeditions to the upper Dnieper, but Muscovy, eager to take the Siverian province for itself, asked the Tatars not to attack it, and they accordingly left Kiev in ruins and turned their attention to the neighboring districts of Volynia and White Russia. Occasionally they were defeated, especially by Michael Hlinsky and Constantine Ostrozky; but more frequently they were successful in committing depredations and carrying away booty. All Ukraine was overwhelmed by oppression, fear, and the plaints of the downtrodden, which echo to this day in the old popular songs. Instead of offering a defense, the Lithuanian government attempted to bribe the Tatars by paying them an annual tribute and giving them gifts. It also encouraged them to attack the territory of Muscovy, and ultimately the Tatars plundered both Muscovy and the Lithuanian lands. They so laid waste the Ukrainian territory that on both sides of the Dnieper the province of Kiev became almost a wilderness. In Polisia, around Ovruch and Chornobil, several villages remained standing, but south of the city of Kiev there were left only a few strongholds in which the people who still remained in this section of the country took refuge, sallying forth to make their living by hunting and farming. This devastation of Ukraine by the Tatars was worse than that inflicted by Batu, and the country did not recover from it for many generations. The lower Dnieper became completely vacant, and for several decades was abandoned to the wild animals.

This rich wilderness had gained the name of Ukraine, which means borderland, because it was the borderland of the civilized Christian world. It attracted people for the very reason that there were no landlords or masters there. Written accounts of the sixteenth century are full of wildly exaggerated tales regarding the natural wealth of the region, describing the soil as being so unbelievably fertile that it yielded a hundredfold. There was no need to sow seed every year; a harvest sown in the autumn yielded two and three crops the next summer. When the plow was left in the field for three or four days it was lost in the fast-growing grass which grew so high in the pastures that it almost hid the grazing oxen and sometimes even covered the tips of their horns. Bees stored their honey not only in old trees but in caves, and springs of honey were common. The rivers were full of fish. Sturgeon and other varieties swam up from the sea; when one thrust a sword into the water, it would stand upright in the mass of fish as it might in the ground. Buffaloes and horses were killed for their hides and the meat was thrown away. Wild goats that migrated to the forests in winter could be killed by the thousand; while in spring boys were able to fill their boats with the eggs of wild ducks, geese, cranes, swans, and the like.

Though these stories were exaggerated, they are indicative of how the region of Kiev was regarded. The country attracted brave souls who dared to occupy the steppes in spite of the danger of the Tatar sword, and to fight for the sake of freedom, the wealth of the soil, and land without a landlord. Every spring emigrants from Kievan Polisia, northern Volynia, and White Russia moved to the unoccupied southern country, where they lived by fishing, hunting, and bee keeping. As the inhabitants increased in number, they organized themselves into armed bands, and in the early spring went on "expeditions" into the steppes, farming there until late autumn, and then returning to their permanent homes with great supplies of honey, fish, hides, horses, and cattle. On their return they were promptly met by government officials who demanded the best of the supplies in payment for the privilege they had enjoyed. As a result of this the more daring did not go home for the winter, but remained in the steppes, or wintered in the vacant castles of the lower Dnieper, and only the less courageous returned. Thus some people lived on their farms, spending only the summers in the southern steppes, while others made the steppes their permanent dwelling place. For many this mode of living provided the sole means of livelihood, with the castles and the steppes offering them protection.

This way of living was called "the Kozak life" (kozatstvo), and the people who adopted it were known as Kozaks. Originally it meant expeditions to the wilderness, fishing, hunting, and the keeping of bees, but the meaning of the word changed into "fleecing the Turkish or Tatar shepherds." Constantly on guard against Tatar attacks,

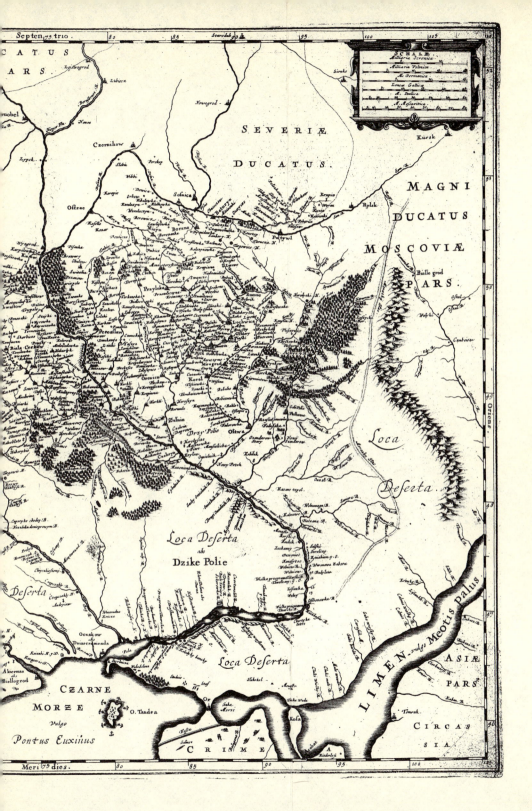

these Ukrainian pioneers attacked the Tatars whenever they felt strong enough. They seized Tatar herds of sheep, attacked the caravans of Turkish and Armenian merchants, seized Lithuanian or Muscovite messengers on their way with "gifts" for the sultan, and frequently attacked and plundered the small towns of the Turks and Tatars. It was, in fact, among these steppe people that the name of Kozak had originated, the word being widely known among people of Turkish extraction, and in use among the earlier Polovtsians to denote one who lived on booty. At first it was applied chiefly to nomadic Tatars, but was later transferred to Ukrainian freebooters.

Although the name as applied to the Ukrainian steppe dwellers was new, first appearing in this sense in Ukrainian historical sources at the end of the fifteenth century, freebooting in the steppes had been a very old practice. The ancestors of these Ukrainians were the ancient tribe of the Antae, who, with the aid of Bolgars and Avars, had plundered Byzantium. They were the rovers of the steppes at the time of the Polovtsians; they were the "exiles from Galicia" who roamed in the Dniester and Dnieper regions during the twelfth and thirteenth centuries, living by fishing and fighting; they were the "brave warriors" of the frontier praised in the *Song of the Legion of Ihor,* where King Vsevolod says of his soldiers:

> But my men of Kursk are tried warriors—
> Swaddled to the sound of trumpets,
> Lulled beneath helmets,
> Nursed from the point of the spear.
> Known to them are the roads,
> Familiar the vales.
> Their bows are strung, their quivers filled.
> Their swords are keen.
> Like gray wolves they plunge through the steppe,
> Seeking glory for themselves and honor for their prince.

So immense an area of land could not be subjected to regulation by the government or by the nobles, and the

old custom of freebooting was now resumed on a large
scale.

The Kozak Host and the Early Kozak Expeditions: The
Kozaks who lived in the Black Sea steppes in the fourteenth and fifteenth centuries were probably Tatars, but
their racial origin is not definitely known. The first authentic information regarding the Ukrainian Kozaks
dates from the last decade of the fifteenth century; in
1492 the khan of Crimea complained that the Kievans and
Cherkasses (Kozaks) had seized a Tatar ship near Tiahinia, and the Lithuanian Grand Duke Alexander promised to make an investigation among the Kozaks in
Ukraine regarding the seizure. In the next year, when
Prince Bohdan Hlinsky, the governor of Cherkassy, destroyed the Turkish fortress at Ochakiv by the estuary of
the Dnieper River, the khan called him and his followers
Kozaks. In the charter granted Kiev in 1499 the Kozaks
are described as migrants from the northern part of
Ukraine who went into the steppes to fish and then returned to Kiev with abundant supplies of both fresh and
salted fish. It is evident that the Kozaks engaged in many
kinds of activity; they were known as steppe traders,
as freebooters, and as soldiers hired by the governors
of frontier towns for use in expeditions against Turkish
forts, and are often mentioned in records of the beginning
of the sixteenth century in connection with such enterprises.

The Kozaks were not widely known at this time, primarily because the term referred to an occupation and
not to a distinct class of people; in their ranks were included townspeople, farmers, officials, and even a few nobles and princes. The total number of those who were
Kozaks and nothing else was comparatively small, and
they had only a few villages on the Dnieper highway south
of Kiev.

Later tradition connected with the Kozaks the names
of a few noted frontier officers, the most important being

Ostap Dashkovich and Predslav Lantskoronsky. The former was governor of Kiev and Cherkassy from 1510 to 1535, the latter governor of Podolia at about the same time. These men were regarded as the first hetmans (leaders) of the Kozaks, but in reality they were high-ranking frontier officials who used Kozak volunteers in expeditions against the Turkish and Tatar settlements in the steppes. Various frontier governors, important officials, prominent Ukrainians, and even some Polish lords of Podolia participated in these expeditions under the experienced leadership of Prince Constantine Ostrozky. They were not regular Kozak freebooters; indeed, they frequently annoyed the regular Kozaks by demanding special contributions in payment for freedom of action in the steppes under threat of depriving them of their booty and other property. We hear more about these officials at the time, however, than we do about the real Kozaks, who were only incidentally mentioned in connection with their daring expeditions against the Tatar settlements and Turkish cities. Among the leaders mentioned by Ukrainian sources of the 1540's were Karpo Maslo of Cherkassy, Yatsko Bilous of Pereyaslav, Andrushko of Braslav, and Lesun. The chroniclers were evidently not greatly interested in these maraudings, for the attack on Ochakiv by Karpo and his forces is not even mentioned; they were however deeply concerned with Lantskoronsky's expedition against Ochakiv and that of Dashkovich against the Tatars. Later historians considered these two expeditions the first undertaken by the Kozaks, though contemporaries made no mention of the Kozaks as such.

The real Kozaks were not the wealthy lords and officials who wished to gain fame as ''Kozaks'' and undertook expeditions into the steppes against Tatar settlements in the spirit of the big-game hunter of today, but were poor, exploited, homeless people—courageous Ukrainian frontiersmen. They tried by all possible means to free themselves from the heavy hands of frontier governors and other officials along the steppe borders, for under the rule of these officials the people were not free; but their revolts were usually unsuccessful because the number of freedom-loving Kozaks was small. Unable to organize freely in the up-river frontier region known as the Townships (*volost*), the Kozaks settled in the steppes, adapted themselves to the new way of living, and formed organized bands. As early as 1550 the governors of border towns complained of the reduction in tax receipts because these people had moved out to the steppes, "living there on meat, fish, and honey," without paying for the privilege. Actually, however, life in the steppes was hard, even with frequent starvation. Sometimes the Kozaks were killed by Tatars or taken as slaves:

> Oh, three years and three weeks have passed
> Since the Kozak was killed in the woods;
> Under the green maple tree
> Lies the young Kozak.
> His body is blackened;
> It is withered by the wind.
> Over him stands his mournful horse,
> Sunken to his knees in the ground.

Founding of the Sich: Under these difficult conditions the number of noble Kozaks did not increase but the common folk did; they were recruited from people enslaved by the landlords and oppressed by the city officials, who were ready to face the hardships of the steppes if only they could be free. For protection against the attacks of the Tatars, the Kozaks built little forts known as *siches*, strengthened the organizational ties among themselves, and gradually established themselves in a great Kozak union as masters of the lower Dnieper region with their center in the Zaporozhe, "below the rapids." The Dnieper rapids were a safe location for the Kozaks, for there they were unapproachable by the officials of far-off Lithuania or Poland from one side, and on the other thick forests, whirlpools, and waterfalls prevented Turkish boats from coming up the river.

About 1550, Dmitro Vishnevetsky, one of the petty Ukrainian princes living among the Kozaks, began to build a strong permanent fortress in the Zaporozhian region, to serve as a protection for all the Kozaks and as a center of political power that would be respected by the neighboring governments. Vishnevetsky began his career about 1540 as a gentleman Kozak of the frontier. Other wealthy nobles had tried the life as a diversion, but had abandoned it in order to attend to other affairs. Not so Vishnevtsky, who wished to make the Zaporozhe so strong that it would protect the Kozaks against the Tatars and enable them to make themselves masters of the Dnieper valley by expelling the Turks and Tatars.

The plan of building a fortress was not new. As early as about 1520 the Ukrainian frontier governors had proposed to the government that it take the Kozaks under its protection and into its service for use as a border guard against the Tatars, but since the government had no money available for such a project, it failed of adoption. Again in the 1530's Dashkovich reminded the Polish-Lithuanian government that for the protection of Ukraine the rapids of the Dnieper should be fortified and a Kozak garrison stationed there. Again nothing was done. Finally, the task which the government had failed to accomplish was undertaken and completed by the Ukrainian frontiersmen.

In about 1552 Dmitro Vishnevetsky built a fort at Khortitsia and stationed there a Kozak garrison. He asked the Polish king and the Lithuanian Grand Duke Sigismund August to aid him with supplies, and at the same time attempted to arrange an understanding with Turkey. He himself went to Turkey, probably either to seek her aid or to dissuade her from protecting the Tatars of Crimea, on whom he intended to make an attack. Whether he was successful in his diplomatic mission to

Turkey is not known, but one thing is certain—the Polish-Lithuanian government did not raise money for the project because it feared the Tatars. Instead it attempted to divert Vishnevetsky's ambitions elsewhere, by sending him and his Kozaks on a campaign against Livonia.

Vishnevetsky then sought an alliance with Muscovy, suggesting that with their united forces they destroy the Crimean horde, which had been plundering their territories and collecting tribute from them. The government of Muscovy accepted and in 1556 sent an army to aid the Kozaks in an attack upon the Tatars in Crimea. The Kozak and Muscovite armies went down the Dnieper and attacked the fortified towns of Aslam-Kermen and Ochakiv. They failed to capture the towns, but killed a large number of Turks and Tatars and took others prisoners. This so angered the khan that he determined to destroy the Kozak headquarters. He first invited Vishnevetsky to come to see him, but as the latter failed to accept, the khan marched in winter with all his forces to attack the fort of Khortitsia. For three weeks he unsuccessfully besieged it, returning home empty-handed. Vishnevetsky notified the king of the Turkish failure and asked him for men and ammunition, but the king still feared to intervene. In summer the khan came again, and this time besides a powerful Turkish army which came up the Dnieper in boats, he had the Wallachians as allies. Together they besieged Khortitsia, this time with greater success. Vishnevetsky's supplies ran short, the bulk of his Kozaks were put to flight, and he retreated with the remnants to Cherkassy.

Realizing that he could expect no aid from the Lithuanian government, Vishnevetsky went to Muscovy to arrange an alliance against the Tatars. It was an auspicious moment for him, and in 1558 he was able to lead a Muscovite army against Crimea, whereupon the khan lost courage and retreated beyond Perekop with the entire horde. Vishnevetsky spent the whole summer in the Tatar city of Aslam-Kermen and planned to follow the Tatars

beyond Perekop with his Kozak and Muscovite army.
Muscovy, however, unwilling to let Vishnevetsky stay in
the Dnieper region, withheld its approval of the plan and
sent its own officers to lead the attack on Crimea, advising
Vishnevetsky to attack the peninsula from the side of the
Caucasus, and finally dropping the campaign completely.
Muscovy and Lithuania again failed to agree but became
involved in new quarrels over Livonia which ended in
war; and again each sought the aid of the Crimean khan.
When Vishnevetsky learned that he could not rely upon
the aid of Muscovy, he returned to Ukraine in 1561.
Shortly after this there was a revolution in Wallachia,
and one of the factions asked aid of Vishnevetsky; but he
was betrayed and imprisoned by the Wallachians, who
sent him to Constantinople, where he was put to death.
Many stories were circulated in Ukraine and the neighboring countries about his violent end. According to one
version he was hung by a rib and remained suspended for
three days; he did not complain or ask mercy, but reviled
them and cursed Mohammed, until the Turks shot him in
anger. The memory of his life and deeds has been preserved in popular songs in which he is known as Baida.

Though Vishnevetsky died without having carried out
his plans, his activity was not in vain: the Kozaks continued the struggle at the point where he had left off. His
policy was continued by his successors, and whenever the
Kozaks gained sufficient strength they began to take advantage of wars among neighboring countries. During the
second part of the sixteenth century their forces rapidly
increased, and their increase in numbers, their military
and political activity developed in scope; they became a
self-conscious group, widely known for their daring and
bravery.

The Kozak Organization: One cannot sufficiently appreciate the courage of this handful of Kozaks who, lacking
ammunition and money, almost with their bare hands attacked the fierce Turks who were bleeding Ukraine white

and keeping the powerful neighboring states in subjection. Not only Ukraine but all Eastern Europe lived under the terrible menace of Turkish conquest and Tatar devastation. The Tatars subjected to themselves all southeastern Europe and carried away thousands of people to the market places in Crimea, where they were sold into slavery and taken to Turkey, Italy, France, Spain, and the Barbary coast. "They are selling slaves in all the Crimean cities, but especially in Kaffa," says a Lithuanian author of the middle of the sixteenth century; "herds of these unfortunate folk sold into slavery are driven onto the boats in the harbor of Kaffa. Because of this practice the city of Kaffa may well be called a heathen giant who feeds on our blood."

The sufferings and the longing of the prisoners and slaves for their native land were popular literary topics. Man became a plaything of fate, which could change him in a moment from a wealthy lord to a poor slave, or from a pious Christian to an unbelieving Turk. A tale was told of a sister enslaved by her Ottomanized brother, and another of an aged mother sold into slavery to her son, who had become a Mohammedan and forgotten his native land. For generations the accounts of the conditions under which Ukrainians lived excited national feeling; the Ukrainian *kobzars* (minstrels) called them the psalms of slaves.

A poor slave in Turkey sends greetings
From the land of Mohammed to the Christian cities,
To his father and mother;
He cannot greet them,
But he greets the gray pigeons:
"O thou gray pigeon
That fliest high and wanderest far!
Fly thou to the Christian cities, to my father and mother,
Fly down into their yard and make a mournful sound,
Remind them of my Kozak fate:
Let my father and my mother know my troubles,

Let them sacrifice their wealth
To free my Kozak head from wretched slavery.''

Such songs always end with a prayer:

Free, O God, a poor slave;
Permit him to land on the shores of Holy Ukraine—
That beautiful country—
Among Christian people!

An adventurous young Kozak suddenly appears. Though poorly clothed and armed, he boldly faces the infidel Turk, attacks and puts to flight the enslaver of Ukraine.

The wealthy Turkish and Tatar slave traders of the cities along the coast of the Black Sea were accustomed to lending money to the Tatar bands and collecting the interest in slaves. The Kozaks were dedicated to the task of expelling such Tatar slave hunters and traders from the Ukrainian steppes, scattering their herds over the plains, and later on, to attacking the Turkish cities and the palaces of those who had become wealthy from the slave trade. Freeing the people from Turkish slavery gave the Kozaks their greatest satisfaction.

These activities of the Kozaks gave new hope to the downtrodden Ukrainian people. At first, as has been said, the expeditions were organized and equipped by frontier officials; but in the middle of the sixteenth century the Kozaks, in the face of the opposition of these officials, went to fight the Turks independently and of their own volition. It was known to the Lithuanian and Turkish governments, however, that the Ukrainian frontier officials and lords continued to encourage, aid, and protect the Kozaks, and to share their booty as the Turkish merchants did that of the Tatars; but such assistance was secretly given and did not play an important part in the Kozak expeditions.

The masses began to gain new faith in the power of the Kozaks, who became popular heroes, and whose deeds were commemorated in many songs and stories. As the

Kozak movement grew in favor, recruits flocked from all sides to join it. Without intending to do so, the government itself aided the development of the Kozaks by trying to put restrictions in their way.

For a time the Polish-Lithuanian government, following the advice of the frontier governors, intended to undertake a struggle against the Tatars with the aid of the Kozaks. It wished to station the Kozak forces on the lower Dnieper and with their aid to stop the Tatar attacks; but when the horde protested against the frequent Kozak expeditions and began to justify its own attacks on the ground that the Kozaks had sacked the Tatar cities, the government soon grew timid. Beginning in 1540 it sent repeated orders to its frontier officials in Ukraine not to aid the Kozaks, and made serious efforts to register the members of the Kozak organization and to subject them to strict supervision. They were denied the right to enter the steppes for booty, and punishment was imposed on anyone who possessed booty taken from the Tatars.

The frontier governors, however, paid little attention to these orders; they knew that the Tatars feared the Kozaks, and that if anyone could tame the horde, it was the Kozaks. The officials therefore did not attempt to discourage their expeditions, and even claimed a share in the booty. Whenever attempts were made to restrict their activities, the Kozaks left their frontier strongholds and moved farther south to the heart of the steppes, where they were altogether free. The government also failed in every attempt to take a census of these people, as there were as yet few who lived regularly as Kozaks; indeed when the first registration was made in 1552 there was difficulty in finding five hundred persons who were clearly in this class, so many varieties of people—city dwellers, farmers, and gentry—were now included in it.

The government, however, persisted in its attempt to control the Kozaks and determined to create a special administration for them. About 1560 the Turks again com-

plained to Poland and Lithuania about Kozak attacks on
their cities, and as a result the king commanded the Kozaks to move up the Dnieper into the border forts, where
they would be in the service of the government and would
receive pay. In order to stiffen their discipline, the king
also appointed a Polish hetman and judge, since the province of Kiev, where most of the Kozaks lived, had by this
time been annexed by Poland. These two high officials
were authorized to keep order not only among those Kozaks in the royal service but among the free ones as well,
that is, those not registered for service, and unpaid. The
newly appointed officers, however, were helpless because
the government failed to pay the registered Kozaks, while
the large number of unregistered Kozaks refused to submit to governmental control, and lived as they pleased. At
the same time a lively struggle was proceeding at the
frontier. The Tatars continually raided the Ukrainian villages and cities, and the Kozaks, following in the path of
Vishnevetsky, retaliated by attacking the Tatar camps
and Turkish cities and by interfering in the Wallachian
civil wars. To fill the place left vacant by the death of
Vishnevetsky, there now appeared a new leader, Bohdan
Ruzhinsky, one of the Volynian local princes. Like his
predecessor, he tried to induce Muscovy to aid him with
military supplies for fighting against the horde, and he
became known throughout Ukraine for his wars against
the Tatars but died in the capture of Aslam-Kermen.

Among the military chiefs who led the Kozaks against
Moldavia the most outstanding was Ivan Pidkova, who
conquered that country in 1577. To satisfy the Turks, who
enjoyed sovereignty over the Tatars, the Poles captured
and beheaded him in Lviv; but his loss failed to intimidate or dissuade the Kozaks from their expeditions
against the Tatars.

The Polish government sent written orders to the Kozaks to cease their expeditions under threat of punishment, and continually appointed new officials to enroll the

Kozaks in the service of the king, gain control over all of
them, and put a stop to their attacks on the Turkish and
Tatar lands. Of special importance among these royal
commands was one by King Stephen Batory, from which
new and unforeseen developments arose. His orders, on
the whole, did not differ greatly from those of his predecessors and were no better obeyed; but by appointing special governors for the Kozaks, he removed them from the
supervision of the civil authorities, both provincial governors and municipal officials. The Kozaks then developed
the theory that there was no government over them save
the Kozak government, and refused to recognize the officials sent them by the Poles, submitting only to those
whom they themselves elected. Other difficulties arose
when the government, taking Kozaks into its service,
promised to pay them but failed to keep its word. Acting
on the theory that they were an army of the king, the Kozaks insisted upon the same rights as those enjoyed by the
Polish army, or upon such rights as they specified for
themselves. They soon demanded a number of privileges,
basing their claims on the proclamations of the king, and
interpreting them in their own way and for their own
benefit. As a result the idea developed that a Kozak was a
free man, subject to no one but the elected Kozak officials,
and with no other responsibility than to fight frontier
enemies. All those who joined the Kozaks claimed these
same privileges.

The Kozaks defended these rights and claims in every
possible way. As their numbers continually increased, and
as everyone in Ukraine feared them and also needed them
to defend the country from the Tatars, their privileges
gradually came to be recognized by the local nobles and
government officials. By the close of the sixteenth century
a powerful Kozak organization was developing, augmented by large numbers who entered its ranks in order
to benefit by what were coming to be known as "Kozak
rights and privileges." The Kozak Host had become a social force of great significance.

CHAPTER X

NATIONAL REVIVAL IN THE STEPPES

Reunion under Poland of Eastern and Western Ukraine:
While the Kozak Host was beginning to gain in prestige
and to lay claim to various rights and privileges, the
course of events in western Ukraine was driving Ukrainians by the thousands across the Dnieper to the eastern
or Kozak side, thus bringing new support to the Kozak
Host and a remarkable growth in its numbers. With the
incursion of these newcomers the national life which had
begun to develop in western Ukraine but was being stifled
under the weight of rule by the Polish gentry found a new
opportunity for growth under the aegis of the Kozak
Host.

The first important event to encourage a migration of
Ukrainians into the Kozak steppes was the political reunion of the two long-separated parts of Ukraine; this occurred in 1569 when Poland annexed from Lithuania the
provinces of Volynia and Kiev and also the lands beyond
the Dnieper. The reunion was a complete surprise to the
Ukrainian inhabitants and its implications were at first
not clear even to the Polish government itself; only after
many years did its results become fully apparent.

After the old quarrel over Volynia was forgotten, Lithuania and Poland had experienced no great changes in
their relations to one another. The Lithuanian landlords
enjoyed their connection with Poland but insisted that the
independence of the grand duchy of Lithuania should be
maintained in order that they might manage their estates
as they had been accustomed to, without interference by
the government. During the reign of Grand Duke Alexander, who from 1501 to 1506 was also King of Poland,
the Lithuanian landlords, taking advantage of the fact
that Poland needed Lithuanian aid in a war with Turkey,

forced Poland to annul the old Act of Union between the two countries and to sign new terms, in which the clauses providing for the incorporation of Lithuania into Poland were omitted. The Grand Duke of Lithuania thereafter continued to rule as King of Poland, but the two countries were regarded as separate. It was to the advantage of the Lithuanian ruling dynasty for Lithuania to be independent, because in Lithuania the crown was hereditary, while in Poland the all-powerful gentry elected the king and no one could be sure of the outcome of an election. As long as Lithuania had competent rulers this policy of independence worked well.

The situation remained unchanged until the 1560's. The King of Poland and Grand Duke of Lithuania was then Sigismund August, who having no heirs gave no thought to the question of a successor. Lithuania was at war with Muscovy, and the grand duke thought that his country would gain in security by becoming more firmly bound to Poland. Even the Lithuanian petty gentry, who had not long before gained the right to sit in the Lithuanian parliament, favored such closer union, hoping to receive not only military aid to lessen their own burdens, but also the freedom from duties and obligations to the state which the Polish gentry had received. The king and the gentry accordingly did all in their power to persuade the great nobles of Lithuania not to object to a permanent union between Poland and Lithuania. From 1562 on, the king time and again convoked the parliaments of the two countries in joint session and insisted upon the participation of the Lithuanian lords. But the latter held themselves aloof, profited by their influence over the deputies of the gentry in preventing them from taking direct part in the discussions, and after finally participating in the parliament of 1564, withdrew their concessions. When they learned at the parliament called to meet in Lublin at the end of 1568 that the king, under pressure from his Polish advisers, was planning to force them to sit in joint session with the

Polish representatives, they quietly withdrew during the night of March 1, 1569, expecting in this way to "break the parliament" and to delay the issue. The result was unexpected.

The Poles ignored the withdrawal and persuaded their king that the Lithuanians had affronted him by their illegal boycott of parliament and that questions at issue should therefore be settled without them. They finally took a different tack, however. Seeing that the Lithuanian lords were unwilling to sacrifice the independence of their country, the Poles decided to put an end to Lithuania as soon as possible and to begin by annexing to Poland such lands as Lithuania claimed. Accordingly, they begged the king to seize the provinces of Volynia and Pidliashe, which they asserted rightfully Poland's, even though the Lithuanian nobles had been allowed through the generosity of King Casimir to govern them. This statement was untrue: the Poles had attempted several times to seize these lands but had always failed; Polish princes had merely been allowed by the Lithuanian grand duke to govern them on two occasions for short periods, and the Poles, as a result of this concession, had come to view the territory with covetous eyes as their property. The king approved the project of the deputies, declared that Volynia and Pidliashe belonged to Poland, and at once commanded senators representing these provinces to take seats in the Polish parliament. The recipients of this command did not approve; but as this was not an age when representatives of the people decided issues, but an age ruled by force and deceit, they appeared when the king threatened to punish them by confiscating their property and offices and by removing them from their positions. They were unwilling to take an oath of allegiance to Poland, but the king repeated his threat, and they were forced to take their seats. At the end of May the annexation was carried through, and thus what the Polish nobles had not been able to accomplish by stronger measures was now done by mere proclamation of the king. Weakened already by the loss of its provinces, Lithuania was reduced by this blow to complete impotence, and the Ukrainian nobles no longer cared to fight for the country, because even the Lithuanian nobles had lost all their influence and power.

When the Poles observed how helpless Lithuania was, they decided to deprive it of more of its Ukrainian territory, and were encouraged to do so by Volynian deputies who, having fallen under the rule of Poland themselves, did not wish to be separated by an international boundary from the other Ukrainian lands.

First they annexed the province of Braslav, which after its separation from Podolia had been united to Volynia and where Volynian nobles had acquired property. The Polish king at once commanded the senators and deputies of the annexed province to meet with the parliament and to pledge their allegiance to Poland, as had been done in the case of Volynia. There was no opposition, and within two weeks the annexation of Braslav was completed.

More opposition was encountered when the annexation of Kiev was proposed by the Polish deputies, the king and many of the senators raising objections. The great extent of the province of Kiev, adjoining both Moscow and Crimea, caused apprehension, for it was feared that the defense of such a large and thinly populated area would be too great a burden and that Poland, with its poor financial system, its always empty treasury, and its small army, would be unable to protect it. For these reasons the king and the senators resisted the temptation for a while, but finally yielded; and on June 3, 1569, the king proclaimed his intention of joining the province of Kiev to Poland. He ordered the governor of Kiev—Prince Vasyl Constantine Ostrozky—to pledge his allegiance, and signed the Act of Union in which it was assumed that Kiev, too, had formerly belonged to Poland.

The Lithuanian lords, fearing that in their absence Poland would swallow all Lithuania, returned to the parliament, but did not dare protest vigorously against the partial dismemberment of their country which had already been accomplished, and merely implored the parliament not to destroy it entirely. For a time the Poles were moved by these pleas. Later in the same year it was decreed that in future Lithuania would have neither a separate grand duke nor a separate parliament, but its representatives would sit in the Polish parliament; it was, however, to retain its own ministry, treasury, and army.

After 1569 Lithuania lost its importance and became a mere part of the joint Polish-Lithuanian state. With Kiev gone, it retained of its former Ukrainian lands only Bereste and Pinsk, and even these were strongly subjected to Polish influences.

As to the other areas of Ukraine, Siveria was seized by Muscovy, Bukovina remained subject to Moldavia, while Carpathian Ukraine continued under Hungarian rule. Forty years later, however, Poland took Siveria from Muscovy; and for a short time nearly the whole of Ukraine, with the exception of the small provinces of Bukovina and Carpathian Ukraine, was ruled by Poland.

Social and Political Effects of Polish Annexation: The great historical significance of the acquisition of the bulk of Ukraine by Poland is due to the social and political changes which it brought into the internal structure of the annexed lands, similar to those which earlier annexation by Poland had brought to the Ukrainian provinces of Galicia, Kholm, and Podolia. In these provinces Polish law and social organization had been formally introduced in 1434, but even before this time the many Polish nobles had introduced Polish forms as they moved in. In the Ukrainian provinces which had been subject to Lithuania since the first Act of Union with Poland in 1385, the Lithuanian government had gradually introduced customs and laws modeled after those of Poland. The *Lithuanian Statute,* a collection of laws in force in the grand duchy of Lithuania and first published in 1529, retained in its first edition many characteristics of the old legal system of Ukraine and White Russia that had existed there from the time of the Kievan kingdom, but by the time of the second edition of the *Statute* in 1566 many Polish features of both general administration and the enforcement of local justice had been introduced.

It is true that the Act by which the Ukrainian lands were united to Poland in 1569 left many features of the old system undisturbed: it recognized the Ukrainian language as official in the courts and in formal communications with the government, permitted existing laws to remain in force, including the *Lithuanian Statute,* and created a separate court of appeals for Ukraine. These provisions, however, did not remain long unchanged, partly because as soon as Poland secured a strong grip on the country there was sent in a swarm of Polish officials who in various ways acquired large estates and introduced a program of Polonization. Before 1569 the Poles had been forbidden to hold offices or to own large estates in these Ukrainian provinces, but now they could—another important innovation.

Ukrainian life became closely patterned after the Polish model; hardly a stone was left untouched in the whole structure of life, and Ukrainians who clung to their native ways felt isolated and helpless.

Some of these changes and their influence upon Ukrainian customs must now be noted. The princes and magnates—great landowners who prior to this time had controlled the government and held the whole administration of justice in their hands—were now reduced to the same level as the lesser nobility; because of their wealth, however, they continued to dominate this group and often had large numbers of poor gentry in their employ. The gentry had no responsibilities but enjoyed many privileges: they were freed from military service and the payment of taxes; they possessed legislative power and made selfish use of it; they elected judges and other high officials

from among their own number; they were given the crown
lands for life use, to be managed like personal estates;
they alone could hold political or ecclesiastical offices.
They administered everything and, of course, they administered in their own interest, even the king being forced
to submit to their dictation. The king's authority, like all
public authority, was very weak; the gentry were utterly
irresponsible, and as there was no law or court which
could function against them, they did what they pleased,
fearing no punishment for even the most atrocious acts.
Even crimes which they committed against each other, to
say nothing of those against the common people, went unpunished. In the absence of law and justice, they were
accustomed to settle everything by force; they kept armed
bands on their estates and frequently waged wars among
themselves, but these private wars brought injury to all
the people because all were at their mercy.

The cities, which had previously been the centers of political life, had completely lost their political importance.
With the introduction of self-government on the German
model, each city had become shut off from the rest of the
country as a little self-governing republic; this was true
in theory, but in practice this parceling of authority
placed the townspeople entirely at the mercy of the landlords. The cities had no influence on legislation because
they were forbidden representation in parliament; law-
making remained exclusively in the hands of the landowning gentry, who systematically exploited the urban
centers for their own advantage. In the course of time,
therefore, the cities declined both culturally and economi-
cally, and the country was deprived of the benefits which
they had offered in normal circumstances. Before long the
towns were filled with foreign immigrants, especially
Jews, who could adapt themselves better than others to
the almost unbearable conditions in which government by
the gentry placed the townspeople. Ukrainians in the
cities faced a particularly difficult situation because they

were not permitted to enjoy even the ordinary privileges of city dwellers.

Most Ukrainians were farmers, and they suffered even more than the townspeople. The old system of slavery had gradually disappeared in the fifteenth and sixteenth centuries, but in spite of this, conditions were so wretched that they resembled those of the former slavery. The farmers lost title to their farms and were regarded as living on and farming the land of the king or of the nobles, among whom the crown lands had been distributed. The peasant was required to stay on the estate where he was born, and his children were deprived of the right of departure except by special permission of the landlord. If a peasant secretly deserted his farm, he could be pursued as if he were a slave of former times. The landlord had entire control over the life and property of his subject; he could put him to death or dispossess him of his property, and there was no recourse for the oppressed, because the nobles were above the law. Even the king himself had no legal right to interfere between the landlord and those subjected to him. Only the peasants on the royal estates had the right to take their cases to the king's courts; but it was difficult to obtain justice there because one was obliged to go to the capital, where the courts were likewise in the hands of the lords, and even if a case went against a noble, he ignored the decision. Since the peasants could not obtain justice in the royal courts, the people of Galicia seldom appealed to them, and those from more distant estates even less frequently.

Thus the peasants were deprived of all their rights, civil and personal as well as political. In their desperate position there was no legal recourse; two alternatives were left to them—rebellion or flight, and of these they chose the latter.

Political Changes and the Growth of Population in Eastern Ukraine: In addition to the enserfment of the peasants and the loss of their civil rights through the in-

troduction of Polish law in the first half of the sixteenth
century, there began in the last half of the century an un-
exampled exploitation of their physical strength. During
this period a sharp increase in the demand for wheat and
other grains occurred, and as a result the need for more
labor on the great estates. Hides, honey, wax, fish, and
livestock had previously been exported to Western Europe from Ukraine; and beginning with the early part of
the fifteenth century large herds of oxen had been driven
to Silesia, oxen becoming a medium of exchange in western Ukraine. Somewhat later a heavy demand had arisen
for Ukrainian timber in the regions adjacent to rivers
flowing into the Baltic Sea; as this timber began to be exhausted in the second half of the sixteenth century, the
logs were cut into planks, and in the more distant regions
converted into potash: the peasants were now forced by
the landlords to transport lumber and potash to the near-
est navigable streams, often many miles distant. In the
middle of the sixteenth century and still more in the latter
half, Ukrainian grain was in demand for export to the
Baltic provinces from the regions along the rivers Vistula, Sian, Buh, and Niemen. From the Baltic ports both
grain and forest products were shipped to England, the
Netherlands, France, and Spain. With the increase in demand for grain and the accompanying increase in prices,
it began to be carted from the more remote parts of
Ukraine to the river docks.

This demand for grain for export brought about drastic changes in farming. Prior to the time when this outside demand had arisen, grain was raised only in sufficient
quantities for domestic consumption. Accordingly, the
landlords did not cultivate the whole area of their large
estates, or require a great amount of labor from their
peasants, but instead took payment of dues in the form of
honey, hides, forage for their livestock, and grain. When
the foreign markets were opened for grain and grain raising became profitable, the landlords put more land into

cultivation, and in order to increase the size of their estates seized the small farms from the peasants and added
them to their own land. The peasants were then given
smaller strips of land, and instead of other payment, the
landlords demanded that they work on their estates; as
the peasants valued their labor less than money or goods,
they accepted the change on account of the lower dues in
money and grain. Many became serfs on the estates of the
nobles, and in time were reduced to virtual enslavement.
Serfdom made its initial appearance in western Ukraine,
where the demand for grain first appeared, in the latter
half of the sixteenth century.

All these events—the abolition of the boundary between
Galicia and the Ukraine beyond, the development of large
estates, the enserfment of the peasants in western
Ukraine, the seizure of peasant holdings and the oppression of the serfs by the landlords—all these caused a great
wave of migration from western Ukraine and also from
the closely populated northwestern region of Polisia to
the expanse of eastern Ukraine, which not long before, in
the census reports of 1552, had been described as completely deserted except for a few scattered castles. In the
last quarter of the sixteenth century and the first half of
the seventeenth the appearance of the area changed so
completely as to make it scarcely recognizable: towns appeared on the sites of old Tatar encampments, villages
were widely strewn among the recent Kozak retreats, the
castles and manor houses of Polish landowners sprang
up. Polish law and Polish customs became established
where shortly before wild horses had pastured and the
steppe grasses had rustled in the winds.

The fifty years of determined struggle between the Kozaks and the Crimean horde had not been in vain, for they
had proved that the Tatars could be repulsed and subdued; and following the trail of the Kozaks the peasants
had come and planted grain, pushing gradually farther
and farther away from the fortified castles. The Tatar at-

tacks, to be sure, continued; and farming was thereby hindered, for the peasant had to be constantly on the alert against them. A traveler by the name of Erich Lasota, who crossed the province of Braslav in 1594 on his way to visit the Kozaks, saw forts where the farm population sought refuge in time of Tatar attacks. While he plowed the soil, the peasant carried a gun on his back and a sword at his side, because the Tatar bands still frequented the country and no one felt safe without weapons. The Ukrainian national songs contain many descriptions of peasants taken captive on their land by Tatars.

Constant danger, however, merely made the people more daring. Dissatisfied by the expansion of serfdom in Galicia and the loss of their farms, the inhabitants fled to Volynia and Podolia, or even farther east to the province of Braslav. The farther south and east they went, the more freedom they found; and the news of entirely free land at the frontier attracted the largest number of people to the lower Dnieper region, though it was most exposed to danger. Here they settled down and farmed under the protection of the Kozaks, tilling what soil they could and engaging in bee keeping; whenever the Tatars did not molest them they were happy and contented.

But in a short time these happy settlers suffered a great disappointment. The nobles, like a plague or a swarm of mosquitoes, followed them to the frontier, and as soon as the land was well settled and relieved of raids by the Tatars, began to claim it. Those who believed that they had freed themselves forever by settling on "God's land" found that the nobility and the institution of serfdom had followed them even here.

The landlords who held official positions and lived near the frontier began as early as the close of the sixteenth century to learn from their subordinates of the new settlements in the Buh and the Dnieper regions. As they observed the steady influx of people, they realized how valuable this land would be as soon as it was inhabited, and at once petitioned the king to give them title to it. Where farms were already established in the wilderness, they forced the owners to sell their rights and then asked for royal sanction of the transfer. Among those who thus acquired estates were rich nobles, provincial military governors, city governors, and army officers, who because of their many employees and their control of armed forces had the power to oblige the people to surrender not only their land but themselves. Whenever they decided to "buy" a farmer's land, he had of necessity to give up his rights for any payment offered him.

The first to take action were the local nobles of near-by Volynia; for instance, one of the princes, Vishnevetsky, forced the heirs of Hlinsky to sell him their rights to the land along the River Sula. Then he gained the approval of the king and acquired title to "that wilderness, known as the region of the Sula, Udai, and Solonitsia rivers," which extended from the boundary of Muscovy to the mouth of the Dnieper. Thus the Vishnevetsky family acquired a great tract of land, on which were built Lubny and many other cities. Vast territories were acquired by the nobles of the Ostrozky, Koretsky, Zbarazki, and Ruzhinsky families. Following their examples, Polish nobles petitioned the king to give them title to land in Ukraine; and as soon as they obtained it, nobles of the Zolkiewski, Kazanovski, and Potocki families emigrated there, and forced out the smaller nobles; the result was that within a short time this one-time wilderness had become the possession of powerful nobles, who governed their immense lands through swarms of officials, in complete independence, like "kinglets," as Khmelnitsky called them.

After they had gained title to these territories, the nobles were in no haste to introduce oppressive measures but waited until the land had become populated. They even ceased to collect taxes, but were satisfied with selling timber for making potash and turning over to government monopolies the rights to river fishing, bridge tolls, taverns, and flour mills, the peasants being forbidden to buy liquor or beer except in these taverns; they could neither brew their own beer nor have their flour privately ground. Before long the landlords imposed a tax of one tenth of the bees and the livestock. As compared with serfdom in the west, this was not at all bad; but the peasants who had fled from the oppression of the lords and had migrated here to face the dangers of the Tatars and the wilderness viewed these special claims of their new oppressors with great dissatisfaction. While crossing the other parts of Ukraine they had learned that after making these initial claims the nobles would impose serfdom. Therefore, occasionally, on the very first attempt to limit their freedom, the peasants revolted, left their farms, and sought free land at the outermost frontier. But as the nobles pursued them everywhere, they began to join the Kozak organization.

Growth of the Kozak Host at the Close of the Sixteenth Century: As already indicated the Polish kings—Sigismund August, Stephen Batory, and Sigismund III—had attempted to establish discipline among the Kozaks. In consequence the Kozaks had made the assumption that, being in the service of the crown of Poland, they were subject to no other authority than that of their own elective officials, and that they were free from any responsibility but that of military service. They claimed that they did not have to pay any taxes, work for the nobles, or humble themselves before the power of the nobles or their courts. Moreover, they believed that they had the right to collect from the rest of the population, including the townspeople and the servitors of the nobles and of the king, all the supplies needed for war.

The government recognized some of these claims of the Kozaks who were registered for service as a paid army; but as the administration failed to pay them, the registered royal Kozaks mingled with the general Kozak Host most of the time. After the first registration in 1572 the government made many others—in 1578, 1583, and 1590 —but these were quite ineffective; as registered and un-registered Kozaks both fought against the Tatars and were both called upon by the government and its officials in time of war, the Kozak Host recognized no differences in the "rights and privileges" of the two groups, and any Kozak who performed his duty was a free man, subject only to the Kozak Host and its courts. This meant that if any man joined its ranks and performed his military duty, he was not subject to any other authority, whether that of noble or frontier governor or city warden. Accordingly, once this principle was established, the towns-people and the peasants who did not wish to submit to the landlords became Kozaks. They recognized the Kozak officials as their superiors, proclaimed themselves Kozaks, and refused to obey the nobles. Formerly many people who had lived as Kozaks had not called themselves by that name because theirs was a dishonorable occupation; now, on the contrary, in their search for freedom they enrolled in the Kozak ranks in order to escape oppression by the nobles, even though they had no liking for war. The Kozaks at this time consisted mostly of "disobedient" towns-people and peasants. No earlier census than that of 1616 has been preserved in full, but there are fragments from preceding decades which make it evident that the population of eastern Ukraine had for a long time increased rapidly, expanding north to the very boundary of Muscovy and south to the "wild steppes." There were cities where for every "obedient" person there were dozens of others who were "disobedient." The whole area surrounding such cities was dotted with Kozak farms, whose inhabitants recognized the authority of no lord and fulfilled no obligation to anyone.

In consequence of this movement, the nobles began to treat the "obedient" inhabitants more considerately and to make smaller demands upon them; in some of the cities, for example, the townspeople were merely required to serve in the army, and even then the people fulfilled their terms of service in the Kozak army, where discipline was lighter. Conditions of life were such that practically everyone had to be ready to fight at all times and carried arms regularly for his own protection. Accordingly, the people assumed the duties of Kozaks as a matter of course and took part in their campaigns, preferring to obey the officers of the Host rather than any other authority.

This alteration in national life increased the number of the Kozaks and their importance, and they became a great social force, powerful enough to oppose the whole manorial system of Poland and to hold promise of freedom for the masses of the Ukrainian people and destruction to the gentry. While this revolution made the Kozaks very popular and gave their army a great attraction for the masses, at the same time it laid the foundation for a long struggle with the Polish government and the gentry who supported it. The Poles were unwilling to accept the Kozaks' own interpretation of their rights and privileges, and even less did the government recognize the claims of those who had freed themselves from their landlords by accepting the protection of the Kozaks. But to stop the movement was very difficult because of the increasing rate at which peasants and townspeople poured into the Kozak organization during the last quarter of the sixteenth century and the first quarter of the seventeenth.

The increase in the number of purely military Kozaks, who considered war their chief means of livelihood, is shown by the size and frequency of their campaigns against the Turks and Tatars. They were no longer content with frontier warfare and raids into the steppes for plunder, but took possession of the Black Sea region. Their early expeditions were made by land, but later they carried out attacks by sea, first on the Crimean cities and then past the Danube to Constantinople, as well as along the Anatolian coast of the Black Sea. Whenever the Polish government was not making use of the Kozaks for a war, they were fighting on their own account against the Turks, the Tatars, or the Wallachians. For example, as soon as Stephen Batory dismissed the Kozaks after the war with Muscovy in which they had been aiding him, complaints at once arrived that they had captured the Tatar envoys on the Samara as these men were carrying money from Muscovy to their khan.

In the spring the Kozaks attacked Wallachia, bringing with them a candidate for the throne. Batory, fearing that war with Turkey might result, ordered them to return home; but the Kozaks then captured the Turkish city of Tiahinia (Bendery) on the Dniester, plundered the entire vicinity, and carried away with them Turkish cannon and rich booty, which they were said to have sold at the annual fair for fifteen thousand gold pieces. The Polish royal army pursued the Kozaks, who abandoned their own cannon and fled beyond the Dnieper. In order to appease the Turks, a few of the Kozaks, presumably the chief offenders, were captured and beheaded in Lviv in the presence of the Turkish envoy. An order was then issued that the number of Kozaks registered in the royal service be enlarged. Six hundred were enlisted in 1583, but this measure failed to improve the situation, for during the same year the Kozaks burned the city of Ochakiv and inflicted great losses upon Turkey. When the Poles sent an investigator to seek the offenders among the Kozaks, they drowned him in the Dnieper River.

Stephen Batory died without punishing the Kozaks for their last act of aggression, and they continued to harass the Turkish and Tatar settlements within their reach. They took pay from Muscovy for their attacks upon the Tatars, and at the same time informed the Tatar khan that they were ready to help him in a war against the Turks. When Tatar forces invaded Ukraine in the spring of 1586, the Kozaks blocked their way up the Dnieper, de-

feated them, and forced them to retreat. As further punishment, the Kozaks again attacked Ochakiv, slaughtered
the garrison, and set the city on fire. Then they undertook
another campaign against Wallachia, but the hospodar received aid from the Turks in time to force the invaders to
retreat. Before long they were arming boats and seeking
adventure on the Black Sea; they captured a few Turkish
craft at Kozliv (Eupatoria) and plundered the city. In a
battle with the Tatars their losses were small and they departed for Ukraine laden with spoils. On their way they
stormed the city of Bilhorod (Akkerman) and set it afire,
whereupon the enraged sultan gathered a large army to
invade Ukraine, but the Kozaks annihilated the Tatars
who were coming to aid the Turks, and the khan himself
was killed. After this the Turks lost their desire for war
and made peace on condition that Poland prevent further
Kozak depredations.

In 1590 the government enlisted a thousand Kozaks to
remain on the Dnieper and guard the border. The unregistered Kozaks were commanded to leave the lower Dnieper
region and never to return there or to the steppes; no one
was allowed to sell them supplies, and any caught with
booty were to be severely punished. No attention was paid
to these orders, while those who were taken into the royal
service were not paid and so continued their activities in
company with the free Kozaks, who lived on plunder from
the Turkish and Tatar countries. This warlike energy led
to further expansion of Kozak authority over Ukraine.

After it was once recognized that the Kozaks were a
free people, their control spread from the frontier to the
interior of the country. Their bands, under the leadership
of their hetmans, colonels, and other officials, pitched their
camps in the midst of the estates of the landlords in the
provinces of Kiev and Braslav and far beyond. Before
long the nobles began to complain against them, for they
collected military supplies from the landlords and attacked the estates of those who opposed them, while the

inhabitants of all the surrounding country joined the Kozaks and refused obedience to their overlords, frequently revolting against them. In Braslav the townspeople and the Kozaks together captured the citadel, seized the cannon, and lived independently, governing the province for several years. Such unwelcome events aroused the gentry, who continually called upon the government to subdue the Kozaks and to prevent them from inciting the serfs to rebel. The government, however, was so preoccupied with other affairs that for several years almost the whole of southeastern Ukraine as far as Polisia was in the hands of the Kozaks. Whenever the nobles antagonized them, regular war broke out, and the Kozaks made the lords feel their power and authority.

The Kozak Wars: The leader in the first important Kozak war was Christopher Kosinsky. In 1590, together with other distinguished Kozak officers, he was given an estate on the Ros River for his services, but Yanush Ostrozky, the district governor of Bila Tserkva (White Church), added the territory to his military district. Angered by this seizure, Kosinsky and his Kozaks attacked Bila Tserkva and seized and plundered the property of Prince Ostrozky and his administrator, destroyed other castles belonging to the prince, carried away the cannon, and went to live in the castle of Tripillia. The king commissioned several nobles and their local regiments to subdue the Kozaks. Kosinsky, however, prepared for battle, whereupon the commissioners departed, not daring to face the Kozaks. After this successful venture the Kozaks carried on other campaigns, attacking and seizing the castles of Ostrozky and other landowners who antagonized them, and capturing Kiev, Pereyaslav, and other cities. As soon as they had become masters of nearly all the Kievan region, they went into Volynia, conquering cities and compelling the landlords to recognize Kozak authority over their estates and subjects, give them supplies for their army, and prevent no one from submitting to or joining the Kozaks. When Prince Vasyl Constantine Ostrozky realized that the Kozaks were reducing him to ruin, he and his sons and other wealthy nobles made preparations for war. The Polish government, however, was enraged at these nobles because they were not supporting it in matters of religious faith, and refused to assist them, so that they had to fight their battles alone. They therefore hired an army in Galicia and Hungary, solicited the aid of the nobles of Volynia, and with these combined forces defeated the army of Kosinsky and his Kozaks near the town of Piatka. The Kozaks then promised to return the cannon and other munitions, depose Kosinsky from the office of hetman, and leave the landowners in peace.

As soon as the Kozaks returned to their encampment in the Zaporozhian region, "below the rapids," they made fresh preparations and in the spring of 1593 set out again, this time against Cherkassy. They bore a grudge against Prince Vishnevetsky, who had aided the nobles against them in a previous war, and who, as the frontier governor of Cherkassy, had often closed the chief Kozak highway to them. As they approached his capital, Vishnevetsky attacked them from ambush; Kosinsky and many of the Kozaks were killed. The others retreated for the time being, but in the summer of the same year renewed their attack. As Vishnevetsky feared that eventually the Kozaks would overwhelm him, he made an agreement with them that in future they should enjoy free passage through his province and suffer no oppression of any kind. As he alone controlled the main Dnieper highway and had practically promised that he would enforce no laws against them, the Kozaks after this agreement were actual masters of all eastern Ukraine. The most powerful of the nobles, like the Ostrozkys, were humbled and forced to respect the Kozak organization and its freedom of action. Inwardly they raged against the Kozaks, because the latter had thwarted their plans, had stirred up the spirit of revolt among the serfs, and had freed many of the "disobedient" by accepting them for enlistment; but they remained silent and obeyed the orders of the Kozaks because the government, involved in other struggles, was unable to help them, and they were forced to await a time when the Polish army could come to their aid.

The Kozaks had become masters of eastern Ukraine, but as the power had come to their hands easily and quickly they did not know how to adjust themselves to the new circumstances and to strengthen their position there. Occupied with foreign expeditions and plundering raids, they neglected the government of Ukraine and likewise failed to establish sound foundations for their Kozak organization. Since they made no preparations for defense against the Polish government, the Poles were able in due time easily to undermine their power. After the death of Kosinsky, his place was filled by another Kozak chief, Gregory Loboda, who was a highly respected and experienced warrior but lacked an effective political program, a thing which, as a rule, developed slowly among the Kozaks. Besides the Zaporozhian Kozaks of the Dnieper valley, another group had been independently organized on the boundary of Volynia and Braslav by Semerin Nalivaiko, a native of the city of Ostroh, a brave and skilful warrior whose family had become widely known there as staunch Ukrainians; a brother of Semerin, the priest Damian, was a distinguished member of a Greek Orthodox brotherhood in Ostroh. Semerin had decided to be a Kozak and, being young, ambitious, and eager for glory, was well fitted for the life. He failed, however, to take pains to work in harmony with the other group of Kozaks, and there even existed occasional animosity between the two; the Zaporozhian Kozaks complained to Nalivaiko that he had aided Prince Ostrozky against them in Kosinsky's war, while Nalivaiko tried to justify himself by saying that the war had begun unexpectedly when he was connected with Ostrozky and that he had not been able to leave him. Nalivaiko agreed to submit himself to a military tribunal and the case was amicably settled, but the two groups remained aloof, neither showing any desire for coöperation with the other.

At this time the rulers of Western Europe, especially the Pope and the German emperor, were preparing for war against the Turks, who had just conquered Hungary. Realizing that the Kozaks could be of great help, the Pope on one hand and the emperor on the other sent special deputies to Ukraine with money and other gifts in an attempt to interest the Kozak Host in this war. The papal representative, a Croatian priest named Komulovich, was unable to reach the Kozaks themselves, so that the negotiations were carried on indirectly through one of the Polish officials, whom the Kozaks ignored. Lasota, the representative of the German emperor, was more successful. He went in 1594 to visit the Kozaks at their Zaporozhian Sich, and has left an interesting account of his impressions. He presented gifts from the emperor—a flag bearing the imperial emblem, silver horns, and eight thousand marks—with the understanding that the Kozaks were to furnish aid in the war against the Turks. A delegate from Muscovy with money for the Kozaks also attempted to persuade them to lend help to the project, because the German emperor, not knowing to whom the Kozaks were subjected, had communicated with Muscovy to obtain permission for their services. The Germans expected them to hasten to Wallachia to prevent the Tatars from advancing to Hungary; and although dissatisfied with the small amount of money given them, the Kozaks promised their aid. But instead of attacking the Wallachians, they made a raid upon the Mohammedans living along the coast of the Black Sea in the Turkish cities of Perekop, Kilia, and Babadah. Meanwhile Nalivaiko's Kozaks also became interested in the German project and entered Wallachia, capturing Tiahinia and plundering Turkish and Wallachian estates. Nalivaiko retreated when a

large Turkish army arrived, but attacked the Turks
again soon after with the aid of the Zaporozhians. It was
estimated that twelve thousand Kozaks took part in this
expedition. They devastated Moldavia, set fire to the city
of Jassy, and forced the Moldavian hospodar to break
with the Turks and join the Germans. The German emperor was highly pleased and asked his new ally to continue the struggle against the Turks, whereupon the Kozaks, with the aid of the Moldavians, sallied forth again to
plunder the Turkish cities.

The Polish government, eager to take advantage of this
situation in order to gain advantages for itself, appointed
a Polish sympathizer named Jeremiah Mohila as hospodar of Moldavia and ordered the Kozaks to attack the
Tatars and to leave the Wallachians in peace. As the Kozaks had no desire at this particular time to fight against
the Tatars, they returned to their homes to rest. During
his return to Ukraine with his Kozaks in the autumn of
1595 Nalivaiko reached Lutsk in Volynia at the time of
the annual fair when the nobles were holding court. The
frightened townspeople and nobles came out beyond the
city limits to meet him and agreed to pay him a ransom if
he would leave the city undisturbed, but he was not satisfied with the sum given him and plundered the outskirts
of the city. From there he went to White Russia, captured
the fortress of Slutsk, carried off its cannon, and forced
the townspeople to pay a ransom of ten thousand gold
pieces, after which he and his army kept on north, conquering and plundering estates on the way and levying
tribute. He sacked the important city of Mohilev, but
when he learned that a Lithuanian army was awaiting
him, he retreated to Volynia well supplied with artillery.
Meanwhile the Kozaks of the Dnieper valley had been
making themselves at home in Kiev and Polisia, and as
soon as Nalivaiko returned to Volynia, they too set out to
pillage White Russia. After this, both the Kozaks under
Nalivaiko and the Zaporozhian bands took advantage of

every opportunity to participate in the quarrels and warfare among the nobles and aided the Greek Orthodox nobles, including Ostrozky, by threatening and otherwise disturbing their enemies the Uniate bishops and any others who were friendly to Roman Catholicism.

CHAPTER XI

THE FIRST KOZAK UPRISINGS AND THE CHURCH UNION

The War of 1596: As long as the Kozaks were attacking the Orthodox nobles, the Polish government refrained from interference, but it refused to tolerate raids upon those who, under its protection, were propagating Catholicism, and it did not look calmly upon the plundering of the cities in Volynia and White Russia. Depleted by the Moldavian war, the Polish army was not at this time engaged in any struggle, and the king early in 1596 ordered the commander-in-chief of the army, Stanislaus Zolkiewski, to undertake a punitive expedition against the Kozaks, at the same time urging the nobles of Galicia and Volynia to assist him. The Kozak regiments were scattered, Nalivaiko being in southern Volynia, Loboda and his forces at Bila Tserkva, and the Zaporozhians in White Russia. Zolkiewski decided to act quickly and to surprise and defeat each army separately. He first attacked with his light cavalry the forces of Nalivaiko, who barely escaped capture but who hastened in good order to take refuge among his former friends in the province of Braslav, whither Zolkiewski followed him, slaughtering and taking captives as he went. Nalivaiko opened negotiations with the Polish general, at the same time keeping in touch with Loboda and his Kozaks. He was expecting a message from Braslav that he would be received there, but the people of that city, fearing a massacre by the Polish army, had recently surrendered and refused to admit him. Zolkiewski almost captured him near Braslav, but Nalivaiko destroyed the dam at one of the fords, thus delaying the Polish army; he then threw his cannon into the river, buried the powder in the ground, and easily escaped into the steppes beyond the River Sob, where Zolkiewski was unwilling to follow him. After a halt in the Uman forest he proceeded to Kiev. While Zolkiewski was pursuing Nalivaiko, Loboda united his Kozaks with a band led by Shaula, but both were for a long time undecided as to whether to admit Nalivaiko to their group. Zolkiewski attempted to keep them apart by assuring Loboda that he wished to destroy only Nalivaiko, who was the chief offender, and that the Zaporozhian Kozaks might depart unpunished down the Dnieper. Because the ideal of unity had become supreme among them, the Kozaks rejected the Polish proposals and admitted Nalivaiko to their ranks. Shaula joined him near Bila Tserkva, and together they almost annihilated the advance forces of the Polish army under the command of Kyryk Ruzhinsky, a petty prince who had been until recently the chief of a Kozak band, but who now desired to take vengeance upon them because they had caused an insurrection among the peasants on his estate at Pavolotsky. Zolkiewski arrived just in time to save Ruzhinsky and the army, and the Kozaks retreated, followed by Zolkiewski, who attacked them in a battle at Hostry Kamin. The Kozaks fortified their camp by encircling it with interlocked wagons, through which the Poles were unable to penetrate. Many of the Kozak officers faced the enemy in the front lines and were killed, and Shaula himself lost an arm. The Poles, however, had sustained such heavy losses that Zolkiewski did not dare to advance, but retreated to Bila Tserkva to appeal to the king for additional troops and supplies. In April, after receiving reinforcements, he renewed the struggle.

By this time the Kozaks had mobilized and concentrated their forces at Pereyaslav, where they assembled their wives and children for fear that they might be taken captive by the Poles. Various courses of action were proposed, especially in view of the fact that their families were with them. Some suggested that they move east of the Dnieper toward the border of Muscovy, others wished

to seek the protection of the khan and resist Poland with
his aid, while still others were ready to remain where they
were for a fight to the finish. There were even a few who
were willing to surrender to Zolkiewski, but they found
no support. While the Kozaks were holding council, Zolkiewski was considering how to cross the Dnieper. In this
feat he was aided by the Kievans, who had built boats and
hidden them from the Kozaks, and who now aided the
Poles to cross in order to win favor for themselves. The
Kozaks across the river unlimbered their cannon for action, but were outwitted by Zolkiewski, who sent a few of
his boats to Tripillia, where he made a show of crossing.
When the Kozaks went downstream to guard the river
bank, he crossed the Dnieper just below Kiev. The Kozaks
decided to march toward the frontier of Muscovy, expecting that Zolkiewski, who had not followed Nalivaiko,
would not dare to follow them. Zolkiewski, however, was
determined at all costs to destroy them. As his army had
been reinforced by the arrival of Lithuanian regiments,
he now felt that his forces were stronger than those of the
Kozaks, his only fear being that the Kozaks might escape
over the Muscovite border or across the Don. Because of
this fear he again opened negotiations with them, meanwhile sending part of his cavalry ahead under Strus to
cut them off from the steppes; this order was given so
secretly that even the Poles themselves did not know
where they were being led. Keeping a lookout for Zolkiewski, the unsuspecting Kozaks crossed the Sula between the Solonitsia and the Lubny with the intention of
destroying the bridge behind them as soon as their scouts
gave notice of the arrival of the Polish army, and of escaping over the border into Muscovy while Zolkiewski
was preparing a crossing. But Strus blocked their path of
retreat at Lubny until Zolkiewski arrived and attacked
them from the rear. The panic-stricken Kozaks decided to
remain at the Solonitsia River and to defend themselves
there.

The place where they took their stand was well suited for defense, situated as it was upon hills overlooking a broad expanse on all sides. On one side it was unapproachable because of the marshes of the Sula and on all other sides the Kozaks fortified their position with wagons, earthworks, and trenches; in the center they built mounds of logs and sod for protection, and behind these they stationed their cannon. As the position was strong and its seizure by storm impossible, and the Kozaks still had an experienced army of about six thousand men and an equal number of women and children, and others unfit for military duty, Zolkiewski decided to wear them down by siege. He opened fire and at the same time carried on negotiations intended to cause dissension in their ranks. The intrigues of the Poles had some effect, for the old animosity between the Zaporozhians and the followers of Nalivaiko was revived and developed into quarrels and even bloodshed. In the course of a fight at one of the council meetings Hetman Loboda was killed. Instead of Nalivaiko's being elected his successor, Krempsky was made hetman; the Zaporozhian Kozaks never forgave Nalivaiko for having, as they believed, killed their leader. The besieged Kozaks suffered great hardships, but Zolkiewski too encountered difficulties; and, unable to obtain military supplies and food for his weary troops, he became convinced that they would die of starvation sooner than the Kozaks. Meanwhile, in the Dnieper region new Kozak regiments were mobilized under the leadership of Pidvisotsky, who ravaged the countryside with the intention of forcing Zolkiewski to abandon the siege, while Kozaks from below the Dnieper rapids came up the Dnieper and Sula rivers toward Lubny to relieve their hard-pressed comrades. Zolkiewski made futile attempts to persuade them, as he had attempted to persuade Loboda, that he was not their enemy, but his efforts failed; and if the Kozak reinforcements had arrived in time, he would have had difficulty in dealing with them. Fortunately for him, however, the besieged Kozaks did not know that aid was approaching.

Zolkiewski decided to make one final attempt to force the Kozaks to surrender. He opened a terrific bombardment and began preparations for taking their position by storm, but at the same time continued his negotiations, promising that if they would give up their leaders he would permit the others to leave unharmed. On account of the sufferings of their wives and children, the Kozaks felt that they could hold out no longer, and after two days of Polish bombardment, and without waiting for the reinforcements to arrive, they accepted Zolkiewski's terms, which included the surrender of their leaders, their guns, and their ammunition, and the banners and gifts which they had received from the German emperor. Nalivaiko attempted to escape with the aid of his followers, but the other Kozaks seized him and turned him over to the Poles; Shaula and several others suffered the same fate.

As soon as the Kozaks had accepted the terms offered by Zolkiewski, he treacherously demanded in addition that each Polish lord should be at liberty to take back from the Kozak army those formerly subjected to him, but to this the Kozaks refused to agree, since nearly all of them would have been placed at the mercy of their former lords. The Polish army then savagely attacked the disarmed and defenseless people who had already met the terms of surrender, and slaughtered them "so savagely that for miles one could see nothing but dead bodies," according to a Polish eyewitness.

Only a part of Krempsky's Kozaks succeeded in fighting their way out and departing for the Zaporozhian region, to which Pidvisotsky's contingent also returned. Zolkiewski, not having sufficient troops to carry out his intention of completely destroying the Kozaks, determined to wreak his vengeance upon the prisoners. The most severe punishment was inflicted upon Nalivaiko, who was tortured in prison for over a year before being beheaded and quartered. Legends regarding his treatment soon spread to the most distant corners of Poland and Ukraine, including a story to the effect that he had been seated upon a hot iron horse and crowned with an iron crown because, it was said, he had intended to become king of Ukraine and had called himself "King Nalivai" (drunkard).

Decline of Ukrainian National Life and Efforts at Revival: Although the Kozaks were not wiped out by Zolkiewski's slaughter, their power was temporarily lessened and they were forced to move to the lower Dnieper, with serious results not only for the Kozaks themselves but for the whole Ukrainian movement. The Ukrainians suffered this blow at a critical time, when the Polish government was attempting to force Roman Catholicism upon them and they needed and were seeking the support that the Kozaks had previously given them. Their enemies took advantage of the Kozaks' loss of prestige to accuse the adherents of Greek Orthodoxy of having abetted Nalivaiko and the other Kozak insurgents. There was no truth in this assertion, for the Ukrainian and White Russian non-Kozaks, the so-called "civilians," had merely been seeking aid against their Polish oppressors in whatever quarter they could find it. Nevertheless, if they had not lost the battle of Lubny, the Kozaks would no doubt have played as early as the close of the sixteenth century the important part in the Ukrainian national movement which they actually filled a quarter of a century later. Meanwhile the Ukrainian civilians were forced to carry on alone their bitter struggle against Polonization. It has already been seen to what a deplorable condition the Ukrainian people had been reduced by the Polish government, which had brought economic ruin and serfdom to the peasants, had caused the decline of the cities, and prevented Ukrainian townspeople from engaging in commerce and trade. The only class of Ukrainians to whom the laws permitted a voice in political life was the gentry, and the Polish landowners saw to it that even their rights were rendered ineffective. Being unorganized, the Ukrainian gentry were beaten from the very beginning and overwhelmed by the flood of Polish gentry; in western Ukraine they were soon driven from their offices and deprived of their property. As it was only by becoming Polonized and adopting Roman Catholicism that they could enjoy any real equality of rights and privileges with the Poles, most of the more important and ambitious gentry of Galicia, Kholm, and Podolia had by the end of the fifteenth century taken this step. In the sixteenth century the same process took place in Volynia and along the Dnieper. Though the Act of Union of 1569 had promised to the local Orthodox landlords equal rights with the Catholics, the promise had not been kept, and it was not long before they realized that all roads were closed to them unless they adopted Catholicism and became Polonized. Since the landowners, especially those of Volynia—the stronghold of Ukrainian landlords, petty princes, and landed magnates—gradually submitted to the pressure, the Ukrainian population lost the only influential and important class which could have served as a foundation for a healthy Ukrainian national life.

Under the Polish-Lithuanian rule of the fifteenth and sixteenth centuries, Ukrainian culture, connected as it was with the Church, suffered a serious setback. The Church and its Orthodox clergy had been accustomed to enjoy the special care and protection of the government; now that the Ukrainian government no longer existed, and the Lithuanian government, and to an even greater extent that of Poland, were oppressing the Orthodox Church, it fell into a decline and with it went the old culture so closely connected with it. Fewer educated men were to be found among its clergy, and the old schools foundered; literary and artistic creativeness died out. It is true that in places where the Orthodox aristocracy of landlords and merchants persisted they supported the life of the Church and of the culture associated with it, but even these landlords and merchants were helpless in the face of the dissension brought into Ukrainian religious life by hostile governments. Both the Grand Duke of Lithuania and the King of Poland assumed the privilege of "patronage," or appointment to Church offices, and since prospective bishops and abbots required their approval, they were able to disregard the qualifications of the candidates and auction off the offices to the highest bidders, or to those who would be of service to them. In this manner the chief offices in the Orthodox Church fell into the hands of men who neither were qualified for them nor wished to lead pious lives, but who made use of the wealth of the Church to enrich themselves and their families. As neither the lords nor the people could eradicate this evil, they lost all desire to contribute to the Church when they learned that money intended for education and charity was being spent by drunkards and spendthrifts who even appropriated the Church treasures for their daughters or spent them on mistresses.

Although the Ukrainian landlords implored the king not to interfere in their religious affairs, their prayers were in vain. Because of this system of royal interference the sixteenth century witnessed great dissension and decline in the Orthodox Church; and as the Orthodox Church was the symbol of Ukrainian national unity, the only organized representative of Ukrainian nationalism, and the foundation stone of its culture, Ukrainian culture could not meet the competition of the officially promoted Polish culture and thus lost its preëminence. The Polish culture of the fourteenth and fifteenth centuries was on no very high level, being only a weak and outmoded copy of the German and Italian culture of the time. If it won the upper hand over Ukrainian culture, it did so chiefly because it was the official culture of the government and was better suited to the civic and administrative life of Poland, and also because behind it stood the powerful and

closely related Latin-Catholic culture of Germany and
Italy which was disseminated by means of schools teaching the language and literature written in the Latin
tongue. The Ukrainian-Byzantine culture was, in the new
circumstances of Polish-Lithuanian official life, of less
value than it had been formerly. It was static rather than
dynamic, and in fact of no use whatever except for Church
life, its Byzantine models having long since become outmoded. Its conservatism weakened the possibility of its
competing with the Polish-Latin culture, especially when
the life of the Polish Church began to experience a regeneration.

In the sixteenth century, at least up to the last quarter,
the Polish Church had been badly disorganized, but there
developed within it under the influence of the German Reformation a lively secular and anticlerical literary and
cultural movement restricted to the gentry, which many
Ukrainians were unable to resist. The Ukrainians never
experienced an independent anticlerical reformation, but
those who accepted the basic ideas of the German Reformation withdrew from the Greek Orthodox Church,
adopted Polish culture, including Catholicism, and gave
up their Ukrainian nationality. The mass of Ukrainians
felt instinctively, however, that the only platform upon
which all classes and sections of Ukrainians could unite
was that of the ancient Greek Orthodox Church, upon
which platform they had stood unitedly since the very beginning of the life of Ukraine, or, as the saying went, ''in
accordance with the tradition of the kingdom of Rus and
the life of Rus.'' For the upper classes of Ukrainians,
however, faced by the competition of this new aristocratic
Polish culture, it was difficult to remain true to the
Church, shaken and crushed as it was under Polish rule
and at the lowest ebb of its fortunes.

The marked development of farming and the export of
timber, grain, and cattle had enriched the landlords during the second half of the sixteenth century. The writings

of the time contain many complaints against the extravagant life of the nobles, who had been accustomed to living
modestly or even poorly, but now in addition to their previous sources of income were collecting large sums of
money from their serfs and were thus enabled to live lives
of luxury, spending their money not for the improvement
of farming or for the promotion of culture, but for display, amusements, and liquor. What little was spent for
cultural purposes by the petty aristocracy of Ukraine and
White Russia went toward aping Polish customs and Polish styles, and the nobles sent their children to schools in
Poland, where they became accustomed to foreign ways,
abandoned their faith, and became thoroughly Polonized;
many went abroad to be educated.

Educational Progress: Ukrainian patriots observed
with apprehension this decline in their national life; they
realized that it would mean the loss to the national cause
of its more intellectual and wealthy elements, and saw
with shame that their country had become an object of
contempt and was considered ignorant and backward. As
a result, here and there in Ukraine and White Russia a
few individuals began at the close of the sixteenth century
to devote their efforts to education, literature, and civic
progress, following the old path marked out by the Orthodox Church. This program did not satisfy the people as a
whole, who desired a secular education adapted to the
civil and political needs of the Polish-Lithuanian state;
but patriots considered the Greek Orthodox faith the only
platform upon which the remaining Ukrainian and White
Russian cultural leaders could make a stand, and in their
eyes, all who cut loose from Greek Orthodoxy were lost
to the national life.

Toward the latter half of the sixteenth century there
appeared various signs of a revival of cultural progress,
of which little is known except for a few examples. On the
frontier of Ukraine in Zabludiv, on the estate of a Ukrainian landowner named Gregory Khodkevich, a printing

press was set up in the decade of 1560, and from it there issued the first books printed in the Ukrainian language. The printers were Ivan Fedorovich and Petro Mstislavets, two young refugees from Moscow whose lives had become so endangered by the alarm and anger aroused there by the appearance of a printing press that they had been forced to flee. In 1569 they published a collection of sermons and in 1575 a book of Psalms, but after this Khodkevich lost interest in the project and Fedorovich departed with him and went to live in Lviv. Another exile from Moscow, Prince Kurbsky, who had fled from the Tsar Ivan the Terrible and had settled in Kovel in Volynia in 1560, gathered about him a circle of educated men, translated the writings of the "Greek Fathers," and carried on correspondence with people of distinction in Ukraine and White Russia, to whom he appealed to hold fast to their own religion and not be greedy for Catholic culture. A third cultural group was organized in Slutsk by Prince George Slutsky, a descendant of the Kievan princes of the dynasty of Olelko; at his estate there gathered a number of people interested in literature, and by 1581 a printing press and a school had been established there.

An even more important and permanent center of this new cultural movement appeared at Ostroh in Volynia, on the estate of the princes Ostrozky, who were descendants of an old Kievan family noted for its patriotism. Prince Constantine Ivanovich Ostrozky (d. 1530), an officer in the Lithuanian army, had been considered an outstanding champion of the Ukrainian people and the Greek Orthodox faith, and his son, Vasyl Constantine Ostrozky, governor of Kiev and like his father a wealthy man, continued the tradition by giving generous financial support to the Orthodox Church and to Ukrainian cultural projects.

Information regarding the work at Ostroh is meager. Before this time there had evidently lived in Ostroh a few highly educated Greek Orthodox clergymen who had conducted a primary school and in 1570 had attempted to set up in connection with it an advanced school on the model of a Polish academy, which contemporaries called by various names—a "trilingual lyceum," since courses were taught in Slavonic, Latin, and Greek; a "Greek school"; a "Graeco-Slavonic school"; or an "academy." Because of the small size of the faculty it was impossible to introduce many advanced courses. Qualified teachers could not be found at home or in countries where Greek was spoken, and it was feared that non-Orthodox teachers from Western Europe would bring in Roman Catholic influences. It would have been possible for the school to secure teachers from the ranks of its own graduates by sending them for training to western universities, but apparently the idea of doing this did not occur to anyone. Only occasionally did it attract a Greek with a modern Western European higher education, like, for instance, Lucaris, who was later a patriarch, or Nicephorus; but it was nonetheless an institution of higher learning and a refutation to those who had scorned the Orthodox Church and said that education could not grow under its shadow; its establishment marks the beginning of higher education in Ukraine.

Both in connection with the school and outside its walls there settled at Ostroh a number of educated people who organized a kind of intellectual brotherhood, which numbered among its members Herasim Smotritsky and his son Maxim, whose monastic name was Meletey; Vasyl, the author of the important theological treatise, *The Only True Orthodox Faith;* Filalet-Bronsky; Klirik Ostrozky; and other talented authors. The first important act of this circle of educated men was the printing of the Bible; and the group received new strength when, in 1575, Ivan Fedorovich came to Ostroh from Lviv to operate the printing establishment. The printing of the Bible was an ambitious project, for at that time only separate parts of it existed in Slavonic, and no complete manuscript could be found. Ostrozky sent out agents in all directions to locate Greek texts and Slavonic translations; the translating took several years, the editing and printing several more; but in 1580 there appeared the greatest product of a Slavonic press. In the following two decades the intellectuals of the Ostroh group devoted their writings to the defense of the Greek Orthodox faith, to a struggle against the new Gregorian calendar which the Polish government was attempting to force upon the country, and finally to the question of the Church Union.

Ukrainians highly valued the work of the Ostroh circle and the Ostroh school, and were grieved to learn how uncertain was the existence of the latter. The sons of Prince Constantine Ostrozky were Catholics, with the exception of Alexander, who was of the Orthodox faith, but who died while his father was still alive. The oldest son Yanush, who was to inherit his father's great wealth, became a Roman Catholic, and as a reward received a high position from the Polish government, and there was but little hope that he would continue the educational work of his father. This prediction came true; with the death of Prince Constantine the cultural work at Ostroh suffered a severe setback, as did that at Slutsk, where, after the death of Prince George, his wealth passed into Roman Catholic hands and the educational projects which he had initiated were abandoned. Little hope could be placed in the gentry, for the educational activity had begun too late to take root widely, and it could not be established on a secular basis. The children of the gentry continued to be sent to Catholic schools, and especially to the Jesuit schools which were opened toward the close of the sixteenth century in Vilna, Yaroslav, Lublin, and other cities, in which schools they became ardent Catholics.

"Place no reliance upon the princes," said the townspeople, who now put forth their own efforts and contributed from their own funds in an effort to preserve the national culture. It was the inhabitants of the cities—of

Lviv in Ukraine and of Vilna in White Russia—who led the new movement.

The Brotherhoods: It has been noted that as early as the 1530's and 1540's the Ukrainian and White Russian townspeople, in an effort to gain legal recognition for their organizations, had been making use of the old religious brotherhoods for the purpose. They now reorganized these associations on the model of the craft guilds and thus fitted them to the new municipal organization introduced by the Polish annexation. The apparent purpose of a brotherhood was to assist the church to which it was attached and to care for its poorer members, but in reality the organization fought for Ukrainian national rights, especially in Lviv, where the Ukrainians felt the foreign yoke most heavily.

In the middle of the sixteenth century there began a struggle in Lviv for the revival of the Greek Orthodox diocese to which the Roman Catholic archbishop of Lviv had laid claim; and later, after 1570, the townspeople of Lviv began a new campaign for equality, for toward the close of the sixteenth century they began to feel more keenly than ever the limitations on their national rights, since by then the population had increased and people were also becoming better educated. Through these efforts they won a slight relief from discrimination, but most of the former inequalities remained. The inhabitants of Lviv next began a campaign against the Gregorian calendar, the introduction of which the Orthodox looked upon as an attack upon their Church, and they declared that no one could force it upon them against their will. The question aroused great excitement among the Ukrainians, and violence on the part of the Catholic nobles, clergy, and police; brawls and arrests followed, but the Ukrainians remained firm to the end and won recognition of their religious and cultural autonomy.

When the Ukrainian townspeople realized the need of national and cultural education, the movement was again led by the members of the brotherhood of Lviv, who were among the most ardent advocates of education and literary work, seeking above all to protect their Ukrainian school as the only bulwark against national destruction. It was not enough, they said, to work for the Church alone; without learning, that is, without a school, the Church was helpless.

In the 1570's the printer Ivan Fedorovich, who had left Zabludiv, sought the aid of the Lviv brotherhood, but as the brothers were occupied in building a new brotherhood church in place of one which had burned down and were unable to give him material aid, he was forced by financial need to mortgage his printing press to Jews, and he himself, after printing one book, *The Acts and Epistles of the Apostles (Apostol)* in 1574, went to join Ostrozky. Before long he returned to Lviv and tried once more to establish a Ukrainian printing house there, but died in 1583 without completing his task. Foreigners attempted to buy the press from his heirs, but the people of Lviv were unwilling to let it go, and Gedeon Balaban, the bishop of Lviv, bought it with the aid of the brotherhood, though they had to borrow money from the Jews to pay for it, and in order to pay off the notes and retain this "precious treasure," had to collect contributions from all Ukraine.

Though they had limited financial resources, members of the brotherhood gave thought not only to the printing press but to a beautiful brotherhood building in which they could accommodate their school, their press, and a home for the poor. When the Patriarch Joachim of Antioch came to Lviv at the close of 1585, the brotherhood handed him a petition in which he was asked to make an earnest appeal to the Ukrainians for financial aid in establishing a school for the "education of children of all classes, in order that they may not remain ignorant of letters and learning." The Patriarch granted their request and issued a written appeal for this purpose; at the same

time Bishop Balaban appealed to the whole Greek Orthodox world for aid.

In accordance with these lofty aims, the brotherhood
decided to raise the standard of its organization. The annual banquets were abolished; from now on the brotherhood meetings were to be devoted to religious and secular
education; after regular business was attended to the
members would proceed to the reading and discussion of
good books; the moral life of the members was to be carefully watched over and corrected and unworthy members
expelled. The constitution of the brotherhood was based
on the principles of faith and self-sacrifice.

When this new constitution was presented to the Patriarch Joachim, he was overjoyed by the high motives of
the brotherhood, for he knew only too well the disorder
existing at the time in the Ukrainian Church. He not only
praised its intentions but entrusted to it unusual duties;
it was, for example, to watch over the priesthood and to
report all abuses to the bishop, who, if he should offer opposition and conduct himself contrary to regulation, was
to be treated as an enemy of the faith. Joachim also decided that all other organizations of a similar character
should be placed under the supervision of the main body
in Lviv. These responsibilities conflicted with the regular
discipline of the Church, and had been conferred upon
the brotherhood unnecessarily and carelessly. Sooner or
later they were sure to cause conflicts with the clergy, but
in spite of this danger, they were confirmed by the Patriarch Jeremiah of Constantinople when he visited Ukraine
two years later. The brotherhood of Lviv was thus given
unusual prestige and its activities received the highest
praise, resulting in a burst of enthusiasm among the
townspeople of Ukraine; in large cities and small the inhabitants began to organize new brotherhoods or to reform the old on the model of that in Lviv, the supremacy
of which they recognized, and to establish schools staffed

with teachers from the Lviv school, or to send students there to be educated. Such brotherhoods, it is known, were founded in the large cities of Peremyshl, Rohatyn, Horodok, and Bereste (Brest), and in smaller centers of the type of Holohory and Sataniv. All of these brotherhoods regarded education as their chief aim.

Because of financial limitations the literary and publishing activity of the brotherhood in Lviv did not develop to any great extent; the circle at Ostroh, however, distinguished itself at the beginning of the seventeenth century by its publications and writings, while in the second decade of the century the leadership in these fields passed to the circle at Kiev, which had at its disposal the wealth of the Monastery of the Caves. Although it was not the outstanding institution of its kind in Ukraine, the school at Lviv nonetheless enjoyed a high standing, its teaching staff including not only local savants but also such visiting Greek authors as metropolitan Arseney, Stephen Kukil ("Zizania"), and his brother Lawrence; likewise connected with the school were the noted educator and author Stavrovetsky and the future metropolitan of Kiev, Ivan Boretsky. The success of the school in Lviv, which like that at Ostroh could be regarded as an institution of higher education, made it very popular and led to the organization of smaller local schools to prepare students for it. When the local bishop and townspeople in Peremyshl, for instance, founded a brotherhood there, they had chiefly in mind the opening of a school. "Our vicinity and the district [povit]," they wrote to the Lviv brotherhood, "have fallen to a very low educational level, but the people of good family [the petty Ukrainian gentry] greatly desire a teacher who can give their children letters." They begged for some of the Lviv graduates as teachers, presumably desiring some of those whose homes had originally been at Peremyshl.

Education, both in schools of the lower and of the higher type, was mainly of a religious character, begin-

ning with a study of the Church books and having for its
objective a knowledge of the Scriptures and of other
Christian teachings. Some Ukrainians, however, believed
that these schools were departing from the approved Orthodox tradition because, in addition to strictly religious
instruction, a part of the time was devoted to secular subjects similar to those taught in the Catholic schools, while
others, believing it proper to use in religious instruction
only the formal Old Slavonic Church tongue, criticized
because the teachers, in explaining the Church writings,
made use of the Ukrainian vernacular. Among the defenders of antiquity was the most prominent author and
publicist of the time, the monk Ivan Vishinsky of Galicia,
who carried on a polemic with the brotherhood in Lviv
and in his writings fought against the new ideas, but regardless of his popularity and his silver tongue, educators ignored his criticisms. They all held the conviction
that the only kind of education able to hold its own against
that of the Jesuit schools was a practical one, capable of
being understood by the people and given in the vernacular, and they all believed that such an education alone
could save the Ukrainians from national ruin. This spirit
was clearly expressed in a powerful tract published by the
Lviv brotherhood under the title of *The Warning* (*Perestoroha*).

The Church Union: The success of the brotherhood
movement was hampered by conflict with the priests and
bishops, for the extensive privileges granted to these organizations were, as already pointed out, a dangerous and
unnecessary gift because they led to disagreement with
the clergy. There were unpleasant incidents and as a result several Orthodox bishops sought protection in the
Catholic Church. From the earliest times the bishops in
the Orthodox Church had been privileged to manage the
affairs of their bishoprics as almost complete masters,
only slightly subject to oversight by the metropolitan or
patriarch, but during the last hundred years the authority

of the metropolitan had weakened, the Orthodox princes
had disappeared, there had been few episcopal assemblies, and bishops who purchased their offices from the
king had become accustomed to governing their bishoprics independently and without supervision by any authority but that of the government. Accordingly these
bishops, many of whom came from the gentry class, could
not accept dictation from the townspeople, the "ordinary
peasants, shoemakers, saddlemakers, and furriers," as
they called the members of the brotherhoods, the bishops
considering it an insult for commoners to tell them how
to conduct their offices.

As soon as the Lviv brotherhood attempted to carry out
the wishes of the Patriarch Joachim in reforming the local priesthood, there followed an entirely unnecessary
quarrel with Bishop Balaban. Gedeon Balaban was a
highly educated clergyman, a man of good intentions who
supported the educational policy of the brotherhood but
who could not tolerate taking orders in religious matters
from "ordinary peasants"; he told the brotherhood that
the Patriarch Joachim had nothing to do with the Ukrainian Church and that his decisions regarding it were worthless. The brothers, however, took their case to the Patriarch of Constantinople, who, after being informed by
Joachim of the religious irregularities in Ukraine, approved his orders, rebuked Gedeon for his dispute with
the brotherhood, and threatened him with an anathema if
he continued his opposition. Gedeon disregarded the order, rebuked the members of the Lviv brotherhood, and
continued to oppose their projects. When the Patriarch
Jeremiah himself arrived in Ukraine and looked into the
situation, he gave full support to the brotherhood, which
action of his so incensed Gedeon that he at once appealed
to his former enemy, the Catholic archbishop of Lviv, to
free the Ukrainian bishops from their "enslavement to
the patriarchs"; Gedeon was thus becoming the first of
the Ukrainian bishops to break with them.

This quarrel was largely the outcome of the careless instructions given by the patriarchs, but it was not the only occasion upon which these dignitaries had showed a lack of tact in dealing with the affairs of the Ukrainian Church. Ukraine had been for a long time free from any such interference in its local church affairs, most of the former patriarchs having left the Ukrainian Church completely in the hands of its own church officials, until the patriarchs unexpectedly appeared, one from Antioch in 1585 and another from Constantinople in 1588. As they were on their way to Moscow to obtain relief from financial difficulties, they were only slightly interested in Ukrainian affairs and issued hasty orders without studying the local situation, placing too much importance on petty irregularities with which the Ukrainian Church could have continued for a thousand years with no great injury, and picking out for severe condemnation local church practices which they considered of high importance. In Ukraine, for example, men who had been twice married were regularly ordained into the priesthood and other Church offices, but this local custom was not permitted by the rules of the Greek Orthodox Church, and the patriarchs considered the priests so ordained unlawful and threatened to punish the bishops who retained them. Patriarch Jeremiah, a man of violent temper and little judgment, even deposed the metropolitan, Onisiphor Divochka, because prior to ordination he had been married twice, though he was a capable Church official. In all his dealings with the Ukrainian Church Jeremiah was injudicious and quarrelsome; he regularly threatened the bishops with deposition, and even after his departure continued to meddle in Ukrainian Church affairs by issuing instructions, appointing Byzantine supervisors over Ukrainian bishops, and attempting to collect funds through special Byzantine agents, and in general causing confusion. The bishops, accustomed as they were to an independent Church life, considered these actions by the Byzantine Patriarchs an infringement upon the rights of the Ukrainian Church, and in order to free themselves from Byzantine control, decided to follow the course which the government and the Catholic authorities had long wanted them to take, namely, to break with the Patriarchs and submit themselves to the Pope.

From the beginning of Polish rule in Ukraine, the Polish government had made efforts to unite the Ukrainian and White Russian churches to Rome. King Casimir had believed at first that this could be done simply by appointing Catholic bishops in place of Orthodox bishops, but the Galician nobles resisted; after that Casimir requested of the Greek patriarch the establishment of a separate metropolitan see in Galicia for the Orthodox Church there and left it at that. Beginning with Yagello and Vitovt, the Polish-Lithuanian government made fresh attempts to induce Ukraine to accept Catholicism, attempting to fill the dioceses with docile men of Catholic inclination, requesting them to attend Catholic councils, and urging them to send to the Pope petitions to be accepted under his authority. A few of the bishops attempted to carry out the desires of the Polish-Lithuanian government, but at once became convinced that the clergy and the people would not only refuse to follow but would boycott them. Consequently, when the government insisted that these pro-Polish bishops should bring about the submission of their Church to the Pope, they replied that although they heartily approved of the plan, it would be more appropriate for the matter to be decided by a Church council. No action was taken until the meeting of the Council of Florence in 1439, where it appeared that the Ukrainian Orthodox Church would end its existence as such, since the metropolitan of Kiev, Isidore, gave his approval to the union with Rome, as did nearly all the Byzantine bishops and the emperor of Byzantium, who was eager to obtain papal aid against the Turks. Neither in Byzantium nor in Isidore's eparchies, however, was this act approved. All the efforts of Yagello's son Casimir failed, and although Casimir's successor, Alexander, was enthusiastic for the union with Catholicism, Muscovy, in answer to an appeal by the Ukrainian Church officials and profiting by "the bonds of the Orthodox faith," began to annex the Lithuanian provinces one after another, which action so frightened the Polish-Lithuanian officials that they abandoned the project.

For several years the question was dropped; then in the second part of the sixteenth century the Catholic Church in Poland restored its internal discipline and, noting dissension and weakness in the Orthodox Church, decided to take fresh action. Even among the Orthodox believers there were those who thought that the best way of settling their internal troubles would be to unite with the Catholic Church, since otherwise their Catholic rulers would continue to appoint metropolitans and bishops under whom the Orthodox Church would experience only dissension and difficulty; among those who favored this solution of the problem was Prince Vasyl Constantine Ostrozky, but he and his supporters maintained that it should be carried out with the approval of the patriarchs and of the whole Orthodox world.

The bishops who now decided to submit themselves to Rome believed, however, that the patriarchs would not approve their action and that such a move would mean a break with them, and they also knew that the people would not follow them. They therefore decided to handle the matter secretly in the belief that once they had carried out their plans the Polish government would force the other bishops and the people to follow them. Balaban, angered by the fact that the patriarch had treated him so unreasonably, was the first to take definite action; he communicated with a few other bishops, and by the end of 1590 three of them had joined him in drawing up a secret written agreement. In the course of time they secured the adherence of the other bishops, the metropolitan Rohoza alone being slow to make up his mind, for he had been offended by a false document purporting to be an anathema issued by Jeremiah against him; after long deliberation, however, he too joined with the others. At the close of the year 1594 these bishops wrote a joint declaration to the Pope and to the king, informing them of their decision to submit themselves and the Ukrainian Church to papal authority on condition that the discipline of the Orthodox Church remain unchanged and the Orthodox bishops be given the same rights in all respects as the Catholic bishops. The king was highly pleased and promised them favors, aid, and protection, and at the close of 1595 the bishops Terletsky and Potiy went to Rome, where, on December 23, at a sacred convocation of all the cardinals and the Pope, in the name of all the bishops they pledged their loyalty to the Pope and to the Catholic Church and were formally received into Catholicism.

The Struggle against the Church Union: Though the bishops had carried out their plans secretly, the news of their efforts spread rapidly. Greek Orthodox believers, nevertheless, were not alarmed, for they supposed that the bishops would not put their plan into execution at once, and they expected to have an opportunity to pass on the matter in the national synod. Ostrozky implored the king to permit the Orthodox people to convoke this synod, but was unable to secure his consent. As the acknowledged Orthodox leader, Ostrozky now counseled his supporters in a circular letter not to follow the leadership of the traitors, but to stand by their faith and to oppose the Union with all their strength; this letter, distributed in printed form throughout Ukraine and White Russia, made so deep an impression that when Balaban became aware of the popular antagonism against the bishops he hesitated for a time, then finally abandoned the project and withdrew from the Union, claiming that his name had been signed to the declaration of the bishops without his knowledge; and Bishop Kopistinsky of Peremyshl followed his example. The king was now more determined than ever to support the Uniate bishops, and, to make matters worse, the patriarchate of Constantinople was in such a state of anarchy after the death of Jeremiah in 1594 that the Orthodox Ukrainians could expect no aid from there. They begged the patriarchal vicar, Nicephorus, to come to Ukraine, but while crossing Wallachia he was arrested and imprisoned by order of the Polish government. Many counted for help on the Kozaks who had attacked the adherents of Church Union in Volynia in 1595, and the government itself feared them to such an extent that when, in the spring of 1596, the Orthodox groups decided after long deliberation to take up arms against the Uniate bishops, Zolkiewski himself was sent with the entire Polish-Lithuanian army to keep an eye on the Kozak bands.

The Greek Orthodox finally succeeded in spiriting Nicephorus out of prison; he convoked the synod and with the aid of a few high Church officials from Byzantium led a movement against the Union. On October 6, 1596, the king convoked a general council of the Greek Orthodox Church in Bereste for the purpose of publicly proclaiming the union of the Roman Catholic and Greek Orthodox churches. Adherents of Greek Orthodoxy appeared in large numbers— clergy and laymen, deputies from the brotherhoods, the towns, and the gentry, and a few of those nobles and princes who still clung to the Orthodox cause, headed by Ostrozky himself and his son Alexander, who was military governor of Volynia. The Roman Catholic clergy and the royal delegates as well as the Uniate bishops met in the cathedral, but the Greek Orthodox delegates refused to convene in this church, as it was under the jurisdiction of the Bishop Potiy, who was a Uniate adherent; they held a separate meeting in a private hall. For several days the two assemblies exchanged messages of invitation to each other's meetings, but finally each began to consider its own business separately, the Uniate bishops voting in favor of the Union and anathematizing all the clergy who would not follow them, while the Greek Orthodox delegates under the leadership of Nicephorus anathematized and deposed all those who had accepted the Union and requested the king to depose the bishops who had voluntarily gone over to it.

The king, however, had no intention of approving the pleas of the Greek Orthodox, but, on the contrary, he and the Roman Catholics maintained that the bishops were following the right path, that it was their duty to decide religious problems, and that both the lower clergy and the people should submit to their leadership. A literary polemic on the subject developed, the Orthodox group attempting to prove that the bishops could not decide religious questions without the approval of all the faithful and that such decisions were the function of a synod, by which they meant that the Uniates had acted illegally and had therefore lost all rights to their bishoprics. Many important pamphlets were written, among the more scholarly being the "Apocrisis," by Filalet-Bronsky, a member of the Ostroh circle, while the works of Vishinsky became famous for their eloquence. Although considered old fashioned in his views on education Vishinsky had extraordinary talent as a publicist and was endowed with the zeal of a prophet, so that his words sank deep into the hearts of the people as with mighty blows he attacked the bishops who had "fled into the Union," charging that their immoral lives and their desire for aristocratic luxuries and self-satisfaction had led them to bow to the will of the king, and that in doing so they had betrayed the townspeople, the brotherhoods, and the serfs. In writing of the abuses suffered by the serfs he employed the most eloquent pen of his time, and in spite of the fact that his works were not printed but were circulated in manuscript, his writings must have had far-reaching effects.

While the Orthodox could fight only with words, their enemies had on their side all the agencies of government. The king, the administrative officials, and the Polish no-

bles all maintained that the Orthodox must respect the
authority of their "legal" bishops, that is, those who had
accepted Catholicism, and used the full force of their official positions to compel them to do so, confiscating their
churches, taking Church lands from the Orthodox and assigning them to Uniates, and in other ways making as
many difficulties as possible, a policy which, it is true, had
been followed to some extent even before the Union, but
was now put into full operation. Among the Uniate bishops the most powerful and energetic, as well as the most
ruthless, was Potiy, who did not hesitate to imprison and
otherwise deal out punishment to the disobedient. After
the death of the metropolitan Rohoza, who was not as ardent a Uniate as he, Potiy took over his see in 1590 and
for fifteen years made every effort to exterminate Greek
Orthodoxy, begging for the support of the Polish government and urging the gentry to appoint only Uniate priests
to the livings on their estates, as well as forcibly to drive
the Orthodox clergy into the Union on pain of losing their
churches.

Taking advantage of the difficult position in which the
government found itself, the Orthodox deputies forced it
in 1607 to enact a law providing that in future all bishoprics and other offices in the Orthodox Church should be
given to Orthodox clergy only. Realizing that it was impossible to deprive the Uniate bishops of their bishoprics,
they were content for the time being with this small victory; King Sigismund, however, a devout Catholic, failed
to keep his word; and although he gave his approval to
the law, he continued his old practice of assigning Orthodox bishoprics to Uniate bishops, to whom he gave all
possible support, while subjecting the Orthodox clergy to
their authority.

The Orthodox fought on, refusing to recognize the Uniate bishops as their superiors or to accept the priests appointed by them. In the province of Galicia in western
Ukraine, where Polish oppression was felt most severely,

the Orthodox Church was fortunate in that both of its
bishops, the one in Lviv and the other in Peremyshl, remained true, but in Kholm and in Pobuzha, which were in
the hands of Catholic landowners and Uniate bishops, the
worst conditions prevailed. In Volynia and in Kiev the
local landlords lent aid to the struggle against the Catholic bishops, and when the king decided to dispossess Nicephorus Tur, the Orthodox abbot of the Monastery of the
Caves—the wealthiest monastery of Ukraine and the
strongest bulwark of Ukrainian Orthodoxy—Vasyl Constantine Ostrozky, who was governor of the province of
Kiev, disregarded the king's orders. The king then sent
an official of his court to seize the monastery from the
Orthodox and to give it to the Uniate metropolitan, but
Tur defended the monastery itself by force of arms and
installed armed garrisons of "Nalivaikans," as the Uniates called them, to protect the estates of the monastery
which the king had wished to take from it. In Volynia the
monastery at Zhidichin was defended in the same way.

The Orthodox, however, were apprehensive as they
thought of the future. What would be the outcome if the
king continued to fill all the positions with Uniate clergy?
After the present Orthodox bishops and abbots died, who
would succeed them? Who would dedicate the churches?
Who would defend the faith after the death of the powerful patrons who had remained true to Orthodoxy and the
Ukrainian nation? For a long period of time the king
had been giving all the important offices to Catholics
alone, and in the long run little reliance could be placed
upon parliament, for the gentry were becoming Polonized
and Catholicized, and the number of Orthodox nobles was
decreasing not only in the senate but in the chamber of
deputies as well.

This conversion of Ukrainian nobles and gentry struck
at the root of all the hopes and plans of the Orthodox. In
his *Threnody, or the Plaint of the Eastern Church,* published in 1610, the noted theologian Meletey Smotritsky

painted in strong words the deplorable position in which
the Church had been placed by the loss of the most important Orthodox families. Without the support of the
princes and gentry, the townspeople and their educational
and national organizations felt insecure. At Bereste the
brotherhood was completely destroyed by the king with
the aid of the local bishop, Potiy, and in Vilna, the chief
center of White Russian cultural and religious life, the
churches were taken by force from the Orthodox, soldiers
breaking in the doors, taking possession of the buildings,
and turning them over to the Uniates. The king happened
to be in Vilna at this time, and the Orthodox people—men,
women, and children—surrounded him on the street, knelt
on the cobbles, and implored him not to destroy their faith
by force and not to deprive them of their churches, but
their pleas were in vain.

Despair filled the hearts of the Orthodox people, whose
only ray of hope was that the Kozaks might some day
come to their aid. These warriors were recovering from
their defeat at Lubny and by the beginning of the seventeenth century were beginning to exhibit new life. After
the annihilation of the Orthodox organization at Vilna,
Potiy attempted to destroy in like manner the metropolitan see at Kiev, and sent a vicar there in 1610 for that
purpose, but the Kozak hetman Tiskinevich warned him
against any attempt to enslave the clergy or to subject
them to his authority since he, the hetman, had already
given orders to the Kozaks that if any such attempt were
made they were to kill the vicar "like a dog"; the warning had an immediate effect on Potiy's agent, who refrained from interfering in the local affairs. In 1612 the
Greek archimandrite Neophite came to Kiev under the
protection of the Kozaks and performed the duties of a
bishop, dedicating churches and ordaining priests, but
neither the metropolitan nor the government dared to intervene, as they did not wish to be shorn by the Kozaks.

The Ukrainian civil population now felt that with Kozak support they were treading on firm ground, and that here, far out on the frontier of Ukraine, under the protection of the Kozak banner, they would be able to carry on their national life without interference.

CHAPTER XII

THE KOZAKS AND THE REVIVAL
OF KIEV

The Kozak Host after the Battle of Lubny: Sorrow pervaded Ukraine when news was received of the disastrous
defeat of the Kozaks at Lubny in 1596. Though Zolkiewski
had not succeeded in carrying out his intention of completely destroying the Kozak Host, he had inflicted upon
it a great loss; driven from their settlements on the upper
Dnieper the Kozaks were forced to move below the falls,
where they were deprived of supplies, while laws passed
by the parliament abolished all the rights of the Kozak
army and even the organization itself. Worst of all, as a
result of the defeat an internal conflict broke out within
the Kozak Host, which split into two groups, the bolder
element entering into a struggle with the more conservative faction, which favored conciliation with the government in order to regain the lost Kozak rights. This quarrel was a continuation of the old dissension between the
Zaporozhian Kozaks and the followers of Nalivaiko, but it
now assumed a more serious aspect, leading to strife and
bloodshed, with one party even seeking from the Polish
government aid against the other. The Poles were delighted and hoped that after the Kozak factions had decimated each other, the remnant would be more submissive.
The state of anarchy among the Kozaks did not, however,
last any great length of time, for in 1599 the famous hetman Sameilo Kishka succeeded in restoring unity by undertaking several expeditions into the Black Sea region
and against Moldavia, which expeditions revived the old
Kozak spirit to such an extent that the Polish government
itself turned to the Kozaks for support.

Following the defeat at Lubny the succeeding hetmans

—Vasilevich, Nechkovsky, and Baibuza—sought for the Kozaks the favor of the government by keeping it informed as to the activities of the Tatars, but as Poland was not at the time engaged in a war, more important aid from the Kozaks was not required. In the spring of 1600, however, Hospodar Michael of Wallachia attacked Hospodar Mohila of Moldavia, who was friendly to Poland, with the intention of seizing his province, whereupon the Polish government took steps to defend Mohila and asked for support from the Kozaks. Kishka is remembered in popular tradition as the hero of an insurrection of Kozaks in a Turkish prison, which resulted in their liberation, but he deserves greater renown as an astute Ukrainian statesman who knew how to take advantage of events to regain for the Kozaks the rights which they had possessed prior to their disastrous war with Poland. When the Polish general Zamoiski appealed to the Kozaks to go to the aid of Moldavia, Kishka paid no attention to him but waited for a request by the king himself, since it was he who had attempted to destroy them and had proclaimed them traitors. The king was now forced to address an appeal to the "traitors," and although Kishka replied as hetman that he would gladly be of assistance, he showed no haste in taking action. In Polish circles there was much anxious search for someone influential enough to induce the Kozaks to furnish military aid, until finally the hetman informed the king that the Kozaks would fight on condition that they be exonerated of all blame for past acts, that all their former rights be restored, and that the government protect them in future against oppression by the governors and other officials in Ukraine. At the same time he declared that the Kozaks would take to the field at once without waiting for the fulfillment of these conditions because they trusted the king to carry out the terms. The campaign in Moldavia proceeded without serious difficulties, but before it came to an end a new and more serious war between Poland and Sweden broke out in Livonia. Again the Polish government sought the aid of the Kozaks and again Kishka presented the grievances of the Host, this time with complete success, for the parliament passed a law repealing the dissolution of the Kozak Host, canceling the punitive measures taken against them, and with a few exceptions restoring to them all their former rights.

As this was an important beginning, Kishka used all his prestige and authority to induce the Kozaks to take part in this unpopular and distant war and to persuade them to keep on until it was over. The Kozaks suffered great hardships in their campaign in the devastated Baltic province, losing men, horses, and supplies, Kishka himself being killed at the siege of Fellin. After his death the Kozaks changed hetmans several times in quick succession, as their officials were unable to keep them contented in the difficult circumstances under which they were fighting, but the regiments fought on patiently until the end of the war in order to remain "in the royal service," and thus to acquire more rights for themselves and for Ukraine. Upon its return to Ukraine in 1603 after the close of the war, the Kozak army demanded equal treatment with that of the Poles and a guarantee that no Polish troops be garrisoned in Ukraine; as a reward for its services it further demanded full self-government, all the privileges and rights enjoyed by the gentry, and the same mastery of the Dnieper region as it had enjoyed before 1596.

The documents of the time contain many complaints by the gentry that the Kozaks were gaining the upper hand, and that no one was able to control them.

The gentry appealed to the government to subdue the Kozaks, but this the government was not free to do. At this time many nobles of Ukraine and Poland were carrying on negotiations with the so-called Tsarevich Dmitri, who was in Ukraine, and who was claiming as the son of the deceased Tsar Ivan the right to seize for himself the tsardom of Muscovy; the nobles and the king himself were on the lookout for any advantages they might gain from disturbances in Muscovy in this connection. They did not, however, intend to involve Poland openly in this affair, and made it appear that individual nobles of their own accord were assisting Dmitri and that it was they who were seeking aid of the Kozaks. From 1604 on, time and again various nobles incited the Kozaks to undertake campaigns into Muscovy by describing the rich plunder to be had; time and again bands of thousands of Kozaks raided Muscovy and returned laden with spoils. Muscovy was experiencing its "Time of Troubles," which began in 1604 and lasted nearly ten years, devastating the country and making of the once powerful tsardom the prey of various bands of soldiers and Kozaks. One after another various claimants to the Muscovite crown appeared, marched back and forth across the country, and with the aid of Polish or Lithuanian soldiers and Ukrainian and Don Kozaks collected money and captured cities. The cities of Muscovy went up in flames, the snows of Muscovy were reddened with bloody tracks, and the raiders carried back to Ukraine, to Lithuania, and to Poland barrels of money and cartloads of rich clothes—brocaded caftans and sable mantles.

At last the king of Poland, unable to stand by and see the complete destruction of Muscovy, decided to lead a campaign to Moscow in an attempt to make himself tsar. The Polish parliament, however, refused to give him financial support, and again, in 1609, royal courtiers went to the Kozaks to ask them to take part in the expedition. Volunteers appeared, not in hundreds or in thousands, but in tens of thousands. As before, those who entered the Kozak ranks believed that by thus fulfilling their service to the king they had made themselves free men, and that they, their families, and their property were thereafter subject to no one, and they recognized the authority neither of the nobles nor of anyone else than the Kozak officers. With every new appeal for volunteers for the royal service, vast numbers responded by joining the Kozaks.

Not content with their campaigns against Muscovy, the Kozak Host attacked the territories of the Turks, the Tatars, and the Wallachians, and even took to the sea. Information about these campaigns is rare and accidental. We hear, for instance, of a famous Kozak expedition in 1606 against the Turks, in the course of which they captured the city of Varna and took booty valued at 180,000 gold pieces. In the autumn of 1608 the Kozaks captured the Tatar city of Perekop, plundered it, and set it afire, and in the next year sailed to the mouth of the Danube in sixteen boats, sacking and burning the cities of Izmail, Kilia, and Bilhorod, but were forced to depart without booty when the Turks attacked them and put them to flight. The Kozaks displayed great energy, which was annoying to the neighboring lands but developed an independent spirit in Ukraine and broke the chains of bondage.

During the period when the Polish government was attempting to secure the largest possible number of Kozak soldiers from Ukraine, the number of "disobedient" townspeople and farmers increased beyond all previous records, and in consequence a vast portion of the country became semimilitarized, while the people, by joining the Kozak organization, freed themselves from the yoke of the landlords.

The Kozak Organization: By this time the social and political system of the Kozaks was becoming well established. There was nothing complex about it; it was simple and free, but capable of such great strength that it could command the allegiance of the Kozak brotherhood, body and soul. In the Kozak Host the Ukrainian people displayed great aptitude for organization and an ability to carry out extraordinary projects with simple and limited means.

The center of gravity of the Kozak organization remained in the lower Dnieper region beyond the reach of the Polish lords and their armies, where the organization could develop in freedom; its heart was the Zaporozhian Sich, or headquarters, which was transferred from one island in the Dnieper River to another. This camp had at its disposal all the Kozak forces scattered along the lower Dnieper and farther up in the older settlements; there were as yet no castles or regular fortifications in the Sich, but the records mention trenches and ambuscades. The small but mobile cannon and other materials for war were kept hidden in secret caches, there was a military band, for trumpeters and drummers are mentioned, and there were also carefully guarded army flags, a war treasury, herds of horses, and many boats and galleys captured from the Turks.

In the 1590's the combined forces of the Kozaks was reputed to be twenty thousand men. The defeat of 1596 at the hand of Poland reduced its numbers, but within a few years the membership reached its old level and continued to grow. The majority of the Kozaks lived and farmed in the Townships (*volost*), as the more settled country above the falls was known, but in the spring and summer several thousands migrated down river to prepare for their campaigns or to engage in various occupations—fishing, hunting, salt extraction, or trading with the Turks and Tatars in settlements along the frontier. In winter they returned to the Townships, leaving several hundred Kozaks at the Sich to guard the munitions and other war supplies. It was no easy matter to spend the winter in a Kozak hut, poorly constructed out of willow withes or logs, and those who wintered there for several seasons were regarded as experienced and hardy members of the brotherhood.

The Kozak army was divided into regiments. The official record indicates that the Polish government had in its service at the beginning of the seventeenth century four regiments of five hundred men each, but in reality there were more regiments at the time and more men in each regiment. Sometimes the Kozak regiments contained several thousand men, and in the Khotyn war, for example, the Kozak army had eleven regiments, some of which numbered four thousand men each. At the head of the regiment (*polk*) was a colonel (*polkovnik*). Each regiment had its own banner, trumpeter, and drummer, and was divided into companies (*sotni*, "hundreds"), which in turn were subdivided into squads (*desiatki*, "tens"; or *kurini*, "tents"). The chief officer of the squad was the *ataman*, while the captain (*sotnik*) was in charge of the company. Orders issued by the hetman were carried out by the adjutant (*osaul*). The chief ordnance officer (*obozny*) watched over the cannon, which were officially stored at Terekhtemiriv, a town given to the Kozaks by Stephen Batory to be used as a hospice for pilgrims and for miscellaneous military purposes; as Terekhtemiriv, however, was within reach of the Polish government, the cannon were as a rule stationed in some other location more convenient for the Kozaks. All the military correspondence was in the hands of a secretary (*pysar*), letters written in the name of the army being confirmed by stamping with the army seal. In its communications the army usually called itself the "Zaporozhian Host," but also made frequent use of the name of "Zaporozhian Order of Knights," and in negotiations with the German emperor the Kozak delegates were authorized to use for their army the official title of "Free Host of the Zaporozhe." Members of the organization addressed each other as comrade (*tovarish*); the army as a whole was called a fellowship (*tovaristvo*).

At the head of the Kozak army was an elected officer commonly known as the "hetman," and the holders of this office frequently used this title in their official communications, though the government called them "elders," "officers," or "officers of the Zaporozhian army." Khmelnitsky was the first to receive the official title of hetman, which had previously been applied only to the highest rank of Polish and Lithuanian military officers.

The Kozaks placed a high valuation upon their right to elect their chief officer, this privilege being considered the keystone of Kozak autonomy; and although it is true that after the first reorganization in 1570 the Polish government appointed various officials to supervise the Kozaks, the Kozaks themselves considered such Polish appointees merely commissioners sent to keep in touch with them, and refused to permit them to participate in any of the decisions of the army. There was an exception to this rule immediately after the loss of the battle of Lubny, when internal dissension prevailed and the Kozaks requested the government to appoint an "elder" for them; but when, between 1617 and 1619, the government gave indications of intending to appoint their chief officer, the Kozaks protested vigorously. Except for permitting the government to accord recognition to the hetman whom they had elected, the Kozaks excluded the government from any hand in their affairs, and even considered their own elections and depositions as final, paying little attention to whether the Polish government recognized their hetmans or not, though the government was eager to have some authority in this connection.

Important problems were acted upon at a meeting of all the higher officers (*starshina*) or at an assembly (*rada*) of the whole army. The character of this joint government by hetman, officers, and army is made clear from the terms used in the military dispatches, where authority issues not only from the hetman, but also from the officers and the army, as, for example, in a letter from the hetman Kishka to the king in 1600, signed "Sameilo Kishka, hetman; the colonels; the captains; and your royal grace's entire knightly order, the Zaporozhian Host."

In practice the relation of the hetman to the army was not always the same, but depended upon circumstances, and especially upon the personality, the ability, and the influence of the hetman—the more competent he was, the less important being the assembly, but whenever the army began to hold meetings to debate every petty detail, especially in time of war, it was clear evidence that he no longer had its full confidence. A hetman who knew his own strength and had confidence in himself brought before the assembly only such problems as he himself wished to present, and outside the assembly ruled like an autocrat, with power of life and death over each soldier and with the army in absolute obedience to his commands. The combination of such extensive Kozak self-government with such unusual discipline was a feature which foreigners had difficulty in understanding; on the one hand there was the stern hetman, able to dispatch the army by a word to any destination, even to its doom, while on the other hand there was the assembly, which could deal without ceremony with the officers and with the hetman himself, and before which these officers humbled themselves. The meetings were conducted informally and were noisy and disorderly, the soldiers shouting, quarreling, throwing their caps on the ground, and offering at the first impulse to depose the hetman, who groveled before them.

This procedure, however, was a holdover from early times, and the Kozak organization as it grew in size gradually became firmer and better disciplined; the authority of the hetman became more highly respected, and was accompanied by formal evidences of esteem, while depositions of the hetman by the general assembly grew less frequent; and beneath the forms of extreme simplicity and democracy, as evidenced by the presentation to the hetman at his inauguration of an ordinary reed instead of a mace, there developed a knightly spirit of devotion which aroused the wonder and admiration of foreigners. "There is nothing common about the Kozaks except their uniforms," said the Frenchman Beauplan, who was in the service of Koniecpolski, an archenemy of the Kozaks, and added, "they are energetic and sagacious, not greedy for wealth but valuing freedom immeasurably; they are powerful of frame and easily endure heat and cold, hunger and thirst. In war they are noted for their endurance and courage, but are lighthearted, for they do not value their lives; they are of handsome appearance, alert and strong, and nature has endowed them with good health, for they are seldom subject to any diseases, rarely dying of sickness unless in very old age, and in the majority of cases they end their lives on an altar of fame—killed in war.''

The Sea Raids: The attacks on Muscovy, the rich booty gained there, the mobilization of the Kozaks by high-born freebooters for expeditions against that country, and, finally, the encouragement of the government, developed the military strength of the organization to an unprecedented degree. According to a statement of Zolkiewski, thirty thousand Kozaks came to the aid of the king in 1609 when he was besieging Smolensk, and later even more arrived; while another eyewitness estimated the number of Kozaks who wandered about in Muscovy that winter at more than forty thousand, with their number continually increasing, and leaving the country below the Dnieper rapids almost deserted, though they rendered useful service to the king. Not all of them, of course, took part in the invasion, but the forty thousand or more mentioned give an idea of their great number and strength in Ukraine at this period.

By the end of 1612 the troubles in Muscovy were coming to a close, and in 1613 the Muscovites began to drive out the Kozaks and other freebooters; the soldier-adventurers, accustomed to warfare and plundering, now sought a new field of operations in the Turkish possessions in Wallachia and along the coast of the Black Sea. Kozak expeditions to sea had been carried on even before this time, but they were now vastly increased, the years 1613–20 marking the heroic era, when the Kozaks in their primitive boats known as chaika* cruised all about the

---

* The word is said to be derived from the Turkish word, *chay* (river): hence, a river boat. *Chaika*, in Ukrainian means ''pewit.''

HAUTE VOLHYNIE, ou PALATINAT DE LUSUC;
tire de la Grande Carte d'Ukraine;
du Sr. le Vasseur de Beauplan
Par le Sr. SANSON d'Abbeville Geogr. ord.ie du Roy
A PARIS
Chez Pierre Mariette, Rue St. Jacques, a l'Esperance
Avecq Privilege pour Vingt Ans.
1665.

HAUTE VOLHYN

RUSSIE

PALA TIN

NOIRE.

LU

PO

HAUTE PO

Eschelle

Mille Pas Geometriques

Lieües communes de France

Lieües d'Allemagne et de Pologne

OCCIDENT

SEP

PO

Lohiseyn

Iastolda R.

Pinch
Pina

Ster R.

Pohost
Pohost

Dobrinia
olim
Ducatus

Ratno
Serredrohosee
Libiaz

Peresopie sr.

Rntemspra

Czatorisho olim
Ducatus

Horin R.

Stepan

Melce

Kamen

Wolodimirow Kolades

Nisechwies
Nissacheissa

Kowel Duc.

HAUTE
VOLHYN

Borowis
Kolki

Silno
Derazina

Czetwiza
Mon.
Tresseniec

Olyka

Sakalma

Klewan

Horin

Alexandra

Kora
Tuczyn

Krupa

Biclow

Zuchow
Rowna

Teskowa

Dorohobuss
Dorohobuch

Macielow
Freiwalt

Lubomle

Kossor

Tureszk

Mikolauow

Kirielin

Lokacz

Torczin

Lucko P.
Lusuc G.
Luceonia L.

Markofsinska

Perzemil

Dorosłay

Zornawno

Wignanca

Przemil

Targunowica

Morawiku

Wachowiecz

Mrdgrzeec
Ostrog Duc

Scurowice

Lesnioui

Dubno

Rochmonow

Suraß

Besing

Stanislawow
olim
Nowiez.

Kozin

Ihua R.

Szumsl
Bialagrodka

Podhorce ali
Tarnopie

Prenten
Orlace
Urla
Radziwilow

Kremieniec

Iampol
Horin R.

Ulowece
Ulaneca

Torgas
Peicza

Lachow

Seyten
Horzuko

Ozohowka

Tiporow

Broodi

Podhorcainci

Wesmiunoca

Olesko
Wiegrodeck

Olezniec

Czarna R.
Seluch

LU

Matopole
Horolieze
Zaloscie

Osdzicowica

Basilia

Krasilou

NOIRE.

Zbaras
Dui

Sopronowka
Wolodeissa

Trohuisie

Czarne Ostrow

Bor

Klebanowhas
Czernowiha

Romanuwha

Romanui Starcy

Foduski

Zalotnoe
Feletyn

Klinkosce

Plodyrof

Bawarow

Franuczolu

Tutonow
Shalat

Octopie

Romanoce

Iankasie

Kapustince
Porchanka
Michaka

Terinpol
Mikul
nice

Josfcow

Grzymolw

Krasyne

Loubia
Otahopsec

Ostahopsse

Leuczkoce

HAUTE
PO

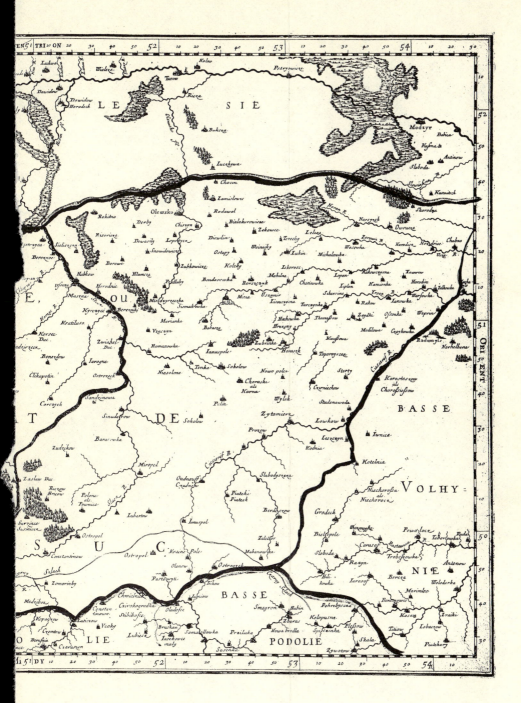

Black Sea, inflicting upon the Turkish empire at a time when all Europe was trembling in fear of it such damage that the sultans, even in their palaces at Constantinople, did not feel safe from attack.

The Ukrainian Kozaks gained world fame by their great courage and military skill, a contemporary Turkish historian thus describing their campaigns: "One can safely say that in the entire world one cannot find a more daring people, more careless for their lives or having less fear of death; persons versed in navigation assert that because of their skill and boldness in naval battles these bands are more dangerous than any other enemy." The French minister at Constantinople, who himself witnessed the Kozak expeditions, spared no words of praise for the bravery of the Kozaks, and advised his government to have no hesitation in spending fifty thousand thalers on the Ukrainian forces in order to keep the Turkish fleet occupied and to prevent it from entering the Mediterranean Sea, where the Turks were at this time fighting against Spain, the ally of France.

An especially impressive feature of this Kozak naval warfare was that with their insignificant forces they even attacked the mighty Turkish fleet. In another account of the Kozak naval expeditions Beauplan describes them as follows:

First of all, they send to the Zaporozhe—the region below the Dnieper rapids—all the supplies necessary for the campaign and for the building of boats; then they themselves go there to build them, about sixty men working on one boat and completing it within two weeks, for every Kozak is a jack-of-all-trades. For the frame they use a small boat about forty-five feet long, ten to twelve feet wide, and of the same depth. All around the boat they bind firmly sheaves of reed; they fasten a rudder at the front and another at the rear, and fasten masts for the sails to each side, where they also make provision for ten to twelve oars. There is no deck, but though the waves fill it with water, the reeds around it prevent it from sinking. Five to six thousand Kozaks working from two to three weeks complete eighty to one hundred such boats, each of which accommodates fifty to seventy men. At the sides of each boat they have four to six small cannon, and they carry hardtack, millet, and other victuals in barrels. Each boat is equipped with a compass.

Thus organized and equipped they sail down the Dnieper, led by the hetman with a flag at his masthead, the boats so close together that they almost touch one another. As a rule, the Turks keep their galleys at the mouth of the Dnieper, in order to prevent the entrance of the Kozaks into the Black Sea, but the Kozaks select a dark night before the new moon and steal their way out. When they are discovered on the open sea, all the neighboring countries, including Constantinople, become terror-stricken; the sultan sends couriers all along the sea coast to give warning of the approaching danger, but this is of little use because within thirty-six to forty hours the Kozaks are in Anatolia. Upon their arrival, they leave but two of their number to guard each boat while all the rest with muskets in hand attack the cities, conquer and plunder them, and set them afire. Occasionally they go for plunder a league from the coast, collect booty, and return home.

If by chance they meet Turkish galleys or other ships, they act as follows: As the boats of the Kozaks are only two and a half feet above the water, they see the higher galleys before they themselves are seen; therefore, they lower their sails and approach from the west, headed north, and keeping their eyes all the time on the clearly visible ships of the enemy. At midnight they row with all their might toward these ships, while half of the crew prepares for battle. Then the enemy suddenly discovers that eighty to a hundred boats have surrounded his ships, which are overpowered and captured. From the captured ships they take money, military supplies, cloth, and anything else that does not spoil at sea, after which they sink the ships with the people still aboard.

Whenever the Turkish galleys meet the Kozaks at sea in daytime, the latter have a more difficult time. The Turks open a terrific fire from their cannon and scatter the Kozak galleys like chaff, sinking some and putting the others to flight; but they gather and return to the battle in formation, some Kozaks firing while others load the guns after each shot. The Kozaks are good marksmen, but the Turkish cannon create much havoc among them, and in such battles two thirds of the Kozaks usually perish, while seldom do half of them return home. Those who do, bring with them rich booty, such as Spanish and Arabian money, rugs, bars of gold, and silk cloths of various kinds.

In the popular songs of the Ukrainians there have also been handed down accounts of the Kozak expeditions, often portraying the Ukrainian Kozaks as prisoners at work on the Turkish galleys, where they were chained to the benches as slaves. Several early poets whose names are not known have left vivid and forceful descriptions of the terrible storms on the Black Sea which caused the destruction of many Kozak boats.

The years after the close of the Kozak campaigns into Muscovy were especially marked by frequent sea raids, the Kozak Host going out several times a year, carrying their raids to greater distances than they had ever ventured before and boldly attacking the Turkish fleet itself. According to a report by Zolkiewski, the Kozaks undertook two expeditions in 1613, in the course of which they inflicted great damage upon Turkey. The sultan sent a large fleet of galleys to the port of Ochakiv to intercept them on their way back from plundering cities in Crimea, but instead of being annihilated by the Turks, the Kozaks attacked the negligent Turks at night and slaughtered them. In the spring of 1614, the Kozaks again sought adventure on the sea, this time meeting with disaster because of a storm, but they were apparently not discouraged, for in the summer they went on another raid, with about forty boats and two thousand men, crossing the Black Sea directly toward Trebizond and attacking the city. This portion of the coast was studded with rich cities and villages, the inhabitants of which had long lived in safety, knowing no fear of foreign attacks; "because ever since the Turks had captured Asia Minor, they had suffered no affliction," writes Zolkiewski. Turkish exiles and captives served as guides to the Kozaks, who went inland, attacked the luxurious city of Sinope—the "city of lovers"—captured the citadel, killed the guards, and set afire the large Turkish naval base, in which were ships, galleys, and galleons. Before the inhabitants could organize a defense, the Kozaks departed and returned home laden with rich booty. When the sultan learned of this incident, he became exceedingly angry and ordered the grand vizir to be executed, but finally spared his life because of the pleas of his own daughter and wives. Once more the Turkish ships sailed to waylay the Kozaks at the port of Ochakiv, but the raiders learned of the approaching danger in time and divided their forces into two parts. One half landed on the coast east of the port of Ochakiv, with the intention of moving their galleys on rollers overland to the Dnieper above the city, but being attacked by the Tatars, these Kozaks sustained heavy losses both in men and in booty before reaching home. The other party fought its way through the Turkish fleet at Ochakiv, likewise losing much of its booty, which they were forced to empty into the bay in order to lighten their boats, but this band also returned home. The Turks captured only twenty Kozaks, whom they sent to Constantinople for punishment; when the citizens of Trebizond came to the sultan with their complaints against the Kozaks, he surrendered to them these twenty young captives so that they could avenge themselves.

In 1615, the Kozaks went out with a much larger expedition than they had taken the previous year, this time going in eighty boats to attack the city of Constantinople itself, "to smudge the wall of Tsarhorod with the smoke from our muskets," as they said. They disembarked between the two ports of Constantinople—Mizevna and Archioca—which they destroyed by fire; when the sultan, who was hunting near the city, saw the smoke caused in his capital by the Kozaks' fire, he furiously ordered the Turkish ships to drive away the invaders at once. The Kozaks were not alarmed, but plundered as much as they cared to before taking their spoils and going home. The Turkish galleys overtook them at the mouth of the Danube, but the Kozaks boldly attacked and defeated them, the Turkish admiral being wounded and taken prisoner; he offered a ransom of thirty thousand gold pieces, but died in captivity. The other Turkish galleys fled. The Kozaks brought to the port of Ochakiv a few of the galleys which they had captured and here in derision set them afire in the presence of the Turks of the city; then after attacking Ochakiv they departed home overland, driving cattle before them.

After this disastrous experience, the Turks decided not to permit the Kozaks to enter the Black Sea in future and stationed their ships near the mouth of the Dnieper to stop them there; but the undaunted Kozaks emerged, engaged the Turkish fleet in battle and defeated it, capturing many galleys and about a hundred small boats. Having thus dispersed the Turkish fleet, they attacked the coast of Crimea and pillaged it, capturing and burning the city of Kaffa, the chief market for Ukrainian slaves, and freeing large numbers of Ukrainians who had been held there in slavery; when news of this second disaster to the Turkish fleet reached Constantinople, the inhabitants became terror-stricken and gathered together their Kozak prisoners to ask them by what means the Kozaks could be prevented from making further raids. The reply is not known, but the Turks decided there was nothing left but to send an expedition to capture the forts on the Ukrainian frontier, such as Kaminets, Cherkassy, Kaniv, and Bila Tserkva, and to station in them Turkish garrisons to hold the Kozaks inland.

Meanwhile, in the autumn of the same year, 1616, the Kozaks set out on another expedition by sea, and although only about two thousand men took part, they were unusually successful. Again they attacked the coast of Anatolia, aiming at Samsun, but as the wind carried their boats near the city of Trebizond, they disembarked there, marched along the coast to the city, captured and sacked it, and set it afire. When they were attacked by a Turkish squadron commanded by the Genoese admiral, Cicali, and consisting of six large galleys and many smaller boats, they defeated it, and then, learning that the sultan had sent a fleet in the direction of Ochakiv to intercept them on their return, they sailed off to plunder the defenseless suburbs of Constantinople. After enjoying themselves to the full and making merry over the useless Turkish efforts at defense, they next sailed where they were least expected, into the Sea of Azov, from which they reached the Dnieper by local rivers and portages and so returned to the Zaporozhe, while the Turkish pasha awaited them in vain at Ochakiv. In order to have something to show the sultan, the pasha waited until the Kozaks had left the Sich, and then ascended the Dnieper by boat as far as the rapids, whereupon the few hundred Kozaks who had remained there for the winter retreated, leaving to the Turkish army only their empty huts. The Turks carried off several small cannon and a few Kozak boats, and with this "loot" returned in triumph to Constantinople, leading the sultan to believe that the terrible Kozak Sich was at last destroyed.

Polish Negotiations with the Kozaks; Hetman Sahaidachny: Though the Kozaks made sport of the Turks and gained worldwide renown for themselves by their expeditions, these raids caused the Polish government much difficulty, for after each Kozak attack upon the Turkish cities the sultan issued orders to his pashas to invade Ukraine for the purpose of destroying the Kozak forts along the frontier, to construct Turkish fortresses in their places, to station garrisons all along the Ukrainian border, and to keep the Kozaks in subjection. Hardly a year passed in which the Turkish government did not send forces to the Ukrainian border, or in which the rumor did not at least spread that they were preparing to. The wars with Muscovy had been so costly for the Polish government that it could not afford to pay an army, and had now been practically without one for several years; the entire force under Zolkiewski numbered only from three hundred to five hundred men, as no one wished to serve without pay. Accordingly, rumors of Turkish preparations for war spread terror among the Poles, who attempted to free themselves of blame by declaring that the Kozaks were making their expeditions contrary to the wishes of the government, that the latter had attempted to disperse them, but that new forces had entered the steppes from Muscovy. As a matter of fact, it was unjust to accuse the Kozaks of causing all the trouble for the Turks, for the Polish and Ukrainian nobles had also interfered in the affairs of the Moldavian subjects of the Turks and had entered Moldavia with their troops; it was these raids as much as the Kozak expeditions that had caused Turkish animosity against Poland.

Several Polish attempts were made to reduce the power of the Kozaks. In 1614 Zolkiewski threatened them with war if they refused to submit to authority and made preparations for a campaign against them, but they coolly began to mobilize at Pereyaslav; and since Zolkiewski had no army with which to carry out his threats, they remained empty phrases. The Polish government then sought the assistance of the nobles by sending a group of commissioners to request for Zolkiewski the armed support of the more influential Ukrainian landowners in settling disputes with the Kozaks, after which, from 1614 on, almost every year a nondescript army consisting chiefly of the retainers of the landowners was dispatched to maintain order among the Kozaks, but without result. The Kozaks invariably demanded of the royal commissioners a written statement of the intended changes in their internal government, but when one was produced they disapproved of most of the terms because these would have limited their privileges; they found unacceptable, for instance, demands that they guard the border, leave foreign countries at peace, remain on the lower Dnieper, or—if they did go up the river to the populated Townships—recognize the authority of the landowners there. Then the Kozaks would threaten to send delegates to the king to beg him not to require them to do the impossible in giving up their rights, and there the negotiations usually ended, the king's commissioners departing with their soldiers after ordering the Kozaks to keep the peace and to refrain from attacking foreign countries, and the Kozaks making such promises but continuing to do as they pleased.

It was the policy of the Kozak hetman Peter Sahaidachny to avoid war with Poland, to make promises of good behavior, and to await the time when Poland should need the assistance of the Kozaks in war; meanwhile he attempted to develop the strength of the Kozaks throughout Ukraine. Sahaidachny is first heard of in connection with the sea expedition of 1616, in the course of which he captured the city of Kaffa and freed the Christian slaves there; he must, however, have been made hetman much earlier, for in 1614 there was already visible the pattern in Kozak policy for which Sahaidachny became famous, and it is possible that he had served as hetman at intervals, since Ukrainian information regarding the Kozak hetmans during this period is incomplete. Popular tradition has retained but little about him, though there is a song to the effect that ''he traded his wife for a pipe and tobacco,'' a description that no more does justice to Sahaidachny than another song representing Baida Vishnevetsky as a Zaporozhian strolling dancer does credit to that Ukrainian hero. His contemporaries, on the contrary, considered Sahaidachny a wise and able statesman, capable of placing the Kozak Host at the service of the national cause. The policies which had only germinated in the time of Loboda and Nalivaiko were brought to fruition by Sahaidachny, and it may thus be said that he initiated a new era in Ukrainian history.

Born in the vicinity of Sambir in western Galicia, apparently of a family of local gentry, Sahaidachny was one of those Ukrainians who because of Polish oppression had migrated east to the Dnieper region in the heart of Ukraine, where he became a champion of the national cause. Educated in the school at Ostroh, he later entered the Kozak army, and, according to tradition, participated with it in both the Moldavian and the Livonian wars of 1600–1601, which facts make it probable that he had entered the army as early as the 1590's. Although in his later years, from 1616 to 1622, he was in the forefront of Ukrainian national life, little is known about this early period, except that he had become well known as a skilful and successful Kozak warrior whom Jan Sobieski, his companion on several expeditions, described as always favored by fortune. Several times he seriously defeated the Tatars in the steppes and spread alarm into Crimea; and his prestige was further enhanced by his sea expeditions, in which he was invariably successful and in the course of which he destroyed many of the largest Turkish cities in Europe and Asia and set fire to the suburbs of Constantinople. He was described as a man of high spirits, seeking adventure and fearless for his life, always the first to attack and the last to retreat, alert and energetic, on guard even in camp, where unlike the other Kozaks he slept little and did not carouse, self-controlled at general assemblies, a man of few words, and in cases of disobedience a strict disciplinarian who did not hesitate to impose sentences of death upon the guilty.

Sahaidachny gained the respect and favor of the Polish government during the war with Muscovy in 1617. The aid of the Kozaks was indispensable to the king, while the Kozaks also found it a favorable opportunity to act, and willingly responded to the call of the government. The royal commissioners had been putting increased pressure upon the Kozaks to force them to cease their attacks upon the Turks, to avoid stirring up revolts in Ukraine, and to reduce the Kozak army to one thousand men, all above that number to be returned to serfdom and no newcomers to be admitted. In order to avoid war Sahaidachny and his staff had promised to meet these demands, but presented a few Kozak grievances in order to delay signing; luckily, just before the agreement was made, the king became involved in war with Muscovy, and as the Polish parliament refused to give him financial support for the war, he was obliged to look to the Kozaks for aid. The crown prince Wladyslaw, who had been elected tsar of Muscovy by the boyars there during the Time of Troubles only to be dethroned later, had invaded Muscovy with a small force and needed immediate assistance. Sahaidachny believed that upon his participation in the war the demands of the commissioners would be dropped, and he accordingly began to mobilize the Kozak army. Under cover of mobilization, the Kozak Host ruled Ukraine independently throughout the winter and spring of 1618. In summer Sahaidachny entered Muscovy at the head of twenty thousand picked Kozaks to bring aid to Wladyslaw, and upon his arrival laid waste the land, capturing forts and cities and causing such terror that it was considered a miracle if a city withstood his attacks. Uniting with Wladyslaw, who was greatly relieved by the addition of the Kozak army to his forces, the Kozaks at once attacked the city of Moscow by night, but the Muscovites had expected them and defended the city so stoutly that its capture proved impossible. From this time on, however, the government of Muscovy was less stubborn in its negotiations with Poland; and the commissioners sent by the Polish parliament took advantage of the opportunity to make peace, a decision which was distasteful to both Wladyslaw and Sahaidachny, who favored a continuation of the war, but were helpless to object. The war thus came to an end.

In 1619, as soon as the war between Poland and Muscovy was over, the government again sent commissioners to supervise the Kozaks, this time with Zolkiewski and an army, and again demands were made that the Kozaks reduce their forces, discontinue their sea raids, burn their boats, and so on. After the Polish government had implored the help of the Host and received the support of twenty thousand Kozaks, it was gross ingratitude to send all but one or two thousand back into serfdom, and the Kozaks threatened to go to war over the question; Sahaidachny, however, wished to avoid a clash, and the Host was at length partially mollified by the distribution among its members of twenty thousand gold pieces. At the end of the negotiations, while ten thousand Kozaks gathered to await the result of the deliberations, it was decided that the Kozak army would be limited to three thousand men. An agreement to this effect was signed, the royal commissioners departed, and Sahaidachny bided his time in the expectation that sooner or later the Poles would again be forced to humble themselves before the Kozaks; in the meantime he prepared for the Poles a more damaging blow than had ever been dealt them by the unruliness of the Kozaks.

The Revival of Kiev as the Center of Ukrainian Cultural Life: Among the Poles Sahaidachny had the reputation of being a bold and successful warrior, but in Ukraine he was most justly known as a supporter of Ukrainian education and literature, of the Greek Orthodox Church, and of all else at that time that was a factor in Ukrainian national life. As a former student of the Ostroh school he was in close contact with educational and religious circles in Kiev, where many of his fellow countrymen from Galicia were then living, and in Kiev it was an accepted fact that in time of need Sahaidachny could be depended upon to furnish the aid of himself and his Kozak Host for the Ukrainian national cause.

Under these circumstances an unusually significant era opened for the history of the Ukrainian people. Kiev, which for several hundred years had been lost in oblivion, more and more completely deprived of cultural and religious importance, suddenly burst into new life.

In the sixteenth century Kiev had been merely a frontier fortress in which a military garrison was stationed, and to which a few inhabitants still clung; among the old ruins several monasteries had been left standing as reminders of the former glory of Kiev, the most important of which was the Monastery of the Caves, followed by the Pustinsko-Nikolaevsky and the Mikhailivsky monasteries. Even in these monasteries, however, the memory of the former literary and educational significance of Kiev had been vanishing, for the abbots and priors, as has been noted, had become persons who could afford to buy their positions from the king and who cared little for learning and enlightenment, while the immense material resources of the monasteries, which owned countless estates contributed through the course of centuries, were being dissipated or spent on food and drink for the monks.

The introduction of the Church Union forced the Ukrainian population to concentrate its attention upon the Church offices still in Orthodox hands, which positions it was vitally necessary to free from the influence of the government and to fill with properly qualified men; and since the Monastery of the Caves was the most important and wealthy of the Orthodox institutions, attention was concentrated upon it after Nicephorus Tur had repelled by force of arms the efforts of the Uniates to seize it.

After the death of Tur in 1599, Elisha Pletenitsky, who was known as a true patriot, was elected abbot. The Ukrainian people should be grateful to his memory, as he exerted a tremendous influence upon later Ukrainian life. By birth he was from Zolochiv, Galicia, and of the lesser local nobility; at the time he was elected abbot of the monastery he was about fifty years old. From documents of the time it is learned that he restored order in the monastery and handled the wealth of the institution as a care-

ful steward against whom the monks made complaints because he placed limits upon their expenditures for drink
and other luxuries. As Pletenitsky evidently realized that
a new cultural center could be developed here under the
protection of the Kozak army, which was gaining strength
and had already aided the Ukrainians of Kiev in time of
danger, he therefore devoted his efforts to collecting
funds for this purpose.

With money from the monastery Pletenitsky bought the
Balaban printing press in 1615, brought it from Striatyn,
in the Rohatyn district of Galicia to Kiev, and put it to
work, the first book being printed in 1616. Even before
this time he had attempted to bring educators and writers
from Galicia to Kiev, and by 1615–16 there were in Kiev
many noted savants from Galicia: Ivan Boretsky, a future metropolitan; Zachariah Kopistinsky, a Church historian; Lawrence Kukil, a teacher in the Lviv school and
the noted compiler of a Ukrainian dictionary; Berinda,
the printer; and many others. As the most outstanding
man in Orthodox circles at Kiev, Pletenitsky was able to
place his friends from Galicia not only in offices in the
Monastery of the Caves, but in various other religious positions in Kiev. Having at his side many educated friends
and finding in Sahaidachny a man of similar ideas, he began an extensive cultural activity in 1615–16, just when
Sahaidachny became hetman.

At about the same time as the establishment of the
press, a brotherhood was founded in Kiev, with an endowment of land bequeathed by Halshka Hulevichivna,
the wife of a wealthy nobleman, who earmarked her gift
for the establishment of a monastery and in connection
with it a school "for the children of the gentry and the
townspeople" and "an inn for pilgrims of the Orthodox
faith." According to its constitution, adopted in 1605, the
purpose of the brotherhood was to carry out these aims.
Its membership included "countless" numbers of people
of every class—local clergy, especially Pletenitsky and

his group, who were the prime movers in the plan; Ukrainian gentry; and merchants. Sahaidachny and the entire Kozak army also joined the brotherhood, thus providing armed defense for all its activities; with such a protector at hand the townspeople of Kiev were relieved of anxiety as to the attitude of the government and promoted the cultural work of the brotherhood so zealously that from an isolated and backward community Kiev speedily grew to be the center of Ukrainian national life.

The newly founded brotherhood made use of its endowment to build the Monastery of the Epiphany on a lot bequeathed for the purpose and to establish a school in connection with it. Boretsky, a former teacher in the Lviv school who became the first rector, went at once to Lviv to purchase books and other necessary school supplies, and the school was probably opened in the same year, 1617. Laying aside all other work, the printing press of the Monastery of the Caves at once issued a breviary, the usual first reader at that time, "in order to satisfy the needs of the school in the Orthodox city of Kiev." The school was conducted on the model of that at Lviv, teaching both "Graeco-Slavonic and Latin-Polish letters"; one of the first books introduced was a Graeco-Slavonic grammar published by the Lviv brotherhood. Owing to the support of the Kievan gentry and clergy and of the educated Galicians, the newly founded school was a success from the very beginning. From the verses read at the funeral of Sahaidachny in 1622, it would appear that the pupils were primarily the children of Kievan townspeople, of local clergymen—Greek Orthodox clergy being required to marry before ordination—and of Ukrainian gentry.

The printing press was also active. Prior to this time, the primary position in printing activity in Ukraine had been held by the press at Ostroh, which from 1580 to 1606 had issued more books than any other press in the country, but after the death of its owner, Prince Ostrozky, in 1608, it had fallen into disuse, as his Catholic son Yanush was not interested in this work. Within a period of fifteen years, from 1616 to 1630, the new press at the Monastery of the Caves printed more books than had been printed in all Ukraine up to this time. It was well supplied with money and with competent, devoted workers, the monastery even building a factory to make its own paper and another one for other printing materials. It is true that the books printed were chiefly religious in character, but it should be borne in mind that Ukrainian national life was at that time mainly centered in the Church.

The new brotherhood also manifested an organizing activity which soon made itself felt. One of the first to recognize its strength was the Uniate metropolitan Rutsky, the successor of Potiy, who in writing about the forces impeding the spread of the Union placed first of all the brotherhood, "founded three years ago," and reminded the government that the brotherhood had been organized without royal permission and in consequence should be dissolved. The government, however, dared not oppose it because it was under the protection of its members, among whom were the hetman Sahaidachny and the Kozaks.

The New Hierarchy in the Church: The Kievan brotherhood was the first organization to bring the Kozaks into contact with the higher classes of the Ukrainian people. The Kozaks had long been in close touch with the peasants, who had sought their protection and the opportunity of gaining freedom through them, and it had been natural for the Kozak Host to come to the aid of the common people because most of its members were recruited from this group. Some of the other classes among the Ukrainians, however, still viewed the Kozaks as their foes and considered them to be a destructive element; and accordingly, as soon as the Kiev brotherhood began to work under their protection, it considered itself obliged to explain to the Ukrainian people at large that the Kozaks were not passing adventurers but doughty exponents and preservers of the ancient knightly traditions of Rus:

They are the descendants of the famous people of Rus, of the sons of Japheth, who waged wars against Byzantium both on land and on the Black Sea. They are the descendants of that warlike race which with Oleh, the Rus monarch, attacked Constantinople with wheels under their boats. They are the same as those who with Volodimir, the sainted King of Rus, conquered Greece, Macedonia, and Illyria. Their ancestors, together with Volodimir, were baptized and accepted Christianity from the church at Constantinople, and even to this day they are born and live in this faith.

After their first activities under the protection of the Kozaks had proved successful, the Kievan circles decided to take advantage of the visit to Ukraine of the Patriarch Theophanes of Jerusalem to revive the Orthodox hierarchy. Such a step was imperative, for ever since the death of Bishop Balaban in Lviv in 1607, and of Kopistinsky in Peremyshl in 1610, there had remained but one Orthodox bishop, Tisarovsky in Lviv, for the entire population of Ukraine, and even Tisarovsky had had himself made bishop by trickery, having promised the king to become a Uniate, a promise which he failed to keep. As the king of Poland also did not carry out his promises or those made by parliament but appointed Uniate bishops to Orthodox sees, it is small wonder that the people became apprehensive lest the time might come when they would no longer have in Ukraine any Church heads of their own faith.

Upon learning that the Patriarch Theophanes was passing through Ukraine on his way from Moscow, the Kievans invited him to Kiev and showed him the educational institutions and cultural work there, after which they begged him to renew the hierarchy by ordaining a metropolitan and bishops. The Ukrainian convention which was being held in Kiev in commemoration of the foundation of the Monastery of the Caves strongly supported this plea in an appeal to the patriarch, who hesitated for a long time, "fearing the king and the Liakhs [Poles]," until Sahaidachny declared that he would be

responsible for his safety. Despite the fact that Borodavka had been elected hetman on the lower Dnieper, Sahaidachny ruled the Kozaks above the falls and full dependence could be placed upon his word, while the local
gentry also supported his declaration. The Patriarch finally consented to these requests and during the autumn
and winter of 1620, in various places, secretly ordained a
metropolitan and five bishops to fill all the Ukrainian and
White Russian dioceses, after which, under the protection
of the Kozaks, he departed in safety for Moldavia, ignoring the invitation of the Poles who had asked him to go
through Podolia, where it would have been possible to lay
hands upon him.

Though the bishops were ordained, it was even more
important to find a means of gaining the legal right for
them to perform the duties of their office. How were they
to take possession of their dioceses and begin work without interference on the part of the government? The
Kievans and the Kozaks hoped that the government
would find itself in need of the Kozak Host, and so be
forced to yield in this matter of religion.

Poland was then undergoing a great crisis. Because
Polish guerrilla bands were aiding the Emperor Ferdinand II against the hospodar of Transylvania, who was a
Turkish subject, the sultan became angered and decided
to wage war upon Poland, while the animosity of Turkey
for Poland was increased by the raids of the Kozaks under Borodavka, in which they attacked Constantinople,
plundered the vicinity, and caused such confusion among
the Turkish sailors that the officers found it difficult to
force them to take to the galleys to face the Kozaks. The
Turks were unable to repel the invaders, who after ravaging the region of Constantinople in safety at last departed for Ukraine. The sultan now decided to attack Poland in earnest and sent an army into Moldavia. Zolkiewski marched with the Polish forces which he had at hand,
hoping to unite with the Wallachians for joint defense

against the Turks, but when the Wallachians saw how small his army was, they refused to join him, and he was compelled to return homeward. The Turks fell upon the Polish army near the Dniester River and annihilated it, Zolkiewski himself being killed, his lieutenant Koniecpolski captured, and only a few escaping.

Poland was thus left entirely without an army, and in great fear awaited a Turkish attack in the following year. It was believed that the chief cause of Zolkiewski's defeat had been his failure to obtain the aid of the Kozaks, who knew how to fight against the Turks. Few Kozaks had taken part, for the freebooters under the hetman Borodavka had not marched, and those of Sahaidachny had been devoting their efforts to the religious cause while Zolkiewski was fighting against the Turks. The Polish general had looked upon the Kozaks with contempt, for which carelessness he had paid with his head, but now the Polish government put forth a great effort to gain their services, employing every means at its command and even appealing to the Patriarch Theophanes to win them over. In Kiev it was decided that in return for the participation of the Kozaks the Orthodox Church should receive legal recognition for its new bishops, but the king and his advisers were unwilling to yield on this point, and in vain the noted Ukrainian representative, Lawrence Drevinsky, criticized the Polish government in parliament in 1621 for the abuses and oppression of the Ukrainian and White Russian people, using the following terms:

Throughout the length and breadth of this Kingdom, how is the glory of God manifested with the aid of the newly invented Church Union? In the larger cities churches are already closed and the wealth of the Church is dissipated; in the monasteries, cattle are now kept instead of monks. Let us pass to the kingdom of Lithuania; there we are faced by the same sight, even in the frontier towns along the Muscovite border, where in Mohilev and Orsha the churches are closed and the priests expelled, and in Pinsk, where the Leschinsky Monastery has been made into a barroom. Children die unbaptized, bodies are buried without benefit of Church services, people live together unmarried, and without confession, and die without holy communion. Is not this an offense against God? Will not this anger the Lord? Let us consider other acts of injustice and abuse. Is it not unjust to the people of Rus in Lviv, that those who are not Uniates cannot live in the city or be free to transact business or be admitted to the guilds; that the body of a deceased resident cannot be transported with religious ceremonies through the city, and it is unlawful for a priest to visit the sick? What of the oppression in Vilna? Here the dead bodies of Orthodox Christians cannot be carried through the regular city gate, which is used even by Jews and Tatars, but must be taken in disgrace through the back gate used usually for offal and rubbish.

The king will request the people of Rus to furnish him with the major part of his army, but how can these people fight for a nation that oppresses them? How can we expect peace with our neighbors if we have no peace at home?

The government paid no attention to these complaints; and when Meletey Smotritsky, an Orthodox bishop ordained for the Polotsk diocese, went to enter upon his duties, the Uniates protested vehemently, whereupon the king, disregarding the risks involved, issued an order of arrest for Boretsky, Smotritsky, and all the other newly ordained bishops. Boretsky and the other bishops, being under the protection of the Kozaks, were not alarmed by the royal orders, but at the same time did not dare to enter their dioceses. In White Russia persecutions began, all who gave aid to Smotritsky or treated him as a bishop being arrested, and even threatened with death by the king; and although no one was actually executed, severe penalties were imposed, and Smotritsky himself was obliged to flee to the Kozaks to seek their protection.

Under these circumstances Kievan circles joined with Sahaidachny in a resolution to restrain the Kozaks from taking part in any campaign until the king should "give satisfaction to the Orthodox faith."

CHAPTER XIII

THE KOZAK WARS

The Khotyn War and the Death of Sahaidachny: During the winter, in compliance with the pleas of the patriarch and relying upon the promises of the king, the Kozaks began to prepare for a campaign. Their first step toward preparation was to attack and capture Bilhorod, where they took many prisoners and freed about three thousand slaves; from there they went into the Townships on the upper Dnieper to collect supplies for the campaign—horses, powder, lead, and so on—a call to the service of the king giving them a welcome excuse to make requisitions of all kinds upon the non-Kozak population. Boretsky and Sahaidachny ordered the Kozaks to continue these forced collections until the Kozak demands were met. In spring a great Kozak assembly was convoked for the purpose of receiving a subsidy from the king; and Boretsky, who was present with a large number of clergy, described to the gathering in sorrow and anger the persecutions suffered by the Orthodox Church, reading a letter from Vilna which described the cruelties inflicted upon the bishops there. Sahaidachny then read a communication from the patriarch, kissing it beforehand and placing it upon his head afterward, as a sign of reverence, while the Kozaks shouted approval and swore to defend the faith. On the following day, however, a royal envoy made a speech in which he urged the Host to join in the campaign, and handing them the money sent by the king won their consent in principle, though they decided to dispatch a delegation to Sigismund to declare that they would not go to war until the new bishops were recognized. Ezekiel Kurtsevich, the abbot of the Kozak monastery at Terekhtemiriv, was chosen to accompany Sahaidachny on this mission.

The Kozaks, however, could not resist the temptation to begin the campaign at once; and while Sahaidachny and Kurtsevich were on their way to the king, Borodavka led the Host into Moldavia, where they busied themselves in collecting booty, and many of them were killed in skirmishes. Sahaidachny's mission achieved no definite results, the king being polite but evasive; so having received news that war had broken out, he departed for the front. Upon Sahaidachny's return to the Kozak army, his supporters demanded the punishment of Borodavka on account of his haste and incompetence, which they claimed had caused the loss of too many lives. The unfortunate hetman was deposed from his office, sentenced to death, and executed at Khotyn, while Sahaidachny was reëlected in his place.

Upon receiving the hetman's mace of office for the last time, Sahaidachny decided to make one more appeal to the government to recognize the rights of the Ukrainians as a reward for the services rendered by the Kozaks. He might have threatened to abandon the Polish forces to fight their battles alone until these rights were granted, but he did not wish to deliver an ultimatum. Meanwhile the war continued. The Polish army crossed the Dniester at Khotyn, and was about to attack the Turkish fortress there when a large army of Turks appeared and began to surround them. The Poles feared that the Kozaks, who had not yet arrived, would be prevented from making a juncture, but Sahaidachny skilfully brought his forces through the Turkish lines and succeeded in joining his allies, though he suffered a wound in the arm from the effects of which he was to die in the next year.

The Kozak army numbered about forty thousand men, supplied with few but effective cannon, while the original Polish army consisted of thirty-five thousand men, including eight to ten thousand Ukrainians. The arrival of the Kozaks thus doubled the strength of the Poles, who were delighted, not only by the addition to their number, but because the Kozaks were experienced in fighting against Turks and Tatars. The newly arrived army took its position alongside the Poles and facing the Turks, who concentrated all their forces against the Kozaks in the belief that if they could defeat these troops the Poles would fall an easy prey; the Kozaks, however, not only repelled the Turkish attacks, but threw the enemy back into its camp, Kozak bands several times defeating larger Turkish contingents and at night crawling into the Turkish camp to terrorize it.

Though the Kozak soldiers lacked supplies, they held out under the stern hand of Sahaidachny until the end of the war, though Polish nobles, unable to endure the hardships, deserted in large numbers. The Poles now realized that their fate rested upon the Kozaks, and when the Turkish sultan lost hope of victory and made peace with Sigismund, the Polish government admitted that the Kozaks had saved the country from ruin, Sahaidachny and his men receiving high praise for their valor, endurance, discipline, and skill in the art of war.

Sahaidachny, relying upon the promises of the king, returned to Ukraine and from there sent him another petition, requesting in the name of the Kozak Host an increase in pay from forty thousand gold pieces to a hundred thousand, compensation for the losses sustained in the war, the right to settle on the estates of the crown, the clergy, or the landlords, and a satisfactory settlement of the religious controversy. Realizing how bitterly opposed the gentry were to any privileges for the Kozaks, the hetman worded his requests in almost submissive tones, but in vain; Sigismund now believed that he would have no further need of the Kozaks and was unwilling to waste further time on them. He ordered the government commissioners to renew the statutes of 1619 reducing the Kozak army to two or, in case of need, three thousand men, all the others to be returned to servitude; and as to the religious issue, he retorted that the Kozaks had never

been abused and that matters would remain as before. In
order that the Kozaks might accept this ingratitude more
readily, the king promised gifts to Sahaidachny and the
other officers, in the hope that they would pacify their followers.

Since Poland had no money with which to pay the Kozaks for their services, no one could be found to serve on
the commission to them, but other means were found to
inform them of the king's decision. The situation was thus
left unchanged, the Polish government and the Polish
king having deceived the Kozaks once more.

To the wounded Sahaidachny the king attempted to
show his appreciation by sending money for physicians,
but this belated generosity could not satisfy the dying
hetman, oppressed in spirit by the failure of his hopes
and plans. Feeling that his end was approaching, he drew
up a will leaving his fortune to the brotherhoods of Lviv
and of Kiev, to be used for educational purposes, and died
a few days later, on April 10, 1622. The news of his death
was a heavy blow to Ukrainian patriots, so many memo-
rials to him being composed by students that the educational organization to which he had belonged published
them in a book praising his heroism and his love for the
religion and the educational progress of his people, and
appealing to the Kozaks to emulate him. At the same time
the volume praised the Zaporozhian army and urged it to
follow in his footsteps in defense of the national cause.
The clergy, who kept in close contact with the army, also
used their influence in this direction.

Strife with the Government: The hetmans who succeeded Sahaidachny earnestly desired to follow in his
footsteps, and not only occupied themselves with their
own Kozak matters, but continually put pressure upon the
government to settle the question of the Orthodox Church,
lending their support to the Ukrainian gentry, who protested in parliament against the persecution of the Orthodox people; the king and the Polish nobles, however,

were consumed with hatred against the Orthodox and the Kozaks on account of their opposition to Catholicism, their demands for religious equality, and their refusal to comply with the orders of the king.

The Kozaks were at this time masters of the southern part of the Dnieper valley and therefore paid no attention to the royal orders to reduce their number by returning their surplus members to serfdom; on the contrary, they threatened to increase their army to a hundred thousand men and to force the king to live up to his promises, declaring that otherwise they would make difficulties both for him and for Poland. They continued their sea raids, so terrorizing the Turks that "the news that there were four Kozak boats on the Black Sea gave the Turks more alarm than the Black Death," according to the French envoy at Constantinople. The Polish government was filled with wrath, and the great landholders in Ukraine appealed to it to take some action regarding the Kozaks, since, as they complained, the gentry were unable to control them, lived in constant danger, and could expect a popular uprising at any moment. At this time the Polish landowners were dividing Ukraine among themselves and making efforts to introduce serfdom on a large scale, while the Kozaks who inhabited the land to which the landowners had received title from the king not only "disobeyed" them, but appealed to both peasants and townspeople to arm and expel these "foreign intruders." Because of this agitation the landlords desired to reduce the number of registered Kozaks and to enserf the rest.

After their participation in the Polish wars with Muscovy and Turkey the only means by which Poland could subdue the Kozaks was to slaughter them again as she had done at Lubny, for she did not now have sufficient strength to deprive them of their freedom, no one now caring to serve in the army, since the Polish forces had not yet been paid for their services in the war with Turkey. Realizing that neither the Polish government nor the king would do them justice, the Ukrainians considered various plans for action and attempted to arouse a national consciousness which would either force the government to yield to some of their demands or would support a war for independence. The clergy of Kiev favored the old policy of seeking aid from Muscovy, which was quite feasible, since the struggle involved a question of religion, and the Muscovites had never made any promises to Poland not to interfere in this issue; as soon as Muscovy had recovered from its anarchy, therefore, various groups of Ukrainians sought aid there in their religious difficulties, among those who went to Moscow being a large number of monks from the Hustinsky Monastery on the Vishnevetsky estates near the border. The abbot of this monastery and of two neighboring monasteries at this time was Isaiah Kopinsky, a man highly respected and worthy to be entrusted with the management of these important institutions, since he yielded neither to the government nor to the Uniate Catholics, and, through his friendship with the princes Vishnevetsky and with the powerful Princess Raina Mohilianka, was able to increase the number of monasteries. Both he and his monks were in favor of seeking the protection of Muscovy, and many other religious leaders, especially in Kiev, also hoped to secure aid from the north, the metropolitan sending one of the bishops there in the summer of 1624 to draw attention to the oppression of the Orthodox people at the hands of Poland and to ask the tsar if he would not take Ukraine and the Kozaks under his protection in case they were defeated by Poland in the approaching war. As Muscovy, however, had not yet fully recovered from its civil wars and feared to antagonize Poland, it returned an evasive answer, charging that the Kozaks thought more of their sea adventures and their expeditions than of the struggle with their real enemy Poland, but declaring that, when the people of Ukraine had fully decided that they wished to unite with Muscovy they should make their decision

known, and the tsar and the Patriarch would then take
the matter under consideration. For the Orthodox people
this was a very difficult time; in White Russia persecutions had increased, especially after 1623, when the people
of the city of Vitebsk had revolted against the local Uniate Catholic bishop, Josafat Kuncevich, and killed him,
and in consequence both innocent and guilty had been imprisoned or had suffered death. Many kinds of persecution were being visited upon the Orthodox, especially
upon the bishops, and adherents to the faith were expelled
from their offices, their monasteries, and their cities;
"they seek the blood of the Orthodox faith," wrote the
metropolitan of Moscow. The bishops sought refuge in
Kiev, "under the wings of the Christ-loving Kozak
heroes," and awaited with impatience the outcome of the
imminent conflict with Poland, expecting, if the Kozaks
were defeated as they had been thirty years before at
Lubny, to seek shelter in Muscovy.

The Kozaks, however, conscious of their own energy
and strength, were not perturbed over the outcome and
with great determination continued their sea raids against
Turkey, rejoicing when they found an unexpected ally in
Crimea in the person of the Tatar khan, Mahmet-Gerai,
who invited them to join him in a war against the Turks,
from whom he had revolted. The Kozaks accepted his invitation with alacrity, and while the Turkish ships were
being sent to Crimea in 1624 to install a new khan, they
sailed to Constantinople, where they took the Turks by
surprise and for a whole day plundered both sides of the
Bosporus, destroying rich residential sections and luxurious villas, and in the evening, loading the booty on their
boats, departed before the Turks could organize a defense. When the fleet of the enemy hastened after them,
the Kozaks, unable to attack on account of a contrary
wind, awaited them calmly, at which display of courage
the Turks retired without striking a blow; the Kozaks,
unmolested, also went home. Two weeks later, with much

larger forces, they were ready to attack Constantinople again but were blocked in the Dnieper estuary by a Turkish fleet of twenty-five large galleys and three hundred small boats; after a few days of fighting, however, the Kozaks broke through the Turkish blockade and sailed to Constantinople, this time pillaging and burning the shores of the Bosporus for three days before returning unhindered. The sultan in consternation sent messengers to the commander of his forces in Crimea to leave the Tatars there in peace and to hasten home to defend the capital from the attacks of the Kozaks, an order with which the commander complied willingly, having been helpless to carry out his mission in Crimea, since he had found the Kozaks there, too. When he had invaded the country to punish the disobedient khan, he had encountered the Tatar forces under Mahmet-Gerai reinforced by a Kozak regiment, at the sight of whom his alarm had been so great that he had opened negotiations. The combined Tatar and Kozak armies, however, had fallen upon the Turks, defeated them, and driven them headlong as far as Kaffa, where they were forced to surrender, whereupon the Turkish commissioner recognized Mahmet-Gerai as khan, was given back the prisoners and cannon taken by the Tatars and Kozaks, and departed for Constantinople.

After the successful war with Turkey the Crimean khan, assuming that the Turks would not leave him in peace but would make a fresh attempt to depose him, attempted to make a permanent alliance with the Kozaks. For this purpose he wrote to the King of Poland to beg him to induce the Kozaks to assist the Tatars in future against the Turks, at the same time negotiating with the Kozaks themselves, and in 1624, on Christmas Eve, Khan Shahin-Gerai of the Tatars signed a treaty of mutual alliance with the Kozaks.

The Kozaks had full faith in this treaty with the Crimean horde and expected in case of necessity to receive help, not only in a war with Turkey but also in the inevitable war with Poland. The alliance created a new spirit of confidence among them, as they saw a golden future ahead both for themselves and for Ukraine.

The Ukrainian Project and the War of 1625: In the autumn of 1624, a man by the name of Alexander Yakhea came to Kiev, went to the metropolitan, and introduced himself as the legal son and successor of the Turkish sultan Mohammed III, who had died in 1606. According to his story his Greek mother had stolen him from the court of the sultan and had brought him up in the Orthodox faith, the entire Christian population of the Turkish empire was awaiting him as claimant to the throne of Turkey, he had been promised 130,000 soldiers from Bulgaria, Serbia, Albania, and Greece, whose people recognized him as their rightful sovereign, and he wished to gain the help of Ukraine and Muscovy in breaking up the Turkish empire; he expected aid also from the enemies of Turkey in Western Europe, especially Spain and Tuscany. The metropolitan probably did not believe the whole story but, not knowing the true situation, thought there might be some advantage in assisting Yakhea nevertheless, and accordingly sent him to the Zaporozhe region, where in concert with the Kozaks and Shahin-Gerai he began at once to make plans for a war against the Porte. Since the metropolitan wished to interest Muscovy in the project and at the same time to increase the tsar's interest in the Ukrainian cause, he himself went to visit the Kozaks, and with them and Yakhea selected a delegation consisting of a few Kozaks and an agent of Yakhea named Mark the Macedonian, to go to Moscow, where they were to inform the tsar of Yakhea's plans and alliances and to solicit aid. The scheme, however, collapsed. Though the tsar gave indications of being interested in the affair and sent valuable gifts to Yakhea through the agent, with whom he had a secret interview, he refused to intervene either in the Ukrainian uprising or in the conflict with Turkey.

The ambitious plan for an alliance of Ukraine, Crimea,

and Muscovy which the Ukrainian statesmen in Kiev had
been preparing thus failed to materialize; it is of interest,
however, as a link in a consistent Ukrainian policy, the
negotiations being reminiscent of the earlier plans of
Dmitro Vishnevetsky and the later efforts of Bohdan
Khmelnitsky. In the end, while placing their trust in alliances, the Kozaks found themselves forced to fight alone
against Poland. Muscovy had spoken the truth in saying
that it was useless for her to intervene as long as the
Kozaks themselves were so careless in defending their
own interests, for the Kozaks, believing that Poland would
not dare to attack them while the Crimean khan was their
ally, thoughtlessly continued their sea raids, in complete
disregard of Polish threats and orders to abstain. Three
times they undertook large-scale expeditions to sea which
lasted until late fall while the Polish general Koniecpolski
was mobilizing against them. Koniecpolski not only hated
the Kozaks personally because he was the owner of large
estates in Ukraine which they had often molested, but was
also obliged to take immediate action because there was
danger of war in the near future between Poland and
Sweden, in which case he would be forced to abandon
Ukraine to the Kozaks while he went to fight against
Sweden. Only one obstacle lay in the path of Poland—the
Kozak alliance with Crimea, but in the summer of 1625
Koniecpolski bribed Shahin-Gerai and his brother not to
intervene in the Kozak war with Poland; and then, before
the Kozaks had returned from the sea, he hastily dispatched the Polish army to Ukraine, following it himself
with commissioners from the parliament.

The Polish invasion caught the Kozaks completely off
guard. Koniecpolski crossed Ukraine as far as Kaniv
without encountering opposition, and even at Kaniv there
were only three thousand Kozaks, who, unable to oppose
the large Polish army, retreated to Cherkassy, where they
hoped to join with the main body of Kozaks supposed to
be coming up from below the rapids. In the face of Ko-

niecpolski's swift advance the Ukrainians in northern Ukraine had no opportunity to mobilize the Kozaks there, while in the Zaporozhe Hetman Zhmailo wasted his time waiting for the return of the Kozaks from their sea raid and in corresponding with the khan to beg aid under the terms of the treaty. Meanwhile newly commissioned Polish regiments arrived to assist Koniecpolski, whose army was now larger and better equipped than that of the Kozaks. The Poles demanded that the Kozaks surrender the leaders of the sea raids as well as their booty, that they hand over Yakhea and the delegates who had been sent to Muscovy, and that they meet other specific requirements; but the Kozaks decided to fight rather than to accept these terms, and a battle followed near Krilov, on the River Tsibulnik. Though the Kozaks held their own, they realized that they were in a disadvantageous position and moved secretly farther south toward Lake Kurukiv, leaving small detachments behind to detain the enemy; the Poles, however, destroyed these forces and approached the camp of the main army before the Kozaks could strongly fortify themselves. Unable, however, to capture by storm even the hastily built defenses and realizing that a long war lay ahead of them, the Poles opened negotiations and after lengthy bargaining and the exchange of many notes succeeded in persuading the Kozaks to sign an agreement, according to which their standing army would in future be limited to six thousand men with full Kozak privileges, who were to be registered within twelve weeks, while every Kozak who was not included in the registration was to return to some landowner as a serf.

Even if they had wished to, the Kozaks could not have kept the terms of this treaty, but Koniecpolski and the parliamentary commissioners persuaded them that the war could not be brought to an end or the Polish army withdrawn from Ukraine under any other conditions, while the Kozak officers attempted to console their troops by assuring them that Poland would be unable to enforce the treaty because her army would have to take part in the Polish war with Sweden, which had in fact already begun, and that since the Kozaks would also be called upon for aid, the treaty would remain a dead letter.

With the support of the Kozak officers the newly elected hetman, Michael Doroshenko, who had been chosen during the campaign as a successor to Zhmailo, succeeded without arousing internal conflict in persuading the Kozaks to accede to the demands of the commissioners to register the Kozaks and to exclude from the army all whose names were not in the register, but he made use of every means within his power to delay removing the Kozaks from the estates of the landowners and to avoid fulfilling the other provisions of the Treaty of Kurukiv.

The War of 1630: Doroshenko was an intelligent and able administrator who enjoyed the full support of the officers of the Kozak army in his efforts to induce the Ukrainian civil population to endure their hardships for a time in order to avoid a fresh war, even succeeding in preventing the nonregistered Kozaks from undertaking new sea raids. Fortunately, a war broke out between the Crimean Tatars and the Turks in which the Kozaks took part with the tacit approval of the Polish government, since the latter desired to preserve the alliance with the Tatar khan; the Kozaks went to the aid of Crimea several times, participating in the battles of Kaffa and of Bakhchisarai. Doroshenko himself was killed in the course of one of these campaigns; his death was a serious loss to the Ukrainian cause, for his successors were less skilful than he in controlling the Kozak army, and especially in preventing strife with the government. Nevertheless, for some time peace with the Poles was maintained.

At this period not only the Kozaks, especially their officers, but the Church leaders and the townspeople as well were in a mood for compromise: tired of the unfruitful struggle, a part of the Kievan clergy and of the Ukrainian population in general was ready to submit to the government in order to establish better relations. This movement was led by Meletey Smotritsky, the noted Ukrainian author and theologian, who, driven into exile by the persecution which had befallen him upon his ordination as bishop of Polotsk, had gone to Byzantium and after his return to Ukraine had attempted to induce the Orthodox clergy there to come to an agreement with the Catholics, finally becoming a Uniate himself because of the failure of his efforts at compromise. Cast out by the Orthodox, he died at the Dermansky Monastery in Volynia. He was not the only one now who leaned toward conciliation with the government and the Catholics, other noted leaders who temporarily approved such a policy as the best being Peter Mohila and the metropolitan Boretsky; a great majority of the common people, however, followed the leadership of the ultra-Orthodox Kopinsky and eventually forced the bishops to abandon their position of compromise. Meanwhile the Kozak leaders complained that the government did not place a proper valuation upon their services, though Stephen Chmielecki, Koniecpolski's assistant in Ukraine, endeavored to maintain friendly relationships with them, and by a policy of not enforcing the treaty was able to maintain peace.

As soon as Chmielecki died, the situation again became aggravated, for Koniecpolski, an archenemy of the Kozaks, returned to Ukraine in 1629 after the close of the war with Sweden, bringing with him the unpaid Polish army which he quartered in garrisons throughout the country, where the soldiers continually irritated the Kozaks and the other inhabitants. Many uprisings resulted, which were intensified as he demanded the fulfillment of the Kurukiv agreement and after each revolt ordered "the blood of the serfs to flow." The new Kozak hetman, Hritsko Chorny, who had the approval of the government, tried to obey its orders by requesting the Kozaks of the Zaporozhe to come to the Townships on the upper Dnieper and join the registered army there "for war service," and when the Zaporozhian Kozaks ignored this order, they were excluded from the register. They then marched to the Townships in the spring of 1630, under the leadership of Taras Fedorovich, and having deceived Hetman Chorny by making him believe that they were coming in compliance with his request, they seized him, brought him before a Kozak military tribunal, found him guilty, and beheaded him. When the registered Kozaks learned of this event, they began to flee to the Polish army stationed at Korsun; there the Zaporozhian army attacked them, whereupon the registered Kozak soldiers, deserting their officers and leaving them among the Poles, joined the Zaporozhians; the inhabitants of Korsun of their own accord now attacked the Poles from the rear and forced them to flee to save their lives.

This action marked the outbreak of an insurrection, and the Zaporozhian Kozaks dispatched a call to arms to the whole country, urging everyone to join their army in order to avail himself of the Kozak rights and to defend the faith. Even before this time dangerous rumors had been circulating among the people as to the evil designs of the Polish government against the Orthodox faith; in fact, ever since the synod convoked by the government in 1629, the people had been as bitter against the Orthodox officials who had attended this synod as against the Poles who had been responsible for it. While the civilian inhabitants of Ukraine were being aroused by the rumors of Polish attacks upon their Church, the Kozaks revolted in defense of national rights. The story spread that the Polish army had been stationed in Ukraine to destroy all the Orthodox, that the Hetman Chorny had become a Catholic and had been killed for this reason, and that the Uniates had turned over to Koniecpolski for the upkeep of the Polish army the money collected for the schools; the Kozak insurrection thus became a war in defense of religion, and the Kozaks and the revolting peasants killed Polish soldiers wherever they found them. This time the conditions of 1625 were reversed; it was not the Kozaks but Koniecpolski who was unprepared. Before he had an opportunity to collect his army, which had been carelessly scattered over all Ukraine, the revolution had spread through the entire eastern portion of the country and the Kozak army had swelled in size with extraordinary rapidity.

Unable to muster his army at once, Koniecpolski sent his lieutenant, Sameilo Lasch, into the war zone, where Lasch began "to restrain the people." Even among the Polish nobles Lasch was known as a bandit and robber; reports circulated that he had been condemned for over two hundred crimes and deprived of his title of nobility thirty-seven times. As long as Koniecpolski was alive he was assured of protection, though he and his bands knew no mercy; but so thoroughly was he hated that later, immediately after the death of Koniecpolski, the gentry of the Kievan district were to collect twelve thousand men, attack Lasch and his bandits, and expel them and their families from the country.

Such was the man whom Koniecpolski now sent to suppress the revolt, and it may be imagined how he conducted himself. A contemporary Kievan relates that Lasch came to the town of Lisianka on an Easter morning when the people were in church and slaughtered them all, from the priest to women and children, and that in the city of Dimir the Poles massacred the entire population. Whether these reports are true in all details or not, they do reflect the sentiment of the time and the Ukrainian attitude toward the Poles, and whenever Ukrainians came upon Polish soldiers they repaid them to the best of their ability in their own coin.

Encounters upon a small scale continued during the entire month of April, while the Kozaks were gathering their forces at Pereyaslav to prepare for decisive action, and meanwhile to block the passage along the bank of the Dnieper. Koniecpolski, assembling his troops as best he could, crossed the Dnieper near Kiev and attacked the Kozaks, but barely escaped being taken prisoner and was forced to retreat at full speed. A second time he crossed the river with more care and encamped between it and Pereyaslav, fearing that the Kozaks might attack him from the rear. His forces gradually dwindling away, and all his attacks upon the Kozak encampment failing of success, he decided to await aid from the king, which, however, the latter could not send him, while the small contingents of his own scattered army marching to join him were attacked and dispersed by the Ukrainian rebels, who controlled the entire Dnieper region—the heart of Ukraine—and destroyed the Polish garrisons wherever they could be found. Finally, after two weeks of skirmishing at Pereyaslav, the decisive battle was fought.

It was this battle which the poet Shevchenko described in his well-known poem, *The Night of Taras:*

> With red serpent on the water,
> River Alta brings the word
> That black vultures after slaughter
> May feast on many a Polish lord.
>
> And now the vultures hasten
> The mighty dead to waken.
> Together the Kozaks gather
> Praise to God to offer.
>
> While black vultures scream,
> O'er the corpses fight.
> Then the Kozaks sing
> A hymn to the night;
>
> That night of famous story
> Full of blood and glory.
> That night that put the Poles to sleep
> The while on them their foes did creep.*

* Alexander J. Hunter, *The Kobzar of the Ukraine* (Winnipeg, 1922), pp. 33–34.

The Kievan chronicler states that Lasch and Koniec-polski, observing a Kozak advance guard, attacked and pursued it for some distance, leaving their base far behind; two Polish camp servants now hastened to the Kozak headquarters with the information that Koniecpolski was not in his camp, whereupon the Kozaks sallied forth and fell upon it, defeating the small defending force and destroying everything except the guns and ammunition, which they brought back to their own encampment, Koniecpolski being placed in such difficult straits that he had to sue for peace.

Eyewitness accounts assert that the Poles were overwhelmingly defeated, their camp was destroyed, the recrossing of the Dnieper made impossible, and Koniecpolski forced to ask for terms of peace. As the Kozaks did not deem it the best policy to destroy him completely, it was agreed that the conflict should be forgotten, while the Kozaks who had fought against the Poles would not punish the two thousand who had served with them. The number of registered Kozaks was to be increased to eight thousand, but as no registration was actually made, all continued to enjoy equal rights.

The Interregnum: The Kozak victory at Pereyaslav brought great benefits to the Ukrainian national cause, for the time was approaching when the Ukrainians could carry their battle for national rights to the floor of the parliament itself. It is true that only the gentry could participate there and that few of these were left who still clung to their nationality, but it was important to these few to know that behind them stood the Ukrainian population and the Kozak army, and even more important that the Poles also knew it.

King Sigismund, the implacable foe of Ukrainian hopes, was now old and his reign was nearing its end; accordingly, in Ukraine and White Russia everyone prepared for the great struggle over the election of his successor, and over the *pacta conventa,* the conditions which the new king, according to the Polish constitution, would have to approve before taking office. Even during the lifetime of Sigismund the Ukrainian members of parliament, who realized that they could not win anything from him, had said to the Uniates: "We see that we can gain no rights so long as this king lives, but during the interregnum we shall rise up against you with all our might." When the news spread that the king was dying, the Ukrainian people—nobility, clergy, brotherhoods, townspeople, and Kozak officials—prepared to persuade the new king and the Poles to put an end to the old injustices against them and the repression of their Church and culture.

The king died in April 1632. Though he had sons, and the oldest, Wladyslaw, considered himself the logical successor, he yet, according to the Polish constitution, had to be elected. The election procedure involved three steps: first a "convocational parliament" was convoked to keep order during the interregnum; then an "electoral parliament" was called to elect the king and draw up the pacta conventa; and finally a "crowning parliament" conferred the crown. The convocational parliament came together during the summer of 1632; in it the Ukrainian representatives, especially the older parliamentarians Drevinsky and Kropivnitsky and a young leader named Adam Kisil, endeavored to have the Ukrainian problems settled first of all, and until this was done to discourage all efforts to elect a king. In this policy they were supported by delegates of the Kozak army sent by Hetman Petrazhitsky-Kulaha, who demanded freedom of worship for the Greek Orthodox, and for the Kozaks the same right to participate in the election of the king as that enjoyed by the Polish gentry. Raising of the question of the participation of the Kozaks in parliament and their future role in politics brought up an important problem, and when the nobles opposed Kozak participation in the election, Petrazhitsky-Kulaha, in order to emphasize the demands of his people, took his army into Volynia and be-

gan to plunder the large estates belonging to the enemies
of the Kozaks. The religious issue was finally postponed
until the electoral parliament should meet, but the hostile
attitude of the Polish nobles had further antagonized the
Ukrainians, who determined to present their case more
forcibly at this parliament, which was to be convoked in
the autumn.

The first problem in importance was that of the bishops. The Orthodox attempted to regain the old dioceses,
monasteries, and churches which had been taken away
from them and given to Uniates, but the Crown Prince
Wladyslaw, like others who were willing to grant some religious rights, did not intend to go so far; and even for
the concessions which he was willing to make, he was
obliged to fight the opposition of the Polish clergy and of
the tenacious Catholic members of the parliament. Finally
it was decided to divide the former Orthodox dioceses and
the entire wealth of the Orthodox Church between the Orthodox and the Uniates. According to this arrangement
two metropolitan sees were to be created, an Orthodox
and a Uniate, and each was to share alike; the Orthodox
were to receive the old dioceses of Lviv, Peremyshl, and
Lutsk, and a new one to be created for them in White Russia, while the Uniates were to receive the dioceses of Polotsk in White Russia and the three Ukrainian dioceses of
Volodimir, Kholm, and Turiv-Pinsk; the churches and the
monasteries were also to be divided between them by
royal commissioners. Although the Orthodox were not
satisfied with these concessions, they were forced to accept them; and Wladyslaw himself, in the face of the
strong opposition of the Catholic clergy and of many of
the senators who did not wish to give their consent without the approval of the Pope, which would probably not
have been forthcoming, had to bring to bear all his personal influence to secure the enactment of the law. His
chief argument was the need of satisfying Ukraine, especially the Kozaks, since he intended to attack Muscovy

upon the expiration of the treaty and knew that unless the Orthodox were satisfied, he could expect no aid from the Kozaks, who might, in fact, even join with Muscovy against him, the metropolitan Kopinsky having indeed thrown out hints to the effect that the Ukrainians would never gain any rights as long as they were united to Poland, and should look for protection to the Tsar of Muscovy instead. In the end Wladyslaw succeeded in inducing a sufficient number of senators to approve the concessions to the Orthodox, including a promise to pass laws giving to the Orthodox equal rights in the cities; these proposed laws, however, hardly need further discussion as they were never enacted.

Though the actual gains of the Ukrainians were unimportant, it meant much that they had been secured at all, considering the powerful opposition against them in parliament. This settlement must therefore be considered a great victory—the last parliamentary victory won by the remnants of the Ukrainian gentry.

The Ukrainians decided to strike while the iron was hot, and set about the election of a new metropolitan, since the bishops who had been previously appointed and the metropolitan Kopinsky were not recognized by the government, and on this point the Orthodox had had to yield. Peter Mohila, the archimandrite of the Monastery of the Caves, was at once elected metropolitan. He had many friends and relatives among the Polish landowners, and had formerly favored the union of the Orthodox Church with the Roman Catholic, for which reason the Poles preferred him to Kopinsky for the office. At one time, when he had become prior in 1627, the Ukrainians, particularly the Kozaks, had looked upon Mohila with suspicion, for he had attempted to found a college of his own in Kiev to teach Latin in competition with the brotherhood school; and feeling against the proposed college had risen so high among the more militant Orthodox that some of them, especially among the Kozaks, were ready to slay the teachers of the school as well as Mohila himself, whom they suspected of scheming with the Poles. In the end he had been forced to abandon his project and to merge his school with that maintained by the Kievan brotherhood, after which he had become a member of the educational circle and had reformed the school on the model of the Jesuit colleges so that it would be able to withstand their competition. This concession on his part had satisfied both the Kievans and the Kozaks, while his great energy in educational and religious activities had gained for him high respect among the Ukrainians, who now fully approved his election as metropolitan.

Nor were they disappointed, for as soon as Mohila had united in his hands the immense wealth of the monasteries and the power and authority of the metropolitan's office, he managed both educational and religious affairs with energy and skill. The Monastery of the Caves, with its enormous resources, remained in his own hands, and in addition to it there fell to his care the wealthy Pustinsko-Nikolaevsky and the Mikhailivsky monasteries, in the latter of which the preceding metropolitans had resided; in addition, he still remained an elder and the director of the educational institutions in Kiev. Mohila made good use of his authority and of the wealth entrusted to him to renew and reorganize the activities of the Orthodox Church; he raised the standard of the brotherhood college, which became known first as the Academy of Kiev and eventually as "Mohila Academy" in his honor; he also financed publications and educational and literary enterprises; the educational system, however, was too far removed from Ukrainian national life, it having been adjusted to Church Slavonic influences on the one hand and the Polish and Latin culture of the gentry on the other. There was no clear conception of the national Ukrainian spirit, and in some respects the learning and literature of the new school were of a less advanced type than the livelier conversational style which had appeared prior to this time.

These defects were, however, overlooked, and everyone highly respected the new metropolitan because of his energy and ability.

Mohila displayed this energy immediately after his election by securing the appointment of an Orthodox bishop for the diocese of Peremyshl, where the Uniate bishop Krupetsky was in office and was reluctant to surrender his post, in spite of the fact that the people were eager to be rid of him. Hulevich-Voiutinsky, a Ukrainian nobleman of Volynia who was appointed bishop, was a man of great determination and people expected that he would seize his diocese from the hands of the Uniates, since it had been legally recognized as Orthodox by the new law; he fulfilled this expectation but his bold actions and his use of force injured his cause, for the Poles managed to get a court decision against him, which they permitted to be withdrawn only at a high price—the division of the Peremyshl diocese into two parts, an Orthodox and a Uniate.

Mohila was more cautious. Though he too was obliged to take his Cathedral of St. Sophia by force from the hands of the Uniates, his retainers attended to the task beforehand, and when he arrived the cathedral was his. Such practices were common at this time, and Mohila acquired new prestige as a man who knew how to look after the interests of the Orthodox Church. The Kievans, the clergy, and the Ukrainian gentry of the neighborhood ceremoniously welcomed him with speeches, verses, and scholarly orations, for in his person they were celebrating, after many years of struggle, sorrow, and enslavement, their national victory.

Sulima and Pavliuk: The newly elected king, Wladyslaw IV, thirsted for military glory but, since the Polish gentry were unwilling to support his projects, he placed a high valuation upon the Kozaks and attempted to keep their friendship. Immediately after his coronation he began a war with Muscovy, and even before it started he sent the Kozaks to attack the Siverian region, which at that time belonged to Moscow; with their aid he also attacked Smolensk. The parliament, however, would not permit him to conduct the war as he pleased and forced him to bring it to an end in its second year; although he hoped to wage a new war with Turkey in its place, the Polish senators again intervened and instructed Koniecpolski not to antagonize the Turks but to live on friendly terms with them. A decision was made to fortify the Dnieper near the rapids in order to hinder the activities of the Kozaks, and Koniecpolski engaged the French engineer Beauplan to select an appropriate site. This time the project did not remain on paper as it had so often done previously, but work on a fort was begun at once, and within a few months, to the great indignation of the Kozaks, a Polish garrison was stationed at the rapids to cut off their passage to the Zaporozhian country below, thus preventing not only raids but all kinds of legitimate enterprises on the steppes as well. Even without this new violation of their freedom the Kozaks had been discontented, for they had not been paid for their services in the last war, and now they waited impatiently for an opportune moment to destroy this hated Polish stronghold.

An apparent opportunity for the Kozaks came in 1635, with the approach of a war with Sweden. Wladyslaw, whose father had been related to the Swedish ruling dynasty and for a short time had even ruled over Sweden, had a claim to the Swedish crown and therefore welcomed this war. As he planned to attack the Swedes at sea and recalled the Kozak sea raids, he decided to make use of the Kozaks for a naval campaign, hired Kozak craftsmen to build thirty boats on the Niemen River, and requested the Kozaks to mobilize about fifteen hundred more soldiers than the register permitted. These preparations were made, and on the Baltic Sea the Kozaks displayed the same prowess which they had shown on the Black Sea; the Swedes showered them with cannon balls, but

RUSSIE NOIRE.
divisée en ses Palatinats. &c
tirée pour la plus grande partie
de la grande Carte de l'Ukraine,
du Sr le Vasseur de Beauplan.
Par le Sr SANSON d'Abbeville Geogr. ord.e du Roy.
A PARIS.
Chez l'Autheur
Avecq Privilege pour Vingt Ans.
1665.

their boats were left uninjured, while they in turn attacked a Swedish ship and captured it, thus striking terror into the hearts of the enemy, who were filled with amazement at the skill of the Kozaks in withstanding wind and storm, and, when their boats were scattered, in reforming their fleet. The war did not, however, last long enough to enable them to display their full fighting ability, and at the king's command they returned to Ukraine, where they stored their boats for future use.

Meanwhile the Kozaks in Ukraine, not knowing that Poland was secretly negotiating peace with Sweden and expecting a long war, attacked Fort Kodak, the Polish fort on the Dnieper. Led by Hetman Ivan Sulima, the Kozaks attacked the fortress at night, captured it, seized and shot the commanding officer, slaughtered the garrison, and completely demolished the fort, an act which aroused such great anger in Poland that Koniecpolski, who was just returning to Ukraine from the Swedish war, threatened the Kozaks with dire revenge. In order to avoid war the registered Kozaks decided to surrender the insurrectionary leaders, including Sulima and the other high officers, though Adam Kisil, the government commissioner to the Kozaks, states that his predecessor, Lucasz Zolkiewski, brother of General Zolkiewski, had bribed the Kozaks to desert the hetman. In any case, the Kozaks seized Sulima and five of his friends and sent them in chains to Warsaw, where they were tried by the parliament and condemned to death, to the regret of many, even of the Poles, Sulima having been a noted leader of the Kozaks who had been elected hetman several times, had participated in innumerable battles with the Turks without having been wounded, and had received a gold medal from the Pope because he had captured a Turkish galley and a large number of prisoners, three hundred of whom he had taken to Rome and donated to him. The king himself attempted to save the hetman's life but failed, and attempts were made to induce Sulima to become a Catholic in order to save himself, but in vain; he was beheaded, and his body was dismembered and hung on four corners of the city streets.

When they turned Sulima and his friends over to the enemy, the registered Kozaks begged the king to grant them protection from abuse by the governors and to pay for their past services; the king made promises but as usual the treasury was empty, there not being even money enough on hand to rebuild the razed Fort Kodak. At the same time the Kozaks were ordered to refrain from sea raids and to curb the disobedient; this, however, was becoming increasingly difficult for them to do, as both registered and unregistered Kozaks were in a rebellious mood, complaining of mistreatment by the government officials, curtailment of their rights, and failure to receive pay for their past services. The Polish commissioner, Kisil, attempted to keep order by bribing the officers to hold the Kozaks in check. The hetman, Tomilenko, and his secretary, Onushkevich, did their best to keep these unruly warriors under control, but in spite of all efforts the Kozaks continued to rebel, especially the Cherkassy and Chihiryn regiments in western Ukraine, the chief leader of the malcontents being Pavliuk But.

For a time the Kozaks were occupied with the Crimean question, since the khan, Inaete-Gerai, who was revolting against the sultan as his predecessor Shahin-Gerai had done, was seeking their aid against the Turks. The dissatisfied faction of the Kozaks, with Pavliuk as their leader, departed for Crimea, and their absence prolonged the peace in Ukraine; but as soon as they returned after the war, in the spring of 1637, their leader began to stir them up, and not even the money finally brought by the royal commissioners could alleviate the situation. The registered Kozaks had many complaints to make regarding the government, and Pavliuk urged them to rise and to fight for their rights, threatening that if civil war broke out against them, he would give them no aid or sympathy.

Pavliuk's followers now seized the Kozak cannon and took them to the Zaporozhe. Tomilenko merely urged him not to rebel but did not oppose him in any way, and for this reason was suspected of being a friend to Pavliuk. The registered Kozaks accordingly deposed Tomilenko and elected as hetman the colonel of the Pereyaslav regiment, Sava Kononovich, whom they considered more reliable, but this act marked the beginning of a revolt. Pavliuk sent two of his colonels, Kirpo Skidan and Semen Bichovets, through the countryside with declarations appealing to the Kozaks and the inhabitants of Ukraine in general to revolt against Polish oppression, to join his army, and to give no support to "those traitors who have accepted dinners, festivals, and banquets from Zolkiewski and in return have delivered our comrades into his hands"; they then seized Kononovich, Onushkevich, and the other officers of the registered Kozaks and delivered them to Pavliuk at Borovitsia, where they were tried, found guilty, and executed.

Pavliuk, however, instead of marching at once to the Townships of the upper Dnieper, returned to the Zaporozhe, where, according to rumor, he began to negotiate with the khan and the Don Kozaks for their aid; meanwhile he left his assistant, Skidan, in the upper Dnieper region to spread revolutionary propaganda and to gather an army, soldiers being sent out with circulars appealing to all who were of the Orthodox faith to prepare to fight against the Poles. As a result the people revolted, attacked the nobles, and joined with the Kozaks, especially west of the Dnieper, where nearly all the peasants became Kozaks—"every man a Kozak," as the Poles reported. Pavliuk made a blunder by remaining too long in the Zaporozhe and failing to assume leadership in person; thus the events of 1625 repeated themselves, the Polish army under Nicholas Potocki crossing the province of Cherkassy before Pavliuk had returned from the Zaporozhe so cooled the ardor of the rebels that the revolt subsided, lacking as it did the support of the main Kozak forces. Skidan, who was at Korsun, did not attempt to oppose Potocki, but retreated toward Moshny, calling upon the other bands from the Townships to join him there, while the Kozaks east of the Dnieper, under the leadership of Kizim, hesitated to participate in this unexpected war. When Pavliuk finally arrived at Moshny and appealed to all the Kozaks to fight for the Orthodox faith and their "golden" rights, it was too late; before their forces had united with him a decisive battle was fought on December 6, 1637, between Moshny and the Ros River. The Kozaks attacked the Polish camp near the village of Kumeyko, but the Poles, because of a strong position protected by swamps and well-placed cannon, drove them off. The Poles then successfully counterattacked, the Kozaks being thrown into confusion by the explosion of the powder wagons in their camp; and though the Poles sustained heavy losses they won the battle.

After their defeat, Pavliuk, Skidan, and the other officers, taking with them a few of the cannon, proceeded rapidly to Borovitsia, where they began to assemble a new army, leaving the main forces behind in charge of Dmitro Hunia, who led the retreat in good order, though he was forced to abandon the sick and wounded at Moshny, where they were mercilessly slaughtered by the Poles. Hunia united his forces with those of Pavliuk at Borovitsia and began negotiations for an armistice; Potocki, however, refused to accept an armistice on any other terms than the surrender of Pavliuk, Tomilenko, and Skidan. As Kisil and the other government commissioners gave assurances that no harm would be done these officers, the registered Kozaks could not resist the temptation, and gave up Pavliuk and Tomilenko, while Skidan and Hunia were absent at Chihiryn. When the absentees learned what was afoot they fled to the Zaporozhe, while Potocki appointed Iliash Karaimovich temporary head of the Kozaks, who were obliged to sign a declaration stating that they would submit to the orders of Potocki, would destroy their boats, and would expel the "disobedient" Kozaks from the Zaporozhe. The declaration was signed by Bohdan Khmelnitsky, the Kozak secretary, among others, who appears here for the first time.

After Potocki had thus succeeded in subduing the Kozaks, he entrusted to the registered regiments the task of keeping order in the Zaporozhe, while he himself marched across the provinces of Kiev, Pereyaslav, and Nizhin, punishing all who had participated in the revolt and leaving garrisons scattered throughout Ukraine.

The Ostrianin War and the Oppression of the Kozaks: Though Potocki had suppressed the Kozaks in the upper Dnieper region, he failed to subdue them in the Zaporozhe, where they continued to gather, the followers of Kizim and Skidan also taking refuge there from the registered Kozaks. When Karaimovich arrived with his regiment to execute the orders of Potocki, Hunia, who was the senior Kozak officer in the Zaporozhe, refused to yield, and the registered Kozaks also began to desert Karaimovich and to join the Zaporozhians, so that Karaimovich was obliged hastily to return to the Townships on the upper Dnieper to avoid losing his whole army by desertion.

The Zaporozhians then waited until spring to take revenge for the last war. They began to make preparations early, sending out messengers to arouse the inhabitants and electing as commander an experienced Kozak colonel, Yatsko Ostrianin, who led his army through the country east of the Dnieper, where the people were ripe for revolution. The Polish army attempted to block his way, but Ostrianin skilfully evaded them by marching north of Kremenchuk and advancing to the mouth of the River Holtva near Psiol, where he encamped near the city of Holtva, built fortifications, and prepared for battle in an advantageous position between the cliffs and ravines. The Polish army launched an unsuccessful attack upon Ostrianin, after which the Kozaks in turn attacked the

Poles from two sides and completely defeated them, forcing the remnant to retreat.

In the excitement over his victory, Ostrianin made a fatal error; instead of retaining his strategic position and massing more troops, he failed to wait for the regiments marching to join him, but pursued the Poles to Lubny in the expectation that on the way he would come up with his other regiments, including those from Chernihiv under the command of Skidan and those from Kiev, Putivl, and other districts under Soloma. He missed them, however, and was forced to face the Poles unaided near Lubny, where he was defeated and obliged to beat a hasty retreat to the upper Donets basin. In the meantime the regiments marching from the Don and the Zaporozhe to meet him were unable to find him but came upon the Polish army and had to surrender, the Poles falling upon them during the negotiations concerning the surrender and slaughtering them to the last man. By this time Ostrianin had gathered such a large force from among the inhabitants of the Romen district that he decided to attack the Poles from the south near Sniporod, but again he was defeated and had to retreat south along the River Sula with the Poles in hot pursuit. After losing another battle at Zhovnin, Ostrianin considered his cause lost, and with a few of his followers deserted the army, crossed the Muscovite border and settled down in the Slobidshina, the "Land of Free Communes," in the upper Donets basin near modern Kharkiv. Here Ukrainians had been settling in large numbers since the period when the Polish nobles had introduced serfdom into the country east of the Dnieper, the number of such settlers having increased after each unsuccessful Kozak war. Wherever they settled the immigrants established the same Kozak form of government as existed in Ukraine.

The remnants of Ostrianin's army were rescued by Dmitro Hunia, who had once before saved the Kozak forces from destruction. He defeated one Polish army, but when he learned that Potocki himself was arriving with fresh forces, he retreated to the Dnieper and encamped there on the old battle site where the Kozaks had withstood the governor of Cherkassy, an advantageous position which Hunia fortified so strongly that the Polish engineers recognized that it was impregnable and could be reduced only by starvation. The retreat from Zhovnin and the defensive battle on the Startsi branch of the Dnieper give Hunia a place in the annals of Kozak history as one of the greatest of their warriors.

Potocki besieged the Kozak camp, but opened negotiations upon discovering that he would not be able to capture it by storm. Hunia declared that he would not make a peace like that of Kumeyko but only upon an honorable basis with provision for the restoration to the Kozaks of all their former rights. He intentionally dragged out the negotiations to await help and also in the hope that the Poles might lose their ardor for further war. Though Colonel Filenko, who was coming up from the other side of the Dnieper with supplies, managed to fight his way through the Poles, he lost his supplies to them, and in the end the Kozaks were starved into submission and had to accept the same hard terms as those imposed after the last campaign, except for one concession—the Poles did not demand the surrender of their leaders, and all the participants who had not died in battle or been killed by the Poles were pardoned.

The Kozaks were at last thoroughly subdued. The whole Kozak army consisted of only a few thousand men, for although six thousand were permitted by law, this number was not reached, since few cared to enroll. Many of the registrants, moreover, were not Kozaks but Poles, and the elected officers were all discharged and replaced by new officials appointed by the government; the colonels, and in fact all the higher officers, were now Polish gentry. Polish landlords were allowed to manage the Kozak properties, and Kozaks were permitted to live only in the districts of

Cherkassy, Korsun, and Chihiryn, unregistered Kozaks being subjected to the landowners and officials.

The Kozaks begged the king to remove these strict limitations on their liberties, but without success. For some time they nursed the idea of another war for revenge, but after two unsuccessful wars they had little inclination for a third; Potocki and his army, moreover, were on guard to prevent any new uprisings. Upon the return in 1638 of the unsuccessful delegation sent to the king, the Kozak Host was further reorganized, a new council of officers in place of the old being appointed, including a Polish commissioner and colonels who were "gentry by birth." Only two adjutants and the captains were Kozaks, among these being Khmelnitsky, a captain in the Chihiryn regiment. Fort Kodak was rebuilt, Koniecpolski himself guarding it during the construction and upon its completion leaving a permanent garrison there, with orders to the commandant under pain of death not to allow anyone to go down to the Zaporozhe. In the Zaporozhe itself two regiments of registered Kozaks were to take turns in standing guard in order to keep out the Tatars and to prevent unregistered Kozaks from congregating there, while a Polish army was stationed in the Townships on the upper Dnieper to intimidate the inhabitants.

This time the Poles did not become involved in war for a long period, and consequently did not need the services either of their own army or of the Kozaks, so that the new arrangement enacted into law in 1638 was in force for ten years. The Polish landowners, believing that they had now suppressed forever the "Kozak hydra," felt thoroughly at home in Ukraine, where they lived in luxury while the rest of the inhabitants were reduced to serfdom.

CHAPTER XIV

KHMELNITSKY'S REBELLION AND THE LIBERATION OF UKRAINE

The Revolution of 1648: The severity of the oppression of the Ukrainians did not guarantee the permanence of the settlement, for although those who were discontented suffered in silence, they were merely awaiting the first opportunity to cast off the Polish yoke. There were many dissatisfied people—the registered Kozaks, deprived of their former self-government and placed under the command of unfriendly Polish officers; and the unregistered Kozaks, excluded from the army, reduced to the level of the peasants by the impositions of the Polish landlords, and forced to endure abuse and insult at the hands of the Polish soldiers quartered upon them; the Ukrainian peasants, who had migrated to "the land without a landlord" and had found to their sorrow and horror that the plague of Polish landowners had followed them there; and the Ukrainian townspeople and clergy, bereft of the protection of their friends and patrons the Kozaks. The whole new order of things rested on one foundation—peace in Poland, which made it possible for her to leave her army in Ukraine and to avoid calling upon the services of the Kozaks. The first war to break out would shatter these arrangements in Ukraine, since in case of war the army of occupation would have to be withdrawn, and the Kozaks called upon for aid. It was rare for so long a time to pass without war, but the gentry kept a firm grip upon the king and did not permit him to disturb his neighbors. There was, however, so much inflammable material lying about loose in Ukraine that at last war itself was not needed to set it afire, but the mere rumor that the king wanted war was enough.

Wladyslaw nursed the idea of war with Turkey and was

strongly encouraged by the republic of Venice, which was engaged in hostilities with the Porte and was seeking to draw other countries to her side. Knowing how unwilling the Polish nobles were to undertake a war, the king decided to enlist the aid of the Kozaks in provoking a conflict with Turkey, and in 1646 entered into secret negotiations with the Kozak officers for this purpose. The Polish nobles, however, discovered his project and forced him to abandon it.

Not long afterward the king's aims were even more clearly revealed. Bohdan Khmelnitsky, mentioned above as a captain in the Chihiryn regiment, had suffered wrongs at the hands of the government officials, his family estate in Subotiv being seized, the buildings on it destroyed, the movable property stolen, and his family insulted, but when he demanded justice he was thrown into the prison of one of the gentry and kept there until his friends managed to free him. Outraged and robbed of all his possessions, Khmelnitsky decided to lead a revolt. As one of those with whom the king had been in close secret communication, Khmelnitsky knew that the king favored a stronger Kozak army free from domination by the nobles, and believed that Wladyslaw would not seriously oppose an uprising, his belief in this respect being typical of the Kozaks' confidence in the power of the king, to whom, however, the Polish constitution at that time allowed very little authority. According to one report, in the fall of 1647 Khmelnitsky stole from the pocket of a Kozak officer the confidential letters written by the king and fled with them to the Zaporozhe country, where he preached revolution among both the registered and the unregistered Kozaks, asserting on the evidence of the letters that the king was in sympathy with his cause. Through his friends among the Tatars, Khmelnitsky also got in touch with the khan, whom he urged to join with the Kozaks for an invasion of Ukraine. The khan was at odds with the Poles because they had not paid him their regular contributions;

moreover, he needed war because his country was suffering from a famine and he could not seize supplies in Ukraine so long as there was peace between Crimea and Poland. For these reasons he promised to come to the aid of Khmelnitsky and ordered Tuhai-bey and the Tatar horde to join him.

As soon as the Kozaks in the Zaporozhe learned of this alliance, they decided to raise the standard of revolt. Khmelnitsky was elected hetman, news was sent out secretly that war would begin in spring, and all the secret paths to the Zaporozhe became choked with volunteers going down the Dnieper to join the Kozaks.

The Polish nobles, too, learned of the impending rebellion and sent frantic appeals to Potocki, the new head of the Polish army, to defend Ukraine. When Potocki began to make preparations for a campaign, the king attempted to dissuade him by suggesting that the Kozaks could be permitted to undertake raids on the sea; but Potocki, who stood in fear of parliament, refused to follow the king's advice and wrote to Khmelnitsky to urge him to return to Ukraine. In his reply Khmelnitsky demanded the abrogation of the law of 1638 and the restoration of the former Kozak privileges, but Potocki, who could not meet these demands without the approval of parliament, continued his preparations and invaded Ukraine shortly after Easter.

Sending his son Stephen ahead with the cavalry and a few registered Kozaks and dispatching the other registered Kozaks down the Dnieper in boats, Potocki himself, with Kalinovski and the main Polish army, advanced slowly, picking up as he went the garrisons stationed along his route. Stephen Potocki had meanwhile forged ahead carelessly far into the steppes without resistance from Khmelnitsky, until he suddenly found himself surrounded by the rebels at Zhovty Vody Creek (Yellow Waters). Khmelnitsky had also been devoting his attention to the registered Kozaks coming down the Dnieper to attack him; but many of these were in sympathy with the rebels, and after killing their pro-Polish officers they went over to Khmelnitsky at Kaminni Zaton. The Tatars, who had been watching these events, now joined Khmelnitsky, and the combined forces fell upon Stephen Potocki, whose Kozak troops also changed sides. In the ensuing battle of Kniazhey Bairak, on May 6, 1648, the Polish army was completely destroyed.

Without losing time, Khmelnitsky now marched to the upper Dnieper, while the main Polish army advanced as far as Chihiryn. No word having been received from Stephen Potocki, both his father and Kalinovski began to fear the worst and turned back, laying waste cities and farms as they went. After passing Korsun they received news that Khmelnitsky and the Tatars were approaching, and drew up to meet them in a weak position between Korsun and Stebliv. Upon sight of the large Kozak and Tatar army, however, they took fright, abandoned their camp, and resumed their retreat, only to fall into a Kozak ambush in which Khmelnitsky completely defeated the main Polish army, capturing all the officers, including both generals; these captives he turned over to Tuhai-bey.

Poland was now left without officers and without an army to face the victorious Kozaks. To add to the misfortunes of the Poles, King Wladyslaw died. He had been well liked by the Kozaks who had expected to make peace with Poland through his mediation, for neither Khmelnitsky nor the other Kozaks had expected to gain complete independence by their revolt, their aim being merely to secure the repeal of the unjust law of 1638, the restoration of the Kozak privileges, and an increase in the size of the Kozak Host to twelve thousand men, which the king too had had in mind. After the battle at Korsun, Khmelnitsky had sent delegates to the king and to the influential Polish nobles to beg for forgiveness, meanwhile taking care to advance only to Bila Tserkva in order not to arouse the Poles. At the same time, however, his agents were calling upon all Ukraine to rise in rebellion. No great effort was needed; wherever news arrived that the Polish army had been beaten, the Poles and Jews immediately packed up their belongings and fled for their lives, while the people rose, sacked the manors of the landowners, killed the gentry and the remaining Jews, seized the abandoned estates, and introduced the Kozak system of government. The way lay open for Khmelnitsky to march unopposed through Ukraine, White Russia, Lithuania, and Poland, meeting on his way only masses of oppressed peasants and townspeople eager to join him in putting an end to the rule of the Polish nobles. In many districts of Ukraine the very mention of his name was enough to set off a revolt, but Khmelnitsky had other plans and feared lest the Poles might become thoroughly aroused and crush the Kozaks completely.

While awaiting replies to his petitions, Khmelnitsky learned that the king had died and Poland was without a ruler. There was now less hope for a settlement, since there was no one with whom to negotiate a treaty, for Khmelnitsky and the Kozaks had trusted in the good will of the king but had feared the intentions of the gentry, into whose hands Poland had fallen during the interregnum. The convocational parliament met at Warsaw and discussed means of keeping the good will of the Kozaks but made no provision for meeting their demands, and although Adam Kisil was sent with a commission to negotiate with Khmelnitsky, a new army was mobilized for use against them. As soon as it became evident that the Poles were not ready to make concessions, Khmelnitsky moved with great caution, pretending to be quietly awaiting a reply from the commissioners. His Kozak officers, meanwhile, were busily engaged in raising the countryside, especially in Kiev and Braslav, which they did so successfully that Jeremiah Vishnevetsky, the owner of large estates in Ukraine and an archenemy of the Kozaks, was forced to take flight from Kiev to Podolia, and then into

Volynia, where he attempted to crush the Kozaks who were rallying under the leadership of a man with the picturesque name of Crook-nose (Krivonos), later known as Perebiynis.

Khmelnitsky marched slowly toward Volynia while waiting for the commissioners, but before their arrival a new Polish army organized in southern Volynia set out to attack him. Turning to meet it, Khmelnitsky delayed an encounter until the arrival of the Tatar horde, which joined him at Piliavtsi, a small castle on the bank of the Piliavka River, where he enticed the Poles into an engagement and fell upon them with the full force of the united Tatar and Kozak armies. The Poles lost the battle, but fell back to their camp in good order. During the night, however, a rumor spread among the Polish soldiers that their officers had deserted them, whereupon they fled panic-stricken in all directions. The next morning when the Kozaks found the Polish camp deserted they set out in pursuit of the fleeing army, killing and capturing large numbers and seizing more booty than they had ever before acquired.

The remnants of the Polish army gathered in Lviv and entrusted the chief command to Vishnevetsky, who collected money from the townspeople, the churches, and the monasteries, but doubting his ability to defend the city, retreated to Zamostia. Khmelnitsky continued westward at a slow pace, hoping for news of the election of a new king to bring the war to an end. When he reached Lviv and found the city abandoned by the Polish army, he waited for two weeks before beginning to bombard it; then, deciding to spare the city because of its Ukrainian inhabitants, he collected a ransom and departed for Zamostia. This fortress he could have captured with ease, but instead he besieged it in leisurely fashion until at last a king was elected.

The Kozaks greeted with satisfaction the accession of the new king, Jan Casimir, a brother of Wladyslaw, one of whose first acts was to send the Kozak hetman a letter to notify him of the result of the election, to promise many favors to the Kozaks and other adherents of the Orthodox Church, and to beg them to postpone further military operations pending the arrival of commissioners whom he was sending. Replying that he would submit to the will of the king, Khmelnitsky returned to Kiev.

The Ukrainian War of Liberation: Khmelnitsky hoped that with the end of hostilities a bright future would open before the Kozaks, for the securing of whose rights the war had been fought. Like his predecessors, he had aimed at nothing more ambitious than this, but had looked upon the Ukrainian people merely as a tool to be used in gaining special privileges for the Kozak Host, though the people might incidentally hope that the Kozaks would in turn help them to find partial relief from their burdens. In his eyes the only important national question was that of religious freedom, and in all probability he was not greatly interested even in that. Upon his arrival, however, at Kiev, the center of Ukrainian national life, he had an opportunity to come into close contact for the first time with intellectual circles and to study the plans, desires, and needs of the inhabitants of Ukraine as a whole.

Several years before, in the time of the metropolitan Boretsky, Kievan leaders had held lofty political aims for the nation, but there had been at that time no force capable of putting them into effect, since the Kozak Host had comprised only a small organization. But now, under the leadership of Khmelnitsky, the Kozaks had grown into a powerful army. The Patriarch Paisius of Jerusalem, who was paying a visit to Ukraine, made a number of bold suggestions to Khmelnitsky, even going so far, it is said, as to address Khmelnitsky as the King of Ukraine—the head of an independent Ukrainian state. With this encouragement from Paisius, Khmelnitsky himself began to view his position and its responsibility in a new light, and to make plans not only to enlarge his army and gain additional rights for the Kozaks, but also to promote the interests of all the Ukrainian people and the whole territory of Ukraine. These purposes he outlined to the royal commissioners, one of whom summarized them as follows:

I have hitherto undertaken tasks which I had not thought through; henceforth I shall pursue aims which I have considered with care. I shall free the entire people of Rus [Ukraine] from the Liakhs [Poles]. Up to now I have fought because of the wrongs done to me personally; now I shall fight for our Orthodox faith. All the Ukrainian people as far as Lublin and Cracow will help me, and I shall not abandon the people, for they are our right hand; moreover, in order that you may not subdue the peasants and then attack the Kozaks, I shall maintain two or three hundred thousand soldiers. I shall not draw my sword against the Turks or the Tatars, nor shall I wage foreign wars. I have enough to do in Ukraine—in Podolia and Volynia. When I march toward the Vistula I shall say to the Poles, ''Be still!'' I shall drive the dukes and the princes ahead of me, and if they become too unruly beyond the Vistula, I shall seek them out there, too.

Not a single prince or nobleman shall I permit to set foot in Ukraine, and if any one desires to eat our bread, he must be loyal and obedient to the Zaporozhian Host. I am a small and insignificant man, but by the will of God I have become the independent ruler of Rus.

These words give clear expression to the political aims of Khmelnitsky. His program may have been far from definite, but the essential feature of his new policy was his recognition of the need to defend the whole Ukrainian population, even to the extent of a struggle for the independence of Ukraine. From this point of view all the fighting of the previous year had represented a waste of energy, and as the best opportunity of freeing the Ukrainians had been lost, it was imperative to formulate a more careful plan in order to make up for past errors. When the Polish commissioners arrived in 1649 they found Ukraine fully prepared for war, Khmelnitsky refusing

even to discuss with the Poles the future arrangements
for the Kozak army, knowing well that before he could
speak of the independence of the Ukrainian people he
would have to shatter the Polish state to its very foundation.

This time, however, though successful at first, he was
in the end less fortunate than in the previous war. Immediately after the royal commissioners informed the king
of the warlike intentions of Khmelnitsky, the Polish gentry were called to the colors and began to make preparations for a campaign, while the Polish regular army set
out at once to attack the Kozaks in Volynia. Khmelnitsky
marched to meet them, but when the Poles beheld the superior Kozak army, they retreated to the strong fortress
of Zbarazh, where they were reinforced by the troops under Vishnevetsky, who was given command of the whole
army. Khmelnitsky laid siege to the fortress and harassed
the Poles by repeated attacks and a continuous bombardment, so that their situation soon became desperate, and
they had to send messages to the king to implore him to
dispatch reinforcements, which he, however, was helpless
to do, as the gentry were still in process of assembling
their forces. Finally, in order to save the besieged army,
the king marched toward Zbarazh with what troops he
had, without waiting for the gentry, and there fell into an
ambush, Khmelnitsky and his Tatar allies having hastened secretly in the direction from which the king was
coming in order to block his passage at the ford of Zboriv.
The Kozak army surrounded the king's force so completely that it was unable to move, whereupon the panic-
stricken Poles were on the verge of taking flight as they
had done before at Piliavtsi, when they thought of a way
of escape by breaking the Tatar alliance with the Kozaks.
The Poles wrote to the khan, who was with the horde in
person, to promise him everything he wished if he would
desert Khmelnitsky. The khan consented, and began to
urge Khmelnitsky to make peace with the king, where-

upon the Kozak hetman realized how dangerous it was to place reliance upon the horde, and in order to prevent the Tatars from joining the Poles in an attack upon him, accepted their advice.

Negotiations were opened, and the terms of peace were agreed upon in the early part of August 1649. Under the circumstances, Khmelnitsky could not, of course, demand independence for the Ukrainians, so that this treaty, like the earlier ones, dealt only with questions concerning the registered Kozaks and the Orthodox Church. The treaty did, however, represent an important step forward: the registered army was increased to forty thousand men and the registered Kozaks permitted to live with their families on the land claimed by the king and the gentry in the provinces of Kiev, Chernihiv, and Braslav, where they were to govern themselves without interference by the government or the landowners, and no Polish troops were allowed to live in their neighborhood. In these provinces all the higher offices were to be filled by Orthodox only, while the Kozak hetman was to rule directly over Chihiryn. The Union of the Orthodox and the Catholic churches was to be abolished, and the metropolitan of the Orthodox Church was to receive a seat in the Polish senate.

These concessions were even more sweeping than those which Khmelnitsky had hoped to gain after humiliating Poland in the previous year, but they fell far short of his new aim of independence for the Ukrainians. Though all eastern Ukraine was to be subjected to the authority of the Kozaks and their hetman, it was also true that the power and privileges of the gentry had not been abolished, and that the great majority of the inhabitants were unable to enter the registered Kozak army, and so remained as before in servitude to the landowners, a result which the peasants had not foreseen when they had answered the call of Khmelnitsky's agents. As soon as the gentry learned that serfdom was to be continued, they were eager to return to their properties in Ukraine, while Khmelnitsky, by issuing orders that the peasants should submit to their landlords, lost much of his popular support. Other events also occurred to spread dissatisfaction, among which were raids by the Tatars, who received as a bribe from Poland permission to carry off numbers of Ukrainians to be sold as slaves, this being done, according to rumor, with the consent of Khmelnitsky. The imposition of capital punishment upon those who had participated in earlier revolts also gave rise to much discontent.

Khmelnitsky fully realized that after so ambitious a revolution had come to so unsuccessful an end, the people might easily turn against him. After the futile war for independence, many emigrated in disillusion from Ukraine across the border to the Land of Free Communes under Muscovy, in the area where Kharkiv and Voronizh are now located, while those who remained in the part of Ukraine under Polish rule felt that they had been wronged and were both grieved and angry. Any man bold enough could have led a new revolt, not only against the gentry, but against Khmelnitsky, who had permitted them to return.

Owing to this dissatisfaction a long period of time elapsed before Khmelnitsky dared to register the Kozaks; and when he began to enroll them, he ordered that to the names of each Kozak household there be added the names of neighboring families, thus swelling the roll far beyond the forty thousand permitted; but even this did not satisfy the people. Though he desired to carry out the terms of the treaty of Zboriv, he recognized the fact that the inhabitants of Ukraine would not permit him to do so. On the other hand he saw that the Poles also did not fully approve of the treaty and had failed to fulfill some of its terms; they had not, for example, permitted the head of the Orthodox Church to take his seat in the senate nor had they abolished the Church Union. As it was evident that the Poles were merely awaiting an opportunity to annul the entire agreement, Khmelnitsky and his staff became convinced that they would have to take up arms again if they wished to secure the independence for which they had fought in vain at Zboriv.

Foreign Alliances: Khmelnitsky failed to profit by his bitter experience with the khan, and once more based his plans upon the support of foreign powers instead of relying upon the Ukrainian people. He urged the khan to attack Poland, and at the same time begged the sultan of Turkey, under whose protection he placed himself and whose sovereignty he recognized, to compel the khan to make such an attack. Meanwhile Khmelnitsky entered into contact with Muscovy, doing his utmost to involve Poland in a war with the tsar, and attempting to persuade Muscovy to welcome it, for which purpose he promised to recognize the sovereignty of Muscovy over Ukraine. His neighbors the Hospodar of Moldavia and the Prince of Transylvania, both of whom were subject to the sultan of Turkey, also played a part in his schemes; and he actually reached an agreement with Vasyl Lupul, the Moldavian ruler, according to which the latter was to give his daughter in marriage to Khmelnitsky's oldest son, Timosh. When Lupul, however, delayed carrying out the agreement, Khmelnitsky attacked Moldavia, devastated it, and sacked the capital of Yassy, forcing Lupul to pay him a heavy ransom and to make a definite promise that Timosh could marry his daughter.

Of all these negotiations the most significant for future Ukrainian policy were those carried on with Muscovy. The Kozaks had long been in close relations with this northern neighbor, either in friendship or in war. The two powers had waged war jointly against Crimea, and as early as the 1530's the Crimean khan had complained to the Grand Duke of Lithuania that despite an alliance between Crimea and Lithuania the Ukrainian Kozaks subject to the latter were giving aid to his enemies. Later on, Vishnevetsky had proposed an alliance between Muscovy and Ukraine for a struggle against the khan, who had by now become their common enemy; and various Kozak chieftains afterward made the claim that they had fought against the Mohammedans in the interests of Muscovy as well as those of Poland and Lithuania, and had asked compensation for their services from both the Polish and the Muscovite rulers. This friendship, it is true, had not prevented the Kozaks from attacking Muscovy at the request of the Polish government or from making such attacks of their own accord, for their leaders considered war their vocation and rendered good service to anyone who paid them, as was the practice of all military officers in Europe at this time. Because they defended the Ukrainian frontier, which was claimed by Poland, the Kozaks, however, gave their primary obedience to orders received from the Polish government.

The negotiations carried on by Kievan circles with Muscovy in the 1620's were of a different nature from the earlier ones, the aim now being to liberate Ukraine from Poland and to establish a Muscovite protectorate over the Kozak army and all Ukraine, by which they meant the Dnieper region. This the Ukrainian revolutionary leaders had attempted to do in the fifteenth and sixteenth centuries, and there is no doubt that in later times similar plans for submission to Muscovy had been discussed by both Kievan and Kozak circles. Khmelnitsky, who had at first relied upon Crimea, now began to correspond with the government of Muscovy, which he begged to aid the Kozaks and to accept a protectorate over "all Rus"—all Ukraine. The Muscovite statesmen understood this to mean that Ukrainian Rus, as the old state ruled over by the dynasty of Volodimir, would be united to the Muscovite tsardom and would recognize the claimant to Volodimir's legacy—the Tsar of Muscovy—as their "tsar and autocrat." Khmelnitsky, reading their thoughts, suggested as much through his envoys. For a long time he had carried on intrigues in the old Kozak fashion, in an attempt to draw as many neighboring countries as possible into his struggle against Poland by telling each what it was eager to hear, and he now sent a message to the tsar to say that he would willingly recognize him as tsar and autocrat, the Muscovite envoy having evidently informed him that he would win his objectives by using this form of expression. Nevertheless, at the same time Khmelnitsky recognized the supremacy of the sultan, who accepted him as a vassal, according to a letter dated in 1650, in which the Turkish ruler informed him of this fact and presented him with a caftan in token of protection and sovereignty; he also carried on correspondence with the Prince of Transylvania to urge him to become the king of Ukraine. Later he submitted himself to the protection of the King of Sweden, while simultaneously signing treaties with the King of Poland, whom he recognized as overlord.

Khmelnitsky had political talent and undoubtedly loved his Ukraine and was devoted to its interests, but he schemed and intrigued too freely, and, as has been said, placed too great reliance upon foreign powers rather than awakening the strength and energies of the people themselves. Although in his speeches in Kiev in 1649 he had proclaimed that his aim was to free all Ukraine, he apparently did not keep this program clearly in the forefront of his plans, but remained for some time a Kozak, placing purely Kozak aims and interests above the new, national, all-Ukrainian ideals. In the course of time his ideas would have matured and become clarified, but life did not stand still, and the fate of Ukraine had to be decided at once. It was no easy task to direct the ignorant popular masses or the unruly Kozaks, who thought nothing of changing hetmans every few months; furthermore, it was not advisable to submit important national problems to the Kozak assemblies for decision. Khmelnitsky ruled the Kozaks with an iron hand, but he had little faith in their perseverance and still less in that of the people as a whole, and it was for these reasons that he sought help from foreign powers.

For Khmelnitsky personally, and for all Ukraine, it was highly unfortunate that just at the moment when Ukrainian national aspirations had reached their highest point the treachery of the Tatars had forced the signing of the unfavorable treaty of Zboriv. As a result the masses of the people were so disillusioned and discouraged that it was difficult henceforth to arouse in them any interest in revolution. The rebels had not been professional soldiers, but peasants who had hoped to free themselves from subjection to the Poles, to become owners of the product of their toil, to live in liberty and the pursuit of happiness, and to improve their economic and cultural lot. When the revolution had failed to give them their expected freedom, they had migrated in large numbers beyond the Dnieper toward the outermost frontier of Ukraine and over the border itself into Muscovy, thus depriving Khmelnitsky of their support and forcing him to look abroad for aid in liberating Ukraine.

Keeping a careful watch upon Khmelnitsky's dealings with foreign powers, the Polish government also began to make preparations for war as soon as the treaty had been signed. The first Polish attack, however, had an unexpected result, General Kalinovski falling upon the Kozaks in the province of Braslav in the winter of 1650, only to suffer at Vinnitsia another crushing defeat like that of Korsun. Poland was not yet fully prepared for war, but Khmelnitsky, instead of following up his victory, wasted time by insisting that the Tatars come to his aid. When the khan finally appeared, he was in an angry mood because the sultan, at the request of the Kozak hetman, had forced him to undertake the campaign, and he avenged himself at the first possible occasion by deserting the hetman in a decisive battle at Berestechko and taking flight with his army. Khmelnitsky followed in an effort to persuade him to return, but was seized by the Tatars and

carried off. The Kozak officers, abandoned by their hetman and knowing how jealous he was of his authority, did
not continue their advance but began to fall back. While
crossing a field of deep mud behind their camp the army
became disorganized, whereupon the Poles attacked and
overwhelmed them. Potocki then marched across Volynia
from the north with the main Polish army, while a Lithuanian contingent went south and captured Kiev. Khmelnitsky escaped from the khan and began to mobilize an army
at Korsun, but the Kozaks had now lost all desire for further conflict, and the peasants were more bereft of hope
than ever. The Poles, too, had finally learned to appreciate the courage of the Ukrainian people in defense of
their rights and were willing to call a halt. Kisil was
again sent to arrange terms of peace with the Ukrainians,
and in the middle of September 1651 a new treaty was
signed at Bila Tserkva.

This second treaty placed limitations upon the rights
granted to the Ukrainians by the treaty of Zboriv, the
number of registered Kozaks being now reduced to twenty
thousand, who were to reside and to enjoy Kozak privileges only in the province of Kiev. No mention was made
of the abolition of the Church Union, and the nobles and
the government officials were to return to their estates,
though the collection of taxes was postponed for several
months. Khmelnitsky was to send home the Crimean horde
and was henceforth to carry on no negotiations with foreign powers.

This time Khmelnitsky apparently did not consider the
treaty binding, but merely accepted it so that he and his
soldiers could recuperate. In the spring of 1652 he again
summoned the Tatars to accompany him and his son
Timosh to Moldavia, where the latter was to be married,
the hetman apparently suspecting a Polish attempt to
prevent Timosh from crossing the border. Kalinovski,
who was in fact waiting in Podolia with a Polish army to
block the passage of Timosh, was surprised by the elder

Khmelnitsky with the main Kozak army and the Tatars and suffered a crushing defeat, the Polish general himself being killed in the battle, in which the Kozaks took ample vengeance for their defeat at Berestechko in the previous war. After the battle the war dragged on in desultory fashion, as both the Ukrainians and the Poles were exhausted and on the verge of starvation as a result of the long conflict. The chief center of operations was in Moldavia, which was invaded by the Poles; they laid siege to Timosh in the city of Suchava, and in the course of the siege he sustained a wound from which he died. Khmelnitsky, who had not arrived in time to relieve his son, met the Poles in Podolia not far from Zhvaniets, where the two armies faced each other for a long time, neither wishing to attack. Finally the khan again deserted the Kozaks and made a separate agreement with the Poles, according to which Poland was to restore to the Kozaks all the rights specified in the treaty of Zboriv.

This time, however, Khmelnitsky did not accept the terms of a treaty made without his participation, for he had received news that his new ally the Tsar of Muscovy was beginning hostilities against Poland, the Muscovite government having decided, after long hesitation, to establish a protectorate over Ukraine.

The Muscovite Protectorate: Muscovy was eager to take part in the Kozak war in order to regain for herself the territory she had lost during the "Time of Troubles," and if possible to gain additional land. She had hesitated for a long time to risk involvement because of the defeats she had in the past suffered from Poland; but the Muscovite statesmen believed that if the Poles conquered Khmelnitsky, their next aim would be to turn the Kozaks and Tatars against Muscovy. Accordingly, after Khmelnitsky's defeat in 1651, the tsar decided to take part in the Ukrainian struggle and to justify his intervention by the old and customary grounds of defense of the Orthodox faith and protection of the Orthodox people. For the sake of formality a delegation was sent to Poland to demand the restoration to the Kozaks of all the rights guaranteed in the treaty of Zboriv; but when Poland refused to comply, the estates general (*zemski sobor*) which met in Moscow in the autumn of 1653 decided that the tsar was entitled "to accept under his high hand Hetman Bohdan Khmelnitsky and the entire Zaporozhian Host, with its cities and lands," and authorized him to take these by force from Poland.

Khmelnitsky was immediately informed that Muscovy would afford him the protection which he desired and would send an army in the spring to attack Poland, a decision which was most welcome, as he had no other allies at the time, Turkey being unwilling to intervene, the khan and his Crimeans having proved untrustworthy, and negotiations with Moldavia and Transylvania ending without result. The government of Sweden, which had long been hostile to Poland and to the Polish kings, had been making efforts since the 1620's to enter into close relations with the Kozaks, but had not indicated any willingness to make war, and in any case the Kozaks now wished to break away completely from Poland. When Khmelnitsky learned that a delegation of important Russian nobles had come to Ukraine to administer an oath of loyalty, he ceased to be disturbed over the Poles or the Tatars, but designating Pereyaslav as the meeting place, left the scene of the war and went there.

When Khmelnitsky met the tsar's delegates in the early part of January 1654, they at once requested him to call an assembly of the entire Kozak Host to give formal recognition to the sovereignty of Moscow. Unfortunately there is little detailed information regarding the assembly, except for a report by the Muscovite envoy, Buturlin, according to which Khmelnitsky placed before the Kozaks the question of submission to the tsar and received their assent. Then there was read a declaration from the tsar promising to maintain friendly relations with the Ukrainians and to defend them from all their enemies. The Muscovite delegates now proposed that the whole assembly should go to the Cathedral to swear allegiance to the tsar, but a dispute arose when Khmelnitsky requested the tsar's representatives first to take an oath in the name of the tsar that their ruler would not surrender Ukraine to Poland, would defend the land from its enemies, and would leave intact the Ukrainian rights and privileges—such an oath as the Polish kings upon assuming office were accustomed to take in their pacta conventa. This proposal the Muscovites refused to accept, since their tsar, they said, was an autocrat who ruled according to his own will and did not make pledges to his subjects. Though this reply caused great displeasure among the Kozak officers, they finally swore unconditional allegiance in order to avoid breaking off negotiations; and after they had sworn the envoys sent agents to all the cities and villages of that part of Ukraine which was under Kozak rule to administer the oath of allegiance to the local inhabitants.

Khmelnitsky began to be disillusioned as soon as this question of the oath was raised. When, however, he sent his own envoys to the tsar to present a petition from the Kozak Host regarding the future relations between Ukraine and Muscovy, to his great satisfaction nearly all the points in the petition were approved, the most important being as follows. The rights and liberties of all the people living in Ukraine were recognized. All the Kozak judges and the elected city bailiffs were to be free to perform their functions without interference. The Kozaks were to elect their hetman, but were to inform the tsar of the result. The hetman and the Zaporozhian Host were to be permitted to receive foreign envoys, but were obliged to notify the tsar's government of any circumstances which might lead to conflicts. And finally, the Kozak army was to number sixty thousand men. It is upon this so-called treaty of Bohdan Khmelnitsky or treaty of Pereyaslav that all later Ukrainian claims to autonomy were based.

To some extent these terms, for example the one regarding foreign envoys, gave Ukraine new rights by recognizing it as an independent and autonomous state, bound to Muscovy only through the person of the tsar. But the tsar, in applying the treaty, did not grant complete self-government to the Ukrainian people, who were not permitted to elect their higher officials in a democratic manner, nor did he allow the locally elected officials to collect all the Ukrainian taxes for deposit in the Ukrainian treasury and expenditure for local needs. Although the Ukrainians disliked these infringements upon their autonomy, they could present no strong opposition for fear the tsar might lose his interest in Ukraine and neglect their cause in his war against Poland. Nevertheless, the opposition of Muscovy to Ukrainian self-government and democracy left a painful impression, especially as it became evident that Muscovy intended to send her own officials to take the place of the hated Poles, a few being sent to Kiev at once, where they built a new fortress, stationed a garrison, and acted like absolute masters, paying no attention to the rights of the hetman, and in time similar military governors made their appearance in other cities. Moscow also refused to recognize the autonomy of the Church in Ukraine, but attempted to subordinate the Kievan metropolitan and bishops to the authority of the Patriarch of Moscow.

Khmelnitsky and the Kozak officers (*starshina*) realized how different these arrangements were from those which they had hoped to receive from Moscow and in what direction they were leading. What they had wanted was aid in their struggle for independence from Poland and freedom from the landlords, but Muscovy appeared to look upon Ukraine as a new territorial acquisition for herself, over which she wished to gain complete control. It is true that she began to wage war against Poland, but it was with the aim of annexing White Russian lands, for which she had long been greedy; and she now requested Khmelnitsky to dispatch his army to White Russia to assist the Muscovites. He complied with this request, and in return the government of Muscovy sent an army to Ukraine to join Khmelnitsky there for a march to Volynia and an eventual juncture with troops from White Russia. Khmelnitsky, however, lost his desire for aid from the Muscovites when he discovered that they were becoming firmly entrenched in Ukraine and were making use of every ill-considered word and every careless act to gather the reins of Ukrainian life in their hands. He began to fear that the only result of the Muscovite campaign would be new claims to domination.

The campaign was a dismal failure. In spite of reprimands from the Muscovite government, Khmelnitsky did not even leave the province of Kiev, his chief aim now being to extricate himself from the difficult position into which he had fallen by joining Muscovy. He was giving his full attention to the new developments in international relations which, once set in movement, now took an entirely different turn.

Between Muscovy and Sweden: In the early part of the war in White Russia, the Muscovite and Kozak armies had gained easy successes, for most of the cities had voluntarily surrendered to them. The Kozaks conquered the part of White Russia that lay along the border of the Kozak lands and organized there a new Kozak regiment, while the Muscovite forces overran the country as far north as Vilna. This overwhelming victory over Poland encouraged other countries to take advantage of the opportunity; and in Sweden the newly crowned king, Charles X, decided to renew the old conflict with Poland, Charles to act in concert with the Prince of Transylvania, who had been for many years allied to Sweden as a member of a coalition of Protestant states against Catholic Austria and Poland. The two allies now invaded Poland, where they expected to receive aid from the Protestant land-owners who had suffered as severely as had the Orthodox from oppression by the Catholic gentry and the government; they also had in mind Khmelnitsky, since he had for years been carrying on friendly negotiations with both Transylvania and Sweden in an attempt to incite them against Poland. Up to this time his efforts had met with no success, and he had therefore been forced to seek help in Moscow; but now, just when the Ukrainians were becoming disgusted by the aggression of the Muscovites, Sweden and Transylvania were making preparations to attack Poland and of their own accord willingly joined Ukraine. Khmelnitsky relied upon this new alliance to aid him not only in freeing the Ukrainians from Poland, but in breaking his ties to Muscovy; he therefore joyfully accepted the invitation of the Swedish king to join in a common war against Poland and withdrew from the Muscovite campaign to await a move by Sweden, though still keeping with him the Muscovite army.

During the winter of 1654–55 Khmelnitsky fought a defensive campaign against Poland, which had gained an ally in the Crimean khan when the Kozaks had joined with Muscovy. The Polish forces and the Tatar horde invaded the province of Braslav and then the province of Kiev, where Khmelnitsky and the Muscovite army met them at Bila Tserkva, near Okhmativ. The Muscovite army proved weak, but Colonel Bohun arrived in the nick of time with a Kozak regiment to drive back the Polish-Tatar forces, whereupon the khan abandoned his allies. Khmelnitsky did not press the campaign further, until in the spring of 1655 he received a letter from King Charles notifying him of preparations for an invasion of Poland and appealing to him to attack at the same time. The hetman then marched to Kaminets in Podolia (Kaminets-Podolsk), and from there to Lviv and on to Lublin, but as he was accompanied by the Muscovite forces under the command of Buturlin, his hands were tied, and he was not free to make use of his own troops as he wished. After the defeat of Potocki at Horodok, all Galicia lay open before him, but he was unwilling to capture the Galician cities for Muscovy to occupy with her troops. Instead of seizing Lviv he accepted a ransom from the city; and during the negotiations with the townspeople there, Vyhovsky, the Kozak secretary and an intimate friend of Khmelnitsky, begged them not to deal with Buturlin or to recognize the sovereignty of the tsar, while Khmelnitsky himself wrote to the King of Sweden that in order to exclude Muscovy from western Ukraine he had made no conquests there. The Swedish king advised the Kozaks to break off their alliance with Moscow, warning them that Muscovy, with its autocratic form of government, "would not tolerate a free people," would not live up to her promises of independence for Ukraine, and would enserf the Kozaks. Khmelnitsky at first attempted to persuade Sweden to avoid a rupture with Muscovy, he and his officers having apparently decided to make of Ukraine a neutral state under the protection of Muscovy and Sweden, and perhaps even of Turkey, with whom he had renewed diplomatic relations as soon as he had lost faith in the Muscovites. As it was, however, difficult to maintain neutrality with both Sweden and Muscovy, circumstances compelled him to make a choice among his neighbors. As Sweden began to gain victories in the war and soon occupied all northern Poland, the Poles made efforts to incite a quarrel between Sweden and Muscovy, giving the tsar to believe that Poland would elect him as king and thus unite the whole country to Muscovy. In the end he made an armistice with Poland and attacked Sweden, a shift which both improved the position of Poland and aroused the fears of Khmelnitsky, who complained that Muscovy would now give Ukraine back to the Poles in violation of her pledge. What angered him most was that the negotiations between Muscovy and Poland had been carried on in secret, without his being informed, without the participation of the Kozak envoys, and without anyone's knowing for what purpose, except that it probably boded no good to Ukraine.

As soon as the Polish king had made a truce with Muscovy, he began efforts to recover Ukraine, employing secret diplomacy, deceit, and extravagant promises, even offering a guarantee of complete self-government; Khmelnitsky, however, refused to commit himself. Moscow now insisted that he break off relations with Sweden and join in the war, but the hetman valued his alliance with Sweden more highly than that with Muscovy, the government of which was revealing more and more clearly its imperialistic aims. He was aroused to anger by dictatorial efforts to direct his activities from Moscow and also disapproved of attempts to lessen Ukrainian autonomy by placing military governors in the Ukrainian cities, becoming more and more convinced that for the best interests of his country he would have to break off relations. According to a story told by Vyhovsky to the Muscovite nobles in an attempt to gain their favor, Khmelnitsky was moved to such anger by his officers' complaints against Moscow during a Kozak council that he "shouted like a madman" that there was no way left open but to part with the tsar and seek aid elsewhere.

In 1656 Khmelnitsky concluded a close alliance with Sweden and Transylvania in which he promised to assist the Swedes with his Kozak army against any of their enemies, including Muscovy, and agreed to partition Poland with them. Early in 1657 the combined forces of Sweden, Transylvania, and the Kozak Host attacked Poland in spite of opposition by the tsar. Khmelnitsky himself was too ill to lead his army, but he sent Zhdanovich, the colonel of the Kievan district, into Galicia with three regiments. These Kozaks united with an army brought by Prince George Rakoczy from Transylvania, and together they marched in the direction of Warsaw with the intention of joining the Swedish forces there. If successful, this war was intended to destroy Poland, give western

Ukraine to the Kozaks, and free the hetman from subservience to Moscow. The campaign, however, failed. The
Poles defeated Rakoczy and then dispatched the Tatars
against him, so that he was obliged to make peace with
Poland; Zhdanovich, who had no greater success, was endangered by a mutiny in his army; while the Kozaks,
learning that their hetman was dying, feared the difficulties that might arise after his death and announced that
they would not fight against Poland without the approval
of the tsar. Meeting with the Muscovite envoy in the
course of their campaign, they begged him to inform his
master of their decision, whereupon Zhdanovich, faced
with this resistance, gave up the campaign and returned
to his home.

Even before this blow fell, Khmelnitsky had been a
very sick man. Distressed by the news, he summoned
Zhdanovich to his side, became hysterical, and suffered a
paralytic stroke, from which he died six days later, on
July 27, 1657. Just at the moment when the future of
Ukraine was being decided, she had lost the only person
capable of directing her affairs. Bohdan Khmelnitsky was
succeeded by his inexperienced and incompetent son
George, who was elected because of his father's great
name while the latter was still alive.

The Hetman State: The great national movement set in
motion by Khmelnitsky resulted in the establishment of a
new institution of government, the Hetman state (*Hetmanshina*). Even during the first decades of the seventeenth century the military Kozaks had been settling
down on the land, while at the same time the civilian settlers—peasants and townspeople—originally subject to
the ordinary government, were accepting the rule of the
Kozaks and becoming members of the Kozak organization. The division of the Kozak Host into regiments led
to a division of their territory into corresponding regimental districts, there existing as early as the decade of
1630 the Chihiryn, Cherkassy, Kaniv, Korsun, Bila

Tserkva, Pereyaslav, and Lubny regiments, though the
Lubny district was nominally the property of the nobles
and not at the disposal of the crown. Even at that time the
Kozak colonels, captains, and squad leaders were not
merely military officers in time of war, but had begun to
perform in time of peace administrative and judicial functions for the whole Kozak populations of their respective
districts, in which they replaced every other organ of authority.

During the period of Khmelnitsky's leadership, the Kozaks had established their system of government throughout an extensive area in eastern Ukraine, especially in the
provinces of Kiev, Braslav, and Chernihiv, where they had
driven out all other governing powers, there remaining
of the old officials only the elected wardens in the towns
and the old administration and courts on the monastic
and church estates, the population outside these areas
being freemen, most of whom became Kozaks. Those who
did not enlist with the Kozak Host registered as townspeople, regardless of whether they lived in cities or in the
peasant villages, and from these people various taxes
were collected for the benefit of the army treasury. The
Kozak population was not subject to taxation, but performed military service, and during the endless wars the
Kozaks endeavored to enlist as large numbers as possible,
while the freemen also considered it wiser to register with
them in order not to be forced back into serfdom.

The number of regiments in Khmelnitsky's army was
not always the same, but according to the registration
records of 1649–50 there were nine west of the Dnieper—
those of Chihiryn, Cherkassy, Kaniv, Korsun, Bila
Tserkva, Uman, Braslav, Kalnik, and Kiev; while east of
the river there were only seven—those of Pereyaslav,
Kropivna, Mirhorod, Poltava, Priluki, Nizhin, and Chernihiv. The regiments, composed of companies of about
one hundred men each, were not always equal in size,
there being in some less than ten companies, though others

contained as many as twenty; furthermore, the number
of Kozaks in each company varied considerably, several,
according to the census of 1649–50, including as many as
two or three hundred men each, and others less than a
hundred. The colonel (*polkovnik*) governed his regimental district with the assistance of a regimental staff—a
regimental chief ordnance officer, a regimental judge, a
regimental adjutant, and a regimental secretary—while
the captain (*sotnik*) administered his company district,
and the squad leader (*otaman*) ruled over a Kozak community. In theory the military authorities had jurisdiction over the Kozak inhabitants only, but in practice they
enjoyed a general power of control over the whole population, except in the larger cities and on the estates of the
nobles and the Church, which were less dependent upon
the lower Kozak officials, being directly subject to the hetman. There were at first very few estates left in the hands
of the nobility, as many of them had been abandoned during the popular uprisings.

The military type of organization, although theoretically restricted in its jurisdiction to the Kozak army, began as early as Khmelnitsky's long hetmancy to assume
the character of a territorial government. In the course
of his negotiations with Muscovy, Khmelnitsky declared
that the Kozak army would govern Ukraine according to
ancient usage, and that the Muscovite government would
assume the functions formerly held by the Polish authorities; but when Muscovy began to install military governors (*voyevoda*) in Ukraine and attempted to collect taxes
from the non-Kozak population and otherwise to control
them, the Kozak officers, who had for many years been accustomed to ruling over all the inhabitants, at once felt
that there was no room for a foreign power which might
weaken the importance of the Kozak Host. The hetman,
under the new order, became the real ruler of the country
and the chief executive of the Ukrainian government,
everyone in the land being forced to submit to his au-

thority. However, as he was also the head of the military organization, his regional army representatives likewise acquired a general jurisdiction over the whole population. The army staff became the hetman's cabinet of ministers; thus the council of general staff officers, made up of the chief ordnance officer, the general judges, the general adjutant, and the general secretary, formed a ministerial council attached to the hetman for discussion of all matters of general or political significance, each general officer exercising supervision over the officers who filled corresponding positions in the regiments. The Officers' Council, which included the general officers, the colonels, and the army staff, met for important deliberations and made decisions in problems pertaining to the general welfare of Ukraine.

The Kozak officers and the Ukrainian civilians both felt the imperative need of an autonomous body able to act for all classes and for the whole area, and the Kozak army organization performed this function. The basic principles of the constitution of the new self-governing Ukraine were not, however, carried out to a logical conclusion or put into formal effect. An effort to do so was made at the time of the Hadiach Union with Poland in 1659, but the proposed constitution was never ratified. This absence of clear definition as to the relationship of the civil government to the Kozak administration laid the way open to claims by foreign powers, especially by Muscovy, the interference of which caused confusion and irritation. It was, moreover, poor policy to admit to the councils which governed the whole country only Kozak army officers to the exclusion of the other classes of the population—the clergy, the townspeople, the peasants, and the gentry— whereas the very fact that the Kozak type of government was unfamiliar made it difficult to apply and evoked both misunderstanding and opposition.

The new arrangement, connected as it was with the army, savored too much of caste rule, and this characteristic hindered the transition to a new territorial and national government. The old military autonomy under a general army assembly (*rada*), which was called into session by any one of the Kozaks on any occasion and which could unceremoniously depose the hetman or other officers, was not suited to the new conditions of life, which demanded a strong and permanent authority able to direct the destinies of the nation, especially in these difficult and critical times. Khmelnitsky, blessed with talent and good fortune, had succeeded in exalting the personal authority of the hetman, and under him the army assembly had met only at such times as the hetman felt the need for it; these times occurred rarely, and the meetings were chiefly for the sake of form. Problems had been debated in the Officers' Council only when the hetman chose to lay them before it, but this limitation on the freedom of the council had been an innovation and had caused discontent among important Kozak factions, especially that of the Zaporozhians, while the successors of Khmelnitsky often failed to maintain their control over the general assembly of the whole army. Any such weakening of the hetman's power both lowered the importance of the office itself and threatened the efficiency of the whole Kozak system as a general territorial government.

It was not easy to uproot at once the old understanding which had grown out of the past history of the Kozaks to the effect that the center of Kozak activity and organization was below the rapids in the Zaporozhe country, at the central fortress or Sich, where the hetman was traditionally elected and Ukrainian policy formulated. As early as the decade of 1620–30, when the Kozaks were making themselves masters of the Townships on the upper Dnieper and were creating a strong organization there, the Sich had begun to lose its significance as the Kozak capital. Under the new Kozak regime the center of Ukrainian life came to be the residence of the hetman and his staff, at which place all matters were dealt with by the army court or the military chancellery, while the claims of the Sich to its former rights now appeared obsolete. During the time of Khmelnitsky's hetmancy the Sich had become a mere refuge for the men who formed the frontier guard of Ukraine and had failed to retain any political importance, but after his death the Kozaks of the Zaporozhe began to insist that they should again have the privilege of electing the hetman and the officers; they also complained against the usurpation of power by the Officers' Council at the expense of the Sich.

These internal conflicts contained the seeds of destruction. If Khmelnitsky had lived longer or if Ukraine had enjoyed a few years of peace after his death, the discontent could not have grown so swiftly, for the Ukrainian people displayed great organizing ability. They were making rapid political progress and if left to themselves could undoubtedly have made the new regime stable and enduring, settling their internal disputes and adapting themselves to the Hetman state. Unfortunately what they lacked was an opportunity to live in peace long enough to establish the new government on a firm foundation, for Ukraine existed under perpetual threat of war, surrounded by selfish neighbors who constantly interfered in its internal affairs and thus undermined the props of the Ukrainian political system.

Besides all these difficulties, there was one more—the sharp social conflict between the mass of the people and the Kozak officers' government. The ordinary inhabitants had rebelled in order to free themselves from the oppression of the nobles, to expel the landlords, and to become owners of the products of their labor. Above all else the people feared the return of the gentry to Ukraine and the restoration of the old serfdom, and for this reason were unwilling to make any compromise with Poland, while viewing with suspicion any effort to restore the old aristocratic tradition. Meanwhile, however, the Kozak officers, after gaining political power, began to take the place of

the former gentry in other respects, evincing a desire to
gain possession of the abandoned estates, to seize the
villages, and to people them with their serfs. Having
grown up under an aristocratic system, they knew no
other way in which to advance their material interests;
and accordingly at the earliest opportunity, with the dispatch of the first mission to Muscovy in 1654, they began
to beg the Muscovite government to give them titles to
various estates and the privilege of colonizing these with
serfs. It is true that, knowing well how antagonistic the
people would be, they feared even to show these titles in
Ukraine; but the Ukrainians heard rumors to the effect
that the new officials were following the old path of aristocracy and, suspecting them of selfish intentions, developed a hostility toward them, which is evidenced by a
poem of the time which contains the phrase:

Ah, dukes, you are indeed dukes! To you belong meadows and
    pastures;
Nowhere can my poor brother the landless Kozak, stop to graze
    his horse.

After the death of Khmelnitsky this animosity to the
Kozak officers became general, the lower classes of both
Kozaks and civilians coming to distrust their officials
more and more. This lack of popular support, which un-
dercut the authority of the officers and hindered them in
carrying out their policies, was highly unfortunate, for
the officers really had the political interests of all classes
at heart and were working for the liberation of all
Ukraine.

The Union of Hadiach: In a situation fraught with such
difficulties the election of Khmelnitsky's weak and inexperienced son George was a fatal mistake which the officers did not dare to oppose in the presence of the dying
hetman but intended to correct later. After Bohdan's
death young Khmelnitsky was in fact recalled and replaced as hetman by Ivan Vyhovsky, who had long been

the Kozak army secretary and an intimate friend of the late ruler. Charges were later made that he was elected only as acting hetman pending the time when George should finish his studies and come of age, and that he had illegally seized the Kozak mace of authority and made himself the regular hetman. Contemporary documents do not, however, mention any such arrangement, and the facts in the case are that Vyhovsky was given a regular appointment from the very first; but since the officers feared that the "Kozak rabble" who were in favor of George Khmelnitsky might protest, they had elected him at a meeting of the Officers' Council and not in a general army assembly.

The newly elected hetman was intellectually the superior of George Khmelnitsky, being not only a man of experience and wisdom but also a passable statesman as well as an undoubted Ukrainian patriot and a convinced believer in Ukrainian self-government, in which respect he saw eye to eye with the Kozak officers; but he was not as popular as his great predecessor, Bohdan Khmelnitsky, had been. He was of petty Ukrainian gentry stock from Kievan Polisia; in his early years he had held various positions of a clerical nature and never had special military aspirations, but had found himself in the army quite by accident, having, according to rumor, fallen into the hands of the Tatars after the battle of Zhovty Vody and having been ransomed from them by Khmelnitsky. Moreover, the circumstance that he had not been elected in a regular assembly, but in opposition to the general will, aggravated the difficulties of the position in which he had been thrust at a critical period in national history.

In his initial acts Vyhovsky attempted to continue the policy of Khmelnitsky of maintaining as far as possible neutrality with Muscovy and Sweden, Crimea and Poland, and thus to preserve the peace of Ukraine, to uphold order and good government, and to strengthen his own position. He gained the alliance of the Crimean horde, which had previously been on the side of Poland, and also brought to a conclusion the negotiations already begun with Sweden. The result was a treaty according to which the King of Sweden bound himself "to recognize and proclaim the Zaporozhian army with all its territories a people free and subject to no one," to defend their rights and liberties against encroachment by any hostile power, and in particular to demand of Poland the recognition of the freedom and independence of the "Zaporozhian army," that is, of eastern Ukraine, and to expand its area to include western Ukraine. These were important promises, but they were given too late, when Sweden was already losing ground. Almost immediately the King of Sweden was forced into a war with Denmark, obliged to withdraw his army from Poland, and thus prevented from aiding Ukraine. There were still Poland and Muscovy to deal with, the former of which continued its negotiations with the Kozaks, begging them to return to submission to the Polish crown and promising them extensive privileges which even included Ukrainian autonomy. Muscovy, however, having decided to profit by the death of Khmelnitsky, made efforts to extend her authority over Ukraine by collecting taxes, installing military governors in other Ukrainian cities besides Kiev, and planning to abolish the independence of the Ukrainian Church. All these acts were in violation of Ukrainian rights and provoked to anger both the inhabitants and the Kozak officials, but Vyhovsky was strongly under the influence of Muscovy and did not protest because he was not sure of his own position and expected that in return for his loyalty the tsar would protect him against his enemies in Ukraine, who were becoming more numerous. His hopes in this regard did not materialize.

Because Vyhovsky had been elected by the Officers' Council and not by a general assembly, various opponents of the officers exploited the situation for their own purposes, especially in the Zaporozhe, which was most hostile to the new regime and favored the old democratic army practice, according to which the army assembly, centered at the Sich, had full authority. The Zaporozhian Kozaks were supported by the regiments of Poltava and Mirhorod, who were neighbors and close friends, and among whom a wave of hostility to Vyhovsky now surged up, of which the colonel of the Poltava regiment decided to avail himself in order to force the hetman from office and to be elected in his place. In addition to the common complaints against Vyhovsky that he had been fraudulently elected by a few officers without the vote of the assembly and without the support of the Zaporozhe, word was spread that he was not a Kozak but a Pole, and that he was not working for the welfare of the people and the army, but wished to sell Ukraine to Poland. In order to put an end to these malicious lies Vyhovsky summoned a new assembly consisting of representatives of the different regiments. Although he was reëlected by this gathering and then officially recognized by the Muscovite government as legal hetman, his opponents were still not satisfied; and Pushkar, together with Barabash, the custodian of the Zaporozhian Sich, sent agent after agent to Moscow with the complaint that he had been illegally elected, that he was a traitor, that he was not wanted by the army, and so on. Vyhovsky expected that because of his loyalty the government of Muscovy would support him against his enemies and would aid him in suppressing the hostile faction by ordering his opponents to obey him or even by giving him armed assistance in subduing them; the tsar, however, maintained contact with Vyhovsky's attackers, who appeared in the guise of loyal servants of Muscovy. He received their agents, sent them letters, and extended to them a number of favors, so that they were able to begin a whispering campaign that Moscow had sided with them and did not consider Vyhovsky to be the real hetman.

When Vyhovsky realized that Muscovy was not supporting him, he decided to take steps to curb his opponents.

Though he was directed from Moscow not to use force, but to wait and see if Muscovy could not persuade his opponents to stop their criticism, it was impossible for him to delay action; and in the spring, with the aid of the Tatars, he undertook a campaign across the Dnieper and defeated the Poltava regiment. Pushkar himself was killed, the province of Poltava conquered, a new colonel placed in command, and all the leaders of the mutiny punished severely. After this clash, Vyhovsky and his followers considered that relations with Muscovy were severed. The metropolitan, Dionysy Balaban, who had been appointed by the Ukrainians without the consent of Moscow, now moved to Chihiryn, while the champions of Ukrainian autonomy spread propaganda among the people against Muscovy, warning them that if the tsar once established his control over Ukraine, he would transport the inhabitants to Muscovy and Siberia, as was actually being done from White Russia, would carry off the Ukrainian priests, and would send Russians to take their places. The following declaration was sent to the European powers to explain the reasons for breaking off relations with Muscovy and for declaring war against her:

We declare and testify before God and the entire world that our last war with Poland had no other cause or motive but defense of the Holy Eastern [Greek Orthodox] Church and the liberty enjoyed by our ancestors, the love of which liberty gave us strength to follow our immortal leader, Bohdan Khmelnitsky, and our secretary, Ivan Vyhovsky. We laid aside our private affairs in order to do the will of God and of the people, and for this purpose entered into cordial relations with the Tatars, with Christine, the august Queen of Sweden, and later with His Majesty Charles Gustavus [Charles X], the King of Sweden, to all of whom we have been loyal. We never gave Poland any reason to violate her treaty with us, for we religiously observed our obligations set forth in it. We had no other motive when we accepted the protection of Muscovy but to preserve and increase our liberty with the aid of God and the shedding of our blood. Muscovy made many promises, while our army expected that because of the similarity of religion and our willing submission the Grand Prince [tsar] of Muscovy would be just, friendly, and sympathetic to us, would treat us fairly, and would not attempt to take our liberties from us, but would rather increase them in accordance with his promises. In these hopes we were deceived. The ministers of the Grand Prince won over their august master within the year, when negotiations were entered into between Poland and Muscovy, and in the hope of gaining the Polish crown it was decided to oppress and to enslave us, while they carried their intentions so far as to attempt to involve us in a war with Sweden and thus oppress and enslave us the more easily. . . .

The most serious offense charged against the Muscovite statesmen was that they had betrayed Ukraine by entering into an alliance with Poland, another accusation being that they had brought dissension and anarchy into Ukrainian political life by supporting various rebellious leaders, the manifesto closing with the declaration:

Thus are revealed the cunning and deceit of those who at first by means of internal strife and later by open use of their own forces prepared for us a yoke of slavery without provocation on our part. In order to preserve our liberty we are forced to defend ourselves and to throw off the hated yoke, and in this task we appeal to our neighbors for aid. We are not to be blamed for the approaching war; we have been loyal and remain loyal to the Grand Prince, and take up the sword against our will.

Sweden, which was to have been an ally of Ukraine against Muscovy, had been reduced to impotence; in the 1660's she withdrew from the war and made formal peace with both Poland and Muscovy. In order to secure another ally besides the Crimean horde, Vyhovsky decided to conclude the lengthy negotiations with Poland. In the summer of 1658 the Ukrainian representative, Colonel Paul Teteria, of the Pereyaslav regiment, and the Polish representative, Stanislaus Bieniowski, signed a treaty at

Hadiach on September 6 (September 16 Gregorian calendar),* according to which Ukraine was to return to Poland, but as a separate and autonomous state to be known as "The Grand Duchy of Rus." This treaty was known as the Union of Hadiach.

Though the treaty never went into effect, it is nevertheless interesting as an indication of the aims of Vyhovsky and his friends, who were the leading Ukrainian statesmen of the time. Under what was known as the Union of Hadiach, eastern Ukraine—the provinces of Kiev, Braslav, and Chernihiv—was to become a separate state, with its own ministers, treasury, and coinage, similar to the grand duchy of Lithuania. It was to have a joint parliament with Poland and Lithuania, and was to be ruled by a hetman elected with the participation of all estates or classes of the inhabitants, who would nominate candidates, one of whom the king would appoint as hetman. The Kozak army would consist of thirty thousand men, and in addition the hetman would have at his personal disposal ten thousand mercenaries. The Orthodox faith was to enjoy equal rights with the Catholic, and the metropolitan and bishops were to have seats in the joint senate. The Academy of Kiev would have the same privileges as the Academy of Cracow, and another academy was to be opened in one of the cities of Ukraine.

The treaty was hurriedly prepared, and many of the points in it were not carefully considered or explained. A petition to include western, as well as eastern Ukraine in the grand duchy of Rus was sent with the treaty to the

* With Ukraine linked to Russia, the author has from this point on employed the dates of the Julian or ''Old Style'' calendar in use there, until with Ukrainian independence the Ukrainian National Rada reverted as of February 16, 1918, to the Gregorian calendar in use in Central and Western Europe. While the original dates have been retained in this translation, the Gregorian dates have been added in parentheses in the case of a few of the more important events. Gregorian dates are derived by adding to the dates of the Julian calendar 10 days in the seventeenth century, 11 days in the eighteenth, 12 days in the nineteenth, and 13 days in the twentieth (Editor).

parliament, which was to ratify the document. Vyhovsky lost no time in signing the treaty in order to secure armed aid from Poland against Muscovy.

The War with Muscovy: War began with an unsuccessful attempt to expel the Muscovite military governor from Kiev, whereupon the government of Muscovy proclaimed Vyhovsky a traitor and ordered the Kozaks to elect a new hetman. Upon learning of the treaty with Poland, however, the Muscovites were so dismayed that they prepared to abandon their aggressive policy and sent Prince Trubetskoy to open negotiations with Vyhovsky in which they promised him exoneration from all charges and to make many other concessions, including the removal of the Muscovite governor from Kiev if Vyhovsky so desired. Vyhovsky, believing that the tsar was not in earnest, refused to turn back.

Early in 1659 the hetman led his army east across the Dnieper to subdue his opponents, who no longer concealed their hostility once Muscovy had declared against him. When the Muscovite army was dispatched to block him he retreated across the Dnieper, but the Muscovites began to overrun Siverian Ukraine and laid siege to Colonel Hulianitsky in Konotop. Vyhovsky waited for the Tatars, upon whose arrival he again marched to eastern Ukraine to relieve Konotop. The Muscovite army, lacking exact information as to his strength, came out to meet him, was caught in a crossfire between the Kozak and Tatar armies, and was annihilated, two Muscovite commanders being taken prisoners. Trubetskoy abandoned Konotop and evacuated Ukraine, leaving it in the hands of Vyhovsky.

Vyhovsky, however, was incapable of making good use of his victory. He failed to expel the Muscovite garrisons from the Ukrainian towns and withdrew westward across the Dnieper, since the hostile Zaporozhians under Sirko, the custodian of the Sich, had attacked Crimea, forcing the Tatars to abandon him, and had then gone on to storm his capital of Chihiryn. The pro-Muscovite faction beyond the Dnieper again raised its head to spread charges that Vyhovsky had offered submission to Poland, charges which were the more readily believed as the details of the Union of Hadiach were not known and the people feared Polish landlordism so thoroughly that they wished to have no further contacts with Poland. The Polish reinforcements stationed in the province of Siveria recalled to their minds so violently the old hatred against the Poles that the regiments hostile to Vyhovsky revolted, killing not only Poles but also George Nemirich, a cultured Ukrainian nobleman who was a supporter of Vyhovsky's views and was by many considered the real author of the treaty of Hadiach. The revolt spread west of the Dnieper as well, where the aroused Kozaks declared they would not endure Polish rule, Colonel Michael Khanenko of the Uman regiment joining with the Sich Kozaks under Sirko to proclaim that they wished George Khmelnitsky as hetman instead of Vyhovsky.

Early in September 1659 the armies of George Khmelnitsky and of Vyhovsky met at Hermanivka, but Vyhovsky's Kozaks went over to Khmelnitsky, leaving him only his mercenaries and his Polish allies. The Kozaks now held an assembly at which they shouted that they did not wish to submit to Poland or to fight against Muscovy and evinced such hatred for Vyhovsky that he was forced to leave the meeting for fear of being killed on the spot. Then, in an atmosphere of rejoicing and enthusiasm, the Kozak Host elected George Khmelnitsky as hetman and demanded that Vyhovsky surrender the hetman's mace, which he gave up together with the other insignia of office.

The Officers' Council, consisting of supporters of Vyhovsky, realized that the Union of Hadiach was dead, since the army was stubbornly opposed to Poland. They accepted the fact that they would have to return to submission to Moscow but decided to make the best of matters and to force Muscovy to promise that in future she would not interfere in Ukrainian internal affairs. They persuaded the new hetman to be in no haste to begin negotiations with the tsar.

Encamping on the Dnieper near Rzhishchev, the Kozaks awaited action by Moscow. When Trubetskoy presented an appeal to recognize the sovereignty of Muscovy on the old basis, the new hetman, upon the advice of the officers, sent Peter Doroshenko to present new demands, which included provisions that in future all Ukraine should be free of Muscovite military governors except for the city of Kiev, and that any Muscovite army sent to Ukraine should be placed under the command of the hetman. It was further asked that the Muscovite government should not address any communications directly to the officers of the army or receive any from them, and that in general the authority of the hetman should not be infringed upon. The hetman was to be permitted to carry on correspondence with foreign countries independently, and if the Muscovite government entered into any discussions with foreign countries involving Ukrainian questions, Ukrainian delegates were to participate in the transactions. The Ukrainian clergy were to remain under the authority of the Patriarch of Constantinople, as had been decided at the time of the election of the metropolitan Dionysy Balaban.

Trubetskoy made no reply at the time, as the instructions from his government contained entirely different terms, but he invited the hetman and the officers to come to his headquarters to conclude the negotiations. When they arrived at Pereyaslav in compliance with his request, they discovered that they had fallen into a trap; for Trubetskoy now informed them that there was no basis for negotiating since it was necessary to call a general assembly of the Kozak army. He not only called the assembly, which was hostile to the officers, but also brought up the Muscovite army. Under these circumstances Khmelnitsky's officers could not even present their demands, and without opposition Trubetskoy revealed that his government had instructed him that the old "treaty of Bohdan Khmelnitsky" had been revised and supplemented. Under the new terms the hetman was obliged to send his Kozaks wherever the tsar directed and was forbidden to send them anywhere against his will, while hetmans could be changed only with the tsar's permission. Members of the Muscovite faction were not to be punished without an investigation by Muscovy, the associates of Vyhovsky were forbidden to attend meetings of the assembly or to accept high offices under penalty of death, and lastly, Muscovite military governors were to be stationed in Pereyaslav, Nizhin, Chernihiv, Braslav, Uman, and Kiev.

These alterations limited and in fact destroyed Ukrainian autonomy, but faced by a hostile assembly and the Muscovite army, Khmelnitsky and his staff were at the mercy of Trubetskoy and did not dare to protest. Moscow had upset all their plans, but there was nothing they could do but accept the humiliation and conceal their anger at the deception. They made no effort to seek the real cause of their own weakness and the victory of the enemy, which had in fact resulted from their living too far removed from the masses and from basing their policy, as Bohdan Khmelnitsky had done, upon the aid of foreign alliances rather than upon their own people. They continued to make these old mistakes, seeking the aid of Poland whenever they faced the shrewd and deceitful policy of Muscovy, or turning to Moscow when the people revolted because of fear of Polish landlordism. After each such futile attempt, new troubles fell upon the shoulders of the Ukrainian population, until they were too disheartened to continue the struggle, lost all faith in the officers and their policies, and at the same time lived in terror of the extension of the power of Muscovy and Poland over their lives.

Within half a year a new dispute arose between Mus-

covy and Poland, and in the summer of 1660 the Muscovites decided to invade Galicia in order to force Poland
to evacuate White Russia. The Muscovite general, Sheremetiev, led several Ukrainian regiments into Volynia,
while George Khmelnitsky marched through the southern
part of the same province to protect it against an attack
by the Tatars. The Polish generals, however, received aid
from Crimea and attacked Sheremetiev's army at Lubar,
enveloping it so completely that not even a message could
be sent through to Khmelnitsky. After a few days the
harassed Muscovite general began to retreat in the hope
of joining the other Ukrainian army and with this intention marched as far as Chudnov. Meanwhile the Poles
were attempting to persuade Khmelnitsky to sever his
relations with Muscovy and to unite with Poland on the
terms of the Union of Hadiach of 1658. Vyhovsky, too,
was eager to renew this treaty and urged the hetman to
accede. Unable to effect a juncture with Sheremetiev and
faced by Polish and Tatar forces more powerful than his
own, Khmelnitsky hesitated to act, though his officers,
provoked at Moscow because of the deception of the previous year, raised no objections. The Poles, however,
were no more farsighted than the Muscovite statesmen,
and perceiving the critical position of the Ukrainians decided not to renew the treaty of Hadiach in its original
form but struck out of it all clauses referring to the grand
duchy of Rus. The Kozaks were at first unwilling to accept these alterations, but as this was not the time to object, they finally gave their assent. Sheremetiev was now
forced to surrender his ammunition and supplies to the
Poles and to promise to withdraw all the Muscovite
troops from Ukraine. Unmoved by pity for the Kozak
army under his command he turned it over to the Poles
and Tatars in order to prevent them from plundering his
Russian forces and taking them captive. This detestable
act aroused in Ukraine great indignation and anger
against Moscow.

CHAPTER XV

DISSOLUTION AND DECLINE

The Partition of Ukraine: Even now the Muscovite statesmen were not farsighted enough to abandon their old policies, satisfy the few demands of the Ukrainians, and thus regain the friendship of the people and win them over from Poland. Instead, the tsar continued the old practices toward Ukraine, depriving the inhabitants of their rights, stationing garrisons in the towns, and attempting in other ways to gain complete control of the country. It was Moscow's good fortune that the Poles did not take full advantage of their victory at Chudnov, but left the Muscovite garrisons undisturbed in Ukraine to suppress the Ukrainian uprising which broke out against Muscovy after the battle; later Polish campaigns across the Dnieper failed to win the support of the local inhabitants and merely turned them against their old Polish oppressors. Finally the Kozaks in eastern Ukraine, led by Jacob Somko, a relative of George Khmelnitsky, and Vasyl Zolotarenko, the colonel of the Pereyaslav regiment, agreed to submit themselves to Muscovy, of whom they asked permission to elect a hetman in place of Khmelnitsky, each of the leaders expecting to receive the appointment as a reward for his services.

The tsar, however, delayed the election because he wished to bring under his authority the Kozaks of the western part of Ukraine as well. Young Khmelnitsky could not decide what action to take, since the Kozak officers had no wish to return to the "yoke of Moscow" after the Muscovites had failed to permit the promised autonomy of Ukraine, and at the same time neither the rank and file of the Kozaks nor the civilian population desired Polish sovereignty. The hetman had begged Poland to dispatch a large army into Ukraine in order to strengthen his government, but Poland was too poor to send a strong contingent and the small detachments sent from time to time merely aggravated the situation. Moreover, the Polish nobles were again swarming into Ukraine and attempting to force the Kozak families to surrender to them the estates to which they laid claim, which action not only irritated the inhabitants but so provoked the Kozaks that George Khmelnitsky finally gave orders to his army to expel these nobles from Ukraine and never permit them to return. In addition to these difficulties the young hetman was discouraged because the Crimean horde, under the pretense of aiding him, was plundering the countryside, carrying off the inhabitants as slaves, and even claiming that Ukraine should be under the protection of Crimea. Some of the higher officers were disgusted with both Poland and Muscovy because they had made promises to Ukraine which could not be kept, and these officers saw no objection to recognizing the supremacy of the khan; the ordinary people, however, were violently opposed to such a step.

Before long George Khmelnitsky realized that the Ukrainians everywhere were becoming dissatisfied with his policies, and, losing courage, he resigned from office in 1663 to become a monk. In his place the Kozaks elected as hetman his brother-in-law, Paul Teteria, who had the reputation of being a shrewd politician, it being rumored that he had purchased his office by lavish gifts to the Officers' Council. Since he leaned definitely to the side of Poland in his policies, his election forced the statesmen of Muscovy to postpone their project of annexing western Ukraine.

In the eastern half of the country beyond the Dnieper, where the two colonels, Somko and Zolotarenko, were competing for the hetmancy, a condition of anarchy prevailed, with the Muscovite government supporting now one and now the other. It was not long before a third candidate appeared and became a serious threat to the other two. The new claimant was Ivan Brukhovetsky, the chief (*koshovy*) of the Zaporozhian Sich, who opposed the Kozak officers as Pushkar and Barabash had done. In the fall of 1659, when he received his appointment, he assumed the hitherto nonexistent title of koshovy-hetman, and playing cleverly upon Zaporozhian ambitions advocated the theory that in accordance with old traditions the office of the hetman belonged to the Sich and that the Zaporozhians should have the decisive voice in elections. Brukhovetsky took full advantage of the disordered conditions in the Zaporozhe to promote his interests, and living among Kozaks who came from the poorer classes he portrayed himself as one of them, a man of the people and an opponent of such "dukes" as Somko and Zolotarenko. He became the subject of the epic poem *Fesko Hanzha Andiber, the Hetman of the Zaporozhe,* in which, disguised as a poor Kozak, he is described as strolling about the Kozak country. On one occasion he entered a tavern where there were three rich "dukes," "Havrilo Dovhopolenko of Pereyaslav, Veytenko of Nizhin, Zolotarenko of Chernihiv"—in other words, Somko, Zolotarenko, and the other officers—all of whom ridiculed the poor Kozak. But when he pulled out his wallet and covered the whole table with gold coins they changed their tune. He made no effort, however, to be admitted to their company, but ordered his comrades to beat the "dukes" in order to teach them respect for the ordinary Kozaks.

The essence of this poem is its description from the point of view of the Zaporozhian Kozaks of the struggle of their koshovy-hetman with the city colonels, in which in the end Brukhovetsky emerged as victor. He did not win his victory, however, by fighting in the knightly fashion appropriate to an epic but by falsely accusing his opponents of treason to the Muscovite government. By this vicious propaganda he was unwittingly digging the grave of the liberties of the Ukrainian people; for although his activities were beneficial to Moscow, they did great injury to the Ukrainians. He recommended himself to Muscovy as the most docile man to carry out her plans and thus undermined the power and influence of his chief opponent, Somko. Realizing the seriousness of the situation Zolotarenko at the last moment joined with Somko, but it was now too late; Brukhovetsky appeared at the last assembly in Nizhin in June 1663 with the support of a large number of Zaporozhians and of nonregistered Kozaks of the southern regiments who sided with them. Somko, too, brought his regiment to the meeting as well as a cannon, and a brawl developed which was not halted until Brukhovetsky had succeeded in persuading Somko's troops to rebel against their officers, who were obliged to flee with Somko to the Muscovite camp, only to be arrested as insurgents. After this disturbance the meeting continued without further interruption, Brukhovetsky being elected and receiving the approval of the Muscovite commissioners, while Somko, Zolotarenko, and a few others were condemned as traitors and, though innocent, were beheaded. After gaining control, the followers of the new hetman began to persecute the officers of Somko's regiment who had joined them, and according to the Ukrainian chronicles the people suffered serious oppression as a result of the election.

Doroshenko's Aims: With the elections of Teteria and Brukhovetsky the hetman's office was split, and there were now two hetmans, one of whom ruled over Right Bank Ukraine west of the Dnieper under Polish protection and the other over Left Bank Ukraine to the east under the sovereignty of Muscovy. This partition so weakened Ukraine as to make almost hopeless the prospect of liberation. It had been difficult enough to secure independence when the army was united under a single hetman; it was a much more serious problem now that the country's forces were divided, especially with the two parts quarreling with one another. To make matters worse, as a result of the many uprisings and the ensuing anarchy selfish leaders were enabled to seize control, which they used only for their own personal gain with no thought for the rights and welfare of Ukraine itself.

Even the adventurers who gained the upper hand by means of intrigue found it impossible to remain in power. Teteria was the first to sense the weakness of his position, and as soon as he became hetman, advised the Polish king to send a strong army across the Dnieper to annex Left Bank Ukraine. The king decided to make one last attempt and after the close of the year crossed the Dnieper with a large Polish force supported by Tatars, and burned and pillaged the smaller towns, avoiding the fortified cities. He marched as far as Hlukhiv, which he besieged but failed to take, abandoning the siege upon learning of the approach of a Muscovite army. Since the Ukrainians showed great hostility to the Poles and since this last Polish effort to conquer eastern Ukraine had proved both futile and costly, the Poles gave up the attempt and returned to their side of the Dnieper.

During the invasion of eastern Ukraine much opposition to Poland had developed in western Ukraine as well, which Vyhovsky was accused of having incited. He was illegally tried by a military tribunal and executed, but the revolts continued, and when the Russian army accompanied by Brukhovetsky and his Kozaks pursued the Poles into western Ukraine the hatred for Poland became even more intense. Brukhovetsky could easily have conquered western Ukraine but he neglected his opportunity; and the Muscovite government, tired of war with no hope of being able to regain this area, was even less eager. The Polish army, especially the forces of the ferocious Czarniecki— he who caused the bones of Khmelnitsky to be burned— attempted to put down the revolt by savage repression, but the insurrections continued and spread ever more widely. Finally the Polish army was withdrawn for use elsewhere, leaving the hetman, Teteria, in a more difficult position than ever; and early in 1665 he was disastrously

defeated by a revolutionary leader named Drozd, whereupon he packed up his goods and departed from Ukraine.

Western Ukraine had thus succeeded in gaining freedom from Poland, but had no desire, after the earlier experience, to submit to the rule of Muscovy. Again it was
suggested that the protection of Crimea be sought, the
first to take steps in this direction being an officer named
Opara, who with the approval of the khan proclaimed
himself hetman in the summer of 1665, but was shortly
afterward arrested and deposed by the Tatars. The Crimean horde now gave their support to another candidate,
Peter Doroshenko, whom the Kozaks accepted as hetman
in August 1665. The new hetman was well known and
highly respected among the soldiers, and spoke of himself as a "fourth generation Kozak." He had been a colonel during the period of Khmelnitsky's hetmancy and
after his own election continued to play a leading part
in Ukrainian national life for several years.

A man of great energy, Doroshenko worked heart and
soul for the independence of Ukraine. Though he had accepted the hetmancy from the hands of the Tatar khan, it
was his chief desire to carry on Khmelnitsky's old policy
of making Ukraine a neutral state among Poland, Muscovy, and Turkey, in order to ensure complete freedom
and self-government. Dissatisfied by the protection af-
forded by the Tatars he followed the example of Khmelnitsky and went over the head of the khan to enter into
negotiations with the sultan of Turkey, from whom he
received assurances of assistance in case of need; he
recognized the sultan as his protector and the Porte in
turn promised to aid Ukraine to free herself within her
ethnographical borders—from Peremyshl to Sambir,
from the Vistula to the Niemen, and from Sivsk to Putivl
on the Muscovite frontier. The khan of Crimea now received orders from his suzerain the sultan to aid Doroshenko on all occasions. The hetman did not at once attack Poland but had no hesitation in expelling the Polish

military detachments from Ukraine wherever he found them, even forcing them out of the province of Braslav and occupying it.

Thus Right Bank Ukraine became free and neutral. As soon as Doroshenko was firmly entrenched there and had gained the support of the head of the Ukrainian Church, Metropolitan Joseph Nelubovich Tukalsky, whom the Poles had held for two years in prison at Marienburg and had then finally released, he decided to liberate eastern Ukraine also, in this case from the grip of Muscovy. Observing that Brukhovetsky was losing his influence, Doroshenko and Tukalsky entered into negotiations with him. While attacking Moscow from their side of the river, they gave him to understand that Doroshenko was even ready to resign as hetman of western Ukraine in his favor in order to restore the old unity of the hetmancy. In spite of his hopeless position Brukhovetsky now began to incite an insurrection against Muscovy in the expectation of receiving aid from Doroshenko and the Tatars.

Brukhovetsky, like Teteria, soon came to realize that having gained his office by means of intrigue, he could not hold it securely. He tried to please Muscovy as best he could in order to keep her support, even going to Moscow in 1665 to pay homage to the tsar, an act which had been demanded without success of previous hetmans. While in Moscow he asked for a Muscovite maiden in marriage and received a favorable reply, the daughter of Saltykov, an official of the court, being wedded to him amid great festivities. He requested of the government a residence in Moscow and promised to keep a nephew there as hostage. In compliance with the desires of the Muscovite statesmen and in the names of himself and of the Officers' Council he also begged the tsar to rule over Ukraine, to collect all the taxes for his own use, to send in military governors and garrisons, and to appoint a Muscovite metropolitan to administer the Ukrainian churches. As a reward for his services Brukhovetsky was given a title of nobility and

many rich gifts, including a large estate in Siveria. Upon
his return to Ukraine, however, he discovered at once that
he had gained the hatred of the people. The clergy, the
army officers, the common people, and even the Zaporozhian Kozaks rose against him, the clergy protesting because he intended to subordinate them to the Muscovite
authorities, while the Officers' Council was indignant because of his destruction of Ukrainian self-government
and even more so because he had sent all his opponents to
Moscow to be dispatched into exile. The people hated him
because he permitted Muscovy to collect taxes, but they
also complained because upon his return to Ukraine he attempted to collect from the people as much as he could for
his own army treasury before the foreign tax collectors
arrived. At once a vehement outcry went up against the
corruption of the hetman and the oppression suffered by
the Zaporozhians, who after examining the situation protested against their recent representative, but Brukhovetsky retaliated according to ancient custom by accusing
the Kozaks of treason to Muscovy. When the census tak-
ers arrived from Moscow and began to record the population and their property, and to lay heavy taxes for the
account of the tsar, and when the tax collectors began to
appear, the hatred against Brukhovetsky and his Muscovite supporters increased. Never had the people heard
of such high taxes. Moreover, the Ukrainians complained
that when Muscovy had approved the grant to Poland of
western Ukraine in the treaty of 1667, this partition was a
violation of the promises made when Ukraine submitted
to the protection and sovereignty of the tsar.

Revolts began to break out. Brukhovetsky requested
Muscovy to send an army to Ukraine to deal severe punishment to the disobedient, and to raze, burn, and destroy
the revolting cities and villages. Even Muscovy, however,
was unwilling to comply with this brutal request, and the
hetman now realized that if the Ukrainian movement
against him continued he would lose the support of the

tsar in spite of all his efforts to gain it. Accordingly, he decided to accept Doroshenko's offer of aid for a revolution against Muscovy and thus regain his former popularity. He entirely failed to understand the extent of the cunning of the western Ukrainian hetman, who, while inciting Brukhovetsky against the Muscovites, was at the same time carrying on negotiations with them. Doroshenko also made peace with Poland, it being agreed that all the Polish garrisons should be recalled and that Right Bank Ukraine would recognize the sovereignty of the Poles. He now desired to reach an understanding with Muscovy under which she too would be satisfied with a nominal protectorate over Left Bank Ukraine while permitting him to rule it in fact. Unaware of Doroshenko's plans, Brukhovetsky led a revolt against Muscovy early in 1668. His Officers' Council supported him and all over the country people slaughtered or expelled the oppressive Muscovite officials, while Brukhovetsky sent out letters urging the people to drive out the Muscovites and notified the Muscovite garrisons that they must withdraw from Ukraine under threat of attack, which they did except in Kiev and Chernihiv. In the spring Brukhovetsky made preparations for defense against the Muscovite army which had invaded Ukraine under Romodanovsky. The Tatars came to his aid; and Doroshenko was on his way from across the Dnieper, supposedly to bring him assistance, but during the march Doroshenko sent messengers to Brukhovetsky ordering him to surrender his office and the hetman's insignia in return for the province of Hadiach, over which he could rule as long as he lived. This demand struck Brukhovetsky like a bolt from the blue and, deciding to resist, he arrested Doroshenko's agents. But when Doroshenko arrived with his army at Opishnia, the suppressed hatred of the Ukrainians toward Brukhovetsky came into the open, even his revolt against Muscovy having failed to gain him popular support. The Tatars at once deserted him. The Kozaks, proclaiming in unison that they would not resist Doroshenko, then began to plunder Brukhovetsky's supply train and finally seized him and delivered him to Doroshenko, who ordered him chained to a cannon, after which the Kozaks beat him to death "as if he were a mad dog." At Doroshenko's orders he was buried in Hadiach in a chapel which he himself had built. His conqueror then moved eastward to attack the Muscovites, but Romodanovsky evacuated Ukraine without fighting.

By the spring of 1668 all that part of Ukraine which had formerly composed the Hetman state was in the hands of Doroshenko. Fortune was with him. With a strong army at his command he was in a position to deal with the tsar and to force him to respect the Ukrainian rights and liberties, and his plan of autonomy for Ukraine under the sovereignty of Moscow and the protection of Poland and Turkey had come near to being realized. His course, however, followed that of Vyhovsky after the victory at Konotop; he failed to consolidate his gains. Called home to Chihiryn, reputedly by a family scandal, he appointed Demko Mnohohrishny, the colonel of the Chernihiv regiment, as acting hetman of eastern Ukraine, and left. His departure cost him all that he had gained.

As soon as Doroshenko was gone, the Muscovite army invaded the frontier province of Siveria, and the pro-Muscovite groups there at once became active. The inhabitants realized that the Muscovites would not evacuate the area of their own accord but were unable to oppose them and so remained quiescent. The metropolitan of Chernihiv, Lazar Baranovich, who ruled the eastern dioceses, now came to the fore as a champion of the cause of Muscovy and used his influence to persuade Mnohohrishny to surrender to Romodanovsky. Mnohohrishny waited for some time for Doroshenko to send reinforcements, but as they were not forthcoming, he finally gave up Chernihiv to the Muscovites. The Kozaks were then summoned to Novhorod-Siversky, where they elected

Mnohohrishny as hetman and resolved to recognize a protectorate by Muscovy on condition that the autonomy of Ukraine be guaranteed. The newly elected hetman assumed the title of hetman of Siveria, and asked Baranovich to become a mediator between him and Muscovy. Mnohohrishny requested the tsar to renew the old treaty of 1654 signed with Khmelnitsky at Pereyaslav and to remove his troops from Ukraine, in return for which concessions the Kozaks would recognize his sovereignty and sever relations with the Tatars, threatening in case of refusal to defend their rights until they perished or were driven from their native land into Poland. These were courageous words but uttered too late. Mnohohrishny could have negotiated with Muscovy and still remained loyal to Doroshenko, but now that the Muscovite statesmen had taken possession of the country they intended to keep it; they continued their intrigues until they had gained their objective.

The Downfall of Doroshenko: The election of Mnohohrishny undermined the power of Doroshenko, to whom it came as a complete surprise. For some time he ignored his opponent, thus placing the latter in a precarious situation and forcing him into greater submission to Muscovy, while the tsar carried on negotiations with both hetmans in an effort to discover which would be the more docile. Both hetmans held the same conception of Ukrainian autonomy, but the position of Mnohohrishny was the more difficult because he was hetman in Siveria, which was occupied by Muscovite troops, and he could therefore not press his demands. Nevertheless he displayed a high sense of patriotism in defending the rights of his people.

The Muscovite government was informed by its officials that the demands of Doroshenko and Mnohohrishny reflected the attitude of the Ukrainian people in their refusal to permit the presence of Muscovite garrisons or to be ruled by Muscovite governors. Since this information was sent to Moscow by Sheremetiev, the military governor of Kiev and the most distinguished and trusted representative of Muscovy in Ukraine, Mnohohrishny was enabled to press his demands. The tsar, however, had no intention of yielding to the claims of the Ukrainian people but on the contrary made use of every crisis in Ukrainian affairs to extend his authority, confident that Mnohohrishny would have to yield, which he finally did. In March 1669 at an assembly held in Hlukhiv, Muscovy proposed a new treaty to replace the original agreement between Ukraine and the tsar, that of Khmelnitsky of 1654. Mnohohrishny, the Officers' Council, and Metropolitan Baranovich vigorously protested against the armed encroachment of Muscovy upon Ukrainian privileges and opposed the acceptance of the new treaty, and several days passed before they accepted it on March 6. In addition to the military governor already in Kiev, others were to be stationed with Muscovite garrisons in Pereyaslav, Nizhin, Chernihiv, and Oster, but they were not to interfere with the courts or other local administration. The treaty, the so-called Hlukhiv Articles, was signed, and Mnohohrishny was recognized as hetman.

At first Mnohohrishny held only Siveria and Kiev, but later on the Priluki and Pereyaslav regiments were added to his domain. The southern regiments were at first loyal to Doroshenko, but before long new hetmans were elected by the Kozaks of the Zaporozhian region, Peter Sukhovienko in 1668, and Michael Khanenko in 1670, after Doroshenko had defeated his predecessor. The Zaporozhian hetmans introduced confusion into the frontier regiments and undermined Doroshenko's influence by attempting to win over the khan, so that from 1669 on he was obliged to send repeated punitive expeditions against them; and when Doroshenko became involved in a dispute with the Polish government because it refused to renew the Union of Hadiach and so recognize the Kozak right to rule over western Ukraine, Khanenko opened negotiations with the Poles. As he did not demand any rights whatever for the

Ukrainian people, the Polish government readily recognized him as hetman in place of Doroshenko, and although the Poles were unable to assist him, Khanenko and his limited forces placed new obstacles in the already difficult path of Doroshenko.

As soon as Mnohohrishny was approved as hetman Doroshenko became reconciled with him, though he still continued to make complaints about the "frontier hetmans." Both Mnohohrishny and Doroshenko held similar political views as to their relations to Muscovy and made no attempt to interfere with each other. Both were deeply grieved by the partition of Ukraine between Muscovy and Poland in 1667 by the treaty of Andrusovo, and were particularly concerned over the arrangement with regard to Kiev, which was to remain in the hands of Muscovy for two years and then be transferred to Poland. When the time for the transfer came, however, Muscovy did not surrender the city, and this alteration in the original terms gave rise to great uneasiness in Ukraine and many complaints against Moscow.

Unable to secure justice from either Poland or Muscovy, Doroshenko began to place hope in Turkey; but as his people hated the Turks and would not tolerate his policy in this respect, he was obliged to carry on his negotiations with the sultan in secrecy. The plundering of Ukraine by his Tatar allies caused great dissatisfaction, but Doroshenko could see no other possible source of support and so appealed to the sultan to make good his promise to assist the Ukrainians in freeing themselves from Poland. His appeals, however, went unheeded until at length, in 1671, the Sultan Mohammed IV decided to invade Ukraine in fulfillment of his agreement. He informed Poland that he was about to attack her in behalf of Ukraine in retaliation for Polish attacks upon his vassal, Doroshenko, and in the spring of 1672 he invaded Ukraine with a large army, sending the Crimean khan ahead to join the hetman. The joint Tatar and Kozak

forces scattered the Polish contingents stationed in
Ukraine as well as Khanenko's Kozaks. The sultan himself laid siege to the poorly supplied fortress of Kaminets-Podolsk, which quickly surrendered, and from there
he marched to Lviv and besieged it. Poland lacked courage to resist such a powerful army and hastened to sign
the treaty of Buchach in which she surrendered her claims
to Podolia in favor of Turkey and promised to pay an annual tribute. "Ukraine within her ancient boundaries"
was given to Doroshenko, and Poland promised to remove
her garrisons.

Thus one part of Doroshenko's project had been accomplished—the liberation of Ukraine from Poland. It
appeared that he would experience no great difficulty in
carrying out the other part—that of uniting the whole
Ukraine under the protection of Muscovy but with a full
guarantee of Ukrainian autonomy, since the tsar, frightened by the sultan's victory, was ready to make liberal
concessions to Doroshenko to prevent the Turks from occupying eastern Ukraine, there being rumors to the effect
that the sultan was planning to return in the next year to
conquer that region. The tsar summoned the estates-general, which decided to receive Doroshenko and western
Ukraine under the protection of Muscovy; Poland by the
treaty of Buchach having abandoned her claims to the region. It was understood that Muscovy would fulfill the demands of Doroshenko, which repeated those of 1668: all
Ukraine including the Zaporozhe was to be united under
one hetman, all Muscovite garrisons were to be removed
from Ukraine, even from Kiev, and the government of
Muscovy was to defend Ukraine but was not to interfere
in her internal affairs.

Though Muscovy was prepared at the time to accept
these terms, this conciliatory attitude was of short duration. In the first place, Doroshenko no longer had as ally
east of the Dnieper a man of similar political views. Mnohohrishny had been unable to maintain the support of his

officers, who looked upon him with contempt as the son of
a peasant, while he, suspecting them of intrigues, ruled
them with a heavy hand. This severity caused his downfall. The offended officers entered into secret negotiations
with a Muscovite regiment and in March 1672 seized him
and sent him to Moscow under accusation of treason; then
they asked permission to elect a new hetman. Though
Mnohohrishny was not guilty the Muscovite boyars tortured him, stripped him and his family of their property,
and exiled them to Siberia. There they lived in poverty
for many years, but he outlived all the enemies who had
had a share in exiling him. The Officers' Council was permitted to elect a new hetman, the election taking place on
Muscovite soil under the protection of a Muscovite army,
since the officers feared that the people might avenge their
exiled leader. The newly appointed hetman, Ivan Samoilovich, known as ''Popovich'' (the son of a priest), was
forced to promise that he would not remove officers except
after trial by a military tribunal; and the Hlukhiv Articles were renewed, but so amended as to omit the right
of Ukrainian delegates to participate in deliberations
with foreign powers concerning Ukrainian affairs, thus
removing the last vestige of Ukrainian autonomy.

Doroshenko was on no such friendly terms with the new
hetman as he had been with Mnohohrishny, for Samoilovich was very subservient to the Muscovite authorities,
in whom he had great faith. Fearing that Doroshenko
might succeed him, and wishing to further his personal
ambitions, he dissuaded the tsar from entering into any
understanding with his rival, advised him to fight rather
than to yield, and finally succeeded in persuading him to
go to war.

Another difficulty for Doroshenko arose from the fact
that Poland had abandoned her claims to western Ukraine
only under pressure from the Turks but had never become
reconciled to this loss, had not removed her garrisons,
and now supported Khanenko against Doroshenko, de-

claring that if Doroshenko were accepted under the protection of Muscovy this would be looked upon as a breach of the armistice. As the tsar was not eager to become involved in a war with Poland, Doroshenko's project of uniting Ukraine under Muscovite auspices was blocked.

Meanwhile, as the Turks did not repeat their invasion in the next year the Poles lost their fear of them, and the Polish general Sobieski took the initiative by attacking and defeating them at Khotyn, an exploit which proved that the Turks were not greatly to be feared and that they could give Doroshenko little protection, while he for his part had lost prestige among the Ukrainians by inviting them to assist him. Prior to this time his vassalage to Turkey had been kept secret, but it now became known; and rumors circulated that the Turks had changed the Christian churches in Podolia into mosques, had destroyed the religious relics, and had forcibly converted Christian children to Mohammedanism, for all of which outrages the inhabitants laid the blame upon Doroshenko, since it was he who had invited them in. His enemies made use of these rumors to incite the people against him, and even his close friends accused him of responsibility for the Turkish atrocities.

Samoilovich rightly judged that his opportunity had come and urged Muscovy not to make peace with Doroshenko but to attack and conquer him. The tsar finally ordered Romodanovsky to join Samoilovich and to cross the Dnieper in order to come to an agreement with Doroshenko, but not to begin hostilities. Samoilovich, however, desired to destroy Doroshenko's power completely so that he might not become a source of danger in future, and instead of negotiating, invaded western Ukraine with his own army and that of Muscovy. The campaign set out from Kaniv, and everywhere Doroshenko's enemies welcomed the invader. Doroshenko appealed in vain to the Turks and Tatars for aid; the khan, however, angered because he had appealed to the sultan to force the Crimeans to come to his aid, stubbornly refused to assist him. Almost all his friends and soldiers deserted him, and he remained helplessly at his headquarters in Chihiryn. Samoilovich, disregarding him completely, stationed his own garrisons in Kiev and Cherkassy. Deputies of the ten regiments then existing in western Ukraine recognized the rule of Samoilovich and the sovereignty of Muscovy, and being summoned to Pereyaslav, on March 15 (25), 1674, in response to a proposal by Romodanovsky, "with willing and quiet voices," according to the report sent to Moscow, they approved Samoilovich as their hetman. Khanenko, who also attended the assembly, surrendered his claims and pledged support to the new Kozak chief, who was thus proclaimed sole hetman of united Ukraine.

"The Ruin": Doroshenko was so taken aback by this sudden change in his fortunes that he was ready to give in. He sent a young agent, Ivan Mazepa, to congratulate Samoilovich, whom he rebuked, however, for using force instead of negotiating, and he was on the verge of according the hetman recognition when couriers arrived from Sirko, the chief of the Zaporozhian Sich. This famous campaigner, who had previously been on friendly terms with the Muscovites, had returned from exile as their bitter foe. He now advised Doroshenko not to go to Samoilovich or to give himself up, and promised to bring him the support of the Zaporozhian Kozaks, who refused to acknowledge the authority of the new hetman. News also came that Sobieski, who for many years had been counseling Doroshenko to break off relations with Moscow and to recognize the protection of Poland on his own terms, was about to be elected King of Poland. When in addition word reached him that the Tatars were coming to his aid, Doroshenko decided to continue the struggle, which turned out to be a bitter one.

Doroshenko sent Mazepa to Crimea to hasten the aid of the khan, and at the same time sent other messengers to the sultan to complain that the khan was reluctant to help him; he begged for immediate assistance, pleading that if relief was not forthcoming within a month or two, he would have to abandon Ukraine and take refuge in Turkey, though as a matter of fact he had no means of maintaining himself in power and should have yielded for the best interests of his unfortunate country. When the Tatar horde arrived, Doroshenko began to regain command of his old cities by intimidation, punishment, and the surrender of the miserable inhabitants into slavery to the Tatars; but as soon as the Tatars had left, Samoilovich led an army across the Dnieper, and the inhabitants of western Ukraine again deserted Doroshenko. Samoilovich laid siege to Chihiryn and placed Doroshenko in a desperate situation, for his Kozaks went over to the enemy, only five thousand, according to reports, remaining at his side, many even of these being dissatisfied because of his Turkish policy. The story goes that Doroshenko was about to commit suicide when tidings arrived that both the Turks and the Tatars were coming to his assistance. Samoilovich abandoned his conquests and retreated back across the Dnieper, thus freeing Doroshenko, who was not, however, at the end of his difficulties. Though the Turks came up they were of little aid, as their punishment of the disobedient inhabitants of Podolia and Braslav injured the cause of Doroshenko, and the fear of the Turks spread far and wide through the country. Samoilovich made little effort to gain Right Bank Ukraine; and the year 1675 also passed in civil strife, the villages being sacked and the people punished by Doroshenko or receiving the same treatment from his opponent. Finally Polish regiments also appeared on the scene and attempted to subject the people to the rule of Poland. The period is aptly known as "The Ruin."

As a result of this strife and the depredations committed by the Turks, Tatars, Muscovites, and Poles, as well as through local anarchy, the inhabitants became so disheartened that they began to emigrate. Even before this time, as a consequence of the first Kozak war, which had been conducted chiefly in western Ukraine, many people had moved eastward beyond the Dnieper, the movement assuming mass proportions after the unsuccessful uprising of 1648–49, when not only individuals but whole villages, unable to endure oppression by the nobles and the ravages of constant warfare, deserted western Ukraine. The migrants had penetrated to the eastern frontier of Ukraine and even across the border of Muscovy into the so-called Land of Free Communes about modern Kharkiv and Voronizh. The movement had continued for many years, growing in the 1660's and reaching a peak during the years 1674–76, by which time the provinces of Kiev and Braslav west of the Dnieper had again become quite deserted and people were moving across the Dnieper from even farther west. At last Doroshenko realized that if this emigration continued, his plan of a united Ukraine would end in futility, as there would be no one left for him to govern. He employed every possible means to halt the flight, issuing proclamations, cajoling, and threatening, and at last resorted to force, attacking the lands of the emigrants and turning the people over to the Tatars. All was in vain, and by 1675 Samoilovich could write to Moscow that there were few people left in western Ukraine. Because of this movement, however, eastern Ukraine and the Land of Free Communes had become thickly settled.

Though Doroshenko saw that his plans had miscarried, he still hoped to gain some concessions from the government of Muscovy—at least a hetmancy in some part of Ukraine—and he therefore held out stubbornly. The "last of the Kozaks" presented a pathetic picture as he appeared on his deserted mound of Chihiryn with a handful of loyal hired Kozaks, his desolation weighing more heavily upon him from day to day. Samoilovich opposed any compromise, while the Muscovite government maintained its position that there was but one hetman, Samoilovich, for the entire country of Ukraine, whose authority Doroshenko and his regiment must recognize. The negotiations continued, however, since the Muscovites wished to conclude matters peacefully in order to avoid a clash with the Turks, while Doroshenko continued to appeal to the Turks to come to his rescue, but without success. Since Sirko was making efforts to defend his ally by submitting the old Zaporozhian theory that only the Zaporozhe had the right to elect a hetman and settle disputes, Doroshenko sent his hetman's mace and his other insignia to the Sich, where the koshovy attempted to convoke a Kozak assembly to reëlect him. Samoilovich of course refused to recognize the claims of the Zaporozhians and in the spring of 1674 sent Colonel Borkovsky of Chernihiv across the Dnieper to make a settlement; but Doroshenko still refused to surrender, and Borkovsky did not have the courage to lay siege to Chihiryn. In the fall Samoilovich himself, at the head of a large army partly provided by the Muscovites, crossed the Dnieper to put an end to Doroshenko's claims once and for all. The latter again appealed for aid to the Turks and Tatars, but help failed to arrive; and when in September 1676 he surrendered, his political career came to an end. He begged only for permission to spend the remaining days of his life undisturbed, but in spite of promises and regardless of the personal intercession of Samoilovich the Muscovite officials sent him to Moscow, where he was kept in prison for several years, then given a military position at Viatka from 1679 to 1682, and after this the village of Yaropolche in Volokolamsk.

Doroshenko was never permitted to return to Ukraine, and died in 1698, after outliving both his ally Sirko who died in 1680, and his enemy Samoilovich, who ended his life in 1687, an exile in Siberia.

The Great Eviction and the New Kozak State in Western Ukraine: The surrender of Doroshenko did not solve the problem of western Ukraine. Samoilovich expected to become hetman of united Ukraine, but his hopes were doomed to disappointment, for Turkey, though unwilling to aid Doroshenko, had not abandoned her rights over the land west of the Dnieper, and Poland renewed her claims to it.

When the Porte learned of Doroshenko's capitulation, it decided to fill his place with the weak George Khmelnitsky, whom the Turks had captured on their Ukrainian campaign in 1672 and had carried to Constantinople. The sultan now ordered the Patriarch to release him from his monastic vows and then sent him with an army to Ukraine as the new hetman. In the spring of 1677 the Turkish army under Khmelnitsky pushed as far north as Chihiryn, but when Samoilovich and Romodanovsky arrived to relieve the Muscovite garrison there the Turks withdrew. In the next year they made preparations for a fresh campaign and demanded from Muscovy that she abandon her claims to Ukraine west of the Dnieper. The Muscovite government was prepared to accede to this request, but Samoilovich refused his consent. Romodanovsky was given secret instructions that if the Turks attacked again he should march with Samoilovich to Chihiryn, but avoid a conflict, and after persuading the Turks to agree not to build forts beyond the Dnieper, he should destroy Chihiryn and remove its inhabitants. In the summer of 1678 the Turks laid siege to Chihiryn, the garrison of which, ignorant of the secret instructions from Moscow, defended it stubbornly until orders were received from Romodanovsky to evacuate and destroy the fortress. Preparations for blowing up the powder were made and the garrison departed, the ensuing explosion destroying the fortress and killing a large number of Turks who had hastily rushed in to occupy it. The inhabitants were driven eastward across the Dnieper.

The people of Ukraine were greatly aroused and justly complained that Muscovy had plundered the country and given it to the Turks instead of defending it. Samoilovich intended to settle the migrants in the Land of Free Communes with the understanding that this area should be attached to the Hetman state, but the Muscovite government objected because the Land of Free Communes was under the jurisdiction of Muscovite authorities. Samoilovich finally used them to colonize the frontier region along the River Orel, and the forced migration went down in tradition under the name of ''the great eviction.''

After his election in 1676 the newly elected Polish king, Jan Sobieski, decided to attack Turkey in order to regain Podolia and on this account renounced Poland's claims to Kiev forever in favor of Muscovy upon payment of two hundred thousand rubles. In 1680 he signed a treaty of perpetual peace with Muscovy in an attempt to gain her assistance in a war against Turkey, and simultaneously opened negotiations for a Polish-Muscovite alliance against Turkey. The nobles of Muscovy asked Samoilovich for his advice; he counseled them to distrust the Poles but to make peace with Turkey, on the basis of obtaining the portion of Ukraine from the Dnieper to the Dniester, or at least the Buh. His counsel was followed; but as the khan objected to the proposal it was finally agreed to set the boundary at the Dnieper, while the vast area between the Dnieper and the Buh was to remain a no-man's land. The treaty was signed between Muscovy and Turkey in 1681, but at the time of its ratification the clause pertaining to the land between the Dnieper and the Buh was struck out, Turkey having decided to appropriate this fertile area.

Turkey had great difficulty in executing her project. After their futile campaign against Chihiryn in 1677–78 the Turks had authorized George Khmelnitsky to govern western Ukraine in the expectation that the prestige of his name would attract the inhabitants to him. But George had no other qualifications and was unable to accomplish anything important in the critical circumstances. In 1681 the Turks removed him and entrusted the government of the country to Duka, the Prince of Moldavia, who made efforts to colonize the territory by promising a long period of freedom from taxation. Large numbers responded to his invitation and returned from eastern Ukraine after discovering that all was not milk and honey there; Duka, however, was captured by the Poles in 1683, and his efforts came to an end. According to the Ukrainian chronicler Velichko, George Khmelnitsky was again sent to Ukraine to succeed Duka but was executed by the Turks at Kaminets because he had killed a wealthy Jew, a story which is, however, of doubtful authenticity and is reported in no other source. In any event, the Turks had little success in colonizing the region, though they made repeated attempts in later years.

While the Turks were attempting in vain to settle the land between the Buh and the Dnieper, the colonization of western Ukraine was proceeding with great rapidity under the auspices of the Poles, for Sobieski desired the aid of the Kozaks in his wars against Turkey and entrusted to various chieftains the task of mobilizing them. He was aided by Kozaks in his campaign in 1683 to raise the siege of Vienna, and finding them of great value he wished to settle the southern part of the province of Kiev with a large population capable of furnishing soldiers for a Kozak army. In 1684 he issued a proclamation urging the Kozaks to occupy the land south of the Ros, promising generous rights and privileges, and the Polish parliament approved this declaration in the next year. The Ukrainian leaders now appealed to their people to return to the vacant lands, among those who received the title of colonel in these regimental districts being Iskra in Korsun, Samus in Bohuslav, Abazin in the Buh region, and most famous of them all, Semen Hurko, known as Paliy, who took over Khvastiv, between the Ros River and the border of the Hetman state. Thousands followed them from all the provinces of Ukraine, especially from Polisia, Volynia, and Podolia. The former eastward trek was now

reversed, and great numbers migrated westward, all efforts to halt them failing. The authorities in eastern
Ukraine were at this period levying high taxes, introducing serfdom, and oppressing the inhabitants in other
ways; therefore the people responded to the call of Paliy
and the other colonels and emigrated to a freer country.

In three or four years a considerable number of settlements had been established west of the Dnieper, and the
Kozak army there had acquired great importance, aiding
Sobieski in his wars with Turkey but being unwilling to
live under Polish rule. As early as 1688 Paliy and other
colonels were making efforts to unite their forces to those
of the Hetman state east of the Dnieper.

Events in the Hetman State: While the western part of
the country was undergoing "the Ruin"—experiencing
serious changes and suffering terrible calamities, passing
from Polish to Muscovite and then to Turkish hands, becoming deserted and then repopulated, dying and returning to life, enduring executions and repression—political
life in the Hetman state in eastern Ukraine was proceeding at an uneventful pace. Ever since the uprising of
Brukhovetsky in 1688 there had been no serious disturbances there. The army officers had conspired to rid themselves of the hated "peasant boy," and had filled the office of hetman with the submissive Samoilovich, of whom,
in the same manner, they would rid themselves fifteen
years later to elect Mazepa. They paid little attention to
the fact that Muscovy was continually encroaching upon
Ukrainian political rights and loyally complied with all
the demands of the Muscovite ministers.

Having before him the example of Mnohohrishny, who
was writing from Siberia in his appeals for pardon that
he was "driven from door to door and dying of starvation," Samoilovich took great care not to antagonize the
Muscovites. He sent his sons to Moscow, where they won
the favor of the officials and looked after his interests;
later he made them colonels, one in Starodub and a second

in Chernihiv, while his nephew became colonel of Hadiach. His daughter he married to the Muscovite noble Fedor Sheremetiev, for whom he begged appointment as governor of Kiev. Moscow placed a high valuation upon the services of the loyal hetman, followed his sage advice, ignored all accusations against him. From all appearances his position was secure; he had overthrown his enemies, filled the important offices with relatives, and gained the good will of the tsar.

It is true that in return for this good will the hetman was obliged at times to perform unpleasant tasks, and that his appeals regarding Muscovite policies in Ukraine went unheeded. It has already been pointed out, for example, that his petition to have the frontier regiments of the Land of Free Communes placed under his control was refused, and there were other instances of a similar nature. Furthermore, he was obliged to do for the government of Muscovy what no one else before him had been willing to do, namely, permit it to appoint the metropolitan of the Ukrainian Church. When Tukalsky died in 1684 the Muscovite government entrusted Samoilovich with the task of finding as his successor a man who would accept ordination by and recognize the authority of the Patriarch of Muscovy. He found such a person in a relative, Prince Gedeon Sviatopolk-Chetvertinsky, the bishop of Lutsk, and the appointment was made in spite of the objections of Baranovich, the metropolitan of Chernihiv, whom Samoilovich disliked. The hetman merely asked the officials at Moscow to settle the dispute by laying it before the Patriarch of Constantinople; this was done, but the Patriarch protested that he could not decide a matter of so great importance without the consent of the other Patriarchs. The Muscovite officials then referred the matter to the sultan's vizir, who brought pressure to bear upon the Patriarchs to make them approve the usurpation by Moscow, Turkey being at this time eager to curry favor with Muscovy in order to prevent her from joining the

alliance with Sobieski. The autonomy of the Ukrainian
Church was thus destroyed; it fell under the control of
the religious authorities of Muscovy and with it went
Ukrainian cultural and educational life.

These humiliating services to the Muscovite government failed to save Samoilovich from a sad fate. Relying
upon the favor of Moscow, this son of a village priest,
once known as "kind and well-intentioned toward all
men," began to lose his sense of proportion. He ruled arbitrarily, without the advice of his officers, and when they
objected, he treated them with disdain; he took bribes
from the administrative officials, lorded it over all, and,
they suspected, intended to turn the mace of office over to
his son and make the hetmancy hereditary in his family.
In these ways he antagonized the officers, who merely
waited for an opportunity to intrigue against him as they
had done against his predecessor. The opportunity came
quite unexpectedly.

Disregarding the advice of Samoilovich, Muscovy finally joined Poland in an alliance against Turkey, and in
1686 the two governments signed what was termed a
treaty of perpetual peace. Muscovy paid the balance of
146,000 rubles due for the cession of Kiev and promised
to attack the Crimean horde while Poland, Austria, and
Venetia were attacking Turkey. Samoilovich looked with
disapproval upon this agreement, the more so as Poland
did not retract her claims to the Ukrainian lands west of
the Dnieper as he had insisted she should be forced to do.
He was, however, unable to hinder the course of events
and was obliged to undertake a campaign against Crimea
in company with the Muscovite army under the leadership
of Prince Basil Golitsyn, the chief Muscovite minister,
and the favorite of the Tsarevna Sophia, who was ruling
as regent for her infant brothers, Ivan and Peter.

Samoilovich, who was well acquainted with the conditions of steppe warfare, recommended a start in early
spring with a large army, but his advice was disregarded

and the expedition set out in summer when the grass was already dry. The campaign was a fiasco, for the Tatars set the steppes afire, and the army was forced to return empty-handed. Golitsyn, fearing that the failure of his expedition would undermine his position, was looking about for a scapegoat, when on his way home he was told by the Kozak officers hostile to Samoilovich that the hetman had brought about the failure of the expedition because he did not approve of the Muscovite alliance with Poland or the war with Crimea. Though this was a pure lie, the Tsarevna and Golitsyn, disregarding the valuable services rendered by the old hetman, decided to place the blame upon him. Golitsyn was authorized to depose Samoilovich on the basis of the dissatisfaction of the Kozak officers, to send him and his family to Moscow, and to elect another hetman in his place. In Moscow Samoilovich and his eldest son were arrested and exiled to Siberia without trial, and his property was confiscated, one half going to the royal treasury and the other to the Kozak war chest. His younger son, the colonel of Chernihiv, who had opposed his father's arrest, was tried for treason, condemned to death, and unmercifully executed in Sivsk. Two years later the deposed hetman died in exile in Tobolsk.

As soon as the news of the arrest of Samoilovich reached the Kozak army, a mutiny broke out against the Officers' Council. In the camp at Fort Kodak the Priluki regiment threw its colonel and its judge into a fire and covered them with earth, several officers were killed at Hadiach, and in other regiments even the officers who had been supporters of the old hetman were attacked by the soldiers. Because of this anarchy the officers were eager to elect a new hetman in place of the temporary appointee, Borkovsky. Ivan Mazepa made preparations for the election by promising Golitsyn ten thousand rubles if he were elected, and under the powerful influence of the Muscovite minister his candidacy was unopposed. The government of Muscovy laid before the general assembly of the army the Hlukhiv Articles of 1672, with several clauses inserted in favor of Moscow: the right of the officers to the estates given to them by the tsar or the hetman was recognized, members of the Officers' Council could be removed by the hetman only with the consent of the tsar, marriages between Kozaks and Muscovites were encouraged in order to bind Ukraine more closely to Muscovy, and it was suggested that Ukrainians migrate to Muscovy and make their homes there. Golitsyn then advised the officers to elect Mazepa, which they did on July 25 (August 4), 1687.

The newly elected hetman, Ivan Stepanovich Mazepa, was of Ukrainian petty gentry stock in Bila Tserkva. He was born about 1640 and had spent his boyhood years at the court of the Polish king, from which he was being sent on various diplomatic missions to Ukraine as early as 1659–63. After this he left the court, reputedly because of the love affair described by Byron and other poets, and settled in Ukraine, where he entered the Kozak army and became a close associate of Doroshenko. In 1675 he was captured in eastern Ukraine while on his way to Crimea on a diplomatic mission, and remained in the Hetman state. Here he found favor with Samoilovich and with Muscovy, and at the time of the hetman's downfall held the post of inspector general (*asaul*).

CHAPTER XVI

IVAN MAZEPA

The Officers and the People: The change of hetmans brought with it little alteration in the living conditions of the Ukrainian people. Mazepa followed the policy of his predecessor, the path trodden by all the officers of the eastern half of the country, who were eager for peace after ten years of fruitless struggle. The downfall of Doroshenko, the last warrior and statesman of Khmelnitsky's type and the last loyal representative of the policy of Ukrainian independence, had been a vivid lesson in the new circumstances. The hard feeling which resulted from the radical measures which he had employed to execute his projects and the misfortunes which had attended him, together with the fact that he was deserted by all and hated by the masses, led his contemporaries to believe that, with him politically impotent, there was no hope that Ukraine could ever free herself from Muscovy; and the officers decided that it was useless to resist the forces of the enemy as long as the people themselves, weakened by social cleavages, failed to assist them. Even the Zaporozhe could not be depended upon. It was easy to follow the line of least resistance and to seek personal favors at the hands of the tsar.

With new aggressiveness the Muscovites continued their policy of penetration, demanding additional political concessions from the Ukrainian officers and rewarding them, at the expense of the people, with large estates and lucrative offices. The tsar desired to create in Ukraine a new class of landed nobility, to enserf the peasants, and to bring Ukraine into line with Muscovy, where serfdom was in force. The carrying out of this program caused animosity between the Ukrainian masses and the political leaders, the breach becoming wider and wider as time went on. The freedom-loving Ukrainians were subjected to new oppression, while, in the words of Baranovich, "the people longed for liberty." The attitude of the masses toward the Muscovite system had been indicated by the rebellion of 1668, but after enserfing the Ukrainian people the tsar began to oppress their officials as well, understanding clearly that whenever it became convenient he could terrorize the Ukrainian leaders by threatening to incite the people to revolt against them.

The government of Muscovy made it a policy to bestow large estates upon the Ukrainian officers as rewards for loyal services, and also approved similar gifts made by the hetman, for the Kozak officials were thus made dependent upon its pleasure. The officers accepted these gifts and gradually became the owners of extensive lands which had previously been ownerless or had belonged to the army as a whole. They reduced the inhabitants to serfdom and loyally served the tsar. Samoilovich and Mazepa, who had been elected by the Officers' Council, supported the Muscovite program and promoted the interests of the officers, whom they aided in acquiring land and enserfing the inhabitants, failing to realize or ignoring the fact that these practices were destroying all political activity by the Ukrainian people.

The hetmancies of Samoilovich and Mazepa spanned a period of nearly forty years, years of great importance, when the free institutions won by the Ukrainian revolution of 1648–49 were on trial. Unfortunately, during this critical period the incompletely developed system of democracy was replaced by an autocracy which destroyed the last remnants of national freedom.

After Khmelnitsky's uprising, when the landlords had for the most part been killed or expelled, great areas in eastern Ukraine had been immediately taken over by free people, who had settled down on the ownerless land, built themselves homes, and cultivated as much soil as they could work. Although it seemed as if the entire system of landlordism had been "abolished by the Kozak sword," fragments of the old order survived the storms of revolution and eventually began to expand, hampering the new democratic social order. The large estates of the Orthodox monasteries and churches had remained intact to carry on the old practices, while a few noble landlords who had joined the Kozak Host as officers had also retained their properties and had obtained confirmation of their titles by the tsar. Following their example, other Kozak officials begged the government to grant them title to land in various inhabited regions.

The Kozak officers who had replaced the Polish gentry began to consider themselves the social equals of the ousted nobles. They began to trace their ancestry back to princes of earlier times, and to create for themselves new titles of nobility and family crests. Since there were no laws to favor their class, they searched the old Lithuanian Statute and the Magdeburg Municipal Law, which gave them bases for the aristocratic system which they were introducing into Ukraine, and on the authority of these ancient laws claimed ownership of the land and villages of the non-Kozak population.

The officers appropriated for themselves without formality the free and uninhabited land much as the ordinary Kozaks and the peasants had done, except that the officers acquired great areas and expected it to be cultivated, not by themselves, but by their serfs. Dissatisfied with the land alone, they appealed to the hetman and his colonels, and even to the tsar, to grant them ownership of the villages inhabited by free people who were cultivating their own soil, and the villagers thus suddenly found themselves and all their belongings in the hands of an army officer who called himself a "noble." When an officer succeeded in gaining the approval of the tsar the people and their land became his property forever; this practice of giving away free property resembled the old custom of the Polish kings of giving villages and their inhabitants to the gentry. In 1687 the government approved all the grants hitherto made to officers by the hetmans, but the officers demanded that the government also give blanket approval to all future grants by the hetman or the colonels instead of considering each case separately. Muscovy, however, disapproved of this plan and made it necessary to petition for each new concession, and, of course, to exhibit a proper servility.

The lower army officers, who could not boast to the tsar of their great services, increased their holdings by purchasing the land from the peasants and the Kozaks at nominal cost, either by taking advantage of the poverty of the people or by using armed force to oblige them to sell, the bargain frequently being one in name only. Because the Kozaks themselves were not permitted to sell their land, they were made serfs, though this step came later, after the death of Mazepa, when there was no more unoccupied land available.

By these means the Kozak officers appropriated a great amount of land, and it became true that the poor Kozak had "nowhere to graze his horse." Meanwhile the revolutions and wars of the decades of 1660 and 1670 had driven into the Hetman state many people from west of the Dnieper, and these refugees, unable to find free land, were obliged to settle on the properties of the gentry, of the Church, or of the officers, where they became serfs by accepting various obligations in dues or in labor. At first these new settlers were known by the modest name of share croppers, but before long were openly called "serfs."

During the period of Samoilovich the officers already spoke openly about the "servile duties" of the peasants. The special obligations imposed upon the new settlers were likewise applied to the older ones who were living on their own land, but were now assigned, together with their land, to the holders of certain governmental offices known as "ranks," each such position carrying with it the right to the use during the term of office of a definite piece of property. Following the example of the old Polish landlords of the pre-Khmelnitsky era, the new landholders attempted to prevent the peasants from joining the Kozaks. After the revolution of 1648 everyone had been free to register, and those who could afford to and wished to, were allowed to serve voluntarily in the army at their own expense. Now registration in the Kozak army was made compulsory, and all who were excluded were considered "common people," or villagers. Before long they too were subjected to various taxes, those who refused to pay being deprived of their farms to make room for new settlers. All the people were thus gradually forced into submission to the gentry.

During the time of Samoilovich, when peasants were first invited by the thousands from western Ukraine and later brought in by forced migration, the Hetman state also began to impose upon the so-called common people the "regular obligations of serfs." At first these feudal duties were few in number—assistance in the haying season, work on dams for the millpond, and so on—but once the new landlords had seized the villages and forbidden the immigrants to return to the west side of the Dnieper, they lost no time in imposing more burdensome terms. A proclamation ("universal") issued by Mazepa in 1701 refers to forced labor as being legal in Ukraine, the peasants being compelled to work two days a week for their landlords and in addition having to pay a tax in oats, these obligations being extorted from people who lived on their own farms and were not share croppers.

Woe unto us! It is not the Hetman State
But the accursed labor that troubles us;
We eat while walking, sleep while sitting:
When I go to work, I carry my bread,
When I leave my work, none is left, and my bitter tears flow.

This new serfdom, of course, enraged the villagers who still remembered that they or their fathers had settled upon free land, and, most of all, they hated the officers who had so quickly and cleverly enslaved them. Especially did they loathe Mazepa, whom they called a nobleman and a Pole, because he insisted upon introducing the Polish system of large estates into Ukraine. They were suspicious of all his acts and those of his officers but failed to see in them the hand of Muscovy, and were even ready to believe that these oppressive practices were enacted against the will of the tsar. The people were sympathetic, however, toward the leaders of the Kozaks west of the Dnieper, especially toward Paliy, whom they looked upon with respect as a loyal representative of the liberty-loving free Kozak Host in contrast to Mazepa.

Mazepa and his officers either did not understand the significance of this hatred or could not mend matters. They were aware of the popular grievances and lack of confidence in them; they could not even trust their own Kozak followers, and had to keep regiments of mercenaries in addition to them, as well as ask to have Muscovite troops garrisoned in their country. They took no steps, however, to remove the causes of discontent and estranged themselves more and more from the common people and from the Kozak rank and file. In the end this neglect had serious results for the officers at a time when they were forced to make a stand against Muscovy, whose leadership they had followed for many years.

Mazepa's Administration: Now that serfdom had been introduced and legalized with the aid of Muscovy, Mazepa's hetmancy appeared in its initial years to be only a continuation of that of Samoilovich. The struggle in Moscow between the faction which supported Peter as tsar and that which backed his sister, the Tsarevna Sophia, caused some uncertainty, the Ukrainians finding it difficult to decide whom to support; but Mazepa succeeded in escaping from the dilemma without incurring enmity. His patron, Prince Golitsyn, had been removed from office as a result of a second unsuccessful expedition against Crimea a year after the first, but Mazepa, in spite of his participation in this second campaign, did not suffer any loss of prestige; on the contrary, he won special favors from the young tsar and recovered from the estates of the fallen Golitsyn the entire sum which he had paid for his election, besides securing many grants for his family and relatives and large estates for his officers. In consequence he urged his officers to serve the tsar faithfully.

These events strengthened the position of Mazepa in Ukraine. Meanwhile he was making use of the great wealth which he had inherited from the downfall of Samoilovich and from his income as head of the Kozak army to build churches and to promote religious and educational work, largely for the purpose of counteracting rumors that he was a Catholic and a Pole. His building of magnificent churches and his donation of money and property to the larger Ukrainian monasteries and churches also impressed the people with his piety and respect for Ukrainian culture, as well as with his own glory, power, and wealth. It is interesting to note that despite Mazepa's rich endowment of the Ukrainian Church, this institution was later forced by the tsar to issue an anathema against him and to efface all inscriptions and seals reminding the people of him. Nevertheless, to this day the Ukrainians speak of Mazepa's philanthropy and point to his monumental work for the Church and for Ukrainian education in general.

Mazepa remodeled the Monastery of the Caves and built around it a stone wall which still delights the eye of the visitor; he also constructed beautiful gateways with miniature churches over them, the so-called Holy Gate and the Steward's Gate, and therefore it is easily understood why until recently his portrait was kept on the wall of the altar room of the Monastery. On the grounds of the Pustinsko-Nikolaevsky Monastery he erected the lovely

Church of St. Nicholas, which was confiscated by the government in 1831 and converted into an army church. He rebuilt the brotherhood Church of the Epiphany, and erected a new building for the Academy, besides raising a large church in Pereyaslav, described by Shevchenko in his *Panorama of Ukraine*. Space is lacking to enumerate all the monuments left by Mazepa in Ukraine and elsewhere. In the Church of the Holy Sepulchre in Jerusalem there is still used on all great holidays a large silver platter bearing the inscription, "Donated by His Highness, Ivan Mazepa, Hetman of Rus."

The clergy, the officers, and the whole group of what might today be called the Ukrainian intelligentsia praised him as a benevolent hetman, and had it not been for his later misfortunes he would have lived on in Ukrainian memory as a great patron of religion and culture. His achievements in these fields of activity could not but impress the masses and increase his prestige among them, but did not lessen the discontent and antipathy toward him caused by the many abuses to which they were subjected. Mazepa did not display ability to penetrate the popular mind and to gain its favor, though the many mutinies and revolts both within the Kozak army and outside its ranks against the officers who had forced Samoilovich out of office should have made him aware of the deep undercurrent of popular dissatisfaction. Mazepa and his officers attempted to ensure the obedience of the people by intimidation, all of those connected with the uprisings being seized and severely punished, in many cases flogged to death, after which, according to a contemporary, the chronicler Velichko, "there was silence and fear among the people." It cannot be said that Mazepa paid no attention to the causes of the popular discontent, but the only action he took to remove them was to abolish the special taxes which had been imposed by Samoilovich in 1678, with the consent of the tsar, for the upkeep of the mercenaries hired to protect him against the hatred of the common people and the poorer Kozaks. He leased to private concerns the manufacture and sale of liquor and the sale of tobacco and axle grease, and though the people were given a limited right to make *horilka* (liquor) for home use—the Kozaks being allowed a double quantity—complaints continued and on this account it was decided to find other sources of income and to abolish the monopolies. As no other special source of revenue could be found, however, and as it was feared that if general taxes were levied the people would be even more antagonized, the concessions and monopolies were continued, for both the hetman and the officers considered it unsafe to live in their residences unguarded by the soldiers hired with the funds thus received.

The hetman and his officers were satisfied but the people were not, though they did not dare to revolt against the system because it was protected by Muscovite troops and the hetman's mercenaries.

One sign of the people's discontent was the abortive revolt led by Petryk Ivanenko in 1692–96. Petryk was an army clerk, who for some reason had fled to the Zaporozhian country in 1691 and had attempted to persuade the Kozaks there to attack Mazepa in order to free the Ukrainian people from the "new landlords," the Sich being, as in the time of Samoilovich, hostile to the hetman's government and to the sovereignty of Muscovy. An officer in the Zaporozhian army named Husak complained in letters to Mazepa that in the Hetman state the poor people were suffering more severely than under the Polish rule, because even those who had no need for them acquired serfs to haul hay and timber, chop wood, and clean the stables, exactly the same complaints that had been made against the Poles before Khmelnitsky's rebellion. Petryk, counting on the disaffection of the Zaporozhians, hoped to induce them to rebel against these abuses and hoped also to obtain military aid from Crimea. The Muscovite government, and with it the Hetman state, was still hostile to

Crimea and Turkey; and the khan accordingly recognized Petryk as hetman of Ukraine and promised assistance for a war of liberation, guaranteeing to defend Ukraine from her enemies on condition that the Kozaks should not interfere with an invasion of Muscovy. Petryk told the Zaporozhians, "I am for the common people, for the poor. Bohdan Khmelnitsky freed the Ukrainians from slavery to Poland, and I will free them from the Muscovites and their own landlords." He assured the Zaporozhians that the whole Ukrainian nation would join him in revolt:

I will risk my head, and you may cut me to pieces if all Ukraine, from Poltava on, will not bow down before you. If we can get at least six thousand men of the horde, we can begin. Do you not believe our poor brethren will help us, who in these times are unable to make a living because of the extortion of the landlords and the new dukes who have received estates from the tsar? When they hear that you are coming with the army of the Sich, they will rise up and kill the devilish landlords, and we shall arrive to see the deed accomplished. The hetman will flee to Moscow, where his heart and soul are: here in the Zaporozhian army there is only his shadow.

The news of Petryk's rebellion spread over Ukraine and alarmed Mazepa and his officers. The people boasted, "When Petryk comes with the Zaporozhian Kozaks we will join them, kill the oppressive officers and landlords, and restore the old order; abolish the aristocracy, and permit all the people to be Kozaks." Mazepa in dismay asked for the support of a Muscovite army, fearing that if he moved alone the revolt might break out at once. His apprehensions, however, were unfounded; the Zaporozhians, though they hated Mazepa, were not eager to join Petryk in an uprising, nor did they wish to become allies of the Tatars. In the summer of 1692 Petryk received a band of Tatars from the khan and with them invaded Ukraine, calling upon the Zaporozhians to join him in freeing Ukraine from the tsar, who, he said, was sure completely to enslave the Ukrainian people and had already permitted the hetman to subject them to new lords, "in order that our people will not be able to protest when they attempt to take their final step of stationing their colonels everywhere and reducing us to everlasting servitude." The Sich Kozaks did not join Petryk as a body; and although they permitted volunteers to join his movement not many went, while the circulars which he sent out to the frontier Ukrainian cities were of no effect. Mazepa's army awaited him at the border, and when the people learned of Petryk's insignificant forces, they did not dare to revolt. He was thus forced to retreat, and after this paltry beginning the people had little hope of a successful rebellion. In 1693 and in 1696 he again attempted to lead uprisings in Ukraine, but only the Tatars were with him, and during his last campaign he was killed by a Kozak who wished to collect the price set on his head by Mazepa.

Conditions did not improve. Many of the unemployed and the poor fled to the Sich, though Mazepa and his officers made vain efforts to stop them. Threats were again sent from the Sich that the Kozaks would kill the landlords, and Mazepa complained to the tsar that "the Zaporozhians are not as dangerous as the Ukrainian civilian masses who are imbued with the rebellious spirit of freedom" and were ready at any moment to join the Zaporozhians. When the hetman wished in 1702 to send his regiments to attack the Sich Kozaks, who under their new custodian Hordienko were threatening to "find a new master for themselves," the colonels feared a rebellion and objected to the hetman's plan.

West of the Dnieper large numbers of people joined the Kozak army led by Paliy, and from 1689 on made sporadic attacks upon the neighboring landlords, threatening to "expel the hated Poles beyond the Vistula and not to leave a trace of them here." They succeeded in extending their activity to all parts of the territory, driving out the gentry. The Poles attempted to subdue the Kozaks; and after 1699, when the war with Turkey came to an end, they decided to do away with them completely, but Paliy and the other colonels defended themselves bravely, capturing the most important Polish forts at Nemiriv and Bila Tserkva and preparing to carry the war in earnest against Poland. This success attracted the support of all those who were dissatisfied with Mazepa's rule, and Paliy was on the way to becoming a national hero, whom Mazepa feared more than he had Petryk, as he thought that the revolution might be carried across the Dnieper to his Hetman state. "All the people have but one thought, to cross the Dnieper, and serious troubles may be brewing," he wrote to Moscow; "both the Kozaks and the civilian population dislike me, and all cry out in unison, 'We shall perish in the end; the Muscovites will swallow us.'"

On the Eve of the Break: Hoping to win the appreciation of the government of Muscovy, Mazepa informed the tsar that the popular dissatisfaction against him was due to his faithful services. It was unwise of him to complain, however, because all previous experience indicated that as a rule loyal services were promptly forgotten when there was antipathy in Ukraine against a hetman and it had become embarrassing to Moscow to support him. Apparently Mazepa failed to realize the seriousness of the situation and hoped with the aid of Muscovy and his own mercenaries to maintain himself safely regardless of popular sentiment. Meanwhile his loyal services to Muscovy brought fresh hardships upon the Kozaks and the rest of the population, while the people "lost their respect for the Great Tsar," no longer wished to submit to his protection, and, moreover, hated the hetman because he was subservient to Muscovy.

The new Muscovite government of Peter the Great renewed the war with Turkey and Crimea in 1695, and for four years the Kozak armies were obliged to go time and again wherever the tsar sent them, either against the Turkish strongholds or against the Tatars, while Ukraine itself suffered from Tatar raids. These misfortunes, however, were negligible compared with those to follow. As soon as Peter had ended his war with Turkey he joined Poland in an attack upon Sweden in order to open a way to the Baltic Sea. From 1700 on, the Kozaks were again forced to fight for Peter for several years at their own expense, not only receiving no pay for their services but perishing in great numbers in the far north because of the rigors of the unaccustomed climate. They suffered terrible hardships, and those who lived to return home were barefooted and in rags; but in return for their services they received from the Muscovite agents only insults and curses, bodily punishment, and mistreatment of many other kinds.

Besides using them for fighting, the tsar employed the Kozaks continually as laborers in the building of fortresses, a large number of men being forced to work on the new Pechersky fortress at Kiev in 1706–07, when Peter feared a Swedish invasion of Ukraine.

There the Kozaks labored summer and winter under the eyes of Muscovite overseers who treated them without mercy. Meanwhile the tsar's troops roamed about the country, their officers abusing the inhabitants, taking supplies without compensation, and lording it over all Ukrainians alike, whether common people or officers. In all parts of the land even those most subservient to Moscow declared that they could endure this mistreatment no longer.

A letter written by Philip Orlik, secretary of the Kozak Host and an intimate friend of the hetman, gives the following vivid description of these conditions:

The task of building the Pechersky Fortress having begun, the people of the Ukrainian cities have witnessed a stream of both recruits and officers to the hetman to complain that the Muscovite overseers beat the Kozaks over the head with clubs, cut off their ears, and abuse them in other degrading ways. Those Kozaks who have left their homes, their haymaking, and their harvesting have suffered from heat and been worn out by hardships in the service

of His Majesty the Tsar. Meanwhile the Russians have robbed
their homes, plundering and burning, assaulted their wives and
daughters, carried off horses, cattle, and everything else of value,
and beaten Ukrainian officers to death.

Two brave Ukrainian colonels, Apostol of Mirhorod
and Horlenko of Priluki, said to Mazepa: "The eyes of
all the people are fixed upon you, and in case you die,
which God forbid, and we are left in this slavery, only the
chickens will be left to bury us." Horlenko added: "As
we pray daily to God for the soul of Khmelnitsky, so will
we and our children curse your body and soul if you as
the hetman leave us in our slavery!"

These words must have inspired a gloomy fear in Mazepa's heart. Until now he had relied upon the support of
Muscovy; but by the end of 1706 the tsar was on the losing
side in the war with Sweden, whose intrepid king, Charles
XII, had by this time settled accounts with his other enemies, Denmark and Poland, broken up the faction supporting Augustus II in Poland, held a new election there,
and compelled Augustus to make peace with Sweden and
give up his claims to the Polish crown. Peter was thus left
unaided to face an opponent who had gained fame as an
invincible warrior. The Swedish army might be expected
at any time to enter Ukraine, and no reliance could be put
upon the tsar; when Mazepa discussed with. Peter the
danger of a Swedish invasion, the tsar retorted that no
help could be looked for from him and he could supply no
troops because he needed them all himself. It was clear
that Mazepa with his own forces could not hope to withstand the King of Sweden, and that as soon as the Swedish troops entered Ukraine and the Muscovites withdrew,
a popular uprising would follow. The people, annoyed by
the indignities suffered at the hands of Muscovy, would
join the Swedes, and in all probability even the Kozaks
would follow their example. It should also be remembered
that there had been a treaty between Sweden and Ukraine
made in the time of Khmelnitsky and Vyhovsky, accord-

ing to which Ukrainian rights and independence had been guaranteed under Swedish protection. This agreement had raised high hopes, which had remained unsatisfied because of a change in Swedish policy, but now the King of Sweden was on his way to Ukraine and the Kozak officers felt that upon them rested the responsibility of completing the task begun by their predecessors, the task of attempting with the help of Sweden to free Ukraine from the rule of Muscovy, which within the last few years had become so oppressive.

On the other hand, Mazepa had had many opportunities to convince himself that Muscovy was unreliable. In the restless brain of Peter new projects were continually developing, and among them were many harmful to Ukraine. At one time he considered the abolition of the Kozak army and the establishment of regular army recruiting stations in Ukraine; and another plan called for making Ukraine a principality for someone who could be of use to him, like the Duke of Marlborough, for instance, through whom he hoped to win the friendship of England. In order to gratify Mazepa Peter had procured for him from the German emperor the title of prince, and the documents and insignia were ready to be conferred. But knowing Peter intimately, Mazepa saw that if the tsar should hit upon any useful scheme in his plans for Ukraine, he would pay no heed to past loyalty and services. As it was impossible to rely upon Peter, Mazepa had to think of himself.

In addition to other acute problems, there was that of western Ukraine, where the colonels had decided to revolt against Poland and now desired to unite with the Hetman state in order to get help from it. From 1688 on Paliy and the other colonels had time and again besought Mazepa to take them under his rule. Though Mazepa himself was eager to annex western Ukraine, the tsar, who was allied to the King of Poland, objected because he could not accept land to which Poland laid claim. Meanwhile the future looked dark for the Kozaks in western Ukraine, where in 1703 the Polish General Sieniawski attacked the Kozak regiments in the province of Braslav and on the frontier, where they were weak, defeating them and ruthlessly suppressing the revolt. Though the Poles did not venture to attack Paliy because of his superior forces, nevertheless he did not feel safe and begged Mazepa to come to his protection. The tsar not only refused Mazepa permission to do this but promised the Poles that he himself would subdue Paliy, whereupon Mazepa, unwilling to desert the cause of western Ukraine, decided to take a decisive step regardless of what the tsar might have to say about it.

In the summer of 1704 the tsar ordered Mazepa to enter western Ukraine to crush those nobles who were supporting the Swedish cause. Mazepa decided to use this opportunity to unite Ukraine, but fearing that Paliy might become a dangerous opponent because of his popularity among the Kozaks, he treacherously arrested him and installed in his place one of his own relatives, Colonel Omelchenko. Paliy's Kozaks at one time or another had served in Mazepa's army, and those who were at Bila Tserkva decided to defend themselves; but the inhabitants of the city, fearing disorders, surrendered it to Omelchenko, who became governor there. To Peter, Mazepa falsely accused Paliy of having been in communication with the Swedish faction with the result that Paliy was exiled to Siberia. The people put this incident into a ballad and remembered the exiled chieftain in story and legend.

Thus Mazepa became ruler over the Kozaks of western Ukraine and apparently over their country as well. This was the first occasion on which he dared to oppose the will of the tsar. At first all went smoothly: he attempted to justify himself by saying that as long as there was a pro-Swedish faction in Poland, the western Ukrainian territory should not be surrendered to the Poles, an explanation which the tsar accepted. Under Mazepa's leadership the western Kozaks in a short time increased rapidly in number, but finally in 1707 the tsar requested him to return this part of Ukraine to the Poles. Mazepa disobeyed, offering various excuses and continuing to govern the country, because he valued it highly and wished to keep it united to his original domain.

The Alliance with Sweden: Among the numerous accusations brought against Mazepa was his composition of a song exalting the independence of Ukraine. As the accusation was brought by Kochubey, who was an intimate friend of the hetman, he may be believed when he said that the words were those of Mazepa. This song contained the gist of Mazepa's policy: he desired to create for the hetman great authority based on loyal service by his officers, to engender respect for his office in the eyes of the people, to put an end to democratic methods of administration, and to unite all the people in the person of the hetman as monarch. He spent a score of years working toward this end, but when the proper time came the hetman, now grown old, lacked the courage to lead Ukraine in the revolt of which he had written, but continued to wait and to speculate until the last moment. The risk, it is true, was great, and the punishment to be faced in case of failure too terrible to contemplate.

While he was awaiting with anxiety the victories of Charles XII, Mazepa had for long been making efforts to protect both his flanks by maintaining his connection with Muscovy and at the same time by keeping in communication through friends with Charles's supporters in Poland. In 1707 he entered into direct negotiations with King Stanislaw Leszczynski, whom the Swedes had placed on the throne of Poland. No detailed account of these negotiations is available, for Mazepa conducted them in the utmost secrecy, not revealing them to even his most trusted friends, so that some of the Ukrainian leaders insisted that he should enter into relations with Charles, not knowing that he had already done so. Through this excess of prudence he destroyed the factor that would have brought him the most assistance in time of need, for he failed to indicate to his people in any public way his disapproval of the abuses of Muscovy and continued to send his troops wherever the tsar demanded. When the Don Kozaks under Bulavin revolted against Muscovy in 1707 Mazepa not only refused them aid but even assisted the tsar in suppressing the uprising, though this occurred only a short time before he himself rebelled against Muscovy.

It is true that because of this caution he succeeded in keeping his plans hidden from Muscovy, and the tsar continued to trust him implicitly. In the spring of 1708 Kochubey, the general judge of the Kozak army, became angered at Mazepa because of the hetman's love affair with his daughter. The judge, together with a relative, Colonel Iskra, placed before Peter an accusation against Mazepa in which he claimed that the hetman was in communication with the Swedish party, but the tsar refused to place credence in the charges and ordered both accusers brought before a military tribunal where they were condemned to death. Mazepa, however, had gained but little from this success. He apparently continued to believe, as Brukhovetsky had done, that the Ukrainians hated Muscovy so bitterly that they would revolt whenever the signal was given. It soon became evident that he had overestimated their hatred and had injured his cause by failing to take sufficient pains to prepare them for the uprising.

In the autumn of 1708 Charles attacked Peter in Lithuania along the border between Ukraine and Muscovy, and it was still uncertain in which of these two countries the war would be continued. If Charles had marched into Muscovy Mazepa could have continued to act as an observer and could finally have thrown his weight to the side of the victor. It is difficult to believe reports to the effect that Mazepa had actually invited Charles to enter Ukraine, for such an act would have been contrary to his own interests. Almost nothing is known about his agreement with Charles, but the king's movements are a matter of history. Charles had intended to attack Smolensk and to march on through Muscovy, but becoming aware that in this devastated country he would find no supplies for his army, he crossed the border into Ukraine at Starodub, in September.

The Swedish invasion took Mazepa completely by surprise. Only shortly before this time he had sent most of his Kozak regiments out of Ukraine into Lithuania and westward against the Poles, while Peter had sent a Muscovite army to the heart of Ukraine in response to the hetman's complaints of unrest among the Ukrainian people. Upon learning of the march of the Swedish army and its location at Starodub, the tsar sent an army there and ordered Mazepa to send his Kozaks there too, and following close upon this order Peter himself entered Ukraine and ordered Mazepa to see him in person. This was a critical moment for the hetman, who was now forced to decide which army he would support. He was helpless to move against the tsar, but he and his officers were united in their burning desire to grasp this opportunity to liberate Ukraine, an aim which apparently had taken so strong a hold upon them that they could not realize that circumstances were against them. They decided to support Sweden, and day after day Mazepa's officers urged him to notify Charles of their decision and work out with him a joint plan of campaign against Muscovy. At length the hetman decided to take their advice and entered into open negotiations with Charles, whom he begged, according to Orlik, to cross the Desna and unite with his army. In the latter part of October he stationed a few Kozaks at his capital of Baturin to protect it, and with the remaining troops and the officers went to the Swedish camp near the Desna. There is no exact information of the agreement which he drew up with the Swedish king, but later documents furnish information as to what Mazepa and his officers expected to gain from the alliance. The Ukraine, on both sides of the Dnieper and including the Zaporozhians, was to be free forever from any foreign rule. Neither Sweden nor any other allies were to use any pretext such as freedom, protection, or any other aim to extend their authority over Ukraine and the Zaporozhian Kozaks, to claim any right to collect tribute or taxes, or to occupy the Ukrainian fortresses which might be taken from Moscow by capture or by treaty. Sweden was to preserve the integrity of Ukraine and prevent other nations from enslaving her in any way, and religiously to respect the Ukrainian boundaries as well as the liberties, laws, rights, and privileges of the people, in order that Ukraine might live in peace and enjoy her freedom forever.

Though these were the gains which Mazepa and his associates expected to secure from their joint operations with Sweden, they were soon forced to recognize that their hopes were pitched too high.

Mazepa's Defeat: Mazepa conducted his negotiations with such great secrecy that even the Kozaks whom he was leading to unite with Charles knew nothing about his plans, and first learned of them during their march. Peter, in fact, discovered the existence of the alliance before the Ukrainian people did; and before Mazepa had acquainted his fellow citizens with his union with the King of Sweden, the tsar laid his heavy hand upon Ukraine, making any action impossible. The Muscovite army immediately laid siege to Baturin and captured it through the treachery of its defenders, seized Mazepa's supplies, his treasury, and his cannon, and visited terrible punishment upon the inhabitants, massacring the townspeople, destroying the city, and putting the officers to torture. In other places the Muscovites likewise imposed savage retribution upon those suspected of adherence to Mazepa and the Swedes, except upon the officers, whom they treated with consideration in order to retain their loyalty to the tsar. Circulars were distributed in the tsar's name to tell the Ukrainian people that Mazepa had joined the Swedes for the purpose of giving Ukraine to Poland and of introducing Roman Catholicism as a means of destroying the Orthodox faith. Mazepa was portrayed as an atheist, a secret Catholic, and an enemy to the Ukrainian people, as well as the person responsible for the extortion of the heavy and illegal taxes from the people, while the government of Muscovy promised the Ukrainians consideration and favors of various kinds. The Kozak officers were ordered to meet at Hlukhiv to elect a new hetman in place of Mazepa.

To counteract this Muscovite propaganda Mazepa and the Swedish king also distributed to the Ukrainian inhabitants open letters in which they appealed for popular support and gave assurances that Charles did not intend any harm but desired "to defend Ukraine from the tyranny of Muscovy." They claimed that it was his purpose to return to the people their former rights and liberties, but Muscovy, on the contrary, desired to enslave Ukraine; the people would be doomed to destruction if they did not take immediate steps to prevent this threat to their freedom.

It is difficult to say whether the people, if they had been free to choose, would have accepted the promises made by Mazepa or those by the tsar. The Ukrainians undoubtedly had many serious grievances against Moscow and the Muscovites, but at the same time they neither liked nor trusted Mazepa, whom they considered a faithful servant of the tsar. As it was, however, the people had no choice in the matter; the Muscovite army was in the heart of Ukraine, where it was punishing without mercy the followers of Mazepa and threatening dire vengeance upon the inhabitants if they dared to support the Swedes. Most of the Kozak troops were absent with the Muscovite army, and Mazepa had with him only about four thousand men. Under these conditions Ukraine was powerless to move.

The Kozak officers arrived humbly at Hlukhiv and in

their presence Mazepa was formally deposed from the hetmancy, publicly denounced, and hanged in effigy. In the election that followed, the wishes of Muscovy were heeded and the docile Ivan Skoropadsky was elected in his place. The clergy obediently pronounced an anathema against the deposed hetman, who had done more for the Ukrainian Church than any of his predecessors; and in order to free themselves from suspicion the Ukrainian townspeople declared their loyalty to the tsar and begged for the bounties he had so graciously promised. The Kozak officers received estates which the tsar had confiscated from Mazepa and his followers, and many of the officers who had followed Mazepa to the Swedish camp now returned, the most noted being Apostol, Sulima, and Galagan. Mazepa himself hesitatingly entered into correspondence with the tsar, but feared to trust his word, and was, moreover, carefully kept under surveillance by the Swedes.

It was clear that Mazepa's hopes had failed to materialize, but he continued to delude himself with the expectation that matters would eventually turn out in his favor. He persuaded Charles to winter in Ukraine and thus exhausted the strength of his ally; his only real accomplishment was his winning over of the Zaporozhian Kozaks to the Swedish cause. Formerly they had been hostile to Mazepa, whom they looked upon as a tool of Muscovy and of the landlords; and Hordienko, the custodian of the Sich since 1701, had been a bitter enemy to Moscow, Mazepa, and serfdom. Now that the hetman had joined the Swedes against the tsar, Hordienko went over to him, but several months passed before he succeeded in inducing his Kozaks to follow him, since the Zaporozhian officers had for a long time maintained neutrality toward Mazepa and Skoropadsky. Early in 1709 they began to drift to the side of Sweden and sent representatives to Mazepa, and in March the custodian and his Zaporozhians arrived in the Swedish camp and greeted Charles in a speech delivered in Latin. The Swedes expressed their delight at the accession of the Zaporozhian troops and praised their military accomplishments, but the reinforcement was of little material benefit to them, and even less advantageous for the Zaporozhians. The Swedish king, in order to assure his communications with the Zaporozhians, moved deeper into Ukraine but was halted in the province of Poltava, which refused to submit and blocked his way to the Sich. Meanwhile a Muscovite army had captured the Sich with the aid of a former Kozak, Galagan, who had deserted Mazepa and was eager to win the favor of the tsar. The Zaporozhian garrison surrendered because of promises made by Galagan and the Muscovite officers, but the latter failed to keep their word and mercilessly punished the rebels, beheading and hanging many of those still alive, and exhuming and defiling the bodies of the dead, both Kozaks and civilians. The remnants of the Zaporozhian Kozaks moved their headquarters to Oleshky in the Tatar territory, not far from the mouth of the Dnieper River, where their new Sich continued to exist for nineteen years.

The surrender of the Sich in May 1709 was followed by the defeat of Charles a month later in the decisive battle of Poltava. The remnants of his forces attempted to cross the Dnieper into Turkish territory, but the Muscovite army pursued them and only Charles and Mazepa succeeded in making the crossing with a small part of the army, while the rest were overtaken and forced to surrender. Although most of the Ukrainian officers who had been with Mazepa surrendered immediately after the battle, a few of his intimates followed him, including the general secretary Philip Orlik and Mazepa's nephew Andrey Voinarovsky. All the refugees fled with the Swedish king across the steppes to Tiahinia (Bendery), where they remained for several years. Charles made efforts to incite Turkey to attack Muscovy, and finally succeeded, but Mazepa did not live to see the attack. Weary and despairing of his life, since Peter had offered the Turks 300,000 thalers to give him up, he fell ill, died on August 22 (September 2), 1709, and was buried in a monastery at Galatz on the Danube.

Philip Orlik: The officers who were with Mazepa and the army under Hordienko did not lose hope but continued to plan to free Ukraine from Muscovy with the aid of Sweden and Turkey. In April 1710, after lengthy negotiations, they elected Orlik hetman to succeed Mazepa. An interesting set of regulations was drawn up at this time to outline the future government of the Hetman state; though they never went into effect because the authors never succeeded in conquering Ukraine, they are nevertheless of interest as indicating the aims of those who were attempting to liberate the country. In many respects the document represents a distinct advance, for it provided the germ of a parliamentary system and called attention to the fact that in later years the hetman had usurped "autocratic authority and legalized it by the motto, My wish is my command!" Accordingly the constitution provided that a "general assembly" was to meet at the hetman's capital three times a year—at Christmas, Easter, and in the autumn—to decide important issues. The assembly was to consist of officers of the general staff, the colonels, their regimental staff officers, and captains, "general councillors" elected by the Kozak rank and file, and deputies of the Zaporozhian Sich. In case any tendency harmful to the people should appear in the hetman's rule, the councillors were to be free to "notify" the hetman, who was not to take offense or to punish them. He was to have permission to handle without awaiting a decision of the general assembly urgent issues which could not be delayed, but even in such events he was to seek the advice of the general staff. He was not to carry on secret negotiations or correspondence, nor was he to have control of the military treasury, for which a general treasurer was to be elected, but the hetman was to have a definite amount at his disposal for his "official and personal needs.'' Another provision specified that he must guard against oppression of the soldiers or civilians, and against such corruption as had forced people to abandon their homes and seek freedom in foreign lands. The Kozak officers were forbidden to use for work on their estates Kozaks or civilians not dependent upon them, to seize land or acquire it by forced sale, to enserf people for any misdemeanor or use their subjects for labor, and so on.

The constitution was an excellent one, but it never went into effect, for the men who planned it and drew it up never succeeded in returning to Ukraine.

From time to time a ray of light appeared. The King of Sweden promised that he would not make peace with Russia until he had won freedom for Ukraine, and the same promise was made to the Zaporozhians by the Crimean khan, while Turkey, which was in constant fear of Russia, joined Sweden in the fall of 1710. Early in 1711 Orlik marched into western Ukraine with his own Kozaks, a Tatar army, and the regiments of Polish nobles belonging to the pro-Swedish faction, and captured the cities of Uman, Bohuslav, and Korsun. He defeated Butovich, who was sent to oppose him; but when he laid siege to the fortress of Bila Tserkva he was less successful and lost many of his soldiers. Meanwhile the Tatars had begun to plunder the countryside, the inhabitants turned against him, and he was forced to withdraw.

In the summer of 1711 Peter declared war against Turkey. Expecting aid from the Moldavians he advanced to the Pruth with as little caution as that shown by Charles during his invasion of Ukraine; there he was surrounded by the Turks and placed in a desperate situation. Orlik expected that it would now be possible to dictate terms of peace regarding the future of Ukraine, as Peter would be obliged to abandon his claims to it, but the tsar's officers bribed the Turkish vizir, who permitted Peter and his army to depart unmolested. As to the future status of Ukraine, the terms of the treaty now drawn up between the Muscovites and the Turks were so vague that anyone could have interpreted them to his own satisfaction. Orlik claimed that Russia had promised in the treaty to evacuate Ukraine, but the tsar's officials claimed that there was no such obligation. The Turkish government accepted the interpretation of the Ukrainian hetman and declared war against Russia for having failed to evacuate Ukraine, but Muscovite money again changed hands, the treaty of the previous year was ratified, and the clause relating to Ukraine was defined as meaning that Russia had abandoned her claims to all western Ukraine with the exception of Kiev and to the Zaporozhian Sich, but that the region east of the Dnieper was to remain in her hands. These concessions cost the tsar another hundred thousand rubles, and Orlik, in spite of all his efforts to induce the Turks to make provision in the treaty for eastern Ukraine, which had been promised to the Kozaks, had no success. Even in western Ukraine the people did not enjoy their freedom long, for Poland soon renewed her ancient claims to this area.

Several years passed before the tsar removed his troops from western Ukraine, and then only after giving orders that the inhabitants should be forced to migrate to eastern Ukraine, a proclamation to this effect being made in 1711, after which for four years Muscovite soldiers drove the Ukrainians east across the Dnieper; at the close of 1714 they surrendered the fortress of Bila Tserkva to the Poles and departed. Late in 1712 Orlik and the Zaporozhians had attempted to conquer the country west of the river, but their weak forces had been dispersed by the Polish army. In 1713 Russia and Turkey reached a full agreement, after which Charles was obliged to leave Turkey and to set out for home, accompanied by Orlik and a few of his friends. The rest of the Kozaks went back to Ukraine. The Zaporozhians returned to their old villages below the falls and begged the tsar to accept them as subjects, but though several large groups were admitted the tsar refused to take in the entire Sich population because of the treaty of 1712 with Turkey, and it was not until after the outbreak of another war with Turkey in 1733 that they were finally accepted. Orlik and Hordienko attempted to dissuade the Zaporozhians from joining Russia, but failed, and for several years Orlik also made efforts to find new allies against Russia and to interest neighboring countries in the Ukrainian problem, but without success.

CHAPTER XVII

THE DISSOLUTION OF THE KOZAK HOST AND THE DECLINE IN UKRAINIAN NATIONAL LIFE

The Curtailment of the Hetman's Power: The alliance between Mazepa and Charles had a far-reaching effect upon Ukrainian national life, for it gave Peter an excuse to adopt stronger measures against Ukrainian self-government. The Russian* government had long been taking steps in that direction, though until this time it had left Ukraine under the formal control of the hetman and his Officers' Council. It now, however, began little by little to limit the authority of the head of the Ukrainian state and the scope of Ukrainian autonomy. Whenever a new hetman was inaugurated or a crisis in Ukrainian affairs occurred, Russia attempted to bring about a further reduction of Ukrainian rights, accompanying each such seizure of power with a declaration that it was merely a logical outgrowth of the "treaty of Bohdan Khmelnistky," and that Ukraine was in the same situation as at the time of the Union of 1654, though in reality the tsar was consciously violating the terms of this agreement. It is true that after Brukhovetsky's uprising Russia had not at once introduced the Russian system of taxation and administration, but had been content to postpone them to a future occasion, and theoretically the country had been left in the hands of the hetman and the Officers' Council, but Russian governors with garrisons had been stationed in all the larger cities, where they so limited the authority of the hetman as to reduce him in fact to impotence. No important issues could be settled without the consent of Rus-

* As the tsardom of Muscovy expanded by the conquest of its neighbors it had abandoned its old name and assumed that of "Russia," which was a Latinization of "Rus," the ancient name of Ukraine (Editor).

sia, and the Russian government watched with great care all movements in Ukraine, making efforts to gain the loyalty and assure the services of the Kozak officers by giving them estates.

The Russians, however, were not content with control but aimed at the complete abolition of Ukrainian identity and the reduction of Ukraine to the level of an ordinary Russian province, and decided to take full advantage of Mazepa's insurrection for this purpose.

Though Ukraine had quite unintentionally found itself involved in Mazepa's revolt and the masses had not followed the hetman at all, the Russian government decided to punish the whole population, "Mazepa's betrayal" having established in its eyes a presumption of guilt against all Ukrainians, and the tsar determined to deal with them severely in order to prevent revolts in future.

As has been noted, nearly all the Kozak troops had been attached to Peter's army, and the ordinary people had not joined Mazepa when he made his sudden alliance with Charles XII. The new hetman, Skoropadsky, had been immediately elected to provide opposition to Mazepa, but the problem of sanctioning the Ukrainian liberties had been delayed pending a more peaceful era. When the crisis had passed and the Swedes had been defeated, the Kozak officers and Hetman Skoropadsky reminded Peter of the need for this sanction and begged him to protect Ukraine from abuse by the Russian generals and other officials stationed in the country during the Swedish invasion, who under pretext of war conditions had been grievously oppressing the inhabitants. The tsar readily agreed to approve the old rights, but did not restore the hetman's office to its old position of supreme authority, and on July 31 (August 11), 1709, named a Russian, Izmailov, "to be resident minister at the hetman's court with the function of assisting him with 'forceful' advice in settling all issues, because of the recent rebellion in Ukraine and the Zaporozhian uprising." It was Izmailov's duty to assure good administration throughout Ukraine, as well as on the part of the hetman and the Officers' Council, and also to keep a sharp eye upon these officials. A year later another Russian representative was appointed, making two overseers of Ukrainian affairs. The residence of the hetman had been moved from Baturin nearer the Russian border to Hlukhiv, where two Russian regiments were stationed with instructions to arrest him and the officers upon suspicion of taking action contrary to the tsar's desires.

This last step alone completely limited the hetman's authority and destroyed the old importance of the hetman's office. He could take no action without notifying the tsar's representatives, or rather without securing their permission. Everyone perfectly understood that the real power lay, not in the hands of the hetman, but in those of the tsar's representatives, his ministers, and various confidential agents, who ruled Ukraine according to their own will. The garrisons which the tsar stationed in Ukraine lived at the expense of the overburdened inhabitants, while the Ukrainian Kozaks were forced to go to remote regions to dig canals and build fortresses in the vicinity of St. Petersburg, or Astrakhan, or in the Caucasus Mountains—"on the Line," as it was called—where they perished by the thousands, and those who succeeded in returning to their homes were broken in health and stricken with poverty. They received no pay for their services.

Colonel Cherniak, who was present at the digging of the Ladoga Canal in 1722, reported the sufferings of the Kozaks to the Russian senate as follows:

In the construction camps on the Ladoga Canal there are many Kozaks who are sick and dying, and frightful diseases spread with appalling rapidity, the most common being fever and swelling of the feet, which cause many deaths. The officers in charge of the work, in pursuance of orders by Brigadier Leontiev, disregard the sufferings of the poor Kozaks, unmercifully abusing the sick laborers by beating them with clubs and giving them no rest day, night, or holiday, and on this account I fear that the Kozaks there will perish, as they did last year, when only about a third returned home. Wherefore I inform the senate by this modest report, and humbly beseech you in your kindness not to allow all the Kozaks under my command to perish on the canal works, and not to transfer them to other places to undertake new tasks. God is my witness that these poor people are unfitted for further labor, for they have lost their health and strength and are barely alive. Permit them to go to their homes in the early part of September and do not keep them until the rainy season in fall.

The sufferings of the Ukrainians at forced labor on the Russian canals form the theme of many folk songs.

Orlik later recalled to the Zaporozhians their terrible sufferings and declared that "Moscow" was deliberately planning the destruction of the Kozak army, and it was for this reason that "by her ukases she sent tens of thousands of them into hard labor where many died, others were starved to death, and the rest were poisoned by bread made of rotten flour mixed with lime and ground lizards."

Whether intentional or not, the result for Ukraine was the same. No one, however, had the courage to protest against the will of the dreaded tsar, for all feared for their lives and even more so for their positions.

Peter was not satisfied with having placed the hetman under constant supervision, but personally interfered in Ukrainian affairs by appointing colonels and members of the Officers' Council against the wish of or without notice to the hetman. The Russian generals and ministers, ignoring the hetman completely, also gave positions to various parasites in return for gifts, and before long began to distribute offices not only to native Ukrainians but to Great Russians as well. Peter requested Hetman Skoropadsky to give his daughter in marriage to a Great Russian, and when the hetman made inquiry as to a suitable son-in-law his attention was called to a trusted official of the tsar, Peter Tolstoy. After this the tsar, ostensibly as a reward to Skoropadsky for his services, personally appointed Tolstoy colonel of Starodub, the largest of the Ukrainian regiments. After this beginning many such colonelcies in Ukraine were given to Russian "commandants," as the former military governorships came to be called, so that by the time of Peter's death in 1725 there were few Ukrainian colonels left.

The tsar intervened in Ukrainian affairs of all kinds, but if anything went wrong he blamed the hetman and the Officers' Council, and made use of the occasion as an excuse to lessen their power. Peter had approved the elderly Skoropadsky as hetman in the first place because of his age and docility. The Kozak officers had wished to elect a man by the name of Polubotok, but the tsar disapproved of him, remarking, according to reports, that he was too wise and might turn out to be another Mazepa. Skoropadsky surrounded himself with relatives, of whom his beautiful young wife Nastia, of the Markovich family, is worthy of special mention; it was said that she bore the mace while he wore the dresses. His son-in-law, Charnysh, who was made general army judge, introduced corruption, falsehood, and bribery into the military courts, and the tsar, pointing to this mismanagement in the hetman's administration, prepared a new blow to Ukrainian autonomy by appointing in 1722 a council known as the "Little Russian Board," consisting of six Russian senior officers of garrisons in Ukraine, under the chairmanship of Brigadier Veliaminov. The board was empowered to supervise judges and to hear complaints against any Ukrainian courts or any officials having to do with law enforcement, even to the supreme army tribunal and the army, or hetman's, chancellery. It had authority to see to it that officers did not oppress the ordinary Kozaks and civilians and, in case of quarrels with the hetman, to take whatever action against him it saw fit. It could inspect the hetman's chancellery and all incoming and outgoing correspondence, control all Ukrainian income, take funds from local collectors and offices and make payments for army and all other needs. Regarding any irregularities it was to report directly to the senate.

Peter attempted to justify his usurpation and these violations of the treaty between Ukraine and Russia by charging malpractices in respect to the office of the hetman, the courts, the collection of taxes, and abuses by the officers, who, he claimed, were taking land from the Kozaks and civilians and enserfing the peasants. It was in vain that Skoropadsky with tears in his eyes implored the tsar in the name of "all the Little Russian [Ukrainian] people" not to believe the false accusations. The tsar paid no attention to the appeals of the hetman, and in order to present his autocratic measures to the Ukrainians in their best light distributed a printed order throughout the country in which he stated that he had inaugurated the Little Russian Board for no other reason than to prevent the Kozak officers from abusing the people, and that he had ordered the board to hear all complaints in such matters.

The First Abolition of the Hetmancy; Polubotok: Skoropadsky was so affected by this injustice on the part of the tsar that he fell sick and died, in July 1722, thus giving the tsar a fresh opportunity to strike a blow at what was left of Ukrainian autonomy. He now decided to abolish the hetmancy altogether, and upon receiving the news of Skoropadsky's death directed Colonel Polubotok and the Officers' Council to take the place of the late hetman but to make no decisions without the approval of Veliaminov. At the same time he transferred Ukraine from under the ministry of foreign affairs, through which the hetmans of Ukraine—as an autonomous country—had maintained official relations with the tsar's government, to the competence of the senate like the ordinary Russian provinces. When the Ukrainian officers sent representatives to Peter to request permission for the election of a new hetman in place of Skoropadsky they received no answer for a long time; and when they repeated their request, the tsar replied in the summer of 1723 that the matter of the election of a hetman had been postponed indefinitely, adding that his government was seeking a properly qualified and loyal man for the position because "from the period of the first hetman, Bohdan Khmelnitsky, to Skoropadsky all the hetmans had proven themselves traitors," and that they must not annoy him further with this problem, "because at present the Ukrainian government is functioning in an orderly manner." The tsar not only postponed the election but forbade the Ukrainians to make further requests so that to all appearances the hetman's office had been abolished forever.

Events in Ukraine after the abolition of the hetmancy, however, forced the Ukrainian people to mourn for the lost hetmans. Though the Russians attempted to make them believe that all the limitations on the freedom of action of the Ukrainian government were for the best interests of the people, the Ukrainian officers having proved to be corrupt, the new Russian rulers did not bring any betterment of conditions or any relief for the suffering inhabitants, but instead multiplied the abuses and added to the oppression. Everyone complained that there was no one to defend the Ukrainians, no head—no hetman.

Veliaminov, the chairman of the Little Russian Board, acted as if he were the real ruler, issuing orders to everyone and railing at the acting hetman, Polubotok, "What does your position amount to beside mine? Don't you know that I am a brigadier, and chairman of the Board? In comparison with me you are nothing!" He further boasted to the officers that he would bend them until they cracked, and when they reminded him of the ancient Ukrainian rights, he shouted, "Your old system is ordered changed; you are to have a new system—I am your law!" If the Russian officials conducted themselves in this manner in the presence of the acting hetman and his officials, it may be easily imagined how they treated the common people. The board introduced new and higher taxes in violation of old custom and dictated the use of the finances; the Russian generals, relying upon the support of the government, oppressed the Ukrainian inhabitants more than the Ukrainian officers ever had, while the Russian soldiers stationed in Ukraine broke the laws with impunity. Meanwhile the Kozaks were drafted in large numbers for hard labor far from home, where they perished like flies; out of five or ten thousand sent into remote parts of Russia a third or a half died at the scene of employment and the rest returned home broken in health. It has been estimated that within the five years from 1721 to 1725 inclusive about twenty thousand Ukrainian soldiers perished in toil on the Ladoga Canal, in the Caucasus, and along the Volga.

The terrible sufferings inflicted upon his people were more than Polubotok, a man of great energy and lofty patriotism, could endure. Realizing that Peter had given as an excuse for the abolition of the former Ukrainian rights the corruption of the Ukrainian officers, he attempted to restore clean government and to put an end to the abuses which had given the tsar his opportunity. He issued orders forbidding his officers under severe penalties to employ the services of Kozaks for private purposes, reformed the courts by ending bribery and the oppression of the poor, and demanded that in each village and regimental court there should be more than one judge, in order that one might watch the other. He regularized the system of appeals from the lower courts and improved the procedure in the supreme military tribunal.

The Russian government, however, continued to refer to alleged corruption in order to have a pretext "to take Little Russia into its own hands," as Tolstoy later said of Peter's policy. Accordingly the efforts of Polubotok to improve the Ukrainian administration met only with opposition and hostility on the part of Russia, the more so because he and the Officers' Council unceasingly pressed for permission to elect a new hetman, complained of the maladministration and brutality of the Russian officials, and pointed out the breaches of Bohdan Khmelnitsky's treaty—the treaty of Pereyaslav, of 1654—with Russia. When Veliaminov brought charges against Polubotok because the acting hetman had dared to differ with him, the tsar decided to limit the rights of the Ukrainian people still further; he ordered Polubotok and his higher officers to move to St. Petersburg, with the aim of reducing the number of Ukrainian officers and Kozak soldiers in Ukraine; and commanded the Kozak army to be sent to the southern border under pretext of using it to guard Ukraine against the Tatars.

In St. Petersburg Polubotok and his officers petitioned the tsar to restore to Ukraine her old rights, again citing the terms of Bohdan Khmelnitsky's treaty, which forbade all interference with the Kozak courts, whose work was being hindered by the Little Russian Board with its Russian members. Simultaneously, however, a petition arrived from the Starodub regiment to request the introduction of a Russian court and the appointment of a Russian colonel. Polubotok protested that Veliaminov had forged this petition in order to nullify the effect of that presented by the Ukrainians, and that it had been presented to provide an excuse for robbing the Ukrainians of their rights. Upon receiving this statement the tsar sent a confidential agent, Rumiantsov, to Ukraine for the professed purpose of inquiring among the Kozaks as to whether they wished the old Ukrainian system of administration for which Polubotok and his officers had pleaded, or the Russian system requested by the Starodub regiment. His real purpose, however, was to receive complaints by the people against the Kozak officers.

As soon as Polubotok learned of this scheme, he understood what Peter was aiming at and foresaw the consequences, for he knew that Rumiantsov and Veliaminov could easily obtain from the inhabitants the kind of information they desired, primarily because Ukraine was now left without the general officers and there was no one who could prevent intimidation of the populace. The people would be forced to make such replies as the ruthless Russian officials demanded, which meant that they could collect a large number of votes for the Russian system, especially if the Russians suggested that the common people would regain the lost lands which had fallen into the hands of the Ukrainian officers. Unable to leave St. Petersburg himself, Polubotok sent representatives to Ukraine to instruct the people how to conduct themselves during Rumiantsov's investigation and what answers to make to his questions. At the acting hetman's suggestion the Kozak force stationed along the southern border on the Kolomak River sent the tsar a petition complaining against the abuses of its new Russian rulers, in particular of illegal recruiting, the presence of Russian garrisons in Ukraine, and their plundering of the country, and begged for permission to elect a hetman in accordance with ancient custom.

There was obviously nothing illegal about this procedure, but Peter became enraged because Polubotok was blocking his plans and ordered him and all the Kozak officers with him at St. Petersburg to be arrested and thrown into prison, also issuing orders for the arrest of all who had shared in preparing the petition. The Russian government had no grounds for accusation against Polubotok's civil administration, which had been honest and efficient, and accordingly the investigation was directed against him as head of the army. He was kept in confinement for several months, but fell ill before the conclusion of the inquiry and died in the SS. Peter and Paul Prison in St. Petersburg in the fall of 1724. The death of Polubotok was mourned throughout Ukraine, especially by the Ukrainian officers, who acclaimed him as a hero and a martyr for his country.

Revival of the Hetmancy; Hetman Apostol: After the

death of Polubotok Ukraine was left defenseless against the abuses of the Little Russian Board and Veliaminov. The best-known Ukrainian officers were in prison at St. Petersburg and the others remained silent for fear of punishment by the cruel tsar. They dared not protest against the all-powerful Veliaminov, and a few selfish native careerists even aided him in enforcing the Russian administration. A Russian, Major Kokoshkin, was appointed colonel of the Starodub regiment; and another Russian, Bogdanov, was put in charge of the regiment of Chernihiv. For two decades the country swarmed with Russian soldiers, all of whom were maintained in Ukraine illegally and at the expense of the Ukrainian population; in 1722 the Russian government collected 45,000 rubles and great quantities of food for the upkeep of the army, and in 1724 it gathered 140,000 rubles and 40,000 measures of grain. In addition, the government attempted to reduce the Kozaks to poverty by hard labor, sending ten thousand to the region of the Caspian Sea in 1723 to build the Holy Cross fortress on the Sulak River, and filling their places with another ten thousand when the first contingent was sent home in 1724.

Ukraine faced ruin, and the people were in desperation, not knowing whither to look for help. The death of Peter the Great early in 1725 brought about some changes. As his widow and successor, Catherine I, and her chief minister, Menshikov, did not feel as secure as had her dreaded husband Peter, she considered it necessary to relieve Ukraine to some extent from its terrible oppression, another reason being the prospect of war with Turkey, in which the Kozak soldiers would be needed. The despots of St. Petersburg also feared that the Ukrainian officers might rebel in revenge for the ill treatment received from Russia. Accordingly, Catherine and Menshikov promised to permit the election of a Kozak hetman, to abolish the Little Russian Board, to cancel the new taxes, and to restore the former rights to the Ukrainian people. There were some supporters of Peter's policy, however, who strongly protested against these changes, the most bitter of them being Tolstoy, who reminded the authorities that the great tsar had consistently refused to permit the election of a hetman and had reduced the power of the colonels and other officers "in order to get Little Russia into his hands." Much had been done toward that end, and the authority of the Kozak officers had also been undermined by the antagonism of the Ukrainians themselves. There was no prospect of restoring the old rights, and the only apparent improvement was that the officers who had not yet died in prison were released, taxes were slightly reduced for a brief period, and instead of being sent to the Sulak for forced labor the people paid a contribution in money.

In 1727 the Empress Catherine died, and Peter's young grandson, Peter II, came to the throne with the aid of Menshikov, who had acquired many large estates in Ukraine, was opposed to the Little Russian Board, and advocated the restoration of the old rights of self-government. Shortly after the accession, the party of Dolgoruky defeated Menshikov's faction, and the new ministers, who were also opponents of the old policy of Peter, convinced the young emperor that it was best to restore Ukrainian autonomy.

The administration of Ukraine was at once transferred from the hands of the senate to those of the ministry of foreign affairs, the Little Russian Board was abolished and with it all the taxes and charges which it had introduced, the Ukrainian officers who were still in St. Petersburg were released and permitted to return to their homes, and Veliaminov, upon accusation by the Kozak officers, was tried for mismanagement. Most important of all was the decision to elect a new hetman. In the summer of 1727 Privy Councilor Naumov was sent to Ukraine to supervise the election and to reside at the capital of the new hetman. He had secret instructions from the government, however, to permit the election of no one but Danilo Apostol, the aged colonel of the Mirhorod regiment.

The Kozak officers had no intention of opposing the will of the tsar, for they were only too pleased to see the old customs and privileges restored and were willing to accept any hetman whatever. Apostol, moreover, was quite acceptable to the Ukrainians in spite of the fact that he was the choice of the Russian government. He was a Kozak of long standing, seventy years of age or over, who had grown up during the period when Ukraine had known strength and hope and the ambition to fight for a better future. He had been one of the close associates of Mazepa when the latter had planned to free Ukraine with the aid of the Swedes, but had left the ill-fated hetman when he realized that the plan was sure to end in failure. He had won the favor of the government by his tactfulness, but had never been a party to anti-Ukrainian plans, and had a definite Ukrainian policy of his own. He also belonged to that small group of officers whose hands had never been stained by oppression of the common people; in fact, he was a hetman whose election could be welcomed by all.

The Officers' Council announced that it would gladly accept Apostol as the hetman, and on October 1 (12), 1727 he was elected in Hlukhiv amid great jubilation. Naumov arrived before the church where the Kozak army and the populace were awaiting him; after him came the bearers of the insignia of the hetman's office; then there was read the imperial proclamation permitting the election, and finally Naumov asked whom the people desired, whereupon all with one voice shouted "Apostol!" The formula was repeated three times, after which Naumov proclaimed Apostol hetman of Ukraine. The nominee at first disclaimed willingness to accept, but as the people insisted, he withdrew his objections and took an oath of loyalty to the tsar. The people, wrote Naumov in his report, rejoiced exceedingly.

From the reports of the proceedings it is clear that the old Ukrainian rights were not restored in full. At the election of the hetman nothing was said of the statutes which were to serve as the basis for the Ukrainian constitution, nor were the old Ukrainian liberties ratified in the name of the tsar. Naumov, the resident commissioner of the Russian government, was to live at the hetman's side and aid him in settling important issues. From now on the general army court was to consist of three Ukrainian officers and three Russians appointed by the Russian government, while the army treasury was placed under the control of two men, one a Ukrainian and the other a Russian, and in military matters both the hetman and his officers were subordinated to the field-marshal of the Russian army. Though the Russian government trusted Apostol more fully than it did any other Ukrainian officer, nevertheless after the election one of his sons was kept in St. Petersburg as a hostage. The old policies of Peter the Great had not gone with him to the grave, some at least having been retained by the new government.

The Ukrainians, however, were relieved to be freed from Veliaminov's rule and to have a degree of autonomy restored, abridged though it was. Apostol endeavored slowly and cautiously to revive the authority and prestige of the hetman's office and to lessen the influence and the interference of the Russian military and civil authorities in Ukrainian affairs by attempting, as Polubotok had done, to secure good administration in all departments and to defend the people against abuse by the officers. He strove to abolish bribery and insubordination in order to give the Russian government no excuse to intervene, whereas in his relations with St. Petersburg he displayed a loyalty and a willingness to coöperate which eventually led to the restoration of many of the old rights guaranteed by Bohdan Khmelnitsky's treaty.

On the occasion of the coronation of the young emperor early in 1728, Apostol and the Officers' Council went to St.

Petersburg, where they remained at court for more than six months in an effort to gain the favor of the tsar and of the influential courtiers, with the aim of regaining autonomy for Ukraine. In August 1728, in reply to a petition by the hetman, the tsar and his Privy Council approved the so-called "Definitive Articles." Though Khmelnitsky's treaty was not fully upheld, a number of rights were recognized and the people were left with the hope that the government would at last live up to its promises. In reality Ukrainian autonomy remained decidedly limited, the government, for example, admitting that the election of the hetman should be free from interference but stating that one could be held only with the permission of the tsar. The right to appoint the members of the Officers' Council was placed in the hands of the Host, but in reality the privilege applied to the lower officers only. Each company was to nominate several candidates for captain, one of whom would be approved by the hetman, while the regimental officers were to be selected from among the captains and important Kozak soldiers subject to the approval of the hetman. Candidates for the positions of colonel or member of the Officers' Council were to submit their names to the tsar for confirmation. The Ukrainian court was affirmed according to the articles accepted by Khmelnitsky, but with the important reservation that in future the general army court should be composed of three Ukrainian and three Russian members.

It was a serious blow at autonomy, however, that these concessions were made only after many petitions had been submitted and that they accordingly appeared to be favors granted by the government and subject to withdrawal at any time—and in fact they were withdrawn soon after. As there was no force available with which to fight for rights, it was, however, the best that could be done at the time. Previous events had proved the complete lack of strength to resist among the Ukrainian people, and Apostol therefore considered it his duty to petition the tsar, and literally to beat his brow upon the ground before him, in order to make some small gains for Ukraine.

In accordance with the promises made by the Russian government several vacancies in Ukraine were filled by Ukrainians. A special commission of Ukrainian jurists was chosen to collect and codify the Ukrainian laws. In order to put an end to future efforts by the officers to acquire army and Kozak lands, the titles to the land already owned by the officers were checked. The regimental chancelleries which directed regimental business were reorganized, and in 1730 an important set of instructions similar to those prepared by Polubotok was issued to the courts, each of which, from the lowest village court to the general army tribunal, was no longer to be administered by one judge but by a board of several judges. The procedure of appeals was also regulated, from decisions of a company judge to the regimental court, and thence to the general army court which was to hear appeals only.

Another important event was the return of the Zaporozhians. It has been pointed out that the Kozaks were not content to live under the Turkish flag but had appealed to the Russian government to permit them to return to Ukraine. Hordienko and Orlik had attempted to discourage this step, but after the death of the former the Kozaks of the Sich petitioned more urgently for permission to come back. As long as the treaty between Russia and Turkey was in force, the Russian government did not consider it possible to take the Kozaks back, for to do so would have violated the agreement which recognized the Zaporozhians as subjects of the sultan. The Russian government, however, promised that they might return as soon as preparations were completed for an attack on Turkey, and as war clouds appeared early in the decade of 1720 the return of the Zaporozhian Kozaks was expected in the near future. In 1733, when the interregnum began in Poland and it was decided to begin war in summer, a declaration from the tsar was sent to the Sich to

inform the Zaporozhians that they could be admitted to
the protection of the tsar, and promised to inform them
later as to the definite time of their return. It became impossible for them to wait, however, because the khan had
called them to join him in an invasion of Poland, and accordingly they left Oleshky early in 1734 and ascended the
Dnieper to an old Zaporozhian center at Bazavluk. Later,
in Lubny, the Zaporozhian delegates signed a treaty with
Russia, according to the terms of which they were to live
in the old territory they had occupied in 1709 and to remain free from serfdom. They were to be governed by
elected officials and only indirectly by the commander of
the Russian army garrisoned in Ukraine and were to
guard the border and to receive for their services twenty
thousand rubles a year from the Russian government. In
return for these privileges the Zaporozhians took an oath
of loyalty to the empress. At that time they numbered
more than seven thousand men.

Thus there disappeared the last trace left by Mazepa's
insurrection. Only the uncompromising Orlik attempted
to take advantage of chaos in Poland and the war between
Russia and Turkey to arouse among the enemies of Russia some interest in the Ukrainian question, but without
success.

The efforts of Orlik and the simultaneous wars in Poland, Crimea, and Moldavia compelled the Russian government to use extreme caution in its dealings with
Ukraine. When Peter II died in 1730 and his place was
taken by his aunt, the Empress Anna, the old system of
repression applied by her uncle, Peter the Great, was revived. When Hetman Apostol fell sick and became para-
lyzed in 1733, the empress refused to permit the Ukrainian officers to rule the country, but entrusted the government to her resident commissioner, Prince Shakhovskoy,
and a council composed of equal numbers of Russians and
Ukrainians, and thus set up an organ to take over the government after the hetman's death. As recompense for this

injustice the burden of taxes was somewhat lightened and regiments quartered in Ukraine were reduced.

Apostol died shortly afterward, in January 1734. His death was a serious loss to the Ukrainian people, for he had had at heart the best interests of the country and had known how to work successfully for the welfare of the inhabitants. If his policy gave the impression of being humble and yielding, it must be remembered how difficult it was for him to gain anything substantial, surrounded as he was by new generations of Ukrainians who had grown up under Russian influences, who had no hope in the outcome of a struggle for their rights, and who were ready to follow the line of least resistance and seek favors of the Russian government. He had, moreover, to contend with a swarm of worthless individuals not connected in any way with Ukraine or Ukrainian national life, who had been given high positions by the generosity of the Russian government, and whose chief aim was to enrich themselves quickly at the expense of the masses.

The Second Abolition of the Hetmancy: The Russian government took advantage of the death of Hetman Apostol to abolish the hetmancy again. As soon as it learned of his passing it issued a second proclamation declaring that the election of a "capable and loyal man for this important office" required careful consideration, and that until such a man could be found the empress was introducing "a government composed of six persons." These were the imperial resident, Shakhovskoy, with two Russian associates, and three Ukrainians—Colonel Lizohub and two other Kozak officers. They were jointly to direct the affairs of the hetman's office, "in meetings they were to be on an equality, with the Great Russians sitting on the right, and the Little Russians on the left," and they were to govern according to Apostol's Definitive Articles, while the empress promised to accord the Ukrainian people the protection guaranteed by the terms of Bohdan Khmelnitsky's treaty.

The very wording of the empress' declaration indicates that it was patterned after the policies of Peter the Great, the reference to Khmelnitsky's treaty being intended purely to mislead the Ukrainian people, for the secret instructions given to Shakhovskoy clearly specified that the election of a hetman was mentioned only in order to avoid an insurrection but that in reality the government had no intention of electing any hetmans in future. The senate was again to have direct control over Ukraine as if it were one of the ordinary Russian provinces, and the real ruler of the country was now to be the head of the provisional council, Prince Shakhovskoy. The equality of the members remained an empty phrase in view of the authority with which this man was clothed; Prince Shakhovskoy was secretly directed to watch over the Ukrainian members of the council; if he found any grounds for suspicion against any of them, he was to arrest him and fill his place with someone favorably inclined to the Russian government, and in all important cases to pay no attention to formal instructions but to act according to his best judgment.

Under this new plan the head of the council became as truly the ruler of Ukraine as the chairman of Peter's Little Russian Board had formerly been. The government at St. Petersburg was sadly disillusioned, however, by the Russians who now and later were placed in positions of authority, for they proved to be autocratic, lawless, and oppressive, and governed unjustly and corruptly because they could rely upon the invariable support of their government. By their acts they destroyed the faith of the Ukrainian inhabitants in Russian methods and Russian people and in the pleasant sounding but treacherous phrases about justice and protection which were often repeated in Russian proclamations regarding administrative reorganization, Shakhovskoy, for instance, receiving public instructions to appoint to the new administration and to the general army court only capable Russians in order to make the Ukrainians prefer Russian officials and the Russian system of government, while his instructions also attempted to deceive the Ukrainians by explaining to them that this new order had been established primarily to protect them against the abuses committed by their Ukrainian officers, and that the hetman's administration was at fault for all the evils which they had suffered. In order to Russify the members of the Ukrainian upper classes Shakhovskoy was directed to prevent their contact with Poles and other foreigners and to sponsor and encourage intermarriage between them and the Russians.

It may easily be imagined how the Ukrainian people reacted to this new administration. Though the Russian government ordered its officials to put its policy into effect "secretly," "stealthily," and "cunningly," the injunctions soon became known and alarmed the timid Ukrainian officials, and it was not long before the government itself lost its delicacy of touch. It deposed the Kievan metropolitan, Vanatovich, and the priors of the Kievan monasteries, and exiled them because they did not hold church services to celebrate the name days of the tsars. Seizing upon various unfounded suspicions against the officers, it spied upon them and ordered the personal correspondence of all the high officials, even to Lizohub, to be inspected. With such treatment accorded to persons of importance, little thought was given to the ordinary inhabitants. Shakhovskoy considered the conduct of his administration too gentle in its dealings with the Kozak officers, and advised that Ukrainians be deprived of any share in its work, also recommending that a single Russian commissioner be appointed to rule Ukraine, evidently with himself in mind for the task. The Russian government, however, did not follow his advice, but attempted to satisfy its ardent representative with the comment that the Ukrainian members of the board were mere figureheads in any case, but that if they were excluded from participation, the Ukrainians "would become suspicious." An excellent example of how well Russia safeguarded the rights of the Ukrainians occurred in Kiev, where the magistrates were attempting to defend their rights against the abuses and lawlessness of the brutal Russian officers. In 1737 Prince Bariatinsky, who was then in charge of Ukraine as foreman of the board, arrested the entire city council of Kiev, seized the city charter and other documents, and explained to his government that he had taken this action so that the city council would have no legal basis for their claims to rights and privileges.

In addition to oppression by the Russian administration, the Ukraine suffered under the hands of the army officers, especially the Russian military governors in Kiev, who had long since replaced the so-called *voyvods,* and the commanders of the Russian troops, who during the long Turkish and Crimean campaigns and the Polish wars conducted themselves as they wished in southern Ukraine, gave orders to the Ukrainian regiments and their officers, and submitted to no laws or regulations. Terrorized by the harsh rule of the Russian authorities, the Ukrainian officers kept silence, not daring to raise their voices in defense of their rights, even to beg for the promised election of a hetman and the restoration of their ancient privileges. They were satisfied if they could only have the wherewithal to live, and conducted themselves, as the saying goes, "more silent than water, more lowly than grass." How severe was the Russian government, trained in the harsh school of Biron, is indicated by the relief experienced by the Ukrainians when the English General Keith was sent in 1740 to take the place of the Russian administrator. This distinguished soldier left a pleasant memory by his unwillingness to employ torture and cruel punishments; his slowness to impose penalties and his just and kindly manner were a source of amazement to a people to whom such conduct was most unusual in a government official.

While the upper classes of the Ukrainians were suffering insult and abuse, the common people were being mistreated even by their own officers, who had lost their political importance and did not have the courage to protest against the policy of the Russians but did their best to enlarge their estates and to enrich their descendants with vast areas of land. They accepted the program of the Russian authorities, did their share in making it effective, won the favor of the Russian government, increased the size of their holdings, and enserfed Kozaks and peasants alike, certain that the government would disregard any complaints against them. It was impossible for the people to defend their rights through legal channels.

The government understood thoroughly the value of intimidating the Ukrainian officers by spreading rumors from time to time that new orders were about to be issued to defend the inhabitants from them. As a matter of fact, the new Russian administrators made no efforts whatever to lessen the oppression by the Kozak officers, but trained in the Russian school of corruption and serfdom, accepted bribes from the Ukrainian nobles and sided with them and not with the downtrodden people.

The Ukrainians did not find in the Russian officials just and honest administrators, but lawless, selfish, and despotic rulers, who treated the masses harshly and at times even cruelly. There were many scoundrels who threatened people with accusations and drove them into prison, chains, and exile by pronouncing the dreaded phrase, "word and deed"—which meant that they knew of a "word and deed affecting the tsar"—whereupon reports of the accusation were sent to the terrible Russian "secret chancellery" in charge of political investigation. There is the well-known story of a Russian officer who quartered himself and his soldiers in the home of a Ukrainian nobleman. Not content with the hospitality he received he accused the owner of having stove lids decorated with pictures of the Russian two-headed eagle, arrested his host, and sent him to the office of the secret chancellery with the accusation that he was burning the tsar's insignia, "with what intention is not known." Here was a clear case of "word and deed," and the secret police began to question the man as to why he was thus burning the tsar's insignia. Though the defendant proved that the stove lids were of the usual pattern sold in the market and that he had had nothing to do with the design or manufacture, nevertheless it cost him a large number of horses and cattle as well as a goodly sum in cash to free himself from the hands of his corrupt guest.

The Russian officials knew very well that their activities did not endear them to the Ukrainians, and they viewed the inhabitants with great suspicion, imagining plots and treason and arresting them and putting them to the torture for every trifling offense, the innocent as well as the guilty often suffering permanent injury. Rumors of these terrible investigations and trials circulated in Ukraine for many years, as reported, for instance, in *The History of Rus or Little Russia* written by a Ukrainian at a later date:

They did not cease to question, torture, inflict with various machines and especially by branding the unfortunate people who fell into their hands. Today these acts would call forth horror and be looked upon as the result of insanity, but at that time they were important proceedings, held in secrecy, and richly rewarded. People were subjected to excruciating torture on the basis of mere accusations or malicious gossip by migrating or quartered soldiers, or even more frequently by deserters and other scoundrels. For making the accusation, the formula was, "in regard to a word and deed concerning the tsar," this "word and deed" being for wicked and good-for-nothing people a kind of talisman of evil, in which were mingled the three points of the life, the honor, and the welfare of the tsar himself and his family.

Everyone accused, no matter how good his reputation, was put to the torture, even though his accuser was a common thief. The slightest provocation or the failure to stand a treat for a Russian soldier, or vagrant, was sufficient to cause trouble of this kind, for the offended rascal would hasten off to the city or village authorities to shout "word and deed" and "chain us together." The officials, not knowing anything about the case, put both accused and accuser into chains, and rushed them off to the office of the secret police, who made no effort to inquire into the relations of the complainant and defendant, or the reason for the accusation, or whether it was probable, did not inquire, for example, how the defendant by his station or means of living could do any harm to the tsar and his family, whom he had never seen and never would see. They blindly followed their instructions, submitted the accuser to the ordeal, and if he withstood three kinds, his accusation was proved, and the accused person had no further recourse. He was then tortured and put to death.

In addition to persecution by the officials the Kozaks were sent on many campaigns against Turkey, Crimea, and Poland, and the peasants were forced to furnish without compensation transportation and provisions for the army. According to the records of the army treasurer, Jacob Markovich, thousands of oxen were taken from the Ukrainians for the army, "to be paid for later." By its seizures of livestock and other provisions the government brought ruin to the peasants, and many who were forced to transport military supplies lost their oxen and returned home unpaid, with only their whips in their hands.

CHAPTER XVIII

EASTERN UKRAINE

The Hetmancy of Rozumovsky: Under the Russian administration Ukraine was almost completely desolated. When the Russian minister Volynsky traveled through the country in 1737, he wrote to Biron, who was then governor:

Until I entered Ukraine I never realized how desolate the land is and how the population has fallen off, and even now so many are forced to go to war that there are not enough left to raise food for themselves. Though they are suspected of stubbornness because so many farms are left uncultivated, still if one would judge conscientiously, he would have to admit that as a matter of fact there are no people or animals left to cultivate the farms. Last year many oxen died of starvation while transporting military supplies, the Nizhin regiment alone taking fourteen thousand of them, while it is impossible to estimate the exact number confiscated by the other regiments.

As late as 1764 the Ukrainian Officers' Council, writing to the empress to remind her of these seizures, reported:

The fact must be remembered that in the recent war with Turkey Ukraine bore the greatest burden for several years by quartering the army and by furnishing supplies, and that in addition horses, oxen, and peasants were taken by force from the farms for military transportation. Besides this, various taxes were collected from the inhabitants. Several hundred thousand horses and oxen were also confiscated by the army, some owners receiving promissory notes for future compensation, others receiving nothing. During the present war with Prussia horses and oxen have again been seized from Ukraine, which is also maintaining several regiments to be paid for in future. For all of the above, with the exception of a very few instances where small sums of money were paid for oxen and horses taken during the war with Turkey, no payment whatever has been made, and because of this the Ukrainian population, especially the Kozaks and the peasants, is reduced to destitution and starvation.

These conditions caused great dissatisfaction, a warm desire for the restoration of the hetmancy, and great joy when such a revival became a possibility. The Empress Anna died in 1740, several months after the termination of the war with Turkey. After the palace revolution of 1741 Peter's daughter Elizabeth became empress. Her accession was the occasion of important changes in Russian relations to Ukraine. Although Elizabeth considered herself a pupil of her father as far as her policies were concerned, nevertheless in respect to Ukraine her personal sympathies led her to be more considerate than he had been. While she was still a princess and lacking in influence and authority, she had fallen in love with a handsome Ukrainian court singer, Alexey Rozumovsky (Razumovsky). The son of a registered Kozak from the village of Lemeshiv in the province of Chernihiv, Rozumovsky was endowed with a beautiful voice, had sung at first in the local church, and had then been sent to St. Petersburg to sing in the imperial choir, where he attracted the attention of the princess, who fell in love with him. At first she made him the manager of one of her large estates, but as soon as she became empress she secretly married him and thereafter showered favors upon him all through her life. She regarded him highly and besides other indications of her good will bestowed upon him the titles of Field-Marshal and Count of the Holy Roman Empire. Though he was a man of no education, Alexey Rozumovsky was tactful, kind-hearted, and serious, and conducted himself with dignity in his unusual position. He did not interfere in political matters but remained loyal to his fatherland and won for it the sympathies of his wife. At first the Ukrainians received little tangible relief through his influence except that the hetmancy and other Ukrainian institutions were renewed in principle. In 1744 Elizabeth came to Kiev, visited its historic spots, and responded graciously to the warm welcome of the inhabitants with a declaration that she would treat the Ukrainians with consideration and kindness. This attitude, of course, soon became known to the officers, who pledged their loyalty to her and prepared the way for the new Ukrainian policy. Assured of the friendship of the young empress, the Officers' Council and the colonels petitioned her to consent to the election of a hetman, to which request she gave a favorable reply, instructing them to send a formal deputation to St. Petersburg on the occasion of the wedding of the heir to the throne, Peter, whose wife came to the throne later as Catherine II. When the deputies arrived, they were received with high honor and given an affirmative reply to their petition. The actual election, however, was delayed because the person intended to fill the office was not yet qualified. This was Alexey Rozumovsky's younger brother, Cyril, who, born in 1724, had just reached his twentieth birthday and was completing his education abroad. The Ukrainian delegation, duly informed, remained in St. Petersburg patiently to await the arrival of the future hetman, until at last, in 1746, he was brought back and married to Catherine Naryshkin, a relative and a maid of honor of the empress. Many titles of distinction were awarded him, among others that of president of the Russian Academy of Science, after which it was considered appropriate to introduce him to the Ukrainian officers as their future hetman. In 1747 the Russian senate received an imperial order to renew the hetmancy in Ukraine, and at the close of 1749 the empress informed the Ukrainian delegates still waiting in St. Petersburg for an answer that a royal minister, Count Hendrikov, a relative of the empress, was being sent to Ukraine to conduct the election. Overjoyed by this news the members of the delegation departed for their homes.

In February 1750 the royal minister arrived in Hlukhiv

amid great ceremony. He was formally greeted by the members of the Ukrainian Officers' Council and other officers of all ranks as well as the clergy, and the election took place on February 22 (March 5) amid great pomp.

At the head of the procession was a Ukrainian military band, followed by the secretary of the Russian ministry of foreign affairs bearing the imperial authorization, which received a salute from the assembled regiments. Behind him marched a long procession of Kozak officers, led by the "Bunchuk Fellows," holders of honorary ranks granted to members of prominent families who had no regular appointment. They bore on red cushions the hetman's seal, his horse-tail standard (*bunchuk*), and banners, and were followed by the imperial representative, Hendrikov, who rode in a carriage. In the church the declaration was read aloud and a proposal presented to the "army and people" that they elect their hetman, in response to which all present of course shouted their desire for Cyril Rozumovsky, the question being thrice repeated and thrice receiving the same reply. The imperial delegate then proclaimed Rozumovsky hetman of Ukraine. The entire procession then proceeded to the Church of St. Nicholas to celebrate a Mass in honor of this joyful event. The Ukrainian Officers' Council then presented Hendrikov with a gift of ten thousand rubles, a large sum for the time, and his associates with three thousand rubles each, while the Kozak regiments were given more than nine hundred casks of spirits.

After the ceremony, a special deputation was sent to inform the empress of the hetman's election, which she ratified. She issued a proclamation that he should be ranked with the Russian field-marshals, and bestowed upon him the Russian Order of St. Andrew. The Russian officials were removed from their positions in Ukraine, their offices being abolished; the Zaporozhian Sich was placed under the authority of the hetman; and the Ukrainian administration was restored as it had existed before 1722, when the Little Russian Board had been appointed. The affairs of Ukraine were once more placed under the ministry of foreign affairs; Rozumovsky, however, soon became involved in a quarrel with this ministry and at his request was placed under the authority of the senate.

Thus there began the reign of the last Ukrainian hetman, which lasted for almost fifteen years. In the spring of 1751 Rozumovsky received from the empress the hetman's insignia of office and a charter resembling that given to Skoropadsky, and armed with these he went to take up residence in Ukraine. His inauguration resembled the ceremonies previously held, but was more elaborate; Rozumovsky, surrounded by his retinue, rode in a carriage drawn by six horses. The imperial ratification of the election was proclaimed in the church, and then the insignia of authority were taken to the palace of the hetman, where a banquet was held. The Ukrainian chroniclers described these ceremonies in great detail, for they were the final echo of Ukrainian independence, to be recorded in their annals as the last happy moment in Ukrainian life before the final destruction of Ukrainian autonomy.

The new hetman himself was unaccustomed to Ukrainian ways of life, for he had grown up in St. Petersburg and had married into the nobility there. His confidential adviser was his former tutor, Teplov, a cunning and malicious man who had no sympathy for the Ukrainian mode of government, and whose report ''About the Disorders in Little Russia'' later gave Catherine II material to be used against the administration of the hetman and the Officers' Council and helped bring about the repeal of self-government. Subsequently he was considered the chief cause for the abolition of the hetmancy. A story circulated to the effect that when the hetman was journeying over Ukraine a portentous incident occurred in Chernihiv: the wind blew off Rozumovsky's ribbon of the Order of St. Andrew and Teplov picked it up. Rozumovsky's mother predicted that great evil would befall her son at the hands of Teplov, and begged that he be dismissed. Rozumovsky disobeyed her injunction, however, and perished.

Cyril Rozumovsky felt lonely and out of place in Ukraine and made frequent visits to St. Petersburg. He did not consider himself an associate of the Kozak officers but a ruler by the grace of God, even modeling the court at his residence at Hlukhiv after that at St. Petersburg. He paid little attention to Ukrainian affairs but allowed the Officers' Council to govern according to its will and to deal directly with the senate and the Russian administration. Because of Rozumovsky's prestige and his influence in governmental circles, the Russian military and civil officials dared not interfere in Ukrainian affairs. Serious difficulties arose on account of the Zaporozhian region, new complaints arising against the Kozaks there, either because they had built new forts, had recaptured their old forts, or had invaded the Crimean, Turkish, or Polish possessions; and the hetman was continually in receipt of orders from St. Petersburg to keep the Sich under control, but as this proved impossible, the Sich thus prepared its own downfall. Aside from this difficulty, life in Ukraine under the benevolent protection of the empress ran smoothly enough and the Officers' Council ruled without interference; some of its accomplishments outlived the abolition of the hetmancy and survived nearly to our own day. In its activity lies the real significance of the last hetmancy, the holder of the position being himself a person of little importance.

Political and Social Organization of the Hetman State: The origin of the organization of the Ukrainian Hetman state has been described above.* The division of the army into regiments and companies had in time become applied to the land in the form of a division into regimental and company districts; then, when the regimental organiza-

* Pp. 301 ff.

tion was abolished, the Kozak army organization which had taken its place began to be transformed into a general civic administration. It was, however, no easy task for the army organization, more suited to military mobilization than to administration, to change into a system of territorial government. During the transition there was need of a great deal of adjustment, and the more conscientious representatives of Ukrainian officialdom worked hard at the task of making the system function; but it has been seen what difficulties were placed in the way by the Russian government, whose intention was completely to abolish Ukrainian autonomy, giving as an excuse Ukrainian mismanagement but doing nothing to better conditions. Polubotok had fallen because of his attempts at reorganization, and Apostol, in his brief hetmancy, had succeeded in making only a few improvements before the harsh years of Russian administration, when the Russian military and civil officials, by their corruption and their interference, often crude and inefficient, completely disrupted the Ukrainian judicial system.

The central administration of the Hetman state consisted at first of two superior organs, the army or general chancellery, and the general court. The army chancellery supervised army and general (civil) affairs under the general army secretary. After the death of Apostol it was fused with the governing board as the supreme organ of administration under the name of the general army chancellery. The army court was in charge of the general judge, who at first acted alone, until, as has been seen, associate judges were added and thus the later general court evolved. Upon the accession of Apostol as hetman, the army treasury was set apart as a separate board under two treasurers; there were also bookkeepers who had a special treasury chancellery, to which was attached an auditing commission. There was also a separate artillery chancellery, under the direction of the ordnance officer (*obozny*), which supervised the armament of the army and the estates and other sources of income assigned for that purpose.

The army assembly (*rada*) ceased to meet as early as the period of Samoilovich, and the early tradition regarding it lived on only at the election of a hetman, and then purely for the sake of form. All "important" issues were decided by the Officers' Council, called by the hetman, and the "most important" or "most complete" discussions were held in the Hetman's Council, which included both the general officers and the colonels.

From the time when western Ukraine had fallen into the hands of Poland, the Hetman state in eastern Ukraine had been divided into ten regiments, those of Starodub, Chernihiv, Kiev, Nizhin, Priluki, Pereyaslav, Lubny, Hadiach, Mirhorod, and Poltava. These were of unequal size, the Nizhin regiment having in 1723 eight companies totaling about 10,000 Kozaks—6,566 cavalry and 3,379 infantry, while the Kiev regiment also had eight companies, but with less than 3,000 Kozaks—1,657 cavalry and 1,259 infantry. In all ten regiments there were at the time 114 companies and nearly 50,000 Kozaks. In 1735 the government selected for special army service 30,000 "picked" Kozaks from among the wealthier ones, and divided them proportionately among the regiments, assigning the rest as "assistants" to the "picked" group, but later this arrangement was reversed, and the "assistants" performed their services at the expense of the more well-to-do "picked" Kozaks.

The colonel was the officer in command of the regiment, in which there was also a staff of officers whose authority, like that of the colonels, increased greatly in the eighteenth century. From the time when the Russian government undertook to appoint the colonels and forbade the hetman to remove them without the consent of the emperor, they became more independent and only slightly subject to the authority of the hetman and the general Officers' Council. On the other hand, the rank and file of the Kozaks lost their rights of participation in the government, and self-government lingered on only in the Kozak villages. Even the captains were appointed by the colonels, although according to Kozak law each company should have elected its own.

In this manner the old Kozak tradition of democracy disappeared almost completely. Insofar as general self-administration existed at all, outside of the village or city communes, it was in the hands of the members of the officers' families who under the name of "Bunchuk Fellows" and "Army Fellows" formed a privileged hereditary upper class of "gentry," as they called themselves. In fact, the whole administration of the Hetman state in the eighteenth century was restricted to aristocratic landowners.

In complete subordination to this class were the municipalities. The smaller towns were quite simply subjected to the regimental or company administrations, the larger, so-called magistracy towns, which had full-fledged municipal councils as recognized by German law, were supposed to be independent not only of the colonels but even of the hetman himself except in matters of exceptional importance; there were ten such cities in the middle of the eighteenth century. But in the eighteenth century the colonels managed even these cities rather arbitrarily. The clergy, although they were immediately subject to the synod through their bishops, were nevertheless in fact quite dependent upon the Officers' Council. As to the rank and file of the Kozaks and the peasants, they were fully subordinated to the authority of the officer landlords.

The last exercise of authority by the Officers' Council under the rule of Rozumovsky developed and hardened these characteristics of the Hetman state, as one governed by officer landlords, which had just begun to appear at the end of the seventeenth century. In an attempt to strengthen as much as possible the social and political foundations of the Hetman state, the officers erected it on the basis of landlordism and laid stress upon the rights of the officers as landowners, thus completely destroying the remnants of the old democratic system. In these efforts they valued such legislative relics as were taken over from the old system for lack of written law.

It has been pointed out* that the greater part of the national Ukrainian law which guided the decisions of courts of all kinds was not codified, and for this reason the judges frequently looked to the aid of the codes which were applied in the courts of the towns—the Magdeburg Law and the Lithuanian Statute; the latter was consulted not in its first edition, which had been only slightly removed from the native legal practice, but in its later editions of 1566 and 1588, which had been strongly influenced by Polish law and the gentry regime. Although these codes were applied chiefly to private and criminal suits, their seignorial character offered growing protection for the gentry at large in proportion as the Lithuanian Statute itself became more generally accepted.

When the hetmancy was renewed in 1727 on the basis of the Definitive Articles there was appointed a commission of Ukrainian jurists to codify the Ukrainian laws; but this commission, instead of concerning itself merely with the collections of common law consisting of provisions which were accepted as just and legal among the people, also applied themselves to the finished codes of law employed by the Ukrainian courts—the Lithuanian Statute and the Magdeburg Law. It was in this manner that they worked out their code of laws completed in 1743 under the title of "The Law in Accordance with which the Little Russian People Is Judged." Although this code was never confirmed by the government, it increased the importance of the Lithuanian and Magdeburg laws, and the administration of Rozumovsky began to apply the principles of the Lithuanian Statute to the organization and procedure of the courts. A Ukrainian jurist, Fedir Chuikevich, submitted to the new hetman in 1750 a book en-

* Pp. 349 ff.

titled *The Court and Lawsuits in the Little Russian Law,*
in which he criticized the omissions of the Ukrainian law
and the errors of the courts and offered plans for reform
conceived in the spirit of the Lithuanian Statute. At the
close of Rozumovsky's regime reforms were actually
made in this direction, and to the general court were
added deputies from the regiments, after the pattern of
the Polish tribunal. The regimental courts became municipal courts conducted on the model of the Polish district
(*starost*) courts, while for civil and land cases there were
set up county (*povit*) courts, the judges of which were
elected from among the gentry officers. The Hetman state
was divided into twenty such judicial counties.

Although this reform, to be sure, was not in existence
for a long time, it is of value as indicating the general
aims and ambitions of the Kozak officers. Accepting the
Lithuanian Statute as a guide, they attempted on every
occasion to introduce the principles of landlordism taken
for granted by the Statute. The officers looked upon themselves as a class of gentry, the term "Little Russian gentry" coming into more common usage in all Ukrainian
lawsuits in the middle of the eighteenth century; and applying to themselves the provisions of the Lithuanian
Statute regarding the rights and privileges of the gentry,
the officers claimed such rights in Ukrainian administration and private life. Just as formerly the old army organization of the Hetman state was reorganized after the
model of the Polish administrative organization based on
the gentry, so the conceptions of the rights of the gentry
were introduced into the laws concerning landed property, into the relations of the inhabitants to the landlords,
and into the rights of the peasants, or rather, the absence
of such rights. This tendency was greatly furthered by
the abolition of the hetmancy. Various principles of the
civil law taken from the Lithuanian Statute were in force
as local law in the territory of the old Hetman state—the
governments of Chernihiv and Poltava—down to 1917,

while the conception of the rights of the officers as landlords over the inhabitants had a strong influence upon the
whole social system of the Hetman state.

The Land of Free Communes (*Slobidshina*): A weak
and pale copy of the Hetman state in the eighteenth century was the neighboring Ukrainian Land of Free Communes, which contained the territory of the later governments of Kharkiv and parts of Kursk and Voronizh. Reference has been made several times to the settlement of
this region by Ukrainian emigrants, who fled over the
Russian border from the Ukrainian lands under Polish
rule and settled beyond the line of frontier fortresses constructed by the Muscovite government, the so-called Bilhorod line which closed the way to the Tatar bands into
Muscovite territory. Making their homes there along the
old Tatar highways the emigrants assumed the task of
protecting this frontier, and in return for their services
received from the Muscovite government various rights
and privileges.

There are scattered references to these Ukrainian emigrants dating from the latter half of the sixteenth and the
beginning of the seventeenth centuries. In 1638 a large
number, over eight hundred Kozaks, besides women and
children, left with the hetman Yatsko Ostrianin and settled in the region of Chuhuev, where they organized a
separate Kozak army; but becoming dissatisfied there
they revolted, killed Ostrianin, and went back across the
border. Migration on a large scale began in 1651, when
the people became disgusted with Khmelnitsky's government and both large and small groups emigrated and occupied the frontier region; there they built towns and
established a Kozak system of government. In 1652, for
instance, Colonel Dzinkovsky and a thousand Kozaks emigrated with their families and property and settled near
the Sosna River, where they built the city of Ostrohozhsk
and founded the Ostrohozhsk regiment. About the same
time another Ukrainian group founded the city of Sumy

near the Psiol River and organized the Sumy regiment. In 1654 settlers appeared for the first time at Kharkiv, where they founded a city. The migrations continued at intervals through the decades of 1660, 1670, and 1680, and in the course of time a large area became inhabited.

In return for their military services the Ukrainian settlers were exempted from taxation and other obligations and were permitted to govern themselves "according to custom." They organized on the Kozak pattern an army of five regiments, those of Sumy, Akhtirka, Kharkiv, Ostrohozhsk, and Izium. They were subject to Russian control only indirectly, though their dependence upon it was greater than that of the regiments in the Hetman state. The hetmans attempted to persuade the Muscovite government to unite these free Kozaks with those who were under their authority, Samoilovich making particularly energetic efforts in this direction after Russia abandoned her claims to western Ukraine in favor of Poland; the Russians, however, were already planning to reduce the authority of the hetmancy in the near future and disregarded these appeals. Almost from the beginning of settlement, Russian law was introduced into the Free Communes, and since there were a number of Russians intermingled with the Ukrainian settlers, the local officers became Russified more rapidly here than in the Hetman state. The Russian government made use of the Free Communes as a laboratory for the abolition of the Kozak system, changes being introduced there as a rule several years earlier than in the Hetman state.

As early as 1732 Russia attempted to abolish the old Kozak system in the Free Communes and for this purpose replaced the Kozak regiments with regiments of dragoons, into which the more amenable Kozaks were absorbed, while all others were obliged to revert to the status of peasants. Russian officers were placed in command. This arrangement aroused so much dissatisfaction, however, that in 1743 the Empress Elizabeth put a stop

to the experiment and reëstablished the Kozak organization, although in matters of civil administration she subjected the inhabitants of the Free Communes to the rule
of the governor of Bilhorod. This system lasted for
twenty years more, until 1763–64, when the regiments in
the Free Communes were dissolved and replaced once and
for all by hussars.

Social relationships in the Free Communes resembled
those in the Hetman state, but fell under the influence of
Russia somewhat earlier. In place of the old fortresses
and army lands new estates sprang up belonging to officers and inhabited by serfs. In this manner the officers
acquired a position like that of the Russian landowner
(*pomeschik*) and the non-Kozak population that of the
serfs. This transition was aided by the gift by the Russian government of great areas of land to such Kozak officers as had shown special loyalty and submission; Colonel Kondratiev of the Sumy regiment, for instance, received for his faithfulness such large grants that in 1780
his family held 120,000 dessiatines (324,000 acres). When
in 1767 there was some thought given to the enactment of
new laws in Russia, some of the deputies from the Free
Communes demanded the confiscation of the land from
the officers and the freeing of the serfs, but the arrangement of landlords and serfs was too deeply rooted and
they met with no success.

*Culture in Eastern Ukraine—Literature and Educa-
tion:* From the social point of view, both the Hetman state
and the Free Communes were losing their importance.
National self-government and that of the Kozak army
were partially destroyed by the Russian government, and
what elements were not destroyed assumed the character
of self-government by the officers, now become a landed
gentry. Municipal and ecclesiastical self-government were
weakened, and the villagers had become enserfed. The
rank and file of the Kozaks were deprived of all participation in the government and also robbed under various

pretexts of their name of Kozaks and reduced to the class of peasants and even serfs. The Ukrainian courts were swamped with countless lawsuits arising from the illegal abolition of Kozak privileges; and the Kozaks, disgusted with their inability to obtain justice in the courts, frequently rebelled against their aristocratic oppressors.

The loss of self-government in eastern Ukraine was accompanied by a decline in importance from the point of view of national culture. Since Ukrainian culture was chiefly of a religious character, especially during the seventeenth century and the first part of the eighteenth, the transfer of the Ukrainian Church to the jurisdiction of the Patriarch of Russia had important effects upon cultural life. Prior to this time the Church had been nominally under the supervision of the Patriarch of Constantinople, but in fact it had been fully autonomous and independent and had carried on its activities under the direct control of the inhabitants, who filled all important church offices by popular vote. When the Russian government, with the aid of Samoilovich, induced the metropolitan of Kiev to submit himself in 1685 to the "blessing" of the Patriarch of Muscovy, and the Patriarch of Constantinople was forced by the Turkish government in 1677 to recognize this act, the Ukrainian clergy at once felt the heavy hand of Russian oppression. Both the publications and the schools in Ukraine became subject to the ever-suspicious and hostile Russian censorship, the Russians even before this time having looked askance upon the Ukrainian Church and its schools and literature. Although the Muscovite authorities had made efforts in the 1660's to abolish altogether the Academy of Kiev by taking advantage of the political unrest and the resultant decline in the level of learning and other activity in the Academy, they had feared that the closing of the school might arouse great discontent in Ukraine and had abandoned their plan. The publications of the Kievan Academy were frequently forbidden by the Russian government, however, and in the time of the Patriarch Joachim, in the 1670–80's, the campaign against Ukrainian books took on fresh vigor. When the Ukrainian Church became subject to the Patriarch of Moscow and the Russian authorities were able to prohibit Ukrainian publications not only in Muscovy but in Ukraine as well, Russian hostility became fully manifest. At first the government prohibited the publication of Ukrainian books on the pretext that they contained non-Orthodox ideas, but it soon became evident that the prohibitions were made because the books were in the Ukrainian language, and in the decade of 1720 the Russian government issued an order forbidding all such publications except religious ones, and even these were to be reprinted from the old Church books and to follow closely the Russian editions. Large numbers of spies saw to it that this law was strictly enforced, a separate censorship being established to examine Ukrainian publications. It was now impossible to secure a permit from the censor to publish any book in the Ukrainian tongue; in 1726, for example, the metropolitan of Kiev wrote a litany dedicated to St. Barbara, but could not get permission to publish it until it had been translated into Russian. In 1769 a monastery at Kiev petitioned the synod for authority to publish a Ukrainian grammar because the Ukrainians did not wish to buy Russian books, but permission was refused, and the synod even requested the bishops to remove all the old Ukrainian Church books from their edifices and to substitute for them books in the Russian language.

These restrictions seriously hindered the literary progress of eastern Ukraine. The sentiment of nationality, even without these difficulties, had not been very strong in the old Ukrainian literature of the sixteenth and seventeenth centuries. Although the vernacular was occasionally used in the religious books printed during the sixteenth century, there were opponents of this custom who did not wish to see the popular language used for religious purposes, as they considered the popular tongue inferior to the Old Slavonic used in the Orthodox Church and, ignoring the vernacular, sought to teach the students in the Ukrainian schools to write correctly in this old language of the Church. In the seventeenth and eighteenth centuries the Ukrainian writers employed the Church Slavonic in their literary writings but used the vernacular in their daily life, in poetry, in anecdote, and in personal correspondence.

The Ukrainian system of education had developed under the influence of the religious struggle and its whole attention was turned to the study of theological and dialectical subjects, all others such as history, literature, mathematics, and natural science being considered of secondary importance. Printed books were almost exclusively religious. Judging from the manuscripts, however, it appears that the people were intensely interested in history, for they copied old chronicles, composed new ones for more recent times, and preserved materials of historical importance. A considerable number of copies of Galician-Volynian manuscripts have thus been handed down. None of these was put into print with the exception of the *Synopsis,* which was a brief history of Rus composed at the Monastery of the Caves, and it was incomplete and unreliable, almost entirely omitting the Kozak period, the struggle with Poland, and the recent history of Ukraine. Because there was no other book of this type, it went through several editions, the first of which appeared in 1674; other more valuable writings remained in manuscript form. Historical literature was on the whole fairly rich. Among the examples which have been preserved, some of the most interesting are the *Lviv Chronicle* devoted to the events of the first part of the seventeenth century, an eyewitness account of Khmelnitsky's war, a later history of the Kozak Host to the end of the seventeenth century, and many annals and chronicles— the Hustin chronicle, chronicles by Safonovich, Bobolin-

sky, and others. Among the many Kozak chronicles may
be mentioned those by Hrabianka, Lizohub, and Lukomsky; very interesting, though in places inaccurate, is that
by Velichko. These writings frequently reflect with accu-
racy the interests of the Ukrainian people at the time, but
the ecclesiastical officials who had the means did not consider them of sufficient importance to warrant printing
them. None of the remarkable Ukrainian historical songs
was printed, not even those which were composed in the
course of the seventeenth century in a special form, the
so-called *dumy,* which combined subjects of literary content and style with a popular poetic foundation. Purely
literary verses on historical or everyday life were not
printed to any extent, except for those in praise of prominent persons, which, though of little intrinsic interest,
were published for purely financial reasons.

Such books as were not prepared for use in church services had a religious content, but the religious struggle
died down in the latter half of the seventeenth century,
people lost interest in purely religious books, and readers
desired to have something new, more lively, and closer to
their own lives—qualities which the books of the time did
not possess. The chief difficulty was that all the Ukrainian
printing presses were in the hands of the Church; in addition, the Russian authorities prohibited the publication
of Ukrainian literature, especially on modern subjects.

It is true that the authors, being continually subject to
Russian suspicion and severity, often feared to write on
the topics of the day, especially on political subjects, but
despite this hindrance we have inherited interesting manuscripts of the first part of the eighteenth century, both
poems and school dramas. For example, the drama written in 1728 concerning the renewal of the hetmancy and
entitled *God's Grace which Saved Ukraine from the Polish Oppression through Bohdan Zinovey Khmelnitsky* not
only brought to its reader the glories of that period, but
also touched upon the problems of the time and the rela-

tions of Ukraine to Russia. Another drama, *The Resurrection of the Dead* (1747) by George Konisky, was based upon social problems and the position of the serfs. There were also popular interludes written in vernacular Ukrainian in facetious style to amuse the public. The dramatic works of Mitrofan Dovhalevsky in the 1730's and of Konisky in the 1740's which have come down in manuscript form are of great interest; they deal in a witty vein with many contemporary Ukrainian and foreign characters. The Ukrainians of a later period valued these works highly and compared them to the best humorous literature of the world, but could not print them because of the Russian censorship. Gradually Ukrainian literary output fell off, to be carried on in manuscript form only. Russian censorship and other restrictions added to the falling off of Ukrainian literary development, which also suffered from the competition of Russian influences.

Education suffered the same fate. The chief center of Ukrainian education and of culture in general was the Academy of Kiev. After its decline in the decade of 1660, when it was almost closed by the Russian government, it renewed its activity and broadened its program on the model of the Jesuit colleges, and in 1694 received a charter from the Russian government. The period of the hetmancy of Mazepa, the patron of Ukrainian cultural life, was the most progressive in the history of the Academy. Many of its graduates became leaders in literary, religious, and political life in Ukraine and in Russia; and until the middle of the eighteenth century it remained the leading school for the education of Ukrainians, both clergy and laymen. When Hetman Apostol confirmed the endowments of the Academy, he spoke of it as a "school for all needy citizens, where the sons of Little Russia obtain free education." It is true that according to the school roll for 1727 there were registered the sons of almost all of the noted officials and as a rule more laymen than clergy, and the graduates occupied prominent places

in civil life. Because of the excellent scholastic standing
of the Academy of Kiev, it was regarded very highly and
new schools were established on the same pattern, both in
Russia and at Chernihiv, Pereyaslav, Kharkiv, and Poltava in Ukraine.

The decades of 1730 and 1740 were the last bright years
in the history of the Academy of Kiev. Raphael Zaborovsky, the metropolitan of the Ukrainian Church from 1731
to 1747, was a good friend to the Academy, taking great
interest in its work and collecting funds for its upkeep
and expansion. New classroom buildings, dormitories, and
churches were constructed under his leadership. So highly
was his work valued that his name was attached to the institution, and it became known as the "Mohila-Zaborovsky Academy." Among the professors were such gifted
men as Mitrofan Dovhalevsky, George Konisky, and
Michael Kozachinsky, while the students of those years
included many such future leaders and authors as Gregory Skovoroda and the distinguished Russian Lomonosov. There were more than a thousand students in attend-
ance: 1,243 in 1742; 1,193 in 1751, and 1,059 in 1765.

After this last phase of its development, the Academy
declined. Serving the interests of the Church, its cur-
riculum had taken on a theological character; and its
teaching methods were those of scholasticism—antiquated, uninteresting, and behind the European learning
of the period. The school offered little of practical value,
the literary training being based on antiquated models
poorly adapted to the times; therefore, as soon as advanced secular schools were established in St. Petersburg
and Moscow, the Academy of Kiev and others modeled
after it could not stand the competition. The wealthier
Ukrainian citizens and the officials sent their children for
higher education to the schools at the Russian capitals or
to foreign universities. As a result, the Academy of Kiev
and others of its kind remained theological schools and
lost their broad cultural significance. Ukrainians who

were eager to give higher education to their young people consequently desired to establish universities. They petitioned Catherine II to permit them to found, in place of the Academy of Kiev, a university with a theological department in the city of Baturin and colleges in the larger cities, but the Russian government disapproved of such an extensive Ukrainian educational program, and not until the establishment of the University of Kharkiv by the local Ukrainian nobility at the beginning of the nineteenth century did Ukraine gain her first secular institution of higher learning.

National Life in Eastern Ukraine: The political and cultural situation described in the preceding section brought about the decline of nationalism. This was very unfortunate because eastern Ukraine, especially the Hetman state, in comparison with other parts of the country, had enjoyed considerable opportunity for development and self-government. Civic activities here, too, lost their former significance. On the ruins of the joyful, free life of the Kozaks and their political autonomy there grew up an ideal of large estates, wealthy families, and large incomes. The grandchildren of the Kozaks, descendants of those who had risen in rebellion under the leadership of Khmelnitsky and shattered the aristocratic Polish rule in Ukraine by expelling the nobles, now became landed magnates themselves, who by legal and illegal methods gained large areas of land and colonized them with unprivileged serfs. Convinced that the struggle against Russia was futile, they gave up attempts to gain independence for Ukraine, and instead endeavored to keep the land which they had seized, to assure themselves of their rights as landowners, to gain equal rights with the Russian gentry, to open the way to higher offices, and to be absorbed among the nobles of Russia. Three hundred years before, the Ukrainian gentry had attempted to adapt themselves to the Polish rule by accepting Polish laws and becoming Polonized and Catholicized; the Ukrainian aristocrats with equal willingness now obeyed the orders of the Russian government, not only adapting themselves to the new form of administration but accepting the culture and language of Russia.

They paid little attention to the fact that Russian culture was still on a low level. Several decades before this time, during the reigns of Doroshenko and Mazepa, Ukrainians had been in a sense the pioneers of education in Muscovy and had introduced Ukrainian culture there. During the time of Peter the Great almost all the high ecclesiastical offices in Russia were occupied by Ukrainian graduates of the Academy of Kiev, and even in the Russian schools Ukrainian was the introductory language in which Russian boys were taught. But now, just as in the fifteenth and sixteenth centuries, it was not the higher culture, but the superior political power, which won the supremacy. Having no connection with the masses and no confidence in popular support, the Ukrainian officials surrendered their national position in politics and in culture, and thoughtlessly adopted Russian customs, language, and general culture, although they considered the Russians barbarous, half-civilized, and uncultured. Beginning with the reign of Peter the Great, the Russian language came into use more widely, not only for communications with the Russian officials but even for Ukrainian local affairs and literature. Before this time the vernacular had been subordinated to the Old Slavonic language of the Church, but the censorship now forbade the printing of books in the living language of the Ukrainian people, the Russian government attempting to impose its language forcibly upon them and to drive the old Ukrainian books out of circulation and replace them with Russian. As the Russian culture was acquiring western ideas more rapidly than the Ukrainian, it became more attractive to the Ukrainian people. Ukrainians wrote books in Russian and many of them attained places of prominence in Russian literature, but they did nothing to develop the literature or the cultural life of Ukraine.

Such weaklings did these petty hetmans prove to be, descendants though they were of the Kozak heroes who had fought for the freedom and independence of Ukraine! Nevertheless it cannot be truthfully said that the existence of Ukrainian autonomy, though limited and Russified, was a matter in which the Ukraine people took a half-hearted interest. Beneath the powdered French wigs and the modish embroidered camisoles of the new generation of Ukrainian townspeople, and behind the Russian language and the political subservience, there existed an eager and lively Ukrainian patriotism which in time would express itself in quite different and more attractive ways. The new Russian ruler of Ukraine, Rumiantsov, who replaced Hetman Rozumovsky, observed to his surprise that many of the fashionable Ukrainians, although they acquired their higher learning in foreign countries, remained Kozaks, and preserved a deep love "for their own nationality and their sweet fatherland," as they called Ukraine. Disregarding the fact that they were subjected to the influence of Russian culture, they had high hopes for the future of their own people. "This handful of people will not say otherwise, but that they are the first in the world, that there is no one stronger, no one braver, no one wiser, and that nowhere can be found anything better, more useful, more free; everything they possess is of the best," Rumiantsov complained of Ukrainian patriotism in his letters to the empress. When the Ukrainian people, in connection with the making of a new law code for Russia, had an opportunity in 1767 to voice their wishes, they expressed with unexpected vigor their hearty desire for Ukrainian autonomy and for the old laws and privileges, which they wished to renew at the first opportunity.

No doubt the existence of Ukrainian autonomy, even in

limited form, upheld the spirit of nationalism and patriotism—"republican ideas," as Rumiantsov called them. From this point of view the preservation of the autonomous Hetman state was of great national significance. The Ukrainian masses were lacking in extensive political knowledge, and the feeling for nationalism in their culture was negligible, but the maintenance of political separation served as a means of keeping intact and deepening a national patriotism. It is probable that if these Ukrainian governmental forms had not been destroyed, they would have prevented the Ukrainian townspeople, who composed the intelligentsia of the country, from sinking into the sea of Russianism, as they did after Ukrainian autonomy was abolished. The new political and cultural ideas from Europe would have reached the Ukrainian townspeople in the course of time by other channels and would have created for them new interests and new relationships to the people and the life of the nation. If the Ukrainian customs and forms of government had not been destroyed by Russia but had been left undisturbed, the new cultural movement would have developed of itself at the proper moment and future generations would not have been obliged to make a fresh start, as the Ukrainian leaders were forced to do during the renaissance of Ukrainian cultural and political life in the nineteenth century.

Nevertheless, the little that remained of Ukrainian independence in the middle of the eighteenth century, fragmentary and undeveloped though it was, was of the greatest value, and it is for this reason that we have dwelt at such length upon its history. The tradition of independence proved a great impetus to the rebirth of Ukrainian nationalism in the next century.

CHAPTER XIX

THE LAST REBELLIONS

The Decline of Ukrainian Culture in Western Ukraine:
The limitation of Ukrainian autonomy in the Hetman
state of eastern Ukraine was an ominous sign for the
whole country, for the cultural center ever since the middle of the seventeenth century had been at Kiev. From
here education and culture had gone out to supply the
needs of remote sections of Ukraine, especially that part
which was under the rule of Poland. The partitioning of
Ukraine in 1667 between Poland and Russia had dealt a
deadly blow to Ukrainian life by separating Kiev from
western Ukraine, and this act had provoked the Ukrainians to fury against Russia for her betrayal in dividing
their country with Poland. Although they attempted by
every means at their command to preserve their cultural
and national life, they found this extremely difficult. Once
they were politically separated, the two parts of Ukraine
drifted further and further apart, the western section remaining subject to Polish influences while the eastern fell
under the impress of Russia. The subjection of the
Ukrainian Greek Orthodox Church to the Patriarch of
Moscow, which was accomplished against the will of the
Ukrainian clergy and people, severed the connection between the dioceses of eastern and western Ukraine and
enabled Poland to force Catholicism upon the Ukrainians
with greater ease, while the Russification of Ukrainian
schools and literature in eastern Ukraine raised a barrier
against the western portion of the country; in proportion
as the sources of cultural impulse weakened and dried up
in western Ukraine, its separation from Kiev led to a general cultural decline.

It has been noted that the cultural center of western
Ukraine at the end of the sixteenth century was the city

of Lviv with its brotherhood, which gathered about itself and gave organization to not only the Ukrainian townspeople of Lviv but to the Ukrainian inhabitants of all eastern Galicia as well. These people, however, became Polonized, as did the townspeople of Lviv, and all their efforts to gain political equality and freedom for expression and development proved futile. Polish municipal government did not admit the participation of Ukrainians and hampered their economic and commercial freedom, and none of the Ukrainian complaints to the central government brought any relief. Moreover, during the seventeenth century Lviv was losing economic ground because of short-sighted Polish economic policies, and with economic decline the energy of the Ukrainian patriots was weakened. With the advent of depression, the more energetic and active Ukrainians left Lviv and Galicia and moved into eastern Ukraine to join the Kozaks. As has been said, the cultural leaders of Kiev during the third decade of the seventeenth century came chiefly from Lviv, and it was they who made Kiev the center of Ukrainian life, while Lviv and the rest of Galicia, abandoned by the most energetic people, began to lose their former cultural significance. The Lviv brotherhood lost its importance; and its chief glory, the school, declined in the middle decades of the seventeenth century, after which the main activity of the brotherhood consisted in the publishing of Church books, especially liturgies, which it provided to all eastern Ukraine. As its publications provided the chief source of income for the brotherhood, which therefore placed a high value upon this activity and especially upon its monopoly of publication of books for the Church, it permitted no other Ukrainian presses to open in Lviv.

In the second part of the seventeenth century the Ukrainian national movement lost its significance even more rapidly, in part because Khmelnitsky temporarily improved conditions in eastern Ukraine and attracted large numbers of people to move there. In 1648 western

Ukraine, including Volynia, Podolia, and Galicia, revolted in the expectation that with the aid of the Kozaks they could free themselves from Polish oppression. The towns-people, the peasants, and the petty Ukrainian gentry rebelled, joined the Kozaks, either killed or expelled the Poles, and established their own independent Ukrainian government. In all the larger cities of Galicia—Ternopil, Sokal, Rohatyn, Tovmach, Zabolotiv, Yaniv near Lviv, Horodok, Yavoriv, Kalush at the foot of the Carpathians, and Drohobich—there were uprisings on a larger or smaller scale, and the insurrection spread far and wide. The Ukrainian nobles and the city fathers organized the peasants into military bands and destroyed the castles of the Polish nobles.

Khmelnitsky, however, was too engrossed with Kozak problems to support this energetic movement, and when he left western Ukraine, the revolution subsided. The leaders of the revolt and the more energetic people in general went east with the Kozaks, after which migration those who remained behind suffered more seriously than ever from Polish oppression, the Polish nobles having come to realize during Khmelnitsky's rebellion the potential power of Ukrainian nationalism. The remaining Orthodox gentry rapidly became Polonized, not only in Galicia and Podolia, but in Volynia and in those parts of Kievan Polisia which were not under the Kozak banner. Fewer voices were raised in the local parliaments in defense of the Orthodox Church and the Ukrainian people, and in the last quarter of the seventeenth century these voices died out altogether. Left without help from the gentry the urban brotherhoods lost their significance, especially as they languished under the oppressive rule of the nobles.

The Polish government also did its utmost to injure the relations of the region with eastern Ukraine and the Greek Orthodox countries. In 1676 the senate passed a law forbidding the Orthodox to leave or to reënter the country, or to communicate with the Patriarch under penalty of death and confiscation of property. The brotherhoods were ordered to submit to their bishops, and in case of dispute to appeal the case, not to the Patriarch, but to the Polish courts. At the same time the government attempted to induce the Orthodox bishops and other higher clergy to accept Catholicism.

At Lviv Bishop Joseph Shumliansky aided the Polish government considerably in this task. In his early years he became a Uniate Catholic, and later, in order to be made bishop of the Lviv diocese, he reverted to Orthodoxy. As soon as he was made bishop, however, he began to plot with the clergy to convert the Orthodox to Roman Catholicism. The priests who joined him in this plot were Inokenty Vinnitsky, who had failed to secure the Peremyshl diocese, and Varlam Sheptitsky, who was eager to become bishop of Kholm, while Shumliansky himself was desirous of becoming the overseer of the metropolitan estates after the Polish government without reason had expelled and imprisoned the former metropolitan, Tukalsky. When the king learned of this project, he decided to call a congress of the Orthodox in Lviv in 1680 and to force them to accept Roman Catholicism. He issued invitations to both the Orthodox and the Uniates, but Shumliansky and his friends, recalling the events at the similar meeting held in Bereste in 1569, and being unwilling to reveal their plans so openly, pretended a lack of interest in the matter and did not appear at the congress, while the brotherhood of Lutsk protested at the congress that it could make no decisions in the absence of the bishops. Shumliansky, however, informed the king and the government leaders that the conversion must be approached secretly and accomplished by appointing as bishops of the Orthodox Church men who were in favor of the Union and by granting privileges to the Uniate clergy.

The Polish government accepted this clever scheme and thereafter followed the advice of Shumliansky to bestow

Orthodox dioceses upon persons who promised to become Uniates. It made Shumliansky acting metropolitan and gave him and his friends the property it seized from the Orthodox bishops and the monasteries belonging to foreigners. It harassed the Orthodox in many ways such as by limiting certain rights to the Uniates; for example, in 1699 a law was passed by parliament that only Catholics could hold city offices in Kaminets and that Orthodox and Jews were not permitted to live there—a more drastic provision than any enforced in the city by the Turks when they had been in power during the previous year. The government did not demand openly that the Greek Orthodox accept Roman Catholicism, but the bishops appointed pro-Catholics to the better positions in the Church. In the course of several years by these shrewd and treacherous methods the Orthodox Church was so undermined that finally, in 1700, Shumliansky, certain of success, decided to take an overt stand for the Church Union. He now publicly repeated an oath which he had taken secretly twenty years before and began openly to Catholicize his eparchy of Galicia and Podolia. The Orthodox Church was by now so weak that its clergy lacked the courage to oppose the Union. The Lviv brotherhood protested, but Shumliansky appeared with Polish troops, broke open the door of the brotherhood church, and held a Uniate service in it. The brethren, however, were still unwilling to accept Roman Catholicism and complained to the king against Shumliansky's incursion, whereupon the king confirmed the rights of the brotherhood, but the opposition of their bishop and the Poles was too much for them. In 1704, when the Swedes laid siege to Lviv and demanded a ransom, the Polish government forced the Ukrainian brotherhood to furnish it; the members were obliged to part with all the money and valuables in their possession, amounting to 120,000 gold pieces, and were left penniless. In order to deprive them of their last source of income, the printing of books, Shumliansky established a printing press in connection with his Cathedral and became their competitor; the brotherhood could not endure this blow, and in 1708 yielded to Shumliansky and accepted the Union, as did most of Galicia and Podolia, with the exception of the monastery of Veliki Skit in Maniava at the foot of the Carpathian Mountains, which remained Greek Orthodox until it was finally closed by the Austrian government in 1785 after the partition of Poland.

In 1691 Vinnitsky, the bishop of Peremyshl, had already proclaimed the Union in his diocese and had begun to force his parishes to accept it, reporting recalcitrants to the Polish civil authorities and requesting the government to enforce obedience on their part. The number of such recalcitrants decreased every year under the severe punishments and other persecution, until by 1761 Vinnitsky's successor was able to declare with pride that in his diocese there was not a single Orthodox parish. In 1711 the Uniates seized the diocese of Volynia and inaugurated a forceful transfer of the parishes there to the Uniate Church. In the course of the first half of the eighteenth century, the whole of western Ukraine was made Uniate, and the clergy began to carry the movement into the region of Kiev; but here, because of local conditions, it met with less success. Meanwhile, Carpatho-Ukraine (Carpathian Ruthenia or Carpathian Rus) deserves attention because of the religious struggle of the people for and against the Union.

Carpatho-Ukraine: As the Ukrainian mountaineers who inhabited the Carpathian and Trans-Carpathian Mountains were for a very long period politically divided from the rest of their people there are accordingly very few records of their development. Life in the mountains was itself dull and uneventful, and there is no information as to early settlements in this region. For many years people pastured their flocks there in the summer only but in due time settled down and developed farming. Statements have been made that the first settlements were established in the eleventh and twelfth centuries, but they must have been made sooner, for when the Hungarians invaded this region in the ninth century, they found Ukrainians already living in the Carpathian Mountains. Apparently these people were in close contact with the Ukrainians of Galicia for some time, but very little is known about this. It is known, however, that there was a long and continuous struggle between Galicia and Hungary for possession of the country. The Hungarian kings, after they had extended their borders to the top of the Carpathian Mountains, wished to conquer the territory north of them also, and at times were successful for short periods at the end of the twelfth century and the early part of the thirteenth; on the other hand, when Hungary declined at the close of the thirteenth century, the Galician kings attempted to conquer the Trans-Carpathian districts. Finally, after the futile attempts of the Hungarian King Louis I and his family in the 1370's to subject Galicia to Hungary, there was fixed in the 1380's between the two countries the boundary which has remained down to recent times.

Whether or not Carpatho-Ukraine was ever a political unit is not known. There are old traditions which indicate that at one time that may have been the case, but in the twelfth and thirteenth centuries the country was divided into "comitats" or "counties" similar to the districts into which all Hungary was divided, the Carpatho-Ukrainians being grouped into several such districts along the river valleys, most of the Ukrainian settlements falling into the five counties of Sharish, Zemlin, Uzh, Bereh, and Marmarosh. This division into counties further cut up the already scattered and geographically disunited Carpatho-Ukrainian territory, thus broken into fragments, each of which was united to a neighboring non-Ukrainian Slovak, Hungarian, or Rumanian district. There is little evidence that Carpatho-Ukraine was ever a solid unit. It is true that many difficulties stood in the way of unity, for there, as in neighboring Galicia in the sixteenth and seventeenth centuries, the Ukrainian population consisted primarily of enserfed and downtrodden peasants and poor, ignorant village clergy; and the echoes of the great national movement in the rest of Ukraine rarely reached these remote areas. In the early years of the history of this region, various privileged foreign groups began to appear, including Hungarians, Germans, and Roman Catholic clergy. The Ukrainian masses found themselves in the role of serfs, and the same was true even of the village priests, who were forced to perform feudal services, being taken from the altar to do manual labor on the estates of feudal landlords and flogged in the same manner as other serfs. Those who elevated themselves above the common masses did so at the price of denationalization and joined the ranks of the Hungarian nobility.

The only expression of nationalism, and also the only national tie with the other Ukrainians, was religion, as was true in adjacent Galicia. For a long time the lands beyond the Carpathians did not have an organized Orthodox Church of their own, but were apparently under the supervision of the bishops of Peremyshl, who later on frequently exerted their influence over the mountain villages. Little is known about the church life of the region until the time when Roman Catholicism was introduced. The records of the seventeenth and eighteenth centuries indicate that the people of the mountain territories had a spiritual life in close contact with neighboring Galicia, the same books and manuscripts being in circulation in both of these regions. The religious centers of the Carpatho-Ukrainians were the monasteries of St. Nicholas on Monks Hill near Mukachev in Bereh county, and St. Michael at Hrushiv in Marmarosh county. It is believed that Theodore Koriatovich founded the Monastery at Mukachev. After Vitovt deprived him of Podolia, he settled in Hungary, was given Mukachev, became governor of Bereh, and according to the popular tradition of the Ukrainians of this region was considered not only the founder of various national institutions, but of Ukrainian settlement in Carpatho-Ukraine, which was said to have begun under him and his retainers. Not only the settlement, however, but the monastery, too, was much older, founded "from time immemorial," and it was only later that popular tradition accredited it to Koriatovich, in 1360. Neither is there any definite record regarding the foundation of the very old monastery at Hrushiv, the history of which is assigned to the times before the Tatar invasion. At the end of the fourteenth century, it received recognition from the Patriarch, and its abbots were given the right to supervise the churches in Marmarosh and Uzh in the absence of the bishops.

The bishops first appear in Carpatho-Ukraine at the close of the fifteenth century in the monastery at Mukachev. The first such record dates back to the 1490's, and the diocese must have been organized during the second half of the sixteenth century. It led a difficult existence, however, because the monasteries lost their wealth during the revolts of the seventeenth century, and the only income received by the bishops was the installation fees of young priests and their annual dues. In the seventeenth century one eparchy covered entire Carpatho-Ukraine with about two hundred thousand Orthodox inhabitants and about four hundred priests unevenly scattered over the mountain region; there were several villages without any priests, and in others there were several of them. Because there were no sound educational institutions, the clergy were ignorant and had to be supplemented with immigrants from Galicia and Moldavia. The Ukrainian educational movement of the close of the sixteenth century did not take in Carpatho-Ukraine. Mention has been made of the printing press at the monastery in Hrushiv, but there is no definite information regarding it. In the following century the Roman Catholic clergy reported that the people were ignorant in religious matters, and they expected therefore that if the bishop and higher clergy were converted to Catholicism the people would follow blindly without knowing that they had accepted the Uniate religion. To a marked extent this was true, and even in the eighteenth century, during the revolt against the Union in 1760, people said that they did not know that they were subject to Rome; but as soon as they had heard that Roman Catholicism was a bad faith, they had decided to return to the old true religion. Religion was the only sacred thing in their ignorant, almost inhuman, enserfed existence, and they received every attempt to change their faith with extraordinary resistance. "They hate the name of Uniate worse than they hate a snake; they think that it conceals some great evil, and although they unconsciously believe fundamentally in the same principles as the Uniates do, they despise the name," wrote the governor of Marmarosh, whose words furnish an understanding of the previous struggle by these enslaved, poor, and ignorant people in behalf of their religion.

The first struggle broke out during the second decade of the seventeenth century, when one of the local landed magnates by the name of Homonai attempted to introduce Uniate Catholicism on his estates, which contained about seventy parishes, and invited in Krupetsky, the Uniate bishop of Peremyshl. The priests and monks of the Homonai estates were induced to accept Catholicism, but the peasants revolted, attacking with pitchforks the new Uniates and Bishop Krupetsky, whom they wounded and almost killed, thus putting an end to Homonai's plan. The efforts of the Uniates, however, did not cease, for their nobles and clergy continued their attempts to win over the Orthodox bishops and clergy by promising them the right of freedom from serfdom enjoyed by the Catholic clergy if they would become Uniates. The temptation for the enserfed clergy and their poor bishops was great, and without the knowledge of the people they decided to convert the masses to Catholicism. In the 1640's a fairly large number of them were thus attached to the Union, and in 1649 they formally declared for it at Uzhorod, the declaration being submitted to the Pope in 1652 for his approval.

Even after this period the Uniate cause had hard sledding. On the one hand there remained a considerable number of priests hostile to Catholicism, who like the people wished to adhere to their old faith, and on the other there developed revolts and disturbances which characterized the entire second half of the seventeenth century in Hungary. The anti-Austrian Protestant party also stood in the way of the shrewd plans of the Uniates. There were, as a rule, two bishops, an Orthodox and a Uniate, and the priests leaned to one side or the other. The Monastery at Mukachev remained for a long time in the hands of the Orthodox and bore on the walls of its church an inscription regarding its rebuilding with Orthodox funds provided with the help of Moldavian nobles.

In the 1680's, when Austria was well established in eastern Hungary, she helped the Uniates to propagate their beliefs among the Ukrainians in Carpatho-Ukraine and not always in a Christian manner, but with the aid of military force and the application of pressure to those who returned to the Orthodox faith. Finally, in the eighteenth century the Uniate religion became well established and the western part of the country fell into the hands of the Uniate bishops. But in Marmarosh, bordering on Orthodox Moldavia, the old faith held its own until 1735, and in this province the priests even to a later date accepted ordination from the hands of Moldavian and Serbian Orthodox bishops. In the 1760's a last spark of resistance against the Union flared up unexpectedly among the Ukrainians and Rumanians in the Marmarosh region. Publications were distributed among the Orthodox people informing them that the Austrian government would not force them to accept the Uniate faith and that they could remain either Orthodox or Catholic, also hinting that the "eastern rulers" were keeping special watch over the welfare of the Orthodox. These rumors and circulars had an immediate effect. The people did not wish to live under the Pope and returned to the old faith, accepting only priests ordained as Orthodox. The clergy who had become Uniate had meanwhile been sadly disappointed, for their material conditions had not improved, they had remained serfs, and in addition had become dependent upon the Roman Catholic clergy; therefore they too abandoned the Union.

This movement alarmed the Austrian government, which undertook an investigation into the causes of antipathy toward the Union. The Uniate clergy pointed out that the chief reasons for the popular opposition to their religion were the ignorant clergy and their critical economic conditions. As soon as the rebellion was suppressed, the Empress Maria Theresa became interested in these people; she gave serious thought to improving conditions in the Uniate Church and endeavored to provide the priesthood with better education and an improved material existence. At a later date these efforts had important effects for the revival of Ukrainian nationalism.

Western Ukraine: In western Ukraine—the southern part of the province of Kiev and the neighboring districts of Braslav—after a short renewal of Kozak rule by Paliy and other colonels, the reign of the Polish gentry with their system of serfdom began to expand again during the second decade of the eighteenth century.

When the Russians in 1714 drove the Ukrainians from western Ukraine across the Dnieper and gave the country to Poland, the descendants of those landowning nobles whom the Ukrainians had expelled during Khmelnitsky's rebellion returned and either they themselves or their agents and factors began to found settlements in the deserted country in the provinces of Kiev, Braslav, and

Podolia, and to attract inhabitants by promising them freedom from all taxation for a period of fifteen or twenty or more years. They sent agents to the more densely settled side of the river to coax the population there to flee to the free land across the Dnieper, and these agents actually induced many Ukrainians to return to their former homes. Again a large number of people migrated, as 150 years before they had moved away from Polisia and Volynia, so that within a few years the deserted country west of the Dnieper was again studded with thickly populated villages and estates, among which were strewn the mansions and castles of the nobles and Roman Catholic monasteries. The nobles began to develop farming on a large scale, and when the period of promised freedom expired, the farmers became enserfed, were forced to perform various tasks, and were obliged to pay dues and contributions. The nobles, however, were careful not to stretch the string to the breaking point, because life was hard and uncertain; and until the introduction of serfdom by Russia into eastern Ukraine the Polish nobles were not sure of their position in western Ukraine.

After the unfortunate experience of Sobieski with the Kozaks, the Polish government did not permit them to organize again. The people on the other hand remembered the glorious Kozak days; and when Paliy died, following his return from exile in Siberia after the downfall of Mazepa, the masses hoped that Paliy's son-in-law, Colonel Tansky, would continue to work and fight for the rights of his people. At the time of his death Paliy gave his Bila Tserkva regiment to Tansky, in whose home Paliy's widow lived for the remaining years of her life. After the fortress of Bila Tserkva fell into the hands of Poland in 1714, Tansky became colonel of Kiev, and the people of western Ukraine set their eyes upon him as a man who would revive the Kozaks and free them from Poland. But their hopes were doomed to disappointment. Small Kozak companies composed of peasant serfs re-

mained in the service of the nobles on their estates, where
they were freed from taxation, but had no influence over
local conditions, being few in number and too weak to be
of danger to the nobles. Frequently these Kozaks joined
insurrections, but they never began any. Neither did the
people initiate them; they were a reflection of events in
eastern Ukraine, Moldavia, or the Zaporozhian region,
especially after the Zaporozhians had returned to Ukraine
in 1730 and settled down on the Ukrainian side of the Polish border. The people had fresh memories of Kozak liberty, of life without a landlord, and of free, democratic
Ukraine, and the attempts of the Polish lords to introduce
serfdom accordingly caused insurrections in Ukraine and
along the Ukrainian borders. Although the Polish government since the time of Khmelnitsky had lost its power and
political importance, there were now no well-organized
Kozaks in Ukraine to fight against the Polish nobles and
their system. Ukraine was left altogether in the hands of
the local gentry, chiefly great landed magnates, who governed their districts and their immense personal estates,
and who, though very wealthy, devoted but little attention
to their Ukrainian properties and lived on unfriendly
terms with one another.

On this account during almost the entire eighteenth century when Ukraine was under Polish rule and until the
partitions of Poland, there were many insurrections.
Sometimes these took the form of uprisings by robber
bands, and frequently they caused rebellions that extended over a large territory, so that only with the aid of
foreign armies was Poland able to suppress them. Not
only the large-scale revolutions, however, but even the
plundering bands had popular support, especially along
the Russian, Moldavian, and Hungarian borders. Their
attacks were directed against the nobles and the Jews,
who irritated the people because they assisted the nobles in oppressing them and enjoyed commercial monopolies; and the masses therefore looked upon the bandits as

their avengers and defenders, while there is no doubt that
the robbers considered themselves in the same light. The
people sang praises to them in folk songs, described them
in stories as popular heroes, attributed to them super-
human characteristics, or pictured them as warriors
against popular injustice. The Galician Hutsul country
even to this day is rich in stories of the robber chieftains
who were numerous in this mountainous region, along the
rivers, and in the forests. They lived especially along the
rivers Pruth and Cheremosh, on the Hungarian and Moldavian frontiers, where they attacked the merchants and
nobles. The most celebrated chief of the robber bands in
this region was Oleksa Dovbush, the son of a poor laborer
of Petchenizhin, who was widely known as a leader from
1738 to 1745, when he was killed by a bullet from ambush
near Kosmach. His name still lives in a popular song,
Dovbush.

In Podolia, next to Galicia, there were bands called
leventsi and *deineki,* who lived along the River Dniester
and in case of danger fled across it into Moldavia, Braslav, or southern Kiev; frequently they joined similar
bands living along the Dnieper, especially in the Zaporozhe. They were better known as *Haidamaks,* their name
being possibly derived from a Turkish word for brigand.
Their organizations existed either in the Russian territory or in the steppes. Where the Russian border at Kiev
formed a triangle in western Ukraine, there were many
church and monastery villages managed by the monks, in
which the Haidamaks made preparations for their raids
and sought refuge and protection after them. The local
monks, townspeople, and even Russian soldiers looked
upon the Haidamaks as warriors against Polish enslavement and in defense of Ukrainian rights, and consequently
considered it a good deed to aid them in every way possible or at least not to hinder them. When the Haidamaks
appeared in western Ukraine, people of all classes joined
them and frequently followed them back across the bor-

der, while others gave them every possible support in
their raids upon the Polish gentry. Because of the sympathetic feeling toward them, they were able to penetrate
deep into Ukraine, where they gathered large forces and
created havoc on the Polish estates. Occasionally they
were the nuclei of widespread revolutions which spread
throughout the region.

The Haidamak Rebellion: During the Polish interregnum in 1734 the Ukrainians in Poland revolted. The Polish nobles were divided into two political parties, one side
desiring as their ruler the elector of Saxony, the future
Augustus III, son of the late king, whereas the other
party supported the candidacy of Stanislaw Leszczynski,
whom King Charles XII of Sweden had once supported
but had failed to place on the throne. Russia at this time
supported the elector of Saxony, and his followers therefore asked that Russian forces be sent to assist them. A
Russian army had invaded Poland for the purpose of expelling Leszczynski and besieged the city of Danzig,
where he had established his headquarters; and at the
same time, in 1733, Russian and Kozak armies had been
sent to western Ukraine to attack the Polish nobles who
had organized themselves into a military "confederation" for the benefit of Leszczynski. The nobles of the
"confederate" group were themselves occupied in fighting against their opponents, while the Kozak and Russian
armies attacked and fought all Polish nobles alike. During this period of chaos the Haidamak bands were free to
take action, and finally the peasants also revolted, expecting that now, as in the days of Khmelnitsky, they would
succeed in driving the Polish nobles out of the country.
The people believed that the Kozak and Russian armies
had come to expel the Poles and to free Ukraine, rumors
being spread that the empress had issued proclamations
in which she called upon the people to rise in revolt
against the Poles and the Jews, reference being made to
the long-deceased Colonel Samus, an associate of Paliy,

and Paliy's son-in-law Tansky as having been requested
to lead a new Kozak rebellion.

The revolt was most widespread in the province of
Braslav. The Russian colonel sent there captured Uman
and sent out letters to the nobles of the Saxon party asking them to join him and to send their Kozak retainers
and other soldiers to attack the followers of Leszczynski.
Upon receiving a letter of this kind, Verlan, the officer in
charge of Prince Lubomirski's Kozak retainers, spread
the news among the people that the Empress Anna had
issued a manifesto calling upon the people to revolt, to
kill the Jews and the Poles, and to become Kozaks, and
that for this purpose the Kozak and the Russian armies
had come to Ukraine; when they had freed the whole of
Ukraine from the Poles and had introduced the Kozak
form of government, they were to unite western Ukraine
to the Hetman state. This rumor at once so aroused the
people that they revolted, established a Kozak system of
government, and organized a Kozak army. Verlan assumed the title of colonel and appointed the captains and
other officers, and was joined by many Kozak retainers
and Wallachians. As soon as he had collected a considerable army, he went on a campaign into the province of
Braslav, where he plundered the estates of the nobles and
the settlements of the Jews and urged the people to revolt and pledge their loyalty to the empress. From Braslav he went to neighboring Podolia, where he carried out
the same program; then he advanced to Volynia and in a
few battles defeated the small Polish forces there. He now
marched westward to the vicinity of Lviv and Kaminets,
where he captured Zvanets and Brody.

At this moment the conditions that had furnished the
opportunity for a revolution came to an end. In the summer of 1734 the Russian army captured Danzig, and
Leszczynski fled, whereupon the nobles of his party
yielded to Augustus of Saxony and at once appealed to

the Russian army to cease plundering the country and to aid them in restoring order among the peasants. The Russian officials saw no more need for popular revolt; and the Russian armies, which for several months had been urging the people to rebel, now aided the nobles in "taming" them, by capturing, bringing to trial, and punishing all who resisted. With the aid of the Russian army the nobles succeeded in a short time in reducing their serfs to submission. When the peasants and the Kozaks realized that they could not count on the aid of Russia, most of them submitted to their landlords; but the many who did not wish to return to serfdom joined the armed bands and made their way into the Zaporozhian country or to Wallachia, whence they later returned with the Haidamaks to renew their plundering of the Polish nobles.

As a result of the rebellion the number of armed bands increased to a great extent, and with the passage of time they made many incursions into western Ukraine to ravage the estates of the hated nobles. Thus in 1735 and 1736 the Haidamak leaders Hriva, Medvid, Kharko, and Hnat Holy terrorized the Polish nobles, captured towns, villages, and castles, and settled accounts with traitors who had repented of their previous revolts, had joined the nobles, and were now fighting against the Haidamaks. The most dramatic incident was the punishment by the Haidamaks of the traitor Sava Chaley, which was described in popular song and brought renown to an insignificant man. Chaley was of burgher stock from the city of Komarno and was serving Prince Lubomirski as the captain of his company of Kozak retainers when he joined Verlan's uprising, fleeing with other rebels when the Russian army suppressed the revolution. He then begged forgiveness of his lord, was elevated to the position of colonel of the other Kozaks who had returned to the nobles, and was sent out with them to attack their former Haidamak comrades. The latter decided to punish the renegade, and on Christmas Eve, 1741, Hnat Holy and his band attacked Chaley on his estate, killed him, and took his property with them, an act which became the theme of a popular folk song.

The momentum of the revolution of 1734 led the Haidamaks to harry the Polish nobles in Ukraine as late as 1760, their raids becoming the chief occupation of large numbers of people, neither the nobles nor the weak royal army being able to put an end to them. The peasants, continually in a state of unrest because of rumors of impending revolution, supported and aided the Haidamaks in every way possible and the more daring, having once joined the Haidamaks, frequently remained with them for life. By their attempts to propagate Uniate Roman Catholicism in the Dnieper region, the Poles themselves added fuel to the Haidamak movement by inciting the discontented Orthodox to join it against them, while the leaders of the brigands readily aided the townspeople in their struggle with the Uniate priests who were installed in their communities by the Polish nobles; they upheld the Orthodox faith and, in return, all the Ukrainian Orthodox priests and monks considered it their religious duty to aid the defenders of the Church. Although, no doubt, the chief aim of the Haidamaks was frequently merely brigandage, they, like the Kozaks of the sixteenth and seventeenth centuries, had a great influence upon people and events. Since they prevented the Polish nobles from strengthening their hold over the Ukrainian people and defended the local Church, the popular sympathy for them was justifiable. The Poles have failed to understand that the Ukrainians, then and now, have seen in the activities of the Haidamaks something more than mere banditry.* Enemies of the Galician Ukrainians often scornfully referred to them as Haidamaks, to indicate that they were

---

* The Ukrainians, it might be said, view the Haidamaks in something the same light as do Englishmen their ''sea dogs'' of the sixteenth century (Editor).

imitators of those early bands, but they were not disheartened by this epithet and replied in the popular song: "We are Haidamaks, all alike."

Following the revolution of 1734, the Haidamaks increased steadily in numbers and in power as long as conditions favored them, becoming especially active around 1750. For almost a full year Braslav, eastern Podolia, and the province of Kiev as far as the border of Polisia were in their hands and those of local revolutionists. Many towns, villages, and castles were captured and destroyed; and even such larger cities as Uman, Vinnitsia, Letichiv, and Radomisl fell into their hands. But the Haidamak bands and the local revolutionists were not well organized, they failed to establish any centers of operation west of the Dnieper, and after a year the Haidamak peasant revolutionary movement subsided, without either the government or the nobles having made serious attempts to suppress them. The Haidamak leaders quarreled with one another, while the peasants, not seeing any definite results from the uprisings, also began to subside, and in later years the movement reverted to such sporadic and isolated raids and assaults as had been characteristic of the Haidamaks in earlier years.

The Revolt of the Kolii: The revolutionary Haidamak movement surged up anew in the decade of 1760, but this time the chief issue was that of religion. Prior to this the Uniate metropolitans had established themselves in Radomisl, whence they were making serious efforts to spread the Uniate forms of Catholicism into the region of Kiev. The bishops of Pereyaslav, to whom the Orthodox parishes of Kiev were subject, were under Russian rule and could not successfully resist the enemy across the border, but they found an able supporter in the province of Kiev itself in the person of Melchisedek Znachko Yavorsky, who was appointed abbot of the Motronin Monastery near Zhabotin in 1753. Delighted to supervise the Orthodox churches in the southern part of Kiev province, he began with great energy to organize the Orthodox communities, encouraging them to be steadfast in their faith, to refuse to admit the Uniate priests into their churches, and to support the Orthodox priests only. The Motronin Monastery and its neighbors—the Zhabotin, the Moshnohory, the Medvediv, and the Lebedin monasteries—served as refuges and supporters of the Orthodox, and thus in 1760 a stubborn religious struggle broke out between the Orthodox and the Uniates. Aided by the Polish army the Uniate clergy attempted by the use of force to make Catholics of the Ukrainians who refused conversion, but the communities declined to accept the Uniate priests into their churches, the people compelling them to accept the Orthodox faith or expelling them from the village churches and selecting Orthodox clergy in their places. The Uniate authorities resorted to violence, those who resisted being imprisoned and punished in other ways, while Uniate clergy were sent to the recalcitrant communities. The Orthodox opponents of this Polish campaign appealed to the Russian government, as the protector of the Orthodox, to defend them from Polish persecution; and Yavorsky, who journeyed to the empress for this purpose, received various promises of help, the Russian ambassador in Warsaw being instructed to intercede with the Polish government in behalf of the Orthodox. His representations brought no relief. Meanwhile, as soon as the people in the province of Kiev learned of the aid promised by the empress, they became restless and either expelled the Uniate priests or compelled them to accept the Orthodox faith. The Uniate authorities then began to apply stronger methods of intimidation, punishment, and threats. In this chaos, inhuman and dreadful events frequently occurred; for example, the assassination of the churchwarden in Mliiv, which Shevchenko made the theme of a poem. His description was based on tradition and differs from the account recorded by contemporaries immediately after the event. The earlier account states that the churchwarden in Mliiv, Danilo Kushnir, was a righteous man who was persecuted because he hid the chalice at the orders of the townspeople, who did not wish to admit the Uniate priests. Though he kept the chalice piously, he was accused of taking it to a saloon and drinking liquor from it; by way of punishment the Uniates burned off his hands and then beheaded him, nailing his head to a post in the presence of the people, who had been driven by force to witness the act (1766). There were many similar instances of imprisonment, flogging, and the infliction of torture of various kinds.

Acts of this character aroused the people to rebellion; there were many insurrections in which both Zaporozhian Kozaks and Haidamak bands took part, and finally in the spring of 1768 there began on a large scale a popular uprising which was known as the rebellion of the Kolii (Koliivshina). The occasion of its outbreak, like that of the rebellion of 1734, was the presence of Russian troops in western Ukraine. When a revolt against the Polish government broke out at Bar in Podolia early in 1768 because of concessions granted to Russia, Poland begged the Russian government to suppress the uprising, and a Russian army was sent into Ukraine. When the news spread that the Russians had arrived, the people took it for granted that they had come to free them from Poland; again rumors spread that the empress had sent out proclamations, and later on copies of a "Golden Charter" were produced in which orders were given to blot out the very name of the Poles and the Jews in revenge for their abuse of the people and of the Orthodox faith. These purported copies were forgeries, but the leaders of the revolution and the masses believed them to be genuine.

The leader of the Kolii rebellion was Maxim Zalizniak, a Zaporozhian Kozak, who for many years had lived in monasteries, at first in the Zhabotin and later in the Motronin. Other Zaporozhians soon gathered together and planned a revolution. At the end of April 1768, Zalizniak with his band of followers emerged from the Motronin forest, went to Medvedivka, appealed to the people there to revolt, and admitted to his regiment a large number of volunteers. From here he marched through the southern part of the province of Kiev by way of Zhabotin, Smila, Cherkassy, Korsun, Bohuslav, and Lisianka, and into Uman, on his way seizing Polish estates and aiding the villagers to expel Uniate priests, Jews, and Poles. In the Uman district he was joined by Ivan Gonta, captain of the Kozak retainers of the Potocki estate, who had been charged with the defense of Uman. Gonta was a man of distinction and the recipient of many favors from the landlords, but when the revolution broke out he decided to abandon the gentry and join the Haidamaks. He entered into communication with Zalizniak, and when the latter arrived at Uman, Gonta went over to him. With Gonta and other Kozak warriors Zalizniak captured Uman, where the neighboring gentry had gathered. The ensuing massacre was considerably overdrawn by contemporary Polish accounts. Meanwhile, other Haidamak leaders fell upon the Polish nobles and the Uniate clergy in other sections of the province of Kiev, Semen Nezhivy attacking the Poles and the Catholic clergy in Cherkassy, Ivan Bondarenko in Polisia and the vicinity of Radomisl, and Jacob Shvachka and his followers along the Russian border in the vicinity of Vasilkiv and Bila Tserkva. Shvachka became especially notorious among the revolutionary chiefs for his cruelty. The center of his activity was Fastiv, to which place captured Poles and Jews were brought before him, to be condemned and executed. An investigating commission later reported that seven hundred people had been killed there, and the terrible acts of Shvachka became the subject of a folk song.

This time the rebellion was not of long duration. The history of 1734 repeated itself. In the early part of June the insurrectionary confederation formed at Bar was suppressed and the Poles appealed to the Russian authorities to assist them in quelling the Haidamaks. The Empress Catherine II, uneasy about the rumored proclamations which had caused the revolts, issued a manifesto in which she declared that she had had nothing to do with the false proclamation or with the Haidamaks; and she now ordered her army to destroy these revolutionary bands. The Haidamaks, who considered the Russians their comrades, took no precautions against them and were easily captured or dispersed. One Russian colonel, upon his arrival at Uman, invited both Gonta and Zalizniak to come to him, and when they did so he placed them under arrest, while other leaders, Nezhivy and Bondarenko, met with the same experience. Russian subjects were sent to Kiev for trial, and Polish subjects were turned over to their government, which made short shrift of them, some, among them Gonta, being tortured. Polish contemporaries selected for special mention the cruelty of a Pole named Stempkovski. Those who were not executed at once were tried again in the court at Kodno and condemned to various punishments, the most common being death. Thus ended the last great revolution in western Ukraine.

It is true that for some time the Polish nobles were very uneasy, especially when it was rumored that Gonta's son was preparing to massacre them in order to avenge the death of his father, and although there was particularly great alarm in Volynia in 1788, no insurrection broke out. The Zaporozhian organization was destroyed and the Ukrainian movement in eastern Ukraine suppressed, western Ukraine being reduced to passivity under the heavy hand of the gentry.

CHAPTER XX

THE DISPERSION OF THE KOZAKS

The Final Abolition of the Hetmancy: The government of Catherine II of Russia decided at its very institution to abolish the remnants of the Hetman state and the entire Ukrainian system of government. When she made herself empress in 1762 after the short reign of her husband, Catherine instructed the senate to establish a uniform system of administration and law in all those regions, such as Ukraine, the Baltic provinces, and Finland, which still had their own laws and constitutions. She considered it necessary to "destroy the very name of hetman, and not merely to appoint a weakling to the office."

Since Cyril Rozumovsky was one of the closest and most loyal friends of the young empress and she was grateful to him for his many services, she modified her political plans to a certain extent in order to show her appreciation. But an occasion arose to cause Catherine to take action against this loyal supporter. At the close of 1763 she received information from Kiev that the signatures of the Ukrainian officers were being secured to a petition to the empress asking her to make the office of hetman hereditary in the family of Rozumovsky because of its outstanding loyalty to the Russian empire, and citing the case of Khmelnitsky, who had left the office to his son. It is impossible to say whether the officers hoped in this way to strengthen the hetmancy or whether they were merely fulfilling the will of the hetman. In Ukraine it was said that the whole affair was the doing of Teplov, who had induced Rozumovsky to request the officers to initiate such a petition and had then accused him before the government of having appealed to the officers to send the petition to the empress in his behalf. It is true that the petition never reached Catherine because the general officers hesitated to sign it, and the project was dropped since only the signatures of the colonels were secured, but she considered this a good opportunity to abolish the hetmancy. In addition, Teplov also accused the Ukrainian government of corruption and inefficiency. It is quite probable that the government had asked him to compose such an accusation, as it did later in connection with the abolition of the Zaporozhian Kozak organization. Teplov had gathered a quantity of material pointing to mismanagement by the Ukrainian officials and also intended to prove that the Ukrainians were as much "Russians" as the Great Russians, but, through the negligence of the Kievan princes, had become a distinct people whom Russia would encounter no difficulty in Russifying.

Taking advantage of this situation, the empress advised Rozumovsky to resign from the hetmancy. He was unwilling to do this, but put off action until Catherine issued a threat that if he would not quit his office voluntarily, he would be forced from it and in addition would encounter royal disfavor. Rozumovsky finally submitted and begged the empress to free him from "such a difficult and dangerous office," asking as a reward for his resignation grants to himself and his large family. His request was fulfilled and on November 10 (21), 1764 a manifesto to the "Little Russian people" was published informing them that the government had freed Rozumovsky from his hetmancy but failing to mention the election of a new hetman, the empress suggesting only that certain improvements would be made. For the time being a Little Russian Board was created, the president of which, Count Rumiantsov, was to be governor-general of Little Russia. Rozumovsky was well compensated for his humiliation, being given an annual pension of sixty thousand rubles and permission to retain the immense estates which were attached to the office of hetman—the castle of Hadiach and the district of Bikiv. This generosity led the Kozak colonels and other officers to believe that with the abolition of the hetmancy each of them would receive a large estate, and for this reason, according to the author of the *History of the People of Rus,* they did not urge the government to hold an election to fill the office. Their hopes, however, did not materialize. Rozumovsky lived on for forty years, and in spite of his personal worthlessness it was unfortunate that he was not permitted to keep his office during this long period, since this would have prolonged Ukrainian autonomy.

The new Little Russian Board was to consist of four Ukrainian and four Russian members, the president and prosecutor to be Russians. They were to be seated at meetings according to seniority, not as in the time of Anna, when the Russians had sat to the right and the Ukrainians to the left, Catherine fearing that the old system "recognized the Little Russians as a distinct nationality." Having been created for the sake of form the board had little authority, Rumiantsov being the real ruler. The Empress instructed him to carry out her program of destroying the Ukrainian system of administration and law and to replace them with those of Russia.

In her instructions to Rumiantsov the empress pointed out certain phases of Ukrainian life to which she wished him to pay special attention. He was instructed to take a census in Ukraine in order to determine its wealth and to make it possible for the Russians to levy taxes directly. There were several features of the Ukrainian administration especially inacceptable to the Russian government, especially the fact that the Ukrainian peasants were not fully enserfed, being free to transfer their services from one landlord to another, a privilege which had been unknown in Russia for many years. As the empress could not tolerate a special right of this kind in Ukraine, she instructed Rumiantsov to put an end to it. She ordered him to pay special attention to the "inbred hatred" of the Ukrainians for the Russians, especially on the part of the Kozak officers, and urged him to watch for evidences of it and in every possible way to develop the confidence and sympathy of the common people for the Russian government in order to destroy the influence of the Kozak officials over them; for this purpose she directed him to administer affairs in such a way that the people would feel that the new administration was protecting them from the abuses of the gentry and the officers, and that they were better off under the Russian government than they had been under the hetmans.

Although this policy of arousing popular antagonism against the officers was an old one, it was difficult to convince the people of the advantages of the new rule when the remnants of peasant liberty were being destroyed, the officers were receiving the privileges of the Russian gentry, and the despotic Russian system of serfdom and deprivation of civil rights was being introduced.

The "general census" of Ukraine by Rumiantsov has provided an excellent source of information as to life in the old Hetman state, but it did nothing to lighten the burden of the inhabitants. Rumiantsov, the owner of immense estates in Ukraine, looked upon the condition of the peasants from the point of view of the Ukrainian landlord, and the Ukrainian peasants received no relief from him or from the other Russian officials; but on the contrary, all the practices of serfdom, which the Kozak officers had been slowly putting into effect on their estates, were now introduced on a large scale with the support of the government until at length serfdom was legalized by the imperial government and the condition of the Ukrainian peasants had become much worse under the new Russian system of administration and its enforcement by officials who had grown up under the system of serfdom in use in Russia.

Rumiantsov had no difficulty in obeying the instructions of the empress to keep an eye on the Ukrainian officials and their inbred hatred for Russia or, as it came to be called later on, Ukrainian separatism. In this respect he displayed such enthusiasm that even the empress was obliged to check him and to urge him not to become unduly excited. He was especially irritated by the composition of the Ukrainian delegation to the Legislative Commission of 1767; Catherine requested the provinces, including Ukraine, to send to her deputations elected by all classes of the population and to bring with them written mandates regarding the wishes of her subjects and their desires in regard to laws and administration in order that these might be included in the new code of laws to be drawn up for Russia. The entire Ukrainian population—not only the officers, but Kozaks, townspeople, and clergy as well—expressed a desire for the restoration to Ukraine of its old rights and organization, in accordance with the treaty of Bohdan Khmelnitsky, the election of a hetman, and so on. Rumiantsov was enraged. He and his agents attempted to influence the people not to give expression to these desires and urged them to elect as delegates "reasonable" people; he even censored the mandates in cases where he knew the desire for autonomy was strong and prosecuted those who were warmly in favor of self-government for Ukraine. In the Nizhin regiment the "gentry" who composed the regimental Officers' Council elected as deputy a "reasonable" man by the name of Seletsky who, however, was unwilling to accept the mandate given him by the people because it was written in the spirit of autonomy and discussed the renewal of the hetmancy and of the old Ukrainian rights. The officers then elected another deputy, and because of this action, Rumiantsov brought before a court martial all those who had a hand in writing the petition and replacing Seletsky. The court condemned thirty-three men to death, though at the time of confirmation of the judgment the sentence was commuted to eight months' imprisonment.

Disregarding the severe penalties inflicted by Rumiantsov, the population of Ukraine unanimously expressed itself for Ukrainian autonomy. People realized that this was a decisive moment and concluded that it was their duty to give utterance to their desires regardless of the anger and the severity of the all-powerful governor-general. It is true that nothing resulted from the projected code, and the petitions from Ukraine were merely striking evidence of the strivings and aspirations of the Ukrainians, which furnish a faithful picture of the conditions in the country under the rule of the new Russian administrator. It is notable that the empress herself accepted the Ukrainian petitions with less alarm than that felt by her governor-general. As to the angry complaints of Rumiantsov against Ukrainian "stubbornness" she calmly advised him not to pay much attention to it, expecting that in time "the desire for positions and even more for salaries would change these old-fashioned ideas," and that the desire for autonomy and separatism would not be able to withstand pressure by the government and the favors which it could bestow upon the loyal and obedient. Her predictions proved to be true.

In the same manner as in the Hetman state, the desire for the old Kozak rights revealed itself in the neighboring Land of the Free Communes. At the time when the hetman's office was abolished in the Hetman state in 1763–64, the Kozak regimental organization in the Land of Free Communes, which had been similar to that of the hetman state, was also done away with. The "government," or province, of the Free Communes (Slobidska Gubernia) was set up, the Kozak regiments replaced by hussars, and the Kozaks forced to pay a peasant poll tax in place of their former military service. The Kozaks were highly discontented and both during the elections to the law commission and at the time of the reorganization protested against the new order and demanded the restoration of the old. But their resistance was less vigorous than in the Hetman state and met with no success.

Destruction of the Sich: The determination of the government to enforce its new policy in Ukraine was clearly evidenced by the destruction and abolition of the Sich.

It is true that the last Sich, transferred to Russian territory in the 1730's, was but a shadow of the old Kozak center. Permitted in response to their own request to return to Russian vassalage, the Sich Kozaks were obliged to give faithful obedience to the orders of the government, which made use of them as if they were mercenary city Kozaks; the officers realized that they were powerless to struggle against it and attempted to carry out its will. The Zaporozhians suffered hardships in wars against Turkey and the Crimea and performed various other duties imposed upon them by the Russian authorities. In both the first Turkish war in the 1730's and in the second, which began in 1768, the Zaporozhian army participated from beginning to end. Several thousand Kozaks were sent on campaigns with the Russian army, others carried on guerrilla warfare or attacked the Turkish fleet on the Black Sea or served as guards, for all of which services they received certificates of praise from the empress. Nevertheless, they suffered oppression and abuse from the government, one reason being that the Kozak officers could not prevent the Zaporozhians from attacking Turkey, the Crimea, and Poland at a time when Russia was at peace with these countries; another annoyance was the territorial disputes.

Already "the line," as the complex of forts built along the old Ukrainian steppe frontier in 1720–30 was called, had taken in the old "Zaporozhian free lands." In the 1730's the Russian government began to colonize "the line," settling there large numbers of Serbian and other immigrants, the first settlement being made in 1732 and the second in 1751–52. "New Serbia," as the colony was called, occupied the northern portion of the Zaporozhian territory; it was organized in military fashion into regiments and companies, infantry, cavalry, and hussars, and its support was a great burden to the Zaporozhians. Late in the decade of 1750, the government began to colonize the region near Elisavethrad with immigrants of various origin and seized Zaporozhian lands for this purpose. Naturally the Kozaks were greatly aroused by the incursions of these uninvited guests, who came into the steppes owned by their ancestors, deprived them of their old homesteads and their income from fishing and hunting, and had no regard for the Sich or its authority. The Kozaks presented to the Russian government documentary evidence of their historic rights and attempted to destroy the hated settlements by force. Instead of improving conditions, however, they only further antagonized the Russian government, which increased its oppression of the Zaporozhian Kozaks as a hindrance to the colonization of the steppes and the creation of a "New Russia" there. Catherine II aggravated the situation by deciding to create a province of New Russia out of "the line" by adding parts of the Hetman state and the neighboring Zaporozhian lands. The Kozaks refused to allow the boundaries of the new province to be extended into their lands and either dispersed the settlers or beguiled them into their ranks. This resistance aroused the anger of the Russian government, which was at that time occupied with plans to colonize the Ukrainian steppes, to master the shore of the Black Sea, and to annex some Balkan lands and even Constantinople.

The Zaporozhians, during the last decade of their existence, had considerably altered their point of view. The last koshovy, Peter Kalnishevsky, who held the office at intervals from 1762 to the destruction of the Sich, was a man of tact and caution. Realizing that the situation was not favorable, he attempted to prevent his Kozaks from antagonizing the Russian government and endeavored to colonize the Kozak lands with raisers of grain. The entire Zaporozhe region acquired new life; Kozak villages were founded and churches built, not only in the Sich itself, but also in other settlements; and the Russian government had no reason to complain that the black earth steppes were remaining vacant and useless in the hands of the Zaporozhians. Under Kalnishevsky's wise management it was demonstrated that the steppes in the hands of the Sich could become inhabited and productive. The government, however, desired to seize these lands for itself, and having destroyed the old Kozak system in Ukraine, it did not wish to permit to exist such a center of freedom of spirit as an autonomous Sich, modest though it was in comparison with the Sich of the period of Hordienko.

By the close of the 1760's the relations between the Russian government and the Sich had become very much strained. About this time a war with Turkey broke out which the Kozaks were accused ·of having caused by an attack upon the Turkish frontier town of Balta. At the same time the Zaporozhians became deeply involved in the Kolii rebellion; the Russian government aided the Polish gentry in suppressing this uprising and boasted that it would also suppress the uprising in the Sich, from which Haidamaks were carrying on raids into Polish Ukraine. Moreover, according to reports by the Russian officials, the Zaporozhians were disturbing the settlers in the newly created province of New Russia and establishing their own settlements there. The Russian government accordingly decided to destroy the Sich; fearing revolution, however, it concealed its purpose in order to strike when the Zaporozhians were unprepared. In 1775, at the close of the Turkish war, the government sent out secret military orders to disarm the Kozaks in the steppes; after the disarming was completed, General Tekeli arrived in the Zaporozhe with a large Russian army, occupied the entire region, and unexpectedly laid siege to the Sich stronghold itself. After his artillery had been brought up and placed in position, he informed the garrison on June 5 that the Sich could no longer exist and that the Zaporozhians must surrender, abandon the fortress, and disperse, under threat of attack. Overcome with confusion, the Kozaks were at a loss as to what to do. There were many who preferred to fight rather than to surrender, but Kalnishevsky and the other officers, supported by the army chaplain, attempted to persuade them to yield, for resistance was futile. The Zaporozhians assented and surrendered, the Sich was destroyed, and on August 3 the empress issued her famous manifesto which "abolished the very name of the Zaporozhian Kozaks." The government made public the reasons for its sudden destruction of the Sich, but its motives appear contradictory. On the one hand it accused the Zaporozhians of not making good use of the land, of keeping it in a wild condition, and of preventing the development of agriculture and commerce, but on the other hand it accused the Kozaks of departing from their former way of living during the last few years and of having permitted some fifty thousand farmers to settle on their land and raise grain. They were also accused of developing the raising of grain to such an extent that they were losing their dependence upon the Russian government, as they could live from their own produce and become entirely independent "under their own disloyal government."

The most contradictory incident in the fall of the Zaporozhe was that the officers who had persuaded the Kozaks to surrender and to submit to the will of the empress were arrested and sent into exile at hard labor. For a long time nothing was heard of them, and it was believed that they had perished, until it was unexpectedly revealed that Kalnishevsky had been exiled to the Solovetsky Monastery in the White Sea, where he had been locked in a small cell for twenty-five years. The pilgrim eyewitnesses who saw him in the first years of the nineteenth century stated that he was permitted to leave his confinement three times each year to attend the annual festivals of the monastery —at Christmas, Easter, and on Transfiguration Day. He inquired who was emperor and if all was well in Russia, but the guards did not permit him to talk long. He looked aged and feeble, but still wore his Kozak uniform with its buttons shining. He died in 1803, at the age of a hundred and twelve. Hloba, the Kozak secretary, died earlier, in 1790, in one of the northern monasteries; and at about the same time Paul Holovaty, the army judge, passed away in the Tobolsk Monastery in Siberia.

Out of the Kozak land large estates were carved and distributed among the Russian nobles, while the Kozaks were obliged to become carbineers in the Russian army or to enter civil life as townspeople or peasants. In 1776 the imperial commissioner Potemkin informed the empress that the problem of the Zaporozhians had been solved; some had moved to the towns and villages, and the rest had joined the Russian army as carbineers, of whom two new regiments had been organized, the property of the Kozak officers had been confiscated for the benefit of settlers, and so on. In reality this report was far from the truth. The majority of the Zaporozhians did not wish to become serfs again and had decided to do now what they had done after the first destruction of the Sich—live under Turkey. An old Zaporozhian, Mikita Korzh, relates how the Kozaks outwitted the Russians. Because the border and all the main highways leading out of the Zaporozhe were in the hands of the Russian army, the Kozaks asked Tekeli to permit them to go out fishing on the Tilihul and to seek other employment. Whenever a pass for fifty men was received, a few hundred emigrated, and before long more than half had moved to Turkish territory, so that by the summer of 1776, Kozaks to the number of seven thousand had settled near Ochakiv.

When this fact became known in St. Petersburg, it caused some concern to the government, which sent various agents to the Zaporozhians to persuade them to return; at the same time Russia requested the Turkish government to give them up, but the Kozaks did not care to go back and the Turks were unwilling to surrender them.

This migration is described in many popular songs and epics, although there is not one which deals with the abolition of the hetmancy.

In order that Russia might not oppress the Kozaks, the sultan gave them land at the mouth of the Danube; but the Zaporozhians were not eager to move there and for several years lived at "both limans," as the silted estuaries of the region near Ochakiv were called. In 1778 they were formally recognized by the Turkish government, permitted to build a new stronghold and to live and carry on commerce without restraint, in return for which favors they were to serve the sultan in infantry and cavalry regiments. But as the Russian government insisted that they should not be kept near the Russian border, the sultan ordered them to migrate to the Danube. This the Kozaks did not wish to do, and some of them returned to live under Russian sovereignty. In order to prevent further migration by the Kozaks to foreign countries, Potemkin then decided to renew the Zaporozhian army under the name of the "Black Sea Army," and in 1783 asked Anton Holovaty, Chepiha, and other Zaporozhian officers to call for volunteers, whereupon more of those who had emigrated returned and joined this army.

The other Ukrainian Kozaks petitioned the Hapsburg Emperor Joseph II to permit them to settle in his empire. They were granted permission and established their Sich in 1785 on Hapsburg territory in the Banat on the lower Theiss. Eight thousand Ukrainians emigrated there but did not stay long. There is no definite information as to their final destination, but it is probable that some of them returned to Turkey and the rest to Ukraine. In Turkey they were settled at the mouth of the Danube near the town of Dunavets, where the émigré Russian (Don) Kozaks under Nekrasov had lived until they were forced out by the Zaporozhians. At the close of the Russo-Turkish war of 1792 the Russian government set aside as a reward for the services of the Black Sea Army the land in the lower Kuban basin between the Kuban River and the Sea of Azov, where they were permitted to establish a democratic Kozak government, to reëstablish the Kozak army organization, and to have their own courts, and to enjoy freedom of trade. Altogether there were seventeen thousand Kozaks in this Black Sea Army, the members of which were the founders of the Ukrainian colony in the Kuban region. The first chief of this army was Kharko Chepiha.

The Sich on the Danube lasted until 1828. Relations with the Turkish government were good, but the Kozaks were uneasy at having to assist the Mohammedans in fighting against Christians.

The Russian government did not cease its agitation to induce the Danubian Kozaks to return to Ukraine, but only a small number took advantage of the invitation, until in 1828 war broke out again between Russia and Turkey and Osip Hladky, the leader of the Danubian Zaporozhians, decided to lead his Kozaks back to Russia. For this purpose he spread rumors that the Turkish government intended to force the Kozaks to emigrate and settle in far-off Egypt, and he urged them to avoid this fate by returning to Russian rule. Since not all volunteered, he tricked them by leading them out, ostensibly to fight against the Russians, but informed them, when he reached the Russian border, that they would have to give up and live under Russia. Since it was too late to turn back, they agreed. When they were ready to join the Russian army, Hladky appeared before the emperor and informed him that he was surrendering to Russia. He participated in the war and after it was over selected as a home for his followers the coast of the Sea of Azov, where they settled between Berdiansk and Mariupol; there the small "Azov Army" lived until 1860, when it was forced to migrate to the Kuban region.

Hladky's treason brought great misery to the Kozaks who had remained on the Danube. The Turkish government disbanded their army, destroyed their settlement, and scattered the Kozaks throughout the empire. It was reported that many of them were killed by the Turks, and those who survived lived to curse Hladky.

The Last Years of the Hetman State: As soon as the Russian government had disbanded the Kozaks of the Dnieper Sich, it turned its attention to those of the Hetman state. In the fall of 1780 a proclamation by the empress was issued, establishing a Russian form of government in Ukraine. The whole of eastern Ukraine was to be divided into provinces organized on the Russian model, Rumiantsov being authorized to inaugurate this "reform." The next year the Little Russian Board, the general court, and the general and regimental administrations were abolished and the Hetman state was divided into the three provinces of Kiev, Chernihiv, and Novhorod-Siversky, in which new governors were appointed and courts established, all of the Russian type. In place of the former army courts, Russian civil and criminal courts were established; municipal and district courts were replaced by circuit courts; in place of the military treasury, a department of internal revenue was established; city and town administration was placed in the hands of magistrates, and so on. The Little Russian Board was permitted to exist for a short time to wind up its affairs, and Ukrainian officials were also retained until the government could make further changes.

Subsequent orders supplemented the alterations already made for replacing the Ukrainian system with the Russian. In 1783 the Ukrainian Kozak regiments were abolished and the Kozak regiments transformed into regiments of carbineers. Their leaders, the colonels, were retired from service with the rank of brigadier, and other Kozak officers were permitted either to join the new carbineer regiments or to retire from military service. The Kozak rank and file were to remain as a separate social unit of military peasants to be organized into new regiments later on. All other peasants were reduced to the level of the Russian peasants by being made serfs. Even before this time, in 1763, the Russian government had issued a proclamation forbidding the Ukrainian peasants to change freely from one master to another on the pretense that this freedom was harmful to them, and declaring that such migrations made prosperity impossible it forbade the members of this class henceforth to change masters without the written consent of their landlords. By this regulation the authority of the landlords over their peasants was greatly strengthened; but the villagers, alarmed by this step in the direction of complete serfdom, began to move about more freely than ever in order to flee from their masters. Then by the law of 1783 which introduced new taxes the peasants were forbidden to leave their places of residence from the time that the law went into effect. The peasants of Ukraine were thus completely enserfed and fell under the jurisdiction of the "general ordinances of the empire," that is, subject to the laws under which the harsh regime of serfdom had long existed in Russia.

In the same year the administration of the Ukrainian cities was made uniform with that of the Russian cities, and the Ukrainian officers received rights equal to those of the Russian nobles, a list being drawn up of the Kozak ranks and positions which assured the rights pertaining to the nobility, thus separating the Kozak officers sharply from the rank and file. Finally, in 1786 the remnant of the autonomy of the Ukrainian Church was abolished by the confiscation of episcopal and monastic estates, each monastery being allotted by the state a definite number of monks, who were to receive salaries from the state treasury, to which the monastic estates reverted.

The Ukrainians accepted without protest this final abolition of their old social and political system. Some of the changes appealed to the Ukrainian officers, especially the recognition of their rights as nobles and the complete en-

serfment of the peasants; and many of them grasped
eagerly at the new rights and bounties which accompanied the change or sought for appointment to lucrative offices in the new system. Little by little the landowners forgot their Hetman state and thought only of the wealth
which they had gained as a result of the new laws regarding serfdom, and even those who looked back with nos-
talgia to the old order consoled themselves by seeking
personal careers under the new government. What the
Empress Catherine had predicted had come to pass: the
officers ceased to strive for national rights and thought
only of themselves.

The mass of the Ukrainian people had nothing with
which to console themselves. The Russian government
promised them freedom from the old maladministration
of the officers and from "the petty tyrants"—the landlords; but in reality the new order strengthened beyond
anything which had existed in the past the power of the
landowners over the peasants, who faced a future of unrelieved gloom with a disillusion and bitterness reflected
in the folk songs of the period.

CHAPTER XXI

THE NATIONAL RENAISSANCE

The Austrian Annexation of Galicia and Bukovina: While the old Ukrainian order was being destroyed in eastern Ukraine in the last half of the eighteenth century, there were being created in western Ukraine new circumstances and new bases for Ukrainian life. Just as Poland was attempting to destroy the last national movements among the Ukrainians in western Ukraine and completely to weaken the national culture by introducing the Church Union, an unexpected end came to the existence of Poland herself as an independent state. In the course of a few years the country was partitioned by the neighboring powers, and all efforts by the Polish nobles to regain its independence were unsuccessful.

The extensive areas claimed by Poland in Ukraine and Lithuania did not prove to be of lasting benefit, for her efforts to conquer them and to subjugate and enserf the inhabitants had so weakened and exhausted her that she herself fell prey to her equally aggressive but more powerful neighbors. The Polish gentry, upon getting control of the government, enserfed the rest of the population, lessened the importance and the authority of the king, and deprived the government of all its powers in order to prevent it from limiting their independence and their privileges. Poland had neither money in its treasury nor an army nor a strong organization. All authority had been seized by the great landed proprietors, who cared nothing for their country, but only for their own luxuries and their selfish interests, frequently being paid by foreign powers to conduct the policies of Poland in accordance with the demands of those countries and not those of Poland.

Khmelnitsky's revolution of 1648 dealt Poland a blow

from which she never recovered. After the beginning of the eighteenth century, Polish affairs were not directed solely by her own rulers, but by foreign governments who prevented her from inaugurating reforms which might strengthen her, interfered at every possible occasion in her internal affairs, raised revolts ("confederations") by her corrupt landowners, and in general did as they pleased. And meanwhile from time to time there developed schemes to break up the large but weak country— such schemes as have been observed in the time of Khmelnitsky.

After the death of the Polish King Augustus III in 1763, the Empress Catherine, in agreement with her supporters in Poland, sent in an army, placed her friend Stanislaus Augustus Poniatowski on the throne, and intended to rule the country under cover of his name. The chief occasion for this intervention was the problem of the Orthodox faith in Poland, which Russia claimed the right to protect, a claim supported by the fact that the Orthodox clergy in Poland called upon Russia for aid. The Polish government was eager to free itself from Russian influence and took advantage of the outbreak of a Russo-Turkish war in 1768, at which time Austria supported Turkey in order to prevent Russian expansion toward the Austrian border. Russia wished to place Crimea and Moldavia under her control and demanded that Turkey recognize these states as free and independent, but Austria, who desired to expand into Moldavia, disapproved of the Russian policy. Poland was hoping to take advantage of these strained international relations, when the King of Prussia gave events a new turn. Deciding to take advantage of the tense situation between Russia and Poland, he suggested that Russia expand at the expense not of Turkey, but of Poland, and that Prussia and Austria should at the same time annex some Polish lands near their borders. Catherine was far from eager to accept this plan, as she desired to keep Poland intact for herself, but since Austria was beginning to take the side of Turkey, she gave her approval to the project of Prussia in order to retain its support. Negotiations were begun and it was finally agreed that Russia should give up her designs on Moldavia, although Turkey was obliged to recognize the independence of Crimea, which Russia annexed in 1783 without the necessity of a war and with the approval of Austria. In place of Moldavia, Russia took from Poland some White Russian border territory, Austria annexed Galicia, and Prussia acquired Polish territory along the Baltic Sea. An agreement was reached in August 1772, and the armies of the three nations proceeded without a war to occupy their respective allotments, while the Polish parliament and administration, either from fright or through bribery, were compelled to recognize these losses.

Austria took the western Ukrainian territories, that is, almost the whole of Belz and parts of Podolia, Volynia, and Kholm, claiming that all these districts had belonged to the former kingdom of Galicia-Volynia and had at one time been subject to the kings of Hungary. As has been noted,* the dependence of Galicia upon Hungary had been very short-lived, existing only during the boyhood days of King Daniel, but from that time the Hungarian kings had entitled themselves "Kings of Galicia and Volodimiria"; and since the Hungarian crown had fallen into the hands of the Hapsburgs in the sixteenth century the Empress Maria Theresa now claimed the right to annex this "former Hungarian province" of Galicia. She encircled the Ukrainian districts with neighboring Polish territory and attached the whole acquisition not to Hungary, but to the Austrian lands. With the upper basin of the Pruth River in their hands, Maria Theresa and her son, Joseph II, were eager to add to it the neighboring portion of Moldavia. While visiting near-by Transylvania in 1773, Joseph observed how important it was for Austria to annex northern Moldavia in order to have a high-

* Pp. 98–101.

way between Galicia and Transylvania and decided to seize it from Turkey. In 1774 the Austrian army crossed the Moldavian border and occupied Chernivtsi, Seret, and Suchava—present-day Bukovina.

In this case too the Austrian government attempted to justify itself by claiming that Bukovina had formerly belonged to Galicia. It was true that during the thirteenth century the many settlements along the middle courses of the Pruth and the Dniester had belonged to the principality of Galicia. Later the region had fallen to the Tatars, and in the middle of the fourteenth century, when the principality of Moldavia was formed, the Moldavian princes had seized for themselves the land along the Dniester and Seret, the so-called Land of Pokutia and the Shipin district. Later, as has been seen,* there were several wars between Poland and Moldavia for the possession of these lands until they were finally divided; and Moldavia kept northern Bukovina until 1774, when it was occupied by an Austrian army. The province was settled with Ukrainian peasants, who occupied the lands of the prince, the nobles, and the monasteries. Since peasant obligations were light, numbers of oppressed serfs immigrated from Galicia. This northern Ukrainian Bukovina formed the Chernivtsi district, but Austria annexed at the same time the southern part of the province, Suchava, which was inhabited chiefly by Rumanians, so that in the same way that the new Galicia under the Austrian government was composed of both Ukrainian and Polish lands, new Bukovina was of a mixed Ukrainian-Rumanian character, the north being Ukrainian and the south Rumanian.

The Prince of Moldavia urgently protested against this Austrian aggression; but his sovereign, the Turkish sultan, failed to support him, and in 1775 agreed to allow Austria to keep the northwestern part of Moldavia. Commissioners were appointed to locate the boundary of the

* Pp. 144–149.

new province, which was given the name of Bukovina because of its dense beech forests, the name meaning "Beechland" in the Ukrainian language. For some time it was under military rule, until in 1786 it was united with Galicia; it remained so until 1849, when it was made into a separate province.

The Destruction of Poland and the Annexation of Western Ukraine by Russia and Austria: After the heavy blow sustained by the first partition of 1772, many people in Poland realized the gravity of the situation and attempted to introduce reforms which might have saved Poland earlier but which were now too late. The neighbors of Poland were hostile toward the projected improvements, the Russian government being particularly aroused because the Poles were making efforts to introduce the reforms without its consent, but Russia's hands were tied by a war with Turkey which broke out in 1787 when the Russians annexed Crimea. The Polish reform party considered an alliance with Prussia, hoped for the sympathy of Austria, and expected to get along without the advice of Russia, but its plans miscarried. As soon as Poland proclaimed a new constitution in May 1791, Russia brought to a close her successful war with Turkey in which she had gained Crimea and the northern coast of the Black Sea, and she moved her army from Turkey into Poland. The Polish grandees who opposed the reforms led an insurrection by forming the so-called Torhovitsa Confederation, and submitted themselves to the protection of Russia, whereupon the Russian army occupied Warsaw. A new parliament was convoked and was forced by Russia to abrogate the reform constitution of 1791 and to return to the old system, while Prussia forsook Poland and supported Russia. In the second partition—that of 1792—Prussia seized additional land in western Poland and Russia annexed the Ukrainian provinces of Kiev and Podolia and a part of Volynia, besides White Russian lands on a line extending from Courland to the Austrian border; the Polish parliament meekly approved the Russian seizure of these lands. Two hundred years before at the Congress of Lublin the Polish rulers had annexed Ukrainian territory without the consent of the Ukrainians and had forced the Ukrainian nobles at the point of the sword to take an oath of allegiance to Poland; now the Poles in the same manner were compelled by Russia to endure an equally bitter experience.

But even the small Polish state now left did not long endure. Because the king was too submissive to Prussia and Russia, a revolution broke out against him in 1794 in which the revolutionists attempted to force him to regain the lost territory. The Russian and Prussian armies, however, suppressed the revolution and Russia occupied both Warsaw and Vilna. The existence of Poland as an independent state came to an end in the third partition in 1795. Russia took the Ukrainian and White Russian lands still left to Poland, with the exception of Kholm and Pidliashe, while Austria and Prussia took other provinces. A slight redistribution of Polish territory was made by the three countries in 1815: White Russia went entirely to Russia, the Ukrainian lands were divided between Russia and Austria, and Poland proper was partitioned among Austria, Russia, and Prussia. This arrangement lasted unchanged down to the World War of 1914–18.

Thus at the close of the eighteenth century Ukraine was divided between two great powers, Russia and Austria, both highly centralized and bureaucratic states provided with strong police forces and large armies and quite lacking in popular self-government. All political distinctions marking the Ukrainian lands were abolished, and self-government was either done away with or greatly limited, while even what self-government was left was of little use to the poor and ignorant Ukrainian townspeople and the uneducated village clergy. All the Ukrainian efforts to secure independence had been in vain: all the sacrifices and the streams of Ukrainian and foreign blood that had flowed on the battlefield had not brought freedom and independence to Ukraine.

"Poland fell, but she crushed us too," wrote Shevchenko. Her downfall did not improve the lot of the Ukrainians, especially in that section of Ukraine which became a part of the Russian empire. In the Ukrainian lands which fell into the hands of Austria, the new Austrian government took some steps to lighten the burden of the Ukrainian serfs and to limit the hitherto boundless rights of the Polish aristocrats over them as well as to offer better education to the people of town and country, and especially to the clergy. The placing of Galicia under Austrian rule was the beginning of the Ukrainian renaissance in western Ukraine. But in the Ukrainian provinces which were taken away from Poland by Russia, the lot of the Ukrainians was not improved, but, on the contrary, the powerful hand of the new Russian administration placed a strength behind the rule of the Polish nobles over the Ukrainian serfs such as they had never known under the weak and decentralized government of Poland. As a rule, every Polish landlord held in the hollow of his hand the lower Russian officials with whom he had to deal; he could easily bribe them and was sure that they would carry out his wishes. Previously the attacks of the Haidamaks and the popular revolts had hampered the growth of the power of the landlords; but under the protection of the powerful Russian army and police system, the nobles had nothing to fear and abused the serfs as much as they pleased. In 1848, because of an insurrection in Galicia, the Russian government attempted to lighten the burden of the Ukrainian peasants, but their spiritual and intellectual life remained in unrelieved darkness for many a year.

Ukrainian national life appeared even more hopeless than it had in the past. The very memory of the great national struggle for independence nearly died out completely. The people retained only the folk songs and legends, of which the vast store was confined to the narrow circle of *kobzars* (minstrels), who went about from place to place singing of the glorious past. The printed word had not preserved those productions in which were described the great movements and stirring efforts of Ukrainian life, and among the upper classes who possessed education there were few who had a clear conception of the history of their country. In western Ukraine, Poland was the dominating force; the Polish or Polonized landowners, the wealthy townspeople, and to an even greater extent the higher Uniate clergy who had become Polonized looked upon the past and the present of their people from the Polish point of view. In eastern Ukraine all the higher classes were Russified. The old literary language had either died out or become Russified, and the native Ukrainian tongue was preserved only among the common people and the village clergy. The masses, crushed beneath the burden of serfdom, remained silent as death; it appeared that they would never awaken from their torpid slumber and that an end had come to national life.

Beneath the ashes of the past, however, the seeds of national life remained alive and gradually and unnoticed they began to germinate.

Beginning of the Renaissance in Western Ukraine: At the close of the eighteenth century, just when the end of Ukrainian national existence seemed imminent, the evidences of new life became visible. In western Ukraine it appeared in the religious movement.

At the time of its introduction, the Uniate Church had hampered Ukrainian nationalism. In deference to the nobles it had been thoughtlessly accepted by many, and those who objected to joining it were forced to do so. But to the new generation which had been born into the Uniate Church this faith was the national Ukrainian religion. Those who had introduced the Union with the intention of making Poles out of the Ukrainians now found that their plans had miscarried. Because the Uniate clergy and the Church in general did not enjoy all the rights of the Catholic Church, it had come to be regarded as an inferior church, the church of the peasants, and became a mirror of contemporary national life; before long it was for western Ukraine as truly a national church as the Orthodox Church had been previously. Accordingly, when the Austrian government, after its annexation of Galicia, made an effort to raise the Ukrainian clergy from their ignorance and degradation, this attempt had an important influence upon the awakening of nationalism. When Austria observed how the Polish nobles had enserfed the Ukrainians, it considered means of aiding them; during the reigns of Maria Theresa and Joseph II the authority of the landlords was curtailed, schools were opened in the "local language" for the peasants and townspeople, and institutions of higher education were established for the indescribably poor and uneducated clergy. This popular educational program had its beginnings in Carpatho-Ukraine, as a result of the agitation there against the Union which alarmed the government (pp. 431 ff.). The Mukachev eparchy was freed from the Roman Catholic bishop of Yahra, an academy for the education of the clergy was founded in the city of Mukachev, and steps were taken to improve the economic conditions of the clergy. The new bishop, Andrey Bachinsky (1772–1809), devoted his energies to elevating his clergy; he gathered around himself a considerable number of educated men, some of whom later became the first Ukrainian professors of the University of Lviv. With the annexation of Galicia, Austria extended her activity to that province, too; immediately after the annexation, Maria Theresa established in Vienna for the education of Ukrainian Uniates a theological seminary which became an open window to western Europe for western Ukrainians and was of considerable benefit to them. Later a seminary was founded in Lviv; and when the University of Lviv was founded in 1784, the government required it to teach some subjects in Ukrainian, and a separate lyceum was established to serve as a Ukrainian preparatory school for the university. Much was also done in Galicia for the betterment of the clergy, a "Religious Endowment" being created for their betterment out of the confiscated church and monastery property; and similar steps were taken in Bukovina, where during the short period of martial rule foundations were laid for elementary secular education and the local "Religious Endowment," which constituted one fifth of the entire territory of the state, provided adequate means for cultural development. Some difficulties arose, however, because the Austrian government did not understand local conditions and complicated matters by interfering in local affairs, thus giving rise to disputes. In its cultural work it proved its lack of power and frequently neglected the Ukrainians, for example, by considering the Rumanian language as the "local language" of entire Bukovina, without any regard to the nationality of its inhabitants.

In Galicia the government used more care, but even there its efforts to elevate the position of the Ukrainian people were obstructed by the resistance of the Polish nobles and by the lack of understanding of local conditions. Unfortunately there were not to be found for the newly established institutions alert men who could use them in a manner advantageous to Ukrainian national development. The instruction was given in the dead language of books, the subjects taught were of little practical or cultural value, and consequently they did not lead to effective results. In the course of time the Ukrainian lectures at both the university and the lyceum were abolished, as Ukrainians prepared to attend the general university lectures began to be graduated from the new high schools (*gymnasia*). The death of the Austrian reforming emperor, Joseph II, in 1790, was followed by a period of reaction; the Polish nobles gained in influence in court circles and in local administration, and by falsely accusing the Ukrainians of leaning toward Russia and the Orthodox religion they attempted to divert the government from its good work on behalf of the Ukrainian people. At the insistence of the Poles, the Polish language was substituted for the Ukrainian, at first in the higher schools and then in the Ukrainian village public schools. Because of the protests of the Ukrainian clergy, Ukrainian villages were permitted to establish private schools in the Ukrainian language, but in order to avoid additional expense the government requested the clergy not to encourage the establishment of such schools, while the clergy themselves apparently underestimated the significance of these institutions and did not take full advantage of the opportunities offered them by the government. As soon as the new intellectuals, chiefly priests, had attained a higher cultural level, they drifted away from the masses whom they considered beneath them; they neglected their native tongue and clung to the old dead literary language which was unsuited to progress, and copied the Polish pattern of life.

Notwithstanding the mistakes of the Austrian government and the ineptitude of the Ukrainian people, whose best intentions were frequently to no purpose, some benefits resulted. The most significant was the new spirit which the Austrian government injected into the Ukrainian people. By opening schools it awakened hopes for a brighter future and the energy for a struggle to gain it, while among the new and highly educated Uniate clergy brought up in better cultural and national circumstances there appeared at the beginning of the nineteenth century men of broad vision who thought not only of the welfare of the church but of the interests of the whole nation, and devoted their efforts to raising the educational and economic level of the people and to developing a national culture.

While Polish attempts to crush the Ukrainians challenged the new patriots to fresh efforts in defense of their rights, the hope of receiving support from the Austrian government encouraged them to fight for the cause. The introduction of the Polish language into the Ukrainian schools as a substitute for the Ukrainian led to the first protest by the Ukrainian clergy in vindication of their language, when Metropolitan Levitsky, under the influence of the distinguished young priest, Mohilnitsky, presented to the Austrian government a petition to permit teaching in the public schools in the Ukrainian tongue. When the school commissioners decided that such teaching should be allowed in private schools only, the metropolitan again protested to the Austrian government against this discrimination and wrote a pamphlet pointing out the value of the Ukrainian tongue and demanding equality of rights for it. Later he wrote an extensive study of the same subject entitled *Information about the Ruthenian Language;** this was the first popular essay in defense of the Ukrainian language. He fought for popular education and organized an educational society in Peremyshl, but it expired because of the strong obstacles put in its way by the Polish priests and the Polonized Ukrainian Uniate monks of the Order of St. Basil. He met with more success in establishing Ukrainian grammar schools to take the place of Polish government institutions, and within a short time a large number of parochial schools had come into existence. For the training of teachers, a seminary was established in the city of Peremyshl. New Ukrainian texts were written for these schools, and in this connection a question arose as to the relation of the popular living speech to the archaic literary language. About 1830 there developed lively polemics among the defenders of the vernacular, of the ancient Church-Slavonic language, and of Russian, a dispute which had great importance in developing the new nationalism.

Thus a new Ukrainian life slowly appeared in western Ukraine. Its first manifestations were insignificant

---

* In Galicia, Ukrainian was then known as ''Ruthenian'' (Editor).

enough, but in the parts of Ukraine that were transferred from Poland to Russia not even such signs were in evidence. The fact that ''Poland had fallen'' brought no relief, since the authority of the Polish landlord over the masses in Ukraine merely became more extensive than ever, while the Russian government had no wish to grant the Ukrainians the rights being granted in Galicia and Bukovina by the Austrian government. Among the higher classes Polish culture continued to prevail; and on the other hand the new schools and institutions being established by the Russian government were used to Russify the people, the language, and the Church. The Russian language was introduced into Ukrainian theological schools, and orders were given for the saying of prayers patterned on the Russian style. The Ukrainian people who had previously been oppressed by Poland alone were now oppressed by both Poland and Russia, and the Russian government attempted to destroy even those phases of Ukrainian life which the Poles had not touched. In this manner Ukrainian nationalism continued to decline and disappear. Its revival under Russian rule began not here but in the old Kozak country beyond the Dnieper, on the ruins of the Kozak autonomy, in what had been the Hetman state and the Land of Free Communes.

Beginning of the Renaissance in Eastern Ukraine: Though the Ukrainian landed gentry found personal advantages in the institution of serfdom and the Russian system of government, and therefore served Russia faithfully, yet among the descendants of the old Kozak officers and of the clergy Ukrainian patriotism and love for Ukrainian life, language, and history did not die out, despite the most drastic attempts at Russification. Sorrowfully they recalled the former glory of the Kozaks, the independence of Ukraine, and the autonomy of the Hetman state and complained of the abolition of Ukrainian rights and customs by Russia. As a rule they concealed their dissatisfaction, considering protests and struggle hopeless; but a few of the more courageous leaders returned to the old policy of seeking foreign assistance in their struggle for the liberation of Ukraine. A search among the secret papers in the Prussian state archives reveals that in 1791, when the relations between Russia and Prussia were strained, a Ukrainian leader by the name of Kapnist visited the Prussian Minister Hertzberg. Kapnist was descended from a distinguished family and was the son of the well-known colonel of the Mirhorod regiment. He informed the Prussian minister that he had been sent by his countrymen, who could not endure "the tyranny of the Russian government and of Prince Potemkin." The Kozaks, he stated, were much grieved at the loss of their former rights and privileges and their conversion into regiments of regulars, and were extremely eager to regain their former organization and liberties. In behalf of his countrymen Kapnist asked the minister if they could count on Prussian help when the time came to rebel against Russia; Hertzberg, however, gave an evasive answer, as he did not believe that the quarrel between Prussia and Russia would lead to war. Kapnist accordingly returned to Ukraine, but informed the Prussian government that if it desired, it might enter into negotiations with Ukraine through his brother, who was traveling in Europe.

At one time the old rights were almost restored. When, after the death of Catherine II in 1796, she was succeeded by her son Paul, he altered many of his mother's reforms and restored the old order because he disapproved of the policy of her government. Among other things, the administration of Ukraine reverted to that of the period before the abolition of the hetmancy; the Ukrainian general court was revived, as well as a few other features introduced during the time of the last hetman, Rozumovsky. It was rumored that Alexander Bezborodko, the tsar's minister and confidential adviser, yet a loyal son of Ukraine, was responsible for this partial restoration of the old Ukrainian rights; and it is probable that if the Russian government had continued its liberal policy, the renewal of the Kozak form of government would have followed. But Paul was assassinated in 1801, and his successor, Alexander I, deciding to adopt the general policies of his grandmother Catherine II, restored the old despotism in Ukraine.

In 1812 there were some hopes for the revival of the Kozak army, and in 1831, when the Russian government was organizing volunteer Kozak regiments in Ukraine to strengthen its forces, the local authorities, in order to encourage enlistments, promised the people partial relief from oppression, it being even rumored that Repnin, the governor-general of Ukraine, was preparing to become the next hetman, as he was a relative of the Rozumovsky family. But all such rumors and hopes soon ended in disillusion, for the government sent the newly organized Kozaks into the Caucasus Mountains, thus beginning the Ukrainian colonization of that mountainous region.

All these hopes and sorrows, though not deep and serious, nevertheless awakened the spirit of nationalism among the more enlightened Ukrainians. They became aware of the past of their country and clung to the national characteristics which distinguished them from the Russians.

The Russified officeholders, who shed their blood for Russia as a fatherland and exerted all their efforts, not out of fear but from conscience, to strengthening Russian institutions in Ukraine, and who promoted the spread of the Russian language and Russian culture and wrote as Russian authors—even they devotedly collected historical information about Ukrainian antiquity, wrote down Ukrainian songs and verses, proverbs and sayings, and in their memoirs and letters praised the former Ukrainian freedom and exalted the heroes who had struggled for it. Even out of the divided loyalties of the Ukrainian intellectuals there appeared in due time evidences of a spirit of nationalism, especially in regard to the Ukrainian language, the living symbol of nationality.

The Ukrainian vernacular had not altogether disappeared from literary use in eastern Ukraine, although it was excluded from printed books and from the schools. On the contrary, after the Russian censorship had prohibited the use of the Ukrainian "book language"—a mixture of Ukrainian and Old Slavonic—the living tongue gained a stronger position as the sole national language, and whoever intended to give a native character to his writing was obliged to use it; all those who valued Ukrainian national traits attempted to make use of the Ukrainian spoken language in their literary works, regardless of the fact that Russian was considered the official literary language. The use in literature of the living tongue won respect for the Ukrainian language, songs, and traditions, and some members of the upper classes began to return to its use. With the development of national self-consciousness among the cultural people there came a Ukrainian national rebirth.

Kotlyarevsky's travesty on the *Aeneid,* published in 1798 without the consent of the author, was the first book to elevate the Ukrainian language in the eyes of the people. It portrayed the glorious past of the Kozaks and the present wretched conditions of the peasants and awakened an interest in the life of the common people on the part of the upper level of Ukrainian inhabitants. The book was significant primarily because it was printed in the pure vernacular and consequently attained a large circulation among the Ukrainian intellectuals. From old letters it is known that the collection of historical Ukrainian writings was a very laborious task, because frequently even the most interesting and significant of these works were not printed but remained in manuscript form and therefore out of circulation. For example, the interesting chronicle by Velichko circulated as an original manuscript in a single copy. The *Aeneid* went through three editions within ten years, each edition being bought up at once; the book marked the beginning of an epoch in the history not only of Ukrainian literature but of the national awakening. It was written in the simple style of the popular tongue, but in such a highly cultured manner that it won the approbation of the reader; in addition, the content was of high value, describing in a humorous way the curious experiences of the Zaporozhian Kozaks and in connection with them calling to the attention of the people many problems, scenes, and memories. It was at this time that the Zaporozhians were wandering over the face of the earth unable to find a home, and the experiences of the Trojan soldiers in Virgil's *Aeneid* reminded the Ukrainians of the similar fate of their own Kozaks. Beyond the gusty humor of the author were pictures of the "everlasting memory of the Hetman State." The life of the people was portrayed with an intimacy and affection which evoked sympathy and love for everything that was native. It is no wonder that the later authors of the Ukrainian Renaissance, including Shevchenko, paid homage to the author of the *Aeneid* and proclaimed him the father of the new Ukrainian literature.

The *Aeneid* was not the last of its kind; it was followed by other talented productions that strengthened the impression made by the first as to the cultural value of the Ukrainian spoken language. The new books became less reticent and presented facts openly, among them being the operetta, *Natalka Poltavka,* by Kotlyarevsky, the poems of Hulak Artemovsky, and the stories of Kvitka, appearing during the second, third, and fourth decades of the nineteenth century. Also of great importance were the anthologies of Ukrainian folk songs by Tsertelev, Maximovich, and Sreznevsky. These collections, whether printed or in manuscript, revealed the unusually rich fund of Ukrainian folk songs and increased the importance of the Ukrainian language by calling the attention of educated people to Ukrainian culture. Important historical works appeared, among them the *History of Rus or Little Russia*—a history of Ukraine brought down to the end of the hetmancy. The author of this work is unknown; although it was long considered the work of George Konisky, historians now believe that it was written by Gregory Poletika or by him and his son—in any case by someone of extraordinary talent. It circulated widely among the Ukrainian cultured classes during the second decade of the nineteenth century because of its warm patriotic feeling, and although it was not put into print until the late 1840's, it was distributed in many manuscript copies and had a great influence upon the development of Ukrainian literature. Shortly afterward there appeared a more substantial though dry history of Kozak Ukraine, written by Bantish-Kamensky. That this book went through three editions within a short period of time is a good indication of the interests of the Ukrainian intellectuals. There also began a dispute concerning the Ukrainian national characteristics, the language, and the poetry—an echo of the new conceptions of the importance of nationality in general and of the influences of the Slavic renaissance, which, transplanted to Ukrainian soil, lent a new importance to the little-known and hitherto lightly valued national accomplishments.

Ideas of Nationalism and the Beginnings of Enlightened Democracy: During the eighteenth century there began a movement in Western Europe known as romantic nationalism; instead of dwelling upon the themes of Greek or Roman literature, the writers turned to native and local tradition and began eagerly to collect popular legends and to draw upon their own national intellectual resources. These had been formerly considered of little value, coarse and unpolished, but now their peculiar beauty began to win appreciation. They began to study their own countries, record national traditions, and interest themselves in national accomplishments. The movement spread among the western Slavs, especially from

England and Germany, and aroused among them a new interest in the popular creativeness and the language of the people. Later on it spread among the Russians and the Russified Ukrainians.

Ukrainians, whether under Russian or Austrian domination, welcomed the new movement. Their intellectuals had looked upon people of their own nationality as an ignorant mass entirely lacking in any cultural ability and condemned to receive spiritual nourishment from their more cultured neighbors; and for this reason they had not visualized any future for their own people, considering the Ukrainian language, customs, and traditions obsolete and, although probably interesting and dear to their countrymen, doomed to perish. Pavlovsky, the author of the first Ukrainian grammar published in Russia, writing during the first part of the nineteenth century, called Ukrainian "not a living, not a dead, but a disappearing dialect," and hastened to write a grammar of it before it had completely died out.

Views of the popular language and the national creative spirit now changed. The inexhaustible treasury of the Ukrainian people and of their literature was revealed in popular songs and legends that took the place of books and testified to the great spiritual wealth and creative energy of the people. "Do you know," wrote Tsertelev, one of the early compilers, "that I value this popular poetry more highly than the major part of our [Russian] romances and ballads and even many of our romantic poems." Owing to their originality, beauty, and richness, Ukrainian historical accounts and traditions attracted the interest of foreigners—Poles, Russians, and others—and this very fact impressed upon the Ukrainians themselves the value of their national character. In the new light of romantic nationalism their uninformed interest in their past and present national existence found meaning and justification, and a desire arose for further knowledge of their nation and its history. The ideas of nationalism and the efforts toward a national reawakening which had started up under their influence among the Slavic and other peoples furnished an example to the Ukrainians. Attempts at literary expression of Ukrainian subjects in the Ukrainian language gave these a new meaning and importance as the highway to the rebirth of Ukrainian life.

Out of this movement there arose the necessity of a change of attitude toward the masses, their interests, and their needs. The previous century had been marked in Ukraine by the struggle of the new-born class of Ukrainian officer-landlords to acquire an aristocratic polish in order to distinguish themselves as sharply as possible from the common people out of whom they had emerged. The economic struggle had created a deep abyss between the masses and the gentry who were seizing the land and enserfing the peasants, and the cultural estrangement had caused even more alienation and animosity. The Ukrainian people had become divided into an ignorant, enserfed, overburdened mass deprived of any possibility of progress, and the aristocrats who, although calling themselves Ukrainians (''Little Russians''), had become entirely uprooted from the Ukrainian soil and in their complete estrangement from the people could see no other future than to identify themselves more closely with the intellectual and national life of Russia. But now the new interest in the Ukrainian language and the Ukrainian popular poetry taught the intellectuals to look upon the Ukrainian people with new respect.

These so-called simple peasants, the serfs upon whom the Ukrainian aristocrats looked down with contempt, were the possessors, it was revealed, of a rich store of poetry and were the creators of literary works that compared favorably with the best of Europe. The turbulent past of Ukraine and the glory of her Kozaks, now lost to the gentry, had been preserved in the memory of these peasants who, most important of all, had kept intact the Ukrainian speech. In the eyes of the new generation of educated Ukrainians the Ukrainian masses were the real carriers of the beauty and the secret of life, and it was necessary to draw near to them in every possible way in order to learn from them the real meaning of literary creativeness. But as the educated Ukrainians came into contact with the people, they not only caught the spirit of their creative power but also gained an understanding of their life and nature and of the sufferings and needs of the peasants.

Kotlyarevsky in his *Natalka Poltavka,* Kvitka in his novels, and other less noted authors in their works undertook to reveal the actual living conditions of the peasants and their hardships, the life of the gentry, and the barriers that separated these two groups from one another. Ukrainian literature became democratic, and after uniting the interests of the educated upper classes with those of the peasants, it began to defend the human rights of the peasant serfs, and came in the course of time to understand the economic and social needs of the people and the method of elevating them. The question of the uplifting of the Ukrainian masses to the rights of a free people became the chief problem in the eyes of the Ukrainian renaissance, because the higher classes had been denationalized, and the common people were the nation and needed freedom in order to develop their creative powers to the full.

CHAPTER XXII

THE NATIONAL IDEA

Ukrainian Literary Circles in Russian Ukraine and the Brotherhood of Saints Cyril and Methodius: Those individuals who were interested in Ukrainian language, literature, and history and sympathized with the people, began to organize themselves into societies. The most important of these organizations to appear in Russian Ukraine was that in the city of Kharkiv, which was the center of Ukrainian literary work from about the 1810's to the 1830's. The local gentry, descendants of the Kozak officers of the Free Communes, financed the establishment of the University of Kharkiv, a school for girls, and a theater, and gave financial assistance to the production of literary work, including the publication of books and journals. Although these schools in Kharkiv and the literature and cultural life as well were Russian, Ukrainian currents made their appearance in Ukrainian poems and articles published in Russian journals, or in the Ukrainian booklets which appeared irregularly once in every two or three years, but which were of high literary value, since they came from the pens of gifted authors. The people who were interested in Ukrainian literature were men of education and distinction, serious in their efforts, who intended to accomplish something worth while. Peter Hulak Artemovsky, a professor in the University of Kharkiv, wrote poems of haunting beauty and translated foreign literary masterpieces into Ukrainian. Gregory Kvitka, a descendant of a noted local Kozak family, a man highly respected by the citizens of Kharkiv, composed light operas and the first novels in which popular Ukrainian characters were ably portrayed. Sreznevsky, the famous linguist, published a collection of Ukrainian historical songs—a kind of Ukrainian history in verse—which made a deep impression upon society. After some time Professor Ambrosius Metlinsky became known as a poet and ethnologist; and a young graduate of the University of Kharkiv, Nicholas Kostomariv, distinguished himself as a historian. Ukrainian literature won great respect in the hands of the Kharkiv literary group, which was imbued with the spirit of romantic nationalism and of the Slavic renaissance and which saw in the literature of Ukraine a new member of the Slavic family, a highly gifted member requiring only time and opportunity to reveal its ability.

There were also significant Ukrainian groups in the Russian capitals of Moscow and St. Petersburg, among whose members there lived about 1840 a talented poet, Hrebinka, and the young Shevchenko, who had already attracted attention as a poet. Shevchenko's first poems were published in 1840 under the title of *The Kobzar,* and shortly afterward were followed by *The Haidamaks;* when these poems appeared, a distinguished Russian critic remarked that since Ukrainian literature had Shevchenko it needed no other recommendation or proof for its existence. It was great good fortune for the young Ukrainian literature that in the short space of forty years following the printing of Kotlyarevsky's *Aeneid,* such a great genius as Shevchenko should appear. In him the Ukrainian renaissance found its strongest supporter.

Shevchenko also played an important part in the development of Ukrainian ideology. In this field the most distinguished place in Ukrainian history was won by the university literary group in Kiev which included such distinguished men as Maximovich, Kostomariv, and the youthful, determined, and energetic linguist Kulish. In 1845, after Shevchenko had come to Kiev, he joined this youthful group. The greatest Ukrainians of the time were assembled here; they were men of distinguished talents and fertile ideas concerning the rebirth of their people. Shevchenko, Kostomariv, Kulish, and several younger men became close friends, frequently gathering to talk about the past of Ukraine and the harsh conditions of servitude and to discuss plans for the liberation of the people. Kostomariv, who was then writing the history of the Kozaks, shared his knowledge of Ukrainian history with his friends, while Shevchenko was the first of the Ukrainian poets to find themes for his poems in the history of the Kozaks and the Haidamaks; he had a deep veneration for the national struggle for liberty and popular rights, gained from the popular legends which he had imbibed in his boyhood. He was now authorized by the Kiev Archeographical Commission to travel in Ukraine to study and draw pictures of the old monuments of Ukrainian history. This journey aroused in him a warm love for the past of his country, and behind the splendor of the hetmans and the quarrels and civil wars, the real heroes of Ukrainian history appeared before him; these were the common people, the people who had revolted in order to make themselves masters of the land which they cultivated and on which they lived, and in order that they might own what they earned. With unprecedented force Shevchenko attacked in his poems the injustice and serfdom which existed in Ukraine and reminded the petty descendants of great Ukrainian patriots of their forgotten but glorious national heritage.

On the other hand the society took an interest in contemporary movements in the west, because life was stagnant in Russia. They carefully watched the renaissance among the other oppressed Slavic peoples, the new cultural movements that had sprung up among the Poles, Czechs, Croats, Serbs, Bulgarians, Slovaks, and Slovenes.

In the 1820's, during the short-lived progressive movement in Russia which brought about the insurrection of 1825 by the "Decembrists," there existed in Ukraine a secret "Pan-Slavic" society, the aim of which was to unite all the Slavic peoples into a federation. Some records indicate that a separate "Little Russian Society" existed which aimed at demanding political independence for Ukraine. Shevchenko and his friends received information concerning the then existing societies and decided to organize a similar society and name it after Saints Cyril and Methodius, "the apostles of the Slavs." The chief objective of this organization was to spread the idea of the need of general liberty and political equality, its members considering it their duty to abolish serfdom in Russia and the other Slavic countries as well as to fight for freedom of thought, conscience, and speech, and against compulsion in religion. Their general program included widespread popular education and their political plan proposed a union of all the Slavic peoples into a federation with an elective head; each Slavic nation was to exist as a separate republic, but common problems were to be decided by a congress composed of delegates of all the nations.

As the organization did not last for any length of time, nothing resulted from its program and the members of the group itself differed so much in their policies that harmonious coöperation was impossible. The leading ideas of the organization, however, left a deep impression on the young members and especially on Shevchenko and his later work, and out of them arose the future Ukrainian movement.

The members of the brotherhood paid a high price for their daring thoughts. In 1847 their conversations were reported to the secret police by a student, and the members were arrested, brought to trial, severely punished, exiled, and forbidden to write. It was not until the late 'fifties that they were permitted to return and resume their literary work and even then not all of them returned, while those who did come back had lost their courage and the freedom of thought and expression which they had displayed before their exile. Several decades passed before any of the ideas of the Brotherhood of Saints Cyril and Methodius were revived, and then it was in Galicia rather than in Russian Ukraine.

The National Rebirth in Galicia and the Year 1848: The first Ukrainian society of intellectuals to devote itself to nationalistic activities appeared in Galicia, in the theological school at Peremyshl at the end of the second decade of the nineteenth century. Its objective was the spread of popular education, and as a result of its efforts there appeared the first known brochure in defense of equal rights for the Ukrainian language and an exposition of its cultural value. This Peremyshl circle, however, did not yet have a clear conception of the character of Ukrainian nationalism, some members favoring the literary Old Slavonic language, while the more youthful members made use of the living Ukrainian in their writings; even in the 1820's they had not come to a definite decision. The authors of the first grammars leaned toward the Ukrainian vernacular for literary purposes, but desired to "purify" it of its popular characteristics and assimilate it with the Old Slavonic Church language. In the 1830's two literary factions came to the fore when there appeared in opposition to the literary tradition the champions of the living language of the people, hotly defending its purity from literary clichés and appreciating its flexibility and grammatical perfection. They were influenced by the Slavic renaissance and even more by the literary efforts to develop a pure national language in eastern Ukraine; since in Galicia the old book language had never been completely suppressed, its existence hindered the literary development of the living language there. Joseph Lozinsky severely criticized both Michael Luchkai, the author of the first Carpatho-Ukrainian grammar, who clung to the literary language of the Church, and Joseph Levitsky, who wished not only to cling to the old Ukrainian language of books but to approach the literary Great Russian; in opposition to them

Lozinsky defended the pure vernacular. Even more determined champions of the Ukrainian popular tongue
were the students of the Lviv theological school in the
1830's.

These young Ukrainians had fallen under the influence
of the reborn Ukrainian literature of Russian Ukraine of
the decades of 1820 and 1830; but under the impulse of
the Slavic renaissance and the Polish revolutionary propaganda they developed in a more progressive and patriotic direction and in the spirit of the Romantic nationalism of Russian Ukraine. They also became interested in
Ukrainian ethnology and history, collecting songs and
legends and testing their powers in literary productions
modeled on Ukrainian forms and feeling the full force of
the unity of the Ukrainian people on both sides of the
Russian-Ukrainian border. The likable poet, Markian
Shashkevich, was the first popular poet in Galicia, and
the later Ukrainian national movement there recognized
him as its leader and patron. Jacob Holovatsky was the
first to receive appointment to the newly established pro-
fessorship in the Ukrainian language at the University of
Lviv. John Vahilevich, the third member of this "Ruthenian triumvirate," devoted his time to history and ethnology. The activity of the group met with obstacles because Austria had changed its attitude toward the
Ukrainian movement; having experienced great difficulties from the Polish revolutionary tendencies, the government did not wish to bring upon itself fresh burdens
through similar unrest on the part of the Ukrainians.

A like spirit prevailed among the Uniate clergy, who,
having the power of censorship in their hands, made use
of it from a reactionary, narrowly ecclesiastical point of
view, unsympathetic and full of suspicion toward the
popular spirit in literature. Books which otherwise met
the conditions of the censorship—religious books or eulo-
gies of the Austrian dynasty—were forbidden merely because the language was not Old Slavonic or because the

civil script was used instead of the Slavonic. The literary efforts of the Ruthenian triumvirate met with opposition and animosity, the ecclesiastical censorship forbidding the publication of the first Ukrainian almanac, *Zoria* (The Star), which was published in 1834 by Shashkevich and his associates. The group, however, made a collection of folk songs and legends to which they added their own poems and scientific articles and published the whole under the title of *Rusalka of the Dniester,* evading the local censorship by issuing the book in Pest, Hungary. When it was brought to Lviv it was confiscated and not released until 1848, and the authors were subjected to harsh treatment. The sickly Shashkevich, unable to endure the persecution, died shortly after as a poor village priest. Vahilevich went to work for the Poles, and those opposed to progress in Galicia believed that they had put an end to the Ukrainian movement.

Then came the stormy year of 1848 to alter the whole situation. The French revolution of 1848 infected the national minorities of the Austrian empire, who began to rebel. In Galicia the Poles set about preparing a revolution for the liberation of Poland. The Austrian government now recalled the Ukrainian movement in Galicia and determined to make use of it for weakening the Poles, considering such proposals as the division of Galicia into a Polish and a Ukrainian section, the introduction of the Ukrainian language into the lower and higher schools of Ukrainian Galicia, and the emancipation of the Ukrainian peasants from the Polish landlords—the same program for the Ukrainian people as that which the government of Maria Theresa and Joseph II had intended to carry out in the 1770's and 1780's but had abandoned under the influence of the Polish gentry and their reactionary Austrian advisers. The Ukrainians in Galicia began to rebel against the abuses of their Polish oppressors. The idea of an independent Poland was not at all to their liking, and only a few of the intellectuals sided with the Poles, while the great majority, relying upon the sympathy of the Austrian administration, began to organize themselves into anti-Polish groups. The Austrian viceroy, the famous Count Stadion, was one of the organizers of the Ukrainian movement in Galicia, and in consequence the Poles later said that he had invented the Ukrainians there, as if they had never existed before. A political society, the "General Council" (Holovna Rada), was organized as a kind of Ukrainian national government, the duty of which was to represent its people and their needs to the Austrian government; its organ was the newspaper, *Zoria Halitska* (Galician Star), and a Ukrainian Guard was formed to oppose the Polish revolutionary bands. In the fall of 1848 a "Congress of Ukrainian scholars" met to deliberate upon the cultural needs of the people and to outline a program for future progress. The congress took a definite stand for Ukrainian nationalism, deciding to free Ukrainian culture from Polish influences and also from Russian forms, which the adherents of the literary "Slavonic-Russian" tongue could not see were clearly distinct from the Ukrainian vernacular. The congress insisted that a uniform grammar and a uniform spelling be adopted "for all the Ruthenians [Ukrainians] in Russia or in Austria," based upon Ukrainian characteristics and free from Polish or Russian tendencies, and demanded further that the Ukrainian language be introduced in all Galician schools. For the encouragement of literature the assembly organized a "Society for Enlightenment" on the model of the Czech "Matica." The delegates emphasized the need of separating Ukrainian Galicia from the Polish part of the province, and prepared other plans for national advancement. The congress was an important milestone in Galician history and received high praise from Antin Mohilnitsky, the dean of Ukrainian authors in Galicia at the time.

The government gave the Ukrainian demands a favorable reception. It promised to introduce the Ukrainian language in all elementary and secondary schools and in the university, gave serious consideration to dividing Galicia, and passed a law which, however, never went into effect. Moreover, serfdom was abolished in 1848, and the Ukrainian people were at last freed from their landlords.

The Year 1848 in Bukovina and Carpatho-Ukraine, and the Reaction of the 1850's: During the fateful year 1848 the Ukrainian people in Bukovina and Carpatho-Ukraine did not remain idle. In the former province, the most neglected in Austria, the spirit of Ukrainian nationalism manifested itself when the Ukrainians demanded equal rights with the Rumanians. The Rumanian deputies in parliament demanded the separation of Bukovina from Galicia and its union with the neighboring Rumanian provinces in Hungary, and the Ukrainians fought for a continuation of the union of their province with Galicia, but demanded a division of Bukovina into Ukrainian and Rumanian sections, an arrangement to which the Rumanians objected. Owing to the fact that the Ukrainian masses of Bukovina were uneducated, the peasant revolutionary movement against the Rumanian nobles was of little consequence.

Carpatho-Ukraine was shaken to its depths in 1848 and never outgrew the effects of its experience in that fateful year. With the help of Russia, the Austrian government succeeded in suppressing the Hungarian revolution, after which suppression the Austrians decided to weaken the future influence of the Hungarians by supporting the rights of the various nationalities, including the Ukrainian, over whom the Magyars had ruled. At about this time there appeared among the Ukrainians a man of great energy, courage, and ability whose activity opened a new period of Ukrainian history in the Carpathian regions; this was Adolph Dobriansky. During the Hungarian revolution, Dobriansky fled from Hungary and lived for a time in Galicia, until the Russian army came to assist Austria, when he joined it as an imperial commissioner of the Austrian government. At his suggestion the Ukrainians of Carpatho-Ukraine petitioned the Austrian government to create separate districts in the land which they inhabited, to permit Ukrainians to hold public office, to allow the use of the Ukrainian language in schools and in dealing with the government, and to establish a Ukrainian academy in Uzhorod. The petition was favorably received and the emperor promised his approval. Dobriansky was appointed governor-general over the district inhabited by the Ukrainians and began to introduce the use of the Ukrainian language in both administrative offices and schools. The outlook was bright, but Dobriansky's Russophile, or "Muscophile," inclinations ruined his efforts. He favored a union with Russia, the program of the so-called "pan-Russian movement," promoted the use of the Russian language in place of the Ukrainian, and supported the influence of Russia in other ways. As soon as the Hungarian aristocrats, who bitterly hated Russia on account of the Russian intervention, had regained their authority in the government, they turned against Dobriansky, who was removed from office, while everything that savored of Russophile tendencies in Carpatho-Ukraine fell under suspicion. Under the influence of Dobriansky all the local intellectuals had taken this Russophile road and now had to abandon their activities. Being unwilling to make use of the Ukrainian vernacular and not being permitted to write in Russian, they, after the stormy year of 1849, remained idle for a long time, and in fact the Ukrainian movement in Carpatho-Ukraine was thereafter always behind that of the other Ukrainian regions.

Almost as complete, but not so long-lasting, was the reaction in Galicia and Bukovina which followed the promising movement of 1848. The loyalty of the local Ukrainian leaders to the government during the revolution disappointed the masses, and the good intentions of Austria of aiding the Ukrainians were in most cases not carried out but remained empty promises. As soon as the revolutionary movement of 1848 was suppressed, the government dropped the promised reforms. The Ukrainian masses had placed too much faith in the administration, and when this failed them, they became disillusioned, while the conservative circles among the clergy and in the government which assumed leadership accomplished little of importance.

In Galicia leadership was taken by the metropolitan consistory in Lviv, the intellectuals in Galicia being largely the Uniate clergy and their families, who naturally looked to the metropolitan and his consistory for guidance. These conservative leaders, however, were unfriendly toward the progressive movement in general and the Ukrainian national movement in particular. Opponents of the use of the vernacular in Ukrainian literature again appeared who considered the living tongue and culture vulgar and "uneducated." Meanwhile, the Polish aristocrats were gaining supremacy in Galicia, where they were in full control of the administration in the time of Governor Count Golukhovski. With official positions in Galicia in their hands, the landlords incited the Austrian government against the Ukrainians, whom they accused of being promoters of Russian political policies and the Orthodox faith.

Thus the revolutionary year of 1848 did not mark the beginning of a new epoch in Galicia, but rather introduced a long period of reaction. Several years had to pass before the Ukrainians resumed the march toward the goal which they had set in 1848 and had come so near to reaching.

The New Movement in Russian Ukraine: As in Austria reaction followed the suppression of the revolution of 1848, so too the abolition of the Brotherhood of Saints Cyril and Methodius was succeeded by years of repression in Russian Ukraine. In Russia, however, the reaction came sooner and ended earlier. After the unsuccessful

Crimean War in 1854–56, the government began of its own accord to reform the outdated and inefficient Russian institutions. The program included the abolition of serfdom and the liberation of the masses from the old regime; in the hearts of the people hope rose high for a new life and the Ukrainian national movement began to revive. The former members of the Brotherhood of Saints Cyril and Methodius returned from exile, gathered in St. Petersburg, and resumed their nationalistic activities. One of them, Kulish, acquired special distinction as an organizer and writer; he published ethnological material, collected the works of the old Ukrainian writers, prepared a new almanac entitled *Khata,* in 1860, and, best of all, discovered the brilliant young author, Maria Markovich, whose works were to appear under the pen name of Marko Vovchok. Finally Kulish and his brother-in-law, Bilozersky, began to publish a monthly magazine, the *Osnova* (Foundation), which appeared for about two years and was published both in the Ukrainian and the Russian languages; it was of great value in uniting the intellectual Ukrainian groups in Russia.

It is true that the bold political issues discussed by the Brotherhood of Saints Cyril' and Methodius were not touched upon in the new organ. It is difficult to say whether it was the severe retribution which befell the members of the brotherhood that changed their approach or whether they considered it useless to draw the attention of the people to these remote problems, which could be discussed in a censored journal only in general terms, when there lay on the threshold issues so pressing and of such importance for the Ukrainians as those of the liberation of the serfs, the political preparation of the new citizens, and the economic and cultural life of the peasants. By its discussions of these topics the *Osnova,* which began to appear just before the liberation of the serfs, performed a task of inestimable importance. The next question raised was that of popular education; Sunday schools were being organized in the cities, textbooks prepared, and funds collected for their publication, and in connection with this activity the problem arose as to whether or not the vernacular Ukrainian was suitable for literary purposes. The language had to be defended from its Russian enemies as well as from the indifferent or Russophile Ukrainians who saw no necessity of using their native tongue if "universal Russian," as the Russian literary language was called, could be employed. At the same time a struggle had to be carried on against the Poles, who were eager to draw the Ukrainians back into the old historical Poland.

Because of these live issues the old plan for the unification of the Slavs was pushed into the background, and in its place the improvement of the wretched conditions of the peasants became the chief problem, as it also was for progressive circles in Russia. In the past the Ukrainians had more than once sided with the conservative Slavophiles and had received unfavorable attention from the Russian progressives, Belinsky, the leading representative of the Russian progressive movement in the 1840's having for instance sharply criticized the efforts of Shevchenko. But now the Russian progressives felt themselves at one with the Ukrainians in many of their enterprises and often supported them in their activities. In 1862 the St. Petersburg Committee on Education petitioned the government to introduce the Ukrainian language into the public schools in Ukraine, and among the list of books which it recommended for popular reading there were more in the Ukrainian than in the Russian tongue. Russian writers took an interest in Ukrainian language and literature and even advised the writers of Galicia to give up the Old Slavonic as a literary vehicle and to use the living Ukrainian.

In a short time, however, this active and beneficial Ukrainian movement met with opposition from the government. Although the Ukrainians were struggling against the Polish landlords, who had a strong dislike for their nationalism, the Russian administration believed false accusations to the effect that the Ukrainians were secretly plotting with the Poles. At this juncture, in 1863, an insurrection broke out in Poland. The government now suppressed Ukrainian freedom of speech; at the close of 1862 the *Osnova* ceased to exist, and the other publications were discontinued by order of the Russian government. The Ukrainian leaders were arrested and exiled, and their books were forbidden to be used in schools or even privately.

Finally the minister of the interior, Valuiev, issued an order forbidding the publication of Ukrainian books in general. The only reason given for his act was that "the majority of the Little Russians prove conclusively that there never was any separate Little Russian language, there is not one now, and there cannot be one," and that the Ukrainian movement was being stirred up by the Poles for their own benefit. Thereafter, he ordered the censor in future to permit the publication in Ukrainian of belles-lettres only, but to deny the right to print scientific works or books intended for popular reading. Golovin, the minister of education, came to the defense of the Ukrainian language and declared that the government should not censor books in such a manner merely because of the language, without examining the contents, but all his efforts failed of success; the prohibition remained in force, the Russian Orthodox Synod furthermore prohibited the publication of the Bible in the Ukrainian tongue, and finally the censors, grasping the intent of the administration, prohibited the publication of all Ukrainian books, including belles-lettres.

Thus the new Ukrainian movement was crippled in its infancy. As a result of suppression of the Ukrainian rebirth in Russia, the literary activities were transferred from the east to Galicia in the west; and for the first time in many years the center of Ukrainian activity, which centuries before had moved east under the pressure of Polish oppression, was once more in western Ukraine.

Nationalism and the Russophile Movement in Galicia: After several years of inertia, the progressive Ukrainian movement was resumed in Galicia in 1859. The last project of Goluchovski, the governor of Galicia, was an attempt to force the Latin alphabet upon the Ukrainian people, which action met with strong and unanimous opposition. The Poles, who now occupied the high offices in Galicia, stood between Galicia and the Austrian government, and the Ukrainians recognized that this attempt at Latinization of the alphabet would lead to complete Polonization of Galician life. They decided to resist with their united strength, but the question arose how best to combat the Polish flood which threatened to overflow Galician Ukraine. The conservative circles of the Ukrainian citizenry—the priests and the government officials—felt powerless to awaken a national movement. Until this time they had relied altogether upon the Austrian government, which now, it was clear, had surrendered Galicia to the Poles and would do nothing for the Ukrainians against the desires of Poland. As a result of this discovery, the conservatives placed their hopes upon Russia.

The pro-Russian orientation had existed to some extent since the eighteenth century, when the conservative Ukrainians in Galicia had come to an agreement concerning the retention of the Old Slavonic Church language, which is closely allied to Russian, as the literary language. The Galician leaders entered into negotiations with such Slavophile Russians as Pogodin, who heartily supported the Russophile movement in Galicia. Russia made a strong impression in 1848 when she sent her army to assist Austria in suppressing the Hungarian revolution; she had already left with the people in Galicia the recollection of an all-powerful nation from the time she had so ruthlessly suppressed the Polish revolt in 1831, the Galicians thereafter looking upon the Russian autocracy of Nicholas I as the ideal system of government. Meanwhile Austria suffered a setback in Italy in the 1850's, and in 1866 was defeated by Prussia; it was believed that her final downfall was near. When, in addition, Austria turned over Galicia to the complete control of the Polish gentry, conservative circles in Galicia began to look to Russia for salvation.

They expected that the Russian emperor would soon seize Galicia from Austria and therefore began to preach Russification. As a result of the Austrian defeat at the battle of Sadowa in 1866, the newspaper *Slovo,* the pro-Russian organ of the Conservative party published in Lviv, publicly declared its political program, attempting to prove from the Russian point of view that the Galician Ruthenians and the Russians were one people and that the Ukrainian language was but a dialect of Russian, differing from it only in pronunciation and that once the Russian pronunciation was learned, a Galician Ruthenian could learn to speak Russian in an hour's time; in other words, there were no Ukrainians, but ''one Russian nation''; also that there was no need to cultivate a Ukrainian literature because a Russian literature already existed.

The pro-Russian movement became so contagious in the Ukrainian provinces of the Austrian empire—Galicia, Carpatho-Ukraine, and Bukovina—that it caught up most of the intellectuals, including many of those who had been Ukrainian nationalists in 1848. Even such Ukrainian patriots as Jacob Holovatsky, a professor in the newly established chair of the Ukrainian language at the Lviv University, now became an ardent advocate of the use of the Russian language and later went to live in Russia. Naturally it was easier for the leaders to adopt the line of least resistance, to look for blessings from Russia, and to avoid quarrels with the Poles—much easier than to labor for the awakening of the Ukrainian people and to create cultural and other foundations for a new life for them.

But the more energetic circles among Ukrainian youth in
Galicia took the road of Ukrainian nationalism, ably
aided by a few representatives of the older generation.
They felt themselves immeasurably closer to the democratic and patriotic movement awakening among the
Ukrainians of Russia than to the official Russia of the
era of Nicholas I which received the blessings of the
priests and the Russophile government employees. The
appearance of the Ukrainian renaissance in Russia gave
courage to the young Ukrainians of Galicia to continue
the struggle. They were animated by the inspiring words
of the greatest Ukrainian genius, Shevchenko, and to
them his *Kobzar* became a Bible and Ukraine a Holy
Land. They loved to read about the glory of the Kozaks;
young people took pleasure in dressing in Kozak costumes and intellectuals ceased to use the Polish speech,
but devoted all their efforts to mastering the details of the
Ukrainian language. Through their publications, the
Vechernitsi (founded 1862), the *Meta* (1863–65), the *Niva*
(1865), the *Rusalka* (1866), and the *Pravda* (from 1867),
they evoked Ukrainian patriotism, love for the common
people, and an attempt to aid them culturally, economi-
cally, and politically.

CHAPTER XXIII

THE NATIONAL STRUGGLE

The Beginnings of National Aspirations in Bukovina: In the course of time the spirit of nationalism developed in Bukovina. Although connected with Galicia by the Austrian administration, it was cut off from its neighbor politically, religiously, and culturally, and was for long hardly touched at all by events in Galicia. But the Galician literary nationalism of the 1860's found an echo in Bukovina, where several highly gifted writers appeared, including the Vorobkevich brothers, especially Isidore, who was a popular poet, and Osip Fedkovich, the most distinguished Ukrainian poet who had yet appeared in Austria. In his poems and legends, Fedkovich revealed to the Ukrainian people in Galicia and Bukovina the magic beauty of the Carpathian region and the mountaineer life of the Hutsuls. Because they could not publish their works at home, as there were no literary magazines, the young authors of Bukovina had them printed in Galicia. The national political movement did not begin in Bukovina until a later time; the local organization, "The Ruthenian Society," which was founded in 1869, was long pro-Russian, and it was not until the 1880's that the Ukrainian nationalists gained control of it.

Much more significant for the morale of the national movement in Galicia than the impulse received from the talented young writers in Bukovina was the sympathy and aid from the Ukrainians in Russia. After the Russian government suppressed Ukrainian publication, many writers sent their works to Galicia to be published. Among the prominent older Ukrainian writers of the time who enriched the literature appearing in Galicia was Kulish, and among the young authors Marko Vovchok, Antonovich, Konisky, and Netchuy-Levitsky. When the journal

Pravda was founded in Lviv in 1869, Ukrainians from Russia took an active part in its publication, as it was the only Ukrainian literary journal in existence at the time.

This assistance by Ukrainians from Russia proved of great value to the Ukrainians under Austria. The Ukrainian or, as they called it, the "nationalist" movement in Galicia was carried on by young people, since the older, more conservative generation was unfriendly to it from the beginning. The pro-Russian faction was in control of all institutions in Galicia and Bukovina, not to speak of Carpatho-Ukraine, while through the 1870's nationalism was represented only by a small group of intellectuals, poor in material and cultural resources. Accordingly it meant much for these young workers that they could count on help from Russian Ukraine—boundless, rich Ukraine, the home of the Kozak heroes and of the leaders of the new movement. This support had another wholesome effect in that it made the nationalist movement in Galicia democratic and progressive and thus counteracted the influence of the old religious and conservative groups. To the oppressed Ukrainians in Russia, Galicia appeared an open window looking out on the free expanse of Ukrainian development and in time of extremity a place of refuge.

The Kievan Hromada *and the Decree of 1876:* Early in the 1870's Russian censorship of Ukrainian books was somewhat relaxed, and for a short time literary and educational efforts became possible. The center of Ukrainian life moved to Kiev, where the work was in the hands of the young intellectuals of the local university. The activity of the Kievan group, known as the "Hromada," differed from that of the Ukrainian nationalists of St. Petersburg in that the members devoted their attention less to the social and more to the scientific field in order to prove on the basis of historical studies the independent character of the Ukrainian people. Among those who figured prominently in this work were Antonovich and

Drahomaniv, the ethnographers Chubinsky and Rudchenko, and the philologists Zhitetsky and Mikhalchuk. In
1872 they succeeded in securing permission to establish
in Kiev a branch of the Geographical Society, which became the center of Ukrainian cultural life. In connection
with it Ukrainian literary activity in Russia was revived;
at the close of the 1860's and throughout the 1870's such
men of prominence in literature as Rudansky, Netchuy-
Levitsky, Mirny, Konisky, and Michael Staritsky were at
work. Nicholas Lysenko was laying a foundation for
Ukrainian music; his collections of songs, his original
compositions, including the opera *Christmas Night,* and
his marvelous concerts made him noted in his field. In the
course of time the Ukrainian theater began to rise, with
wide effects upon the intellectual and semi-intellectual
classes.

Thus the Ukrainian leaders of Kiev directed the attention of the inhabitants to cultural and scientific activity
in order to divert their attention from politics and especially from the contemporary Russian revolutionary
movements. There were even those among the Ukrainians
who complained against such one-sided interest in "culture." No matter how careful the Kiev leaders were, however, not even their cultural activity met with the approval of the Russian government. It was two Russian
landowning governmental officials in Chernihiv, Riegelmann, and Yuzefovich, who adopted the role of guardians
of Russian governmental interests in Ukraine.

After quarreling with the leaders of the Kiev cultural
group, Yuzefovich sent to the authorities repeated accusations regarding the progress of Ukrainian "separatism," as the movement was called, declaring that the
Ukrainians were developing their language and literature
in order to separate from Russia. Early in 1875 the government appointed a commission, of which Yuzefovich
was a member, to investigate the matter. He described the
Ukrainian movement to the commission as a Polish-Aus-

trian intrigue against Russia for the purpose of severing Ukraine, and the members of the commission who represented the censorship affirmed that Ukrainian literature had secret separatist aims. Great danger was feared from the Ukrainians of Galicia who were not subjected to the Russian censorship and were at that time hostile to the Russian government on account of its persecution of the Ukrainians in Russia. The commission decided to watch closely the books which were published in Galicia dealing with the nationalist movement and to prohibit them in Ukraine, to finance and otherwise support pro-Russian publications and the pro-Russian movement in Austria, and to employ all possible means to suppress the Ukrainian movement in Russia. The Kievan branch of the Geographical Society was closed at once, and in the spring of 1876 the government issued a decree condemning the Ukrainian language in general: Ukrainian concerts, plays, lectures, and fiction were entirely prohibited, and only the printing of historical works and belles-lettres—poems, stories, and sketches—was permitted in the Ukrainian language, and then with Russian orthography and under the strictest supervision.

In themselves these prohibitions were not exceedingly severe, but the censorship applied them in an arbitrary manner, and for some time no Ukrainian books appeared at all, except through oversight. The situation was not lacking in humor; Ukrainian words were stricken out of stories written in Russian, and orders were issued that Ukrainian songs should be sung in French or Russian translations. Soon, however, the government officials of the provinces of Kiev and Kharkiv told the imperial government of their own accord that its prohibitions were too severe and merely irritated the people. On account of this intervention, partial relief was granted: for instance, Ukrainian plays were permitted, though with many limitations; performances in the Ukrainian language were prohibited for many years, for example, in the Ukrainian provinces subject to the governor-general of Kiev, while in other cities it was required that plays be presented simultaneously in Russian and in Ukrainian.

Under these circumstances Ukrainian cultural and civic activity was impossible, and as a result the more conscientious and energetic Ukrainians transferred their operations to Galicia even more generally than in the 'sixties.

Ukrainian Activity in Galicia: Even prior to the decree of 1876, several far-seeing Ukrainians had intended to establish an educational institution in Lviv where they could work freely and without constant fear of the Russian censorship which was so oppressive in Ukraine. Money was collected for the Shevchenko Society, which was founded in Lviv in 1873. With its small funds it established a printing house for the publication of Ukrainian books, but so little money was collected that publishing was not actually begun until near the end of the 1880's. Several talented Ukrainians including Drahomaniv and some of his younger associates left Ukraine and moved to Geneva, Switzerland, where with the aid of Ukrainians from Russia they published a journal, or review, *Hromada,* devoted to Ukrainian political and national problems, and established connections with the circle in Galicia. Several Ukrainian authors returned to Galicia, where they remained for a considerable period of time engaged in political and literary activity; to this group belonged Kulish, Konisky, Netchuy-Levitsky, and others.

Drahomaniv and his followers in Geneva were interested in spreading popular education among the Ukrainian people and in effecting a stronger organization to struggle for equal rights, while Kulish, Antonovich, and Konisky in Galicia endeavored to improve local conditions by developing a better understanding with the Polish authorities. All these spiritual and material influences coming from Ukraine to Galicia greatly strengthened the nationalistic development there, and in the decades of

1870 and 1880 the Ukrainian nationalists increased rapidly in number and in strength. They began with literary works, the publication of popular books, and the founding of libraries, but later transferred their activity to politics and organized the small communities into a strong political party that by its energy and high morale snatched the leadership from the old reactionary pro-Russian circles in Galicia; and in spite of its meager funds, as compared with those of the far richer Conservatives who were aided by support from Russia, this small but enthusiastic Progressive group wielded a wide influence in Galicia and Bukovina.

In Galicia, under the Austrian government, there was some freedom for discussion of social, political, or national topics; and because of this liberty many of the most active Ukrainians in Russia, unable to discuss these subjects at home, watched events among the Ukrainian nationalists in Galicia with great interest, especially after 1890, when a struggle arose between the Ukrainian nationalist Galicians and the more progressive radical movement, a conflict which was of value in keeping alive an interest in public questions in Russian Ukraine and in preventing one-sidedness.

In 1882 the Ukrainians in Kiev succeeded in establishing a historical journal, *Kievan Antiquity,* which took the place of the abolished Geographical Society; and around it there formed a group of Ukrainians interested in science and cultural problems. The journal, devoted to ethnographic studies, language, and literature, was published at first in Russian, but about 1890 it began to include articles in the Ukrainian language. The censorship, however, was so strict that very few such articles were printed, and consequently the Ukrainian theater came to take the place of books in serving the masses. The number of these theaters increased rapidly, and although hindered by censorship, they successfully defended patriotism and prevented assimilation. Valuable services were rendered the theater by the plays of Kropivnitsky, Staritsky, and the Tobilevich brothers.

As there was little freedom of speech, the authors could not discuss any civic or political topics; and the popular masses were not interested in ethnographical, ethnological, or historical studies. Therefore some of the more active members of the Kievan group became discouraged, gave up their work in the Ukrainian renaissance movement, which they looked upon as an expression of an outworn romanticism, and joined Russian political parties where there were greater opportunities for work, more freedom for expression, and a risk of punishment which appealed to the bolder spirits.* This tendency led in Russian Ukraine to an increased interest in Galicia, where the Ukrainians could make limited use of the press and of factional ties to participate in open party struggles and in political and civic activity.

The Political Movement in Galicia in the 1890's: The years 1890–95 were noteworthy for the activity of the Ukrainians in Galicia. In the 'eighties, as has been said, the Ukrainian nationalist movement spread widely in that province and, as always happens, attracted the attention of many people who, though not directly interested, followed the majority. As Ukrainian nationalism gained ground, penetrated to the most isolated parts of the country, and began to take form as a political party, the inevitable dissensions began to arise.

The more progressive groups which wished to continue their coöperation with progressive circles in Russian Ukraine and the rest of Europe thought it necessary for the success of nationalism to rebuild the social, political, and economic institutions in the spirit of parliamentary democracy and socialism. The more conservative groups,

* Russian political groups were at that time working "under ground," since no political parties were allowed in the Russian empire before 1905 (Editor).

which included the clergy and the few other representatives of the middle class, accepted the forms of nationalism such as the national language and to some extent national traditions, but under this veneer wished to preserve the old content of life—the conservative system of relationships, the authority of the Ukrainian national Church (in Galicia the Uniate), and religious orthodoxy. Drahomaniv, although he did not live in Galicia, was especially influential in directing the Galicians, through his supporters there, along the first of these roads, and his prestige among the youth and the peasants continued to grow.

In 1890 the decisive moment arrived, when, somewhat under the influence of the Ukrainians from Russia, the majority of the Conservative Nationalists in Galicia broke off relations with the Russophiles with whom they had previously joined to fight the Poles in the Galician legislative assembly and in the Austrian parliament, and developed a better understanding with the governor-general of Galicia, Count Badeni. The more progressive groups, even before this time, had organized themselves into a Radical party. When the new alliance of the Nationalists and the government was announced, the Radicals denounced this policy as one of "submission," their opposition being well justified because in reality it was the Ukrainians who were submitting to the ruling Polish aristocrats, and the agreement was not an alliance, but rather a capitulation to the rule of the Polish gentry. As a result of this act by the Conservatives, the Ukrainians won such trifling rights as permission to have a Ukrainian chair at the university, authority to establish one secondary school, and a few other minor gains. When the Nationalist leaders finally analyzed the situation, under popular pressure they broke off their political relations with the Polish party in control of the government and only a few of the older clergy and the ultraconservatives remained loyal to the alliance, while the Nationalists as a whole determined to oppose the Polish rule in Galicia and to re-

sist the Austrian government because it had given Galicia to the Poles.

Following the example of the Radicals, the Nationalists
too decided to draw as near to the popular masses as possible and to educate the people politically, to organize
them, and to inspire them to carry on the struggle for
their rights, this phase of the Radical program having
valuable results in Galicia by preventing the Nationalists
from following the clericals and Conservatives. In 1900
the Nationalists formally joined the Radicals, accepted
their progressive program, and named the new party the
National Democratic party. The acceptance of the Radical
program, however, did not make these Nationalists progressive except in name, and the more conservative leaders of the group continued to urge peaceful understanding
with the Austrian government and the Polish officials, in
which policy they were restrained by popular opinion and
the influence of the Radical leaders.

Struggle and competition kept the national spirit alive
in Galicia in the 1890's and the 1900's. The national and
political self-consciousness which had been aroused originally by a handful of people now permeated the whole
population; the people learned how to safeguard their
rights and came to appreciate the value of organization
and their own strength. The new movement differed from
the policy of 1848 because the people did not wait and
hope that the government would do something for them;
they learned to build up their own future, to rely on their
own resources, and to go forward regardless of what their
enemies said about them: they learned to be self-reliant.
All that the Ukrainians gained during the last decade before the World War they won by means of organization
and a struggle against the Polish rulers. The Poles, with
the Austrian government supporting them and the political control of Galicia and ownership of the large landed
estates in their hands, utilized these resources against

Ukrainian nationalism in Galicia, but could not stop the forward march of the Ukrainian masses.

National and Cultural Progress in Austrian Ukraine: The last two decades before the war brought valuable gains for the Ukrainians. In the first place Ukrainian educational work was undertaken in a serious way, the Shevchenko Society being renamed the "Scientific Society" in 1892 and in 1898 becoming an academy of science under the name of the "Shevchenko Scientific Society." Its publications immediately attracted the attention of scholars, and Ukrainian education thus won for itself the right of citizenship in the realm of world science. Though the association received very little support from the central or local governments, it carried on a publishing and organizational program which would have been inconceivable a quarter of a century before.

The Ukrainians also demanded of the government the establishment of a Ukrainian university. The Austrian government had promised such a university in 1848 but had failed to keep its promise, and meanwhile the Poles had gained control of the University of Lviv, leaving the Ukrainians only a few courses in the Ukrainian language. At the close of the 1890's the Ukrainians pressed their demand for the foundation of a Ukrainian university, and in the first years of the twentieth century this problem became a live issue and caused many disorders at the University of Lviv. Public opinion supported the insistence upon a Ukrainian university so warmly that its foundation could not be long delayed.

In the field of literature a number of highly gifted pioneers were working in Galicia and Bukovina. Even before 1890 Ivan Franko, the outstanding poet, novelist, and publicist, had won the highest distinctions in contemporary literature. With the appearance of the monthly magazine, the *Literary and Scientific Herald,* and the founding of a publishing society, other talented Ukrainian writers, such as Vasyl Stefanik and Olha Kobilianska, came into prominence.

In popular education and national organization the establishment of public libraries was carried forward on a broad scale by the "Society for Enlightenment" (*Prosvita*), and gymnastic associations were organized under the names of *Siches* or *Sokols*. These activities awakened the masses and developed in them a desire for education, organization, and solidarity.

Since the government officials would not open secondary schools for the Ukrainian people, the Ukrainians of Galicia founded their own private educational institutions and in spite of serious obstacles promoted popular education.

In addition to this progress, during the last ten years of the nineteenth century a great deal of attention was paid to the economic status of the Ukrainians in Galicia. The people desired to free themselves from foreign financial and agricultural institutions, and accordingly organized their own mutual credit associations, coöperatives, and agricultural associations.

These accomplishments helped the Ukrainian inhabitants to feel their strength and convinced them that they would win rights and equality not by means of humble petitions or subservience but by a continuous struggle, knowing that if they were strong enough the Polish rulers would have to respect them and grant them equality. The most important fact about this movement was that it was independent and self-reliant, and in this respect the Ukrainians who were under the rule of Russia had been left behind, though even in Russia too during the last two decades the Ukrainians had made marked progress.

Ukraine under Russia on the Eve of the First World War: During the closing years of the nineteenth century the censorship was somewhat relaxed in Russia, and the Ukrainians were thus enabled to carry on literary work. In St. Petersburg, where the censorship was not as strict as in Ukraine, they organized a philanthropic society which published books cheaply and carried to the masses education in various fields of knowledge. A publishing society was also organized in Kiev at this time. A number of distinguished authors appeared, the most noted of these being Kotsiubinsky, Hrinchenko, Samiylenko, and Lesya Ukrainka. The development of the theater deserves consideration, as its literature increased in quality and was enriched by the playwrights Kropivnitsky and "Karpenko-Karey" Tobilevich. Zankovetska, Kropivnitsky, and the Tobilevich brothers established a high reputation for the Ukrainian stage. Finally a Ukrainian style became known in art and architecture, the most important example of which is the Poltava Zemstvo Hall, designed by the Ukrainian artist, Wasyl Krichevsky.

The prohibition of the Ukrainian language at archeological conventions introduced a new and more vigorous struggle for the rights and equality of Ukrainian culture, whose development in Galicia with the aid of the Ukrainians from Russia encouraged the leaders in Russia to continue their battle for national rights under the Russian regime as well. Before long various political parties modeled after those of the Russians became organized, and party strife began in Ukraine just as it had in Galicia. Ukrainian activity was especially strong during the opening years of the twentieth century in connection with the general Russian restlessness and discontent. The unsuccessful Russo-Japanese War and the revolution of 1905 drew the Ukrainians into the vortex of the general struggle for the liberation of Russia. The peasants were primarily interested in the agrarian problem and the intellectual groups in political problems; and in spite of political differences all Ukrainians united in demanding from the government, by means of the press, petitions, and resolutions, recognition of national equality and the free use of the Ukrainian language.

In December 1904 a special commission of imperial

ministers studied the Ukrainian question and came to the conclusion that the Ukrainian movement "does not constitute, as is claimed, any serious danger" that would justify the government in injuring the Ukrainian people to the extent of depriving them of the right to read their own books in their own language. When asked for an opinion, the Russian governmental bodies expressed themselves in the same spirit, and the St. Petersburg Academy of Science in a long report declared that the opinion that the Russian language could serve the needs of the Ukrainian people was false. Disregarding all these explanations, the government did not revoke its prohibitive laws against the Ukrainian language until they were superseded by others in 1905, when new laws pertaining to periodical publications enabled the Ukrainians to publish newspapers and magazines in their own tongue. The law of 1906 established freedom of publication of books for non-Russian nationalities including the Ukrainian. As a matter of fact even after this time the Russian government censored Ukrainian books and newspapers more strictly than any others, issuing against the Ukrainian newspapers special prohibitions not set up against those of any other nationality in Russia. Ukrainian editors, however, despite the threat of imprisonment, published their newspapers.

In the Manifesto of October 17 (30), 1905, the Russian emperor promised many political rights, few of which were actually realized. The people placed high hopes in the First Duma (parliament), convoked in the spring of 1906, and its membership included many people friendly to the Ukrainian cause who organized themselves into a Ukrainian bloc which expected to play an important part in the meetings. But the First Duma was dissolved before the Ukrainian group had an opportunity to act, and the same fate met the short-lived Second Duma. The third did not contain freely elected representatives of the peasants, and the great mass of the Ukrainians was therefore unrepresented.

The new laws passed by the parliament gave the Ukrainians no relief, the duma even refusing to approve one permitting the use of the Ukrainian language in the schools in Ukraine, although it granted this privilege to some other nationalities. The Russian government, especially the senate and the department of the interior, were hostile to Ukrainian nationalism, every phase of which they looked upon as dangerous "separatism." Optimists who had hoped that a constitutional government in Russia would give the Ukrainians equal rights and that the center of the Ukrainian movement would move to Russia were disappointed, for conditions in Russia gave the Ukrainians there less freedom than that of their kinsmen in Galicia.

Regardless of all the restrictions and persecutions, the Ukrainian movement gained ground during the next few years, and it became clear that the Russian government could not now nullify it. The Ukrainian press, established after the Manifesto of October 17, 1905, included the newspapers *Khliborob, Hromadska Dumka* (Rada), *Ridney Krai, Selo, Zasiv, Rilia,* and several others; the chief journals were *Vilna Ukraina, Nova Hromada,* and *Ukrainska Khata.* The *Literary and Scientific Herald* was moved from Lviv to Kiev. In the face of much opposition and punishment by the government, the press united the masses. In 1907 the Ukrainian Scientific Society was established, its membership including scholars in various fields of research. One of its first acts was to present demands for the establishment of Ukrainian schools. The government laid obstacles in the way of popular education and forbade the founding of local branches of the Society for Enlightenment, but a popular literature reached the masses and large editions of some books were sold.

By the eve of the first World War Ukrainian nationalism had developed to a point where it constituted one of the major problems of the Russian empire, and Ukrainians were looking to the future with faith and hope.

CHAPTER XXIV

UKRAINIAN INDEPENDENCE

The First World War: The marked development of Ukrainian nationalism in prewar times, both in Austrian and Russian Ukraine, exasperated the Polish and Russian enemies of Ukraine, who waited impatiently for an opportunity to put an end to the movement. They expected such an opportunity to arise in the event of war between Austria and Russia, hostile to each other ever since Austria had annexed Bosnia in 1908. In Russia extreme reactionaries, intensely displeased by Ukrainian progress, threatened that in case of war they would hang every Ukrainian, meanwhile appealing to the government to suppress the advance of nationalism. In Galicia, where the Austrian government had persecuted the pro-Russian faction, the Poles saw an opportunity to accuse the Ukrainians of many crimes, and when hostilities actually began the Polish officials in Galicia took advantage of the war emergency to attack the Ukrainian intellectuals. Under the pretense of combating the Russophiles, the Poles arrested other Ukrainians as well, imprisoning and exiling the leaders, especially men of prominence, on mere suspicion, and even executing a few without trial.

In Russian Ukraine at the beginning of the war, the Russian government prepared and put into effect a plan of systematic persecution of the Ukrainian leaders, its activity in this respect becoming more drastic after Russia had captured Lviv, the capital of Galicia. All enemies of the Ukrainians now had some assurance of being able to put an end to the Ukrainian movement by destroying the source of its cultural growth in Galicia, and the motto

---

[*] This chapter was not a part of the original body of the book and is rather in the nature of a political commentary on later events in which the author himself played a leading part (Editor).

of the Russian administration became "death to Ukrainianism." Prior to the war the government had not followed the advice of the obscurantist anti-Ukrainian forces, but it now took the offensive.

At the very beginning of the war, all Ukrainian publications of a political character were suppressed and large numbers of Ukrainian leaders arrested and sent into exile. The censorship in Kiev under the direction of old enemies of the Ukrainians proclaimed that it would permit no Ukrainian publications whatever unless they were written in the Russian orthography, although this act was an illegal application of the law of 1876, which had suppressed Ukrainian newspapers only. Lawsuits were instituted against innocent Ukrainian authors in order completely to suppress the Ukrainian publications in Kiev. To evade the censorship there, editors, authors, and publishers attempted to move to other cities, but everywhere met with the opposition of the officials, their publications being either prohibited outright or placed under restrictions, the censor in Odessa, for instance, demanding that the author submit three copies of the manuscript before printing, under threat of confiscation of the printed matter and padlocking of the press; this procedure was even more harmful than open censorship because it wasted time, energy, and money, and in the end ruined the publisher. Prohibitive activity of this kind reached its zenith early in 1917, a few weeks before the March revolution and the downfall of the Romanov dynasty, when the Russian government issued a secret order to the printers in Kiev to print nothing in the Ukrainian language.

While Russia was making deliberate and skilful attempts to stifle the Ukrainian movement in Russian Ukraine, she was making efforts, from the time of her invasion of the province in 1914, to destroy the Ukrainian culture in Galicia by sheer force. Several weeks after the Russians captured Lviv, they set up a Russian adminis-

tration under Count A. G. Bobrinsky, who began systematically to liquidate all Ukrainian gains thus far made. At
the very outset he suppressed all Ukrainian newspapers,
closed the libraries and reading rooms, and dissolved the
Ukrainian societies; the next step was to arrest and exile
to Siberia all "dangerous" and "suspected" authors.
The use of the Ukrainian language was forbidden in
schools and government. Steps were taken to abolish the
local Uniate Catholic Church and to force the acceptance
of the Russian Orthodox Church. When Ukrainian Uniate
priests could not be found, many being in exile or in flight,
Orthodox priests were sent to take their places, while
such priests as dared to face the Russian invasion were
pressed to accept the Orthodox faith; the officials also
persuaded the people to petition for Orthodox priests.
The Russian administration in Galicia, whose official advisers were Ukrainian renegades and whose unofficial
advisers were Poles, maintained that the Poles should
have special national rights in Galicia, while the Ukrainians and the Jews should not be favored but should be
obliged to accept the Russian language and culture, a declaration to this effect being made by Bobrinsky during his
visit to Russia in the spring of 1915, after the last Russian victory in Galicia and the capture of Peremyshl,
when it appeared certain that Galicia would be annexed
to Russia.

The Russian plans for destruction were bad enough,
but the manner in which they were executed was even
worse. Russian officials later admitted that during their
occupation of Galicia the country had fallen into the hands
of scoundrel officials sent in by the Russian government
who took advantage of war conditions to conduct themselves lawlessly, plundering the homes of the inhabitants,
abusing the Ukrainian and Jewish populace, and wrecking the Ukrainian cultural organizations. In some places
Ukrainian clergy, scientists, and other intellectuals were
expelled from their homes and communities. This was

done in a typically barbarous manner, people being seized as they were and wherever they were found, with complete disregard for human rights, men and women, children and invalids alike being exiled to Siberia. The lives of an incredible number of human beings were thus uprooted, one of the relief committees in Kiev registering fifteen thousand cases, but a fraction of the total. There were instances where insane and deaf mutes were seized, "brought to account," and exiled to Siberia in place of others who had succeeded in bribing the Russian officials.

Ukrainian Galicia was completely desolated by the Russian occupation of 1914–15. When the Russians were compelled to retreat from the sub-Carpathian region, they took with them all the inhabitants they could gather; and many others, fearing Polish persecution, also departed before the Hungarian and German armies arrived. Many thousands of peasants allured by the glowing promises of the Russians voluntarily accompanied the Russian army to Russia. When the German army later advanced toward the Russian border, again it was Ukrainians who bore the brunt of the suffering, especially in the provinces of Kholm, Pidliashe, Volynia, and Podolia, where the Russian military authorities attempted to remove the Ukrainian inhabitants by force into the interior of Russia. Ukraine had not undergone such a depopulation since the "great eviction" of the 1670's. People and livestock died on the way, and trains were jammed with innocent victims transported to Kazan or Perm, or beyond the Ural Mountains.* Before its downfall the Russian government displayed its complete stupidity, its intention clearly being to destroy the Ukrainians as a nation by destroying their culture and their educated leadership and by depopulating their country and colonizing it with Poles, through whom it was to be controlled.

* A doctor told the author in Moscow that he had seen freight and stock-cars overcrowded with children on their way to exile, all of whom either died or became insane.

The Ukrainian exiles were not permitted to organize themselves into war committees or to aid the suffering, nor was anyone permitted to bring assistance. The Russian government forbade Ukrainian children to be kept apart in separate groups and refused to permit the establishment of Ukrainian schools, although such a privilege was granted to the Poles, Letts, Lithuanians, and other nationalities. Even in exile the Ukrainians from Galicia were left under the control of Poles, in order that they might feel their "brotherly hand" in distant Siberia.

The Ukrainians of Russia who had coöperated with the Russian liberals now sought their help, but in vain, and under the pressure of the government there appeared to be complete "unity of thought" in all Russian circles. When Sazonov, the minister of foreign affairs, declared before the Russian duma in 1915 that the Ukrainian movement was being supported by German money, none of the Ukrainian "allies" present dared to raise a protest against this patent lie. All the Ukrainian petitions in behalf of Galicia, suffering under the corrupt Russian rule, were filed away. Even friends of the Ukrainians held the opinion that under the existing conditions it was not safe to oppose Russian autocracy because of such "insignificant" acts as the government's assault on the Ukrainians. Meanwhile, the liberal leader Struve and other enemies hastened to take advantage of the war completely to destroy the Ukrainians as a separate people.

In the dark hour for Russia when her army was compelled to evacuate Galicia a few Russians realized that the acts of repression had not succeeded in destroying the Ukrainian movement but had reacted against the interests of Russia herself, and during the short session of the duma on July 19, 1915, the government was severely criticized by Miliukov for its harshness in Galicia and because it had "rejected our native Ukrainian people and brought disgrace upon the idea that the war was fought for freedom." The government was asked for an explanation. The Ukrainians, in spite of the threat of persecution, again presented as a minimum demand permission to use the Ukrainian language in the schools. In 1915 the newly organized Russian political Progressive bloc, although fearing to include these Ukrainian demands in its program, recognized the necessity of "allowing Ukrainian publications" and of "investigating immediately cases of the inhabitants of Galicia who had been arrested" and were languishing in Russian prisons. The duma, however, was dismissed before action could be taken, and consideration of the Ukrainian problem was postponed. Although the Russian government continued its oppression of Ukrainian nationalism for a year and a half longer, even the Russian Progressives never raised their voices in protest.

While the Russian government was making efforts to destroy the Ukrainian movement in Russia, a new threat appeared to the Ukrainians in Galicia. After lengthy bargaining between Austria and Germany regarding the future status of Poland, Germany gained absolute control of this country by expelling General Brusilov in the summer of 1915, and the arrangement agreed upon between Austria and Germany could be put into effect. It provided that while Germany would dispose of the former Russian provinces of Poland, Austrian Poland would continue to remain in the hands of Austria. Galicia would not be divided, as Ukrainians had hoped, into separate Ukrainian (eastern) and Polish (western) parts, but would be governed as a unit, which in practice meant that it would be ruled by Poles and that the Ukrainian inhabitants would have no direct recourse to the Austrian government.

When Germany and Austria jointly declared the independence of Poland on October 23 (November 5), 1916, the Austrian Emperor Francis Joseph II instructed his chancellor to prepare a constitution for Galicia providing for the broadest possible autonomy. It was officially explained that the province was to become virtually as independent as the Polish kingdom newly restored under German protection.

This arrangement dealt a deadly blow to the aspirations of the Ukrainians in Galicia, especially to those leaders who had remained loyal to Austria during the war and had hoped in this manner to disprove Polish accusations of treason and to be rewarded by freedom from Polish control. Local Ukrainian patriots had urged their followers to support Austria in her struggle against Russia, in the hope that a victory over Russian despotism would end in liberation for Ukraine. The Ukrainian emigrants from Russia who had come to live in Galicia after the unsuccessful Russian revolution of 1905 were of the same opinion and had organized in 1914 in Vienna a "Union for the Liberation of Ukraine" (*Soyuz Vizvolennia Ukrainy*) with the intention of creating a Ukrainian state out of the Ukrainian districts seized by the German armies; they planned to give courses in Ukrainian citizenship to all Ukrainian soldiers from the Russian army who were taken by Austria. To a certain point the Ukrainians of Galicia had followed their leadership, especially at the opening of the war. They had formed Ukrainian volunteer regiments, known as *Sichovi Striltsi*, somewhat on the order of the Polish legions, which undertook to take charge of organizing the conquered Ukrainian districts. A "General Ukrainian Council" (*Zahalna Ukrainska Rada*), organized in 1915, and the Union for the Liberation of Ukraine had presented to the Austrian government a demand that the Ukrainian districts conquered from Russia should be allowed to constitute a separate Ukrainian state, that the province of Kholm should not be given to the new Poland, and that a Ukrainian state should be created out of the Ukrainian districts of Galicia and Bukovina.

Meeting with strong opposition from the Poles, who had great influence over the military authorities, these demands had brought no results; but in spite of this disappointment the Ukrainian statesmen had attempted to encourage their people by assuring them that better arrangements would be made after the war, basing their hopes on the promises of the premier, Stürgkh, and the moderating influence of the German government over Austria. The new Austrian policy regarding Galicia opened the eyes of Ukrainian leaders, however, and they finally realized that Austria had again deceived them.

Even the death of the old Austrian emperor and the accession of another did not promise any relief for the Ukrainians in Galicia, to whom only the Russian revolution of 1917 gave an indication of better days to come.

The Russian Revolution and the Liberation of Ukraine: Russian oppression of Ukraine always reached a high point during the celebration of Shevchenko's name day, and persecutions were unusually severe when the revolution of February 25 (March 10), 1917, suddenly broke out in Petrograd, as St. Petersburg had been renamed. The Ukrainian community in Petrograd played an important part in the uprising. There were several Ukrainians in contact with the commanding officers of one of the regiments which took the initiative, and Ukrainian soldiers and workingmen played a leading part in the actual revolt. In Ukraine the inhabitants received with joy the news of the downfall of the Romanovs as tidings of an event destined to bring about the emancipation of their fatherland.

An old organization of Ukrainian Progressives, which had acted in secret before this time, now brought its program into the open and began to organize a new Ukrainian government in Kiev early in March. Communications were established with all the political groups in Kiev and a Ukrainian national organ of government was set up under the name of "the Ukrainian Central Council" (*Ukrainska Centralna Rada*). The Central Rada, as it was commonly known, was an assembly representing the po-

litical parties and such other groups as coöperatives, work-
ing-class organizations, soldiers, and professional associations, whose members laid aside their political and class
differences and worked with a will for the common cause
of Ukrainian autonomy within the framework of a Russian federal republic.*

Without an adequate Ukrainian press the task of securing unified support made slow progress. The publishing
houses had been disorganized by the government and
their presses damaged during the war, so that time was
required to make the necessary preparations; but by the
end of March 1917 three Ukrainian papers, the *New Council*, the *Labor Gazette*, and the *Will of the People* appeared. Meanwhile information regarding political conditions was sent out by means of the Russian newspapers,
the post office, the telegraph, and by personal contacts. All
these were irregular and undependable, but the people
were so eager that they accepted at once the political revolutionary slogans. As soon as the news had spread that
the Central Rada had been organized in Kiev, provincial
councils were organized which recognized it as the supreme Ukrainian national government and asked for recognition for their representatives and instructions regarding local activities. In order to learn to what extent
Ukrainian nationalism had taken hold of the popular
masses, the new government set March 19 (April 1) as the
date for a national manifestation of patriotism in Kiev;
the immense demonstration and subsequent meetings conclusively proved that Ukrainianism was not a movement
restricted to a few teachers but was the will of the nation.
At a great assembly resolutions were passed that Ukrainian autonomy should be inaugurated at once without waiting for approval by the Russian government, which could
be postponed to a later time, and that the Russian Provisional Government should be asked to issue an imme-

* Professor Hrushevsky, who had returned to Kiev from exile at the outbreak of the revolution, was elected president of the Central Rada (Editor).

diate declaration regarding the need of extensive Ukrainian autonomy in order to gain the coöperation of the Ukrainian people for the new regime.

Following the convention and demonstration in Kiev, many other conventions were held in all parts of Ukraine. The Ukrainian Progressives were reorganized under the new name of Union of Autonomous Federalists. On Easter Day there was a national teachers' convention; and on April 6–8, a Ukrainian National Convention was convoked by the Central Rada in order to plan for new elections to transform the Rada itself into a representative assembly and to secure popular approval of its actions. All Ukrainian parties and national organizations were represented at this convention, which met with great success.

The convention, which was attended by about nine hundred delegates, chiefly representatives of peasants and soldiers, laid the foundation for a permanent government organization. The new Central Rada created by the convention included in its membership representatives of the provinces, of the army, of the peasants, of labor, and of cultural and professional organizations. Its first act was to approve the territorial autonomy of Ukraine within a Russian Federal Republic. All delicate controversial questions which might cause bad party feeling were purposely omitted from consideration, but a month later the Central Rada realized that the economic problem could not be left out of its program, because the new Russian government was devoting a good deal of attention to it and all the political parties joined in declaring that the Rada should protect the economic interests of the country and its laboring population. The Ukrainian Central Rada was now augmented by the addition of a large number of labor representatives and included in its platform planks on social and economic problems; it had become more democratic and had begun to advocate social and economic improvements. Its comprehensive platform exercised a greater influence upon the Ukrainian soldiers than upon any other group, and they, in turn, lent valuable support to the national movement.

It was not extraordinary that the soldiers should be so much interested in the Ukrainian movement, for the army included the most energetic classes in the population, and soldiers had been the most active participants in the Russian revolution. It was more surprising that the Ukrainian soldiers, instead of remaining in the Russian army, demanded the organization of separate Ukrainian military units and the formation of a national army. Since the old Russian government had actually permitted the formation of Polish legions in Ukraine, this precedent served as an incentive as well as a warning to the Ukrainian people to form an army of their own, for the presence of a foreign army in the vicinity of Kiev had greatly irritated the local inhabitants. The newly formed Ukrainian military organization was named the "Polubotok Legion." Demands were also made for the organization of independent Kozak regiments and permission was given for civilians to form an army of this kind; but when the call was issued, thousands of soldiers answered it, several thousand gathering in Kiev at the end of April and declaring that they would not go to the front except as members of Ukrainian regiments.

Both Russian military circles and foreign authorities made too much of this incident by saying that the revolutionists were weakening the strength of the army at the front; their threats merely caused greater hatred for Russia, and the soldiers began to spread revolutionary ideas in the trenches. Many delegations representing soldiers appeared before the Ukrainian Central Rada to present their demands, and at a military convention held on April 5 (18), 1917, representatives of nearly 1,000,000 organized Ukrainian soldiers were assembled. A second military convention, held a month later, had an even more impressive character, representing 1,736,000 armed

Ukrainians, nearly double the number at the first convention. It was composed chiefly of front-line soldiers who sent delegates despite a ban on conventions issued by the minister of war.

These conventions were striking evidence of the proportions of the Ukrainian national movement. The Ukrainian peasant convention of May, which included representatives from more than a thousand districts, gave similar proof of strength, and the Central Rada knew that in demanding broad autonomy for Ukraine it could rely upon the support of the people and the army. The armed Ukrainian forces stationed at the front continued to hold back the Austro-German army, but they evinced a strong determination to support the Central Rada, which was also assured of full backing by the peasants.

The Struggle for Ukrainian Autonomy within a Federation: Neither Russian Democracy nor the Provisional Government properly evaluated these factors. After the first acts of revolutionary fraternizing, the Russians viewed Ukrainian national activities with suspicion and opposed the program of the Central Rada. When rumors spread that the Ukrainians were convoking a National Convention in order to proclaim Ukrainian autonomy and the federalization of Russia, revolutionary circles in Kiev were so aroused that they threatened to disperse the Easter convention. After a conference of Ukrainian leaders with the non-Ukrainian organizations this antagonism subsided, only to reappear on several occasions. Russian revolutionary newspapers often joined the old reactionary groups in fighting against Ukrainian nationalism, either openly or in secret. The Provisional Government of Russia paid more attention to anti-Ukrainian activities than to the demands of the Ukrainian people; its relations with the Ukrainians were directed by the unfriendly "Cadet" (Constitutional Democrat)-Centralist bloc, and all attempts on the part of the Ukrainian government to establish better understanding failed.

Because of the tenseness of the situation, the Central Rada hesitated for a long time over the advisability of entering into official negotiations with the Russian government. Following the convention at Kiev, the government of Ukraine did not send a delegation or a declaration to Petrograd, but a Convention of Soldiers' Deputies a few days later insisted that the Rada present the demands of the previous convention for recognition of Ukrainian autonomy, which the Rada finally agreed to do. The Russian authorities, however, received the deputation of the Rada with indifference, expressing doubt as to the jurisdiction of the Central Rada and assuming an air of antagonism toward the Ukrainians.

This refusal to act, following after the Russian prohibition of a Ukrainian military convention, gave rise to intense feeling against Russia at the Convention of Ukrainian Soldiers and Peasants which took place June 2–10. The army deputies, several thousand in number, meeting in St. Sophia Square at Kiev took an oath not to leave the city until a suitable proclamation had been issued by the Ukrainian government, and demanded autonomy for Ukraine within a Russian federation. When the Ukrainian Central Rada took note of this strong determination on the part of the people and the army, it decided to initiate Ukrainian autonomy on its own authority and regardless of Russian objections, and on June 10 (23), 1917, issued its "First Proclamation" (*Universal*) to the Ukrainian people, in which it declared: "From this day you will create your own destiny." It appealed to them to enter into close relations with the Central Rada, to tax themselves for national purposes, to organize a local Ukrainian government, and to remove from office all who were hostile to the interests of Ukraine.

The proclamation made a deep impression upon the people not only because of its well-planned instructions, but because of its strong and determined tone, in which the native population as well as foreigners could hear the

voice of a future government. Following the issuing of
the proclamation, the Central Rada organized a "General
Secretariat," a kind of cabinet, which became the national
administration for all Ukraine. When the Russian government learned what was taking place in Ukraine and
with what great enthusiasm the people had greeted the
proclamation of the Rada, it changed its attitude. The Socialist ministers refused to follow the leadership of the
Cadets in their policy regarding Ukraine and decided to
make concessions. The Russians at first made only half-
hearted efforts at conciliation, such as the issuance of an
ambiguous appeal "to the citizens of Ukraine," but later
they sent a commission to Kiev to study events there, and
on June 28 (July 11), dispatched a delegation with authority to negotiate with the Ukrainians.

Circumstances favored coöperation at this time, as the
Ukrainian Central Rada had admitted to its membership
representatives of the non-Ukrainian inhabitants of Kiev.
The Socialist cabinet in Russia agreed to recognize the
Ukrainian Central Rada as the Ukrainian government, a
decision which met with no opposition. Then the Rada and
the Russian cabinet joined in preparing the text of a Second Proclamation of the Central Rada to the Ukrainian
people, in which the General Secretariat was recognized
as the official government of Ukraine. Since the war was
still in progress, there was no time to discuss minor details and the proclamation was issued at once. The Cadet
ministers of the Provisional Government of Russia
greeted the arrangement with hostility, but since a majority favored the agreement with Ukraine, it was approved, thereby hastening a ministerial crisis in which
the Cadets resigned from the Russian cabinet, leaving it
in the hands of the Socialists. The new Russian government took a firm stand in favor of coöperation with the
Ukrainian government and on July 3 (16) issued a proclamation to that effect.

Ukraine had finally won autonomy, and all that was

necessary was the preparation of the final details. Such, at least, was the understanding of the Ukrainian people and the Russian minister, Tsereteli, who, upon completion of the agreement, expressed his best wishes for the future of the Ukrainian government and departed for Petrograd. Because of the critical situation of the soldiers at the front where the Germans and Austrians were advancing upon Volynia and Podolia, all the nationalities of Ukraine, whether Ukrainians or not, were willing to cooperate. The Ukrainian Central Rada admitted representatives of the non-Ukrainian inhabitants not only to its own membership but to the General Secretariat, which prepared the "first Ukrainian Constitution," as it was enthusiastically acclaimed, and submitted it to the Central Rada for approval. This was a happy moment in Ukrainian history and a promising one. Even the Ukrainian political organizations abroad which advocated a different solution of the Ukrainian problem gave their recognition to the work of the Central Rada and promised to follow its leadership.

Meanwhile political changes occurred which set up obstacles on what had appeared to be a smooth road to progress. The crisis in the Russian cabinet created by the resignation of the Cadets on account of the Ukrainian issue was utilized by the extreme radical factions on the one hand and by the antirevolutionary on the other. An insurrection broke out in Petrograd which, when suppressed there, reappeared on the battle front, where it precipitated an Austro-German advance on Ukraine. Within a few days the Central Powers reconquered Galicia and Bukovina and began to invade Volynia and Podolia. Anarchy spread within the ranks of the Russian army, which became disorganized and a threat to order; the massacres committed by the retreating soldiers caused great horror. Those who sought to disrupt the battle front were at the same time enemies of Ukrainian nationalism. The Russian Socialists lacked the courage to use force in compelling the lawless groups to submit to discipline and sought the aid of the middle classes. The Cadets returned to the cabinet, where they considered themselves masters, and renewed their hostility to Ukrainian autonomy, the Ukrainian representatives to the Russian government now meeting with suspicion and antagonism. The new cabinet attempted to undo the work of the previous one in regard to Ukrainian self-government and sought to restrict the authority of the General Secretariat by attempting to take from its hands all military powers as well as those pertaining to the courts, roads, post office, and the telegraph. The Russians also tried to limit the territory of Ukraine to the five provinces of Kiev, Podolia, Volynia, Poltava, and Chernihiv, and to reserve special rights for their government even within these areas.

The Central Rada convoked at this time found itself in critical circumstances because of the steps taken by the Russian government in issuing "Instructions" to it, which interfered with the Rada's freedom of action, to the great disgust of both the Ukrainian and non-Ukrainian members. In this way the Russians attempted to destroy what was most needed at the time, namely, the unity of all the civic-minded forces of Ukraine in order to defend the nation against growing lawlessness and anarchy. Indignation rose high among the Ukrainians when the first Ukrainian regiment was mobbed on July 26 as it was leaving Kiev for the front, a clear result of anti-Ukrainian agitation.

On the other hand, the inhabitants of Ukraine were eager to avoid a break with the government or with Russian democracy at this critical moment, and on this account the Central Rada yielded to Russian demands and decided to accept the Instructions for the time being, pending the convocation of a Pan-Ukrainian Congress to determine the future of the country. After considerable parleying the Ukrainian General Secretariat was reorganized on August 20 (September 2) with seven members, and on September 1 (14) this reorganization was ratified by the Provisional Government.

The Ukrainian National Republic: The Russian coalition government had recognized Ukrainian autonomy because of the circumstances at the time and because it feared the antirevolutionary activity of General Kornilov, which had almost overthrown the government. But as soon as the danger passed, the Kerensky government decided to withdraw Ukrainian autonomy, ignoring the Ukrainian administration and attempting to rule Ukraine without it. The Russian Provisional Government appointed high commissioners for Ukraine, refused to give the Ukrainian authorities material support, ignored their declarations and representatives, and ended by offering direct opposition to the work of the General Secretariat while the Russian senate, a relic of the old autocracy, desiring to stress the fact that it still existed, refused to publish the Instructions of the General Secretariat and thus deprived them of legal standing. At length Kerensky's cabinet itself turned completely against the Ukrainian government. It sought to utilize the coming Pan-Ukrainian Congress to indict the General Secretariat and the Central Rada. The Russian prosecutor at Kiev was instructed to investigate these two bodies and to take punitive measures against them. In the meantime the members of the General Secretariat were directed to appear at Petrograd to explain the purpose of the congress.

This action on the part of the Russians aroused the Ukrainians whose opposition was given expression in the Third Legion Convention, which convened on October 20, and in the autumn session of the Central Rada. Unexpectedly, however, circumstances again underwent a change. The Provisional Government fell as the result of an uprising in Petrograd led by the Bolsheviks, who in turn organized a new administration by "People's Commissars," which neither the people nor the army were prepared to

support. For a long time the Russian republic was in a
state of anarchy, the provinces, including Finland and
Ukraine, leading an independent life and resisting the
Bolshevik propaganda which called for "all power to the
soviets," that is, to councils made up of representatives
of labor, the army, and the peasants. The representatives
of the Provisional Government present in Kiev accused
the Central Rada of being in alliance with Bolshevism and
took steps to destroy both alike, making use of Kozaks,
Czech ex-prisoners of war, students of the military acade-
mies, and others; but they failed completely, for their intrigues were disclosed and the representatives of the old
regime and their associates were forced out of Kiev and
its vicinity. The Bolsheviks then decided to disrupt the
Ukrainian government, which they accused of being bour-
geois, and demanded the submission of the Central Rada.
At the close of October the government was in a desperate
situation, caught as it was between two hostile camps. In
Kiev and the other larger cities civil war broke out and
threatened to result in complete anarchy.

Under these circumstances it was no easy task to create
a single strong and authoritative organ of government in
the country, although it was very necessary. Resolutions
providing for such an authority were adopted by the Central Rada, but they were not enough. The only way to
create it was to lay a strong foundation, since the General
Secretariat could not remain suspended in air as the organ of a government which did not exist and which had no
hope of being established. The General Secretariat itself
had to become the government of the Ukrainian state, a
plan which a Legion Convention supported in October
and which was revolved in many debates at the meetings
of the Central Rada. The Rada finally became convinced
that the proclamation of the independence of a Ukrainian
republic must be made without delay but that it must dis-
close the democratic and socialist character of the resur-
rected Ukrainian state. The cabinet established contacts

with the representatives of the Social-Democrat and the Social-Revolutionary parties and with them prepared the Third Proclamation to the Ukrainian people, which was adopted by the Central Rada with reservations, and published on November 7 (20), 1917.

The proclamation announced the formation of a new Ukrainian National Republic, placed a few limitations upon the private ownership of land, introduced the eight-hour day and control over the means of production, and aimed at bringing about a conclusion of the war, amnesty to political prisoners, the abolition of capital punishment, court and administrative reforms, and personal minority rights for the non-Ukrainian inhabitants of Ukraine. This was a splendid program, and the Central Rada and General Secretariat did their best to fulfill at least a part of it, the first step being to hold elections of representatives to a Pan-Ukrainian Congress, which was to build the state not on a revolutionary but on a constitutional basis. This was a difficult task, for throughout this period Ukraine was in a state of anarchy. The Bolshevik government, as soon as it had assured itself of its position in Russia, dispatched its armies, not to the front to fight against the Germans and Austrians, but to Ukraine to fight against the Ukrainian government, which was disarming all hostile forces and sending them out of the country. Because the Ukrainian government would not permit the passage of Bolshevik detachments across the country to the Don, but allowed the Don Kozaks to return home from the front through Ukraine, the Bolshevik People's Commissars, at the end of November, formally declared war on Ukraine.

The Bolsheviks accused the Ukrainian government of counterrevolutionary activity, of an alliance with General Kaledin, the head of the Don Kozaks, and of coöperation with other reactionary factions, and accordingly delivered an ultimatum demanding permission from the Ukrainian government for their forces to march across the country, joint action against the Don Kozaks, and recognition of the soviet form of government—government by councils of soldiers, workers, and peasants—in Ukraine. Since acceptance of these demands would have destroyed all Ukrainian autonomy and placed the country in incompetent hands, the Ukrainian government refused to comply, whereupon the Bolsheviks proclaimed the Ukrainian Rada an assembly of reactionary capitalistic factions and swamped the country with Bolshevik agitators who spread all manner of lies about the Ukrainian authorities. The Bolsheviks next attacked the government finances by preventing the sending of Russian money to Ukraine, thus forcing the Ukrainians to hasten the coinage of their own money. Finally the Bolsheviks collected Russian troops from the front and sent them into Ukraine to disband the Central Rada. Simultaneously a Bolshevik convention was called to meet in Kiev in the first days of December with the object of overthrowing the existing order, a stroke which the government warded off by calling a peasant convention for the same time and place. The peasant convention took a decided stand in support of the Central Rada.

The eighth session of the Central Rada, convoked in the middle of December, revealed the resolute will of the people to defend the authority of the Rada and the sovereignty of independent Ukraine. The earlier plan of a federated Russia was now completely discarded. With the Russian empire in a state of anarchy, the subject peoples were all declaring their independence, partly because they could not form a federation apart from Russia, the largest potential member. Ukraine, too, was obliged to safeguard her political destiny, and in such a chaotic time the only safety lay in a strong and independent statehood.

Independent Ukraine: During the last half of December 1917, the position of Ukraine became even more critical. As Bolshevik agitation began to take effect, the army became disorganized, the soldiers at the front stole military supplies, deserted, and on their way home plundered everything in their path, while the villages were occupied by anarchist bands which gained the support of the weak and terrorized those opposed to them. The plundering and destruction of estates, warehouses, and factories became common, so that the wealth of the country was dissipated and its productive forces weakened.

To the evils of economic depression were added those of political anarchy. A group of Bolsheviks who had failed in their attempt to hold the convention in Kiev called another meeting in Kharkiv, where, on December 13, 1917, they set up a Bolshevik government for Ukraine in opposition to the existing national government. Declaring that the Central Rada did not represent the will of the Ukrainian working people, the convention appealed to the masses to oppose it. These efforts would have had a musical-comedy ending, but unfortunately bands of Russian Bolsheviks made up of soldiers and sailors and vagabonds broke into Kharkiv on the pretense of fighting their way to the Don and remained there. Their coming further encouraged local groups already incited by propagandists, the local population was terrorized, and although the Ukrainian garrison held out for two days, it finally had to give in.

After this, bands of Bolshevik soldiers and Red Guards, consisting of armed laborers and others in the service of the Bolsheviks, instead of going on to the Don to fight against the counterrevolutionists as they had said they would do, began to advance along the railroads into the heart of Ukraine, carrying their poisonous propaganda to the provinces of Poltava and Kherson. Events in Kharkiv repeated themselves in other cities; as soon as the Bolshevik bands arrived, various groups, mostly Jewish and Russian, caused insurrections in the cities and at stations along the railroads. Under the influence of their propaganda revolts broke out in the Ukrainian regiments newly organized or taken over by patriots; the soldiers were told that the struggle was against the capitalistic Central Rada and for the socialization of Ukraine. Many Ukrainian soldiers, or Kozaks as they were called, either joined the Bolsheviks, declared themselves neutral, or simply deserted their regiments and went home, as did a large number at Christmas.

These Bolshevik successes caused even the Ukrainian leaders to waver as the Russian Bolsheviks propounded their system to the Ukrainian radicals, attempting to prove that Bolshevism was the logical development of the program of the socialists, who must adopt the Bolshevik slogans if they did not wish to be wiped out by Bolshevism. They further called for the election of a new Central Rada at a convention of soviets to consist of deputies of soldiers and workers, and the transference to the local soviets of all local authority. Bolshevik propaganda had already been widely spread since the eighth session of the Central Rada, at which the extreme Social Revolutionaries from Kharkiv were present. Revolutionary groups also went to Petrograd to explain to the Russian government the proposal for a Pan-Ukrainian congress, the Bolsheviks and extreme Social Revolutionaries hoping that if the Ukrainian Social Revolutionaries gained control of the government they would bring to a close the Russo-Ukrainian war and put an end to anarchy in Ukraine.

These events brought uncertainty into Ukrainian politics at a critical moment. At the end of December and early in January, eastern Ukraine, the Black Sea region, and such cities as Poltava, Katerinoslav, Odessa, and Kremenchuk were in the hands of the Bolsheviks, who prevented delivery of coal supplies to the Kievan region and advanced on Ukraine from south, east, and north. In Kiev itself there was continuous propaganda against the Ukrainian government and against the Ukrainians in general which almost completely demoralized the local Ukrainian regiments that not so long before had arrived eager to defend their country. The Ukrainian authorities realized the difficulty of their position, and the Central Rada hoped to transfer its authority to the new cabinet to be formed January 9, 1918, in accordance with a Fourth Proclamation. Yet because of the war with Bolshevism the elections, which were to have been held in December 1917, and decisions regarding all important issues had to be postponed.

In addition to the Ukrainian war with Bolshevism, Ukraine continued to hold the front against the Central Powers. From the beginning of the revolution the Ukrainian people in all their conventions had expressed a desire for an immediate termination of the war, into which they had been drawn against their will by tsarist Russia. Until Ukraine proclaimed her independence, however, she was unable to make an appearance in international politics as an independent political unit; and meanwhile the Russian government, both under Prince Lvov and under Kerensky, had not dared to make peace with the Central Powers, but had on the contrary attempted to assist the Allies by holding the eastern front. This effort to continue the war was a great mistake on its part, as it not only destroyed gains won by the revolution but also endangered Ukraine. As soon as the Bolsheviks had overthrown Kerensky's government, they promised to bring the war to a close, and late in November opened negotiations with the Central Powers at Brest-Litovsk (Bereste). The Central Rada of the Ukrainian government, which since the time of the proclamation of Ukrainian independence had aimed at ending the war, decided to take part in this peace conference. The Allied Powers—first France and then England—which had hastened to recognize the Ukrainian National Republic attempted to persuade the Ukrainian government not to make peace with the Central Powers, promising Ukraine generous assistance if she would continue to fight against the Central Powers and threatening her with many ills if she signed a separate treaty. But the Ukrainian government had no military supplies with which to oppose the Central Powers, and furthermore the country was exposed to invasion by the Germans and the people were demanding peace. The Central Rada therefore sent a delegation to Brest-Litovsk, where it was to join the Soviet delegates in making a treaty of peace. When the Soviet delegates began to display their inconsistency, first declaring their readiness to sue for peace and then retreating into Bolshevik phraseology, the Central Rada authorized its delegates at Brest-Litovsk to make a separate peace with the Central Powers, regardless of what the Russians might do.

Amid the endless factional and party discussions that were held in the quarters of the Central Rada while Kiev was being besieged by the Bolsheviks, it was decided at length by a majority of the members to take a definite stand against Bolshevism. On January 9 (22), 1918, the date set for opening the Ukrainian Constitutional Convention, the decision was taken to proclaim the independence of the Ukrainian republic, in order to gain a free hand in international and domestic affairs and to cut the ground from under Russian interference in the internal affairs of Ukraine and make it clear that the struggle with the Council of People's Commissars and the Bolshevik bands was a war against Russia's attempts to destroy Ukrainian independence and not a conflict of political ideas under cover of which real enemies could hide as neutrals. In theory the Ukrainian groups still believed that federation was the best form of state life for the future, but the anti-Ukrainian forces were preaching federation with Russia merely in order to keep the Russian empire intact and to have an opportunity to continue to oppress the non-Russians as they had done in the past. The supporters of federation were promoting, moreover, not only political federation but complete unity of economy and all other functions—the same old Russian policy which had always hampered Ukrainian progress. The Russian Soviet government had dropped from its program the slogan of "self-determination of nationalities, even to complete independence," and openly declared itself for a federation, desiring on this basis to unite the Ukrainian proletariat with the Russian. When the Allied Powers, especially the French, suspected that Ukraine might join Soviet Russia, they had threatened in case of separate peace with Germany to deprive her of the resources which they controlled within her borders. It was necessary, then, for Ukraine to define her policy to the foreign nations, and this was another reason for proclaiming the independence of the Ukrainian National Republic.

In reality Ukraine had been an independent nation to some extent ever since the downfall of the Kerensky regime and more completely since the last session of the Central Rada. This independence had been recognized by the Central Powers and by the representatives of the Council of People's Commissars at Brest-Litovsk on December 30 (January 12), 1917, but it required formal confirmation, which was provided by the Fourth Proclamation, decided upon on January 9. It proclaimed the Ukrainian Republic "an independent and sovereign power of the Ukrainian people, subject to no other authority." The General Secretariat was renamed a "Council of People's Ministers," and its first duties were stated to be the completion of the peace negotiations with the Central Powers, regardless of any objections on the part of any section of the former Russian empire, and decisive action toward defense and clearing Ukraine of Bolsheviks. The demobilization of the army was ordered, to be accompanied by reconstruction of the devastated areas, alteration of the factories and shops from a war to a peace basis, and various measures for satisfying the returning soldiers as to their political rights. A number of social reforms were ordered in the interests of the laboring population, in accordance with the general principles set forth by the Third Proclamation—by transfer of land to the workers, nationalization of the forests, waters, and mineral resources, the creation of work for the unemployed, the introduction of monopolies in commerce in goods most needed by the workers, and control over bank credit.

The Proclamation was approved in its final form and published by the Central Rada on January 11 (24), 1918, although the date of January 9 (22) was retained. There was some opposition in Ukraine, there being a few Ukrainians so enslaved to Russian culture and government and so convinced of the need of a united Russia or the traditional type of federation that they were dissatisfied by independence even as a method of transition to federation. This was even more true of the un-Ukrainian Ukrainians, who had torn themselves free from the Ukrainian soil and considered themselves "Russians," of the Russians themselves, and particularly of the Jews, who failed to realize where the real interests of the Jewish population of Ukraine lay, but protested against being separated from the Jewish organizations of Russia. And this hostile attitude toward Ukraine, which had already made its appearance with such force in the commercial centers and especially in the Ukrainian capital of Kiev, following the declaration of Ukrainian independence culminated in an insurrection in Kiev at this critical moment in the struggle for Ukrainian freedom.

The Insurrection in Kiev: The Fourth Proclamation had been approved by a majority vote in the Central Rada, but as a result of a difference of opinion between the more radical Social Revolutionaries and the Social Democrats, the latter party announced that it was withdrawing its members from the cabinet, thus precipitating a crisis just at the moment when Ukrainian independence hung in the balance.

When the Council of People's Commissars learned that the left Social Revolutionaries were splitting the Central Rada, they sent to Ukraine, and especially to Kiev, new groups of propagandists to prepare the way for a revolt against the Rada and at the same time to intensify the blockade of Kiev from without, being particularly eager to disrupt the Central Rada to prevent it from making peace with the Central Powers. Meanwhile the Bolsheviks themselves refused to continue the war against Germany or to accept the German peace terms; nor would they renounce peace, especially since they had made it one of their chief slogans in overthrowing Kerensky's government. They attempted to undermine the influence of the Ukrainian delegation at Brest-Litovsk by sending Bolshevik agitators there from Kharkiv who called themselves the "real" representatives of Ukrainian democracy because they favored the federation of Ukraine with Russia and the union of Russian and Ukrainian proletarians. When even these attempts failed and the Central Powers continued their negotiations with the representatives of Ukraine, the Bolsheviks decided to destroy the Central Rada at no matter what cost.

These subversive efforts on the part of the Russian Bolsheviks met with a measure of success. Until the middle of January the city of Kiev, besieged by the enemy from all sides, was in a critical position. The Ukrainian soldiers in Kiev, completely demoralized by Bolshevik propaganda, began to make speeches attacking the Central Rada and demanding peace with the Bolsheviks under threat of withdrawing their support from the Rada. To make a stronger impression upon the Ukrainians the Bolsheviks placed at the head of their army George M. Kotsiubinsky, the son of a noted Ukrainian writer. The small Ukrainian forces were helpless against the large Red Russian bands. The heroism of the loyal Ukrainian troops, the legionaries from Galicia, and the high school students, who sacrificed their lives in battles against Bolshevism at Hrebinka and Darnitsia, could not counterbalance the activity of traitors and deserters. The Bolsheviks massed their troops at Zhmerinka, Koziatin, and Fastiv just across the river from Kiev in preparation for a crossing.

The war ministry declared Kiev in a state of siege and appointed a commander with dictatorial powers to defend the city. He called for volunteers, but the foreign and Bolshevik sentiment in the city was too strong.

On January 15 (28), 1918, the Central Rada met in its ninth session to enact such reforms as an eight-hour day and control of industry. The enemies of Ukraine took advantage of this opportunity to attempt an insurrection in Kiev, and during the session one of the Ukrainian regiments which had succumbed to Bolshevik influence approached the building where the Rada was meeting with the intention of dissolving the assembly, but lacked courage and limited its activity to vigorous protests against the use of "free Kozaks"—Kiev workers—in defense of the capital. The following night the Bolsheviks captured the arsenal and instigated a revolt in the city, at once sending news to Petrograd to proclaim to the world that Kiev had fallen into their hands, that the Central Rada had been dispersed, and that the Ukrainian government was in the hands of the revolutionists. Since the Bolsheviks had cut the telegraphic connections with Kiev, the Ukrainian delegation at Brest-Litovsk, ignorant of the exact conditions, was placed in a difficult position until the telegraph lines were repaired and the delegates enabled to discover the truth about conditions in Kiev, which gave them encouragement to continue their work. The Central Powers now recognized the independence of the Ukrainian Republic. They made no efforts to take advantage of the critical position of Ukraine and made many concessions in order to hasten peace, not only recognizing Ukrainian independence but signing a peace treaty advantageous to Ukraine, whose independence they considered essential for their purposes.

The Ukrainian government put forth all its efforts to keep its hold on Kiev in order to maintain its international prestige and to make a satisfactory peace, hoping that the peace treaty with the Central Powers would enable Ukraine to demobilize, restore order, and buy badly needed supplies. The return of the Ukrainian war prisoners who had been under the instruction of Ukrainian teachers for some time was also expected to strengthen the position of the government, the Union for the Liberation of Ukraine having of its own accord undertaken at the very beginning of the war to teach the Ukrainian prisoners of war the precepts of Ukrainian nationalism in order that they might know how to defend their rights in case of war between Ukraine and Russia; these loyal and conscientious soldiers were now to save Ukraine from military disorder. The Ukrainian *Sichovi Striltsi* (Sich Sharpshooters) from Galicia, former Austrian prisoners of war in Russia, also rendered useful service in fighting against Bolshevism. For these reasons the leading members of the Ukrainian administration attempted at all costs to bring the war to a close and to remain in the capital at least until the peace treaty was signed.

To attain this aim the Rada was forced to reorganize in order to avoid dissension. The extreme radicals who desired to compromise with the Bolsheviks gave way; the Kiev commandant arrested a few radical members of the Central Rada, which protested against the arrests made without its consent and appointed a commission to investigate the case but did not place obstacles in the way of the government in its struggle for existence, and because of the common danger all parties agreed to work in harmony. On January 18, accompanied by the roar of cannon fire as the attack on Kiev proceeded, the government passed a land reform bill, leaving its details for future settlement. V. Holubovich, the candidate of the Social Revolutionaries, was asked to form a new cabinet, a crisis was avoided, and internal harmony established; but the city of Kiev remained in a critical position. The Bolsheviks attacked it from the east and the west, and continuous street fighting went on within; parts of the city changed hands several times during the day. All the heroic efforts of several thousand loyal soldiers could not withstand the pressure of the enemy firing upon them with cannon stationed outside the city and with firearms aimed from roofs and windows of buildings, and the treachery which manifested itself at every turn. The people weakened under the extreme nervous tension. Both sides did their utmost, the Bolsheviks to take the city and the Ukrainians to defend it. The terrible results of civil war appeared, and the inhabitants began to complain that the Central Rada desired to save itself by exposing the city to destruction. The heavy guns were destroying the city buildings, and the streets were illuminated at night by the flames of burning houses.

Ten days passed in this manner. The Bolsheviks kept sending news to the world that "the Soviet Army under General Kotsiubinsky has captured Kiev," that the Central Rada had dissolved and taken flight, and that power had passed into the hands of a "Soviet Republic." Nevertheless the Ukrainian government remained in Kiev, struggling against treason of all kinds until January 25 (February 7), when terms were agreed upon with the Central Powers. Then, not wishing to expose the capital to destruction, it gave orders to the artillery and troops to leave the city and march to a suburb, while it moved its seat to Zhitomir. By January 27 (February 9) Kiev had been evacuated by the Ukrainian forces and had passed into the hands of Ukrainian and Russian Bolsheviks. For a few days the Bolsheviks carried on terrible massacres, killing all those who had passports issued by the Ukrainian government and all whom they suspected of being Ukrainians. They boasted that they had massacred five thousand. A more reliable report indicates about two thousand slaughtered, but regardless of the number killed, the character of Bolshevik warfare was revealed. In spite of their claims that they fought for socialist rights against the bourgeoisie and reaction, it was clear that this was a national war, the war of Russian imperialism against national rights; and the war the Bolsheviks waged to preserve the old Russian empire was more savage than any the tsarist governments had ever conducted.

The War for the Preservation of Independence: The Ukrainian government had not made a mistake in concluding peace. On the very day when the Ukrainian army evacuated Kiev a treaty was made with the Central Powers; it was concluded on January 25 (February 7) and signed on the evening of January 27 (February 9). It provided that the western parts of Ukraine—Kholm, Bereste, and a part of Pinsk—which had been occupied by the Germans during the war, should be returned to Ukraine; free exchange of prisoners of war and the barter of goods or the establishment of limited trade were likewise provided for. The German government at once mobilized the Ukrainian prisoners of war and sent them to Ukraine to assist the government in fighting against the Russian Bolsheviks and in addition expressed its willingness to send a German army to assist in clearing the country in order to get from Ukraine the food supplies specified in the treaty.

The prospects were anything but pleasing. It could be foreseen that as soon as the German soldiers invaded the country the Central Rada would be blamed, and wide dissatisfaction among the peasants would result. On the other hand it was not safe to abandon the country any longer to anarchy at the hands of the Bolsheviks and passively await the time when the people would become so disgusted by it that they would welcome the Ukrainian authorities. The most serious of the peasants desired peace and order and a strong government to free them from the Bolshevik Terror; they knew that they were helpless and that lawlessness would continue for a long time if the Ukrainian government had left its people without any organization or government. As the spring season was approaching, it was necessary for the good of the people to have peace and order so that they might cultivate their fields undisturbed. It became evident, however, that it would take time to organize the Ukrainian army, made up as it was of prisoners of war returned from Germany, and meanwhile Austria was slow in sending the Ukrainian regiments and volunteer legions from Galicia to assist the Ukrainian government. Under the influence of the demoralizing Bolshevik propaganda the ranks of the regular Ukrainian army had become depleted, and the task of mobilizing new forces required additional time.

In the face of this situation the Ukrainian government could not afford to refuse the military assistance offered by the German government, although it was of course clearly understood that Germany was acting purely from self-interest in order to secure the grain promised in the agreement. The Ukrainian government accordingly made a formal request for military assistance, and within a week after the treaty was signed a German army had crossed the Ukrainian border. Austria, which had previously hesitated, also promised to aid Ukraine, but instead of dispatching the Ukrainian regiments, sent Czech, Polish, and Hungarian troops, who at once antagonized the local population.

Meanwhile the Ukrainian government, with the meagre military forces which had been reorganized at Zhitomir, was expelling the Bolsheviks from Volynia. When the Bolsheviks learned that the government had established itself in Zhitomir, they sent forces to attack this city and forced the government to move for several days to Sarny in northern Volynia. Rail connections were established with the city of Kovel, where the Germans and the new Ukrainian army made up of ex-prisoners were encamped. With the aid of these additional forces Volynia was freed from the Bolsheviks by the middle of February, and the Ukrainian army advanced on Kiev. As of February 16 the Ukrainian Central Rada adopted for Ukraine the Gregorian calendar. The Bolshevik bands, after plundering the city for three weeks, now evacuated it without a battle when the German and Ukrainian forces threatened to lay siege, and on March 1 the German-Ukrainian army entered Kiev and was received by the local people with a great ovation. A few days afterward the Ukrainian ministry together with the Central Rada also returned to Kiev.

Several days after its departure from Kiev the Central Rada had met in Zhitomir to continue its legislative work, daily receiving information from the ministry concerning events of importance. Laws were passed pertaining to the revival of the old coinage of Ukraine, the boundaries, and the flag. Some of the Rada members who were not present at these meetings and did not meet with the parliamentary group until it returned to Kiev opposed a few of the measures. The radical members and the cabinet accused the government of being not socialist, but too nationalist, and attempted to cause the downfall of Holubovich's ministry.

Again the Central Rada was under fire, and the radicals and the anti-Ukrainian groups which opposed Ukrainian independence attacked the Central Rada and the ministry with the aim of overthrowing the government. They also criticized it because the ministry, which had charge of the Kievan police department, prohibited demonstrations and the celebration of the anniversary of the Russian revolution, and passed a law ordering proclamations and laws to be written in the Ukrainian language. Another subject of attack on the government was the presence of the German army.

On the other hand, the socialist policy, especially the land reform law of January 18 (31), aroused the wealthy classes in Ukraine against the Republic; they attempted to discredit the government in the eyes of the Germans and Austrians and sought their aid against the socialist policies, Polish landlords of Podolia and Volynia appealing to the Austrian government to occupy these provinces, and repeal the local land reform laws. Of their own accord they organized Polish legions and attempted to seize the land of the peasants. The landlords east of the Dnieper likewise attempted to organize themselves in opposition to the land reform laws; appealing to the wealthy peasants and Kozaks for support they adopted resolutions calling upon the Central Rada to abandon its socialist policies, dismiss the socialist ministry, refuse to convoke the Pan-Ukrainian Congress, organize a dictatorship, and dissolve itself; otherwise they threatened it with insurrection. They also sent representatives to the German military authorities to spread propaganda among the officers and urge them to use their influence against the land reform laws and for the removal of the socialists from the government, and planned with the aid of the Germans to reëstablish landlordism in Ukraine.

It was under these difficult conditions that the Central Rada was attempting to expel the Bolsheviks from the country, to reorganize the economic machinery, to restore order, and to preserve independence.

The Rada met with obstacles from without and from within. The military forces of Ukraine were neither strong nor well disciplined, and the land swarmed with anarchist, foreign, and reactionary military bands which ravaged the countryside and opposed both nationalism and the existing government. Likewise, various self-appointed officers, councils, and other unruly forces interfered with the plans of the government. The German and Austrian forces were not coördinated between themselves nor with the Ukrainian forces, and by their independent action frequently obstructed the military plans of the Ukrainian military staff.

Even so the expulsion of the Bolsheviks continued at a rapid pace, and during the month of April almost the whole of the country west of the Dnieper was freed, including the large cities of Odessa, Nikolaev, Kherson, and Elisavethrad. On the east side of the Dnieper, during the same month, most of the territory of the provinces of Chernihiv and Poltava was also cleared of the enemy, although operations there were not so successful because the Czech divisions, instead of proceeding to the western war front in France as they had promised the Ukrainian government they would do, joined the Bolshevik bands and fought against the Germans in Ukraine. Before the Bolsheviks evacuated Katerinoslav they exported to Russia everything of value, practically cleaning out the province. The chief Bolshevik general, Muraviev, an ex-policeman who boasted in January of how many thousands of Ukrainians he had massacred and how much property he had destroyed, was now forced to retreat, and finally, after being expelled from Poltava, he resigned from the command. During the month of April 1918 almost the entire eastern part of Ukraine was freed of Bolsheviks, the Czech-Bolshevik forces being unable to hold their ground against the Ukrainian-German armies in Kharkiv and Katerinoslav, but still retaining the Don region and the Crimean ports.

To establish internal order was an even more serious problem for the government than the expulsion of the Bolsheviks. Such issues were pending as the spring cultivation of the fields, the establishment of better transportation facilities, trade, improvement in manufacture, unemployment, and the organization of a sound, well-disciplined Ukrainian army that would ensure the national defense.

At the time when the Central Rada reconquered Ukraine the country was in a deplorable condition, suffering from four years of war, the general anarchy in the Russian empire, and, finally, destruction by the Bolsheviks. Before the Bolsheviks left the country they robbed the banks for money with which to meet the demands of their soldiers for pay; they also destroyed the railroad system and the bridges. The mines, out of operation for months, were flooded. The Ukrainian government also had to meet the unpaid bills incurred by the Russian regime for work or goods.

From every side there came upon the Central Rada demands for money as well as urgent appeals to restore order. Taking advantage of the critical position of the government, enemies from without and from within attempted to embarrass it, while others strove to win economic concessions for foreign nations, and the local landowners and their agents prevailed upon the Central Powers to insist that it should give in to the demands of the aristocracy. At the same time those who were unfriendly toward Ukraine kept close watch upon the acts of the Central Rada in order to have some reason for accusing it of a reactionary policy and for discrediting it in the eyes of the peasants and working classes, who feared that the government would abolish the land reform acts, return the land to the nobles, and destroy personal freedom.

Under these circumstances it was evident that nothing except the unity of all Ukrainian forces could save Ukraine and its democratic and social gains. Many groups, realizing the significance of the moment, laid aside their factional preferences in order to preserve national independence and hastened to the support of the Central Rada.

The first act of the Rada upon its return to Kiev was the proclamation on Shevchenko's anniversary that it would adhere to the socialist and democratic policies proclaimed in its Third and Fourth Proclamations. In order to carry these out the government obtained the aid of the Germans. The Holubovich coalition cabinet included representatives of all the chief Ukrainian factions and thus avoided a crisis, although the non-Ukrainian factions refused to accept positions in it. After long and heated debate the government ratified the peace treaty with the Central Powers. Although foreigners living in Ukraine remained unfriendly toward Ukrainian nationalism, the calling of the constitutional convention was of the greatest interest at this time, becoming the most popular issue.

The Central Rada had twice before designated the time for the convocation of a constitutional convention, but the Bolshevik invasion had delayed it. It was eager to hold new elections for representatives to be chosen by the people at large and in proportion to the population, after which the Central Rada was to transfer the government to the newly elected popular representatives.

At the last session of the Rada in January, it was decided that the constitutional convention might be convoked as soon as half its members were elected. Some of the people criticized this plan because the election was held during the Bolshevik terror and in a condition of lawlessness, and the members thus elected did not express the will of the people; but finally a majority of the members approved the idea of calling the convention into session immediately after the election, since the people, especially the peasants, were earnestly awaiting the meeting of the convention promised to them by the Central Rada.

The possibility of calling the convention was in prospect immediately after Ukraine was freed of the Bolshevik bands. The people of Ukraine were tired of war, unrest, and nervous tension; they desired peace and order and an opportunity for a better future and believed that a newly elected convention would give them what they needed. Therefore their motto was: "Immediate convocation of the Ukrainian Constitutional Convention." The Central Rada decided by a majority vote to convoke it for the twelfth day of July 1918.*

* Professor Hrushevsky's narrative closes at this point.

CHAPTER XXV

RECENT UKRAINE*

Skoropadsky and the Germans: The constitutional convention planned by the Central Rada, however, was destined never to meet. On April 28, 1918, German soldiers forced an entrance into the council chamber of the Central Rada in Kiev and despite the protest of its president, Hrushevsky, dispersed it. The following day a constitutional convention was held under German auspices. The bulk of its members were landowners of various nationalities, many being Russians to whom the nationalist aspirations of the Rada had been anathema; a large number of these landowners, including Polish and Ukrainian, had either lost their land or feared they were going to, and to them the agrarian policies of the Rada appeared little less extreme than those of the Bolsheviks.

The new head of the government appointed by the convention was the bearer of the old Kozak name of Skoropadsky, and the illusion of a return to Kozak independence was added to by giving him the Kozak title of hetman. A veneer of nationalism was preserved by adopting the Ukrainian tongue as the legal language of the republic for use in the courts as well as for proclamations.

It soon became clear, however, that the German army had no real interest in Ukrainian independence, but was merely intent upon collecting the foodstuffs promised in the "Bread Peace" at Brest-Litovsk. Since order was a prerequisite, laws were passed forbidding strikes, and with German officials in charge they were ruthlessly enforced. In order to revive production the confiscated estates were taken back from the peasants who had occupied them and restored to their former landlords, chiefly

* The following supplementary chapter sketching the chief events in the recent history of Ukraine is based on notes by Dr. Luke Myshuha (Editor).

Russian or Polish, and the hetman was obliged to begin forced collections of grain. Even the complaisant land-owners were not untouched, but were forced to pay the German authorities 10 to 20 per cent of the value of the returned land as a fee.

The way was thus opened for the dissemination of propaganda among the Ukrainian peasants and factory and mine workers, against the new regime and its German sponsors. Passive resistance became widespread, breaking out in riots against foreign landlords and German soldiers, and in the northern province of Chernihiv near the Bolshevik border, into organized rebellion. The German commander Eichhorn was assassinated and in Kiev and Odessa ammunition dumps were blown up. In the provinces bordering on the Black Sea, where the Austrians were installed with their headquarters at Odessa, the chief troublemakers were the port workers.

With the armistice of November 11, 1918, the rule of the Germans came to an abrupt end. The Allies ordered them to continue their occupation of Ukraine as a bulwark against Bolshevism until the future of the country could be decided upon, but the troops were weary of fighting, their governments at home were undergoing revolutions with accompanying loss of discipline, and many of the soldiers were being unsettled by Bolshevik propaganda. Without waiting for orders the soldiers began to return home. Lacking the support of the German troops and with his own small army becoming daily more restive Skoropadsky's regime neared its end. For a time he held on in Kiev with the support of the Russian counterrevolutionists known as the White or Volunteer Army, one of whose officers he made commandant of Kiev.

Western Ukrainian Independence: Meanwhile events in Galicia had resulted in the establishment of a western Ukrainian government there. With the collapse of the Austrian empire in the last weeks of the war, each of its many nationalities began to lay the groundwork for an independent national existence. In Lviv a Ukrainian National Rada was organized under the leadership of Dr. Eugene Petrushevich, which, invoking the principle of self-determination, proclaimed on October 19, 1918, the establishment of a Ukrainian national state comprising all the territories of Austria-Hungary inhabited by Ukrainians, that is, eastern Galicia, northwestern Bukovina, and Carpatho-Ukraine.

On November 1 a Ukrainian Military Command took charge in Lviv, and Huyn, the Austrian governor of Galicia, surrendered his authority to the Ukrainian National Rada, which had already assumed it in the name of the newly proclaimed Western Ukrainian Republic. Poland, however, had also declared its independence and now asserted its intention of reëstablishing a Polish state within its old historic boundaries. As the Polish empire of the sixteenth century had included a good portion of the Ukrainian territories, the Poles laid claim to Ukraine and at once began to overrun eastern Galicia. On November 21 the Ukrainian army was obliged to evacuate Lviv, and the Ukrainian National Rada retired eastward to Ternopil.

Civil War: At this juncture a national revolt broke out in eastern Ukraine against Hetman Skoropadsky. Petlura, the most prominent military officer in Hrushevsky's government, had gathered about him in the no-man's land between Kiev and Galicia an army which included Ukrainian soldiers from Galicia. In coöperation with Vinnichenko he established a headquarters at Bila Tserkva and proclaimed a Ukrainian National Republic governed by a Directory, in opposition to the hetman and as a successor of the defunct Central Rada. There were thus by the beginning of December five forces operating in Ukraine: the White army in the Donets Basin, the Red army with its base at Kharkiv, Petlura's National Republic forces at Bila Tserkva, the Western Ukrainian Republic troops in Galicia, and the Poles near Lviv. Before

the onslaught of Petlura's forces Skoropadsky's resistance collapsed. Abandoned by his Russian White Volunteers, he resigned on December 14, fled from Kiev, and
made his way to Berlin.

Petlura entered Kiev as Skoropadsky left, and prospects now appeared bright for a union of all Ukraine. Petlura sent aid to the government of the hard-pressed Western Ukrainian Republic at Ternopil, which moved to
Stanislaviv and there proclaimed the union of western
and eastern Ukraine. On January 22, 1919, the Directory
accepted the overture and proclaimed at the labor congress assembled in Kiev the establishment of a united
free and independent Ukrainian National Republic by the
merging of the Western Republic and the National Republic, the former being designated the Western Division
of the new state and adopting as its insignia a trident.

The union was, however, short-lived. By this time the
Soviet government was firmly established in Russia and
ready to undertake the reconquest of Ukraine from the
Ukrainian National Republic, and the Whites. Driving a
wedge between Petlura and the Western Division, it
forced the army of the latter into Rumania, where it was
disarmed and interned. Petlura was then obliged to evacuate Kiev, which he did on February 4. In this emergency
he became president of the Directory and also commander-in-chief of the Ukrainian armies, but with actual
control over only a small area northwest of Kiev. He was
joined in July by the army of the Western Division which
had retreated before the Poles to Kaminets-Podolsk,
where a temporary joint capital was established for the
Ukrainian National Republic and its Western Division.

Meanwhile the Bolsheviks had called a convention at
Kharkiv which on May 5 had published the constitution of
a Ukrainian Soviet Socialist Republic as "a free and independent national state." The Red army, however, was
unable to provide a strong defense for Kiev, and on August 31 the city was recaptured by Petlura. Immediately

thereafter, however, the latter had to give up the city to the Russian White army led by Denikin, who was fighting to reëstablish a united Russia and was receiving much aid from the Allies for that purpose. At about this time the spread of typhus decimated the ranks of the Ukrainians. Ravaged by this disease and attacked from all sides by the Whites, the Reds, the Poles, and even the Rumanians in the southeast, the Ukrainian forces began to give way. As a result the administration of the Ukrainian National Republic had to move into Polish-occupied western Ukrainian territory, while the government of the Western Division took refuge in Rumania and eventually settled down in Vienna. And now from its Polish base the National Republic began its so-called "winter campaign."

Meanwhile events of a different character were taking place in southern Ukraine. This area had been the scene of large-scale French investments before the war. Upon the declaration of the Armistice the Austrians withdrew from it, and on December 18, 1918, a French army of about twelve thousand men, having crossed the Black Sea from Rumania, occupied the important port of Odessa. Its announced purpose was to assist the "healthy" forces in restoring order. A White Army officer was appointed as military governor of Odessa. The occupation by the French was a complete failure, as they were unable to aid the Whites to any extent and soon began to quarrel with the landlords who formed the backbone of the White Army government; the French soldiers were also catching the virus of Bolshevism and now that the war was over felt nothing but dislike for their unpleasant duties as police in a country where no one wanted them. To avoid direct war with the Soviets they withdrew on April 6, and the Bolsheviks entered Odessa.

At this time the Bolsheviks were also in possession of Kiev, while in the east they had reduced the Whites to a weak group in the lower Donets Basin. But they still had to suppress new peasant outbreaks that arose under the

actual experience of Soviet rule, and a fresh onslaught set
in motion by the Whites. Through most of 1919 a struggle
went on with the Whites in which the Reds were finally
victorious, largely because Denikin's army made no pretense of hiding its intention to reannex Ukraine to Russia
and reduce it to a mere province. In the path of Denikin's
conquests the Ukrainian language was banned, Ukrainian
newspapers and bookstores were closed, and Russian
alone was permitted in the schools; Ukraine was again
officially named Little Russia. Under simultaneous pressure from Petlura and the Bolsheviks Denikin's movement collapsed.

The most successful of the anarchist peasant bands
which resisted all other forces in southeastern Ukraine
was that of Nestor Makhno, an organizer of extraordinary ability who for many months dominated the Black
Sea steppes from the lower Dnieper to the Don.

It was the Bolsheviks who benefited most immediately
from Denikin's downfall. By the spring of 1920 they were
in control of practically all Ukraine, until Petlura found
a new supporter in Poland. Having reconquered Galicia,
the Poles were eager to put into effect their project of restoring the medieval Polish-Lithuanian empire, and
formed a coalition with Petlura, who saw in the Poles the
only force capable of driving the Bolsheviks from
Ukraine. On April 21 a treaty of peace was signed between Poland and the Ukrainian National Republic which
provided for recognition of Petlura's Directory as the
supreme authority of a Ukrainian National Republic. The
Poles, accompanied by Ukrainian detachments, launched
their "March on Kiev" on April 25, 1920, and at first met
with little resistance. On May 7 the Sixth Division of the
Sichovi Striltsi corps under Bezruchko entered Kiev. The
presence of the Poles, however, proved fatal to Petlura's
cause, for all the quarreling factions in Ukraine united
against these traditional foes.

The Poles had advanced too fast for their supplies to

keep up with them and before the pressure of the Red army they abandoned Kiev and fell back upon Warsaw, followed by the Reds. Although the latter besieged the Poles in their own capital, they too had outrun their supplies; and when the French began to furnish not only materials of war but General Weygand as commander, a deadlock ensued.

A preliminary peace was signed by Poland with the Soviets at Riga, Latvia, on October 12, 1920, which became definitive on March 18, 1921. Two treaties were drawn up. Russia signed one treaty, and the Ukrainian Soviet Socialist Republic, as an independent state, signed another. The line of demarcation between Ukraine and Poland was left about where it had been before the Polish drive was begun, few lives had been lost, and, indeed, as far as Ukraine was concerned the chief result of the whole incident was to ensure the grip of the Soviet government over all eastern Ukraine.

Following the war with Poland a serious rebellion broke out in Ukraine. The peasant anarchist, Makhno, who had assisted the Soviets previously by a revolt against the Whites, now led an uprising against the Reds but was subdued in 1921. Sporadic outbursts continued for a time. But the period of intervention and civil war was past.

The Ukrainian Soviet Socialist Republic: In 1921–22 Soviet Ukraine suffered one of the worst famines in modern history, a result of disorganization following seven years of international and civil war and the resistance of peasants and factory and mine workers to the war communism of the Bolsheviks. One of the periodic droughts which in ordinary times would have meant merely a time of discomfort became the occasion of tragedy. Before aid could be brought by the American Relief Administration and other agencies, several million Ukrainians had died of starvation.

During the civil wars the Bolsheviks tried hard to gain support in Ukraine by promising autonomy, and in fact the treaty of Brest-Litovsk guaranteed Ukraine the status of ''a free and independent country.'' It soon became evident, however, that this was merely a cover for the age-old effort to reduce Ukraine to a Russian province, pushed more strongly than ever by the impact of the Soviet theory of economic centralization.

The first step in the reduction of autonomy was an agreement signed February 22, 1922, by which Soviet Ukraine authorized Soviet Russia to represent it at an international conference at Genoa, after which it became an accepted matter for Soviet Russia to take full control of Ukrainian foreign relations. The next step was to draw up a constitution for a Soviet Union, providing on paper at least for a federal relationship between Ukraine, Russia, and the other members. Adopted December 20, 1922, by the First Congress of the USSR, put into force on July 6, 1923, and finally approved January 31, 1924, it took the form of a treaty among the several states. Although federal in form, the central authority of the Union was assigned much greater powers than the federal government in the United States, and in the parliament Soviet Russia had an overwhelming strength in comparison with Ukraine. Moreover, in the Communist party, which was the real power behind the government, there were comparatively few Ukrainians.

Rumania and Czechoslovakia: While the Soviets were reconquering eastern Ukraine, the other portions had been falling to foreign powers. With the collapse of the Russian empire, Bessarabia became released from its control; and as soon as the Ukrainian Soviet Republic had signed the treaty of Brest-Litovsk on March 3, 1918, Germany and Austria were free to make arrangements with Rumania regarding the future of the province. This was done by permitting Rumania, by the treaty of Bucharest signed in May 1918, immediately to annex Bessarabia with its half-million Ukrainians. With the collapse of Germany at the close of the war a popular revolt broke out resulting in the creation of a Bessarabian Directory which passed resolutions demanding the attachment of Bessarabia to Ukraine. Rumania, however, looked upon Bessarabia as a part of its spoils of war and crushed the revolt.

The other Ukrainian district which Rumania longed to acquire was Bukovina, which had been a part of Austria Hungary. As the Dual Monarchy dissolved, the various nationalities that formed it began to demand self-determination; and on November 3, 1918, the Ukrainians in Bukovina held a huge demonstration at the local capital, Chernivtsi (Cernauti), to demand union with Ukraine. Three days later Ukrainian armed detachments occupied government buildings in the capital and other cities in Ukrainian northern Bukovina, and a Ukrainian Regional Committee was organized which proclaimed Omelian Popovich President of the region. On Armistice Day, however, Rumanian troops pressed in, General Zadik captured Chernivtsi, and Bukovina was declared under official Rumanian occupation.

Neither the Ukrainians of Bessarabia nor those of Bukovina recognized these occupations, and boycotted the Rumanian elections held in the spring of 1919. But when the treaty of St. Germain was signed by Austria and the Allies on September 10, 1919, Rumania received Bessarabia.

The consent of the Allies to Rumanian annexation was made subject to the general guarantees of minority rights common to most of the postwar treaties and the special obligations incurred as a member of the League of Nations: these included promises of equal racial, religious, social, linguistic, and economic treatment of Ukrainians. The Ukrainian population in Rumania was, according to the Rumanian census of 1930, only 452,842, but the figure was quite generally recognized as vastly inferior to the facts, the actual population being probably about a million, divided fairly evenly between Bessarabia and northern Bukovina. It might be added that the guarantees of minority rights by Rumania were honored more in the breach than in the observance; and as the Ukrainian population was less concentrated than elsewhere, it was quite unable to protest effectively or to resist Rumanian efforts at denationalization.

The break-up of Austria Hungary also liberated from Hapsburg rule the half-million Ukrainians of Carpatho-Ukraine, who became incorporated by Czechoslovakia. Consent for this action was obtained by the Czechs from the American Ruska National Rada meeting in Scranton, Pennsylvania, on November 18, 1918. The Ukrainians in Carpatho-Ukraine, however, took a stand for union with Ukraine and published a proclamation to this effect at Hust on January 21, 1919; but on May 5 a National Rada of Carpatho-Ukraine declared itself in favor of incorporation into Czechoslovakia which became an accomplished fact in September by official action of the Czechoslovak government, Carpatho-Ukraine being annexed as an "autonomous unit within the Czechoslovak state."

Poland: By far the most serious Ukrainian problem aside from that of Soviet Ukraine was the question of the relationship of western Ukraine to Poland, involving a struggle between Poland and the Ukrainians in which the Supreme Council of the Allies became an intermediary but with little desire to act. As early as February 28, 1919, an Allied commission under General Berthelmy unsuccessfully made an effort to end the Polish-Ukrainian conflict by suggesting terms of peace; his efforts were resumed by an Inter-Allied Armistice Commission under the presidency of General Botha, which on May 13 drafted a Polish-Ukrainian demarcation line, rejected by the Poles, however. Soon after, General Haller arrived with a Polish army from France, armed and equipped by the Allies, supposedly for use against the Soviets, but actually employed for an offensive against the Ukrainians. On June 25 the Allied Supreme Council authorized the

Poles to occupy eastern Galicia as far as the Zbruch River, but on condition that local autonomy and political and religious freedom be guaranteed the inhabitants. The Ukrainian Galician army then withdrew east of the Zbruch. In November further attempts at settlement were made by a proposal of the Supreme Council that Poland should exercise a mandate over eastern Galicia for a period of twenty-five years, at the end of which time a plebiscite should be held; but Poland flatly rejected this proposal. Shortly after, on December 8, the famous "Curzon Line" was proposed as the eastern boundary of Poland, which would have granted Poland a small Ukrainian area. Again the Poles refused to accede. Meanwhile the Polish authorities conducted mass arrests and trials of Ukrainian participants in the Polish-Ukrainian war, many persons being condemned to death and large numbers sent into concentration camps at Stshalkova, Wadowice, Brest-Litovsk, Dombie, and elsewhere. On January 20, 1920, Poland took a long step toward absorption by abolishing the autonomy of Ukrainian Galicia and the Ukrainian organizations which had existed under Austrian rule there. The very name was changed from Eastern Galicia to Eastern Little Poland.

The boundary established on the Zbruch was broken by the Polish-Soviet war of the summer of 1920, being first overrun by the Poles and then by the Bolsheviks. In September and October it was finally fixed by direct negotiations at Riga* between Poland, Soviet Russia, and Soviet Ukraine.

For a time the Allies refused to recognize this decision regarding western Ukraine taken without their mediation, the Council of the League declaring on February 23, 1921, that "Galicia is beyond the borders of Poland" and that "actually Poland is the military occupant of Galicia," but neither party to the agreement paid any attention. The only concession gained by the Ukrainians was a se-

* See p. 557 above.

ries of guarantees of minority rights similar to those
given by Rumania to the Ukrainians annexed by her, and
equally ineffective. The number of Ukrainians in Poland
was subject to wide variations in estimate, depending
upon the circumstances under which the count was made,
being placed all the way from four to seven millions.

Through 1921 and 1922 feeling among the Ukrainians
under Polish rule ran high, the spearhead of resistance
being the Ukrainian Military Organization (UWO). With
the aid of funds sent by Ukrainian-Americans, a Ukrainian Citizens' Committee was founded in Lviv in 1921 to
provide relief for Ukrainians in internment camps, but in
the autumn it was dissolved and its members placed under arrest. On September 25 a Ukrainian student named
Stephen Fedak attempted to assassinate Marshal Pilsudski and Governor Grabski, and soon afterward Poles
bombed such Ukrainian institutions as the University
Student Home and the headquarters of the Shevchenko
Scientific Society. When a Polish census was taken in November it was boycotted by the Ukrainians, as were elections to the Polish chamber of deputies (*Sejm*) and the
senate. Repressive measures of retaliation were taken by
Poles in the form of terroristic acts. In the summer Metropolitan Andrew Sheptitsky, head of the Ukrainian Uniate Church, returned from a visit to the United States,
was placed in confinement and held from August 22 to October 5. On November 15 the executive committee of the
Ukrainian National Rada, headed by Dr. Eugene Petrushevich, protested to the Allied Supreme Council, the
Council of the League of Nations, and the premiers of
the Allied governments against mass arrests of Ukrainians by Polish authorities, and issued an appeal addressed
to the conscience of the entire civilized world. The introduction of military conscription of Ukrainian inhabitants
by the Polish government met with strong opposition. Finally, in order to obtain the consent of the Allies for the
annexation of eastern Galicia, which was still not forth-

coming, the Polish parliament passed a law on October 26, 1922, providing for limited autonomy for the provinces (*voivodates*) of Lviv, Ternopil, and Stanislaviv, a law which, however, was never really put into effect. The Ukrainian political parties, with headquarters in Lviv, refused to be mollified, and on August 28 unanimously declared their support of the government-in-exile of the Western Division of the Ukrainian National Republic, located in Vienna, under Dr. Petrushevich. It was not until March 14, 1923, that the Conference of Ambassadors representing Great Britain, France, Italy, and Japan made further resistance impossible by recognizing the frontiers of Poland as drawn up in the treaty of Riga and refusing to accept a protest by a delegation from the Ukrainian National Rada of western Ukraine which had hastened to Paris to register objections. Poland was thus confirmed in possession of the Ukrainian districts, not only of eastern Galicia but of all northwestern Ukraine, including Kholm, Polisia, and Volynia. About 35 per cent of Poland was composed of Ukrainian territory.

"Poland thus obtained title to this territory without having to give anything more than a moral pledge in favor of autonomy. No steps have been taken to carry out the unilateral promises made in the autonomy law of September, 1922, and Eastern Galicia is still governed from Warsaw," wrote Raymond Leslie Buell in 1939.[*] A great Ukrainian demonstration against the decision of the Conference of Ambassadors was held in St. George's Square in Lviv, Julian Romanchuk, the dean of Ukrainian leaders, administering to the assembly an oath that the Ukrainian people would never renounce their rights to the independence of their native land.

After the Allies had given their approval to the Polish annexation, the position of Petrushevich and the government of western Ukraine became untenable in Vienna, and because of Polish diplomatic pressure, they moved first to

[*] *Poland: Key to Europe, 1939*, p. 274. Knopf, New York.

Prague and then to Berlin, where they continued their activities chiefly in the form of petitions addressed to the League of Nations. Early in 1924 Petlura moved from Poland to France, where he made his home until his assassination on May 25, 1926, when his place as head of the Ukrainian National Republic in exile was taken by Andrew Levitsky. The Ukrainian Free University was transferred from Vienna to Prague. Here a Ukrainian Pedagogical Institute was founded. Here, too, the Ukrainian Historical and Philological Society and the Union of Ukrainian Physicians of Czechoslovakia became active, while in 1927 a Museum of Ukraine's Struggle for Liberation was established.

Ukraine under the Soviets from the Postwar Treaties to Munich: The civil wars and the famine had left Soviet Ukraine in great need of reconstruction, both material and moral. As a means of restoring production, particularly among the peasants, the New Economic Policy (NEP) of 1921, "a strategic retreat on the economic front," as Lenin called it, was introduced in Ukraine as elsewhere. Even this limited return to capitalism with its restoration of currency, a free market, small-scale manufacturing and trade, and taxes rather than confiscation of grain brought about a startling degree of improvement.

It soon became evident, however, that much of the resistance to Soviet rule was due to the feeling that Ukrainian national culture, for which such high hopes had been raised, was being suppressed. Accordingly a retreat on the cultural front was begun. In 1923 Hrushevsky returned to Soviet Ukraine at the invitation of the authorities, to resume his work as the head of the historical division of the Pan-Ukrainian Academy of Science at Kiev. In 1925 a definite program of "Ukrainianization" was inaugurated along such lines as making Ukrainian the compulsory language of the universities and of the schools. In 1927, however, as an offset to this Ukrainian policy "islands" of Russian, Jewish, German, and Polish national groups were created within Ukraine, and a "Moldavian Autonomous Republic" was established across the Dniester from Bessarabia, where it could serve as an object lesson to Rumanians of the "cultural freedom" permitted by Soviet Russia.

By 1928 the economic crisis which was on the verge of creating great tension in Polish Ukraine had already begun in Soviet Ukraine, where it was artificially stimulated by the export of grains for the purpose of creating balances of foreign exchange with which to buy the machines for the first Five Year Plan. Economic oppression in this and other ways reached such a point that Volobuev, a Russian Communist, protested against the economic exploitation of Ukraine and declared that "the budgetary rights of Ukraine are but a fiction." In the next year economic centralization in the Soviet Union was pushed a step further by the abolition of the Ukrainian Commissariat (Department) of Agriculture and the reduction of the powers of the Commissariat of Education. To all intents and purposes the Ukrainian governmental departments had become mere administrative agencies of the central offices at Moscow. With the introduction of the Five Year Plan for speeding up industrial and agricultural production, rural collectivization was introduced in Ukraine in 1929, great numbers of recalcitrant *kulaks,* or prosperous peasants, being banished to prison camps in the Solovetsky Islands and elsewhere. In the same year the industrial phase of the plan was pushed forward by the beginning of work on the Dnieper electrification project known as the Dnieproges.

The cumulative effect of forced collectivization, industrial speed-up, and economic centralization was an outburst of unrest which the Soviet government attempted to suppress by force. Mass executions without trial took place throughout Ukraine, and a great public trial was held of the Union for the Liberation of Ukraine and its leaders, including Sergius Yefremiv (Jefremov), secre-

tary of the Pan-Ukrainian Academy of Science in Kiev.
"The real reason for bringing a charge against Jefremov,
Czechivsky and others is the desire to destroy the Ukrainian intelligentsia by getting rid of its chief representatives," said the *London Saturday Review* in its issue of
January 18, 1930. "Realizing its failure, Bolshevism has
taken to alternative weapons—terrorism and provocation. By this means it seeks to kill the creative efforts of
Ukrainian culture and that is the real significance of the
present trial." Persecutions of Ukrainian national leaders continued throughout 1932, when a purge of the Academy of Science took place. Skripnik, the Commissar of
Education in Soviet Ukraine, committed suicide in 1933
in protest against Soviet policies there, and in particular
against the export of foodstuffs and the Soviet system of
education.

Again a year of drought coincided with chaotic agricultural conditions; and during the winter of 1932–33 a great
famine, like that of 1921–22, swept across Soviet Ukraine,
again costing the lives of several million men, women,
and children. In the United States Ukrainian-Americans
launched a campaign for the dispatch of an international
commission to report on famine conditions, and protested
against the American recognition of the Soviet Union in
1933.

In 1930 Professor Hrushevsky was arrested and transferred from Kiev to a town near Moscow; he died on November 26, 1934, at Kislovodsk, in the northern Caucasus.
Many Ukrainian intellectuals, especially those who had
worked closely with him, were arrested and thrown into
prison. In the same year the capital of Ukraine was again
removed from Kharkiv to the ancient capital of Kiev.
Even as late as 1937 the suicide of Panas Lubchenko, the
premier of Soviet Ukraine, showed that the Soviet government had failed to achieve a normal status for Ukraine.

*Ukraine under Poland from the Postwar Treaties to
Munich:* Within Poland the struggle for self-government

continued even after recognition by the Allies of Poland's
sovereignty had abandoned them to their own resources;
and before spring Tugut, a member of the Polish chamber, was publicly predicting that unless conditions in Polish-occupied Ukraine improved, a revolt was inevitable.
On February 13 a wave of protest was aroused by the
death in a Polish prison of Olha Bessarabova, a Ukrainian patriot, reputedly from torture and beatings inflicted
by her jailers; in France Painlevé, Herriot, Blum, and
other prominent men protested against the Polish reign
of terror; and a caucus of Ukrainian representatives to
the Polish parliament from Volynia, Kholm, and Polisia
passed a resolution to the effect that "Poland must be rebuilt on the principle of national self-determination." The
reply of the Polish government was a series of laws
passed on July 31 banning the use of the Ukrainian language in central government departments and in those of
autonomous regions.

In 1925 the caucus of Ukrainian delegates in the Polish
parliament, with the backing of the Ukrainian population,
continued its campaign, this time directed against laws
providing for the breaking up of estates and their colonization and settlement, the effect of which was to cause
an artificial inflow of swarms of Polish settlers into the
Ukrainian districts. Late in the summer actual famine
broke out in Polish Ukraine, and Ukrainian-Americans
set up a Hungry Village Relief Committee.

In 1926 the chief project undertaken by the Ukrainians
was the promotion of education. A proposal introduced
in the Polish chamber by Ukrainian representatives for
the establishment of a Ukrainian university was defeated
on February 5, and in the autumn, when Sukovski, the
Polish minister of education, made an interpellation in
the chamber regarding the same problem, he received a
vote of no confidence, as did the minister of the interior,
Mlodzanowski, who had appointed a commission to prepare a political program for Ukraine. By this time one

group of Ukrainians had given up hope of relief through parliamentary processes, and a wave of terrorism was begun by the Ukrainian Military Organization, two of whose members were accused of assassinating a Polish school director named Sobinski in Lviv on October 19.

In Galicia, where Ukrainians had hitherto refrained from public activity, a great Ukrainian Agricultural Fair was held in Striy in 1927, and in the spring of 1928 Ukrainians for the first time participated in elections to the Polish parliament, electing thirty-four representatives to the chamber, where Dr. Dmytro Levitsky, chairman of the Ukrainian caucus, formally declared that the Ukrainian people had not renounced their aspirations for national independence but still clung to the ideal of "a free, independent, and united Ukrainian national state embodying all Ukrainian areas," and that all international treaties and acts in contravention of the right of the Ukrainian people to national self-determination were without legal basis.

Meanwhile organizational activities continued. In 1929 a Ukrainian Scientific Institute was opened in Warsaw. In the same year the Organization of Ukrainian Nationalists (OUN) was founded, which, like its predecessor, the Ukrainian Military Organization, was charged by the Poles with being the backbone of the Ukrainian revolutionary movement.

The year 1930 was one of violence, famine, and repression for Ukrainians both in the Soviet Union and in Poland, intensified by the growing world depression which had particularly affected the peasant populations through the cumulative fall of world grain prices. From the middle of September until the end of November a drastic "pacification" was carried on by Polish authorities in the Ukrainian areas, conducted with the aid of both police and army. Ukrainian libraries and coöperatives were destroyed, the Ukrainian Boy Scout organization dissolved, Ukrainian secondary schools (gymnasia) closed, and thousands of Ukrainians subjected to beatings, torture, and imprisonment. When the Ukrainian Uniate bishopric issued a letter of condemnation of these proceedings, the circular was confiscated by the Polish authorities. In England and America protests mounted.

Frantic appeals by Ukrainian patriots to both the Polish government and the League of Nations under the guarantees of protection to minorities were futile. On January 26, 1931, the Polish chamber rejected an interpellation by Ukrainian representatives regarding the pacification, while the League of Nations withdrew the possibility of support by handing down a decision upholding the Polish authorities on the general grounds that no government could permit violent disobedience, but expressing regret that the victims of pacification had not been reimbursed for their personal injuries and property losses. The struggle, however, had its aftermath. On December 23, two young members of the Ukrainian Military Organization, Vasyl Bilas and Eugene Danylshyn, were sentenced to death and were hanged for their revolutionary activities.

Two years later, on September 13, 1934, Poland officially repudiated the Minorities Treaty signed upon coming into existence, by which she had solemnly pledged herself to respect Ukrainian national liberties, while a group of the British members of parliament sent petitions to the League of Nations requesting relief for the Ukrainians oppressed under Polish rule.

The Organization of Ukrainian Nationalists was the object of attack in 1935, when mass trials of Ukrainian youths were held on charges of membership in the association. Three young Ukrainians were condemned to death for complicity in the assassination of the Polish minister, Pieracki. In spite of an effort on the part of the more conservative Ukrainian groups, organized in the Ukrainian National Democratic League (UNDO), to "normalize" relations with the Polish government, no concessions were won. The plight of the Ukrainians continued to gain sympathy abroad, an interpellation being introduced in the British parliament regarding autonomy for Galicia and Carpatho-Ukraine. The year 1936 saw more mass trials of Ukrainians accused of being members of the Organization of Ukrainian Nationalists, while the Polish authorities took advantage of the conciliatory policy of "normalization" further to harass the Ukrainians, continuing throughout 1937 to close numbers of Ukrainian political, economic, cultural and athletic organizations and introducing a new period of "pacification."

Carpatho-Ukraine: In Czechoslovakia, until the Sudeten revolt the Ukrainians of Carpatho-Ukraine had been regarded as the minority offering the most serious problem for Czechoslovakia, for they had never been granted the self-rule guaranteed at the time of the formation of the state, the Czechs arguing that they were too backward to be given full autonomy for fear of falling under the more developed Hungarians and Jews who had formerly been their masters. By 1928 relations had become so strained that Carpatho-Ukraine was reduced to the status of a province and was renamed "The Province of Sub-Carpathian Rus." It was true that in the field of education the Czechs granted some concessions. In 1935 conditions became very tense, partly as a result of the general economic depression but partly from political causes. In that year Czechoslovakia signed a treaty with the Soviet Union which may well have included an understanding to the effect that Ukrainianism was to be held under check.

The Reunion of Ukraine under the Soviets: During the 1920's and 1930's there had been no single Ukrainian problem but a series of disconnected Ukrainian questions in each of the countries having a Ukrainian minority. Except for the unsettled period at the beginning of the world depression, from 1930 to 1933, when international meddling was blamed for much of the unrest in Polish and Soviet Ukraines, the Soviet Union and Poland and Rumania and Czechoslovakia had each treated its Ukrainian population undisturbed by outside influences. After Hitler's triumph at Munich, however, the large Ukrainian populations of Eastern Europe were thrown into the cauldron of European power politics.

The first Ukrainians to be directly affected by the Munich settlement were those of Carpatho-Ukraine in Czechoslovakia. In October 1938 immediately after the Munich Agreement, the government at Prague granted autonomy to the province of Subcarpathian Rus. A cabinet was appointed by the Prague authorities, at first with Andrew Brody as premier, then under Monsignor Augustin Voloshyn, the leader of the strongest autonomist group, on October 26. Other Ukrainian groups were also given representation. On November 2 the Carpatho-Ukrainians received a staggering blow, when representatives of Germany and Italy met in Vienna to arbitrate the new crisis between Czechoslovakia and Germany; and in addition to making fresh gifts of Czech land to Germany, they turned over to Hungary the heart of Carpatho-Ukraine, including the capital, Uzhorod, and the cities of Mukachev and Koshytsi. Only a part of Carpatho-Ukraine was left free, with Hust as its capital.

Poland not only acquiesced in this seizure but evinced a desire to remove any danger of the remnant of Carpatho-Ukraine from becoming an irredentist focus by annexing it herself. What was left, however, of Carpatho-Ukraine continued its existence for the time being as an autonomous state within a disconnected federation with the other remnants of Czechoslovakia. It received a constitution and restored the name of Carpatho-Ukraine, and the official language of the state and of education became Ukrainian, with Hungarian and Jewish as minority tongues. A private army of twelve thousand men known by the old Kozak army name of the Sich was established.

When Czechoslovakia broke up completely in the spring Carpatho-Ukraine declared its full independence on March 15, 1939, with Voloshyn as president. But on the next day, in spite of appeals to Berlin, Hungarian troops occupied Khust, and in May completed the occupation of the country, meeting with serious resistance by the Sich and by the tough Hutzul peasants who attempted to repeat the terrible destruction they had wrought on Hungarian troops retreating at the close of the World War. Hungary announced the recovery of "Ruthenia," which was assented to by Germany in May, at the time when Bohemia, Moravia, and Slovakia became German protectorates.

President Voloshyn fled with his cabinet into Rumania, to which he offered to surrender his country, but without response. Thus the brief hopes of the Ukrainians of Czechoslovakia for independence came to an unhappy end. The Hungarians are said to have instituted a program of suppression of Ukrainian nationalism, forcing the churches in Uzhorod to carry on services in the Hungarian language and replacing Ukrainian teachers in the schools with Hungarians.

The next Ukrainians to undergo a change of masters were those of Poland, where after Munich the sharpening of nationalist feelings common to all Europe led to further repression of the Ukrainians. The use of the terms "Galicia" and "Galician" was forbidden, and the name of "Little Poland" (Malopolska) was applied in their place; in Lviv Ukrainian Park, the scene of many stirring events in Ukrainian national history, was seized by Polish authorities. The Ukrainian Women's Alliance (*Soyuz Ukrainok*) was dissolved, a proposed Pan-Ukrainian Congress and a Congress of Ukrainian Culture placed under a ban, and the Regeneration (*Vidrozhenia*) Temperance Society visited with persecution. Public demonstrations in western Ukraine on behalf of Carpatho-Ukraine, then undergoing conquest by Hungary, were quelled by a wave of Polish "pacification," against which the Ukrainian Uniate diocese protested. In the Polish Chamber of Deputies a bill introduced by Ukrainian representatives and providing for Ukrainian autonomy under Polish rule was not even considered. In the autumn patriotic meetings were held in the form of a great celebration of 950 years of Christianity in Ukraine.

In the beginning of the year 1939 Ukrainian deputies again introduced a bill for the creation of an autonomous Galician-Volynian state, but the Chamber of Deputies refused to permit even an entry of the bill on its journal. The dissolution of Ukrainian national, cultural, and economic institutions went on apace. From March 28, 1939, when Germany began its threats against Poland, the Ukrainians of eastern Galicia and northwestern Ukraine urged upon the Poles the necessity of ensuring the loyal support of the Ukrainians by putting into effect the long-promised autonomy. The Polish government, however, refused to comply. When Hitler's steamroller drove across Poland in September, one of the chief lines of invasion was through Ukraine, and when the campaign was over his army was in complete occupation of eastern Galicia. On September 28 the Soviets, in accordance with an agreement with Germany for partitioning Poland, occupied western Ukraine. After considerable negotiation Germany and the Soviet Union finally fixed upon a line of demarcation, and the German troops withdrew westward, leaving practically all the Ukrainian districts of Poland in the hands of the Soviet Union. On October 27 the provisional "Popular Assembly" of western Ukraine issued a declaration of union with Soviet Ukraine. On November 1, 1939, at a festive session of the Supreme Soviet of the USSR at Moscow, "representatives" of western Ukraine requested admission into the Soviet Union, which was formally granted, and by the law of the same date these provinces were definitely attached to the Ukrainian Soviet Socialist Republic. On December 24, 1939, elections to local governing bodies were held throughout Soviet western Ukraine. The elections of the deputies from western Ukraine to the Supreme Soviet of the Ukrainian SSR as well as to the Supreme Soviet of the USSR were held on March 24, 1940.

Rumanian Ukraine was still to be accounted for. In

1928 a resurgence of Ukrainian activity had made its appearance in Rumania, where the Ukrainian National party in Bukovina took the lead in the struggle for Ukrainian national rights. Ukrainians began to participate in national elections, and Ukrainian newspapers, hitherto banned, began to appear.

The Munich Agreement had an immediate reaction upon the Ukrainians in Rumania. The publication of Ukrainian newspapers was again forbidden. Nevertheless, it was not until 1940 that a change of boundaries took place, when on June 27 the Soviet government demanded the surrender of both Bessarabia and northern Bukovina, and on the next day Soviet troops occupied both provinces, perhaps to forestall German occupation and use as a springboard for a campaign to free Soviet Ukraine. Only northern Bukovina and northern Bessarabia, however, were formally attached to the Ukrainian Soviet Socialist Republic; this was done on August 2, 1940. The rest of Bessarabia was made into a Moldavian Soviet Socialist Republic. Thus by the autumn of 1940 Ukraine was reunited although under Soviet rule.

A future independent Ukraine can be foreseen only as the result of some great cataclysm shaking Eastern Europe. Nevertheless, it must be borne in mind that the Ukrainian national area, that is, the area in which a majority of the inhabitants are Ukrainians, occupies over 360,000 square miles, with a total population of some sixty million, more than forty million of whom are Ukrainians; of these over thirty-five million are now united in a single Ukrainian Soviet Republic. Illusory though the self-government of these Ukrainians may be, their great number, their patient struggle, and the experience of a generation of recognition of national culture and language make it appear impossible for the legitimate claims of a now fully self-conscious people to be disregarded in the future as they have been throughout their long and tragic history.

APPENDIX

1. KIEVAN PRINCES AND KINGS*

1. Oleh	913? or	914?
2. Ihor	914? –	945?
3. Olha, as regent	946? –	960?
4. Sviatoslav, son of Ihor	960? –	972
5. Yaropolk, son of Sviatoslav	972 –	978
6. Volodimir, son of Sviatoslav	979 –	1015
7. Sviatopolk, son of Volodimir	1015 –	1019
8. Yaroslav, son of Volodimir	1019 –	1054
9. Iziaslav, son of Yaroslav	1054 –	1068
10. Vseslav, of the Polotsk dynasty	1068 –	1069
11. Iziaslav (9), second time	1069 –	1073
12. Sviatoslav, son of Yaroslav	1073 –	1076
13. Iziaslav (9), third time	1076 –	1078
14. Vsevolod, son of Yaroslav	1078 –	1093
15. Sviatopolk, son of Iziaslav	1093 –	1113
16. Volodimir Monomakh, son of Vsevolod	1113 –	1125
17. Mstislav, son of Volodimir Monomakh	1125 –	1132
18. Yaropolk, son of Volodimir Monomakh	1132 –	1139
19. Viacheslav, son of Volodimir Monomakh	1139	
20. Vsevolod, grandson of Sviatoslav (12), of the Chernihiv dynasty	1139 –	1146
21. Ihor, brother of Vsevolod (20)	1146	
22. Iziaslav, son of Mstislav (17)	1146 –	1149
23. George, son of Volodimir Monomakh	1149 –	1150
24. Iziaslav (22), second time	1150	
25. George (23), second time	1150	
26. Iziaslav (22) and Viacheslav (19), jointly	1150 –	1154
27. Rostislav, brother of Iziaslav (22)	1154	
28. Iziaslav, grandson of Sviatoslav (12), of the Chernihiv dynasty	1154 –	1155
29. George (23), third time	1155 –	1157
30. Iziaslav (28), second time	1157 –	1158

* Figures in parentheses in this and the following table indicate the serial number under which the prince is first mentioned.

31. Rostislav (27), second time	1159	– 1161
32. Iziaslav (28), third time	1161	
33. Rostislav (27), third time	1161	– 1167
34. Mstislav, son of Iziaslav (22)	1167	– 1169
35. Hlib, son of George (23)	1169	– 1171
36. Volodimir, son of Volodimir Monomakh (16)	1171	
37. Roman, son of Rostislav (27)	1171	
38. Mikhalko, son of George (23), of the Suzdal dynasty	1172	
39. Rurik, son of Rostislav (27)	1173	
40. Yaroslav, son of Iziaslav (22)	1174	
41. Roman (37), second time	1175	– 1176
42. Sviatoslav, son of Vsevolod (20), of the Chernihiv dynasty	1176	– 1180
43. Rurik (39), second time	1180	– 1181
44. Sviatoslav (42), second time	1181	– 1194
45. Rurik (39), third time	1194	– 1200?
46. Ingvar, son of Yaroslav (40)	1200?	– 1202
47. Rurik (39), fourth time	1203	
48. Rostislav, son of Rurik (39)	1204	– 1205
49. Rurik (39), fifth time	1205	– 1206
50. Vsevolod Chermny, son of Sviatoslav (42), of the Chernihiv dynasty	1206	
51. Rurik (39), sixth time	1206	
52. Vsevolod Chermny (50), second time	1207	
53. Rurik (39), seventh time	1207	– 1210
54. Vsevolod Chermny (50), third time	1210	– 1212
55. Ingvar (46), second time	1212	
56. Mstislav, son of Roman (37)	1212	– 1223
57. Volodimir, son of Rurik (39)	1223	– 1234
58. Iziaslav, son of Mstislav (56)	1235	
59. Volodimir (57), second time	1236	
60. Yaroslav, grandson of George (23), of the Suzdal dynasty	1236	– 1238
61. Michael, son of Vsevolod Chermny (50), of the Chernihiv dynasty	1238	– 1239
62. Rostislav, son of Mstislav (56)	1239	
63. Daniel of Galicia	1240	
64. Michael (61), second time	1241	– 1246
65. Yaroslav (60), second time	1246	

2. PRINCES OF GALICIA AND GALICIA-VOLYNIA

1. Boris, son of Volodimir the Great of Kiev		
2. Vsevolod, son of Volodimir the Great of Kiev		
3. Rostislav, son of Volodimir, grandson of Yaroslav of Kiev, expelled from Galicia	1064	
4. Yaropolk, son of Iziaslav of Kiev	1077	– 1084
5. Rurik, Volodar, Vasilko, sons of Rostislav (3)	1084	– 1124
6. Volodimirko, son of Volodar (5)	1124	– 1152
7. Yaroslav, son of Volodimirko (6)	1152	– 1187
8. Oleh and Volodimir, sons of Yaroslav (7)	1187	– 1188
9. Roman, son of Mstislav, Prince of Volynia	1188	– 1189
10. Volodimir (8), second time	1189	– 1199?
11. Roman (9), second time	1199?	– 1205
12. Daniel, son of Roman (9)	1205	– 1206
13. Volodimir, son of Ihor, of the Chernihiv dynasty	1206	– 1208
14. Roman, brother of Volodimir (13)	1208	– 1209
15. Rostislav, son of Rurik of Kiev	1210	
16. Roman (14), second time	1210	
17. Volodimir (13), second time	1210	– 1211
18. Daniel (12), second time	1211	– 1212
19. Mstislav Nimiy, of the Volynian dynasty	1212	– 1213
20. Volodislav, nobleman (*boyarin*) of Galicia	1213	– 1214
21. Koloman, Crown Prince of Hungary	1214	– 1219
22. Mstislav the Daring, of the Kiev-Smolensk dynasty	1219	
23. Koloman (21), second time	1219	– 1221?
24. Mstislav (22), second time	1221?	– 1227
25. Andrew, Crown Prince of Hungary	1227	– 1230
26. Daniel (12), third time	1230	– 1232
27. Andrew (25), second time	1232	– 1233
28. Daniel (12), fourth time	1233	– 1235
29. Michael and his son Rostislav, of the Chernihiv dynasty	1236	– 1238
30. Daniel (12), fifth time	1238	– 1264
31. Leo, son of Daniel (12)	1264	– 1300?
32. George, son of Leo (31)	1300?	– 1308?

33. Leo, son of George (32)   1308? – 1323
34. George-Boleslav, of the Mazovian dynasty   1325 – 1340
35. Liubart, of the Lithuanian dynasty   1340 – 1349

3. GENEALOGY OF UKRAINIAN PRINCES OF THE KIEVAN DYNASTY

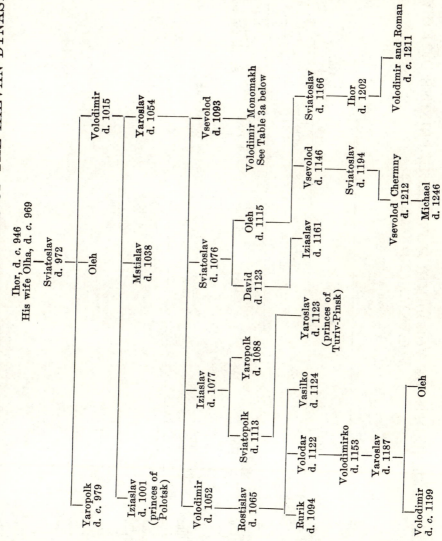

3a. DESCENDANTS OF VOLODIMIR MONOMAKH, PRINCES OF KIEV, VOLYNIA, AND GALICIA

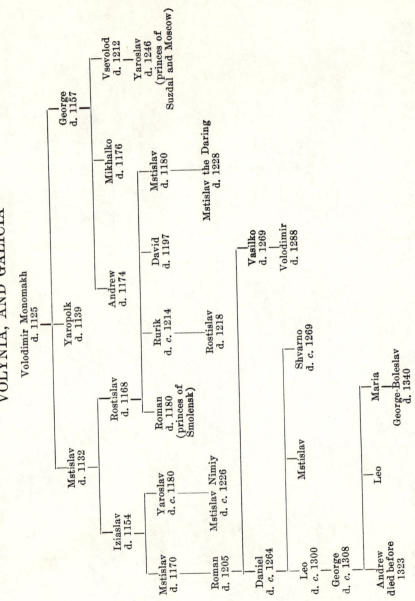

4. GENEALOGY OF UKRAINIAN PRINCES OF THE LITHUANIAN DYNASTY

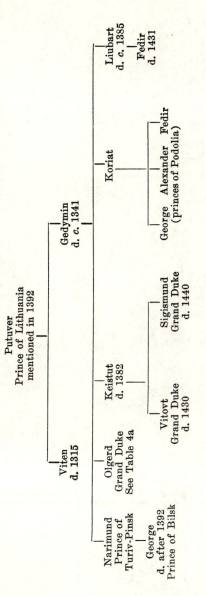

Putuver
Prince of Lithuania
mentioned in 1392

Viten
d. 1315

Gedymin
d. c. 1341

Narimund
Prince of
Turiv-Pinsk

George
d. after 1392
Prince of Bilsk

Olgerd
Grand Duke
See Table 4a

Keistut
d. 1382

Vitovt
Grand Duke
d. 1430

Sigismund
Grand Duke
d. 1440

Koriat

George Alexander Fedir
(princes of Podolia)

Liubart
d. c. 1385

Fedir
d. 1431

4a. DESCENDANTS OF OLGERD

Olgerd
d. 1377

Dmitro
Prince of
Briansk
d. 1377

princes
Trubetskoy

Constantine
Prince of
Chortoreisk

princes
Chortoreisky

Volodimir
Prince of
Kiev
d. after
1398

Olelko
of Kiev
d. 1454

Semen
of Kiev
d. 1470
Prince of
Slutsk

Michael
d. 1481

Dmitro
Koribut
Prince of
Chernihiv
d. after
1404

Fedir
Prince
of
Ratno

Skirhailo
Prince of
Kiev
d. 1397

Yagello
Grand
Duke
d. 1434

Svitrihailo
Grand
Duke
d. 1452

Volodislav
(Wladyslaw)
King of
Poland
d. 1444

Casimir
Grand Duke
of
Lithuania
and King
d. 1492

John Albrecht
King of
Poland
d. 1501

Alexander
Grand Duke
of Lithuania
and King
d. 1506

Sigismund
Grand Duke
and King
d. 1548

Sigismund August
Grand Duke
and King
d. 1572

5. HETMANS OF UKRAINE*

Dmitro Vishnevetsky	1550 – 1563
Bohdan Ruzhinsky, mentioned in the years	1575 – 1576
Shakh	1576 – 1577
Lucian Chorninsky?	1578
Sameilo Zborovsky	c. 1581
Michael and Kirik Ruzhinsky	1585
Zakhar? Kulaha, Bohdan Mikoshinsky, Lucian Chorninsky	1586
Voitikh Chanovitsky	1590
Christopher Kosinsky	1591 – 1593
Gregory Loboda, at intervals	1593 – 1596
Bohdan Mikoshinsky, summer	1594
Fedir Polous, spring	1595
Matvey Shaula, early in	1596
Krempsky and Christopher Nechkovsky, summer	1596
Hnat Vasilevich	1596 – 1597
Tikhon Baibuza and Fedir Polous	1598
Sameilo Kishka	1600 – 1602
Gavrilo Krutnevich, at intervals	1602 – 1603
Ivan Kutskovich	1602
Ivan Kosiy	1602 – 1603
Gregory Izapovich, mentioned at close of	1606
Zborovsky, Olevchenko, Kalenik Andrievich	1609 – 1610
Gregory Tiskinevich, mentioned in May	1610
Peter Sahaidachny, at intervals	1614? – 1622
Dmitro Barabash, March	1617
Yatsko Nerodich Borodavka	1619 – 1621
Olifer Holub	1622 – 1623
Michael Doroshenko, at intervals	1623 – 1625
Hritsko Savich Chorny	1624
Kalenik Andrievich	1624 – 1625
Pirsky, Zhmailo	1625

* Since the power of the hetmans developed spontaneously, there are various dates at which the list of Kozak chieftains can be begun, depending upon one's view of them as the forerunners of the later hetmans. This list begins with Vishnevetsky because little is known of previous leaders and because from his time on, although it is often impossible to distinguish between lesser chiefs and universally acknowledged hetmans, there is nevertheless an uninterrupted succession.

Michael Doroshenko	1625 – 1628
Hritsko Savich Chorny, Ivan Sulima	1628
Hritsko Savich Chorny	1629 – 1630
Taras Fedorovich	1630
Timothy Orendarenko	1630 – 1631
Ivan Petrazhitsky-Kulaha	1631 – 1632
Andrey Didenko	1632
Timothy Orendarenko	1633 – 1634
Ivan Sulima	1635
Vasyl Tomilenko	1636 – 1637
Sava Kononovich, Pavliuk But, Dmitro Hunia	1637
Yatsko Ostrianin, Dmitro Hunia	1638
Bohdan Khmelnitsky	1648 – 1657
Ivan Vyhovsky	1657 – 1659
George Khmelnitsky	1659 – 1663
Paul Teteria, western (right bank) Ukraine	1663 – 1665
Ivan Brukhovetsky, eastern (left bank) Ukraine	1663 – 1668
Stepan Opara, western Ukraine	1665
Peter Doroshenko	1665 – 1676
Sukhovienko, Zaporozhe	1668
Demko Mnohohrishny, eastern Ukraine	1668 – 1672
Michael Khanenko, western Ukraine	1670 – 1674
Ivan Samoilovich	1672 – 1687
Ivan Mazepa	1687 – 1709
Ivan Skoropadsky	1709 – 1722
(Philip Orlik	1710 –)
Danilo Apostol	1727 – 1734
Cyril Rozumovsky	1750 – 1764

BIBLIOGRAPHY

A. History of Ukraine. Works in Ukrainian, English, and other Languages.

1. Ukrainian Historiography and Historical Bibliography

Bahaly, D., *Outline of Ukrainian Historiography* (Нарис Української історіографії). Kiev, 1923-25. 2 vols. (In Ukrainian.)
—— ed., *Bibliography of Ukrainian History for the Years 1917-27* (Бібліографія Історії України за 1917-27). Kharkiv, 1929. (In Ukrainian.)
Czubatyj, N. (Chubaty, M.), "Literatur der Geschichte des ukrainischen Rechtes," *Revue d'Histoire du Droit* January-March, 1930. Lviv.
Doroshenko, D., "Die Namen Rus', Russland, Ukraine in ihrer historischen und gegenwärtigen Bedeutung," *Berichte Ukr. Wissen. Institutes,* Vol 3. Berlin, 1931.
—— *Survey of Ukrainian Historiography* (Огляд Української історіографії). Prague, 1923. (In Ukrainian.)
Hrushevsky, M., "The Traditional Scheme of 'Russian History' and the Problem of a Rational Organization of the History of the Eastern Slavs" (Звічайна схема «русскої історії» и справа раціонального уклада історії східнього славянства), *Symposium of Slavonic Studies* (Сборник статей по славяноведѣнію), Vol. 1. St. Petersburg (Leningrad), 1904. (In Ukrainian.)

2. General Works on Ukrainian History

Allen, W. E. D., *The Ukraine.* Cambridge, 1940.
Antonovich, D., *Abridged Course in the History of Ukrainian Art* (Скорочений курс Історії Українського Мистецтва). Prague, 1923. (In Ukrainian.)
Bidermann, H. I., *Die Ungarischen Ruthenen, ihr Wohngebiet, Erwerb, und ihre Geschichte.* Innsbruck, 1862-67. 2 vols.
Doroshenko, D., *History of the Ukraine.* Edmonton, 1940.
Efimenko, A., *History of the Ukrainian People* (История украинскаго народа). St. Petersburg (Leningrad), 1906. 2 vols. (In Russian.)

Hrinchenko, M., *History of Ukrainian Music* (Історія Української Музики). Kharkiv, 1922. (In Ukrainian.)

Hrouchevskyi (Hrushevsky), M., *Abrégé d'histoire de l'Ukraine.* Paris, 1920.

Hruschewsky (Hrushevsky), M., *Geschichte des ukrainischen Volkes.* Leipzig, 1906.

—— *History of Ukraine-Rus* (Історія України-Руси). Lviv and Kiev. 1898-1937. 10 vols. (to 1658). (In Ukrainian.)

—— *History of Ukrainian Literature* (Історія Української Литератури). Lviv and Kiev, 1923. 3 vols. (In Ukrainian.)

Kripiakevich, I., *History of Ukrainian Culture* (Історія Української Культури). Lviv, 1938. (In Ukrainian.)

—— and Hnatevich, B., *History of the Ukrainian Army* (Історія Українського Війска). Lviv, 1936. (In Ukrainian.)

Krupnyckyj (Krupnitsky), B., *Geschichte der Ukraine.* Berlin. 1939.

Lashchenko, R., *Lectures on the History of Ukrainian Law* (Лекції по Історії Українського Права), 2 pts. Prague, 1923-24. (In Ukrainian.)

Makary, Metropolitan, *History of the Russian Church* (История Русской Церкви). Moscow, 1868-84. 12 vols. (In Russian.)

Pelesch, J., *Geschichte der Union der Ruthenischen Kirche mit Rom.* Vienna, 1879-81. 2 vols.

Sichinsky, V., *Monumenta Architecturae Ucrainae.* Prague, 1940.

Sichinski (Sichinsky), V., *Monumenta Architecturae Ucrainae.* Prague, 1940. (In Ukrainian.)

Tisserand, R., *La Vie d'un Peuple: l'Ukraine.* Paris, 1933.

3. Prehistory

Pasternak, Y., "Brief Archeology of the West-Ukrainian Lands" (Коротка Археольогія Західно-Українських Земель), *Theology* (Богословія), January-February, 1932. Lviv. (In Ukrainian.)

Rostovtzeff, M., *Iranians and Greeks in South Russia.* Oxford, 1922.

—— "Les Origines de la Russie Kievienne," *Revue des Etudes Slaves,* Vol. 2. Paris, 1922.

Spitsyn, A., "The Dispersal of the Ancient Russian Tribes according to Archeological Data" (Разселеніе древне-русскихъ племенъ по археологическимъ даннымъ), *Journal of the Ministry of Public Instruction* (Журналъ Министерства

Народного Просвѣщенія), Vol. 8 (January, 1899). (In Russian.)

4. Early Period, to 1340

Baumgarten, N. de, *Généalogies et Mariages Occidentaux des Rurikides Russes du X au XIII Siècle.* Rome, 1928.

Borschak, E., "Early Relations between England and Ukraine," *Slavonic Review,* Vol. 10 (June, 1931), pp. 138-160.

Chubaty, M., "Western Ukraine and Rome in the Thirteenth Century" (Західна Україна и Рим в XIII віці), *Transactions of the Shevchenko Scientific Society* (Записки Наук. Тов. ім Щевченка), Vols. 123-124. Lviv. (In Ukrainian.)

Golubinsky, E., *History of the Russian Church* (Исторія Русской Церкви), Vol. 1. Moscow, 1901-04. (In Russian.)

Hrushevsky, M., *History of Ukraine-Rus* (Історія України-Руси), Vols. 1-3. Lviv and Kiev, 1898-1905. (In Ukrainian.)

Leib, B., *Rome, Kiev et Byzance à la fin du XI Siècle.* Paris, 1924.

Parkhomenko, V., *Foundations of Historical Governmental Life in Ukraine* (Початок Історично-Державного життя на Украіні). Kiev, 1925. (In Ukrainian.)

—— *Origins of Christianity in Rus* (Начало Христіянства на Руси). Poltava, 1913. (In Russian.)

Sichinsky, V., *Architecture of the Old Kiev Period* (Архитектура Старокиївської Доби). Prague, 1926. (In Ukrainian.)

Taube, M. A., "Rome and Rus in the pre-Mongol Period" (Рим и Русь въ Домонгольскомъ Періодѣ), *Catholic Journal* (Католическій Временникъ), Vol. 2. Paris, 1928. (In Russian.)

Tomashivsky, S., *Ukrainian History* (Українська Історія), Pt. 1. Lviv, 1919. (In Ukrainian.)

Vozniak, M., *History of Ukrainian Literature* (Історія Украінської Літератури), Vol. I. Lviv, 1920. (In Ukrainian.)

5. Ukraine under Lithuanian Domination, Fourteenth and Fifteenth Centuries.

Cherkavsky, I., "The Communal (Kopny) Court in Ukraine-Rus in the Sixteenth to Eighteenth Centuries" (Громадський [Копний] Суд на України-Руси XI-XVIII вв.), in *Transactions of the Commission on Ukrainian Law of the Ukrainian Academy of Science* (Комісія Українського права, Всеукраїнська Академія Наук), Vols. 4, 5. Kiev, 1928. (In Ukrainian.)

Chubaty, M., "The Legal Status of the Ukrainian Lands of the Lithuanian-Rus State toward the Close of the Fourteenth Century" (Правне Становище Українських Земель Литовсько-Русскої Держави пид кінец XIV-го ст.), *Transactions of the Shevchenko Scientific Society* (Записки Наук. Тов. ім.Шевченка), Vols. 134-135, 144-145. Lviv, 1924-26. (In Ukrainian.)

Halecki, O., "L'Evolution historique de l'Union Polono-Lithuanienne," *Le Monde Slave*, 1926.

Hrushevsky, M., *History of Ukraine* (Історія України-Руси), Vols. 4-6. Kiev and Lviv, 1903-07. (In Ukrainian.)

Kolankowski, L., *History of the Grand Duchy of Lithuania* (Dzieje Wielkiego Ksiestwa Litewskiego), Vol. 1. Warsaw, 1930. (In Polish.)

Lashchenko, R., "The Lithuanian Statute as a Monument of Ukrainian Law" (Литовский Статут як памятник Українського Права), *Scientific Collections of the Ukrainian University in Prague* (Науковий збірник Укр. Университету в Празі), Vol. 1. Prague, 1923. (In Ukrainian.)

Liubavsky, M., *Outline of the History of the Lithuanian-Rus State* (Очеркъ Историі Литовско-Русскаго Государства). Moscow, 1915. (In Russian.)

Pfitzner, I., *Grossfürst Witold von Lithauen als Staatsmann.* Brünn, 1930.

Picheta, V., *The Agrarian Reform of Sigismund-August in the Lithuanian-Rus State* (Аграрная Реформа Сигизмунда Августа в Литовско-Русском Государстве). Moscow, 1917. (In Russian.)

Vladimirsky-Budanov, M., "German Law in Poland and Lithuania" (Нѣмецкое Право въ Польшѣ и Литвѣ), *Journal of the Ministry of Public Instruction* (журналъ Мин. Нар. Просвѣщенія). (August, December, 1868.) (In Russian.) In Ukrainian in *Ukrainian Historical Library* (Укр. Истор. Біблiотека), Vols. 23-24. Lviv, 1903-04.

6.   Ukraine under Polish Domination (1340-1648)

Beauplan, Sieur de, *A Description of the Ukraine,* in *Collection of Voyages and Travels.* London, 1704, 1752 eds.

Bednov, V., *The Orthodox Church in Poland and Lithuania* (Православная Церковь въ Польшѣ и Литвѣ). Ekaterinoslav, 1908. (In Russian.)

Chodynicki, K., *The Orthodox Church and the Polish Republic, 1370-1632* (Kosiół Prawosławny a Rzeczpospolita Polska, 1370-1632). Warsaw, 1934. (In Polish.)

Golubev, S., *The Metropolitan Peter Mohila and his Collaborators* (Митрополитъ Петръ Могила и его сподвижники). Kiev, 1883, 1898. 2 vols. (In Russian.)

Hrushevsky, M., *History of the Ukrainian Kozak Host* (Исторія Украинскаго Казачества), Vol. 1. Kiev, 1913. (In Russian.)

—— *History of Ukraine-Rus* (Історія України-Руси), Vols. 4-7. Lviv and Kiev, 1905-09. (In Ukrainian.)

—— *The National and Cultural Movement in Ukraine in the Sixteenth to Eighteenth Centuries* (Культурно-Національный Рух на України в XVI-XVIII вв.). Vienna, 1919. (In Ukrainian.)

Jablonowski, A., *History of Southern Rus to the Fall of the Republic* (Historya Rusi Poludniowej do upadku Rzeczypospolitej). Cracow, 1912. (In Polish.)

Jubilee Book in Celebration of the 300th Anniversary of the Death of the Metropolitan Ipatiy Potiy (Ювилейна книга в 300-літні роковини смерти митр. Ипатія Потія). Lviv, 1914. (In Ukrainian.)

Kamanin, I., "Sketch of the Hetmancy of Peter Sahaidachny" (Очеркъ Гетманства Петра Сагайдачнаго), *Lectures of the "Chronicler Nestor" Society* (Чтенія въ об. Нестора Лѣтописца). Vol. 15. 1901. (In Russian.)

Kharlampovich, P., *West-Russian Orthodox Schools in the Sixteenth Century and the Beginning of the Seventeenth* (Западно-Русскія Православныя Школы XVI и начала XVII вв.). Kazan, 1898. (In Russian.)

Klimenko, P., *Guilds in Ukraine* (Цехи на Україні), Vol. 1. Kiev, 1929. (In Ukrainian.)

Krilovsky, A., "The Lviv Stavropihial Brotherhood" (Львовское Ставропигіальное Братство), *Archives of Southwestern Russia* (Архивъ Юго-Западной Россіи), Pt. 1, Vol. 10. Kiev, 1904. (In Russian.)

Kripiakevich, I., "The Kozak Host and Batory's Grants" (Козаччина и Баторієві Вольности), *Sources of the History of Ukraine-Rus* (Жерела до Історії України-Руси), Vol. 8. Lviv, 1908. (In Ukrainian.)

—— "The Ruthenians at Lviv in the First Half of the Sixteenth Century" (Русини у Львові в І. половині XVI в.), *Transactions of the Shevchenko Scientific Society* (Записки Наук. Тов. ім. Шевченка), Vols. 77-79. Lviv, 1909. (In Ukrainian.)

Levitsky, O. and Antonovich, V., "Studies in Church Relations in Ukraine" (Розвідки про Церковні Відносини на Україні), in *Ukrainian Historical Library* (Українська-Історична Бібліотека), Vol. 8. Lviv, 1900. (In Ukrainian.)

Lewicki, A., "The Florentine Union in Poland" (Unia Florencka w Polsce), *Transactions of the Academy of Science* (Rozprawy Akademii Umiejętności), Vol. 37. Cracow, 1899. (In Polish.)

Likowski, E., *The Union of Brest* (Unia Brzeska). Posen, 1896. (In Polish.)

Linnichenko, I., *Sketches from the Social History of Galician Rus in the Fourteenth and Fifteenth Centuries* (Черты изъ исторіи сословій Галицкой Руси XIV-XV вв.). Moscow, 1894. (In Russian.)

Lozinski, W., *By Law and Lawlessness* (Prawem i Lewem). Lviv, 1903. (In Polish.)

Šmurlo, E., *Le Saint-Siège et l'Orient Orthodoxe Russe, 1609-54.* Prague, 1928.

Szaraniewicz, I., *Outline of Internal Relations in Eastern Galicia in the Second Half of the Fifteenth Century* (Rys wewnętrznych stosunków w Galicyi Wschodniej w drugiej polowie piętnastego wieku). Lviv, 1869.

Vasilenko, N., *Studies in the History of Western Rus and Ukraine* (Очерки по исторіи Западной Руси и Украины). Kiev, 1916. (In Russian.)

Zhukovich, P., *The Parliamentary Struggle of the Orthodox West-Russian Nobility Against the Church Union to 1609* (Сеймовая Борьба Православнаго Западно-Русскаго Дворянства съ церковной Уніей до 1609 г.). St. Petersburg (Leningrad), 1903-12. 6 vols. (In Russian.)

7. The Period of the Ukrainian Kozak State (1648-1782)

Antonovich, V., "Studies in the National Movements in Ukraine" (Розвідки про Народні Рухи на Україні), *Ukrainian His-*

torical Library (Українська Істор. Бібліотека), Vol. 19. Lviv, 1897. (In Ukrainian.)

Bahaly, D., *The History of Slobidska (Free Settlement) Ukraine* (Исторія Слободської України). Kharkiv, 1918. (In Ukrainian.)

Borschak, E. and Martel, R., *Vie de Mazepa*. Paris, 1931.

Doroshenko, D., "Mazepa, Sein Leben und Wirken," *Zeitschrift für Ost-Europäische Geschichte*, July, 1933.

Evarnitsky, D., *History of the Zaporozhian Kozaks* (Исторія Запорожскихъ Козаковъ), Vols. 1-3. St. Petersburg (Leningrad), 1900, 1895, 1897. (In Russian.)

Harasimchuk, V., "Vyhovsky and George Khmelnitsky" (Виговський і Юрій Хмельницький), *Transactions of the Shevchenko Scientific Society* (Записки Наук. Тов. ім. Шевченка), Vols. 59-60. Lviv, 1904.

—— "Vyhovsky and the Hadiach Union" (Виговський і Гадяцький Трактат), *Transactions of the Shevchenko Scientific Society* (Записки Наук. Тов. ім. Шевченка), Vols. 87-89. Lviv, 1909. (In Ukrainian.)

Hrushevsky, M., *History of Ukraine* (Історія України), Vols. 8-10. Kiev, 1922-37. (In Ukrainian.)

—— "A Secret Mission of a Ukrainian to Berlin in 1791" (Тайна Місія Українця в Берліні 1791), *Transactions of the Shevchenko Scientific Society* (Записки Наук. Тов. ім. Шевченка), Vol. 9. Lviv, 1896. (In Ukrainian.)

Kistiakovsky, A., *The Law According to Which the Little-Russian People Are Judged* (Права, по которымъ судится Малороссійскій Народъ). Kiev. 1879. (In Russian.)

Korduba, M., "Der Ukraine Niedergang und Aufschwung," *Zeitschrift für Ost-Europäische Geschichte*, Vol. 4. Berlin, 1932-34.

Kostomarov, N., *Bohdan Khmelnitsky* (Богданъ Хмельницкій), in *Collected Works* (Собраніе Сочиненій), Vol. IV. St. Petersburg, 1904. (In Russian.) In Ukrainian in *Rus Historical Library* (Руська Історична Бібліотека), Vols. XI-XII. Ternopil, 1888-89.

—— *Mazepa and his Followers* (Мазепа и Мазепинцы), *Collected Works* (Собраніе Сочиненій), Bk. 6. St. Petersburg (Leningrad), 1905. (In Russian.) Also in *Ukrainian Historical*

Library (Українська Історична Бібліотека), Vols. 17-18. Lviv, 1895-96. (In Ukrainian.)

———*The Ruin: the Hetmancy of Brukhovetsky* (Руина. Гетманство Бруховецкаго), *Collected Works* (Собраніе Сочиненій), Bk. 6, St. Petersburg (Leningrad), 1905. (In Russian.) Also in *Ukrainian Historical Library* (Українськао Істор. Бібліотека), Vols. 14-16. Ternopil, 1892-94 (In Ukrainian.)

Kostruba, T., *Hetman Ivan Skoropadsky* (Гетьман Иван Скоропадський). Lviv, 1932. (In Ukrainian.)

Kripiakevich, I., "Studies in the Government of Bohdan Khmelnitsky" (Студи над Державою Богдана Хмельницкого), *Transactions of the Shevchenko Scientific Society* (Записки Наук. Тов. ім. Шевченка), Vols. 129, 130, 134-135, 140, 147, 151. Lviv, 1920-31. (In Ukrainian.)

Krupnitsky, B., *Hetman Philip Orlik* (Гетьман Пилип Орлик). Warsaw, 1938. (In Ukrainian.)

Kubala, L., *Historical Sketches* (Szkice Historyczne), Vols. 1-2. Warsaw, 1923. (In Polish.)

Lazarevsky, A., *The Little-Russian Peasants, 1648-1783* (Малороссійскіе Посполитые Крестьяне, 1648-1783). Kiev, 1908. (In Russian.)

Likowski, E., *History of the Uniate Church in Lithuania and Rus* (Dzieje Kosciola Unickiego na Litwe i Rusi). Warsaw, 1914. (In Polish.)

Lipinski, W. (Lipinsky, V.), *Out of the Past of Ukraine* (Z dziejów Ukrainy). Cracow, 1912. (In Polish.)

Lipinsky, V., *Ukraine at the Turning Point, 1657-59* (Україна на Переломі, 1657-59). Vienna, 1920. (In Ukrainian.)

Marshall, J., *Travels Through Holland, Flanders, Russia, the Ukraine and Poland*. London, 1772, 1773, 1792 eds.

Miakotin, V., *Studies in the Social History of Ukraine in the Seventeenth and Eighteenth Centuries* (Очерки Социальной Истории Украины в XVII-XVIII вв.), Vol. 1. Prague, 1924. (In Russian.)

Novitsky, I., "Studies in Peasant Life in Ukraine in the Fifteenth to Eighteenth Centuries" (Розвідки про Селянство на Україні в XV-XVIII вв.), *Ukrainian Historical Library* (Українська Істор. Бібліотека), Vol. 21. Lviv, 1901. (In Ukrainian.)

Okinshevich, L., "The General Council in Hetman Ukraine" (Генеральна Рада на Україні-Гетьманщині), *Transactions of the Commission for the History of Ukrainian Law, Ukrainian Academy of Science* (Праці Комісії Історії Українськаго Права, Всеукр. Академія Наук), Vol. 6. Kiev, 1926. (In Ukrainian.)

—— "The General Officers' Council in Left Bank Ukraine in the Seventeenth and Eighteenth Centuries" (Генеральна Старшина на Лівобережній Україні XVII-XVIII вв.), *op. cit.*, Vol. 2. Kiev, 1926. (In Ukrainian.)

—— "The General Council in the Hetman State" (Генеральна Рада на Україні-Гетманщині), *Ukraine* (Україна), April, 1924. Kiev. (In Ukrainian.)

Slabchenko, M., *The Economic Organization of Ukraine from the Time of Khmelnitsky to the World War* (Организация Хозяйства Украины от Хмельниччины до Мировой Войны), Vols. 1-4. Odessa, 1922—. (Some volumes in Ukrainian, others in Russian.)

—— "The Social and Legal Organization of the Zaporozhian Sich" (Соціяльно-Правова Організація Січи Запорожської), *Transactions of the Commission for the History of Ukrainian Law, Ukrainian Academy of Science* (Праці Комісії Історії Українського Права, Всеукраїнська Академія Наук), Vol. 3. Kiev, 1927. (In Ukrainian.)

Storozhenko, N., "Contributions to the History of the Little-Russian Kozaks at the end of the Eighteenth and the beginning of the Nineteenth" (Къ исторіи Малороссійкихъ Козаковъ въ Конце XVIII и въ Началѣ XIX вв.), *Kievan Antiquity* (Кіевская Старина), Nos. 4, 6, 10-12. 1897. (In Russian.)

—— "Reforms in Little Russia Under Count Rumiantsov" (Реформы въ Малороссіи при гр. Румянцевѣ), *Kievan Antiquity* (Кіевская Старина), Nos. 3, 9. 1891. (In Russian.)

Ternovsky, S., "An Inquiry into the Submission of the Kievan Metropolitanate to the Moscow Patriarchate" (Изслѣдованіе Подчиненій Кіевской Митрополіи Московскому Патріархату), *Southwestern Russian Archives* (Архивъ юго-Западной Россіи), Pt. 1, No. 5. (In Russian.)

Titov, F., *Ancient Higher Education in Kievan Ukraine* (Стара

Вища Освіта в Київській Україні), Kiev, 1924. (In Ukrainian.)

Tomashivsky, S., *The First Campaign of Bohdan Khmelnitsky into Galicia* (Перший Похід Б. Хмельницкого в Галичину). Lviv, 1914. (In Ukrainian.)

Vasilenko, M., "Paul Polubotok" (Павло Полуботок), *Ukraine* (Україна), June, 1925. Kiev.

Vasilenkova-Polonska, N., "From the History of the Last Days of the Zaporozhe" (З Історії Останних Часів Запорожа), *Transactions of the Historical and Philological Section of the Ukrainian Academy of Science* (Записки Истор. Філь. Відділу Всеукр. Академії Наук), Vol. 9. Kiev, 1927. (In Ukrainian.)

Yakovliv, A., *Ukrainian-Muscovite Treaties of the Seventeenth and Eighteenth Centuries* (Українсько-Московські Договори XVII-XVIII ст.). Warsaw, 1934. (In Ukrainian.)

8.   The Nineteenth Century and the Beginning of the Twentieth

Borschak, E., "Le Mouvement nationale Ukrainien au XIX Siècle," *Le Monde Slave*, November-December, 1930. Paris.

Clarke, D., *Travels in Various Countries of Europe, Asia and Africa*. London, 1810-13, 1816.

Doroshenko, D., "Mykhailo Dragomanov and the Ukrainian National Movement," *Slavonic Review*, Vol. 16 (April, 1938), pp. 654-666. London.

Dragomaniv, M., *Historical Poland and Great-Russian Democracy* (Историческая Польша и Великорусская Демократия), Geneva, 1881. (In Russian.)

—— *Literary and Social Parties in Galicia to 1880* (Літературно-Суспільні Партії в Галичині до 1880 р.). Lviv. 1904. (In Ukrainian.)

Franko, I., *Serfdom and Its Abolition in 1848* (Панщина та її скасуванне 1848 р.). Lviv, 1913. (In Ukrainian.)

—— *Young Ukraine* (Молода Україна). Lviv, 1910. (In Ukrainian.)

Hermaize, O., *Historical Sketches of the Revolutionary Movement in Ukraine* (Нариси з Історії Революційного Руху на Україні). Kiev, 1926. (In Ukrainian.)

Hnatiuk, V., *The National Renaissance of the Austro-Hungarian Ukrainians, 1772-1880* (Національне Відродження Австро-

Угорських Українців, 1772-1880). Vienna, 1916. (In Ukrainian.)

Hruschewskyj (Hrushevsky), M., *Die Ukrainische Frage in Ihrer Historischen Entwickelung*. Vienna, 1915.

Hrushevsky, M., *The Liberation of Russia and the Ukrainian Question* (Освобожденіе Россіи и Украинскій Вопросъ). St. Petersburg (Leningrad), 1906. (In Russian.)

Levitsky, K., *History of the Political Ideas of the Galician Ukrainians from 1848 to 1914* (Історія Політичної Думки Галцьких Українців 1848-1914 рр.). Lviv, 1929. 2 vols. (In Ukrainian.)

Lototsky, O., *Pages from the Past* (Старінки Минулого). Warsaw, 1932-34. 3 vols. (In Ukrainian.)

—— A. and Stebnitsky, P., *The Ukrainian Problem* (Украинскій Вопросъ). Moscow, 1907. (In Russian.)

Popovich, O., *The Renaissance of Bukovina* (Відродження Буковини). Lviv, 1933. (In Ukrainian.)

Savchenko, F., *Prohibition of the Ukrainian Language in 1876* (Заборона Українства 1876 р.). Kiev, 1930. (In Ukrainian.)

Terletsky, O., *The Muscophile Movement and the Nationalists in the Seventies* (Москофільство і Народовці в 70-тих роках). Lviv, 1902. (In Ukrainian.)

Vozniak, M., *The Brotherhood of SS Cyril and Methodius* (Кирило-Методиївське Брацтво). Lviv, 1921. (In Ukrainian.)

Wasilewski, L., *Ukraine and Ukrainian Affairs* (Ukraina i Sprawa Ukrainska). Warsaw, 1934. (In Polish.)

9. From the World War to the Present: The Struggle for Independence

Borschak, E., "Traité de la Paix à Brest-Litowsk," *Le Monde Slave*, 1934.

—— "L'Ukraine à la Confèrence de la Paix," *Le Monde Slave*, January-March, 1937; January, 1938.

Choulguine (Shulgin), A., *Le Cauchemar Rouge*. Paris, 1927.

—— *L'Ukraine contre Moscou, 1917*. Paris, 1935.

Doroshenko, D., *History of Ukraine from 1917 to 1923* (Історія України 1917-1923 рр.). (Uzhorod, 1930-32. 2 vols. (In Ukrainian.)

—— "The Uniate Church in Galicia, 1914-17," *Slavonic Review*, Vol. 12 (April, 1934), pp. 622-627.

Kedrin, I., *The Treaty of Brest-Litovsk* (Берестейський Мир). Lviv, 1928. (In Ukrainian.)

Kutschabskyj, W. (Kutshabsky, V.), *Die West-Ukraine im Kampfe mit Polen und dem Bolschewismus in den Jahren 1918-23*. Berlin, 1934.

Levitsky, K., *History of the Revolutionary Uprisings of the Galician Ukrainians during the World War* (Історія Визвольних Змагань Галицких Українців з часу Світової Війни). Lviv, 1929-30. 3 vols. (In Ukrainian.)

Lewicki (Levitsky), E., *La Guerre Polono-Ukrainienne 1918-19*. Bern, 1919.

Mazepa, I., "The Ukraine under Bolshevist Rule," *Slavonic Review*, Vol. 12 (January, 1934), pp. 323-346.

Omelianovich-Pavlenko, M., *The Ukrainian-Polish War* (Українсько-Польска Війна). Prague, 1929. (In Ukrainian.)

Paneyko, B., "Galicia and the Polish-Ukrainian Problem," *Slavonic Review*, Vol. 9 (March, 1931), pp. 567-587.

Tiltman, H., *Peasant Europe*. London, 1934. Chapters on Ukraine.

Tyszkewicz, M. Comte, *L'Ukraine en face du Congrès*. Lausanne, 1919.

—— *Documents historiques sur l'Ukraine*. Geneva, 1919.

Voloshyn, A., "Carpathian Ruthenia," *Slavonic Review*, Vol. 13 (January, 1935), pp. 372-378.

B. COMMENTS ON UKRAINE, IN ENGLISH

1. Books and Pamphlets

Bjorkman, E., Pollack, S. O., Hrushevsky, M., and others, *Ukraine's Claim to Freedom*. 1915. 125 pp.

Coleman, Dr. A. P., *Short Survey of Ukrainian Literature*. 1936. 23 pp.

Cundy, P., *A Voice from Ukraina* (about Franko and his writings). 1932. 74 pp.

Doroshenko, D., *Taras Shevchenko, Bard of Ukraine*, with Preface by Prof. C. A. Manning. 1936. 50 pp.

Ewach, H., *trans.*, *Ukrainian Songs and Lyrics*. Canada, 1933.

"Famine in Ukraine," incl. H.R. 399 intr. in Congress May 28, 1934. 32 pp.

Franko, I., *Moses,* trans. by W. Semenyna, with short biography of Franko by S. Shumeyko. 1936. 93 pp.

Gambal, M. S., *Our Ukrainian Background.* 1940. 31 pp., illus.

—— *Ukraine, Rus and Muscovy and Russia.* 1937. 231 pp.

Halich, W., *Ukrainians in the United States.* 1937. 174 pp., illus.

Hunter, A. J., *trans., The Kobzar of the Ukraine.* Select poems of Shevchenko. 1922. 144 pp., illus.

Kvitka, H., *Marusia,* trans. by F. R. Livesay. Dutton, Ryerson Press, 1940. 219 pp.

Lawton, L., *The Ukrainian Question.* 1935. 36 pp.

Livesay, F. R., *trans., Songs of Ukraina.* 1916. 175 pp.

Manning, Prof. C. A., *Ivan Franko.* 1938. 30 pp.

Myshuha, Dr. L., *Shevchenko and Women,* trans. by W. Semenyna. 1940. 94 pp.

—— *Ukraine and American Democracy.* 1939. 32 pp.

Revyuk, E., *comp., Polish Atrocities in Ukraine.* 1931. 512 pp.

Sciborsky, M., *Ukraine and Russia, a Survey of Soviet Russia's Twenty-Year Occupation of Eastern Ukraine.* 1940. 92 pp., illus., map.

Sembratovich, Rev. L. I., *Strangers Within Our Gates,* with Foreword by Bishop Gallegher of Detroit. 1936. 46 pp., illus.

Shumeyko, S., *Ukrainian National Movement.* 1939. 46 pp.

Snowyd, D., *Spirit of Ukraine: Ukrainian Contributions to World Culture.* 1935. 152 pp., illus.

Turiansky, O., *Lost Shadows,* trans. by Andrew Mykytia. 1935.

2. Periodical Literature*

Alsberg, H. G., "Allied Dog in the Ukrainian Manger," *Nation,* Vol. 110 (March 27, 1920), pp. 392-393.

—— "Situation in the Ukraine," *Nation,* Vol. 109 (November 1, 1919), pp. 569-570.

"Appeal of the Ukrainian Coöperatives," *Nation,* Vol. 110 (February 7, 1920), pp. 184-185.

Attwater, D., "Bolshevist Persecution Marches West," *Commonweal,* Vol. 31 (November 17, 1939), pp. 88-90.

Bakowski, M., "Ukraine's Grievance in East Galicia," *New York*

* From Stephen Shumeyko, "Digest of Periodical Comments on Ukraine," *Ukrainian Weekly,* Vol. VII (Nos. 2–13, January 14—April 22; No. 29, July 15, 1939), Vol. VIII (Nos. 16–18, April 20—May 4; No. 35, August 31, 1940).

Times Current History Magazine, Vol. 16 (June, 1922), pp. 514-515.

Bess, D., "What of the Ukraine" (map), *Christian Science Monitor* (February 8, 1939), p. 3.

"Birth of the Ukrainian Republic," *Literary Digest*, Vol. 56 (February 23, 1918), pp. 7-8.

"Case of the Ukraine," *Nation*, Vol. 108 (April 19, 1919), p. 635.

Conwell-Evans, T. P., "Ukrainians in Poland," *Political Quarterly*, Vol. 3 (October, 1932), pp. 570-580. London.

"Coup in the Ukraine," *New York Times Current History Magazine*, Vol. 8 (June, 1918), pp. 453-454.

"Cry of Ukraine," *Review of Reviews*, Vol. 53 (April, 1916), pp. 485-486.

Davidovich, S., "The Ukrainian Problem," *Nineteenth Century*, Vol. 126 (December, 1939), pp. 717-722. London.

Dickinson, T. H., "What the Reds Did to Ukraine," *New York Times Current History Magazine*, Vol. 16 (July, 1922), pp. 631-636.

"First Congress of a Submerged People," *Survey*, Vol. 35 (November 6, 1915), p. 121.

"Free Speech in Poland," *Nation*, Vol. 120 (June 17, 1925), p. 700.

"The Future of the Ruthenians," *Literary Digest*, Vol. 51 (August 21, 1915), p. 344.

Gibbons, H. A., "Ukraine and the Balance of Power," *Century Magazine*, Vol. 102 (July, 1921), pp. 463-471.

Granovsky, A. A., "Ukraine's Case for Independence," *World Affairs*, March, 1940.

Hallgren, M. A., "The Polish Terror in Galicia," *Nation*, Vol. 131 (November 5, 1930), pp. 508-509.

Johnson, A., "Russia's Ireland," *New Republic*, Vol. 5 (December 11, 1915), pp. 146-147.

Lawton, L., "Ukraina, Europe's Greatest Problem," *East Europe and Contemporary Russia*, spring 1939 issue. London.

—— "Ukrainians Under Poland," *Fortnightly Review*, Vol. 141 (April, 1934), pp. 456-463. London.

"Liberation, Eastern Europe" (map), *Time*, Vol. 33 (January 23, 1939), pp. 15-16.

Livesay, F. R., *trans.*, "Old Folk Songs," *Poetry*, Vol. 14 (April, 1919), pp. 24-29.

—— "Ukraine and Its Songs," *op. cit.*, pp. 36-40.

—— and Crath, Paul, "Religion of Ancient Ukraine — in the Light of Archaeology and Folklore," *Scientific American Supplement*, Vol. 85 (February 23, 1918), pp. 114-115.

Lore, L., "Four Ukraines" (map), *Current History*, Vol. 49 (February, 1939), pp. 31-33.

Lynch, M. C. P., "Ukrainian Pictures," *Catholic World*, Vol. 107 (September, 1918), pp. 820-825.

Malofie, A., "Ukraine's Right to Independence," *New York Times Current History Magazine*, Vol. 17 (October, 1922), pp. 108-109.

Margolin, A., "New Map of Europe and the Ukraine," *New York Times Current History Magazine*, Vol. 16 (May, 1922), pp. 309-316.

O'Dwyer, Sir M., "Soviet and Ukraine," *Saturday Review*, Vol. 153 (April 30, 1932), pp. 437 ff. London.

"Oppression in Poland," *New Statesman and Nation*, Vol. 2 (August 29, 1931), p. 246. London.

Palmieri, O. S., "United Ruthenian Church of Galicia under Russian Rule," *Catholic World*, Vol. 103 (June, 1916), pp. 349-359.

Paneyko, P., "Germany, Poland, and the Ukraine," *Nineteenth Century and After*, Vol. 125 (January, 1939), pp. 34-43. Discussion Vol. 125 (February-March, 1939), pp. 241-242, 378-379.

"Poland 'Freeing' the Ukraine," *Literary Digest*, Vol. 65 (May 15, 1920), pp. 29-30.

Rappaport, S., "Ruthenian Question in Russia," *Contemporary*, Vol. 112 (September, 1917), pp. 300-305.

"Russian Peace," *Times History of the World War*, Vol. 16 (May 21, 1918), Pt. 116, p. 16.

Sands, B., "The Ukrainians (Ruthenians) and the War," *Contemporary*, Vol. 109 (March, 1916), pp. 369-377.

Sheepshanks, M., "Poland's Reign of Terror," *Living Age*, Vol. 339 (February, 1931), pp. 621-625.

Slosson, E. E., "What Happened in the Ukraine," *Independent* Vol. 98 (May 3, 1919), pp. 169-171.

Stoddard, T. L., "Little Russia," *Century Magazine,* Vol. 94 (August, 1917), pp. 569-576.

Tarnavsky, O., "Letters of a Ukrainian Soldier," *New York Times Current History Magazine,* Vol. 14 (July, 1921), pp. 657-663.

——Rev. P., "Ukrainian Case Against the Poles," *New York Times Current History Magazine,* Vol. 17 (February, 1923), pp. 820-823.

"Ukraine," *Review of Reviews,* Vol. 57 (March, 1918), pp. 307-308.

"Ukraine in Literature," *Literary Digest,* Vol. 58 (August 31, 1918), pp. 29-30, reprinted in *Living Age,* Vol. 298 (September 21, 1918), pp. 752-755.

"Ukraine and Its Separate Peace," *New York Times Current History Magazine,* Vol. 7 (March, 1918), pp. 426-437.

"Ukraine Throws Off the Shackles of Serfdom After 263 Years," *Literary Digest,* Vol. 56 (January 12, 1918), pp. 47-50.

"Ukraine's Political Bill of Health," *Literary Digest,* Vol. 62 (September 6, 1919), p. 26.

Ukrainian Federation of the United States, "Mid-European Union and the Ukraine," *Nation,* Vol. 108 (May 17, 1919), p. 813.

"Ukrainian National Chorus," *Nation,* Vol. 115 (November 1, 1922), pp. 477-478.

"Ukrainian People's Republic," *Independent (incorp. with Harper's Weekly),* Vol. 93 (March 2, 1918), pp. 335-336.

"Ukrainians," *Commonweal,* Vol. 14 (June 3, 1931), pp. 116-117.

"Ukrainians in America," *Literary Digest,* Vol. 63 (November 15, 1919), p. 40.

Vishevich, K., "Ukraine's Fight for Freedom," *New York Times Current History Magazine,* Vol. 11, Pt. 1 (October, 1919), pp. 123-126.

Wright, M., "Reign of Terror in Ukraine," *Current History,* Vol. 33 (February, 1931), pp. 681-684.

MAP OF
UKRAINE
Scale of miles

0   50   100   150   200

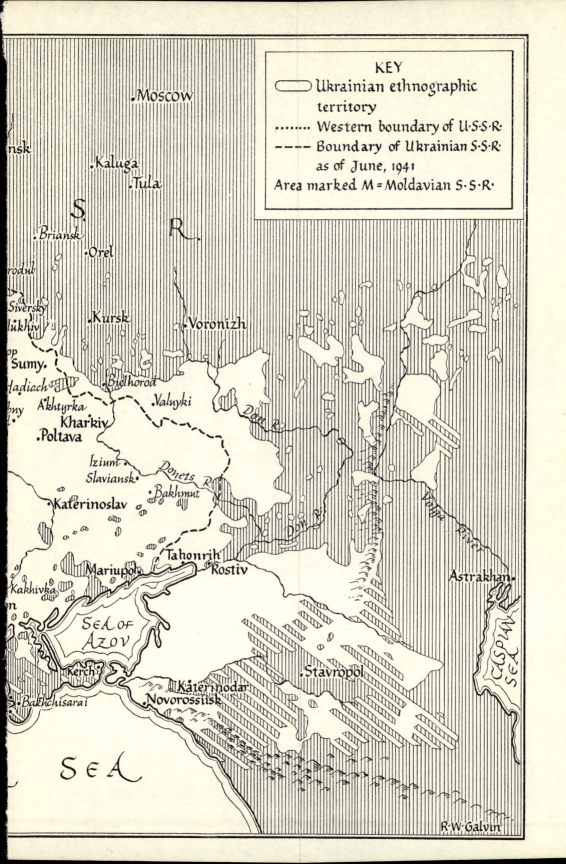

KEY
⬭ Ukrainian ethnographic territory
.... Western boundary of U·S·S·R·
----- Boundary of Ukrainian S·S·R· as of June, 1941
Area marked M = Moldavian S·S·R·

Moscow

Kaluga
Tula

S.
R.

Briansk
Orel

nsk

rodul

Siversky
lukhiv

Kursk
Voronizh

op
Sumy.

Hadiach
bny

Bielhorod

Akhtyrka
Valuyki

Kharkiv
Poltava

Izium
Slaviansk
Bakhmut

Donets R.

Don R.

Katerinoslav

Don R.

Volga River

Tahonrih
Mariupol
Rostiv

Astrakhan

Kakhivka
n

SEA OF
AZOV

Kerch

Stavropol

CASPIAN SEA

Bakhchisarai

Katerinodar
Novorossiisk

SEA

R·W·Galvin

INDEX

Abazin, Kozak colonel, 341
Abii, nomad tribe, 13
"About the Disorders in Little Russia," report by Teplov, 402
Academy of Cracow, 313
Academy of Kiev (Mohila Academy, Mohila-Zaborovsky Academy), 266, 313, 354, 412, 416–419
Academy of Uzhorod, 492
Act of Union of Poland and Lithuania in 1385, 169; of Poland and Lithuania in 1569, 194
Acts and Epistles of the Apostles (Apostol), 202
Administration, 88, 374–376, 381–384, 392–393, 404, 446, 448, 459–461. *See also* Government
Aeneid, by Virgil, 478; travesty by Kotlyarevsky, 477, 478, 484
Africa, 4
Agriculture, 173–175, 196, 197, 434, 565. *See also* Peasants; Serfdom
Akhtirka, 410
Akkerman. *See* Bilhorod
Alans, nomad tribe, 13, 16, 18
Albania, 254
Albrecht, Prince of Saxony, 142
Alexander, Grand Duke of Lithuania and King of Poland, 154–209 *passim*, 582
—— (Olelko), Prince of Kiev, 138, 141, 142, 198, 582
—— Prince of Podolia, 125, 581
—— I, Emperor of Russia, 476
—— the Great, 56
Allied Supreme Council, 560–562
Allies, 536, 538, 539, 552, 555, 559, 560, 562, 567
Alpine area, 9
Alta River, 61, 77
Amadokians, tribe, 17
Amastris, 45
America, 566, 569
American Relief Administration, 557
Amur basin, 102
Anatolia, 180, 228, 231. *See also* Asia Minor
Andrew II, King of Hungary, 97, 99, 100
—— Galician prince, 112, 580

—— Prince of Suzdal, 94, 580
Androphagi, tribe, 17
Andrushko, Kozak leader, 155
Andrusovo, treaty, 331
Anna, Byzantine princess, 66, 68
—— daughter of Yaroslav, 77
—— Empress of Russia, 390, 399, 438, 448
Annals. *See* Chronicles
Annunciation, Church of, in Kiev, 78
Antae, tribe, 20–24, 37, 153
Antioch, Patriarch of. *See* Joachim, Patriarch of Antioch
Antonovich, V., historian, 500, 501
"Apocrisis," by Filalet-Bronsky, 212
Apostol, D., Kozak hetman, 360, 368, 386–388, 390, 391, 404, 416, 584
Arabia, 56, 60, 910
Arabian authors, 31, 43, 46, 59; Caliphate, 36; commerce, 36; cultural influence, 69, 117; money, 37, 229
Arabs, 1, 55
Aral, Lake, 103
Archioca, 230
Architecture, 120, 511
Armenian merchants, 153
Armistice, World War, 555
"Army Fellows," Kozak honorary rank, 406
Arseney, metropolitan, 204
Art, 117, 118, 144, 511
Artemovsky, H., poet, 478, 483
Asaul (Kozak inspector general), 346
Asbiakivna, Persian queen, 53, 54
Asia, 9, 105, 235; central, 13
Asia Minor, 229; Rus raids on, 45, 55. *See also* Anatolia
Askold, Varangian chief, 40–42, 46, 47
Aslam-Kermen, 158, 163
Assumption, Church of the, in Lviv, 148
Astrakhan, 36, 376
Ataman (Kozak squad leader), 223
Augustus II, King of Poland, 360, 361
—— III, King of Poland, 437, 438, 463

Austria, 297, 344, 427, 519–521, 545, 558, 559, 561; annexation of Galicia and Bukovina, 463–466; relations to Carpatho-Ukraine, 432; relations to Galicia, 497–499; partition of Poland, 467; and Ukrainian nationalism, 488; and Ukrainian renaissance, 470

Austria Hungary, 553, 559, 560

Austrian army, 528, 532, 547; parliament, 507; prisoners of war, 542

Austrian Ukraine, 432, 470–474, 488

Autonomy, 311, 319, 330, 374, 385, 387, 404, 411, 420–422, 450, 451, 467, 522–533

Avars, nomad tribe, 22–24, 153

Azov, Sea of, 4, 18–20, 23, 102; coast, 24, 60; steppes, 105

"Azov Army," 458

Babadah, 185

Babylonia, 9

Bachinsky, A., bishop, 470

Badeny, Count K., 507

Baibuza, Kozak hetman, 218

Baida. *See* Vishnevetsky, Dmitro

Bakhchisarai, 257

Bakhmut, 8

Bakot, 125

Balaban, D., metropolitan, 311, 316

—— G., bishop, 202–203, 206, 209–210, 242; press, 239

Balkans, 8, 19–21, 60, 453

Balta, 454

Baltic coast, 17, 19; provinces, 173, 446; region, 126; Sea, 17, 173, 268, 359, 464

Banat, 457

Bantish-Kamensky, N., historian, 479

Bar, Confederation of, 443, 444

Barabash, custodian of Zaporozhian Sich, 310, 321

Baranovich, L., metropolitan of Chernihiv, 328–330, 343, 347

Barbary coast, 160

Bariatinsky, Prince, foreman of Little Russian Board, 394

Basil, Byzantine emperor, 66, 68

—— Christian name of Volodimir the Great. *See* Volodimir the Great

Bastarnians, Germanic tribe, 17, 18

Batory, Stephen, King of Poland, 164, 177, 180, 223

Batu, Mongol khan, 103–108, 151

Baturin, 365–366, 376, 418

Bazavluk, 390

Beauplan, French engineer, 225, 268; quoted, 227

Belinsky, Russian literary critic, 495

Belz, 127–128, 133, 464

Bendery. *See* Tiahinia

Berdaa, 56

Berdiansk, 458

Bereh, 428, 429

Bereste, 100, 142, 169, 544; brotherhood, 204, 215; Council of, 211, 425. *See also* Brest-Litovsk

Berestechko, 291, 293

Berezan island, 36

Berinda, printer, 239

Berlin, 564, 571

Berthelmy, French general, 560

Bessarabia, 7, 558, 559; annexed by Soviet Union, 574

Bessarabian Directory, 559

Bessarabova, Olha, patriot, 567

Besses, 17

Bezborodko, A., Russian minister, 475

Bezruchko, 556

Bible, 496; printed in Ukrainian, 199–200

Bichovets, S., Kozak colonel, 271

Bieniowski, S., Polish general, 312

Bikiv, 447

Bilas, V., revolutionist, 569

Bila Tserkva (White Church), 182, 188, 189, 231, 280, 292, 298, 301, 302, 346, 362, 371, 372, 434, 444, 553

Bilhorod (Akkerman), 181, 221, 246

"Bilhorod line," 406

Bilhorod near Kiev, 73

Bilous, Y., Kozak leader, 155

Bilozersky, author, 494

Bilsk, Prince of, 140

Biron, Russian minister, 394

Black Sea, 3, 34, 36, 180, 452, 453; coast, 1, 8–12, 14, 24, 44, 45, 47, 65, 72, 161, 185 (annexed by Russia), 466; Kozak raids on, 181, 227, 229, 231, 242, 250; region, 103, 179, 217, 534, 552; steppes, 9, 21, 47, 72, 154, 556

Black Sea army, 457
Blue Water, battle, 125
Blum, L., French statesman, 567
Bobolinsky, chronicler, 414
Bobrinsky, Count A. G., governor of Galicia, 516
Bogdanov, Russian colonel, 384
Bohdan, Moldavian *voyvoda*, 145
Bohemia, 572
Bohun, Kozak colonel, 298
Bohuslav, 341, 371, 444
Boleslav, King of Galicia. *See* George-Boleslav
—— I, King of Poland, 74, 76
—— II, King of Poland, 82
Bolgar (near later Kazan), 36, 43, 60
Bolgars, Volga, 31, 60, 65, 103, 153
Bolsheviks, 530–538, 540–545, 547, 548, 550–552, 554–557, 558, 560, 566. *See also* Soviet Union
Bona, Queen of Poland, 147
Bondarenko, I., Kolii leader, 444, 445
Boretsky, I., metropolitan of Kiev, 204, 239, 240, 245, 246, 258, 283
Boris, Prince of Galicia, 64, 74, 577 (1)
Borkovsky, Kozak colonel, 338, 345
Borodavka, Y. N., Zaporozhian hetman, 243, 244, 247, 583
Borovitsia, 271, 272
Bosnia, 514
Bosporus, 51, 55, 252; King of, 16
Botha, South African general, 560
Boyars. See Nobles
Bozh, Prince of Antae, 20
Braslav, 155, 168, 175, 181, 182, 184, 188, 281, 286, 291, 298, 302, 313, 317, 325, 336, 337, 362, 433, 436, 438, 441
Bratchiny (national festivals), 148
Bravlin, Rus prince, 45, 47
Bread Peace, 551. *See* Brest-Litovsk, treaty of
Brest-Litovsk, 536–540, 561; treaty of, 541–544, 549, 551, 558. *See also* Bereste
Briansk, 124, 131
Brody, 438
—— A., premier of Subcarpathian Rus, 571
Bronze, 8

Brotherhood of SS. Cyril and Methodius, 486, 487, 493, 494
Brotherhoods, 147–149, 212, 424, 425; in Kiev, 239, 266, 354; in Lviv, 201–205; in Ostroh, 184; in Vilna, 200
Brothers of the Sword. *See* Livonian Knights
Brukhovetsky, I., hetman of Left Bank Ukraine, 321–323, 325, 326, 364, 374, 584
Brusilov, A. A., Russian general, 519
Buchach, treaty of, 332
Buell, R. L., American author, cited, 563
Buh (Bug) River, northern, 106, 123, 135, 173
Buh (Bug) River, southern, 175, 340, 341
Bukovina, 144, 466, 498, 509, 520, 528, 553, 559, 560; annexed by Austria, 465; nationalism in, 500, 501; northern, annexed by Soviet Union, 574; revolution of 1848 in, 491–493; subjected to Moldavia, 169; Ukrainian renaissance in, 471
Bulavin, K., Don Kozak ataman, 364
Bulgaria, 62, 118, 254; attacked by Sviatoslav, 60, 61; culture, 144
Bulgarians, 19, 21, 60, 485. *See also* Bolgars, Volga
Bunchuk (horse-tail standard), 401
"Bunchuk Fellows," Kozak honorary rank, 401, 406
Burial grounds, 27; mounds, 25, 31
Burundai, Mongol chief, 110
Butovich, Kozak colonel, 371
Buturlin, V. V., Russian boyar, 294, 298, 299
Buzhans, clan, 34
Buzhsk, 34
Bylini (historical ballads), 48
Byron, English poet, 346
Byzantine architecture, 78; authors, 20, 97; Church, 117; culture, 117, 120, 121, 196; emperor, 45, 112, 208; government, 21; interference in Ukrainian Church, 207, 208; markets, 44; marriages, 77; officials, 36; provinces, 21. *See also* Greeks; Greek Orthodox Church
Byzantines, 36, 51, 60, 61, 66, 77, 78. *See also* Greeks

Byzantium, 20–22, 34, 44, 45, 65, 67, 121, 153, 208, 242, 258

"Cadet" (Constitutional Democrat) political party, 525, 527–529
Carol, King of Hungary, 113
Carpathian Mountains, 4, 17, 19, 25, 33, 74, 90, 99, 427, 428; region, 18, 500, 517
Carpatho-Ukraine, 99, 111, 169, 427–433, 470, 498, 501, 553, 560, 570, 571; revolution of 1848 in, 491–493
Carpatho-Ukrainian grammar, 487
Carps, tribe, 17
Casimir, Grand Duke of Lithuania and King of Poland, 138–140, 209, 582
—— I, King of Poland, 77
—— the Great, King of Poland, 113, 114, 126–128, 134, 167, 208
Caspian area, 34; Sea, 4, 13, 18, 36, 46, 47, 51, 54, 60, 103, 384; steppes, 23, 105; towns, 23
Catherine I, Empress of Russia, 384, 385
—— II, Empress of Russia, 400, 402, 418, 445, 450, 451, 453, 461, 463, 475
Catholicism. See Roman Catholicism; Uniates
Caucasian coast, 19
Caucasus Mountains, 4, 14, 376, 381, 476; region, 56, 64, 103; steppes, 13
Celts, tribe, 9
Censorship, 412, 416, 419, 477, 488, 496, 501, 503–505, 510–514
Census of Rumiantsov, 449
Centralist political party, 525
Central Powers, 528, 536–538
Central Rada, 521–551 passim, 553
Cernauti. See Chernivtsi
Chaika (Kozak boat), 226
Chaley, S., Haidamak leader, 439
Charles X, King of Sweden, 297–299, 311
—— XII, King of Sweden, 360–369, 371, 372, 374, 375, 437
Charnysh, Kozak judge, 378
Chepiha, K., Kozak officer, 457, 458
Cheremosh River, 436
Cherkasses, 154
Cherkassy, 154, 155, 158, 183, 231,

255, 270, 271, 275, 276, 301, 302, 335, 444
Cherniak, Kozak colonel, 376
Cherniha, mythological founder of Chernihiv, 40
Chernihiv, 5, 24, 26, 34, 40, 51, 75, 81, 83, 84, 90, 92, 95, 103, 104, 107, 115, 124, 131, 132, 134, 141, 274, 286, 302, 313, 317, 327, 328, 330, 343, 345, 399, 402, 408, 417, 502, 529, 548, 552; dynasty, 90, 141; regiment, 328, 384, 405
Chernivtsi (Cernauti), 465, 559
Chersonesus, 11, 60, 66–68
"Cherven towns," 76
Chihiryn, 272, 280, 286, 311, 314, 328, 335–337, 339, 340; regiment, 270, 276, 278, 301, 302
Chilbudius, Antae warrior, 21, 22
China, 102
Chmielecki, S., Polish general, 258
Chorny, H. S., Kozak hetman, 258, 259, 583, 584
Chortoreisk, 131, 132
Chortoreisky, Prince A., 137
—— Prince J., 137
Christian churches, 334
Christianity, 45, 47, 59, 64, 65, 69, 78, 79, 118, 573. See also Greek Orthodox Church; Roman Catholicism; Uniates
Christians, 65, 458
Christine, Queen of Sweden, 311
Christmas Night, opera by Lysenko, 502
Chronicles, 1, 24, 25, 37, 119, 414; Bobolinsky's, 414; Galician, 97, 104, 105, 108, 109, 120, 137, cited, 125; German, 46; Hrabianka's, 415; Hustin, 414; Kadlubek's, 97; Kievan, 23, 24, 31, 33, 37–42, 44, 46–48, 51, 56, 57, 64, 65, 68, 69, 71, 76, 79, 120, cited, 80, 120; Kozak, 415; Lizohub's, 415; Lukomsky's, 415; Primary, 119; Sofonovich's, 414; Velichko's, 415, 477; Volynian, 119, 120
Chubinsky, ethnographer, 502
Chudnov, 318, 319
Chuhuev, 409
Chuikevich, F., jurist, 407
Church, 78, 88; architecture, 120; books, 205, 413, 423; language,

487; Ukrainian, 412, 413, 417, 460. *See also* Greek Orthodox Church; Roman Catholicism; Uniates

Churches, 69, 105, 121, 453; Annunciation, in Kiev, 78; Assumption, in Lviv, 148; Epiphany, in Kiev, 354; Holy Saviour, in Chernihiv, 75; Holy Sepulchre, in Jerusalem, 354; St. Elias, in Kiev, 65; St. Mamant, in Constantinople, 36; St. Nicholas, in Kiev, 354, 401; St. Sophia Cathedral, in Kiev, 76, 78, 150, 267; Tithe, in Kiev, 39; Volodimir Cathedral, in Kiev, 104

Church Slavonic culture, 266

Church Union, 200, 238, 241, 244, 286, 287, 292, 469; formation of, 205–210; in Carpatho-Ukraine, 431–433; in western Ukraine, 462; resistance to, 210–216. *See also* Uniates

Cicali, Genoese admiral of Turkish fleet, 232

Cimmeria, 12

Circassians, tribe, 102. *See* Kasohi

Cities, 81, 148, 171, 460

"Civilians" (non-Kozaks), 193, 259, 276–278, 304, 319, 349, 357, 358, 371, 378, 411, 449

Clergy, 429, 450, 467, 472, 507; Ukrainian, 148, 412, 422. *See also* Greek Orthodox Church; Roman Catholicism; Uniates

"Comitats" (counties in Carpatho-Ukraine), 428

Commerce, 9, 11, 23, 34–36, 43, 65, 86, 93, 153, 458, 548, 564

Communist political party. *See* Bolsheviks

"Confederations" (Polish legal revolts), 443, 444, 463

Conference of Ambassadors, 563

Congress of Ukrainian Culture, 572; of Ukrainian Scholars, 490; Pan-Ukrainian, 529, 530, 532, 535, 547, 55^ 572

Conservative movement, 497, 498, 501, 507; political party, 498, 508

Conservative Nationalist political party, 507

Constantine, Byzantine emperor, 66, 67

—— Porphyrogenitus, Byzantine emperor, cited, 24, 35, 37, 43, 44, 55, 56

Constantinople (Tsarhorod), 34–36, 45, 55, 60, 67, 77, 159, 227, 228, 230, 232, 242, 250, 339, 453; Kozak raids on, 179, 235, 243, 252, 253; Rus raids on, 47, 50, 54; Patriarch of, 112, 316, 339, 343, 412, 425, 430 (*see also* Jeremiah, Patriarch of Constantinople); patriarchate of, 211

Constitution, first Ukrainian, 528

Constitutional Convention, 528, 537; under German auspices, 550, 551. *See also* Pan-Ukrainian Congress

Convention, Bolshevik (December, 1917), 553; Bolshevik (May, 1919), 554; military (April, 1917), 524; national teachers' (April, 1917), 523; peasant (May, 1917), 525; peasant (December, 1917), 533; soldiers' (May, 1917), 526; soldiers' and peasants' (June, 1917), 526; Third Legion (October, 1917), 530. *See also* Congress

Coöperatives, 510, 522, 568

Council of People's Ministers of Ukrainian National Republic, 538

Courland, 466

Court and Lawsuits in the Little Russian Law, by F. Chuikevich, 408

Courts, 172, 381, 389, 404, 407, 412, 458, 475, 532

Cracow, 111, 129, 284, 313

Crimea, 14, 34, 62, 160, 168, 314, 346, 353, 358, 390, 394, 397, 403, 452, 463, 464, 466; campaign of 1686 against, 344, 345; Kievan expeditions against, 47; Kozak attacks on, 229, 231, 235; relations with Hetman state, 308, 318; with Kozaks, 252–255, 270; with Mazepa, 356; seized by Volodimir, 68

Crimean cities, 179; coast, 45; mountains, 4; peninsula, 19; ports, 548; region, 64

Crimean horde of Tatars, 143, 344, 369, 371, 382, 409, 430, 465; origin, 149; and Galicia, 144, 145, 150; and early Kozaks, 149–158, 161, 162, 174, 175, 177; and Kozak Host under Poland, 178, 180, 181, 185, 186, 218, 221, 222, 230, 235,

245; and Kozak wars, 248, 252–254, 257, 276; and Khmelnitsky's rebellion, 278, 284–289, 291–294, 298, 301; and Hetman state, 308, 311, 312, 314, 318, 320, 323–325; and Doroshenko, 327, 331, 334–336, 338

Crimean war, 494

Croats, 485

Culture, 85, 108, 124, 131, 140, 344, 353, 354, 478, 480, 490, 564, 566, 573; Bulgarian, 144; in Kiev, 68–71; in period of decline, 117–122; in Russian Ukraine, 483, 511; in eastern Ukraine, 412–418; in western Ukraine, 422–427; under Poland-Lithuania, 194–197. *See also* Nationalism

Curzon Line, 561

Cyril Street in Kiev, 39; prehistoric culture site, 5

Czarniecki, Polish officer, 323

Czechivsky, nationalist, 566

Czechoslovakia, 560, 570–572

Czechs, 19, 60, 73, 74, 113, 485, 531, 545, 548

Damian, priest, 184

Daniel, abbot, author, 119

—— Prince of Galicia, 98, 100, 101, 106, 108–111, 113, 120, 123, 464, 577 (12)

Danube River, 13, 14, 18–20, 23, 34, 60, 61, 72, 90, 144, 145, 179, 221, 231, 457; region, 8, 65, 72

Danubian Kozaks, 458; Sich, 457, 458

Danylshyn, E., nationalist, 569

Danzig, 437, 438

Darnitsia, battle, 540

Dashkovich, O., Kozak hetman, 155, 157

"Decembrists," 485

Dedko, D., governor of Galicia, 114

"Definitive Articles," 388, 391, 407

Deiniki (robber bands), 436

Democracy, 549

Denikin, A. I., Russian general, 555, 556

Denmark, 309, 360

Derbent, 102

Derevlians, tribe, 24–26, 39, 44, 57, 58, 61, 63

Dermansky Monastery, 258

Desiatki (squads), 223

Desna River, 5, 24, 37, 365

Diluvial period, 3–6

Dimir, 260

Dir, Varangian chief, 40–42, 46, 47

Directory, 553, 554, 556

"Dispossessed" princes, 83, 84

Divochka, O., metropolitan, 207

Dmitri, so-called Tsarevich, 219, 220

Dmitro, governor of Kiev, 104, 105

Dmitro, Tatar chief, 125

Dnieper River, 8, 11, 13, 17, 20, 24, 35, 37, 39, 41, 44, 47, 51, 62, 68, 72, 75, 103, 104, 106, 107, 151, 154, 158, 165, 176, 180, 189–191, 217, 222, 228, 231, 232, 246, 247, 261, 262, 268, 275, 279, 280, 311, 314–316, 323, 327, 334, 336–342, 350–352, 357, 358, 369, 372, 390, 433, 434, 436, 440, 441, 474, 547, 556; estuary, 11, 36, 253; rapids, 35, 156, 157, 191, 227, 268; region, 64, 73, 85, 108, 112, 115, 149, 151, 152, 156, 175, 194, 221, 226, 235; valley, 106, 157, 183, 186

Dnieper Sich. *See* Zaporozhian Sich

Dnieproges (Dnieper power station), 565

Dniester River, 11, 20, 24, 145, 244, 340, 436, 465

Dobriansky, A., Russophile leader, 491, 492

Dobrinia, regent of Novgorod, 61

Dobroslav, Galician noble, 97

Dolgoruky, V. V., Russian minister, 385

Dombie, 561

Donets basin, 274, 553, 555

Don Kozaks, 220, 271, 364, 457, 532, 533

Don River, 13, 14, 24, 60, 72, 102, 190, 274, 532, 534, 556; region, 47, 64, 548

Dorohichin, 138

Doroshenko, Michael, Kozak hetman, 257, 584

—— Peter, Kozak hetman, 316, 324, 325, 327–339, 346, 347, 419, 584

Dorostol (Silistria), 60, 61

Dovbush, O., robber chief, 436

Dovbush, song, 436

Dovhalevsky, M., dramatist, 416, 417

Dragoons, 410
Drahomaniv, M. P., historian, 502, 504, 507
Drama, 503, 504
Drehoviches, tribe, 24, 34, 44, 74
Drevinsky, L., parliamentarian, 244, 263
Drohobich, 424
Drozd, revolutionary leader, 323
Druzhina. See Retinue
Duka, Moldavian prince, 341
Dulibs, tribe, 23, 24, 34
Duma, Russian parliament, 512, 513, 518, 519
Dumy, 415. *See also* Folk songs
Dunavets, 457
Dzinkovsky, Kozak colonel, 409

Eastern Europe, 70, 129, 160
Eastern Galicia, 423, 519, 561–563, 573. *See also* Galicia; Right Bank Ukraine
Eastern Little Poland, 561
Eastern Slavs, 47
Eastern Ukraine, villages in, 33; separated, 88–92; effort to reunite, 101; acquired by Lithuania, 126; intervention of Muscovy in, 140–143; rise of Kozaks in, 149–164 *passim;* reunion under Poland, 165–174; national revival in, 175–187 *passim;* Kozaks in, 217–245 *passim;* Kozak wars in, 246–276 *passim;* Khmelnitsky's rebellion in, 277–318 *passim;* Doroshenko's attempt to liberate, 325–338 *passim;* Kozak states under Russia in, 343–421 *passim;* abolition of hetmancy and Sich in, 446–461 *passim;* national renaissance in, 474–487, 493–497, 501–504, 510–513; independence, 514–550 *passim;* under Skoropadsky, 551, 552; under Soviets, 557, 558, 564, 566. *See also* Hetman state; Left Bank Ukraine; Russian Ukraine; Ukrainian Soviet Socialist Republic
Education, 69, 79, 117, 118, 144, 197–200, 202, 204, 205, 237, 238, 249, 266, 341, 353, 414, 416, 417, 422, 430, 470, 473, 486, 487, 509, 513, 566, 567

Egypt, 9, 458
Eichhorn, German general, 552
Eimund, Varangian adventurer, 75
Elbe River, 18, 19
Elders, 33, 70, 106. *See also* Officers' Council, Kozak
Elisavethrad, 453, 547
Elizabeth, daughter of Yaroslav, 77
—— Empress of Russia, 399, 400
England, 173, 361, 479, 536, 569
Epiphany, Church in Kiev, 354
Eulogy to Volodimir the Great, by Ilarion, 118
Eupatoria. *See* Kozliv
Europe, 101, 109, 235, 506; Eastern, 70, 129, 160; southeastern, 102. *See also* Western Europe
European powers, 311

Famine, 557, 564, 566
Fastiv, 444, 540
Fedak, S., 562
Fedir of Podolia, 125, 131
—— of Volynia, 131, 132
Fedkovich, O., poet, 500
Fedorovich, I., printer, 198, 202
—— T., Kozak leader, 259
Fellin, 219
Ferdinand II, German emperor, 243
Fesko Hanzha Andiber, Hetman of Zaporozhe, poem, 321
Filalet-Bronsky, author, 199, 212
Filenko, Kozak colonel, 275
Finland, 4, 446, 531
Finns, 17; settlements, 47; tribes, 17, 41
Five Year Plan of Soviet Union, 565
Florence, Council of, 208
Folk songs, 469, 478, 489. *See also* Dumy
Fort Kodak, 268–270, 276, 345
Forts in early Ukraine, 34
France, 4, 160, 173, 227, 536, 560, 563, 564, 567
Francis Joseph II, Austrian emperor, 519, 521
Franko, I., author, 509
Frederick II, King of Prussia, 463, 464
French, 250, 538, 557; army, 555; language, 503; revolution of 1848, 489
Friesland, 142

Funeral fields, 17
Funerals, Rus, 31; Scythian, 15

Galagan, Kozak colonel, 368, 369
Galicia, 8, 17, 25, 63, 64, 87, 89, 90,
    92, 124, 126–129, 133, 144, 145,
    150, 169, 172, 174, 175, 183, 194,
    208, 213, 214, 238, 239, 299, 300,
    318, 424, 426–430, 464–467, 471,
    487–493, 495–499, 501, 503–507,
    511, 513, 514, 519–521, 528, 540,
    542, 552, 553, 556, 561, 568, 570,
    572; kingdom of, 96–122 passim;
    princes of, 577, 578, 580. See also
    Austrian Ukraine; Galicia-Vo-
    lynia; Right Bank Ukraine; West-
    ern Ukraine
Galician Chronicle, 97, 104, 105, 108,
    109, 120, 137; cited, 125
Galician nobles, 90, 96, 97, 99, 101,
    113, 114, 116, 137, 188, 208;
    princes, 109, 111, 112, 115;
    Ukrainians, 440
Galicians, 96, 240
Galician Ukraine, 148
Galicia-Volynia, 98, 100, 108, 109,
    111, 113–115, 131, 134, 414, 464,
    573, 577, 578
"Gathering of Lands of Rus," 64,
    80
Gedymin, Grand Duke of Lithuania,
    124
General army court, Ukrainian, 387,
    388
General Council (Holovna Rada) in
    Galicia, 490
General Secretariat of Central Rada,
    527–531, 538
General Ukrainian Council, 520
Geneva, 504
Genghis Khan. See Temuchin
Genoa, 558
Gentry, 86, 87, 149, 182, 211, 219,
    304, 306, 406, 408, 418, 419, 424,
    435, 474, 481. See also Landlords;
    Nobles; Polish gentry; White Rus-
    sian gentry
Geographical Society, 502, 503, 505
George, Prince of Podolia, 125, 581
George-Boleslav, King of Galicia,
    113, 114, 578 (34), 580
George Monomakh, Prince of Kiev,
    94, 575 (23), 580

George I, King of Galicia, 112, 113,
    577 (32), 580
Georgia, 102
German army, 136, 517, 528, 532, 544–
    547, 551; chronicler, 46; culture,
    195, 196; emperor, 45, 76, 185,
    186, 192; expansion, 123; immi-
    grants, 121; language, 9; law, 121
    (see also Magdeburg Law); mar-
    riages to Kievan dynasty, 77
Germanic area, 19; tribes, 17, 18
Germans, 1, 4, 9, 17, 37, 65, 97, 113,
    127, 128, 186, 429, 537, 544, 547,
    548, 564. See also Teutonic Knights
Germany, 45, 57, 480, 518–521, 538,
    539, 545, 558, 572–574
Glacial age, 4–6
God's Grace which Saved Ukraine
    from Polish Oppression through
    Bohdan Zinovey Khmelnitsky,
    drama, 415
"Golden Charter," 443
Golden Horde, 149
Goldwork, 120
Golitsyn, B., Muscovite minister, 344,
    345, 353
Golovin, Russian minister, 496
Goluchovski, governor of Galicia,
    493, 497
Gonta, I., Kolii leader, 444, 445
Gorodtsov, V. A., archaeologist, 8 n
Goths, 14, 17–21
Government, 33, 70, 115–117, 170,
    171. See also Administration
Grabski, governor of Galicia, 562
Graeco-Slavonic grammar, 240;
    school, 199
Grain, 2, 7, 11, 13, 21, 25, 26, 106,
    173, 196, 455, 564, 568
Great Britain, 563
Great Eviction, 340, 517
Great Khan, 103, 105
Great Rus, 121
Great Russia, 70, 106, 119. See also
    Muscovy; Russia
Great Russian language, 17, 487;
    race, 17
Great Russians, 447. See also Musco-
    vites; Russians
Greece, 11, 242, 254
Greek artisans, 78; authors, 37, 77,
    204; books, 79, 118; cities, 18, 34,
    62, 66, 67; coins, 11; colonies, 10–

12; craftsmen, 11, 12, 120; culture, 118; emperors, 36; fire, 55, 61, 78; historians, 21, 24; influences, 69; language, 12, 118, 199; literature, 479; traders, 72. *See also* Byzantines; Greek Orthodox Church

"Greek Fathers," 198

Greek Orthodox Church, 65, 66, 68, 70, 100, 112, 113, 116, 119, 124, 144, 148, 186, 188, 303, 311, 313, 325, 349, 350, 367, 411, 414, 415, 422, 424, 463, 470; and Church Union, 205–216, 425–427, 440–444 (*see also* Uniate Church); and Khmelnitsky's rebellion, 283, 284, 286, 287; and Kozak wars, 246, 248–250, 252, 254, 258, 259, 263–267, 271; and national revival, 193–201, 203, 205; and revival of Kiev, 237, 238, 241–245; clergy, 66, 70, 103, 118, 121, 240, 258, 304, 354, 406, 416, 425, 431–433, 474; in Carpatho-Ukraine, 429–433; in Galicia, 146–148; nobles, 148, 186, 188; under Muscovy, 293, 296, 298; under Poland-Lithuania, 129, 131–133, 136, 139–142

Greeks, 1, 14, 17, 20, 21, 24, 35, 37, 45. *See also* Byzantines

Gregorian calendar, 200, 201, 313, 545

Gymnasia (high schools) in Galicia, 471

Hadiach, 327, 343, 345, 405, 447

Hadiach Union, 303, 313–315, 318

Hadji-Gerai, Crimean khan, 150

Haidamak rebellions, 436–441, 443–445, 454, 468, 485

Haidamaks, by Shevchenko, 484

Halich, 96, 97, 99, 105, 108, 121, 145

Halichina. *See* Galicia

Haller, Polish general, 560

Hapsburgs, 464, 560

Harold the Bold, Prince of Norway, 77

Hashtovt, J., regent of Lithuania, 138

—— M., Lithuanian noble, 139

Hat of Monomakh, 67

Hendrikov, Count, Russian minister, 400, 401

Henry I, King of France, 77

Hermanaric, King of Goths, 18, 20

Hermanivka, 315

Herodotus, Greek historian, 12–14, 17

Herriot, French statesman, 567

Hertzberg, Prussian minister, 475

Hetman, office of, 223–225, 303–306, 316, 317, 346, 363, 370, 371, 374–378, 380, 385–387, 391, 399, 400, 402, 403, 405, 407, 410, 415, 446–450, 475, 479, 551; origin of title, 155, 223, 224; list of holders, 583, 584

Hetmancy. *See* Hetman; Hetman state

Hetmanshina, 301. *See* Hetman state

Hetman state, 340–342, 346, 350, 351, 410, 453, 474, 478; early organization, 301–307; events under Muscovy, 342–346; under Mazeppa, 347–370 *passim;* under Orlik, 371–373; organization under Russia, 403–409; last years, 446–451, 459–461. *See also* Eastern Ukraine; Left Bank Ukraine

Hippemolgi, tribe, 13

Historical writing, 479, 484, 485, 501, 503; in verse, 483; Ukrainian, 488

History of People of Rus, cited, 448

History of Rus or Little Russia, 479; cited, 396, 397

Hither Asia, 9

Hitler, Adolph, 571, 573

Hladky, O., Kozak leader, 458, 459

Hlib, Rus prince, 64, 74

Hlinsky, Prince Bohdan, 154

—— Prince Michael, 142, 143, 150, 176

Hloba, Kozak secretary, 456

Hlukhiv, 323, 367, 376, 386, 400, 403

Hlukhiv Articles, 330, 333, 346

Hnat Holy, Haidamak leader, 439, 440

Holohory, 204

Holovatsky, J., linguist, 488, 498

Holovaty, Anton, Kozak officer, 457

—— Paul, Kozak judge, 456

Holovna Rada (General Council) in Galicia, 490

Holtva, city and river, 273

Holubovich, V., Ukrainian minister, 542, 546, 549

Holy Cross fortress, 384

Holy Saviour, church in Chernihiv, 75

Holy Sepulchre, church in Jerusalem, 354

Homer, Greek poet, 12

Homonai, Carpatho-Ukrainian magnate, 431

Hontsi, 5

Horde. *See* Crimean horde; Golden Horde; Pechenegs; Tatars

Hordienko, Sich custodian, 357, 368, 370, 373, 389

Horilka (liquor), 355

Horlenko, Kozak colonel, 360

Horod (stockade), 34

Horodla, Charter of, 132

Horodok, 204, 299, 424

Horyn River, 24, 106

Hostry Kamin, 189

Hrabianka, chronicle of, 415

Hrebenev, 74

Hrebinka, battle, 540

Hrebinka, poet, 484

Hrinchenko, B., author, 511

Hriva, Haidamak leader, 439

Hromada, journal, 504

Hromada, society, 501

Hromadska Dumka, newspaper, 513

Hrushevsky, Professor M., 43, 522, 550, 551, 564, 566

Hrushiv monastery, 430

Hulevich-Voiutinsky, bishop of Peremyshl, 267

Hulevichivna, Halshka, benefactress, 239

Hulianitsky, Kozak colonel, 314

Hungarian army, 517; language, 572; marriages to Kievan dynasty, 77; revolution of 1848, 491; rulers, 66; soldiers, 545

Hungarian Mountains. *See* Carpathian Mountains

Hungarians, 60, 69, 96, 108, 114, 132, 570; and Carpatho-Ukraine, 428–433

Hungary, 9, 13, 19, 23, 72, 74, 96, 99–101, 103, 105, 111, 113, 114, 126, 127, 134, 185, 435, 436, 464, 489, 491, 492, 571

Hungry Village Relief Committee, 567

Hunia, D., Kozak officer, 272–275

Huns, nomad tribe, 14, 18–21

Hunter, A. J., cited, 261

Hurko, S. (*pseud.* ''Paliy''), Kozak colonel, 341. *See* Paliy, S. H.

Husak, Kozak officer, 355

Hust, 560, 571

Hustin chronicle, 414

Hustinsky Monastery, 251

Hutsuls, peasants in Carpatho-Ukraine, 436, 500, 572

Huyn, governor of Galicia, 553

Iceland, 75

Ihor, Prince of Kiev, 38, 40–42, 46, 47, 54–57, 67, 72, 575 (2), 579

—— Prince of Novhorod-Siversk, 93, 99, 579

Ilarion, metropolitan of Kiev, 118

Iliad, by Homer, cited, 13

Illyria, 242

Inaete-Gerai, Khan of Crimea, 270

Indentured laborers, 86, 116

Independence, 122, 285, 286, 289, 290, 295, 296, 324, 347, 361, 402, 467, 538, 539

''India,'' 52. *See* Persia

Information about Ruthenian Language, by Levitsky, 473

Ingigerda (Irene), Princess of Kiev, 77

Instructions of Monomakh to His Sons, 120

''Instructions'' of Russian Provisional Government, 529, 530

Inter-Allied Armistice Commission, 560

Iran, 9, 14

Iranian tribes, 13

Iron, 2, 8, 9

Isidore, metropolitan of Kiev, 208

Iskorosten, 58

Iskra, Kozak colonel, 341, 364

Italy, 142, 160, 498, 563, 571; culture, 195, 196

Itil, 36, 43, 60

Ivan III, Grand Prince of Muscovy, 140, 150

—— IV, Tsar of Muscovy, 198, 219

—— V, Tsar of Russia, 344

Iziaslav, Prince of Polotsk, 63, 64, 579

—— I, Prince of Kiev, 80–83, 575 (9), 579

—— II, Prince of Kiev, 92, 96, 575 (22), 580

Izium, 410
Izmail, 221
Izmailov, Russian resident minister, 375

Jacob, author, 118
Jan Casimir, King of Poland, 282, 283, 285, 286, 300, 323
Japan, 563
Japheth, Biblical character, 242
Jassy, 186
Jefremov. *See* Yefremiv
Jeremiah, Patriarch of Constantinople, 203, 206, 207, 210, 211
Jerusalem, 242, 283, 354
Jesuit colleges, 416; schools, 200, 205
Jesuits, 266
Jews, 171, 202, 245, 281, 426, 435, 437, 438, 443, 444, 516, 534, 539, 564, 570
Joachim, Patriarch of Antioch, 202, 203, 206, 207
—— Patriarch of Moscow, 413
Jordanes, historian of Goths, cited, 20
Joseph, metropolitan of Chernihiv, 141
—— II, Hapsburg emperor, 457, 464, 471, 489
Judaism, 65
Julian calendar, 313
Justinian, Byzantine emperor, 22

Kadlubek, Polish chronicler, 97
Kaffa, 160, 231, 234, 253, 257
Kaledin, A. M., Russian general, 532
Kalinovski, Polish general, 279, 280, 291–293
Kalka, 102
Kalmucks, tribe, 13
Kalnik, 302
Kalnishevsky, P., Kozak koshovy, 453–456
Kalokir, native of Chersonesus, 60
Kalush, 424
Kaminets (Kaminets-Podolsk), 125, 135, 231, 298, 332, 341, 426, 438, 554
Kaminni Zaton, 280
Kaniv, 231, 255, 301, 302, 334, 475
Kapnist, nationalist, 475
Karabah, 56
Karaimovich, I., Kozak colonel, 272, 273

Karpo Maslo, Kozak leader, 155
Kasohi (Circassians), 59. *See* Circassians
Katerinoslav, 535, 548
Kayala River, 93
Kazan, 36, 517
Kazanovski family, 176
Keith, English general, 394
Kerensky, A. F., Russian politician, 530, 536, 538, 540
Kertch, 11 (*see also* Panticapaeum); Straits of, 47
Khagan, Avar, 23; title, 46
Khanenko, M., Kozak hetman, 315, 330–333, 335, 584
Kharkiv, 11, 40, 274, 287, 337, 409, 410, 417, 503, 534, 535, 548, 553, 554, 566; university, 418, 483, 484
Kharko, mythological founder of Kharkiv, 40
—— Haidamak leader, 439
Khata, almanac, 494
Khazars, tribe, 23, 31, 36, 39, 46, 51, 59, 65, 72, 75; rulers, 67
Kherson, 534, 547
Khliborob, newspaper, 513
Khmelnitsky, Bohdan, Kozak hetman, 176, 223, 255, 273, 276, 308, 309, 311, 317, 323, 324, 347, 356, 360, 380, 409, 415, 423, 424, 446, 584; rise to hetmancy, 278; War of 1648, 279–282; War of Liberation, 283–287; foreign alliances, 288–291; War of 1650–51, 291, 292; treaty of Zboriv, 293, 294; and Muscovite protectorate, 295–298; campaign of 1654–55, 298–300; government, 301–307
—— treaty of (treaty of Pereyaslav), 294–296, 316, 317, 328, 374, 379, 382, 387, 388, 391, 392
—— rebellion of, recalled, 348, 414, 418, 433, 437, 462, 463
—— George, Kozak hetman, 301, 307, 308, 315, 317–320, 339–341, 584
—— Timosh, 288, 292, 293
Khodkevich, G., landowner, 197
Kholm, city, 111, 128; diocese, 264, 425; province, 127, 133, 169, 194, 214, 464, 467, 517, 520, 544, 563, 567
Kholop. *See* Slave
Khoriv, 39

Khorivitsia Hill, 39

Khortitsia, 35, 157

Khotan, Polovtsian khan, 102

Khotyn, 247, 334

Khotyn War, 233, 246–248

Khust. *See* Hust

Khutor (homestead), 33

Khvastiv, 341

Kiev, city, 5, 6, 8, 11, 17, 24, 35, 37, 39–44, 47, 51, 68, 71–74, 76, 78, 82, 83, 87, 90, 92–95, 104, 105, 132, 150, 154, 182, 190, 204, 208, 214, 237–242, 252, 254, 255, 261, 283, 292, 296, 309, 314, 316, 317, 329, 331, 332, 335, 340, 343, 344, 359, 372, 394, 422, 423, 445, 446, 484, 501–504, 513, 515, 517, 521–531, 533–535, 539–546, 549, 551–557, 564, 566

Kiev, principality and province, 8, 17, 41, 98, 101, 105–107, 115, 124, 138, 142, 146, 151, 152, 155, 163, 165–168, 181, 182, 186, 198, 273, 281, 286, 292, 297, 298, 300, 302, 308, 313, 327, 337, 341, 427, 433, 436, 441, 442, 444, 466, 529

Kiev, regiment, 274, 405, 434. *See also* Kiev, city

Kiev, university of, 484

Kievan Antiquity, journal, 505

Kievan army, 44, 55, 105; brotherhood, 239, 241, 249, school, 240; chronicles (*see* Chronicles, Kievan); clergy, 251, 257; metropolitan, 215, 393, 412, 413; princes and kings, 36, 38, 43–45, 47, 56, 72, 77, 91, 115, 575, 576, 579–582; state, 40, 43, 44, 47, 63–96 *passim*. *See also* Rus

Kievans, 38, 82, 98, 104, 139, 190, 266, 289

Kiev Archeological Commission, 485

Kiev-Volynia, 89

Kilia, 185, 221

Kishka, S., Kozak hetman, 217–219, 224, 583

Kisil, A., Polish commissioner, 263, 270, 272, 281, 292; cited, 269

Kislovodsk, 566

Kiy, mythological founder of Kiev, 39–41

Kizim, Kozak officer, 272, 273

Klym, metropolitan, author, 119

Kniazhey Bairak, battle, 280

Kobilianska, Olha, author, 510

Kobzar, by Shevchenko, 483, 499; cited, 261

Kobzars (minstrels), 160, 469

Kochubey, Kozak general judge, 363, 364

—— Tatar chief, 125

Kodak. *See* Fort Kodak

Kodno, 445

Kokoshkin, Kozak colonel, 384

Kolii (rebels in western Ukraine), 443, 454

Koliivshina (rebellion of Kolii), 443

Kolomak River, 383

Koloman, King of Galicia, 100, 577 (21)

Komulovich, Croatian priest, 185

Kondratiev, Kozak colonel, 411

Koniecpolski, Polish general, 225, 244, 255, 256, 258–262, 269, 276

Konisky, A., author, 500, 502, 504

—— G., dramatist, 416, 417, 479

Kononovich, S., Kozak hetman, 271, 584

Konotop, 314, 328

Kopinsky, I., metropolitan of Kiev, 251, 258, 265

Kopistinsky, bishop of Peremyshl, 210, 239, 242

Koretsky family, 176

Koriat, Lithuanian prince, 125, 581

Koriatovich, T., governor of Bereh, 429, 430

Koribut, D., Prince of Chernihiv, 132, 582

Kornilov, L. G., White Army general, 530

Korsun, 258, 272, 276, 280, 291, 292, 341, 371, 444; regiment, 301, 302; in Crimea. *See* Chersonesus

Korzh, M., Kozak, cited, 456

Koshovy (Sich custodian), 321, 338

Koshovy-hetman, title, 321

Koshytsi, 571

Kosinsky, C., Kozak leader, 182, 183

Kosniachko, Rus commander, 82

Kostoboks, tribe, 17

Kostomariv, N., historian, 484, 485

Kotlyarevsky, I., author, 477, 478, 482, 484

Kotsuibinsky, G. M., Soviet general, 540, 543

—— Mikhailo, author, 511
Kovel, 198, 545
Kozachinsky, M., Professor, 417
Kozak army, 158, 192, 219, 222–226, 313, 342, 382, 476; elders, 223 (*see also* Officers' Council, Kozak); fortress, 35; freebooters, 155; heroes, 501; Host (*see* Kozaks); life, 152; name, 153; privileges, 164, 177, 179, 279, 280, 283, 292, 294, 412, 435, 450, 451, 474; regiments, 524; retainers, 438, 439, 444
Kozaks, 21, 149–421 *passim*, 446–461 *passim*, 531, 535, 541, 547, 551, 571; and Haidamaks, 437; government and organization, 159, 164, 165, 175, 221–226, 274, 276, 281, 382, 438, 454, 409–411; in literature, 475, 477, 481, 485, 499; history of, by Kostomariv, 485; "picked," 405; registered, 163, 181, 256, 257. *See also* Danubian Kozaks; Don Kozaks
Kozatstvo (Kozak life), 152
Koziatin, 540
Kozliv (Eupatoria), 181
Kremenchuk, 273, 535
Kreminets, 134, 135
Krempsky, Kozak hetman, 191, 583
Krevo Union, 129, 130, 132, 134
Krichevsky, artist, 511
Krilov, 256
Kriviches, tribe, 41, 44
Krivonos. *See* Perebiynis
Kropivna, 302
Kropivnitsky, Marko, dramatist, 506, 511
—— Michael, politician, 263
Krupetsky, bishop of Peremyshl, 267, 431
Kuban basin, 458; River, 7
Kukil, Lawrence, author, 204, 239
—— Stephen ("Zizania"), author, 204
Kulaks (prosperous peasants), 565
Kulish, P., author, 484, 494, 500, 504
Kumeyko, 272; treaty, 275
Kuntsevich, J., bishop of Vitebsk, 252
Kura, river, 56
Kurbsky, Prince A. M., Russian exile, 198

Kurini (Kozak squads), 223
Kursk, 153, 409
Kurtsevich, E., abbot, 246
Kurukiv, Lake, 256
Kurukiv, treaty of, 256–258
Kushnir, D., church warden, 443
Kutlubuh, Tatar chief, 125
Kvitka, G., novelist, 478, 482, 483
Kyrilo, bishop of Turiv, 118, 120

Labor Gazette, 522
Ladoga Canal, 376, 381
Land of Free Communes (*Slobidshina*), 274, 287, 337, 340, 343, 409, 411, 451, 474, 483
Landlordism, 348–350, 408, 547, 549
Landlords, 151, 356, 406, 407, 409, 429, 461, 547, 551. *See also* Polish landlords; Russian landlords; Ukrainian landlords
Land reform, 546, 549, 551, 567
Lantskoronsky, P., Kozak officer, 155
Lasch, S., Polish officer, 260–262
Lasota, E., German envoy, 175, 185
Latin alphabet, 497; language, 121, 240, 265, 266, 369
Latin-Catholic culture, 196
Law, 25, 79, 85, 87, 116, 170, 171, 280, 389, 407–410, 420, 460, 546, 551; German, 121 (*see also* Magdeburg Law); Kievan, 87 (*see also* Rus Law Code); Polish, 172, 173; Ukrainian, 446, 448, 450, 451. *See also* Lithuanian Statute
"Law in Accordance with which the Little Russian People Is Judged," law code, 407
League of Nations, 562, 564, 569
Lebed, sister of Kiy, 39
Lebed Stream, 39
Lebedin Monastery, 442
Left Bank Ukraine, 322, 323, 327. *See also* Eastern Ukraine; Hetman state; Russian Ukraine
Legends, 39, 40, 73, 119, 479, 489
Legislative Commission of 1767, 450, 451
Lemberg. *See* Lviv
Lemeshiv, 399
Lenin, V., Soviet leader, 564
Leo, Prince of Galicia, 111, 112, 577 (31)
Leontiev, Russian brigadier, 376

Leschinsky Monastery, 244
Lesun, Kozak leader, 155
Lesya Ukrainka, author, 511
Leszczynski. *See* Stanislaw Leszczynski
Letichiv, 441
Letts, 126, 518
Leventsi (robber bands), 436
Levitsky, metropolitan of Peremyshl, 473
—— Andrew, politician, 564
—— Dr. Dmytro, politician, 568
—— Joseph, literary critic, 487
Liakhs (derogatory name for Poles), 74, 242, 284
Liberals, political party, 518
Liberation of Ukraine, 474
Lieszko, Polish prince, 100
Life of St. George of Amastris, 45
Life of St. Stephen of Surozh, 45
"Line," fortification, 452, 453
Lisianka, 260, 444
Literary-Scientific Herald, 509, 513
Literature, 37, 117–120, 131, 237, 238, 266, 412–416, 422, 477–484, 493, 496, 498, 501, 502, 504, 513
Lithuania, 96, 111, 114, 115, 123–144 *passim*, 149–151, 156, 158, 159, 166–169, 220, 244, 281, 288, 289, 292, 313, 364, 365, 462. *See also* Poland-Lithuania
Lithuanian army, 186, 190, 198; cities, 111; dukes, 115; grand dukes, 117, 195, 581, 582; gentry, 166–168; hetmans, 223; landlords, 165; lands, 47; messengers, 153; nobles, 136, 138–140, 142; princes, 123–126, 131; provinces annexed by Muscovy, 209; soldiers, 220; tribes, 17
Lithuanians, 17, 91, 92, 110, 123, 124, 518
Lithuanian Statute, 88, 169, 170, 349, 407, 408
"Little Poland," 572
Little Rus, 121
Little Russia, 381, 385, 407, 408, 416, 447, 556. *See also* Little Rus; Rus; Ukraine
Little Russian Board, 378–380, 382, 384, 385, 392, 447, 448, 459
Little Russian gentry, 408; language, 496; name, 379; Society, 485

Little Russians, name, 481
Liubart, Grand Duke of Lithuania, 113, 114, 124, 126, 128, 581
Livonia, 159, 218, 235
Livonian "Brothers of the Sword," 126; Knights, 128
Lizohub, Kozak colonel, 391, 393
—— chronicle of, 415
Loboda, G., Kozak hetman, 184, 188, 191, 234, 583
Loess, 3
Lomonosov, M. V., author, 417
London Saturday Review, cited, 566
Louis, King of Hungary and Poland, 127, 128, 428
Lozinsky, J., literary critic, 487, 488
Lubar, 318
Lubche Lake, conference, 84, 85
Lubchenko, P., premier of Soviet Ukraine, 566
Lubech, 24
Lublin, 200, 284, 298; Congress of, 467; Union of, 166, 168–170
Lubny, 176, 191, 274, 390; battle, 193, 215, 217, 224, 250, 252; regiment, 302, 405; River, 190
Lubomirski, Prince, Polish landlord, 438, 439
Lucaris, Patriarch, 199
Luchans, tribe, 24
Luchkai, M., grammarian, 487
Lucian, Greek author, 16
Lukomsky, chronicle of, 415
Lupul, V., Hospodar of Moldavia, 288
Lutsk, 134, 135, 137, 186, 264; brotherhood, 425; diocese, 264
Lviv (Lwow, Lemberg), 112, 146, 147, 163, 180, 198, 242, 245, 282, 298, 299, 332, 423, 438, 489, 493, 498, 504, 513–515, 553, 562, 563, 568; brotherhood, 201, 204–206, 240, 249, 423, 426, 427; diocese, 264, 425; school, 204, 239, 240; seminary, 470; theological school, 488; university, 470, 488, 498
Lviv Chronicle, 414
Lvov. *See* Lviv
Lvov, Prince G., Chairman of Russian Provisional government, 536
Lwow. *See* Lviv
Lysenko, N., composer, 502

Macedonia, 242

Magdeburg Law, 132, 148, 171, 349, 406, 407

Magyars, 72, 491. *See also* Hungarians

Mahmet-Gerai, Crimean khan, 252, 253

Makhno, N., anarchist leader, 556, 557

Mal, Prince of Derevlians, 38, 57

Malopolska (Little Poland), 572

Malusha, Sviatoslav's concubine, 61

Mammoths, 4, 5

Maniava, 427

Manifestation of March 19 (April 1), 1917, 522

Manifesto of October 17 (30), 1905, 512, 513

Manke, Tatar khan, 104

"March on Kiev," 556

March revolution, Russian, 515

Maria Theresa, Hapsburg empress, 433, 464, 470, 489

Marienburg, 325

Mariupol, 458

Mark the Macedonian, agent, 254

Marko Vovchok. *See* Markovich, Maria

Markovich, J., Kozak army treasurer, cited, 397

—— Maria (Marko Vovchok), author, 494

—— Nastia, wife of Ivan Skoropadsky, 378

Marlborough, English duke, 361

Marmarosh, 428–430, 432

Mass trials in Poland, 569

Masudi, Arabian author, 47, 51; cited, 38

"Matica," Czech society, 490

Maurice, Byzantine emperor, 37

Maximilian, Hapsburg emperor, 142

Maximovich, anthologist, 478, 484

Mazepa, Ivan, Kozak hetman, 335, 342, 375, 386, 416, 419, 584; elected, 345, 346; policy, 347–353, 363; and the church, 353, 354; and the Swedish War, 360–369; alliance with Charles XII, 374; insurrection, 375, 390; death, 370

Mediterranean cultural influences, 9

Mediterranean Sea, 9, 227

Medvediv Monastery, 442

Medvedivka, 444

Medvid, Haidamak leader, 439

Meletey. *See* Smotritsky, Maxim

Menander, Greek historian, cited, 22

Mendovg, Lithuanian king, 110, 123

Mengli-Gerai, Crimean khan, 150

Menshikov, Russian minister, 384, 385

Merchants, 86, 240; in brotherhoods, 148; Armenian, 153; Turkish, 161. *See also* Commerce

Meres, tribe, 41

Meta, publication, 499

Metals, 9; tools, 25

Metlinsky, Professor A., ethnologist, 484

Metropolitan of Kiev, 69, 88, 112; consistory in Lviv, 493; see in Galicia, 146

Mezamir, Antae leader, 22, 23

Michael, Hospodar of Wallachia, 218

—— Prince of Chernihiv, 107, 579

—— Olelkovich, 139, 140

Migrations, of steppe tribes, 13, 14; of Antae, 20; of Bastarnians, 18; of Goths, 18; to eastern Ukraine, 154, 165, 174, 274, 287, 291, 337, 372; to Land of Free Communes, 274, 287, 409, 410, 423; to western Ukraine, 72, 434; to Carpatho-Ukraine, 430

Mikhailivsky Monastery, 238, 266

Mikhalchuk, C., philologist, 502

Miliukov, P., Russian Cadet party leader, 518

Mines, 548, 549

Miniatures, 120

Ministry of foreign affairs, Russian, 402

Minorities Treaty, 569

Minority rights, in Polish Ukraine, 562; in Rumania, 559

Mirhorod, 302; regiment, 310, 386, 405, 475

Mirny, author, 502

Missionaries at Volodimir's court, 65

Mizevna (port of Constantinople), 230

Mizyn, 5

Mliiv, 442, 443

Mlodzanowski, Polish minister, 567

Mnohohrishny, D., Kozak hetman, 328, 329, 331, 332, 342, 584

Mohammed, founder of Islam, 159
—— III, Turkish sultan, 254
—— IV, Turkish sultan, 331
Mohammedanism, 65, 334
Mohammedans, 185, 289, 458. *See also* Crimean horde; Turks
Mohila, Hospodar of Moldavia, 186, 218
—— Peter, metropolitan of Kiev, 258, 264, 266, 267
Mohila Academy. *See* Academy of Kiev
Mohila-Zaborovsky Academy. *See* Academy of Kiev
Mohilev, 186, 244
Mohilianka, Princess R., 251
Mohilnitsky, A., author, 490
Moldavia, 8, 144–146, 163, 186, 217, 218, 233, 243, 247, 288, 292–294, 341, 371, 430, 432, 436, 463–465
Moldavian Autonomous Republic, 565
Moldavian dukes, 148; rebellion, 149; wars, 188, 235
Moldavian Soviet Socialist Republic, 574
Monastery, Dermansky, 258; Epiphany, 240; Hustinsky, 251; Lebedin, 442; Leschinsky, 244; Medvediv, 442; Mikhailivsky, 238, 266; Moshnohory, 422; Motronin, 441–443; of the Caves (Pechersky Monastir), 88, 204, 214, 238–242, 265, 266, 353, 414; Pustinsko-Nikolaevsky, 238, 266, 353, 354; Roman Catholic, 434; St. George, 78; St. Irene, 78; St. Michael, 429; St. Nicholas, 429; Solovetsky, 455; Tobolsk, 456; Veliki Skit, 427; Vitebsk, 120; Zhabotin, 442, 443
Mongolian Tatars. *See* Tatars
Mongols, 101, 103, 105. *See* Tatars
Monks, 436
Monks Hill, 429
Monomakh, Volodimir, Prince of Kiev, 26, 67, 83–85, 87, 91–93, 575 (16), 579, 580
Moravia, 105, 572
Moscow, 140, 168, 198, 236, 242, 251, 345, 417, 484, 565, 566; Patriarch of, 296
Moshnohory Monastery, 442
Moshny, 272
Motronin Monastery, 441–443

Mounds, burial, 15
Mozy, 143
Mstislav, Prince of Tmutorokan, 64, 75, 76, 579
—— I, Prince of Kiev, 92, 575 (17), 580
—— II, Prince of Kiev, 96, 576 (34), 580
—— III, Prince of Kiev, 102, 576 (56)
—— the Daring, Prince of Galicia, 100–102, 577 (22), 580
Mstislavets, P., printer, 198
Mukachev, 429, 430, 470, 571; Monastery, 432
Mukha, Wallachian rebel, 145
Munich agreement, 571, 572, 574
Muraviev, Soviet general, 548
Murom, 64
Muscophile movement. *See* Russophile movement
Muscovite dynasty, 93; messengers, 153; princes, 111, 126; tsars, 67
Muscovy, 71, 103, 106, 111, 166, 176, 178, 180, 185, 189, 190, 209, 274, 287, 291, 304, 307, 337, 342, 371, 372, 409, 580; and Crimean horde, 150, 151; intervention in Ukraine, 138–143; early alliances with Kozaks, 158, 159, 163; raided by Kozaks, 219–221, 226, 229, 232, 233; wars with Poland, 235, 236, 250, 264, 265, 267; approached by Kievan clergy, 251, 252, 254, 255; protectorate of Ukraine, 288, 289, 293–297; war with Kozaks, 298–301, 314–318; abandons western Ukraine, 319–322, 324; Brukhovetsky's uprising against, 325–328; and Mnohohrishny, 329–333; and Doroshenko, 331, 334, 337, 338; and Samoilovich, 335, 339–341, 343, 344; and eastern Ukraine, 346, 347, 350, 352; Grand Prince of, 141; name, 374; Patriarch of, 343. *See also* Russia
Museum of Ukraine's Struggle for Liberation, in Prague, 564

"Nalivaikans," 214
Nalivaiko, S., Kozak leader, 184–186, 188–193, 217, 234

Narses, Byzantine general, 22
Naryshkin, Catherine, wife of C. Rozumovsky, 400
Nastia, wife of Skoropadsky, 378
Natalka Poltvaka, operetta of Kotlyarevsky, 478, 482
National Democratic political party, 508
Nationalism, Ukrainian, 201, 214, 221, 237, 240, 241, 262, 266, 283, 284, 374, 412, 413, 423, 468, 490, 498, 499, 514, 522, 528, 542, 550, 564; beginnings, 144; decline after Lubny, 193–197; under Russia, 418–421; revival in Russian Ukraine, 473–487 *passim*, in western Ukraine, 469–474, 487–491, in Carpatho-Ukraine, 429, 491–493. *See also* Romantic nationalism; Ukrainian renaissance
Nationalists, political party, 507, 508
National Rada of Carpatho-Ukraine, 560
Naumov, Russian privy councillor, 385–387
Nechkovsky, C., Kozak hetman, 218, 583
Nekrasov, Don Kozak leader, 457
Nemirich, G., Ukrainian noble, 315
Nemiriv, fort, 358
Neolithic Age, 6, 7
Neophite, Greek archimandrite, 215
Nestor, author, 118
Netchuy-Levitsky, author, 500, 502, 504
Netherlands, 173
Neuri, tribe, 17
New Council, newspaper, 522
New Economic Policy of Soviet Union, 564
New Rome, 66. *See* Constantinople
New Russia, 452, 453
"New Serbia." *See* Serbia
Newspapers, 498, 512, 513, 515, 516, 556, 574
New Stone Age. *See* Neolithic Age
Nezhivy, S., Haidamak leader, 444, 445
Nicephorus, Byzantine emperor, 60
—— patriarchal vicar of Constantinople, 199, 211, 212
Nicholas I, Emperor of Russia, 498, 499

Niemen River, 173, 268, 324
Night of Taras, poem by Shevchenko, quoted, 261
Nikolaev, 547
Niva, publication, 499
Nizami, Persian poet, quoted, 56
Nizhin, 273, 302, 317, 330, 398, 405, 450
Nobles. *See* Gentry; Greek Orthodox nobles; Lithuanian nobles; Polish nobles; Russian nobles; Ukrainian nobles
Nogais, nomad tribe, 13
Nomads, 13, 73, 84, 91, 93, 101, 104. *See also* Steppes, tribes of
Nonregistered Kozaks. *See* "Civilians"
Norse, 44. *See* Scandinavians
Northwestern Ukraine, 563, 573
Norway, 44
Nos, A., Ukrainian prince, 134
Nova Hromada, journal, 513
Novgorod, 41, 42, 47, 56, 61, 63
Novhorod-Litovsky, 125
Novhorod-Siversky, 24, 90, 328; principality, 125

Obozny (Kozak ordnance officer), 223, 404
Obri. *See* Avars
Ochakiv, 158, 180, 229–232, 456, 457
Oder River, 18, 19
Odessa, 515, 535, 547, 551, 555
Odyssey, by Homer, 12
Officers' Council, Kozak, 303, 305, 308, 309, 315, 320, 325–327, 330, 333, 345, 346, 348, 374–379, 381, 386–388, 400–406, 450; quoted, 398, 399
Oka River, 64
Okhmativ, 298
Olaf, King of Sweden, 77
Olbia, 11–13
Old Slavonic language, 205, 414, 419, 487–489, 495, 497. *See also* Church Slavonic; Slavonic
Old Stone Age. *See* Paleolithic Age
Oleh, Prince of Chernihiv, 83, 84, 90, 579
—— Prince of Derevlians, 60, 61, 63, 579
—— Prince of Kiev, 40–42, 47, 48,

50, 51, 54, 55, 58, 59, 72, 242, 575 (1), 579

Olelko, Prince of Kiev, 198. *See* Alexander, Prince of Kiev

Olha (Olga, Helga), Princess of Kiev, 40, 46, 48, 58, 61, 65, 66, 575, 579

Omelchenko, Kozak colonel, 362

Only True Orthodox Faith, by Vasyl, 199

Onushkevich, Kozak secretary, 270, 271

Opara, Kozak officer, 324

Operettas, 483

Opishnia, 327

Orel River, 340

Organization of Ukrainian Nationalists (OUN), 568–570

Orlik, P., Kozak hetman, 365, 369, 370, 389, 390, 584; cited, 359

Orsha, 244

Osaul (Kozak adjutant), 223

Osnova, journal, 494, 496

Ossetes. *See* Yasians

Oster, 330

Ostrianin, Y., Kozak hetman, 273, 274, 409, 584

Ostroh, 184; literary circle and school, 198, 199, 200, 204, 212, 235, 237; press, 240; principality, 132

Ostroh (fortified town), 34

Ostrohozhsk, 409, 410

Ostrozky, Prince Alexander, 200, 202, 210, 211; Prince Dashko, 134; Prince Constantine Ivanovich, 143, 147, 150, 155, 198; Prince Vasyl Constantine, 183, 186, 198, 200, 209, 211, 214; Prince Yanush, governor of Bila Tserkva, 182, 200, 240; family, 176

Otaman, official, 48–50, 303

Ovruch, 61, 63, 143

"Pacification" in Poland, 568

Pacta conventa (conditions accepted by Polish kings), 262, 263

Pagans in Rus, 65, 68

Painlevé, French statesman, 567

Paisius, Patriarch of Jerusalem, 283

Paleolithic Age, 6

Paliy, S. H., Kozak colonel, 341, 342, 352, 357, 358, 361, 362, 433, 434, 437, 438

Pan. See Nobles

Panorama of Ukraine, by Shevchenko, 354

Pan-Russian movement, 492. *See* Russophile movement

Pan-Slavic Society, 485

Panticapaeum. *See* Kertch

Pan-Ukrainian Academy of Science, 564, 566

Pan-Ukrainian Congress, 529, 530, 532, 535, 547, 570, 572

Papal legate, 109

Paris, 563

Parliamentary democracy, 506

"Patronage," 195

Paul, Emperor of Russia, 475, 476

Pavliuk But, Kozak hetman, 270, 271, 584

Pavlovsky, author, 480

Pavolotsky, 189

Peasants, 84, 85, 148, 172, 174, 175, 178, 304, 350, 351, 410, 441, 470, 481, 482, 489, 491, 511, 512, 525, 547, 549–551, 555, 557. *See also* Serfdom

Pechenegs, nomad tribe, 35, 60–62, 71–74, 76, 78, 82

Pechersky fortress at Kiev, 359; Monastir. *See* Monastery of the Caves

People's Commissars of Soviet government, 530, 532, 537, 539

Perebiynis (also known as Krivonos), Kozak leader, 282

Perekop, 158, 159, 185, 221

Peremyshl, city, 89, 133, 204, 324, 473, 487, 516; diocese, 210, 214, 242, 264, 267, 425, 427, 431; province, 100

Peresichen, 57

Pereyaslav, city, 24, 34, 51, 73, 74, 81, 84, 90, 91, 93, 103, 104, 107, 155, 182, 189, 233, 260, 261, 302, 316, 317, 330, 335, 354, 417; treaty of (*see* Khmelnitsky, Bohdan, treaty of); province, 273; regiment, 302, 312, 319, 405; tribe, 34

Pereyaslavets (Preslav), 60, 61

Perm, 517

Persia, 13, 36, 60, 69, 117

Perun, pagan idol, 68

Pest, city in Hungary, 489

Peter the Great, Emperor of Russia,

352, 358–385 *passim*, 387, 390, 392, 399, 419

—— II, Emperor of Russia, 385, 390

—— III, Emperor of Russia, 400

Petlura, president of Directory, 553, 554, 556, 564

Petrazhitsky-Kulaha, I., Kozak hetman, 263, 584

Petrograd (earlier St. Petersburg, later Leningrad), 521, 528, 541

Petrushevich, Dr. E., head of Ukrainian National Rada, 553, 562, 563

Petryk Ivanenko, Zaporozhian leader, 355–357

Phanagoria, 11

Philip I, King of France, 77

Photius, Patriarch of Constantinople, 46

Piatka, 183

Pidkova, I., Kozak leader, 163

Pidliashe, province, 167, 467, 517

Pidvisotsky, Kozak leader, 191, 192

Pieracki, Polish minister, 569

Piliavka River, 282

Piliavtsi, 282, 285

Pilsudski, Polish marshal, 562

Pinsk, 131, 132, 169, 244, 544; River, 124. *See also* Turiv-Pinsk

Pletenitsky, E., abbot of Monastery of Caves, 238, 239

Pobuzha, 214

Podolia, principality and province, 8, 125, 132, 135, 136, 144, 150, 155, 168, 169, 174, 175, 194, 243, 281, 284, 292, 293, 332, 334, 336, 340, 341, 424, 426, 427, 429, 434, 436, 438, 441, 443, 464, 466, 517, 528, 529, 546

Poetry, 481, 483, 489

Pogodin, Russian author, 497

Pokutia, 144, 145; Land of, 465

Polabians, tribe, 19

Poland, 76, 100, 105, 110, 113, 124, 126, 128, 143, 144, 146, 150, 156, 190, 195, 208, 209, 390, 397, 403, 405, 409, 414, 495, 496, 519, 520; unites eastern and western Ukraine, 165–168, 201; and Kozaks, 217–221, 224, 233, 236, 237, 243, 247, 249, 251, 253–257, 270–276; and Khmelnitsky's rebellion, 277–303; and Hetman state, 303–318; attempts to regain eastern Ukraine,

319, 320, 323–331, 334, 335, 340–344; and great northern war, 352, 355, 359, 360, 363–369; rule in western Ukraine, 418, 422–424, 427, 433, 434; loses western Ukraine in partitions, 435, 437, 452, 462, 466–469; reconquest of western Ukraine, 553–557, 560–564; after Munich, 570–573. *See also* Poland-Lithuania

Poland-Lithuania, 123–143 *passim*, 148, 162, 163, 194, 197, 201–211, 582

Poles, 19, 74–76, 89, 92, 97, 114, 123, 127, 146, 163, 267, 485, 489, 498, 507, 510, 514, 516–518, 564

Poletika, G., author, 479

Polians, tribe, 24, 39–42. *See also* Rus

Policarp, author, 119

Polish army, 184, 188, 189, 219, 247, 545, 555; Chamber of Deputies, 562, 572; Church, 196; cities, 111; commissioners, 284, 285; culture, 195, 197, 266; government, 180, 186, 188, 200, 208, 211, 222, 232, 233, 250, 425–427; hetmans, 223; landlords, 179, 194, 222, 250, 275–277, 286, 349, 351, 437, 462, 468, 469, 474, 489, 493, 498, 507, 508, 546, 551, 552 (*see also* Landlords); language, 472, 473; law, 169, 173; legions, 524, 547; nobles, 129, 135, 137, 145, 149, 169, 175, 176, 192, 212, 213, 219, 233, 249, 281, 292, 320, 424, 437 (*see also* Landlords); parliament, 220, 262, 263, 265, 467, 563, 567–569; princes, 98; senate, 424, 562; writers, 97

Polish-Hungarian alliance of 1214, 101, 128

Polish-Lithuanian armistice, 136; empire, 556

Polish-Muscovite treaty of 1681, 340

Polish-Soviet War of 1920, 561

Polish-Ukrainian War, 556, 557, 561

Polish Ukraine, 565–570. *See also* Western Ukraine

Polisia, principality and province, 17, 91, 124, 131, 137, 150, 152, 174, 182, 186, 308, 341, 434, 441, 444, 563, 567; Kievan, 424; on the Pripet, *see* Turiv-Pinsk

Political parties, 432, 498, 506–508, 511, 518, 521, 525, 527, 528, 532, 539, 542, 558

Polk (regiment), 223

Polkovnik (colonel), 223, 303

Polonization, 170, 193, 197, 469, 497

Polotsk, diocese, 245; principality, 63, 75, 82, 88, 136, 258, 264

Polovtsians, steppe tribe, 76, 80, 82–84, 89, 91, 93, 96, 98, 103, 105, 153

Poltava, battle, 369; city, 11, 302, 356, 417, 535, 548; government, 408; province, 5, 311, 534, 548; regiment, 310, 311, 405; Zemstvo Hall, 511

Polubotok, Kozak acting hetman, 378–384, 387, 389, 404; Legion, 525

Pomeschik (Russian landowner), 411

Pomorian tribe, 19

Poniatowski, S., King of Poland, 463

Pope, 100, 109, 110, 114, 127, 185, 208, 210, 269, 432, 433

Popovich, O., president of northern Bukovina, 559

Popular Assembly of western Ukraine, 573

Potemkin, Prince G. A., Russian imperial commissioner, 456, 457, 475

Potiy, Uniate metropolitan, 210, 213, 215, 241

Potocki, N., Polish general, 271–273, 275, 276, 279, 280, 292, 299

—— S., Polish officer, son of above, 279, 280

Potocki estate, 444; family, 176

Pottery, primitive, 6–8

Povit (district), 204; courts, 408

Prague, 564, 571

Pravda, literary journal in Lviv, 499, 501

Prayer of Daniel, prose poem, 120

Pre-Mycenean culture type, 8

Preslav. *See* Pereyaslavets

Press, Ukrainian, 513, 515, 522. *See also* Newspapers; Printing, presses

Priluki, 302, 330, 345, 360, 405

Primary Chronicle, 119. *See also* Chronicles, Kievan

Printing, development of, 240; presses, 197, 198, 423, 427, 430

Pripet River, 37, 123

Privy Council, Russian, 388

Proclamations, of Central Rada, First, 526, Second, 527, Third, 532, 538, 549, Fourth, 536, 538, 539, 549; of Mazeppa, 351

Procopius, Byzantine historian, 21, 22

Progressive political movement, 495, 501, 506, 507, 519; party, 521

Prosvita. *See* Society for Enlightenment

Protestants, 297, 298; political party in Carpatho-Ukraine, 432

Provisional Council for Ukraine, 390, 392

Provisional Government, Russian, 522–530 *passim*

Prussia, 145, 398, 463, 464, 465, 467, 498; Ukrainian project in, 475

Prussians, tribe, 126

Pruth River, 371, 436, 464, 465

Psalms, publication of, 198

Psiol, 273; River, 410

Pushkar, M., Kozak, 310, 321

Pustinsko-Nikolaevsky Monastery, 238, 266, 353, 354

Putivl, 85, 274, 324

Pysar (secretary), 223

Rada (assembly or council), 224, 305, 405. *See also* Central Rada

Radical political party, 507, 508

Radimiches, tribe, 63

Radomisl, 441, 444

Rakoczy, G., Transylvanian prince, 300, 301

Ratno, province, 131, 132

Red army, 553–557

Red Guards, 534

Red ochre burials, 7

Reformation, German, 196

Regeneration (*Vidrozhenia*) Temperance Society, 572

Registered Kozaks, 177, 178, 180, 181, 250, 258, 259, 262, 270, 272, 273, 275, 277–280, 286, 287, 292, 351. *See* Kozaks

Relics, prehistoric, 2–5

"Religious Endowment" in Galicia and Bukovina, 471

Renaissance. *See* Nationalism; Slavic Renaissance

Repnin, governor-general, 476

Resurrection of Dead, drama by G. Konisky, 416

Retinue of Kievan princes, 44, 86, 115

Rhinoceros, woolly, 4

Rid (clan), 33

Ridney Krai, newspaper, 513

Riegelmann, Russian official, 502

Riga, treaty of, 561, 563

Right Bank Ukraine, 322, 325, 327, 328, 336. *See* Western Ukraine

Rix (chief), 37

Rohatyn, 145, 204, 239, 424

Rohoza, M., metropolitan of Kiev, 209, 213

Roman, Prince of Volynia, 92, 96–101, 110, 577, 580; heirs of, 108

—— Prince of Galicia, 123

Roman Catholic culture, 198; landowners, 214; literature, 479; monasteries, 434; schools, 205

Roman Catholicism, 65, 100, 109, 113, 114, 121, 129–133, 136, 139–143, 146, 147, 187, 188, 193, 194, 196, 198–201, 205–209, 250, 258, 313, 367, 422, 425–427, 470, 479, 499; in Carpatho-Ukraine, 429–433

Romanchuk, J., Ukrainian leader, 563

Romanov dynasty in Russia, 515, 521

Romans, 1, 9, 17; coins, 18; provinces, 18

Romantic nationalism, 479, 480, 484, 488, 506

Rome, 269

Romen, 274

Romodanovsky, G., Russian general, 327, 328, 334, 335, 339

Ros River, 26, 182, 272, 341

Rostislav, Prince, usurper of Galician crown, 108

—— I, Prince of Kiev, 92, 94, 98, 576 (62), 580

—— II, Prince of Kiev, 93, 576 (48), 580

Rostov, 11, 64

Rozumovsky (Razumovsky), Alexey, Russian count, 399, 400

—— (Razumovsky), Cyril, Hetman of Ukraine, 400–408, 420, 446–448, 475, 476

Rudansky, author, 502

Rudchenko, ethnographer, 502

"The Ruin," 336, 342

Rumania, 428, 491, 554, 555, 559, 560, 570, 572–574

Rumanian language, 471

Rumanians, 144, 465, 555

Rumiantsov, P. A., president of Little Russian Board, 382, 383, 420, 447–451, 459

Rurik, Prince of Kiev, 89, 93, 94, 98, 576 (39), 580

—— Varangian warrior, 41

Rus (later Ukraine), army, 45, 56, 59, 61, 78; land, 31, 41, 43, 60, 65, 93; name, 40, 42–44; people, 24, 41, 43, 45; princes, 67, 106, 124, 138, 149, 575, 576, 579; state, 43, 115–117, 196, 241, 242, 245, 284, 289, 354, 374

Rus, Grand Duchy of, 313, 318

Rusalka, publication, 499

Rusalka of Dniester, anthology, 489

"Ruska Pravda" (*see* Rus Law Code); and Lithuanian Statute, 88

Ruska National Rada, 560

Ruski (Rus). *See* Kievans, Rus, Ukrainians

Rus Law Code, 79, 87–88

Russia, 313, 372–574 *passim;* name, 373

Russian Academy of Science, 400

Russian army, 517; culture, 419, 516; empire, 506, 513, 537, 548, 558; federal republic, project of, 522, 523, 525, 526, 531, 533, 537–540; imperialism, 544, 545; journals, 483; landlords, 552; language, 413, 419, 420, 473, 476, 492, 494, 495, 498, 503, 516; national groups, 564; nobles, 456; officials, 382, 383, 392–397, 401–404, 517; Orthodox Church, 516; Synod, 496; orthography, 503, 515; Revolution of 1905, 511; Revolution of February 25 (March 10), 1917, 521, 524; senate, 376, 377, 379, 392, 400, 402, 513, 530

Russian Ukraine, 488, 493–497, 500, 501, 510–513, 514, 515. *See also* Eastern Ukraine

Russification, 393, 410, 447, 469, 474, 476, 480, 498

Russo-Japanese war, 511

Russo-Turkish war of 1768, 463; of 1792, 457

Russophile movement, 492, 495, 497, 499, 501, 505, 507, 514
"Ruthenia," name, 473, 572
Ruthenian Society, 500
Ruthenians, 490, 498
"Ruthenian triumvirate," 488, 489
Rutsky, V., Uniate metropolitan, 241
Ruzhinsky, B., Kozak hetman, 163, 583
—— K., Kozak in Polish army, 189
—— family, 176
Rzhishchev, 316

Sadowa, 498
Safonovich, chronicler, 414
Sahaidachny, P., Kozak hetman, 234–237, 239–249, 583
St. Andrew, Russian order, 401, 402
—— Barbara, litany to, 413
—— Basil, order, 473
—— Elias, church in Kiev, 65
—— George, island, 35
—— George, monastery in Kiev, 78
—— Germain, treaty of, 559
—— Irene, monastery in Kiev, 78
—— Mamant, church in Constantinople, 36
—— Michael, monastery in Carpatho-Ukraine, 429
—— Nicholas, church in Kiev, 354, 401
—— Nicholas, monastery in Carpatho-Ukraine, 429
—— Petersburg, 376, 382, 384, 385, 387, 388, 392, 399, 400, 402, 403, 417, 456, 484, 494, 501, 510; Academy of Science, 512; Committee on Education, 495
SS. Peter and Paul Prison, 383
St. Sophia, cathedral in Kiev, 76, 78, 150, 267; Square, 526
—— Theodosius, author, 118
Salt, 96
Saltykov, Russian official, 325
Samara River, 180
Sambir, 235, 324
Samiylenko, V., author, 511
Samoilovich, I. ("Popovich"), Kozak hetman, 333–345, 348, 350, 351, 353, 354, 405, 410, 412, 584
Samsun, 231
Samus, Kozak colonel, 341, 437
Sarai near later Tsarev, 105

Sarmatians, nomad tribe, 13, 16
Sarny, 545
Sataniv, 204
Saxony, 437, 438
Sazonov, S. D., Russian minister of foreign affairs, 518
Scandinavia, 41, 63, 77; warriors, 4
Scandinavians, 44
Schools, in Galicia, 470, 472, 473, 489, 510; in Hungarian Ukraine, 572; in Kharkiv, 483; in Lviv, 204, 239, 240, 488; in Ostroh, 198–200, 204, 212, 235, 237; in Peremyshl, 487; in Slutsk, 198; in Russian Ukraine, 412, 414, 422, 473, 495, 496, 513, 518; in Soviet Ukraine, 564, 568; Roman Catholic, 205; Sunday, 495, 496
Scientific Society (earlier Shevchenko Scientific Society), 509
Scranton, Pa., 560
Scylas, Scythian king, 12
Scythians, nomad tribe, 12–14, 16, 17; chiefs, 15
Sejm. *See* Polish Chamber of Deputies
Seletsky, Kozak officer, 450
Selo, newspaper, 513
Semen, Prince of Kiev, 138, 139, 582
Senate. *See* Polish senate; Russian senate
Separatism, Ukrainian, 449
Serapion, author, 119
Serbia, 118, 254; New, 452
Serbian immigrants, 452
Serbs, 19, 485
Seret, 465; River, 465
Serfdom, 116, 174, 182–184, 197, 212, 250, 256, 274, 276, 286, 306, 342, 347–356, 379, 390, 395, 411, 412, 416, 418, 429, 433, 434, 449, 456, 460–462, 467, 469, 474, 485, 486, 491. *See also* Peasants
Sevastopol, 11
Seym River, 24, 73
Shahin-Gerai, Khan of Crimea, 253–255, 270
Shakhovsky, Prince A., Russian resident commissioner, 390–393
Sharish county, 428
Shashkevich, V., poet, 488, 489
Shaula, M., Kozak hetman, 189, 192, 583

Shek, mythological cofounder of Kiev, 39

Sheptitsky, A., metropolitan, 562
—— V., priest, 425

Sheremetiev, F., Russian noble, 318, 329, 343

Shevchenko, T., poet, 354, 478, 484–486, 499, 521, 549; cited, 521, 549

Shevchenko Society (Scientific Society, 1892–1908, Shevchenko Scientific Society, from 1908), 504, 509, 562

Shipin district, 465

Shumliansky, J., bishop in Lviv, 425

Shvachka, J., Haidamak leader, 444

Shvarno, Prince of Kholm, 111, 123

Sian River, 173

Sianok, 114

Siberia, 311, 333, 338, 342, 345, 362, 434, 456, 516–518

Sich, Zaporozhian (see Zaporozhian Sich); Danubian, 457, 458

Sich, in Carpatho-Ukraine, 572

Siches (fortresses), 156; (gymnastic societies), 510

Sichovi Striltsi (volunteer regiments), 520, 542, 556

Sieniawski, Polish general, 362

Sigismund, Grand Duke of Lithuania, 136–138
—— King of Hungary, 134
—— I, Grand Duke of Lithuania and King of Poland, 142, 143, 582
—— II August, Grand Duke of Lithuania and King of Poland, 157, 166, 177, 582
—— III August, Grand Duke of Lithuania and King of Poland, 177, 210–213, 215, 246, 249, 251, 262, 263

Silesia, 105, 173

Silistria. See Dorostol

Simeon, Tsar of Bulgaria, 60

Simon, author, 119

Sineus, Varangian warrior, 41

Sinope, 45, 230

Sirko, custodian of Zaporozhian Sich, 314, 315, 335, 338

Siveria, principality and province, 142, 150, 169, 314, 315, 325, 328, 330

Siverians (Sivers), tribe, 24, 26, 34, 44, 47

Sivsk, 324, 345

Skidan, K., Kozak colonel, 271–274

Skirhailo, Lithuanian prince of Kiev, 132, 582

Skobeiko, Kievan servant, 137

Skoropadsky, Ivan, Kozak hetman, 368, 375, 378–380, 402, 584
—— Paul, Hetman of Ukraine, 551–554

Skot (cattle), 2

Skovoroda, G., author, 417

Skripnik, Commissar of Education, 566

Slavery, 116, 172

Slaves, 11, 43, 60, 72, 84–86, 231, 234

Slavic countries, 43, 123; peoples, 17; race, 17; tribes, 17, 19, 25, 41, 44; villages, 17; wives, 32

Slavic renaissance, 479, 481, 484, 485, 487, 488

Slavonic books, 119; language, 79, 118, 199, 240, 477

"Slavonic-Russian" language, 490

Slavophiles, 495, 497

Slavs, 17–21, 486; Danubian, 21; western, 479

Slobidshina. See Land of Free Communes

Slobidska Gubernia, 451

Slovakia, 428, 572

Slovaks, 19, 485

Slovenes, 19, 21, 24, 37, 44, 485

Slovo, newspaper, 498

Sluch River, 24, 106

Slutsk, 139, 143, 186, 198; school, 200

Slutsky, Prince G., cultural leader, 198, 200

Smerd. See Peasants

Smila, 444

Smolensk, 63, 143, 226, 365

Smotrich, 125, 135; River, 125

Smotritsky, H., teacher at Ostroh, 199
—— Maxim (Meletey), bishop of Polotsk, 199, 214, 245, 258

Sniporod, 274

Sob River, 189

Sobieski, Jan, King of Poland, 235, 334, 335, 340, 341, 344, 434

Sobinski, Polish school director, 568

Social Democrats, political party, 527, 528, 532, 539

Social Revolutionaries, political party, 532, 535, 539, 542
Socialism, 506, 546, 547, 549
Society for Enlightenment (Prosvita), 490, 510
Sofonovich, chronicle of, 414
Sokal, 424
Sokols (gymnastic societies), 510
Soloma, Kozak colonel, 274
Solona River, 105
Solonchaks (salt swamps), 4
Solonitsia River, 176, 190
Solovetsky Islands, 565; Monastery, 455
Somko, J., Kozak colonel, 319–322
Song of the Legion of Ihor, epic poem, 120; quoted, 90, 93, 94, 153
Songs, 175, 476, 477, 483, 488, 503. See also Folk songs
Sophia, Russian tsarevna, 344, 345, 352
Sosna River, 409
Sotni (Kozak companies), 223
Sotnik (Kozak captain), 223, 303
Southeastern Europe, 160
Southeastern Slavs, 19
Southeastern Ukraine, 59, 182
Southern Slavs, 19
Southern Ukraine, 394
Soviet Russia, 558, 561, 565; delegates at Brest-Litovsk, 537
Soviet Ukraine, 561, 564–566, 570, 573. See Ukrainian Soviet Socialist Republic
Soviets, 555. See Bolsheviks
Soviet Union, 558, 565, 568, 570, 573
Soyuz Ukrainok (Ukrainian Women's Alliance), 572
Soyuz Vizvolennia Ukrainy. See Union for the Liberation of Ukraine
Spain, 142, 160, 173, 227, 229, 254
Sreznevsky, linguist, 478, 483
Stadion, Count, Viceroy of Galicia, 490
Stanislav, Prince of Smolensk, 64
Stanislaviv, 554, 563
Stanislaw Leszczynski, King of Poland, 363, 437, 438
Staritsky, M., author, 502, 506
Starodub, 342, 365; principality, 125, 131, 132; regimental district, 378, 382, 384, 405

Starost (district) courts in Poland, 407
Starshina (Kozak Officers' Council), 224. See Officers' Council
Startsi (elders in early Ukraine), 33
Startsi River, 275
Stavrovetsky, author, 204
Stebliv, 280
Stefanik, V., author, 510
Stempkovski, Polish official, 445
Stephen the Great, hospodar of Moldavia, 140, 144, 145
Steppes, 3, 18, 24, 35, 102, 152, 436, 453, 454; Asiatic, 101; Caspian, 23; Ukrainian, 12–14, 16, 72, 161 (see Black Sea steppes); tribes of (see Nomads)
Stone Age, 34. See Neolithic Age; Paleolithic Age
Striatyn, 239
Striy, 568
Strus, Polish officer, 190
Struve, P. B., Russian Liberal leader, 518
Stshalkova, 561
Stuhna, 73; River, 73, 84
Stürgkh, premier of Austria, 521
Sub-Carpathian Rus, province, 570, 571
Subotiv, 278
Subuday, Mongol leader, 102, 103
Suchava, 293, 465
Sukhovienko, P., Kozak hetman, 330
Sukovski, Polish minister, 567
Sula River, 24, 73, 74, 176, 190, 191, 274
Sulak River, 384, 385
Sulima, I., Kozak hetman, 269, 270, 584
—— Kozak colonel, 368
Sumy, city, 409; regiment, 410, 411
Suzdal, 91, 93, 96, 115
Suzdal-Muscovy, 112, 580
Sveneld, military chieftain, 57
Sviatopolk I, Prince of Kiev, 64, 74, 76, 81, 575 (7)
—— II, Prince of Kiev, 83–85, 93, 575 (15), 579
Sviatopolk-Chetvertinsky, G., metropolitan, 343
Sviatoslav, Prince of Chernihiv, 81–83, 94, 579

—— son of Ihor, Prince of Kiev, 40, 47, 57–63, 72, 575 (4), 579

—— son of Vsevolod, Prince of Kiev, 93, 576 (42), 579

—— son of Yaroslav, Prince of Kiev, 90, 575 (12), 579

Svitrihailo, Grand Duke of Lithuania, 133–138, 582

Sweden, 4, 43, 44, 77, 218, 255, 257, 258, 268, 269, 290, 294, 297–300, 308, 309, 311, 312, 359–371, 375, 386, 426

Switzerland, 504

Synopsis, chronicle history of Rus, 414

Syria, 9

Tabaristan, 46, 51

Tanais, 11. *See also* Rostov

Tangut, 102

Tansky, Kozak colonel, 434, 438

"Tatar people," 106, 110

"Tatar yoke," 109

Tatars, 94, 101, 102, 106–112, 114, 117, 124, 126, 128, 130. *See also* Crimean horde; Golden Horde; Mongols

Taxation, 107, 355, 374, 448

Tekeli, Russian general, 454, 456

Temuchin (Genghis-Khan), 102, 103

Teplov, V. N., Russian official, 402, 403, 446

Terebovl, 89

Terekhtemiriv, 223, 246

Terletsky, Uniate bishop, 210

Ternopil, 424, 553, 554, 563

Tertiary period, 3, 4

Teterev River, 24, 106

Teteria, P., Kozak hetman, 312, 319, 322, 323, 325, 584

Teutonic Knights, 123, 126–128, 133, 136

Theater, 502, 505, 506

Theiss River, 457

Theodore, Prince of Kiev, 125

Theodosia, 11

Theodosius, abbot of Monastery of Caves, 88

Theophanes, Patriarch of Jerusalem, 242–244

Thracians, tribe, 17

Threnody, or the Plaint of the East-ern Church, by Smotritsky, 214, 215

Tiahinia (Bendery), 180, 185, 369

Time of Troubles in Muscovy, 236, 293

Tisarovsky, bishop of Lviv, 242

Tiskinevich, G., Kozak hetman, 215, 583

Tithe Church in Kiev, 39

Tivertses, tribe, 24

Tmutorokan, 47, 64

Tobilevich brothers, dramatists, 506, 511

Tobolsk, 345; Monastery, 456

Tolstoy, P., Russian official, 377, 378, 381, 385

Tomilenko, V., Kozak hetman, 270–272, 584

Torchesk, 84

Torhovitsa Confederation, 466

Torks, nomad tribe, 76, 82

Tovarish (comrade), 223

Tovaristvo (fellowship), name for Kozak Host, 223

Tovmach, 424

"Townships" (*volost,* upper Dnieper region in Kozak times), 156, 222, 234, 246, 258, 259, 271–273, 276, 305

Townspeople, 86, 116, 121, 145, 149, 178, 179, 186, 193, 200, 201, 206–208, 212, 221, 240, 257, 302, 304, 421, 423, 424, 436, 440, 450, 467, 469, 470

Trade. *See* Commerce

Trans-Carpathian Mountains, 427; districts in, 428

Transcaucasia, 102

Transylvania, 243, 297, 465; and Khmelnitsky, 288, 290, 294, 298, 300

Trebizond, 229–231

Trident, insignia, 554

Tripillia, 83, 182, 190

Troki, 147

Trubetskoy, Prince A. N., Russian general, 314, 316, 317

Trubezh River, 73

Truvor, Varangian warrior, 41

Tsarhorod. *See* Constantinople

Tsereteli, I. G., Russian politician, 528

Tsertelev, N., anthologist, 478, 480

Tsibulnik River, 256
Tugut, Polish legislator, 567
Tuhai-bey, Crimean general, 279, 280
Tukalsky, J. N., metropolitan, 325, 343, 425
Tulcea, 60
Tur, N., abbot of Monastery of the Caves, 214, 238
Turiv, 34, 64, 74, 143; tribe, 34; Turiv-Pinsk, 91, 264
Turkestan, 9, 13, 34, 102, 103
Turkey, 144, 145, 150, 160, 243, 250, 254, 268, 277, 278, 288, 290, 294, 299, 324, 328, 331, 332, 334, 336, 339, 340, 342–344, 356–359, 369–371, 384, 389, 394, 397–399, 403, 412, 452, 454, 456–459, 463–466
Turkish bands, 72; cities, 186; language, 436; merchants, 153; tribes, 13, 18, 23; settlements, 186
Turks, 102, 103, 157–159, 163, 179, 180, 185, 186, 208, 221, 222, 226–233, 235, 244, 247, 248, 250, 252, 253, 257, 269, 270, 284, 338, 426
Tuscany, 254
Tyras, 11
Tzimiskes, J., Byzantine emperor, 61

Udai River, 5, 176
Ukraine, eastern (see Eastern Ukraine); name, 41, 151; western (see Western Ukraine)
Ukrainian Agricultural Fair, 568; architecture, 78; army, 545–547, 553, 554; Boy Scouts, 568; Central Council (see Central Rada); chronicles, 33 (see also Chronicles, Kievan); Citizens' Committee, 562; Church, 146, 309, 343, 344, 353, 354 (see Greek Orthodox Church; Uniate Church); dictionary, 239; Free University, 564; gentry, 193, 194, 197, 214, 240, 249, 262, 267; Guard, 490; Historical and Philological Society in Prague, 564; landlords, 195, 481, 551; language, 9, 124, 131, 198, 205, 413, 414, 416, 419, 469, 470, 473, 474, 477–481, 483, 487–492, 494, 495, 498, 499, 502, 503, 505, 507, 509, 511–513, 515, 516, 519, 546, 551, 556, 559, 564, 567, 571; Military Command, 553; Military Organization (UWO), 562, 568, 569; National Convention, 523; National Democratic League (UNDO), 569; National party in Bukovina, 574; National Rada, 313, 553, 562; National Republic, 532, 538, 541, 546, 553–556, 564; nobles, 127, 133, 134, 136, 138, 141, 142, 145, 146, 170, 186, 219, 233, 467; officers, 394, 395; Park in Lviv, 572; Pedagogical Institute in Prague, 564; Progressives, political party (see Union of Autonomous Federalists); Regional Committee in northern Bukovina, 559; representatives in Polish parliament, 572, 573; rights, 374, 375, 380, 382, 385–387, 391, 474, 476; soldiers, 524, 534; renaissance, 468, 478, 499, 506; Scientific Society, 513, 568; Soviet Socialist Republic, 543, 554, 573, 574; tribes, 19, 20, 24, 25, 31; villages, 72; wedding songs, 33; wives, 32; Women's Alliance, 572
Ukrainian-Americans, 562, 566
Ukrainianization, 564
Ukrainians, 1, 19, 21, 23, 25, 34, 88, 91, 115, 133, 136, 139–142, 146, 155, 170, 193
Ukrainska Centralna Rada (Ukrainian Central Rada). See Central Rada
Ukrainska Khata, journal, 513
Uliches, tribe, 24, 57
Uman, 302, 317, 371, 438, 441, 444
UNDO. See Ukrainian National Democratic League
Uniate Church, 252, 258, 469, 470, 507, 516, 562 (see also Uniates); bishops, 187, 211, 213, 214, 242; clergy, 469, 488, 493, 516
Uniates, 213–215, 238, 241, 245, 251, 262–265, 267, 425–427, 440–443, 568
Union for the Liberation of Ukraine, 520, 542, 565
Union of Autonomous Federalists, 523. See Ukrainian Progressives
Union of 1654. See Khmelnitsky, Bohdan, treaty of
Union of Ukrainian Physicians of Czechoslovakia, 564

Universals (proclamations), of Central Rada, 526, 527, 532, 536, 538, 539, 549; of Mazepa, 351
Universities, 564; of Kharkiv, 483; of Lviv, 509
University Student Home in Lviv, 562
Ural Mountains, 517
Usha River, 24
USSR, 558, 573
UWO. *See* Ukrainian Military Organization
Uzh, 428, 430
Uzhorod, 432, 492, 571, 572

Vahilevich, J., historian, 488, 489
Valinana, 38
Valuiev, Count P. A., Russian minister, 496
Vanatovich, metropolitan of Kiev, 393
Varangians, 40–44, 63, 74, 75, 78, 86
Vardas Phocas, Byzantine general, 67
Varna, 221
Vasilev (later Vasilkiv) near Kiev, 68
Vasilevich, H., Kozak hetman, 218, 583
Vasilkiv (formerly Vasilev) near Kiev, 73, 444
Vasilko, Galician prince, 89, 577 (5), 579
—— Prince of Volynia, 98, 100, 108, 110, 111, 580
Vasyl, author, 199
Veliaminov, S., Russian brigadier, 378–380, 382, 384, 385, 387
Velichko, Ukrainian chronicler, 415, 477
Veliki Skit, monastery, 427
Venetia, 438
Venice, 278
Verlan, Haidamak leader, 438
Viatiches, tribe, 59, 63, 107
Viatka, 338
Viche (council), 33, 87, 116
Vid, Lithuanian prince, 124
Vidrozhenia Temperance Society. *See* Regeneration
Vienna, 341, 470, 555, 563, 564; award, 571
Vilkomir, battle, 136
Villages in early Ukraine, 33

Vilna, ·148, 200, 215, 245, 246, 297, 467
Vilna Ukraina, journal, 513
Vinitar, King of Goths, 20
Vinnichenko, V., head of Directory, 553
Vinnitsia, 291, 441
Vinnitsky, I., bishop of Peremyshl, 425, 427
Visheslav, Prince of Novgorod, 64
Vishinsky, I., author, 205, 212
Vishnevetsky, Dmitro ("Baida"), Kozak hetman, 157–159, 163, 234, 255, 288, 583
—— J., landlord, 281, 282, 285
—— M., military governor of Cherkassy, 176, 183
Vishnevetsky estates, 251
Vishorod near Kiev, 74
Vistula River, 17–19, 173, 357
Vitebsk, 252; Monastery, 120
Vitichev, 35
Vitovt, Grand Duke of Lithuania, 130–136, 208, 429, 581
Voinarovsky, A., nephew of Mazepa, 369
Voishelk, Grand Duke of Lithuania, 123
Voivodates (Polish provinces), 563
Volga River, 17, 36, 56, 64, 72, 103, 105, 381; region, 47, 94, 103, 149
Volha Vseslavich, mythical figure, 48–50, 52, 54
Volobuev, Russian communist, 565
Volodar, Galician prince, 89, 577 (5), 579
Volodimir, Prince of Galicia, 96, 97, 577 (8)
—— Prince of Kiev, 125, 126, 131, 132, 582
—— Prince of Volynia, 112, 580
—— the Great (St. Volodimir), Grand Prince of Kiev, 27, 40, 46, 61, 63–74, 76, 78, 81, 94, 117, 119, 289, 575 (6), 577, 579
—— Monomakh. *See* Monomakh
Volodimir, cathedral in Kiev, 104
Volodimir, city in Volynia, 64, 105, 114, 121, 128, 135; diocese, 264; principality, 96, 97, 99, 464. *See* Volynia
Volodimiria. *See* Volodimir, principality; Volynia

Volodimirko, Prince of Galicia-Volynia, 89, 90, 577 (6), 579
Volodislav, nobleman of Galicia, 128, 577 (20)
Volokolamsk, 338
Voloshyn, A., president of Carpatho-Ukraine, 571, 572
Volost. See "Townships"
Volunteer Army. *See* White Army
Volyn, 34
Volynia, principality and province, 17, 23, 24, 89, 91, 96, 97, 99–101, 105, 106, 110, 111, 124, 129, 131, 135–139, 146, 150, 163, 165–168, 175, 176, 183, 184, 186–188, 194, 198, 211, 214, 258, 263, 267, 282, 284, 285, 292, 318, 341, 424, 434, 445 (*see* Galicia-Volynia, Volodimiria); diocese, 427
Volynian Chronicle, 119, 120; nobles, 168, 188
Volynians, tribe, 34, 38
Volynsky, A. P., Russian minister; quoted, 398
Vorksla River, battle, 130
Voronizh, 287, 337; government, 409
Vovchok, Marko, author, 500
Voyevoda (military governors), 303
Vseslav, Prince. *See* Volha Vseslavich
Vsevolod, Prince of Chernihiv and Kiev, 92, 575 (20), 579
—— Prince of Galicia, 64, 577 (2)
—— Prince of Kiev, 80–83, 89, 575 (14), 579
—— Chermny, Prince of Kiev and Suzdal, Grand Duke of Volodimir, 94, 153, 576 (50), 580
Vyhovsky, I., Kozak hetman, 299, 300, 307–315, 318, 323, 328, 360, 584

Wadowice, 561
Wallachia, 134, 140, 145, 159, 163, 181, 185, 211, 226, 243, 244. *See also* Rumania
Wallachians, 17, 132, 150, 158, 180, 221, 438, 439
Wallachs, tribe, 17. *See also* Wallachians
War communism, 557
Warning (*Perestoroha*), tract, 205
Warsaw, 269, 281, 300, 442, 466, 467, 557

West-Slavic tribes, 19. *See* Western Slavs
Western Division of Ukrainian National Republic, 554, 555, 563
Western Europe, 8, 118, 121, 142, 173, 185, 199, 254, 479
Western Galicia, 235
Western Slavs, 19, 36
Western Ukraine, 96, 107, 108, 126, 144, 149, 194, 270, 309, 313, 371, 372, 405, 410, 519, 572; reunited to eastern Ukraine, 165–169; Church Union in, 213, 214; attempts at independence, 319–338 *passim;* new Kozak state in, 338–342; seized by Mazepa, 361–363; decline in culture in, 422–427; in eighteenth century, 433–445 *passim;* national renaissance in, 462–482 *passim;* relations to Poland, 560–564. *See also* Austrian Ukraine; Galicia; Galicia-Volynia; Right Bank Ukraine; Volynia; Western Ukrainian Republic
Western Ukrainian Republic, 552–554
Weygand, French general, 557
White Army, 552–554, 556, 557
White Church. *See* Bila Tserkva
White Russia, 70, 123, 124, 130, 132–134, 136, 139, 140, 143, 148, 150, 186, 188, 193, 201, 210, 215, 244, 245, 252, 262, 264, 281, 297, 311, 318, 464, 466, 467
White Russian Church, 243; churches, 208; gentry, 197
White Sea, 455
Wilhelm, Austrian prince, 219
Will of the People, newspaper, 522
"Winter campaign" of Ukrainian National Republic, 555
Wladyslaw IV, King of Poland, 236, 263–265, 267, 268, 277, 280–282
"Word and deed," 396, 397
Workers, 549, 552
World War, 467, 572
Writing, art of, 1

Yadviga, Queen of Poland, 128
Yagello, Grand Duke of Lithuania, 129–135, 137, 138, 208, 209, 582
Yahra, bishop in Carpatho-Ukraine, 470

Yakhea, A., claimant to throne of Turkey, 254, 256

Yaniv near Lviv, 424

Yaropolche, 338

Yaropolk, Prince of Kiev, 61, 63, 575 (18), 579

—— Prince of Volynia, 89, 579

Yaroslav, Prince of Galicia, 90, 577, 579; sons of, 96

—— Prince of Kiev, 27, 44, 48, 64, 70, 74–80, 575 (8), 579

—— Prince of Kiev, brother of Roman of Galicia, 98, 580

—— Prince of Suzdal, 107, 576 (60), 580

Yaroslav, city, 200

Yasians (Ossetes), nomad tribe, 59, 75, 102

Yassy, 288

Yavoriv, 424

Yavorsky, M. Z., abbot of Motronin Monastery, 441, 442

Yefremiv (Jefremov), S., nationalist, 565, 566

Yellow Waters. See Zhovty Vody Creek

Yuriy. See George

Yursh, Lithuanian officer, 135

Yuzefovich, Russian official, 502

Zabludiv, 197, 202

Zabolotiv, 424

Zaborovsky, R., metropolitan of Kiev, 417

Zadik, Rumanian general, 559

Zahalna Ukrainska Rada (General Ukrainian Council), 520

Zakup (indentured laborer), 85

Zalizniak, M., Kolii leader, 443–445

Zamostia, 282

Zankovetska, actress, 511

Zaporozhe (Dnieper region "below the rapids"), 156, 157, 183, 192, 193, 227, 232, 234, 254, 256, 268, 271–274, 276, 278, 279, 309, 321, 330, 332, 338, 347, 355, 356, 403, 436, 439

Zaporozhian "free lands," 452

Zaporozhian Host, 224, 284, 294, 295

(*see also* Zaporozhian Kozaks, Zaporozhian Sich); Kozaks, 188, 189, 191, 217, 249, 258, 259, 305, 310, 314, 322, 326, 335, 369, 372, 375, 389, 390, 435, 443–445, 447, 478; Sich (fortress and lower Dnieper region), 156, 185, 222, 232, 305, 306, 310, 314, 315, 321, 338, 355–357, 368–373, 389, 401; destruction, 452–459

Zarubsky, G., author, 119

Zasiv, newspaper, 513

Zbarazh, 135, 285

Zbarazky family, 176

Zboriv, 285; treaty of, 286–288, 291–294

Zbruch River, 561

Zemlin county in Carpatho-Ukraine, 428

Zemski sobor (Muscovite estates-general), 294

Zhabotin Monastery, 442, 443

Zhdanovich, Kozak colonel, 300, 301

Zhidichin, 214

Zhitetsky, ethnologist, 502

Zhito (grain), 25

Zhitomir, 143, 543, 545, 546

Zhmailo, P., Kozak hetman, 256, 257, 583

Zhmerinka, 540

Zhovnin, 274, 275

Zhovty Vody Creek (Yellow Waters), battle, 279, 280, 308

Zhvaniets, 293

"Zizania." See Kukil, Stephen

Zolkiewski, Lucasz, Polish commissioner, 269, 271

—— Stanislaus, Polish general, 188–193, 211, 217, 226, 229, 233, 237, 243, 244; 269

—— family, 176

Zolochiv, 238

Zolotarenko, V., Kozak colonel, 319, 320

Zoria (Star), almanac, 489

Zoria Halitska (Galician Star), newspaper, 490

Zvanets, 438

Zvenihorod, 89